ARMED STRUGGLE

ARMED STRUGGLE

The History of the IRA

RICHARD ENGLISH

OXFORD
UNIVERSITY PRESS
2003

OXFORD
UNIVERSITY PRESS

Oxford   New York
Auckland   Bangkok   Buenos Aires
Cape Town   Chennai   Dar es Salaam   Delhi   Hong Kong   Istanbul
Karachi   Kolkata   Kuala Lumpur   Madrid   Melbourne   Mexico City   Mumbai
Nairobi   São Paulo   Shanghai   Taipei   Tokyo   Toronto

Published by Oxford University Press, Inc.
198 Madison Avenue, New York, New York 10016

www.oup.com

Oxford is a registered trademark of Oxford University Press

Library of Congress Cataloging-in-Publication Data

English, Richard, 1963-
Armed struggle : the history of the IRA / Richard English.
p. cm.
Includes bibliographical references (p.) and index.
ISBN 0-19-516605-1 (alk. paper)
1. Irish Republican Army--History. 2. Political violence--Ireland--History--20th century.
3. Guerrilla warfare--Ireland--History--20th century. 4. Ireland--History, Military--20th
century. 5. Political violence--Northern Ireland. 6. Ireland--History--20th century. 7.
Northern Ireland--History. I. Title.

DA914.E55 2003
941.60824--dc21

2002044699

1 3 5 7 9 10 8 6 4 2
Printed in the United States of America
on acid-free paper

FOR

Mab, Jas and B

The author would like to thank:

Paul Durcan, for permission to quote from
'The Minibus Massacre: The Eve of the Epiphany';

Blackstaff Press, for permission to quote from
Padraic Fiacc's 'Elegy for a "Fenian Get"';

Cormac O'Malley, for permission to quote from
Ernie O'Malley's 'To a Comrade Dead'.

Every effort has been made to contact copyright holders of material
reproduced in this book. If any have been inadvertently overlooked, the
publishers will be pleased to make restitution at the earliest opportunity.

Contents

List of Illustrations

List of Abbreviations

ADUCD   Archives Department, University College, Dublin
AP   *An Phoblacht*
AP/RN   *An Phoblacht/Republican News*
ARP   Air Raid Precautions
ASU   Active Service Unit
BT   *Belfast Telegraph*
CAB   Records of the Cabinet Office
CBS   Christian Brothers' School
CIRA   Continuity Irish Republican Army
CLMC   Combined Loyalist Military Command
CO   Colonial Office
CSJNI   Campaign for Social Justice in Northern Ireland
DAAD   Direct Action Against Drugs
DCAC   Derry Citizens' Action Committee
DEFE   Records of the Ministry of Defence
DJ   *Derry Journal*
DO   Dominions Office
DT   *Daily Telegraph*
DUP   Democratic Unionist Party
FARC   Revolutionary Armed Forces of Colombia
FRU   Force Research Unit
GAA   Gaelic Athletic Association
GAC   General Army Convention
GFA   Good Friday Agreement
GOC   General Officer Commanding
HMP   Her Majesty's Prison
ICA   Irish Citizen Army
IICD   Independent International Commission on Decommissioning

IN	*Irish News*
INLA	Irish National Liberation Army
IP	*Irish Press*
IPP	Irish Parliamentary Party
IRA	Irish Republican Army
IRB	Irish Republican Brotherhood
IRSP	Irish Republican Socialist Party
IT	*Irish Times*
LHL	Linen Hall Library (Belfast)
LHLPC	Linen Hall Library, Political Collection (Belfast)
LVF	Loyalist Volunteer Force
MLA	Member of Legislative Assembly (Northern Ireland)
NAD	National Archives, Dublin
NICRA	Northern Ireland Civil Rights Association
NIO	Northern Ireland Office
NLI	National Library of Ireland
OC	Officer Commanding
OIRA	Official Irish Republican Army
OSF	Official Sinn Féin
PD	People's Democracy
PIRA	Provisional Irish Republican Army
PREM	Records of the Prime Minister's Office
PRO	Public Relations Officer
PROL	Public Record Office, London
PRONI	Public Record Office of Northern Ireland (Belfast)
PSF	Provisional Sinn Féin
PUP	Progressive Unionist Party
QUB	Queen's University, Belfast
RIC	Royal Irish Constabulary
RIR	Royal Irish Regiment
RIRA	Real Irish Republican Army
RN	*Republican News*
RSF	Republican Sinn Féin
RTÉ	Radio Telefís Éireann
RUC	Royal Ulster Constabulary
RUCR	Royal Ulster Constabulary Reserve
SAS	Special Air Service
SDLP	Social Democratic and Labour Party

TCD	Trinity College, Dublin
TD	Teachta Dála (member of the Dáil)
TUAS	Tactical Use of Armed Struggle
UDA	Ulster Defence Association
UDR	Ulster Defence Regiment
UFF	Ulster Freedom Fighters
USC	Ulster Special Constabulary
UUC	Ulster Unionist Council
UUP	Ulster Unionist Party
UVF	Ulster Volunteer Force
UWC	Ulster Workers' Council

IRELAND

UNITED
KINGDOM

SCOTLAND
NORTHERN IRELAND

Islay
Jura
Kintyre

Atlantic Ocean

Coleraine

Derry/Londonderry

LONDONDERRY

DONEGAL

Donegal

TYRONE

Omagh

ANTRIM

Belfast

Lisburn

FERMANAGH

Enniskillen

Armagh

ARMAGH

DOWN

Sligo

LEITRIM

Monaghan

MONAGHAN

Newry

SLIGO

CAVAN

LOUTH

Dundalk

MAYO

ROSCOMMON

LONGFORD

Irish
Sea

MEATH

WESTMEATH

GALWAY

Galway

OFFALY

DUBLIN

Dublin

LAOIS

Portlaoise

KILDARE

WICKLOW

CLARE

TIPPERARY

Limerick

CARLOW

KILKENNY

WEXFORD

LIMERICK

Tipperary

Tralee

WATERFORD

Wexford

KERRY

CORK

St George's Channel

Cork

Celtic Sea

| 0 | 25 | 50 | 75 | 100 kilometres |

| 0 | 25 | 50 | 75 miles |

—·—·— International boundary

– – – Province boundary

········· County boundary

NORTHERN IRELAND

- ▬·▬·▬ International boundary
- ·········· County boundary

UNITED KINGDOM

SCOTLAND
NORTHERN IRELAND

Kintyre

Portrush

Ballycastle○

○Coleraine

○Ballymoney

Derry/Londonderry○

COUNTY
LONDONDERRY

COUNTY
ANTRIM

Dungiven ○

○Ballymena

REPUBLIC
OF
IRELAND

○Strabane

Carrickfergus○

Bellaghy○

○Antrim

COUNTY TYRONE

Cookstown○

*Lough
Neagh*

Belfast○

○Bangor

○Omagh

Coalisland○

Dungannon○

○Lisburn

Belleek○

Enniskillen○

○Fivemiletown

Portadown○

Lurgan○

COUNTY
DOWN

COUNTY FERMANAGH

○Lisnaskea

○Armagh

COUNTY
ARMAGH

Banbridge○

○Downpatrick

Newcastle○

Crossmaglen○

○Newry

○Warrenpoint

○Kilkeel

*Irish
Sea*

| 0 | 25 | 50 kilometres |
| 0 | | 25 miles |

Glossary

An Phoblacht/Republican News (*AP/RN*) – *An Phoblacht* (*AP*) was the Provisional republicans' Dublin-based newspaper during 1970–9; *Republican News* (*RN*) was their Belfast-produced paper during the same period. In the autumn of 1978 it was decided that the southern *An Phoblacht* and the northern *Republican News* would amalgamate as *An Phoblacht/Republican News*. In January 1979 the new paper appeared, *Republican News* having effectively absorbed *An Phoblacht*. The early editors of *AP/RN* were Danny Morrison (1979–82), Mick Timothy (1982–5) and Rita O'Hare (1985–90).

Ard fheis – Convention.

Christian Brothers' Schools (**CBS**) – Schools run by the Irish Catholic lay teaching order initially established by Edmund Rice (1762–1844).

Clan na Gael – Irish American revolutionary organization, founded in the nineteenth century to pursue Irish independence from Britain.

Cumann na mBan – Literally, 'the league of women': a twentieth-century Irish women's republican organization.

Fenians – Members of a revolutionary movement active in Ireland and in Irish America. Emerging in the mid-nineteenth century, the Fenians sought Irish independence from Britain and aimed to achieve this through the use of force.

Gaelic Athletic Association (**GAA**) – Founded in 1884, a cultural nationalist organization which promoted Gaelic games such as hurling and Gaelic football.

Gaelic League – Set up in 1893, an organization pursuing the revival of the Irish language.

Irish Republican Brotherhood (IRB) – A revolutionary, conspiratorial secret society which emerged out of the Fenian movement in the late-nineteenth century, and which – through violence – pursued Irish independence from Britain.

Irish Volunteers – An Irish nationalist militia set up in 1913.

Ulster Workers' Council (UWC) – Loyalist body set up in Northern Ireland in 1974 to oppose the power-sharing Sunningdale Agreement.

United Irishmen – An organization set up in 1791: initially pursuing parliamentary and constitutional reform through propagandist means, it developed during the 1790s into a conspiratorial, insurrectionary movement which aimed to bring about Irish separation from England through force.

Acknowledgments

As with my previous books, I have been greatly helped by many people during the writing of this one. The staffs of numerous libraries and archives have made the process both possible and enjoyable, by sharing their expertise and enthusiasm with me over the years. I am heavily indebted to those who have helped me at the following: the Linen Hall Library, Belfast (and especially Yvonne Murphy and her colleagues at the Linen Hall's wonderful Political Collection); the Library of Queen's University, Belfast, especially its invaluable Special Collections section; the Archives Department of University College (Dublin), especially Seamus Helferty; the British Library (London); the General Register Office (Belfast); the Public Record Office (London); the Public Record Office of Northern Ireland (Belfast) – in particular, Marian Gallagher; Belfast Central Newspaper Library; the National Archives in Dublin (especially Tom Quinlan); the National Library in Dublin.

Many friends have provided wise advice and invaluable support during the years it has taken to produce the book. It is a great pleasure to thank: Roy Foster; Tim Bartlett, Rob Tempio, George Morley and Bruce Hunter have provided invaluable advice; David Eastwood; George Boyce; Charles Townshend; Alvin Jackson; successive heads of the School of Politics at Queen's University (Bob Eccleshall and Shane O'Neill); Joe Skelly; Peter Hart; Patrick Maume; Gordon Gillespie; Graham Walker; Adrian Guelke; Elizabeth Meehan; Rick Wilford; Eugene McKendry. In addition, many others have enriched the book by offering their time and insights (often through interview) or by providing other help during the course of the research. I am deeply grateful, in various ways, to: Danny Morrison, Anthony McIntyre, Tom Hartley, Patrick Magee, Declan Moen, Jackie McMullan, Tommy McKearney, Liam O'Ruairc, John Gray, Christine Fearon, George Harrison, Roy Johnston, Cormac O'Malley, Jeffrey Donaldson, Sean Garland, Tommy Gorman, Dessie O'Hagan, Laurence McKeown, Ian Paisley, Anthony Coughlan, Niall O'Dowd,

Marian Price, Sean Nolan, Sheila Humphreys, Frankie Quinn and Davy Adamson. The Economic and Social Research Council (Award Number R000223312) and the Arts and Humanities Research Board provided funding for different aspects and phases of the project. Queen's University, Belfast, also provided valuable research funding.

The book's dedication reflects my deepest and most precious debts of all.

Richard English
Belfast, October 2002

Preface

Funerals. The first was for IRA man Thomas McElwee, on 10 August 1981, in the small County Derry town of Bellaghy in the north of Ireland. Thousands attended. Throughout the day there was a heavy police presence in the town and six British Army helicopters hovered overhead. McElwee had died on hunger strike, and was the ninth Irish republican prisoner to do so in that tragic 1981 sequence occasioned by their battle for political status. He had died on 8 August after refusing food for an incredible sixty-two days. And he had died young, only twenty-three years old. The funeral reflected understandable, personal grief at his death – at one stage his eight sisters carried the Irish-tricolour-draped coffin, and his twenty-one-year-old brother (also a prisoner) had been released to attend the Catholic funeral. One of the priests at the graveside was a cousin of the dead man, and he was buried only a few feet from the grave of another cousin, Francis Hughes – a fellow IRA hunger-striker who had died just three months earlier. For McElwee's funeral was an IRA as well as a personal occasion. The coffin was flanked from his parents' home by six men and six women in paramilitary uniform. Before the cortège moved off, three IRA men fired volleys of pistol-shots over the coffin.

Thomas McElwee had been in prison for the manslaughter of Yvonne Dunlop in 1976. On the afternoon of Saturday 9 October, Mrs Dunlop had been looking after the family shop in Ballymena, County Antrim, with her eight-year-old son. At 1 p.m. an IRA bomb – the first of at least fifteen in Ballymena that day – exploded in the shop. Yvonne had shouted at her boy to get out; he did so and his screams drew the attention of passers-by. Firemen and others tried vainly to rescue Yvonne from the blazing building as her son looked on. His mother, trapped inside the shop, burned to death.

So in October 1976 there had been another funeral, this time in Ballymena. And this time the graveside service had been conducted by a Presbyterian minister, assisted by a Congregational clergyman who was a cousin of Mrs

Dunlop. The large cortège included the dead woman's father, brothers and sister. In his grief, Yvonne's father commented hauntingly about the killers of his daughter: 'All I would ask of these people is why, why take the life of an innocent young girl, and leave three innocent youngsters without a mother?'[1] Yvonne Dunlop was twenty-seven years old, her two younger children aged six and four; Thomas McElwee was a member of the IRA team that carried out the Ballymena bombings.

This book does not argue that these two deaths neatly mirrored one another. Ultimately, Thomas McElwee had responsibility for both of them, in a way that Yvonne Dunlop had for neither. But both deaths were tragic, poignant products of a conflict at whose centre the Provisional Irish Republican Army has found itself for over thirty years: to make sense of these deaths (and of thousands of others arising from the conflict) one must understand this revolutionary organization. Aspects of IRA history from earlier generations have been studied in admirably rigorous fashion,[2] and the *pre*-Provisional IRA has been impressively contextualized in wide-angled thematic surveys of Irish history.[3] But the Provisionals themselves – easily the most sustained, and arguably now the definitive, exemplars of the IRA tradition – have been treated much less carefully, and have received much less in the way of serious analysis. Despite the existence of numerous – often fascinating – books on the subject, much writing about the Provisionals has lacked rigour: it has sometimes relied on patchy research and a shaky grasp of Irish history, and much of it has been marred either by a hazily romantic approach or an unhelpfully condemnatory spirit. Indeed, there remains no full[4] study of the Provisional IRA, no genuinely authoritative, accessible book which – through exhaustive, original research – systematically addresses the questions: what has the IRA done, why, and with what consequences? *Armed Struggle* is intended to fill that gap. The aim has been to produce a rigorously argued book – based on thorough, innovative research – and one that avoids both romantic indulgence and casual, simplistic condemnation in analysing the true nature of the Provisional IRA.

The book is based on the widest range of sources ever used to study the Provisionals: interviews, correspondence, archives (including those only recently released), memoirs, newspapers, tracts, parliamentary records, organizational papers, films, novels – as well as a mass of books and articles relating to the subject – all testify to the wealth of material available, ironically, for an examination of this secret army. Much of the material has not previously been examined or published. But, while the book is thus based on comprehensive scholarly work, it is intended also to be accessible and readable. The Notes and References and the Bibliography are there for those who want to pursue details; but readers who find such things distracting can approach the book purely as a dramatic narrative. In structure, it is precisely that: a chronological story, albeit one layered with argument and analysis. Part One, 'History 1916–63', builds historical foundations on which to base an under-standing of the modern-day Provisionals. The pre-twentieth-century Irish physical-force tradition, with its rebellions and its secrecy; the dramatic events of the 1916 Easter Rising and of the 1919–21 guerrilla war; the partitioning of Ireland in the early 1920s and the Irish Civil War of 1922–3 – all will be considered, since all provide important points of reference for Provisional thought and action. So, too, the IRA campaigns in Northern Ireland and Britain during the 1930s, 1940s, 1950s and 1960s provide an important line of descent for modern Provisional republicanism.

Part Two, 'Protest and Rebellion 1963–76', examines the birth of the Provisionals out of the turbulence generated by the 1960s civil rights move-ment, and it does so with unprecedented detail and precision. It looks at the loyalist reaction to civil rights agitation, the escalating violence of the late 1960s, the introduction of British troops to the streets of Northern Ireland, the split in the IRA which produced the Provisionals, the introduction of internment in 1971, the tragedy of Bloody Sunday in 1972, the appallingly high levels of killing in the early 1970s and the battle within the northern Catholic community between the Provisionals and rival political forces. Bombings in Britain and bloody conflict in the north of Ireland figure prominently in these years.

Part Three, 'Prisons and Politics 1976–88', looks at the dramatic prison war over political status, which culminated in the 1980–1 IRA hunger strikes. It builds on much new archival and interview material to detail this pivotal phase in the IRA's struggle. It also analyses their shift, in the late 1970s, to a different organizational and strategic approach, with the army adopting an attritional long-war policy towards their conflict with Britain. And it deals with the IRA's military campaign during a period that included the 1979 killing of the Queen's cousin, Louis Mountbatten, and the 1984 attempted killing of the then Prime Minister, Margaret Thatcher. This section of the book also scrutinizes the Provisionals' emergence as a more committedly political force in the 1980s, one influenced by – and increasingly significant within – Northern Irish and Anglo-Irish political developments.

This politicization of the Provisional movement, embodied in a more dynamic Provisional Sinn Féin party, made possible the changes addressed in Part Four, 'Peace? 1988–2002'. The latter details the Provisionals' gradual immersion in the 1990s Northern Ireland peace process: their talks with constitutional nationalists such as John Hume; their initially cautious dialogue with the British authorities; and the evolution of a process involving milestones such as the 1993 Anglo-Irish Joint Declaration, the IRA ceasefires of 1994 and 1997 and the 1998 Belfast Agreement. This section also offers the first fully researched consideration of why the IRA so dramatically shifted ground during the peace process of the 1990s.

Having told the story, from history through to the present day, the book's Conclusion then offers an analysis of this organization. Who were its victims? What were the motivations of its Volunteers and leaders? How plausible were its arguments, and what have been the achievements, consequences and legacies of its violence? The IRA themselves have repeatedly claimed that their violence was necessitated by the irreformability of Northern Ireland, and by the extremity of injustice there; are such claims justified by serious interrogation of the evidence now available? The IRA have claimed that only their revolutionary, aggressive politics could end sectarianism in Ireland; has such a claim been borne out by events in the last thirty years? How democratic were Provisional politics, how sectarian, how appropriately considered within an anti-colonial or a socialist framework?

The Provisional IRA has embodied what have been arguably the most powerful forces in modern world history: the intersection of nationalism and violence, the tension between nation and state, the interaction of nationalism with socialism, and the force of aggressive ethno-religious identity as a vehicle for historical change. The Provisionals have been vitally important in the interwoven histories of Ireland and Britain; but their full significance reaches far beyond the politics of those islands, and into the world of non-state political violence once again so prominent today. The IRA has been a much richer, more complex and layered, more protean organization than is frequently recognized. It is also one open to more balanced examination now – at the end of its long war in the north of Ireland – than was possible even a few years ago. As one of the republican movement's ablest political strategists recently and persuasively suggested, 'You see, war is easy. You have to remember that. War is easy because there are the baddies and the goodies. And you don't ever have to engage, or think about, or find out the reasons why people act in the way they do.'[5] This book, in a sense, is an attempt to do precisely that: to find out the reasons behind – and the consequences of –

the Irish Republican Army. It attempts to understand the organization in its many overlapping contexts: Northern Irish, Irish, United Kingdom, international; intellectual, historical, social, communal, personal. It aims to study the Provisionals in a systematic and measured fashion, and to offer the fullest, most balanced and most authoritative treatment of one of the world's leading revolutionary movements.

NOTE

The Provisional IRA was founded in December 1969. In this book, the title 'IRA' – when applied to any date from then onwards – will refer to the Provisionals. Other groups claiming the title IRA after that date will be clearly distinguished as such, including the Offical IRA (OIRA), Continuity IRA (CIRA) and Real IRA (RIRA). (Some observers have referred to the Provisional IRA as PIRA.)

The term 'Army' will refer to the British Army, while 'army' will refer to the IRA.

PART ONE

HISTORY

1916−63

ONE

THE IRISH REVOLUTION

1916–23

1

'The Republic which was declared at the Rising of Easter Week, 1916, was Ireland's expression of the freedom she aspired to. It was our way of saying that we wished to challenge Britain's right to dominate us.'

Michael Collins, one of the Irish rebels of 1916[1]

In literary evocation and political argument alike, the 1916 Easter Rising has been presented as a watershed in Irish history and politics. From W. B. Yeats's 'terrible beauty',[2] to the Provisional IRA's first public statement in December 1969,[3] to the sexual adventures of Roddy Doyle's unorthodox Irish rebel Henry Smart,[4] the rebellion at Easter has been told as a central part of the story of Ireland.

It was a truly dramatic event. The eyewitness account of Dublin-born poet James Stephens (1880–1950) vividly suggests as much: 'The sound of artillery, of rifles, machine guns, grenades, did not cease even for a moment. From my window I saw a red flare that crept to the sky, and stole over it and remained there glaring; the smoke reached from the ground to the clouds, and I could see great red sparks go soaring to enormous heights; while always, in the calm air, hour after hour there was the buzzing and rattling and thudding of guns, and, but for the guns, silence.'[5] Another recollection was equally evocative: 'Over the fine building of the GPO floated a great green flag with the words "Irish Republic" on it in large white letters. Every window on the ground floor was smashed and barricaded with furniture, and a big placard announced "The Headquarters of the Provisional Government of the Irish Republic". At every window were two men with rifles, and on the roof the parapet was lined with men.'[6]

And it deeply changed many lives, especially with the subsequent British execution of Irish rebel leaders. 'Then came like a thunderclap the 1916 Rising,' recalled medical student turned IRA leader, Ernie O'Malley, in 1923; 'Previous to this I had heard a little of the Irish Volunteers, but at home we always laughed at them as toy soldiers. Before [Easter] Week was finished I had changed. When I heard of the executions I was furious.'[7] One of O'Malley's fellow IRA men from the 1916–23 revolution, Tom Maguire, presented the Rising in equally life-transforming terms: 'The Easter insurrection came to me like a bolt from the blue, I will never forget my exhilaration, it was a turning point in my life. To think that Irishmen were fighting England on the streets of Dublin: I thanked God for seeing such a day.'[8] Yet another legendary IRA figure, Tom Barry, reflected of his own response that 'through the blood sacrifices of the men of 1916, had one Irish youth of eighteen been awakened to Irish nationality. Let it also be recorded that those sacrifices were equally necessary to awaken the minds of ninety per cent of the Irish people.'[9]

The seamless identification of self and nation here is telling, for it has been a persistent part of the Irish republican story. IRA man Liam Deasy typically recalled: 'In consequence of the events that occurred in the decisive week of the Easter Rising of 1916, and more particularly of the events that followed it, thousands of young men all over Ireland, indeed thousands of men of all ages in the country, turned irrevocably against the English government and became uncompromisingly dedicated to the cause of obliterating the last vestiges of British rule in Ireland. I was one of them.'[10] Much more weightily, the very leader of the 1916 Rising – the poetic and charismatic Patrick Pearse – engraved himself and his band of rebels permanently into Irish national history. The Proclamation that Pearse read out at the start of the Rising (in Dublin on Easter Monday, 24 April) pointed the way, identifying the rebels with 'the dead generations' of Ireland: 'In every generation the Irish people have asserted their right to national freedom and sovereignty; six times during the past three hundred years they have asserted it in arms. Standing on that fundamental right and again asserting it in arms in the face of the world, we hereby proclaim the Irish republic as a sovereign independent state'.[11]

A dramatic military statement against British rule in Ireland, the 1916 rebellion was also a profoundly First World War event. Serious planning for the Rising began after the commencement of the war, which provided the opportunity for (and, in rebel eyes, the necessity of) an insurrectionary gesture against Britain. With the latter preoccupied and vulnerable, it seemed an ideal time for Irish rebels to strike. And the 1916 rebels had expressed pro-German views, had looked for German help and had been promised it. (In both twentieth-century world wars, militant Irish republicans backed Germany.) Of the specifically Irish ingredients themselves, the Rising had been planned by figures within the Irish Republican Brotherhood (IRB) and the Irish nationalist militia, the Irish Volunteers, and the rebel ranks also contained people from the labour movement's Irish Citizen Army (ICA), whose able leader James Connolly had been admitted to the revolutionary conspiracy in January 1916. In the event, the Rising which began on Easter Monday was essentially a Dublin affair. The General Post Office and other buildings in the Irish capital were occupied by well over a thousand rebels, who were then militarily crushed within a week.

The 1916 Proclamation came to be an emblem of modern Irish republicanism, and for many a kind of national Irish poem. But, poetic or not, those behind the Rising were also (in the words of a later Irish republican, Gerry Adams) 'deadly serious revolutionaries . . . anxious to exploit by military means Britain's involvement in the World War'.[12] And the 1916 gesture did indeed help to recast much Irish – and therefore also British – history. The hundreds killed during the Rising (most of them civilians)[13] represented small-scale tragedy when set against the dreadful context of the First World War. But Easter Week none the less significantly helped to define later Irish politics. For the executions helped to achieve what the rebellion itself had not – an intensification of nationalist feeling well beyond the rebel ranks. Together with the post-Rising arrest and internment of many people, the executions produced sympathy for that rebel cause which they were supposed to undermine (a persistent later theme in British responses to Irish republicanism, as it turned out). The dead rebels became martyrs. Masses, postcards and badges all honoured them in the post-Rising period. A cult had come into existence, with a quasi-sacred quality quickly attaching itself to the rebel leaders after the Rising had entered the popular imagination. Catholic Ireland had found new heroes, and their celebration – unsurprisingly – possessed a markedly religious flavour.

Along with the ever-compelling Roger Casement,[14] the seven signatories to the rebel Proclamation were themselves among those subsequently executed by the British authorities. Though undoubtedly born of wartime exigency, these executions movingly and lastingly haunted political Ireland. It was an awful, poignant sequence. Thomas Clarke (born 1857), long-time Fenian revolutionary; Thomas Mac-Donagh (born 1878), poet and teacher; Patrick Pearse (born 1879), Dublin-born poet, educator, cultural nationalist and revolutionary. All three were executed on 3 May 1916. Joseph Plunkett (born 1887), another poet, an IRB man and an Irish Volunteer: married in his prison cell a few hours before being shot on 4 May. Éamonn Ceannt (born 1881), educated by the Christian Brothers, a Gaelic League enthusiast, Sinn Féiner, IRB man and Irish Volunteer: executed on the 8th. Seán Mac Diarmada (born 1884), a tram conductor and barman, a Gaelic Leaguer, IRB man, Sinn Féiner and Irish Volunteer; James Connolly (born 1868), Scottish-born socialist, former British soldier, talented radical organizer and writer. Both were shot on 12 May.

These deaths had a momentous effect. As one County Clare IRA man from the ensuing conflict (Sean Clancy) later recalled: 'The papers carried the news, and you could see the change of heart in the people. Each day, the British shot two or three, dragging it out over a few weeks. When they shot McDermott [Mac Diarmada], who was basically a cripple, and then put James Connolly into a chair to shoot him because his leg was gangrenous and he couldn't stand, well, that was it for me. I was utterly appalled and just had to do something.'[15] The British government's own Commission of Inquiry into the causes of the rebellion, itself observed 'that there is always a section of opinion in that country [Ireland] bitterly opposed to the British connection, and that at times of excitement this section can impose its sentiments on largely disinterested members of the people'.[16] If this was so, then the authorities' own actions in the wake of the Rising helped to reinforce precisely such a process. And close inspection of the rebels' last days helps explain their resonance. Patrick Pearse, on the morning of his execution, wrote movingly and tellingly to his mother: 'I just received Holy Communion. I am happy, except for the great grief of parting from you. This is the death I should have asked for if God had given me the choice of all deaths – to die a soldier's death for Ireland and for freedom. We have done right.'[17]

What *did* the Rising indicate regarding Irish republican political thinking? According to one of the most eminent survivors, Michael Collins, the rebellion had marked a departure from a doubly flawed Irish nationalist parliamentary strategy: a strategy wrong both for its suggestion that Ireland was a part of the United Kingdom (rather than an independent nation), and for its implication that the Irish should look not to themselves but to England for improving government or for the gift of freedom. Crucial to republican thinking in 1916 and long afterwards was this key notion: that parliamentary politics had been ineffective, and unavoidably so; that constitutional politics were of necessity compromising and compromised.

Indeed, one of the vital things to recognize about this most celebrated of Irish rebellions is that 1916 was as much about the battle between competing Irish political traditions as it was about Ireland's struggle against Britain. While there is no crisp boundary dividing militant Irish separatism from constitutional Irish nationalism, the sometimes blurred overlap between the two should not obscure the fact that their respective centres of gravity exist some distance from one another. And in the battle between these two traditions 1916 was a crucial encounter. In a powerful series of pamphlets written shortly before the Rising (a kind of political Four Last Songs: 'For my part, I have no more to say'),[18] Patrick Pearse had identified his own revolutionary politics with the destiny of the Irish nation, by incorporating iconic and inspirational nationalist figures into his favoured separatist tradition. Eighteenth-century United Irishman Theobald Wolfe Tone (1763–98, 'the greatest of modern Irish separatists'),[19] together with nineteenth-century Irish nationalists Thomas Davis (1814–45), James Fintan Lalor (1807–49) and John Mitchel (1815–75), were presented by Pearse as the four crucial people in developing the conception of the modern Irish nation. In the argument of these Pearsean pamphlets (*Ghosts*, *The Separatist Idea*, *The Spiritual Nation* and *The Sovereign People*), the four heroes embodied a continuous separatist tradition – of which Pearse's 1916 rebels were shortly to become the latest contingent. Against the proper standards of Tone, Davis, Lalor and Mitchel, the most recent political generation in Ireland (dominated by constitutional nationalists) had, in Pearse's view, failed most appall-ingly; but he and his conspiratorial comrades would soon and utterly change all that.

In creating this separatist Valhalla Patrick Pearse had necessarily constrained a more complex historical reality into a compellingly simple argument: that the authentic Irish political attitude was sep-aratism from Britain.[20] Here he and his 1916 comrades were firmly in the nineteenth-century Fenian tradition. In 1858 James Stephens (1825–1901) had launched a secret revolutionary group in Dublin, dedicated to the establishment of a democratic Irish republic. The fog of Conradian mystery here is nicely reflected in Stephens's organiza-tion being known initially precisely as that: 'The Organization', or 'The Brotherhood'. But the term 'Fenian' came to be used to refer to this group – in Ireland and also in America, where a large immigrant population provided it with fertile ground for growth. Though drawing on a Catholic constituency and overlapping, at times, with constitu-tional nationalist projects, the Fenians clashed with the Church and with constitutional political forces. And they were emphatically defiant rather than deferential. As one leading Irish historian has remarked, 'the real importance of Fenianism lay less in its ideas than in its attitude (with a capital A, as it were): it embodied an inspirational sense of character-building, a posture of self-respect, and the repudia-tion of servility. The Fenian, even without an actual rebellion, was a mental revolutionary.'[21]

But the Fenians could also engage in actual revolutionary violence, as in their 1867 Rising or their activities in Britain. In December 1867 a fatal Fenian explosion in Clerkenwell, London – part of an unsuc-cessful attempt to rescue imprisoned Fenians – earned them the scorn of Marx and Engels (Marx: 'Dear Fred, The last exploit of the Fenians in Clerkenwell was a very stupid thing'; Engels: 'The stupid affair in Clerkenwell was obviously the work of a few specialised fanatics').[22] Yet the Fenians, despite their overriding priority of Irish national independence, displayed more than a hint of social argument and grievance too. And they held a significant appeal: within a decade of their foundation, they appear to have attracted well over fifty thousand members. In their attitudinal defiance, their bombings, their primary focus on independence and their flirtation with social radicalism, the Fenians perhaps provide a pre-echo of later Irish republican politics.

They certainly represent a reservoir from which the 1916 rebels drew. For it was the Fenian IRB whose members planned the 1916 Rising, and that rebellion had deep roots in this clandestine, conspiratorial tradition of Irish republicanism.

But, much to Patrick Pearse's annoyance, it had not been this Fenian revolutionism that had dominated late-nineteenth- and early-twentieth-century Irish nationalist politics. Instead, the agenda had been set by the more moderate approach of the Irish Parliamentary Party (IPP), with their goal of Home Rule or limited autonomy for Ireland; the zealous politics of Patrick Pearse and his 1916 comrades were deeply atypical in the Ireland of that period. Indeed, pre-Rising Irish politics were built upon the pervasive expectation that Home Rule would come – one of those many anticipated Irish futures which surprised people by not occurring.[23] Shortly after the outbreak of war in 1914 an Irish Home Rule Bill was passed in London (its implementation suspended for one year or until the end of the war). The constitutional tradition had, it seemed, gained its objective. Catholic Ireland broadly favoured the anticipated Home Rule Ireland, a self-governing place in which their own power would be increased, their own culture more prominent. (As an IRA novelist, Peadar O'Donnell, later sneered, 'with Home Rule on the doorstep, middle-class Ireland queued up for the offices that were to be given out'.)[24] The expectation of John Redmond, IPP leader 1900–18, was that Home Rule would produce a benign era of good relations in Ireland (certainly one of those futures that did not happen). Redmond, the less famous successor to Charles Stewart Parnell in the constitutional tradition, exhibited a comparatively inclusive and moderate approach to Irish nationalist politics. He was emphatically non-revolutionary, eschewing extremes and devoting himself to peaceful and democratic political methods.

But his Home Rule ambitions were fiercely resisted by Irish – and especially Ulster – unionists. The neurotic and brilliant Edward Carson helped to lead this resistance, and unionism emerged as a lasting obstacle to the achievement of Irish nationalist goals. For while 1912 had seen the introduction of the Third Home Rule Bill, it had also witnessed the unionist Ulster Solemn League and Covenant, by which thousands pledged themselves to oppose Home Rule. This gesture was underlined with the formation in early 1913 of the Ulster Volunteer Force (UVF), a body which offered the prospect of paramilitary muscle deployed in defence of unionist politics. So both Ulster unionism and Irish nationalism showed themselves in the early twentieth century to involve constitutional and extra-constitutional strands and strategies. Ambivalence towards at least the possibility of some kinds of violence (specifically, one's own) now emerged as a key and durable aspect of twentieth-century Irish politics.

In a charmingly ironic instance of the Manichean relationship between Ulster unionism/loyalism and Irish nationalism/republican-ism, it was the creation of the aggressive UVF that prompted the formation of what was to become the IRA. Witnessing unionists bearing arms in opposition to Home Rule, nationalists responded with a similar gesture in Home Rule's defence. Thus in November 1913 in Dublin the Irish Volunteers were established, a militia whose Irish title was to be that of the IRA into which the Volunteers later evolved: Óglaigh na hÉireann (Volunteers of Ireland). Major players in the creation of the new body included scholarly patriot Eoin Mac-Neill (1867–1945), prosperous County Kerry figure Michael Joseph O'Rahilly (1875–1916) and northern nationalist Bulmer Hobson (1883–1969). The interrelation and timing of these rival – unionist-versus-nationalist – militias reinforce a point later made by one talented IRA man of the post-Rising era, George Gilmore,[25] namely that it would be wrong to assume that the threat of violence entered Irish politics with the 1916 rebellion: 'The Rising, as we know, failed in its objective, but it did not, as we are sometimes told, "bring the gun into politics". The gun was always in politics.'[26]

But the guns of 1916 – many of them held by militant Irish Volunteers – nevertheless had a powerful effect. For one thing, they helped to sink the Home Rule project of constitutional Irish nationalists like John Redmond. The latter's enthusiasm that Irish nationalists support Britain in the First World War ultimately damaged his party in Ireland, as wartime disaffection vis-à-vis the British cause grew during that conflict. And where Catholic Ireland in 1914 had been dominated by the IPP, post-1916 politics witnessed deep change: constitutional nationalism became eclipsed by an aggressive, revolutionary version of nationalist politics, embodied by those who endorsed the revolutionism of 1916. The IRA of 1919–21 were to be at the centre of this revolution-ary approach. Redmond himself had certainly felt that the Rising was aimed at destroying Home Rule and the IPP ('even more an attempt to hit us than to hit England', as he put it),[27] and the rebellion must be seen as a gesture against the Irish parliamentary tradition as much as against British rule in Ireland. By 1918, with Home Rule still not implemented, Irish nationalist politics had been radicalized, and the 1916 Rising had been a vital step along that path.

For its celebrants saw 1916 as having achieved more than much longer periods of constitutional nationalist activity had done; and as having done so in an entirely appropriate, defiant, proud spirit. To those who believed in an innate national consciousness, it seemed that the Rising had caused the awakening or rebirth of the Irish nation. In the view of one Easter rebel and later IRA man, Florence O'Donoghue, 'The military failure of the Rising proved to be less significant than the effects of its impact upon the nation's mind ... In Easter week the historic Irish nation was reborn.'[28] But it was not a stand-alone event as much as a marked accelerator of trends that can be seen prior to and after Easter Week itself. Yes, 1916 increased nationalist disaffection vis-à-vis the British war effort; but such disaffection was evident before Easter's drama. Yes, the Rising deepened sectarian animosity in Ireland, the vast majority of Irish Protestants being appalled by an overwhelmingly Catholic rebellion which they perceived as back-stabbing wartime treachery. But pre-1916 Ireland was already a deeply sectarian place. In response to perceived and actual discrimination against them by Irish Protestants, Irish Catholics had produced numerous assertive bodies aiming to promote Catholic interests. Perhaps understandably, many Catholics had looked to dominate the new Ireland which they had expected Home Rule to inaugurate; the domination that they had experienced at the hands of Irish Protestants would be replaced by their own pre-eminence.

Yes, 1916 helped give birth to a period in which an alternative, more aggressive brand of Irish nationalism replaced that of the IPP, with Sinn Féin ('Ourselves') enjoying successes in a number of by-elections in 1917 and ultimately coming to triumph throughout nationalist Ireland. But Sinn Féin's success was by no means due exclusively to the 1916 Rising. The 1918 conscription crisis – when Britain threatened to impose conscription upon a significantly unwilling Irish population – considerably strengthened Sinn Féin's hand as that party reaped the benefit of understandable anti-government feeling, amid a campaign in which the Catholic clergy were prominent and significant. Prior to the conscription crisis, small numbers of determined Irish Volunteers had looked for confrontation; with the threat of conscription, the militant nationalist cause seemed attractive to many more than these small numbers. IRA man Peadar O'Donnell underlined this point, disputing the view 'that the Tan War [the 1919–21 War of Independence] and the Sinn Féin struggle arose out of the 1916 Rising'. Even the post-rebellion executions, he argued, did not 'promote the national uprising': 'I don't believe that the executions of 1916 would have passed into ballads like '98 [the 1798 rebellion] only that the threat of conscription came on its heels and that it was the threat of conscription that forced the people onto their feet.'[29] Even Sean Clancy, that 1916 celebrant from Clare, stressed the importance of the 1918 crisis: 'The British government wanted to introduce conscription ... but nobody here wanted to get involved. We'd fight in our own country, for our own country, but not in an army we detested.'[30] So the Rising of 1916 helped to destroy the constitutional IPP and to reshape Irish nationalist politics; but its role was as an important part of a wider, longer process of demolition and change.

One kind of change which emphatically did not occur in the post-Rising years, or for some time to come, was the recreation of Ireland or of Irish nationalism along socialist lines. Yet one of the most talented and prominent of the 1916 rebels had indeed been a revolutionary socialist: James Connolly. Shelves of work have been devoted to the study of this strikingly able radical,[31] and in particular many pages to the question of Connolly's involvement in the rebellion itself. There have been many detractors, and also those – like the talented socialist republican historian, C. Desmond Greaves (1913–88) – who have celebrated Connolly's involvement in 1916. (Greaves judged the Rising 'militarily sound',[32] and considered Connolly the Irish labour movement's 'greatest leader, thinker and hero'.)[33] A number of points seem clear. Though he remained committedly socialist himself, James Connolly's socialism did not define the ideology of the 1916 rebellion as a whole. The Proclamation certainly lacked his definitive commitment to class conflict; and the respective ideologies of Connolly and Pearse clearly diverged on significant points. Connolly had defined the republican struggle in terms of revolutionary class conflict; Pearse had not done so, preferring instead a multi-class, communalist approach. Connolly had read Irish history in emphatically material terms: 'As we have again and again pointed out, the Irish question is a social question, the whole age-long fight of the Irish people against their oppressors resolves itself, in the last analysis, into a fight for the mastery of the means of life, the sources of production, in Ireland.'[34] By contrast, Pearse had explained Ireland's past in terms more spiritualized, more ethereal and less determined by the changing nature of economic relations. Pearse and Connolly were the two giants of the 1916 rebellion; but it was the former rather than the latter who had the more defining influence on the politics of the Rising. The durable and powerful legacies of 1916 did not include a socialist definition of the Irish republican struggle.

2

'Our only regret was that the escort had consisted of only two Peelers instead of six. If there had to be dead Peelers at all, six would have created a better impression than a mere two.'

Dan Breen, on the January 1919 republican ambush at
Soloheadbeg, County Tipperary, which killed two RIC men[35]

Thus 1916 has to be painted on a broad historical canvas; the battles between nationalism and unionism, between competing brands of the former, between Ireland and Britain, all preceded and all continued long after the heroic statement of Easter Week. Certainly, there is a case to be made for seeing the events of the Rising as umbilically tied to those of the years leading up to 1921, when a measure of Irish independence was attained after the War of Independence. That war is usually seen to have begun in 1919, but its roots clearly went much deeper. And many of those who emerged prominently in the 1919–21 struggle had been identified by the authorities in the immediate post-Rising period. Richard Mulcahy,[36] 1916 rebel and later Chief of Staff of the Volunteers, was after the rebellion put in the Class A category of interned rebels: people who were 'prominent extremists and most disloyal'. Mulcahy was an important figure in the IRA's 1919–21 war;

so, too were the Brennan brothers, Michael and Patrick from County
Clare – after 1916, considered by the authorities to be 'most disloyal
and extreme'.[37] For the Rising was an important reservoir of revolutionary enthusiasm, and one upon which later republicanism drew
heavily. Lines of influence or inspiration were not necessarily neat.
Dan Gleeson, a County Tipperary IRA man who joined the Irish
Volunteers in 1917, recalled having been impressed, during the
1914–16 period, by the politics of Sinn Féin founder Arthur Griffith's
Nationality, an Irish nationalist newspaper which first appeared in
1915.[38] Griffith's own brand of nationalist politics was far from clear-
cut republican, and his own preference was not for the use of political
violence. Thus distinctions between the various wings of Irish nationalism during these crucial years were far from clear; there could be a
separatist, revolutionary tinge to politics not always seen in that light.

What happened during 1916–21 was that this complex political
painting came, gradually, to be cast in more lurid, aggressive, violent
colours. There was, for one thing, a very great change in what
membership of republican groups actually meant and involved during
the five years after the Rising. Between 1916 and 1921 the Volunteers/
IRA[39] changed from a body of largely non-violent protest to one of
extremely violent anti-state activity. After 1916 there were Volunteer
attempts to obtain arms by raiding civilians as well as Crown Forces
(the problem and importance of weapon-acquisition being a priority
for the embryonic IRA as it was to remain one for the organization's
later incarnations). The reaction of the British authorities in Ireland
to such operations produced a frictional dynamic which led to the
escalation of the Anglo-Irish conflict. Yes, in 1917 and 1918 Volunteer
activity mostly involved gestures of public defiance. But these years
also saw Volunteers in prison, being rendered more militant and
zealous as a result; and the police frequently raided and searched the
houses of Volunteers and of members of the nationalist political party,
Sinn Féin; arresting such people raised rather than lowered the political
temperature, as a largely quiescent Irish nationalist people gradually
became host to a major revolutionary movement. Following raids,
imprisonment, confrontations with police and warders, incremental
immersion in greater and greater activity, the state (already of dubious
legitimacy in Irish nationalist opinion) was increasingly defined as
hostile. Arrests were often counterproductive, pushing people into the

next stage of commitment, anger and involvement. Prison played a key role here: from 1916 onwards, incarceration helped to cement people together as Irish republicans, to intensify their anti-British convictions and to produce exactly the opposite of the authorities' intended effect.

In 1917 Sinn Féin – originally a non-violent, non-republican nationalist party – was reorganized and committed itself (slightly ambiguously) to an Irish republic. In the post-Rising period this party harvested most of what had been sown in 1916, and by the time of the UK general election in December 1918 Sinn Féin was set to triumph within nationalist Ireland. Although it won under half of the total vote, the party nevertheless gained seventy-three seats to the IPP's dismal six and the twenty-six won by unionists. This was a resounding and very impressive success for the party claiming inheritance to the 1916 legacy and, following their victory, Sinn Féin set up an alternative parliament in Dublin – Dáil Éireann – which comprised those Sinn Féiners elected in 1918 and not imprisoned. This First Dáil became, for republicans, the truly legitimate authority in Ireland.

A kind of rebel government was formed, with the Dáil choosing a cabinet which included leading military men such as Michael Collins, Cathal Brugha[40] and Richard Mulcahy – men who would play a major role in leading the IRA's 1919–21 war against the British. Sinn Féin's rebel government was in part political propaganda. It was far from being a fully functioning government, but it did represent a striking way of questioning British legitimacy in Ireland. If such a rival parliament could be elected, renouncing British rule, then where did that leave British legitimacy? Irish republicans were trying to produce a kind of republic within the old British order, and they fiercely proclaimed the superior legitimacy of their post-1918 regime. As the quixotic Erskine Childers put it in 1919, the Dáil was 'composed of the elected representatives of the Irish nation, and the only authority in Ireland with the moral sanction of a democracy behind it'.[41] And as the republican chronicler Dorothy Macardle lucidly expressed it: 'The Irish people had applied the principle of self-determination to their own case with an unequivocal result'; the 1918 election 'had recorded an overwhelming demand for independence'.[42]

It was on 21 January 1919 that Dáil Éireann first met in Dublin. A Declaration of Independence was read and endorsed, proclaiming the Irish a free people committed to complete independence from Britain.

A democratic programme was adopted, a statement of social and economic policy almost certainly more radical than the actual views of most Dáil members. On the same day, by chance, a Volunteer ambush in County Tipperary saw two Royal Irish Constabulary (RIC) men fatally shot. The coincidence of timing might give an impression that parliamentary and military republican forces were seamlessly one at this point; in fact, the Soloheadbeg ambush in Tipperary was the product of local initiative rather than political or central command. Indeed, the operation was conceived precisely because of a fear by local republican military men that they were (in the words of Dan Breen, one of the Soloheadbeg ambushers) 'in great danger of becoming merely a political adjunct to the Sinn Féin organisation'.[43] There was no major violent action by republicans for two months after Soloheadbeg; there was no sudden, pre-planned escalation to war, and such activity remained at low levels during 1919, with many ordinary Volunteers understandably reluctant to get involved in violence.

Political movement had, however, occurred. In April 1919 Eamon de Valera[44] (dramatically sprung from Lincoln Jail two months earlier) was elected by the Dáil as President of the Council of Ministers. De Valera was now head of the Irish government, in republican eyes, and as such he appointed a new cabinet: Arthur Griffith (Home Affairs), Count Plunkett (Foreign Affairs), Cathal Brugha (Defence), Michael Collins (Finance), W. T. Cosgrave (Local Government), Constance Markievicz (Labour), Eoin MacNeill (Industries). Of these newly prominent figures, Collins was to run a kind of revolution-within-the-revolution. Dáil Minister of Finance, Volunteer Director of Organization then Intelligence, he had also (in May 1919) become President of a revivified IRB, a position that he held until his death three years later. This IRB, as a secret organization that continued after the foundation of Dáil Éireann, reflected the tendency of these years towards overlapping revolutions, towards conspiracies within the revolutionary conspiracy.

Collins and the other cycling revolutionaries (Richard Mulcahy later recalled that 'For [Collins] as for the rest of us the bicycle provided mobility; this was our main protection')[45] were to witness a gradual growth of violence during 1919, with the IRA during that year becoming rather more of an army: guns and fighting now became a more significant part of what it involved, and in mid-1919 the organization was duly proscribed. The logic of these years was frequently that of an escalatory, tit-for-tat dialogue of violence.[46] Sometimes the tit-for-tat cycle burned out quickly; sometimes it continued; and sometimes it resulted in violence becoming more widespread. In the last two situations, the appropriate image is one of violence as a self-sustaining phenomenon. From 1918 onwards, the British response to republican subversion frequently involved punishing the wider population for IRA activities: this had the unintended – indeed, counterproductive – effect of strengthening the very IRA that it was intended to undermine. Republican action provoked state reaction; violence was followed by revenge then counter-retaliation and then war. British reprisals undermined British legitimacy in Irish nationalist (and other) eyes; 'Their campaign of terror was defeating itself', as Ernie O'Malley wrote of 1921.[47] Leading County Clare IRA man Michael Brennan wrote of the same year that 'the British reprisals, instead of turning the people against us as the cause of their miseries, had thrown them strongly behind us'.[48] Crown Forces, frustrated at not being able to convict those responsible for attacking, injuring and killing their comrades, resorted to reprisals targeted against violent opponents, but affecting (and causing disaffection among) much wider numbers than that. And to republican enthusiasts such actions were the inevitable, necessary consequence of malign British involvement in Ireland: 'A war of conquest, such as England's war against Ireland, develops, inevitably, into a campaign of terrorism against the people.'[49]

Provocation, retaliation and counter-revenge between the opposing sides produced sequences of interlocking reprisals and cycles of violence which – once ignited – could prove nastily self-fuelling. The local nature of such dynamics is important: here, as so often, it was local impulses and attrition rather than centralized planning that drove the War of Independence. IRA activity in these years was unevenly spread: it was especially intense in the south-west of Ireland (Cork being a particular fire-centre) and in Dublin city, and local revolutionism was the prism through which national republicanism tended to be viewed. Linked to this was the vital role played by certain individuals in attracting people to the IRA, in leading them and stimulating action, in determining the pace of local war. The IRA operated very much at local level according to spontaneous local initiative, much less a centralized army than an aggregation of varied local groups, with

Headquarters following the localities at least as much as the other way round.

In 1920 the war escalated; in the spring the first IRA flying columns came into existence, spontaneously, in active areas. These units came in a variety of sizes and types: as ever, the IRA did not conform to one neat pattern. The emergence of bodies of committed men in these columns was very important. Physically detached from home communities, these full-time soldiers on the move could engage in ambushes over wide areas; having broken with their former lives, they lived life on the run amid an atmosphere of utter commitment and of deepened contact with comrades. Until autumn 1920, most IRA Volunteers still lived at home, and were brought into action for IRA activities that did not involve violence; only a small number of IRA people had at this stage gone beyond this. But those who *had* left their home areas were much more likely to engage in offensive violence. Once active IRA men became separate from the restraining influences of their community, then killing became easier. These were the people who drove the war, just as their image came to define a much later memory of the IRA: the romantically alluring, trench-coated gunman, living the outlaw life of insurrection.

Romantic images abound from these years, whether in later creations (such as writer Ronan Bennett's television drama, *Rebel Heart*)[50] or in evidence from the IRA's own activities, such as one Westmeath IRA man's revolutionary honeymoon in 1920, during which his wife carried a Mills bomb and a Parabellum (a pistol)![51] But, romantic or not, the 1919–21 war undoubtedly grew vicious. During 1920–1 there was much violence which would have shocked most Irish people only a few years before. Many of those killed during the conflict – on all sides – were in no position to defend themselves. Just as in later phases of Irish republican-British conflict, the deaths often came less out of battle than out of the armed killing of undefended opponents. The sequence of killings was a gruesome one. In March 1920 Tomás MacCurtain (1884–1920) – Cork 1916 rebel, and subsequently IRA leader and Sinn Féin lord mayor of Cork – was shot dead in front of his wife (probably by the police). In October of the same year MacCurtain's fellow 1916 Cork rebel, fellow IRA man and successor as Sinn Féin lord mayor of Cork, Terence MacSwiney (1879–1920), died in a London prison on hunger strike after a brave seventy-four days.

And the following month saw more dreadful violence. On 1 November 1920 the IRA's youthful Kevin Barry was hanged in Mountjoy Jail for his part in an IRA raid in Dublin in which three (youthful) British soldiers had been killed. It seems that the execution was partly intended to prevent Army reprisals for IRA attacks.[52] But Barry none the less entered popular Irish republican memory, not least because a famous ballad was to focus upon him. Heroic, self-sacrificing and unquestionably dignified in the face of execution, Barry was in death deployed to help discredit British government in Ireland: his youth and bravery offered valuable publicity for the anti-British cause.

Then on 21 November 1920 – the original Irish 'Bloody Sunday' – the IRA in Dublin struck at the British intelligence network, killing over a dozen people and wounding six (some of these victims not, in fact, being intelligence agents). Later in the day more killings took place: two arrested IRA men (Dick McKee and Peadar Clancy) were killed – allegedly while trying to escape; and at a Gaelic football match in Dublin's Croke Park, Crown Forces (searching for wanted men, and perhaps coming under fire) killed twelve people. Those responsible for the Croke Park killings were Auxiliaries, a Division recruited from among demobilized British Army officers and first arriving in Ireland in the summer of 1920 (owing to the rising temperature of the war there). The Auxiliaries gained a reputation – often deservedly – for brutality and reprisal. (They too suffered, of course: a week after Bloody Sunday, eighteen Auxiliaries were killed by the IRA at an ambush in County Cork.) The Black and Tans (British ex-servicemen recruited to reinforce the police in Ireland, and initially decked out in mixed uniform) became similarly notorious for retaliatory excesses:[53] 'a body whose unsavoury record stinks in the nostrils of the civilised world',[54] as they were described by one republican opponent. In September 1920 the killing of a police officer in Balbriggan prompted the Black and Tans to terrorize the County Dublin town, in a spree of burning and violence which left two men dead. The sack of Balbriggan became, justly, famous. But even comparatively minor acts by the Tans could become etched into lasting Irish nationalist memory as evidence of their unambiguous villainy. County Donegal poet Pat Doherty thus recorded a 1921 Tan raid on Carrowmenagh which was rough but far from lethal, the concluding lines of his poem declaring:

But on the general judgement day,
When they stand at God's right hand,
There will be little mercy for the military,
And a damned sight less for the Black and Tans.[55]

The inability of the RIC to deal with the IRA had prompted the introduction of Crown Forces, who intensified the conflict and who helped to undermine the British cause in Ireland. And the British authorities were plagued (as they were to be in the north in the late twentieth century) by a refusal to acknowledge how widespread Sinn Féinish sympathy actually was.

It was not only in Ireland, however, that the IRA were active during the War of Independence. IRA units active in Britain itself were formed in 1919 and 1920, with notable groups in Liverpool, London, Manchester and Newcastle. Perhaps a thousand men enrolled in the British IRA during the period July 1920–July 1921, most of them born or brought up or permanently settled in Britain, and there were hundreds of IRA actions in Britain during 1920–1.[56] In the words of one IRA man and Sinn Féiner active in England during the revolution, 'There is no doubt that by the activities of the IRA in Britain much uneasiness was created.'[57] But the centre of IRA gravity lay, of course, in Ireland itself. And here the battle between the IRA and the police, the RIC, was a vital one. One County Galway IRA activist of this period, Pádraig Ó Fathaigh, held the RIC to be 'the most bitter and most potent enemies of Irish national movements',[58] and certainly they were a potentially destructive opponent. The pre-First World War RIC had been local figures of some importance, experiencing deference and respect in the community; as one leading historian has neatly put it, 'Pre-war policemen touched their caps less often than other caps were touched to them.'[59] These men were Irish and most of them Catholic. But their local knowledge and activities were dangerous for those very different Irish people who comprised the IRA. So republicans set about excluding the RIC from Irish society through systematic social ostracization, with the consequence that the RIC's sources of local information tended to dry up and render them less effective in countering republican subversion.

Delegitimizing and ostracizing the local law-enforcers – brutal though it frequently was – made considerable revolutionary sense. De

Valera himself had favoured the social ostracism of the police, and the Dáil decreed a peaceful boycott in April 1919: social contact, and those places frequented by the RIC, were to be avoided. So, during 1918–20, efforts to isolate the force spread across nationalist Ireland. People were warned, as in County Roscommon in June 1920, 'to have no intercourse with the RIC, that there was a general boycott of that force'. Such efforts yielded results. In the same month the authorities noted, in relation to similar notices in County Mayo, that the boycotted police were 'only able to obtain supplies through friends, who smuggle them in in the early hours of the morning'. On 26 June of the same year, at Drumshambo, County Leitrim, police discovered a notice warning people against further dealings with the RIC; subsequently, the police were refused supplies. Anti-police activity could be more menacing still, embodying darker attitudes and actions. On the 28th an RIC constable was shot and wounded while home on leave in the Tralee district of County Kerry, the authorities noting that the motive was 'to deter the constable and compel him to resign'.[60] People were individually and brutally targeted for their dealings with the police. In July 1920, a woman who cooked for the RIC (Mary Duffy of Carrickmacross, County Monaghan) was 'threatened with death if she does any police cooking'.[61] Girlfriends of policemen and soldiers were frequently subjected to the brutal removal of their hair.

There were IRA attacks on outlying RIC barracks. Police officers were therefore moved to larger barracks, with the IRA then destroying those that had been evacuated.[62] By the end of 1919 the physical separation of police from people had developed a long way; by mid-1920 the RIC was in deep crisis. Ostracizing the police was a crucial precondition to shooting them, and the RIC were a major target for the IRA during this war (165 being killed in 1920 alone).[63] Representatives of the British state in Ireland, and local opponents of some value if interwoven into the community, their isolation was a symbolic and practical strategy for the IRA.[64]

By mid-1921 a stalemate had emerged in this localized, often brutal war. Many Volunteers felt that the weak position of the IRA effectively forced upon republicans the decision to accept what the British were to offer in the Treaty later that year; but it is far from clear that the IRA were in fact defeated by the summer of 1921. They were certainly possessed of an intense republican commitment. But what did this entail in practice? What *was* the IRA's thinking in the 1919–21 War of Independence? The political foundation of their thought was self-determination for Ireland: British rule in Ireland denied the Irish right to independence; as such it was profoundly illegitimate. To the aristocratic Irish republican and former 1916 rebel, Constance Markievicz, English law in Ireland in 1919 was 'but legalised oppression';[65] to the IRA's Tom Barry, it was the Crown Forces of 1920 that were truly 'the terrorists'.[66] After the 1918 general election and Sinn Féin's success, republicans considered they had been given a powerful mandate. Speaking about that election, the fiery Dan Breen observed: 'It was the greatest manifestation of self-determination recorded in history. On the principles proclaimed by Britain and her allies, our claim to complete independence was unanswerable.'[67] Britain's difficulties with Catholic Ireland had long existed: the 1800 Act of Union had created the United Kingdom of Great Britain and Ireland, and had been followed by a century during which much Irish political energy had gone into movements espousing some form of nationalist cause. Now there was an aggressive, combative republican movement, with a military wing, demanding full sovereignty and independence from Britain as an absolute right.

Not that these revolutionaries set out neatly defined blueprints of the Ireland they sought. Far from it. For their capacity to hold together a broad-based movement during 1919–21 depended on their *not* defining too precisely the kind of end-product they desired. Even Sinn Féin's 1917 commitment to a republic had been equivocal and ambiguous: 'Sinn Féin aims at securing the international recognition of Ireland as an independent Irish republic. Having achieved that status, the Irish people may, by referendum, freely choose their own form of government.'[68] For it was not just strict republicans who were in the republican movement, and cracks would start to become clear once definite political possibilities were discussed. For the period up until 1921, however, an ill-defined republic was offered as the goal of a united republican movement; and the IRA claimed to represent everyone and every creed in their avoidance of overly specific – and therefore divisive – political programmes.

In a sense, the simpler the politics, the better. For the IRA of these years – a prototypical guerrilla force – was primarily in the business of soldiership, and it was military thinking on which it focused. Just as

Patrick Pearse had ultimately decided upon a hostile view of parliamentary compromises, so likewise did the IRA of 1919–21. They held that force was essential to the achievement of progress and freedom for Ireland. It did not matter to the IRA that in the 1918 general election Sinn Féin had not campaigned for a mandate to use force in driving the British out of Ireland. For, just as in 1916, no prior electoral mandate was deemed necessary for the use of violence in freeing one's country. And while sheer survival was the primary task for IRA units in the localities, the republican army did have aims which nicely combined the rational and the visceral. One could hit back at Britain – for immediate and longer-standing wrongs inflicted upon the Irish – while simultaneously pursuing a rational strategy: namely, to raise the costs of British engagement above the level at which Britain judged them worth paying. If British government were to be paralysed in Ireland, if British forces carried out reprisals that undermined the authorities in Ireland (and embarrassed them in Britain and abroad), then some kind of leverage might be gained over a far more powerful enemy than could be defeated in the field. Revenge and rationality could be served with the same rifle. So it was the principles of General Clausewitz, rather than those of Wolfe Tone, that ultimately guided the IRA of 1919–21: 'If our opponent is to be made to comply with our will, we must place him in a situation which is more oppressive to him than the sacrifice which we demand.'[69]

Armed with this premise, small groups of people could indeed change the world – provided that their own intense views produced echoes among a wider population. If nationalist Ireland was already sceptical about the legitimacy of British rule in Ireland, then the state violence stimulated by the IRA would be seen as oppressive and illegitimate, and the IRA's strategy might work, with Irish nationalist hostility to British rule being deepened by experience of the conflict. And violence offered not merely a means to the achievement of a political end, but an appropriate stance, attitude and posture in itself: the IRA were not asking for Ireland's freedom, but defiantly grasping it in their self-reliant, self-respecting hands. Like the Fenians before them, these were attitudinal revolutionaries, defined as much by their defiant attitude as by their actions.

*

What of the relations between the IRA and their political republican counterparts in Sinn Féin? In some cases they were the same people, and there are those who have denied any tension or separation between the 1919–21 military and political wings of the movement. Richard Mulcahy – eminent IRA soldier and also Dáil minister – was one: 'there was no clash of any kind either of thought or feeling or action between any of the members of the government or members of the parliament, and those who were conducting the Volunteer work, either at top or throughout the country'.[70] Yet this probably presents too cosy and neat an image. The IRA long retained an ambivalent attitude towards the Dáil, and not until August 1919 was a serious effort made to bring the Volunteers under its control. The Volunteer Executive then agreed that their soldiers had to take an oath of allegiance to the Dublin Dáil, but the military and political wings of the movement continued substantially separate lives. It was not until the spring of 1921 – by which time the War of Independence was almost over – that the Dáil agreed that it should publicly accept responsibility for the IRA's actions. It would, in fact, have been difficult for the Dáil (as it was at times even for the IRA's own central authorities) to impose control on the army throughout the country.

Thus for a long time the soldiers were not over-keen to be subject to the Dáil, while the politicians were hesitant to claim authority over the army. The IRA's own paper, *An t-Óglách*, presented the organization as 'a military body pure and simple', asserted confidently that 'the successful maintenance of the Irish Volunteer is the one thing essential to the triumph of the cause of the Irish Republic' and stressed that IRA men 'should not allow their political activities to interfere with their military duties'.[71] There was, at times, an anti-political quality to the IRA's thinking, if politics are held to imply constitutional-style practice. For if the IPP's parliamentarianism was seen as useless (or worse), embodying betrayal and compromise, then there might also be grounds for anxiety about even republican politicians. It was 'as a soldier'[72] that Ernie O'Malley saw himself, and his IRA comrades shared that self-image (Dan Breen: 'I was a soldier first and foremost';[73] Tom Maguire: 'I always had what I will call military leanings. I loved reading about battles, both at home and abroad').[74] And while their violence was clearly political violence – arising from a political conflict, and reflecting political beliefs and goals – it was emphatically violence rather than politics that defined the army's self-image. The IRA had, in the words of one of their eminent figures – Liam Lynch – 'to hew the way for politics to follow'.[75] And for many of these men the 1919–21 struggle, and their soldierly career during those years, represented something of a mythic period in their lives: the most successful part of their career, and a glorious high-ground which their post-revolutionary experience would never succeed in recreating or recapturing.

And if there were political and military dimensions to the IRA's thinking, there was also an important cultural argument there too. No simple causal connection existed between cultural nationalism and IRA enthusiasm, but during the War of Independence there was considerable overlap in membership and allegiance between the IRA, the IRB, Sinn Féin, the Gaelic League and the Gaelic Athletic Association (GAA). The latter two organizations – both late-nineteenth-century creations – provided the IRA with a reservoir of recruits and cultural resources upon which to draw. Many Gaelic enthusiasts considered Ireland's cultural and political wars to be interwoven, and nationalist cultural involvement could strengthen militant republican commitment. Defiantly non-English, the Gaelic League, for example, saw the Gaelic language as a symbol of Irish cultural distinctiveness. Such a view reinforced the kind of arguments that lay at the heart of the IRA's own thinking: Ireland should properly be seen as an independent culture and polity, fully separate from a Britain that had oppressed and obscured it for centuries. Authentic Irishness would be restored by a process of de-anglicization; if the IRA fought to free Ireland politically from Britain's grip, then they also looked to emancipate Irish culture from an ill-fitting British one (Michael Collins: 'English civilisation, while it may suit the English people, could only be alien to us';[76] Ernie O'Malley: 'We had fought a civilisation which did not suit us. We had striven to give complete expression to the genius of the race').[77] A free Ireland would be a Gaelic one.

What of the broader cultural and social thinking of the IRA? They were overwhelmingly Catholic in background, and the profoundly religious sense evident among the republican revolutionaries[78] was one that was deeply Catholic.[79] Irish Catholicism was a powerful, pervasive influence on the intellectual formation of the revolutionary generation: a disproportionately large number of those involved in 1916 and beyond had been educated at Christian Brothers' Schools, which tended more than others to stress the importance of Irish history and of the glories of a distinctive Gaelic civilization. In the post-Rising years many Catholic clergy were sympathetic and practically helpful to the republican political cause. By the early twentieth century, indeed, Irish nationalist grievance had effectively become the grievance of Irish Catholics against those (British and Irish Protestants, for the most part) who had wronged them. Certainly, for many in the IRA itself, religious identification and national identification were inextricably interwoven, with a clear interlinking of national with religious faith.[80] Similarly, the soul of the nation was tied to the spirit of sacrifice. In the staccato reminiscences of leading republican Frank Gallagher (1898–1962), 'Strange what life death gives ... It seems that only by tragedy the soul of a people may be saved ... From the beginning of this awakening, tragedy, or the shadow of it, has been the dominant motif ... The executions in 1916; [Volunteer Thomas] Ashe's death in 1917 [after hunger strike]; the solemn preparations in 1918 to fight conscription to the death ... The murder of the lord mayor of Cork.'[81]

The Irish Republican Army was also a male affair, with the role of women in the struggle generally celebrated in what a later age would read as very conservative terms. From Easter Week 1916 to the early 1920s, female republicans, in bodies such as Cumann na mBan (Irishwomen's Council), were emphatically auxiliary to the boys' own struggle. 1916 rebel Frank Henderson (1886–1959: CBS-educated, with a career involving the GAA, Gaelic League and Irish Volunteers) recalled Cumann na mBan women in the Dublin Rising in terms of the medical and culinary help that they had offered the men ('They cooked our food and served it to us').[82] By 1922 little, apparently, had changed: 'The Cumann na mBan ... are providing comforts for prisoners as far as their resources allow.'[83] The IRA's Tom Barry praised the women's organization as having been invaluable to the IRA in the War of Independence; but in doing so he set out their decidedly auxiliary role: the Cumann na mBan 'were groups of women and girls from town and countryside, sisters, relatives or friends of the Volunteers, enrolled in their own organisation, for the sole purpose of helping the Irish Republican Army. They were indispensable to the army, nursing the wounded and sick, carrying dispatches, scouting, acting as intelligence agents, arranging billets, raising funds, knitting, washing, cooking for the active service men and burying our dead.'[84]

The boys themselves tended to be young (Ernie O'Malley: 'we saw things through the eyes of youth').[85] They represented a broad class spectrum, though with a bias towards the middling classes and with least representation at the upper and lower extremes, among the very rich or the very poor.[86] Some scholars have argued that a key ingredient in the IRA's 1919–21 war was a sense of social or status resentment among a Catholic lower-middle class. On this reading, anger at the existing order would have sprung from a mismatch between educational attainment and available employment opportunities, and the key battle was one between differing sections of the Irish middle class.[87] There is certainly something in this, but it is also true that the IRA themselves claimed to represent a comprehensive community of all classes and creeds in Ireland. 'The boys', 'the lads', 'the organization', presented themselves as embodying an inclusive nation, their own brotherhood band a microcosm of the new Ireland that they sought to create. IRA men often joined as part of a group, informal networks of friendship and camaraderie being carried over into the army.

Yet clearly any definition that made membership of the republican group meaningful for those inside it, carried also the probability of excluding those who did not possess the keys to inclusion. If this was a Catholic organization redressing Catholic grievances, then what of Irish Protestants? If this was a group that equated anti-separatism with anti-Irishness, then what of those many Irish people – unionist *or* nationalist – who disapproved of the IRA? (Even Ernie O'Malley noted that a 'good number' of Irish nationalists themselves had reservations about IRA violence.)[88] And for those outside the IRA's community or group, the Irish revolution could involve dreadful experiences. With the significant exception of the north-east, Protestants across much of Ireland had, by 1919, become a rather vulnerable group with little political power. In County Clare, with an overwhelmingly Catholic population, republican attacks on Protestants included the burning of churches, and were motivated by more than the pursuit of land or arms. But while Clare Protestants during the War of Independence had reason to fear for their property and security, it should be said that the IRA did not kill Protestant civilians there. The same cannot be said of revolutionary Cork. Here, during the Irish revolution, the IRA did indeed shoot some people because they were Protestant. For Protestants were seen as outside the community: what bound the IRA together necessarily excluded Protestant neighbours. It was not just a question of shootings: the seizure of farms and the burning of homes were overwhelmingly targeted at Protestants in County Cork, an ugly part of the wider sectarian violence that plagued these years in Irish history, on all sides.[89]

Police, Protestants, ex-soldiers, tramps, tinkers could all be targeted by the IRA for the crime of being outside the community in this vicious political war. Thus the IRA's revolutionary thinking was many-layered. They fought for Irish self-determination, for political freedom from British rule. They espoused the politics of violence and intended to force Britain to yield, while simultaneously hitting back in revenge at the old enemy. They wanted cultural as well as political freedom, an Ireland authentic and Gaelic. They were Catholic revolutionaries, young, male, cross-class and bound by ties of friendship and local allegiance. The ideological and the non-ideological interacted here. Self-determination appealed to the IRA, but so too could the excitement of glamorous, clandestine adventure, and the release from quotidian dullness. These young men were fighting to free themselves from Britain, but in their defiant fighting they also often freed themselves from tiresome parental restriction. One owed allegiance to Ireland, but also to individual leaders and friends whose example could sometimes be the decisive factor in one's revolutionary path. The rebels of the IRA fought out of conviction; but many of them also drew a salary and found in the alternative republican army a form of professional satisfaction and reward for which they looked elsewhere in vain.

3

'Sooner or later in political life one has to compromise. Everyone does.'

Oscar Wilde[90]

July 1921 brought a truce between the stalemated forces of the British Crown and the IRA. These were ambiguous days. As writer and republican Frank O'Connor put it,

> No one who lived through it is ever likely to forget the summer of 1921. To some it seemed a triumph; to some, a disaster. Volunteer headquarters began upon an intensive campaign of organisation, recruiting, drilling and arming. All over the country summer training camps were established at which Volunteers were put through the usual paces of regular soldiers. British headquarters prepared for real war, gigantic concentration camps, wholesale roundups ... Yet, for all the preparations for war, there was throughout the country far too great a feeling of confidence. It was only natural that this should be so; it was the British who had asked for peace.[91]

But what precisely *was* the position at the time of the truce? The IRA were probably far from beaten, at least in the sense of being on the verge of utter collapse; but they had no sign of imminent victory. So with neither the IRA nor the British close to landing a knock-out blow, the logic of stalemate pointed towards compromise.

Certainly, this would make sense for the IRA at some stage. There had never been any chance of formal military victory over their imperially powerful opponent, nor – in practice – of the British recognizing an Irish republic.[92] And it remained far from clear just how many people – even among Irish nationalists – actually favoured or would continue to favour an IRA campaign. There was no short-age of broad republican sympathy – Sinn Féin gained 124 seats unopposed in the southern Irish elections of May 1921. But Sinn Féinish sympathy did not automatically mean enthusiasm for IRA violence. Still, in August a Second Dáil was formed and in October 1921 a republican delegation (including Michael Collins and Arthur Griffith) went to London to negotiate with the British (for whom the main delegates included Lloyd George and Winston Churchill). De Valera – President of the Dáil and leading symbol of the revolutionary movement – decided to remain in Ireland. He insisted that the Irish delegation should consult with the Dublin cabinet before concluding any deal with the British. His thinking was that his own formulation (Irish external association with, but not membership of, the British Commonwealth) should be the limit of Irish compromise on the question of relations with the British Crown and empire. He knew it to be unlikely that external association would be granted by the British, and he anticipated that their refusal would lead to the brink of a renewed conflict. Believing this to be a conflict that the British would, in fact, be reluctant to renew, de Valera anticipated that at this point he himself would step in and make a compromise deal, the best one available to the Irish at that moment. His strategy was thus to retain a veto on any proposed settlement in London, with a view to his own, personal, last-minute conclusion of a deal.

But on 6 December 1921, under intense British pressure, the Irish delegates scuppered their leader's plan by signing an Anglo-Irish Treaty; they had failed to hold out until the point at which de Valera could intervene. De Valera and his cabinet were thus presented with a Treaty already accomplished, and Irish revolutionary nationalism was to split violently as a consequence.

The 1921 Treaty involved the setting up of an Irish Free State, comprising twenty-six of Ireland's thirty-two counties (broadly speaking, the nationalist, southern portion of the island). It offered qualified autonomy, demanded inclusion in the British Commonwealth, witnessed the formal partitioning of Ireland and meant that the new Ireland had to stomach symbolic remnants of the British Crown with an oath of allegiance and a Governor-General. This deal amounted to more than the Home Rule offer of 1914, though whether the difference between the two was great enough to judge it worth all the intervening death, pain and division is a question on which opinion has long varied. The divide between Irish nationalist and Ulster unionist had been – perhaps irrevocably – deepened by the events of 1916–21; but so too now there was to open up a bloody schism between nationalist and nationalist in Ireland.

The terms of the Treaty were announced on 7 December 1921. Seven days later the Dáil began to debate it, a debate which continued until 7 January 1922 when the epochal Anglo-Irish Treaty was accepted by sixty-four votes to fifty-seven. Republican Ireland – Dáil, cabinet, IRA, IRB, the Sinn Féin party – was profoundly divided over the Treaty. In this split, some followed particular leaders and friends, some were motivated by pre-existing animosities and antagonisms, and all were focused on the momentous argument that raged. For the Treaty, spoke the charismatic Michael Collins: a compelling leader, a revolutionary administrator and improviser of striking ability; a man who has latterly become a figure of mythic stature in modern Ireland, commemorated in book and film alike,[93] but one who was contemporaneously celebrated too (he was offered £10,000 in the early 1920s to write his memoirs). This hero and signatory to the Treaty considered that the deal represented Irish nationalists' achievement of 'the substance of freedom',[94] and the best deal then attainable. The Treaty did not give the revolutionaries all that they had sought; but it could be the foundation on which the construction of the full republic could be built, the stepping-stone towards the ultimate goal.

Arthur Griffith, like Collins an eminent signatory to the Treaty, took a similar approach. Griffith presented it 'not as the ideal thing', but rather as a deal that guarded key Irish interests; it was, he said, 'a Treaty of equality': 'We have brought back the flag; we have brought back the evacuation of Ireland after 700 years by British troops and the formation of an Irish army. We have brought back to Ireland her full rights and powers of fiscal control.'[95] Batt O'Connor (who had been close to Collins during the War of Independence) read the terms of the Treaty 'with profound thankfulness, both for what they gave in fact, and for what they held in promise for the future'.[96] Piaras Béaslaí, one of the IRA's leading publicists, also supported the Treaty, recognizing both the difficulties and the attractions of the new deal:

Although nobody seriously expected the Treaty to recognise an independent republic, separated from the British empire, yet the terms of the Treaty, when published, seemed a bitter pill to separatists ... To the ordinary people, whose vague national aspirations had not crystallised into reasoned doctrines, the Treaty appeared in the light of a big victory, a great advance in national status; and the older generation, remembering their thirty years['] support of the Parliamentary Party in a struggle for 'Home Rule', saw embodied in the Treaty enormously more powers for Ireland than were ever dreamed of in any Home Rule Bill.[97]

The Treaty was not the republic; but it offered significant freedoms, and if it was rejected then how long would the IRA be able to hold out, if faced with intense war? Such pragmatic reflections made little impression on some. Eamon de Valera, speaking in Limerick on the day before the signing, had argued that it was 'for complete freedom that they in Ireland were struggling';[98] once the compromise deal had been struck, many republicans considered that it fell too far short of that sense of complete freedom. Austin Stack, a leading IRA man and Sinn Féiner from County Kerry, stated forthrightly that even if the Treaty 'gave Ireland full Canadian powers, he, for one, would not accept that status for Ireland. This country had never been "a child of England's". Membership of the empire, an oath to the English king, a contract by which Irishmen would acknowledge themselves British subjects, was abhorrent to him. "Has any man here," he asked [the Dáil], "the hardihood to stand up and say that it was for this our fathers have suffered, if it was for this our comrades have died on the field and in the barrack yard?"'[99]

To many of those who opposed the 1921 deal, it was important that much had been suffered in pursuit of a goal now apparently to be betrayed. Mary MacSwiney – whose brother Terence was among the IRA's famous dead – saw the issue as simply 'between right and wrong': 'Search your souls tonight [she told the Dáil in December 1921] and in the face of every martyr that ever died for Ireland take an oath in your own hearts now that you will do what is right no matter what influences have been brought to bear on you.'[100]

Interestingly, it was not on the partitioning of Ireland into north and south that opponents of the 1921 Treaty focused their attention; even in those southern counties close to the new border, the partition issue was not prominent.[101] Nor was it true that a person's opposition to the Treaty automatically implied that they would accept only the full republic. During the Dáil's private session to discuss the Treaty, de

Valera introduced his own alternative 'Document No. 2' (Document No. 1 being the Treaty). His alternative was essentially the Anglo-Irish Treaty plus his own formulation of external association with the Commonwealth. Although this proposal elicited no great enthusiasm, and was therefore withdrawn by de Valera, it did show his preparedness to accept something less than absolute republican separation. Yet many anti-Treatyites wanted just that: the full republic rather than some emotionally unsatisfactory compromise. Though it is doubtful whether IRA zealots' own aspirations and hopes had ever been fully represent-ative of wider nationalist opinion, many of these republican soldiers understandably found it difficult to travel down from their millenar-ian mountain-top to the less enthralling lower pastures of practical compromise.

No deal was going to satisfy all shades of opinion within the revolutionary movement: it had been far too diverse a phenomenon for that. And there were attractive arguments on both sides of this increasingly bitter split. Pro-Treatyites could claim that a substantially free Irish state, with an Irish government in Dublin, deserved to be recognized as a major achievement; and that the endorsement of this new world by the Dáil and – more emphatically – by the electorate demanded that the Treaty dispensation be acknowledged as legitimate. For if the stepping-stone thesis was key to the Dáil's acceptance of the Treaty, then it seems to have had an even more persuasive impact upon wider popular opinion. For the June 1922 general election saw anti-Treaty candidates win only thirty-six of 128 seats, and no anti-Treaty candidate headed the poll in any constituency; in contested constituencies, pro-Treaty candidates averaged 5,174 votes, anti-Treatyites only 3,372.[102] Irish nationalists had overwhelmingly rejected anti-Treatyite politics, and in doing so it might be argued that they were merely recognizing that the realities of power – British versus Irish – were likely to lead, at some point, to the compromise of full Irish republican ambition.

Vitally important though these points are, however, there remains no simple equation possible between the 1921 Treaty and democracy on one side, and anti-Treatyite politics and opposition to democ-racy on the other. For the context of the 1921 deal was the very real threat that, if it was not accepted by the Irish, then Britain might go back to ruthless war in Ireland. The British threat of force meant that

Irish nationalists were not making their decision about their future in the context of a fully free choice. Moreover, the anti-Treaty IRA could reasonably suggest that their pro-Treaty opponents' adherence to electorally expressed majority opinion was inconsistent with the republican struggle of 1916–21 in which they had all been engaged. If majority Irish endorsement of something short of full independence was acceptable in 1922, then where did that leave the legitimacy of the 1916 rebels? If one required an electoral mandate for the pursuit of IRA violence, then why had they fought from 1919 onwards at all? Many in the IRA saw their role as that of a vanguard protecting the prior rights of the Irish nation, an army that led rather than followed popular opinion. As Ernie O'Malley pithily put it: 'If [we had consulted the feelings of the people] we would never have fired a shot. If we gave them a good strong lead, they would follow.'[103]

Anti-Treaty IRA argument, then, had a certain measure of consistency to it. Not reliant on prior mandates – indeed, sometimes rather scornful of them – the IRA anti-Treatyites felt justified in fighting on for the full republic. Unlike the majority of the Irish people, the bulk of the IRA went anti-Treaty. And the painful disintegration of the revolutionary movement – epitomized in clashes between rival groups of IRA soldiers over who should inherit RIC barracks[104] – often involved bitter personal divisions and the intensification of pre-existing antagonisms. The Treaty conflict was a palimpsest, with ideological and personal layers at times obscuring one another. The sharp division between pro-Treatyite Michael Collins and Richard Mulcahy, and anti-Treatyite Cathal Brugha and Austin Stack, long predated arguments over the 1921 Treaty; throughout the country, personal allegiance frequently mattered more than strict attachment to ideological principle.

In March 1922 the anti-Treaty IRA rejected the Dáil's authority – in their view, the Dáil had made the wrong choice – and the following month a section of the anti-Treaty forces took over the Four Courts building by the river Liffey in the centre of Dublin. Having acquired this military headquarters, some of the IRA's ablest irreconcilables (Liam Mellows, Rory O'Connor, Peadar O'Donnell, Ernie O'Malley) now defiantly challenged the new regime; other buildings in the capital were also occupied. The strategy hardly made any practical sense, though with its echoes of 1916 it had considerable symbolic power.

The pro-Treaty authorities were not going to allow this Dublin defiance to persist indefinitely, however, and on 28 June 1922 the Irish Civil War effectively began when Free State forces (using guns provided by the British) attacked their former comrades in the Four Courts. 'What's artillery like?' Peadar O'Donnell asked his comrades, shortly before the bombardment was to begin. 'You get used to it' – replied a GPO veteran from 1916 – 'It's not bad.'[105]

But the Four Courts garrison was quickly defeated, and in truth the Civil War anti-Treaty IRA were poorly led throughout a conflict which was to last less than a year and which was to end in their defeat. In December 1922 the Irish Free State – the product of the Treaty – came into formal existence. Irish independence, of a sort, had been achieved. For whatever the objections of the anti-Treaty IRA, most people in the new state viewed its government as legitimate, and this allowed the Free State regime to achieve greater success against their former comrades than the British had been able to do. Where British reprisals had undermined an already shaky British legitimacy, the Irish government of 1922–3 could rest on its indigenous credentials while employing considerable ruthlessness against its diehard republican opponents. The IRA lost out as a result. There were periods of turmoil during 1922, and no certainty that the pro-Treatyites would win. Yet the pro-Treaty government was determined to maintain order amid the chaos of division ('It is the duty of the government, to which the people have entrusted their defence and the conduct of their affairs, to protect and secure all law-respecting citizens without distinction, and that duty the government will resolutely perform').[106] Within a couple of months of the start of Civil War, serious anti-Treaty resistance was largely restricted to south and south-west, and the Free Staters enjoyed the huge advantage of British backing. The anti-Treatyites were faced with a larger, better-organized force, and one drawing upon British material support of a kind simply unavailable to the IRA. Thus poor IRA leadership – together with governmental legitimacy, ruthlessness and superior weaponry and supplies – resulted in Free State victory. In May 1923 the IRA's Chief of Staff, Frank Aiken, gave the order for republicans to cease fire and dump arms.

The Civil War was over, and the anti-Treaty IRA had lost, but not before Valhalla had welcomed more dead warriors. In July 1922, during the early days of the war, the feisty Cathal Brugha had been fatally shot in Dublin; 'Cathal Brugha was a man of kindliest nature, a sincere friend, gentle in manner, but ... as firm as steel, and as brave as a lion.'[107] The following month, Brugha's great opponent Michael Collins was killed in an anti-Treaty IRA ambush in County Cork. In April 1923 Liam Lynch (the then anti-Treaty IRA Chief of Staff) was shot dead, prompting a commemorative poem from Ernie O'Malley:

To a Comrade Dead

Dead comrade! You who were a living force
Are now a battle cry, on our long roll
To nerve us when our hearts grow faint
At thought of the long odds and thorny path
Which still confront us. You, who in life,
Have shown us how to live and now have
Taught us how to die, teach us still.
We children of unbeaten hope who oft have lacked
Courage and strength to further the cause
Of our endeavour – a nation free![108]

The Civil War which led to such deaths was largely a guerrilla one, with assassination and reprisal and considerable viciousness on both sides. As ever with the IRA's story, jail formed an important chapter. One early-1920s anti-Treatyite prisoner, Frank O'Connor, delightfully suggested that for an Irish republican to say, '"Yes, he and I were in gaol together," ... is rather like the English "He and I were in Eton together" but considerably more classy'![109] Classy or not, large numbers of republicans were incarcerated by the Free State during and immediately beyond the Civil War. Some IRA men remembered this in comparatively jolly terms, as in Peadar O'Donnell's marvellously Wodehousean memoir, with its optimism, japery and boyish good humour in the prison wings, amid the sport and the educational classes.[110] But others presented a gloomier version of early 1920s prison life. Like Peadar O'Donnell, Ernie O'Malley was after the revolution to become something of a bohemian writer. But, unlike O'Donnell, his writings on his 1922–4 imprisonment were heavy in mood. (Indeed, O'Malley's prison letters from those years even depressed that ebullient republican of a later generation, Danny Morrison, during the latter's own incarceration during the early 1990s.)[111]

And there was indeed much reason for gloom. On 7 December

1922 (the day after the Free State came formally into being) two Dáil deputies, Seán Hales and Pádraic Ó Máille, were shot in Dublin by the anti-Treaty IRA. Hales died, Ó Máille was injured and panic gripped the newborn regime. Would there be further assassinations? Would the resolve of people to stand by the Free State survive any more such attacks? Something had to be done and it was decided, ruthlessly, to kill four anti-Treatyites held in jail. So on 8 December the IRA's Liam Mellows, Rory O'Connor, Dick Barrett and Joe McKelvey were executed in reprisal for the shooting of Hales and Ó Máille. For those fellow IRA men in the jails, especially, this was a dark episode. Peadar O'Donnell recorded Joe McKelvey as having been 'an unyielding opponent but not a dangerous enemy for he was quite incapable of deep hatreds. He was predestined to be a martyr in a revolutionary movement that failed for he would not dodge and he could not bend.'[112] For the unbending outside, however, the reprisals appear to have had the effect of putting an end to the shooting of elected Free State representatives; in their awful fashion, the killings of 8 December helped the new state to survive.

The imprisonment of IRA republicans extended beyond the IRA defeat of the spring of 1923. In October of that year there occurred a mass hunger strike, thousands of republican prisoners courageously refusing food with the aim of securing unconditional release from jail. The strike collapsed the following month, its strategy of simultaneously involving so many men making it more difficult to sustain than was the later, shrewder, Provisional IRA approach which involved far smaller numbers. But the resilience and bravery of the 1923 hunger-strikers should not be ignored, and their suffering was an emblem of their profound republican commitment. IRA Chief of Staff Frank Aiken wrote to the hunger-strikers in early November of that year: 'we know that if one Volunteer . . . succeeds in setting the example to his fellow citizens by voluntarily suffering long drawn out tortures of the flesh and mind, and offering his life and sufferings to God for the Republic of Ireland, that the might and wiles of our enemies will be powerless to subdue the spirit that such a heroic sacrifice will awaken in her citizens'.[113]

Profoundly though their politics were infused with religious think-ing, the anti-Treaty IRA none the less suffered clerical condemnation in the Civil War for their violence against the new state. The Catholic

Church excommunicated them and denounced the Civil War IRA cause. This prompted impish scepticism from Peadar O'Donnell. To the Church he wrote, 'The issue was simple: God versus the republic. The embarrassing thing was that the vast majority of the nationalist population insisted on standing by the republic in the name of God.'[114]

O'Donnell was exaggerating here. As the August 1923 Free State general election demonstrated, most people in nationalist Ireland endorsed the new order: the pro-Treaty party (Cumann na nGaedheal, formed in April 1923 and led by W. T. Cosgrave) emerged victorious, with anti-Treaty republicans winning only forty-four of the 153 seats. This was still a significant body of opinion. But clearly the majority of people in the Free State favoured that state's continued existence. What of that other part of the country, the six counties of the newly created Northern Ireland? In 1921 James Craig had succeeded Edward Carson as unionist leader, and later in the year a parliament opened in Belfast with a comfortable unionist majority.[115] This had been intended. For, faced with the longstanding objection of Ulster unionists to separation from the UK, London had in desperation opted for the partitioning of Ireland into two jurisdictions (effectively set out in the 1920 Government of Ireland Act, and solidified during the next two years). The northern portion remained in the UK and covered territory containing a deliberate unionist majority of approximately two-thirds.[116]

And the unionists were resolved not to be subsumed in a nationalist Ireland. Speaking in London in November 1922, Lord Carson himself suggested that 'any idea of driving Ulster under a southern government was absolutely out of the question. It was a harmful and a dangerous dream.' But he also addressed another key point, appealing to Ulster to show herself 'just and fair to those who were entrusted to the care of her government'.[117] For the north-east of Ireland had long been the setting for sectarian competition, the new state of the early 1920s was born amid dreadful intercommunal violence,[118] and northern Catholics were understandably alarmed at being the main losers in the 1921 Irish settlement. From early 1922 Michael Collins tried to establish a strong relationship between the northern IRA and pro-Treatyite GHQ; and in that year Belfast Volunteers were paid by Dublin to defend Catholic areas during rioting – reflecting a defensive role which was long to be a part of the IRA's self-image in the north. Despite this, neither pro- nor anti-Treaty southern forces did much to improve the position of northern Catholics once partition took effect.

In part, this was because they had urgent priorities in the southern conflict. But it was also true that to most non-Ulster IRA men, the north was not in fact a great priority or a place much understood. Michael Collins himself displayed a sense, as he saw it, of the north-east's non-Irishness, when he outlined a rather disdainful attitude towards that part of the island: 'A large portion of her fair province has lost all its native distinctiveness. It has become merely an inferior Lancashire. Who would visit Belfast or Lisburn or Lurgan to see the Irish people at home? That is the unhappy fate of the North-East. It is neither English nor Irish.'[119] Ulster unionists might have retorted that it was Britishness, rather than Englishness, that was at issue; and northern Catholics might reasonably have felt that – however unappealing to southern romantics – the north contained urgent realities for them, and ones that Irish republicanism should address. True enough, the IRA held that partition was unnatural, illogical, unfair and absurd. As Dublin-born IRA man and writer Brendan Behan (1923–64) charmingly put it: 'Like millions of others, I believe in the freedom of Ireland and to me the border is completely nonsensical. In one place it actually partitions a farmhouse and you could be having a shit in the south and your breakfast in the north by simply walking a few steps.'[120]

But it was the day-to-day experience of Catholics in the north that was to prove historically crucial. In April 1922, the Northern Ireland Special Powers Act gave the authorities extensive powers to do what they considered necessary for the maintenance of order. Fearful of Catholic disloyalty within Northern Ireland, of Catholic irredentists in the neighbouring state and of British unreliability, Ulster's unionists built a state largely in their own image. Unionist, like nationalist, politics were neither monolithic nor fixed. But the broad pattern for northern Catholics was to prove that of people in a state which was markedly unwelcoming to their political traditions.

At the birth of Northern Ireland, this was sharply evident in the violence which both preceded and followed the formal founding of the state. During the period July 1920–July 1922, 557 people were killed: 303 Catholics, 172 Protestants and 82 members of the police and British Army.[121] Notably, there was serious intimidation of Catholics in Belfast[122] and large-scale loss of life there: between July 1920 and June 1922 in the city 267 Catholics, 185 Protestants and three other people were killed.[123] It should, however, be stressed – as these very figures demonstrate – that the violence and intimidation of these days were not all in one direction. There were attacks on unionists (including the castration and other mutilation of goats owned by County Antrim unionists who lived in nationalist areas,[124] a powerful image of low-level sectarian hatred and viciousness). And there were unpleasantly personalized threats: in August 1920, for example, a series of threatening letters from Sinn Féin's Dublin headquarters included one sent to a Mary Harte, intended to prevent her (a Catholic) from marrying a Protestant.[125]

The violence had a self-sustaining, cyclical quality – an all too durable feature of northern conflict in Ireland. On the afternoon of 23 March 1922 two Special Constables were killed in Belfast by the IRA. Early the following morning, in apparent reprisal, a number of men (said to have worn a kind of uniform) smashed open the door of Catholic publican Owen McMahon's north Belfast home. The occupants of the house were in bed, but the raiders took the men to the sitting room and shot them. Five people were fatally injured (Owen himself, his sons Jeremiah, Patrick and Frank, and a barman named Edward McKinney); two other sons (John and Bernard) were wounded; and one son escaped. Mrs McMahon and her daughter – who had been ordered to stay in another room – arrived on the dreadful scene after the shooting, to see seven bodies in pools of blood. The wounded John McMahon recalled poignantly of this appalling episode: 'I heard my mother plead with the men not to do any harm to the family.'[126] And the spirit of revenge was not confined to Belfast. On 19 May 1922 the walls of Cookstown, County Tyrone, together with the doors and windows of Catholics' houses and offices, were covered with copies of two printed notices. The first stated that if there were any more attacks on police or loyalists, then 'reprisals at the rate of ten to one will be made on prominent and well-known Sinn Féiners. God save the King.' The second (which was also served on Protestant farmers of the district who had engaged Catholic employees) said bluntly: 'You are hereby required, within forty-eight hours after the service of this notice, to clear out of your employment all Sinn Féiners and Roman Catholics. Herein fail not at the peril of your life.'[127] And if the killing of Catholics was seen as retaliation for Sinn Féinish mischief, then it could itself provoke terrible revenge. In the early hours of 17 June (in reprisal for the killing of two Catholics a few days earlier), five men and a woman – all Protestants – were killed by the IRA in the south Armagh townlands of Altnaveigh and Lisdrumliska.

Northern Ireland in the early 1920s witnessed IRA attacks in which a number of police officers were killed, and the years 1922–4 saw hundreds of republicans interned by the northern authorities.[128] Moreover, the IRA's role in these days could be bloody in terms of suffering as well as infliction. The case of Séamus Blaney provides an example. A Downpatrick IRA Volunteer, he had joined the IRA's youth wing, Fianna Eireann, in May 1918 and was by July 1920 serving as Battalion adjutant in East Down. On 23 May 1922 he was captured by military and police, as one of ten men in possession of revolvers, ammunition and explosives. Two of the ten were wounded, one of them being Blaney; an attempted IRA rescue was unsuccessful, and he died on 18 January 1923.

So, too, in a sense did the northern IRA during these years, or at least their hope of undermining the new Ulster state. For the IRA were defeated in the Northern Ireland of the early 1920s. While nationalists felt the border to be a scar on the Irish island, unionists considered partition a reasonable response to profound pre-existing differences in Ireland. Even Sinn Féin's triumphant 1918 general election had shown the potential problem for Irish nationalism posed by a concentrated north-eastern unionist mass (and one recent scholarly study of working-class life between 1880 and 1925 has concluded that 'in many important ways the developing working-class culture of Belfast had more in common with Glasgow, Manchester or Bristol than with Dublin, Cork or Galway').[129] Yet the nationalist perception that the north was an illegitimate creation was lastingly retained by northern Catholics; it was also, understandably, reinforced by the discriminatory unionist actions that it had helped to encourage.

TWO

NEW STATES

1923–63

1

'Twelve years after Easter Week Ireland remains, unfree and unredeemed, still bound to the British empire . . . It is twelve years since Clarke and Connolly and Pearse proclaimed the Irish republic. It is five years since the last shot was fired in its defence. Cowardice, treachery and war-weariness have prevailed; Ireland is again held in the British empire.'

IRA man, Frank Ryan (1928)[1]

By the summer of 1924, Civil War disorder was largely over and the two new Irelands – north and south – began to settle into their partitioned life. The IRA was in something of a tattered state after its defeat, north and south. Its zealous members had aspired to a united, fully independent Irish republic; they now witnessed instead a partitioned Ireland, part of which was firmly within the UK, and the other part of which was still vestigially tied to Britain and ruled over by the IRA's treacherous and compromised Civil War adversaries. In the aftermath of the Civil War, the IRA's mood was low. As one of their most talented figures, George Gilmore, put it: 'The morale of the army was not of the best . . . We had suffered a thorough defeat in 1923, and were finding it no easy task to pull things together again and to restore confidence in the army leadership.'[2]

Yet the army still contained some very able activists, and was to exude considerable vibrancy during the post-revolutionary years. In November 1925 the organization regrouped, adopting an amended constitution which set out its aims and means. The IRA's four objectives were to guard the republic's honour and uphold its sovereignty and unity; to establish and uphold a legitimate Irish government with total control over the republic; to secure and defend citizens' civil and religious liberties and their equal rights and opportunities; and to revive the Irish language and promote the best characteristics of the Irish race. The existing Free State order was clearly felt to be illegitimate, and awaiting replacement by the appearance of the true Irish republic, free and united. But how was this new day to be reached? The IRA's 1925 constitution set out emphatically military means: '1. Force of arms. 2. Organising, training and equipping the manhood of Ireland as an efficient military force. 3. Assisting as directed by the army authority all organisations working for the same objects.' This newly adopted constitution described the IRA's General Army Convention (GAC) as the organization's supreme authority, with the Army Council exercising this role when a GAC was not in session. Should a proper, full Irish republic be established, then the IRA would hand over the power of legitimate authority to that regime: 'The Army Council shall have the power to delegate its powers to a government which is actively endeavouring to function as the de facto government of the republic ... When a government is functioning as the de facto government of the republic, a General Army Convention shall be convened to give the allegiance of Óglaigh na h-Éireann [the IRA] to such a government.'[3]

That the IRA still posed a threat during the post-Civil War years was evidenced by episodes such as the dramatic escape of nineteen IRA prisoners from Mountjoy Jail in Dublin in November 1925. Even more alarming for the Free State authorities were the persistent threats to, and attacks upon, jurors and witnesses in trials involving republicans during the late 1920s. The IRA might still be trying to recreate itself from the wreckage of Civil War defeat; but the state's difficulty in obtaining convictions against them in jury trials represented a significant victory of a sort. They also engaged in other violent activity. In November 1926 the IRA attacked garda (police) stations in Tipperary and Waterford, two police officers being fatally injured. The army's actions were not part of a systematic, sustained campaign, but they could be brutal for all that – as is evident in the casual reflections of one 1920s veteran: 'Some silly things happened; I suppose that is inevitable at times. [An IRA] Volunteer went to disarm a Free State

soldier, and shot dead the girl who was with him. Then there was a
raid on pawn shops, for binoculars of all things, and a pawn shop
assistant was shot.'[4]

This sporadically active IRA had, however, a regular and compelling
mouthpiece in *An Phoblacht*, the organization's official paper. From
the mid-1920s for a decade, the paper put the IRA's argument with
energy and clarity. But while the late-1920s IRA was undoubtedly
gaining some confidence, some of its menacing acts could help to
undermine its ultimate cause. This was spectacularly so with the killing
of Kevin O'Higgins, one of the most talented and important figures in
the Free State regime. Vice-President of the government, O'Higgins
was hated by many republicans as a symbol of the triumph of one
kind of nationalism – procedural, moderate and firm in defence of
the state – over the IRA's more revolutionary version. On Sunday
10 July 1927 O'Higgins was on his way to Mass in County Dublin
when three IRA men (Archie Doyle, Bill Gannon, Tim Coughlan) saw
him – apparently by chance – and killed him in hate-filled rage. As
one of the killers recalled: 'seeing him and realising that it was not a
mistake, we were just taken over and incensed with hatred. You can
have no idea what it was like, with the memory of the [Civil War]
executions, and the sight of him just walking along on his own. We
started shooting from the car, then getting out of the car we continued
to shoot. We all shot at him; he didn't have a chance.'[5]

O'Higgins had been unarmed; he was shot many times and left to
die. So old Civil War hatreds claimed another victim, this time one
ruthlessly committed to Irish parliamentary, democratic government.
And in this instance IRA violence unintentionally helped to secure
those very political structures for whose defence its victim had been
shot. In the wake of O'Higgins's death, the Free State authorities
legislated that prospective Dáil candidates must swear to take the (to
republicans, despised) oath of allegiance to the British Crown, once
elected. The republican political party, Fianna Fáil (founded in Dublin
in 1926 by Eamon de Valera), had resisted participation in the oath-
contaminated Dáil. Post-O'Higgins, the possibility of entering parliamentary politics without taking the oath was narrowed; and so in
August 1927 de Valera (who had himself condemned O'Higgins's
killing) led his party into the Dáil and consolidated the Free State by
his effective sanction of its parliamentary politics. By his death, Kevin

O'Higgins therefore helped to ensure the survival of that state to which he had determinedly committed himself in life.

And the state thus consolidated was to be a cold place for the IRA that had taken O'Higgins's life. During the 1920s Cumann na nGaedheal governments resolutely devoted themselves to building up that southern Irish state which the IRA despised as a British-imposed compromise. Independent Ireland was built by a regime that attempted, not to inaugurate the millennium of the revolutionary imagination, but rather to rescue the nation from the chaos of revolution. Indeed, against the continuing threat of IRA anti-state activity, and following the violence and chaos of the War of Independence and Civil War, the Free State's achievement of stability by the early 1930s was a striking (though, to IRA republicans, a disagreeable) achievement. That stability had remained shaky as long as those in the anti-Treaty tradition stayed aloof from the structures of the state. But when de Valera and Fianna Fáil gradually brought anti-Treaty opinion within the constitutional fold, during the late 1920s and the 1930s, the prospects for IRA momentum were diminished. If those who wanted movement towards fuller republican freedom could progress through politics and Fianna Fáil parliamentarianism, then where was the role for the IRA?

And progress there seemed to be. Fianna Fáil had been born of de Valera's impatience with the make-believe world of post-Civil War Irish republicanism. It was all very well maintaining that legitimate authority in Ireland rested with those members of the 1921 Second Dáil who had opposed the Treaty and the Free State, or that such authority lay within the IRA itself. But de Valera knew that real power and serious authority lay in the structures of the new Irish state. As one of his Fianna Fáil colleagues described the pre-1926 situation, 'De Valera was still president of the Irish republic, a shadow government which governed nothing. He was president of Sinn Féin, a shadow political party which took no part in practical politics. He decided that this situation must end.'[6] The 1926 foundation of Fianna Fáil, in a split from Sinn Féin, thus marked the beginning of the death of the southern IRA as a serious political force. With its twin interlinked goals of economic and political independence from Britain, and its deft use of Free State structures to forward its goals, de Valera's party drew in, year by year, the bulk of anti-Treaty opinion. In doing so, it effectively constitutionalized southern Irish republicanism and squeezed the IRA out of powerful existence.

De Valera saw Fianna Fáil less as a political party than as a revivification of the national movement, and as the embodiment of the Irish nation. The party dismissed the IRA's late-1920s efforts to establish IRA–Fianna Fáil–Sinn Féin unity. The IRA's numbers had suffered, post-revolution: in August 1924 the army had around 14,541 members; by November 1926 membership had fallen to 5,042.[7] And when Fianna Fáil came to power after the 1932 Free State election, the party was even less in need of its extra-constitutional former friends. Not that the division between the two republican groups was immediately neat. The IRA had looked to Fianna Fáil to beat their own old pro-Treatyite enemies, Cumann na nGaedheal, in the election; and in the wake of de Valera's victory, IRA people imprisoned by the former regime were released. But any cosiness in the army's relationship with the new government was to prove short-lived. There was a very different emphasis to the two bodies' approaches, as was evident from a series of meetings between de Valera and the IRA's Sean MacBride shortly after the former had come to power through majoritarian electoral process. In Wildean fashion ('One should always play fairly ... when one has the winning cards'),[8] de Valera now demanded from everyone the recognition of majority rule within the southern state: 'once the oath [of allegiance to the British Crown under the 1921 Treaty] was removed there could be no objection to such a recognition of majority rule and to recognising the Free State parliament as a legitimate body'.[9]

The post-1932 cabinet comprised the Civil War rebels of a decade earlier; when power peacefully transferred from Cumann na nGaedheal to Fianna Fáil in March 1932, the new government became the establishment within a state against which they had initially fought, but which they now consolidated through their accession to power. They were keen to woo republicans, and through their mixture of social and symbolic policies – together with their offer of pensions to ex-IRA men – they substantially managed to do just that. De Valera during the 1930s undid most of what republicans felt to be unacceptable about the 1921 Treaty – land annuity payments to Britain, the oath of allegiance to the British Crown, the office of Governor-General, the right of appeal to the Privy Council, British access to Irish naval facilities, the 1922 Free State constitution. In doing so he proved, ironically, that the stepping-stone argument of his pro-Treaty opponent, Michael Collins, had been right. He also undermined the rationale, in many southern Irish people's eyes, for continued IRA activity there. During the 1916–23 revolution itself, much of the IRA's competition had been with other Irish nationalists. So, too, in independent Ireland in the 1930s it was fellow nationalists in Fianna Fáil who closed down the space for the republican army's activities.

Initially, the IRA exuded confidence that it was they, rather than de Valera's constitutional party, who resonated with wider opinion. In early 1933 the Army Council proclaimed, 'There is a fine spirit everywhere, and Fianna Fáil people all say that their policy was far behind the enthusiasm of republicans and what they expected. There is frankly great disappointment amongst a large section of Fianna Fáil supporters.'[10] The IRA tended to maintain their belief that, if only the Irish people properly heard the arguments, and had these explained to them, then they would of necessity understand and sympathize with and indeed support the army. In this light, the IRA considered the question of increasing the circulation of their paper, _An Phoblacht_ – for 'no wonder the policy of the army is so badly understood since the people know so little'.[11] And the IRA of the 1930s retained some romantic allure. As one recruit from these days proudly recalled, 'I joined the IRA in November 1934. To me it was the fulfilment of all my aspirations, for to be sworn in as a soldier of the Irish Republican Army had glamour, and there was a thrilling sensation in belonging to it which only a secret, oath-bound society can give.'[12]

But the 1930s arrival of Fianna Fáil in government – for what was to be a sixteen-year period in office – had undoubtedly changed the context for the IRA, and they sensed as much. The Army Council itself acknowledged early in the decade that 'the advent to power of the Fianna Fáil party has made a difference, not fundamentally, but in regard to the tactics which must be followed'. For Fianna Fáil had not yet 'taken any positive action detrimental to the republican cause; theirs are sins of omission'. The propaganda of de Valera's party was more republican than its actions, and if this continued then they would be exposed; but, for now, the IRA distinguished between the two main Free State parties – de Valera's and Cumann na nGaedheal: 'A time may come when it would be immaterial to us which Treatyite party is in office, but that time is not yet.' If Fianna Fáil was not hostile to republican ideals or organizations, then the IRA should make the most of that new situation.[13] The difficulty was that progress by the constitutional de Valera undermined in many people's eyes the rationale for IRA support. As one republican activist ruefully recalled, 'There were a lot of people that thought [de Valera] was going slowly, but he was going somewhere – and they were happy with it.'[14]

One ingenious attempt to differentiate the IRA's approach from that of the Fianna Fáil leadership came from the army's Connollyite left. Prominent among the late-1920s and early-1930s IRA was a circle including Peadar O'Donnell and George Gilmore, who sought to weld together the arguments of socialism and Irish republicanism. Their thesis was that the struggle of the oppressed nation (Ireland) against the oppressor nation (England) was inextricably interwoven with the conflict within Ireland between the oppressed classes and their social oppressors. England ruled Ireland ultimately for economic advantage, and the mechanism for this was the capitalist system which English rule maintained there. Thus, those disadvantaged under capitalism, and possessing an interest in seeing it removed, were those with an economic imperative to pursue full freedom from England as a means to their social emancipation. Likewise, those benefiting from capitalism had an imperative to support the connection with England, as this would maintain the economic system under which they flourished. If, according to this intriguing argument, one wanted to identify those in Ireland with a genuine impulse and commitment towards republican separatism, then one should look to the working classes.

These left-wing IRA thinkers lamented the social conservatism of the 1916–23 revolution.[15] As Gilmore later suggested, 'The form that a struggle takes is bound to have a determining effect on its outcome';[16] the IRA's revolutionary war had not been defined in Gilmore's preferred terms, and so the disappointing outcome was unsurprising. To avoid a repetition of this difficulty, the leftist republicans proposed that post-revolutionary IRA politics be founded on what Gilmore referred to as the 'oneness of the struggle against national subjection and social oppression in a subject nation'.[17] Gilmore was aided in this cause by his inner-circle IRA ally, Peadar O'Donnell, who had become *An Phoblacht* editor in 1926. In 1931 O'Donnell was prominent in the establishment of the largely paper-thin IRA offshoot, Saor Eire: an organization exhibiting rhetorical commitment to socialist revolution. Saor Eire's literature, largely produced by O'Donnell and by County Tipperary IRA man David Fitzgerald, was indeed strikingly to the left. The new group's primary objectives were to 'achieve an independent revolutionary leadership for the working class and working farmers towards the overthrow of British imperialism and its ally, Irish capitalism', and to establish 'the possession and administration by the workers and working farmers, of the land, instruments of production, distribution and exchange'. Its primary method was to be the organiz-ation of 'committees of action among the industrial and agricultural workers to lead the day-to-day struggle of the working class and working farmers'.[18] In practice, however, the IRA as a whole was not committed to these goals and methods, and when the government and Catholic Church turned on the young movement the army quickly abandoned it.

But the socialist republicans within the IRA continued to adhere committedly to their Connollyite vision, and to seek that the IRA as an organization should define its republicanism in terms of necessary class conflict. The O'Donnellite argument set the IRA left a consider-able distance away from Fianna Fáil's capitalist approach to Irish nationalism. As O'Donnell himself put it, his quarrel with de Valera was that the latter pretended to be a republican 'while actually the interests for which his party acts – Irish capitalism – are across the road to the republic'.[19] In this view, one could not be a true republican unless one was – as part of the same struggle – committed to the destruction of capitalism. The IRA in the 1930s refused to allow its thinking to be defined in this way, and so O'Donnell, Gilmore and other talented figures such as Frank Ryan left the army in 1934 to form the short-lived, fissiparous Republican Congress. This group's manifesto lucidly set out in April that year the guiding principle of sincere Irish socialist republicanism: 'We believe that a republic of a united Ireland will never be achieved except through a struggle which uproots capitalism on its way.'[20]

Unfortunately for such left-wing activists, most Irish nationalists did not believe this to be the case, and the socialist republican cause went into comparative obscurity after the collapse of the Congress in the later 1930s, and after the brave gesture of those Irish left-wingers who went to fight against fascism in the Spanish Civil War. Just as

James Connolly had been unable to stamp the republicanism of the
1916 rebellion with the definition of class conflict, so too the IRA of
the 1930s proved ultimately resistant to definition along the lines of
thoroughgoing socialist-republican fusion. The schismatic republican
left exasperated the more traditional comrades: Mary MacSwiney
winningly suggested in a letter of 1935 that 'It would be a good thing
if P[eadar] O'D[onnell] and F[rank] R[yan] had their heads knocked
together until they learned sense.'[21] And their spectre could provoke
anxiety among those outside the movement too: pro-Treaty ideologues
such as James Hogan and Desmond FitzGerald wrote alarmedly about,
as the latter put it, the fear 'that the country may go Bolshevist'.[22] In
truth, such fears were exaggerated, and the Ireland of the day was an
inhospitable place for the republican left. Catholic anti-communism
was a powerful force in independent Ireland, the 1933 establishment
of the Communist Party of Ireland providing a telling example: its
inaugural congress took place in a room that had had to be hired
under a false name because of the anti-communistic atmosphere of the
times. (Veteran communist Sean Nolan recalled that the premises had
in fact been booked under the name of a total-abstinence group,
noting wryly that most of the communist delegates *were* indeed total
abstainers – not through principle, but because 'we had no bloody
money!')[23]

Yet the problems of the 1930s republican left went far beyond
this, and sometimes arose from the unpersuasive nature of their
own arguments. For, despite the obvious intelligence of people like
O'Donnell, Gilmore and Ryan, it could be argued that their reading of
history, of the relation between class and nation, of the mechanisms
of political power within the state, of the politics of land, of political
violence and of Irish unionism, reflected a less than firm grasp of Irish
political realities.[24] Certainly, the majority of Irish republicans thought
as much: the legendary Tom Barry and others objected to the IRA
placing too much emphasis on the social side of the Irish question,
and not enough on the military. And as the political historian Henry
Patterson has observed in his fine study of the relationship between
socialism and modern Irish republicanism, 'For almost thirty years
after the collapse of the Republican Congress, physical force separatism
was the overwhelmingly dominant form of republican activity.'[25]

Not that the interwar IRA lacked a working-class basis. At the army's March 1934 General Army Convention, the Belfast OC observed: 'The bulk of our members are unemployed ... We have 460 men in Belfast but only about 150 working.'[26] But the interwar army's centre of gravity lay within conspiratorial military action rather than class-based, mass revolutionism. In the Free State (after 1937, Eire) their list of violent acts made quite a gruesome catalogue. In January 1931 Patrick Carroll, allegedly an IRA informer, was shot dead in Dublin. In March the IRA shot and killed in Tipperary a police superintendent who had been too energetic in his anti-IRA activities for the organization's taste. In July they killed John Ryan at Oyle, County Tipperary, a placard round his neck proclaiming: 'Spies and informers beware. IRA'. Ryan had given evidence in a prosecution for illegal IRA drilling, and had in April received a threatening letter stating that he had been found guilty of treachery, and that he would be killed if found in the country after 17 May.

Yet these incidents should not suggest that the IRA's military machine was in great working order. In November 1932 the Army Council wrote to their American allies, Clan na Gael, that when it discussed 'the cold reality of the situation, and its military possibilities, it finds itself in a very strange position. The difficulty it is confronted with is lack of ammunition principally, and of effective arms generally.'[27] In February 1933 the situation was still depressing: 'It is a matter of urgency that ammunition ... should be sent along. Every unit is demanding some for training and practice.'[28] In the same month the Army Council stated that the IRA's aim was to assert the republic of Ireland's sovereignty and unity, but its capacity to do this with any degree of success was limited by numerous problems. One was finance. At the army's March 1934 GAC, Chief of Staff Moss Twomey observed amid a discussion of finance that 'Many things which are good for the IRA are often left undone because the cost which may be only £50 cannot be expended.' The IRA's shortage of funds prompted a successful proposal by the soon-to-depart Peadar O'Donnell, to the effect 'That each unit shall as a minimum be responsible for an amount equal to one penny per week per member, arrears not to exceed three months without special sanction of Army Council.'[29]

If money was a concern, then so too was security. At the same 1934 GAC Moss Twomey observed – again, almost poignantly – that the

IRA had 'endured frightful humiliation' from the actions of its own men, who had, when questioned, given 'all the information at their disposal to the police'. Yet while their conspiratorial politics therefore faced obstacles, they remained deeply sceptical of more conventional, constitutional politics. Sean MacBride (who was to leave the IRA four years later, and who subsequently became a constitutional politican) in the same year stated: 'If we are a revolutionary organisation, it is futile our going into parliament.'[30] But figures like MacBride also recognized how much ground had been lost by this stage to Fianna Fáil, and acknowledged that the IRA had to attempt to win over those who had backed, but who might now be disillusioned with, de Valera's party. Admittedly, the IRA could still embarrass the government. On 17 March 1936, while de Valera was delivering his St Patrick's Day broadcast over the radio, a voice was heard, saying: 'Hello, everybody, this is the IRA.' The speaker was then cut off and a second line put into use; but the latter was also interfered with, apparently through a tapped line.

And more deadly activities also preoccupied the army. In March 1936 Vice-Admiral Henry Boyle Townshend Somerville, a Protestant who had helped local lads with joining the British forces, was killed by the IRA in County Cork. Nobody was convicted for the killing, which was authorized by Tom Barry and apparently carried out by Tadgh Lynch, Angela Lynch and Joe Collins.[31] The following month, former IRA man John Egan was shot dead in Dungarvan, County Waterford, by the IRA, having been suspected of giving the police information that had led to the discovery of an arms dump and the imprisonment of a number of IRA members. (Egan was apparently shot by order of the Army Council, which perhaps makes Moss Twomey's 1934 GAC comments look, after all, rather less poignant.)

Though its origins and its government ministers had IRA roots, the independent Ireland over which de Valera presided in these years was now one deeply at odds with the IRA's anti-majoritarian conspiratorialism. Young states are frequently concerned with challenges, internal or external, to their sovereignty, and southern Ireland was no exception: de Valera's regime came to pursue what they saw as an illegitimate republican army, and they did so with marked determination. In May 1936 four members of the IRA in County Tipperary (Michael Conway, William O'Donoghue, Edmund Carrigan and John Tobin) were arrested in connection with John Egan's murder and brought before the state's Military Tribunal in July. In June 1936 the IRA was proscribed and its Chief of Staff, Moss Twomey, himself arrested and brought before the Military Tribunal; he was sentenced to three years' imprisonment for membership of an unlawful association. In Weberian style, the independent Irish state defended its monopoly of the legitimate use of force within its territory; and it did so at the expense of former comrades, some of whom were to pay the highest price during the Second World War, as the ex-revolutionaries of Fianna Fáil eclipsed and defeated the IRA.

2

'Today England is locked in a life and death struggle with Germany and Italy. From what quarter shall the government of the Irish Republic seek for aid? The lesson of history is plain. England's enemy is Ireland's ally.'

The IRA's *War News*, 16 November 1940

During 1939–45 there were four key contexts for IRA activity: within independent Ireland, in the army's bombing campaign of Britain, in their dealings with Nazi Germany and in their activities in Northern Ireland. In the first of these, wartime exigency further hardened the state's resolve to oppose subversives within its boundaries. Effectively defenceless itself, neutral Eire relied on Britain for air and sea defence; IRA activities against Britain or in favour of her enemies could dangerously antagonize the neighbour on whom a vulnerable Irish state depended, and towards whom de Valera's neutrality benevolently leaned.[32] The 1939 Offences Against the State Act strengthened the authorities' hand: it allowed for the establishment of special criminal courts, prohibited seditious activities (including membership of proscribed organizations), and increased the state's powers of search, arrest and detention. A 1940 amendment to the state's 1939 Emergency Powers Act was also significant for the IRA, providing as it did for the summary trial of certain offences by a military tribunal with the sole sanction of execution upon conviction. Thus, not only were hundreds of republicans lengthily detained during the war, but a number of IRA men were also executed in the 1940s. The Royal Ulster Constabulary (RUC) in Belfast noted of de Valera that 'His government was and is as strongly opposed to the IRA as that in the north, and has passed legislation to deal with it far more drastic than anything introduced here.'[33]

In September 1939 raids by the Irish authorities against the IRA captured most of that organization's HQ officers and some of its money. But the favour could be returned. On 23 December that year the IRA raided the (state) Irish Army's Magazine Fort in Phoenix Park, Dublin, and stole most of the Army's reserves of small-arms ammunition. Much of the material was quickly recovered; but the embarrassment took longer to deal with. At the subsequent court of inquiry into the raid, the officer in charge of the Magazine Fort stated that he had repeatedly protested to his seniors regarding the strength of the guard, but that he had been 'informed that there were no men available'.[34] It appears that late in 1939 a Department of Defence civil servant had presented to the IRA a scheme for raiding the fort, a scheme which clearly appealed to an army itself very short of ammunition. On 23 December, therefore, an IRA man came up to the gate of the fort with (as ever!) a bicycle, on which there was a parcel. Addressing the military policeman (Daniel Merrigan) on the gate, the raider said that the parcel was for the officer commanding the fort. Merrigan opened the lock and was about to open the gate itself when the man produced a revolver, pointed it at Merrigan's face and said – in classic B-movie style – 'Stick them up.' The IRA thus entered the fort at around 8.45 p.m., were in complete control of it ten minutes later and had completed their job and departed by around 10.30. They took with them 471,979 rounds of .303 machine-gun ammunition, 612,300 rounds of Thompson gun ammunition, 12 rounds of .45 revolver ammunition, 3 bayonets, 4 scabbards, 7 rifle magazines, 3 rifle slings, 3 oil bottles, 3 pull-throughs, 4 Lee Enfield rifles and 1 Webley revolver.

But the authorities themselves hit back some days later when, on 29 December, the IRA's broadcasting station and radio transmitter, which had been used for broadcasting propaganda, were captured by the police in Dublin, along with IRA men Jack McNeela, Jack Plunkett,

James Byrne and James Mongan. Early in the New Year, IRA man Tomás MacCurtain fatally shot a detective while resisting arrest in Cork. The police had become aware that there was a certain amount of trafficking in firearms in which MacCurtain was involved; on 3 January two detective officers accosted him and informed him that he was under arrest. Fatally shooting one of them, MacCurtain was none the less overpowered and sentenced to death for the officer's killing. The sentence was commuted to life imprisonment, of which he served eight years. MacCurtain neatly encapsulates some of the ironies of IRA experience in these years. Born in 1915, he was the son of the similarly named IRA man and Sinn Féin lord mayor of Cork, killed in 1920; MacCurtain junior had joined the IRA in 1932, aged only seventeen, and was now incarcerated in the tradition of his father, by a regime presided over by his father's revolutionary comrades. Others in the diehard tradition were also locked up, with the authorities during wartime interning large numbers of IRA men in detention camps at the Curragh in County Kildare.

Some incarcerated republicans protested vigorously. In February 1940 Tomás MacCurtain, Thomas Grogan, Michael Traynor, Tony D'Arcy, Jack McNeela and Jack Plunkett went on hunger strike in Dublin's Mountjoy Jail. Their principal demand was to be able to walk around the prison freely, rather than being confined to their cells at 4 p.m. each day. Wanting free association for all prisoners, their gesture was effectively a protest against IRA men being treated as criminals, as non-soldiers, in a battle that modern readers will recognize as pre-echoing the protests of a later IRA. There were resonances too in the authorities' preparedness to allow hunger-strikers to die, which D'Arcy did on 16 April, McNeela following him three days later. In September of the same year the authorities executed two IRA men, Patrick McGrath and Thomas Harte, in Mountjoy. These were cold days in what the IRA scorned as a deeply unfree Irish state.

But their difficulties in independent Ireland were partly internal too, as their wartime conspiracy became engulfed in a paranoid darkness. The most striking example of this was the case of Stephen Hayes. Born in Enniscorthy (County Wexford) in 1896, Hayes had taken part in the 1919–21 War of Independence and had remained an IRA man beyond the revolution. Appointed the army's Adjutant-General in October 1938, he had been left in charge of the IRA by the late-1930s Chief of Staff, Sean Russell, when the latter went to the United States in 1939. This was itself a reflection of the IRA's paucity of talent (as the heavy-drinking Hayes himself recalled: 'I only took over from Russell when he went to America because there was no one else and Russell begged me to do it');[35] and when Russell died in 1940 without having returned to Ireland, the IRA was in very shaky hands. In an attempt to reorganize the disoriented army, Hayes fatefully appointed two Belfast men to IRA GHQ Staff in the spring of 1941, Sean McCaughey becoming Adjutant-General, Charlie McGlade Quartermaster-General. By midway through that year, however, suspicion had arisen of treachery within the IRA. The large-scale arrests of Volunteers in Ireland and England had helped convince some senior army figures (including McCaughey, McGlade and fellow northerners Liam Burke and Liam Rice) that Hayes himself was the traitor.

In this Dostoyevskian world of suspicion, the northerners of the disunited Irish Republican Army captured Chief of Staff Hayes at his County Dublin home on 30 June 1941 and took him to an isolated cottage in the mountains near Dundalk for interrogation. In the IRA's own words, Hayes had been 'arrested and charged with treachery and conspiracy to betray the republic, and imprisoned'.[36] An Army Council was formed (Sean McCaughey, Eoin McNamee, Charlie McGlade, Sean Harrington, Jack Lynch, Tom Mullally, Stephen Rynne, Andy Skelton, Joe Atkinson), and this body convened a court-martial, with McCaughey as prosecutor. Hayes had been moved to a house in Rathmines, Dublin, and it was there that the court-martial was held on 23 July. It consisted of McCaughey, Pearse Kelly, Charlie McCarthy and Tom Farrell, with Charlie McGlade, Liam Rice and Liam Burke also in attendance. In Hayes's own account, this court-martial 'was really a mixture between a schoolboy rag and an American gangster film'.[37] Gangster film or not, it possessed lethal potential for the suspected traitor. Hayes was court-martialled on the charges, first, that he had 'conspired with the "Irish Free State government" to obstruct the policy and impede the progress of the IRA' and, second, that he was 'guilty of treachery by having deliberately forwarded information, of a secret and confidential nature concerning the activities of the IRA, to a hostile body, to wit, the "Irish Free State government"'. He was found guilty on both charges and sentenced to death, 'the president of the court stating that the accused was a party to the most heinous conspiracy of crime in Irish history'.[38]

The discredited leader then volunteered (or was forced) to write a confession, and in this document he admitted having been involved in a conspiracy with the Dublin government 'to wreck the IRA'.[39] Thus the execution of sentence was deferred while Hayes slowly wrote confessional page upon page of inculpatory material, trying – as he later said – to buy himself time. Sean McCaughey took extracts of this confession as it was being produced to show to former IRA man, Sean MacBride – who had not yet embarked upon his future role as an international human rights campaigner – while awaiting the moment when the IRA would shoot their court-martialled leader. The confession-writing continued until 8 September 1941, when Hayes managed to escape and give himself up at the nearby Rathmines garda (police) station, where he identified himself and asked for protective custody. In June 1942 he was sentenced to five years' penal servitude by the Special Criminal Court, for maintenance of an illegal force.

But his captors had themselves not escaped cleanly from the episode. Armed detectives raided the house in which Hayes had been held. On their approach they were fired upon by Liam Rice, who was wounded when the police returned fire. Rice was charged with attempted murder, and in April 1942 was sentenced to twenty years' imprisonment. Sean McCaughey was also arrested by the authorities in Dublin, and charged with the unlawful imprisonment and mistreatment of Hayes; found guilty, he was sentenced to death. This was then commuted to penal servitude for life, with McCaughey being incarcerated in Portlaoise Prison until his death on hunger strike in May 1946. He had refused to wear criminal clothes, therefore wearing only a blanket, and had embarked on his hunger strike in an attempt to win unconditional release. And there was a painful sadness to his bleak demise: even the far from sympathetic Noel Browne – who, as a later Minister for Health, inspected the deeply underground cell in which McCaughey had died – observed that this was 'a truly awful place in which to die, hungry or not'.[40] As the later Provisional republicans were to put it, in de Valera's 1940s Ireland, 'Many who remained faithful to the republic proclaimed in 1916 ... were now suffering the untold torture of years of solitary confinement in the dungeons of Portlaoise prison.'[41]

Hayes himself lived until December 1974, and maintained his innocence right up to his death. He claimed that the confession was not a genuine account of events, that his captors had tortured and starved him (and there is no shortage of evidence concerning the IRA's use of brutal interrogation methods during this period towards those whom they suspected of informing).⁴² Whatever the reality, most IRA members had been unaware of Hayes's capture and were understandably dismayed when news of the sorry events did emerge. Either the IRA Chief of Staff had been a traitor, or a loyal Chief of Staff had been imprisoned and brutally treated by paranoid officers near the top of the army. Neither story was good for the organization's morale, as feuding, suspicion and conspiracy theses divided the ineffective IRA. As one republican of this period later put it: 'For the IRA the Stephen Hayes case was a Catch 22 situation. If he was guilty it did them harm in a public relations sense, if not it was even worse.'⁴³

Yet, notwithstanding such farcically tragic episodes, the IRA retained a striking sense of its own role and importance in Ireland's destiny. In 1942 the organization issued a special manifesto which restated 'the national principles actuating the IRA', and outlined its 'attitude in relation to the present world situation in the light of those principles'. The manifesto contained much that was traditional:

> The IRA is determined to obtain *and maintain* the right of the people of Ireland to the unfettered control of Irish destinies, guaranteeing civil and religious liberty, equal rights and equal opportunities to all its citizens. The maintenance of sectarian strife forms no part of the policy of the IRA . . . In view of the fact that the free consent of the Irish people has not been obtained for the present occupation of north-east Ireland by British and allied forces, the IRA reserves the right to use whatever measures present themselves to clear this territory of such forces . . . The occupation of a part of Ireland by British and American forces is in itself an act of aggression.⁴⁴

And the army deployed not only rhetoric. On 9 September 1942 Detective Sergeant Denis 'Dinny' O'Brien was shot dead by the IRA in Rathfarnham in Dublin. O'Brien had been seen by the army as an overly keen anti-republican. He had, in fact, been a long-time IRA man until the 1930s when – like many other Irish nationalists – he had

become convinced of the legitimacy of de Valera's state. His ambush
was organized by Archie Doyle (one of the killers of Kevin O'Higgins
in 1927), and in December 1944 Kerry IRA man Charlie Kerins was
executed in Dublin for the killing.

Again, in late 1942, during the police searches following O'Brien's
death, the IRA killed a detective-garda in a Dublin shoot-out. Another
Kerry IRA man, Maurice O'Neill, was executed in connection with this
killing; also involved in the fatal skirmish was Harry White, one of the
IRA's leading figures in the 1940s (and the uncle of latter-day republican, Danny Morrison). Born in Belfast, White had joined the IRA
young. Only released from the Curragh earlier in 1942, he escaped
from the shoot-out and was not captured for several years. He was
eventually tried before Dublin's Military Tribunal in December 1946
and sentenced to death; in the event, the charge was commuted to
manslaughter and he served only a fraction of this twelve-year sentence.
In the 1940s Harry White was OC IRA Northern Command, and
during 1944–6 he was also the army's Chief of Staff.[45]

But the decade of his prominence was a dark one for the IRA in
independent Ireland. The army had considerable damage inflicted
upon it, with episodes such as the July 1943 machine-gunning of
Jacky Griffith in Dublin by the Special Branch. And it also, despite
the confused and divided nature of the Eire IRA, caused some serious
damage. On 10 March 1943 Dublin IRA man Eamon Smullen had very
seriously wounded (by shooting him in the back) a man who had
given evidence in the Special Criminal Court resulting in the conviction
of the IRA's Sean Gallagher on a charge of armed intimidation.
Smullen himself was then arrested and sentenced to fourteen years'
imprisonment. Before his trial, armed IRA members tried to intimidate witnesses into not giving evidence; after it, a boy whom the IRA
suspected of having given information leading to Smullen's arrest was
fired on and wounded in the groin. Such low-level, ineffectual brutality
characterized the army's dismal Eire performance during the war years.
Their violent intentions (which apparently even included a plot to kill
the poet John Betjeman, who as press attaché to the British ambassador
in Dublin sent back regular intelligence briefings to London during the
war), amounted to little in terms of their gaining any momentum.
De Valera's state rested on the support of the vast majority of the
population, and the government showed ruthless resolve in suppressing

an alternative army fighting in the name of the tradition from which they themselves had emerged.

What of the IRA's second theatre of operations, Britain itself? In October 1938 the army set out their aims and self-image, as 'an active, effective bulwark against the submergence of Ireland by British imperialism'; as 'an all-Ireland force' aiming 'to assert the sovereignty and unity of the republic proclaimed in Easter Week 1916; to enable a government of the republic to function freely, and to destroy the power of British imperialism in Ireland'. There was here little doubt about the identity of the enemy: 'England is the enemy of Ireland's freedom. The English have partitioned our country. They enforce partition by bayonets and are responsible for the persecution and victimisation of Irish citizens in north-east Ulster.'[46] Following this logic, the obvious target for IRA violence might be thought to be the old enemy itself. In order to rest on secure republican foundations, however, the IRA first sought to gain possession of truly legitimate authority. In the late 1930s this, in their view, rested with the remnant of the 1921 Second Dáil – those who still embodied what to diehard republicans remained the last authentic, uncorrupted authority in Ireland. Thus in December 1938, before launching its bombing campaign in Britain, the IRA Army Council approached the Executive Council of the Second Dáil,[47] looking to have the latter's authority passed directly to it. On 8 December this handover of legitimacy took place, with the IRA Army Council taking over 'the government of the republic of Ireland'.[48] The IRA leadership could now (in their own view, at least) speak to the British as one government to another.

The central figure behind the forthcoming British campaign was Sean Russell, who had become Chief of Staff in 1938.[49] He had already publicly announced his plan to bomb Britain while in the USA in 1936; and his enthusiasm for attacking Britain directly was shared by leading Irish-American republican Joseph McGarrity, whom Russell had known since the 1920s. McGarrity controlled Clan na Gael in the USA and was an important ally of Russell, whose British campaign was funded with US Irish republican money. A GAC in Dublin in April 1938 had approved the British endeavour, and from that October onwards groups of IRA men were brought back from England to Dublin for training, the main bomb-making instructors being Patrick McGrath and Jim O'Donovan. It was O'Donovan who drew up the

S-plan, as the bombing campaign's blueprint was called, with the targets including military installations, BBC transmitters, communications centres, bridges and aerodromes.

In December 1938 key IRA men were sent to various British centres (Glasgow, London, Manchester, Liverpool and Birmingham) and found the IRA organization to be in a poor state when they arrived. But on 12 January 1939 the army none the less sent an ultimatum to the British, calling for withdrawal from Ireland. Four days later, an IRA declaration (signed on behalf of 'The Republican Government and the Army Council of Óglaigh na hÉireann (Irish Republican Army)' by Stephen Hayes, Peadar O'Flaherty, Laurence Grogan, Patrick Fleming, George Plunkett and Sean Russell) pointedly referred back to the 1916 Proclamation and the 1919 Declaration of Independence, and outlined the IRA's intention of completing the republican task: 'The armed forces of England still occupy six of our counties in the North . . . We call upon England to withdraw her armed forces, her civilian officials and institutions, and representatives of all kinds from every part of Ireland.'[50] The British failing to do the necessary, there began an IRA bombing campaign with explosions on 16 January in London, Liverpool, Manchester and Birmingham. The IRA's Volunteers had taken the war to England, armed with what one of their teenage number referred to as his 'Sinn Féin conjuror's outfit': a suitcase 'containing Pot. Chlor., Sulph. Ac., gelignite, detonators, electrical and ignition' – the ingredients for making bombs.[51]

In July 1939, measures were introduced in the London House of Commons to try to deal with the republican threat. By that month, as the British Home Secretary Samuel Hoare informed the House, there had been 127 IRA incidents in Britain since January: it was clear, he said, 'that in the early chapters of the campaign the attempt was intended against property and not against human life'. None the less, 'during the period of these outrages one man was killed in Manchester, one man lost his eye in Piccadilly . . . and fifty-five persons have been seriously or less seriously injured'.[52] The most horrific incident was yet to occur: on 25 August a bomb in Coventry killed five people and injured many more. The person planting the bomb had panicked and left it in an unintended and crowded part of the city. Two people – neither of whom had planted the device – were hanged in February 1940 in connection with the bombing (one had helped with the process of preparing and carrying the explosives used; the other had assembled the bomb).

Shortly before the bombing campaign, Sean Russell had claimed that it was 'very clear' to him that reasonable success would be achieved.[53] In reality, however, the IRA's endeavour was markedly ineffective, and fizzled out without any real positive achievement. It trickled over into 1940, but had by then not much life in it. Even a comparatively sympathetic observer of IRA history could describe the bombing campaign as 'appallingly ill-conceived',[54] and it is unclear precisely how the IRA had anticipated that it *would* produce the desired result. There was little likelihood that the rather inept and low-level IRA attacks that occurred would determine UK policy regarding Ireland. Yet, shambolic though it was, the IRA's campaign reflected the persistence of a neo-Fenian, activist tradition which pointed backwards as well as forwards in the IRA's story. Danny Morrison's uncle Harry was active in this campaign, going to London in 1938 and subsequently planting incendiaries there. County Tyrone's Eoin McNamee (who was to side with the Provisional IRA when they emerged several decades later) was another of those key IRA men sent to Britain (in his case, London) in the December in preparation for the campaign. Packie Connolly also was involved in 1939: arrested in London late that year, he was sentenced to seven years for possession and control of explosive substances and spent his incarceration in Brixton, Maidstone and Albany Prisons. He was born in 1915; his grandfather had been killed by the brutal Black and Tans in 1920, and his uncle had been killed in action against Free State forces in 1922. He himself had joined the IRA in 1931 and had continued his republican activism after emigrating to England in 1936.

If there was in the British campaign drama overlain with ineffectiveness, then the dramatic qualities of the IRA's third arena – that involving its international links – were at times flavoured by something more sinister. American support had been crucial to the British campaign, and, as noted earlier, some IRA and former IRA men had courageously gone to fight against fascism in Spain during the 1936–9 civil war there (though a far larger Irish contingent, more representative of contemporary Irish nationalist opinion, had gone to fight on the other side).[55] The most famous Irish volunteer in Spain, Frank Ryan, had led a body to join the International Brigades in 1936.

Captured in 1938, he was in 1940 handed over to the Germans and taken to Berlin. There was considerable irony in Ryan's having gone to Spain to fight fascism, only to end up as a 'distinguished guest' in Nazi Germany, 'drawing double rations'.[56] Much sadness too, as his health deteriorated and he died in Dresden in June 1944 of pneumonia. But Ryan's unfortunate fate reflected the fact that, during the Second World War, Nazi German and Irish republican interests seemed to coincide. Both the German authorities and Ryan himself envisaged a wartime synergy between their respective anti-British projects just as, from a different republican tradition, Sean Russell himself had sought help from the Nazis. Russell had arrived in Berlin in May 1940, and while in Germany underwent bomb-making and sabotage training. He had sought German support for IRA activities since as early as 1936, and engaged in talks with the German Foreign Office regarding IRA-German cooperation. The Germans apparently thought that, given the IRA's attitude towards Britain, this army constituted their natural wartime allies. Russell was supposed to return to Ireland with a view to fomenting an uprising in the north, which would benefit Germany during the war. With Frank Ryan – with whom he had been reunited in Germany – Russell therefore set out in 1940 on a U-boat, on which he died (apparently due to a perforated stomach ulcer); he was buried at sea, wrapped in a swastika.

Thus neither Russell nor Ryan was to see his country again, and yet the German liaison in which they had, in different ways, become involved demands some attention. During the late 1930s there had been repeated IRA contacts with Nazi Germany: England's enemies were perceived to be the army's obvious friends, a point which grew sharper with the onset of war. In November 1940 the IRA set out its thinking lucidly enough: 'In every generation when an effort was about to be made to break the connection with England, Irishmen sought the help of those who strove for the downfall of England.' Instances were offered of Irish rebellions from the past: 1798, 1803, 1848, 1867, 1916. 'Today [the IRA continued] England is locked in a life and death struggle with Germany and Italy. From what quarter shall the government of the Irish Republic seek for aid? The lesson of history is plain. England's enemy is Ireland's ally.'[57]

Earlier in the year, the army had proclaimed confidently that 'With the assistance of our victorious European allies, and by the strength and courage of the Irish Republican Army, Ireland will achieve absolute independence within the next few months . . . England is now on her last legs!'[58] Some months later, the IRA – the self-styled 'mailed fist of the Irish people' – explicitly refused 'to recognise the present neutrality of Eire, because of the fact that the aggressor has already invaded Ireland. Consequently, the [Irish Republican] Army declared war on the aggressor, which is being waged since January 12, 1939. In spite of the assertions of neutrality made by the present Irish government, the army will continue its warfare against Britain until the ultimate victory is won.'[59] For their part, the Irish authorities were certainly anxious regarding IRA-Nazi links: 'A constant problem is the question of the possibility of cooperation between the IRA and Germany . . . The IRA in their propaganda have repeatedly stated that any enemy of England is their friend and will obtain their cooperation.'[60] And the links went beyond the rhetorical, and far beyond Russell and Ryan. German agent Oskar Pfaus had arrived in Ireland in February 1939 in order to liaise with the IRA. He established contact with the Army Council and arranged for the IRA's Jim O'Donovan (the man behind the British bombing campaign S-plan) to visit Germany, which he did repeatedly between February and August that year. During these visits plans were made for the IRA to assist Germany against Britain through sabotage and espionage in Britain and Northern Ireland.

Abwehr agent Herman Goertz arrived in Ireland in May 1940 (one of his aims being to prompt northern republicans into rebellion) but was detained the following year. He had himself quickly become disillusioned with the IRA and had pursued his goals without them, by trying to obtain intelligence inside Northern Ireland. Achieving little success, Goertz poisoned himself rather than face deportation to Germany. Shortly after his capture, Jim O'Donovan (the primary Nazi-republican link) was interned and, as a consequence, the IRA-German connection was greatly weakened. More feeble still was the career of *Abwehr* agent Ernst Weber Drohl (a former circus strong-man: 'Atlas the Strong'). He arrived in Ireland in February 1940, but mislaid his radio transmitter when landing from the U-boat. Quickly taken by the authorities, he epitomized the ultimately fruitless alliance between the IRA and the Nazis.

The IRA of the mid-twentieth century contained people with a range of ideological instincts (though Catholic nationalism was prominent: in the words of one member, 'many understood themselves as good and holy men for good and holy causes, à la Terence Mac Swiney').[61] But it is important to note where anti-Britishness had led the IRA during the Second World War: ostensibly fighting oppression and tyranny, they here sided with a force far more oppressive and tyrannical than Britain. Clearly, the IRA's primary motivation was simply alliance with their enemy's enemy (though, in the case of the legendary hero of the Irish revolution, Dan Breen, pro-Nazi sympathy lived on beyond the Second World War itself).[62] And the fact remains that, faced with one of the twentieth century's genuinely world-threatening tyrants, the IRA had opted for alliance rather than opposition. As one republican later reflected of her wartime sympathy for Hitler: 'At the time, anyone that was beating the English, we were for them. We thought that way. But how wrong we were. How wrong we were.'[63]

What of the fourth field of operations, Northern Ireland? Stephen Hayes's prosecutor, Sean McCaughey, had pressed from 1940 for the IRA to take action in the north against the British and to seek military, material German aid in doing so. As with the British bombing campaign, there was a certain IRA logic to attacking the north: for it was in the north that British control of Ireland stood out most clearly and painfully. If both Irish states had, after the revolution, settled down to a quasi-confessional order (Catholic in the south, Protestant in the north), then that in the north left a more significant internal minority disaffected from the state's arrangement. Where southern Protestants comprised a mere fraction of the population by mid-century, in the north a third of the population could understandably feel that they were on the wrong side of the border, in a state emphatically at odds with their traditions and culture. Northern Catholics were the main losers from partition, paying the price for the political exigencies and interests of others (Ulster unionists, southern nationalists, the British state). But anxious about a hostile neighbouring state to the south (whose 1937 constitution laid claim to Northern Ireland's territory), and about potential betrayal from London, unionist governments in Belfast also felt concern about the sizeable nationalist minority within their borders, who did not think Northern Ireland a legitimate political entity. A division was drawn between those loyal and those disloyal; but in Ireland confessional background and political

orientation had long overlain one another, and 'disloyalist' in Northern
Ireland all too frequently meant merely Catholic. Thus the northern
state was one in which power and opportunity were far from equally
distributed (a tendency reinforced as unionists looked with increasing
anxiety at the development of a more and more separatist, Catholic,
Gaelicized Ireland under de Valera, south of the border).[64]

The partition of Ireland had reflected the failure of the UK to
accommodate Catholic Ireland satisfactorily, and simultaneously that
of Irish nationalism to attract Irish Protestants; its aftermath in
Northern Ireland echoed such failures, especially in the incapacity of
the northern state to absorb its Catholic population in a fair or
adequate way. Sectarianism in Ireland was not born with partition: the
former long predated, and helped to cause, the latter.[65] But Northern
Ireland was to witness an intensification of sectarian division, and this
was to prove one vital context for the IRA's story. Arguments about
discrimination under the 1921–72 Belfast regime have been lengthy
and frequently bitter. But such debates have generally concerned the
extent, rather than the very existence, of anti-Catholic discrimination.
In truth, the British desire to insulate itself from the Northern Irish
problem allowed persistent anti-Catholic discrimination to occur in
the north. For while Irish sectarianism was not the preserve of one side
alone (Catholics discriminated against Protestants north and south, on
occasions), the fact remains that power in the north was so heavily,
and deliberately, placed at Protestant disposal that the main weight of
discriminatory practice fell from that direction. As authoritative scholarly judgment has it, 'Northern Ireland was created and defined so as
to guarantee a perpetual Protestant and unionist majority. As the new
state became established, so Protestant power became entrenched
within all the major institutions.'[66]

In housing, in electoral practices and in employment, Catholics
were frequently and seriously disadvantaged. They were more likely
than Protestants to be in the lower reaches of the socio-economic
order, and more likely to be without a job; as late as 1971 Catholic
men were more than two and a half times more likely to be unemployed than were their Protestant counterparts. Discrimination was
not the only cause for all this – Catholic occupational and educational
choices also played a part – but it was a profoundly significant one.[67]
Ironically, unionist anxiety about the threat posed by 'disloyalists' itself

led to discriminatory practice which was likely to create or reinforce disloyalty to a state that treated people in this way. No sustainedly imaginative or magnanimous approach was adopted towards winning over the Catholic minority. So, while Ulster unionism was far from monolithic or straightforward in its complexion in the 1921–72 period, the actions of the unionist state did create grounds for serious disaffection on the part of northern nationalists.[68]

What of the IRA in these circumstances? In the 1920s they had been called upon to defend Catholic communities in the sectarian clashes surrounding the birth of the northern state, a role they again sought to adopt amid the intense, fatal sectarian violence of 1935. But 1920s and 1930s Irish republicanism in the north was frequently characterized by defeat and disillusionment. Mid- to late-1920s IRA activity in Northern Ireland was at a low level, although the 1930s Belfast IRA were at least attempting to keep in military shape (Charlie McGlade: 'We were very much a military organisation. We attended parades where you'd be drilled, and as well as that you'd be getting lectures on the different guns: rifles, grenades of course, Webley, Colt, Colt automatic, Thompson sub-machine gun.')[69] And they had used their weapons in more than just drill. In July 1937 the IRA burned customs huts along the Irish border, to coincide with King George VI's visit to Belfast. In the late 1930s also the idea emerged of an IRA Northern Command, which was created to cover the six counties of Northern Ireland (Antrim, Derry/Londonderry, Tyrone, Fermanagh, Armagh, Down) together with Donegal from the southern state. Within this territory there was sporadic but often brutal activity, with the IRA as both victims and agents. On Remembrance Day 1938, the two minutes' silence was broken by four explosions in different parts of Belfast. Early in September 1939 forty-six republicans were arrested and interned by the authorities, 'as a safety measure'.[70] Then on 10 February 1940 an IRA raid on Ballykinlar military camp, County Down, gained them about thirty rifles.

Towards the end of 1941, what was left of the IRA leadership decided to concentrate some of the organization's energies on the north. Significant sabotage and intelligence-gathering might have caused the British considerable wartime nuisance in Northern Ireland, where the republican army might perhaps have constituted a genuine fifth-columnist cause for anxiety; but the IRA's achievements there were, in the event, distinctly unimpressive. The memoirs of Paddy Devlin (later a constitutional nationalist politician, but in the Second World War a youthful IRA man) present a humorous rather than lethal army. On the outbreak of war, the IRA were instructed to paint on gable walls the republican maxim, 'England's difficulty is Ireland's opportunity'; in fact, Falls Road walls were mistakenly daubed with the rather less menacing 'England's difficulty is Ireland's opera tune'. Devlin himself, a teenager at this stage, was instructed on one occasion to commandeer a car in Belfast for IRA use. 'I want your car for the IRA,' Devlin said, but received the crushing reply: 'Fuck off, you wee bastard, or I'll give you a toe up the arse!'[71]

Not that there was no IRA violence at this time. On 4 April 1942 in Dungannon, RUC Constable Thomas Forbes (married, with ten children) was fatally shot by the IRA. On the following day (Easter Sunday) – as a diversion, intended to draw police away from an illegal 1916 republican commemoration – the IRA ambushed an RUC patrol car in Kashmir Road in the Falls area of Belfast ('another dastardly attempt . . . made on the lives of members of the police force', in the RUC's view).[72] Eight IRA members were involved in this, including Tom Williams (nineteen years old and the group's leader), Joe Cahill (twenty-one), Billy Perry (twenty-one), Harry Cordner (nineteen), John Oliver (twenty-one) and Paddy Simpson (eighteen). In the dramatic gunfight that ensued in the kitchen of a house in Cawnpore Street, Williams fatally shot RUC Constable Patrick Murphy – twice in the chest and three times in the stomach – and was himself wounded. Murphy was married with nine children; Williams, and the five comrades named above, were sentenced to death (ex-IRA man Francis Stuart passed on German sympathy in one of his broadcasts via the Third Reich's radio propaganda service for Ireland);[73] and the date of execution was fixed for 2 September.

All but Williams had their sentences commuted to life after great clamour for a reprieve, and would be released from prison in October 1949. Joe Cahill (later famous as a Provisional IRA man) reported back to IRA duty. But on 2 September 1942 Tom Williams was hanged in Crumlin Road Jail. Large crowds assembled in the streets near the prison: Catholics knelt in prayer as the execution approached; Protestants cheered and jeered, and sang their traditional anthem 'The sash my father wore'. Williams had been born in Belfast in 1922, joining the IRA when he was only seventeen; he walked steadily to his death and, in the words of the priest who attended him, 'could not have been braver'.[74] Remembered by Joe Cahill as 'a man of great determination, courage and bravery',[75] Williams – through his death – became a celebrated part of Belfast republican folkloric and balladic culture, a lasting icon from grim years for the IRA.

Early in 1942 an IRA convention had agreed to renew its campaign in the north, but the army faced numerous setbacks. At the end of August that year the police raided a farm just outside Belfast and found there a huge IRA arms dump; in the raid, nineteen-year-old IRA man Gerry O'Callaghan was shot dead. On 5 September a sixteen-year-old Gerry Adams – whose son of the same name was to become the more famous republican of the two – was (as a member of the IRA's Belfast Brigade) involved in a shooting incident in the Falls area of Belfast, in which he wounded an RUC man slightly in the foot, and in which he himself was wounded and arrested. Adams was incarcerated in Belfast's Crumlin Road Jail, and released in 1946. His brother Dominic – IRA Chief of Staff for a time – had been involved in the IRA's 1939 British bombing campaign. Another leading figure in these years in the north was Derry-born Hugh McAteer (1917–70), whose experiences were emblematic of the frustrations and excitements of this period of IRA history. In 1936 he had received a seven-year sentence for possession of explosives. Released in October 1941, he became active again in the army and, shortly after his release, was appointed Chief of Staff. But in October 1942 he was again arrested, charged with treason felony and given a fifteen-year sentence. Then on the morning of 15 January 1943 (together with fellow IRA men Patrick Donnelly, Ned Maguire and Jimmy Steele) he escaped from Crumlin Road Jail. A reward of £3,000 was offered for information leading to the four escapees' recapture, and much excitement followed the break-out:

Car loads of police throughout the day dashed through various parts of the city, while the area in the immediate vicinity of the gaol was completely encircled and houses searched. Hundreds of pedestrians and city workers were stopped in the streets in all parts of the city and questioned. Cars were stopped and examined, trams and buses were boarded and passengers questioned, cinemas, cafés and public-houses were visited. Even breadvans and other covered vehicles came under the police surveillance.[76]

Less than three months after the dramatic escape, McAteer was again appointed Chief of Staff. But later in the year the RUC rearrested him and he was not released again until several years after the war. (McAteer's brother, Eddie, epitomized another strain of northern nationalism: he was a Nationalist Party politician – leader of the parliamentary party in the 1960s – and committed to constitutional, rather than his brother's violent, brand of politics; the two brothers remained close, but 'Eddie maintained that only a patient, peaceful and constitutional approach would eventually lead to [Irish] reunification.')[77]

Though quiet by later northern standards, therefore, the 1940s northern IRA were not entirely silent. On 5 September 1942 they shot dead Constable James Laird and Special Constable Samuel Hamilton in a gun duel near the border in County Tyrone. The following month Special Constable James Lyons was fatally wounded in Belfast in a gun-battle with the IRA: a bomb had been thrown at the RUC's Donegall Pass barracks; the police had opened fire across the street towards the place from which the bomb had been thrown; the IRA had answered fire as they retreated up Donegall Pass towards Botanic Avenue in the Queen's University area of the city. The police gave chase, and in the ensuing gunfight Lyons was shot.

By the end of the war, however, the IRA's fitful northern campaign had drawn to an ineffective close and in July 1945 the authorities even saw fit to release the last of those republicans interned during the conflict. Indeed, the IRA's wartime record in the north was one of low-level brutality and of largely directionless violence. They were a notable presence, activities such as their January 1942 robbery outside Belfast ARP headquarters (which netted £4,750 in cash) keeping the republican flame at least burning; on this occasion one of the seven raiders, together with the ARP chief wages clerk, was injured. Again, at the start of October 1943, the RUC's Patrick McCarthy was fatally shot while on pay-escort duty at a Belfast flax mill. Armed IRA men raided for the cash; McCarthy was ordered not to move; he went for his gun and was shot. But for all the sincerity and the genuine anti-Northern Irish grievance involved in the army of these years, some observers also saw less pleasing traits. F. L. Green's 1945 novel, *Odd Man Out* – itself focusing on the aftermath of a fatally botched IRA raid – referred to Belfast IRA men's 'hatred, fanaticism, and murder, within a tiny island beyond which they had never ventured, and outside of which their stunted imagination could not extend'. It also suggested the role played in IRA members' formation and thinking by embittered teachers and personal envy; and described the Chief of Staff's life as 'small and vicious and stupid'.[78] Though perhaps unduly harsh, these comments might serve to offset some observers' tendency towards a simplistically romanticized reading of the Irish Republican Army of these dark years.

3

'The movement remains intact and is in a position to continue its campaign in the occupied areas indefinitely.'

IRA statement, February 1962[79]

The aftermath of the Second World War appeared to offer little promise for the IRA. Their wartime campaigns in Eire, Northern Ireland and Britain alike had produced little progress, and their alliance with the Nazis had proved equally fruitless. Moreover, with Northern Ireland's wartime participation contrasting favourably in British eyes when set against Eire's neutrality, the leverage enjoyed by the Belfast unionist regime in London had been significantly increased. Ironically, postwar unionism looked set for a strengthened future.

And the immediate postwar situation for the IRA in the south was hardly more inspiring. Morale was low, the public largely indifferent and the state authorities well informed about this supposedly clandestine organization. The IRA opted to eschew formal campaigns against the southern state (which from 1948 became the Republic of Ireland): its General Order No. 8, prohibiting acts of aggression in the twenty-six-county state, was originally drafted in 1948. But in the early postwar days, the IRA looked in no position to mount a forceful campaign anyway. For one thing, splits were occurring. Brendan O'Boyle, who in

1940 had joined the IRA while a student at Queen's University, Belfast, went in 1952 to New York looking for support for an Irish campaign: the Americans were supposed to raise money, purchase arms and ammunition, and arrange to have the material shipped to Ireland. Back in Ireland, O'Boyle tried to gain control of younger sections of the IRA, with a view to his campaign. Little headway was made (and O'Boyle blew himself up on a bombing mission in the summer of 1955), but his schismatic instincts were echoed by Liam Kelly, a County Tyrone republican who in the early 1950s established Saor Uladh (Free Ulster) and its political wing Fianna Uladh. In November 1955 Roslea RUC station in County Fermanagh was attacked in a raid led by Kelly – one police constable was seriously, and one raider fatally, injured. Early reports blamed the IRA for the raid. But a senior army figure soon made a statement to the contrary: 'We wish to state that the Irish Republican Army had no connection with the incident at Roslea (County Fermanagh) and no member of the army was involved.'[80] Kelly's group differed in outlook from the IRA in significant ways, for example accepting the legitimacy of the Dublin parliament; seeing the latter as the sole legitimate authority in Ireland, they focused exclusively on the occupied north.

Joe Christle too wanted IRA action against the north, but doubted that they would offer it. Having joined the IRA in 1949 and Sinn Féin in 1952, Christle had displayed a tendency towards unauthorized actions. In June 1956 he was therefore dismissed from the IRA, his supporters leaving with him. In August that year Christle's and Liam Kelly's groups reached agreement, and on Armistice Day they burned down border customs huts. Christle, who had qualified as a barrister, saw himself as a socialist revolutionary, and he favoured the idea of bombing cafés and bars frequented by British soldiers – an idea with which Liam Kelly disagreed. (Christle did, however, leave his destructive mark in a striking way, when he and some dissident colleagues blew up Nelson's Pillar in O'Connell Street, Dublin, in March 1966.)

What of the mainstream IRA itself? In the early and mid-1950s they pursued one of their longstanding goals with a series of arms raids, in Derry, in Essex, in Armagh, in Omagh, in Berkshire. But arms were for use, and the IRA's next major military venture came during 1956–62: the border campaign. The idea of a northern-focused campaign had long roots, with Tom Barry having espoused it forcefully in (and before) the 1930s. Now, in the mid-1950s, Sean Cronin enthused over a similar strategy for the army. He gave Charlie Murphy (a Dubliner who had joined the IRA in 1950, aged nineteen) a plan entitled 'Operation Harvest'. Cronin had drawn this up at the start of 1956, and it outlined a scheme for attacking military installations, communications and public property in the north with a view to paralysing the place.

The ultimate aim of the IRA's ill-fated border campaign was a traditional one: 'an independent, united, democratic Irish republic. For this we shall fight until the invader is driven from our soil and victory is ours.'[81] The method was to be guerrilla warfare, following on from recognition of the profound inequality between the respective forces of the UK and the IRA. The plan was still ambitious: to use flying columns from the Republic of Ireland to attack targets in the north and, hopefully, to set up liberated areas. From April 1956 the army planned for the campaign, despite some in the leadership (Tony Magan, Patrick MacLogan, Tomás MacCurtain) being less than enthusiastic about the project. Four mobile attack columns were set up, intending their attacks to be on northern military targets in rural border areas. Around twenty organizers were sent in August 1956 to north Antrim, Derry city, south Derry, south Fermanagh, south Down and south Armagh. Their job was to train Volunteers, to do intelligence work, to select targets and to report back regularly to Dublin.

Initially planned to begin in November 1956, it was not until the following month that the campaign actually commenced, with over a hundred IRA Volunteers involved in the operations. In the early morning of 12 December an explosion in Derry destroyed the BBC relay transmitter there; this was followed by an armed raid on Gough barracks in Armagh (a British Army spokesman at the barracks commented: 'There was a raid but it was definitely not successful. The men didn't even get in').[82] Following these incidents, Northern Ireland's Prime Minister (Lord Brookeborough) commented, 'We do not underestimate the seriousness of the attacks',[83] and the Northern Irish authorities did indeed respond to the IRA campaign by introducing internment without trial (which lasted until April 1961, when the last of the detainees were released). Jail for republicans in these years could be grim, as one 1957–60 prisoner in Crumlin Road recalls: 'Single cells ... Talk about doing solitary confinement: you were locked up from

7 o'clock at night to 7 o'clock in the morning; then you slopped out; and then you went for breakfast about 9; once you slopped out you were locked up again, so 7 o'clock to 9, it was fourteen hours. And then, you were locked up immediately after lunch for another hour or so. Fifteen hours. And then on a Sunday it was even worse: you were locked up for something like twenty hours on a Sunday.'[84]

The IRA attacks spread. In the early morning of 14 December four bombs exploded outside Lisnaskea RUC station in County Fermanagh. On 1 January 1957 the IRA attacked Brookeborough RUC station in the same county: among those involved in the raid were later Provisional IRA leader Daithi O Connell, as well as Fergal O'Hanlon and Sean South – two newly minted martyrs, killed in the assault and subsequently celebrated in balladry and romantic imagination. Emotion briefly ran high enough in the Republic for Sinn Féin (now the IRA's political wing, having been reactivated as such in the late 1940s) to secure four seats in the March 1957 general election there. Not that the southern state was any friend to the IRA: in July 1957 internment was introduced there too, and there were sweeps that trawled republicans in to spend much of their campaign locked up. (The northern authorities had recognized immediately the value of southern effort against republican rebels: upon the start of the border campaign, Brookeborough had at once urged that action be taken to make sure that Dublin took effective steps to suppress the IRA.)[85]

Meanwhile, the violence continued. In August 1957 RUC Sergeant John Ovens was killed by an IRA booby-trap bomb in County Tyrone. An anonymous telephone call had lured police and troops to an unoccupied house, with the claim that suspicious men had been seen entering it. When searching the property, Ovens (forty-four years old and married with two young daughters) kicked open the kitchen door – his legs were blown off by the blast and he was fatally injured. November that year saw the awful Edentubber explosion in County Louth, five republicans being blown up when a landmine exploded prematurely. The campaign dribbled on, but explosions along the border (such as those of July 1958) showed little sign of undermining Northern Ireland, given the lack of popular sympathy for the IRA among the nationalist population there.

Yet blood was, none the less, still being spilt. In January 1961 RUC

Constable Norman Anderson was killed near the border by the IRA (machine-gunned in the back from close range); so, too, was another RUC man, William Hunter, in a south Armagh ambush and gun-battle in November of the same year. Commenting on Hunter's death, Northern Ireland's Minister of Home Affairs Brian Faulkner observed: 'This attack was premeditated and cold-blooded murder.'[86] Despite these killings, however, the campaign had still not gained any real momentum, or – significantly – any hold on popular Irish nationalist imagination. Thus in January 1962, with public support for the border campaign virtually non-existent, the IRA Army Council, Army Executive and GHQ Staff met and unanimously voted to end it. A special army order on 5 February 1962 directed all IRA units to dump arms, an order which came into effect three weeks later; and an IRA statement of 26 February announced the end of the border campaign, proclaiming that the movement remained intact and 'in a position to continue its campaign in the occupied areas indefinitely', but also acknowledging that foremost among the reasons for calling off the project had been 'the attitude of the general public whose minds have been deliberately distracted from the supreme issue facing the Irish people – the unity and freedom of Ireland'.[87]

The Irish people had never, in fact, seemed sufficiently interested in this phase of IRA activity. Within a short time of its commencement, it had become clear that the IRA's 1956–62 border campaign was not going to succeed. Unionists, clearly, would oppose it; but Irish nationalists, north and south, failed also to rally at all significantly to the bugle call on this occasion. The initiation of the campaign might have jolted the schoolboy Seamus Heaney:

> When I heard the word 'attack'
> In St Columb's College in nineteen fifty-six
> It left me winded, left nothing between me
> And the sky that moved beyond my boarder's dormer[88]

But it did not have the same impact on the northern state. As a leading republican of the next generation aptly put it, 'The IRA had decisively lost the 1956–62 border campaign, and while republicans were respected in the areas they lived, no one saw them as delivering the promised land. It had all been tried before and had ended in defeat. Unionism was solid.'[89]

None of this should, of course, lead us to dismiss the endeavour as trivial. There were over five hundred incidents, and there was much awful violence inflicted and suffered. This included, of course, republican casualties. Fergal O'Hanlon from Monaghan town (only nineteen at the time of his death) and the devoutly Catholic Sean South from Limerick city became memorialized in song and in republican memory. But less famous republican comrades also gave their lives. Twenty-year-old County Monaghan man Aloysius Hand was shot dead by the RUC in a County Fermanagh gun-battle on the border in July 1958; Hand had been in a group of a dozen men whom a police patrol had called upon to halt – he opened fire with a Thompson sub-machine gun, but was fatally shot when the police fired back. One month later, Cavan man James Crossan was shot dead when police fired on him at Mullan, County Fermanagh; he was one of a group which had been heading towards the British customs hut on the border – the police called on them to halt, and shot Crossan as he ran towards the border with the Irish Republic.

Tragedy had been accompanied by at least a measure of farce, with the IRA's poor organization contributing to their difficulties. But other factors contributed also to their defeat: successful garda–RUC liaison and the effective use of internment north and south helped scupper the IRA; and the overriding problem for this army was that, while they claimed to act for the Irish people, the Irish people seemed not to be interested in their doing so. When the Republic of Ireland released the last of its internees (before the campaign had even ended) and the last of its IRA prisoners (once it had done so), it appeared that the IRA was no particular threat to anyone.

Could there, indeed, have been a new era opening up at this point in Irish politics? If militant republicans could make no progress, did that mean that there was room for less zealous figures to establish benign relations between Ireland's warring groups and states? Two thoughtful observers (writing at the end of 1961) suggested that to those living in Northern Ireland, 'the tension between Protestants and Catholics seems to be a cause of disunity so ancient and all-pervading that a change is difficult to imagine'; but they also noted that 'The two communities in Northern Ireland live side by side, generally at peace.'[90] Could day-to-day peace at last provide the context for the amelioration of unionist-nationalist relations in Ireland? When Eamon de Valera

was succeeded as Fianna Fáil leader and Taoiseach (Prime Minister) in
1959 by Sean Lemass,[91] such a possibility might have seemed likely.
Lemass – 'as hard-headed a man as there is in Ireland',[92] in Sean
O'Faoláin's estimation – helped begin a thaw in north-south relations
which many understandably took to imply movement towards a
resolution of ancient quarrels. In March 1963 Terence O'Neill[93] had
become Northern Ireland's Prime Minister and better days seemed
heralded when the two premiers met in January 1965 in Belfast, and
again the following month in Dublin; following Lemass's Belfast
visit, the nationalist leader at Stormont (Eddie McAteer) became for
the first time official leader of the opposition.

There has been much argument about the degree to which Terence
O'Neill wanted to combat sectarianism in Northern Ireland (and
certainly his priority seems to have been rather to ensure unionist
political solidarity and strength). But he did make benign noises about
the divisions within his troubled state. In February 1965 he gave an
interview to the Republic of Ireland's Telefís Eireann, in which he set
out an ameliorative vision regarding discrimination in the north: 'by
having improved relations between the two communities in the north
of Ireland, then the feelings are better between those two communities and the likelihood, the ability to discriminate must therefore be
lessened'.[94] Sean Lemass too offered novel-seeming strategies in regard
to Ireland's long-fought battle. There was some ambiguity in his
utterances: sometimes he seemed to break with Irish nationalist orthodoxy on the north, moving away from traditional anti-partitionism
and approaching the question of northern discrimination in more
subtle, nuanced ways than had hitherto typified Dublin politicians.
Yet, while he made such moves and pursued north-south cooperation,
he at times also took a more traditional stance, by questioning the
legitimacy and permanence of the northern state.[95]

Whatever these ambiguities, Lemass did help to improve Anglo-
Irish relations, and during these years there were indeed noises being
made in the south which called into question traditional Irish republican assumptions about the ending of partition. The 1960s saw significant nationalist voices call for a rethinking of orthodoxy regarding the
north. One such was Fianna Fáil veteran and ex-IRA man, Sean
MacEntee – one of the ablest of the revolutionaries-turned-politicians.
In November 1969 MacEntee urged the Taoiseach, Jack Lynch, that

Dublin's best policy was to recognize the de facto position of the northern government, and to cooperate with it wholeheartedly in all areas of common interest:

> Is it politic to claim a sovereignty [over the north] that one is powerless to assert? . . . the frontal attack on the northern position, in which governments on this side of the border engaged themselves for almost fifty years, has failed dismally. The time, I feel, has come when another approach should be considered. And here I think full account must be taken of the hard fact that the unionist party in north-eastern Ireland does represent the traditions and deeply-held convictions of a large majority of the people in that area.[96]

Could such voices indicate the birth of an era in which Irish political harmony would render the IRA superfluous? Had the last been heard of the republican enthusiasms and certainties of Patrick Pearse and James Connolly, of Ernie O'Malley and Tom Maguire, of Peadar O'Donnell and George Gilmore, of Gerry Adams senior and Harry White?

PART TWO

PROTEST AND REBELLION

1963–76

THREE
THE BIRTH OF THE PROVISIONAL IRA
1963–72

1

'Now, rightly or wrongly, I grew up with a clear perception of discrimination practised by the state against myself as part of a community. And it wasn't the type of discrimination that would be excessive in terms of, perhaps, the South African situation or some of the obscenities that are performed in south America. But there was a very, very real, tangible perception, and I would argue that it was more than a perception.'

Tommy McKearney, who joined the IRA in 1971[1]

The Provisional Irish Republican Army was born in December 1969. Its birth is frequently understood as part of a narrative that runs as follows. The old IRA was a spent force by the end of its 1956–62 campaign; there emerged during the 1960s a civil rights movement in the north which was separate from Irish nationalism and which sought only equal treatment for Catholics; this civil rights movement was met by the violence of Protestant loyalists who, in the summer of 1969, attacked a Catholic community left defenceless by a moribund IRA; as a consequence the Provisionals emerged as necessary defenders of the Catholic community. The death of the IRA; a non-nationalist civil rights movement; loyalist aggression; the birth of the Provisionals.

There is much that is important in this account. But close inspection of the evidence suggests that there are also, alongside this story, significant – at times, ironic – continuities between the pre-Provisional IRA on the one hand, and on the other both the civil rights movement and the Provisionals who emerged from the turbulence which that movement provoked. Through its maintenance of a perceived military threat, and its inauguration of a radical civil rights initiative, the old IRA unwittingly helped to produce the conditions from which the new one was to spring. For it was not just that key Provisionals possessed an old IRA pedigree. Nor was it merely that the commemorations and celebrations marking the fiftieth anniversary of the 1916 Easter Rising – activities in which the IRA played a significant part – frequently appear in later Provisionals' accounts as having stimulated their republican interest or enthusiasm.[2] At a subtler, far more important level there were also deeper links between the 1960s IRA and the Provisionals who broke away from them and eventually replaced them. The key connection concerns the 1960s Northern Irish civil rights movement, which (for the most part, unwittingly) destabilized Northern Ireland and created the circumstances from which the Provisionals emerged. This movement was based on perfectly reasonable demands for fairer treatment for Catholics in the north of Ireland. But as we shall see, it was also an initiative which originated from within the old IRA, and which – as far as those old-IRA republicans were concerned – did so with the explicit intention of bringing down the Northern Ireland state. Through its generation of this anti-unionist civil rights campaign, the 1960s IRA inadvertently helped to produce the conditions from which both the Provisional IRA and the Northern Irish troubles emerged.

After the closure in 1962 of their border campaign, Cathal Goulding replaced Ruairí Ó Brádaigh as the IRA's Chief of Staff. Ó Brádaigh had been born in 1932 in County Longford; an intelligent, articulate commerce graduate from University College, Dublin, he had built a career as a teacher in Roscommon. But it is his republican career that makes him historically important. He had joined the two wings of the Irish republican movement as a young man: Sinn Féin in 1950, and the IRA in the following year. He gained his first military experience during the 1956–62 campaign during which he served as Chief of Staff. An IRA Army Council member in the 1960s, he was later to become one of the leading figures in the Provisional movement (despite the unflattering description offered by one fellow Provisional: 'His teeth protruded, his hair stood up spikily – he looked more like Bugs Bunny than anyone else').[3] But in the 1960s Ó Brádaigh's role was largely eclipsed by that of his replacement as Chief of Staff, Cathal Goulding (1922–98). A friend of the boisterous Brendan Behan (and, like Behan, both a house-painter and an IRA man), Goulding possessed a family tree that most Irish republicans can only dream about. His grandfather had been a member of the Fenians, his father had participated in the 1916 Rising, and both his father and an uncle had had IRA careers. Goulding himself had been involved in the army since the 1940s. Indeed, he had joined Fianna Eireann (the junior wing of the IRA) in 1937, aged only fifteen. Imprisoned during 1953–61, he was to be IRA Chief of Staff in 1962–9, and later held the same position in the Official IRA during 1969–72 after the Provisionals had broken away.

Goulding could be attractive, bohemian, witty, charming (and on occasions eccentric: a friend of mine recalls meeting him in later life, anticipating insights perhaps into the republican veteran's political thinking. In fact, the only thing Goulding wanted to tell my friend was how to catch, kill and skin a goat). One of Goulding's own former radical comrades remembered him thus: 'The first thing that struck anybody about Goulding was not his politics but his physical attractiveness . . . he had the head of a Greek god: curly hair, laser-blue eyes set in lizard-lazy lids that would suddenly blaze out at you, backed by a boyish grin that broke women's hearts and made men want to follow wherever he led. Sexual attraction is not to be sneezed at in politics. When it came to charm Goulding was like [Bill] Clinton with character.'[4] Attractive or not, Goulding in 1962 inherited an IRA that was in a weak condition. Funding had dried up, they were short of weapons and there were not enough Volunteers coming through to replace those who had been imprisoned or killed. In this attenuated state some significant rethinking emerged. It was not that violence was rejected. Goulding long continued to believe in the appropriateness, in certain circumstances, of using 'the bomb and the bullet';[5] he was himself charged in 1966 regarding illegal possession of a gun and ammunition; and he long remained 'in the market for arms'.[6]

The IRA during the 1960s drew up at least preliminary plans for another military campaign,[7] and at the end of 1965 the Northern Irish government publicly stated its belief that the organization was about to renew violent attacks. In 1966 the government in Belfast was clearly anxious concerning disorder and outbreaks of violence,[8] and in that year the IRA's ruling Army Council did set up a special military council to plan a new northern onslaught. IRA strength was then around a thousand, compared to approximately 650 four years earlier; and in Belfast the IRA had grown significantly in number between 1962 and 1969.[9] All of this should caution against too simplistic an assumption that the organization was militarily dead in the 1960s; and all of this helps explain (though not at all to justify) the anxiously alarmist Protestant reaction to the events of the 1960s in Northern Ireland.

In part, however, such martial noises as the IRA made during that decade were required precisely because Goulding did indeed want his army to embark on a new departure into radical politics. As one LSE-educated comrade of Goulding's observed, 'Cathal was a Marxist: that was one of the things that didn't endear him to many people' – whether Catholic Irish republicans or Irish-American republicans – but he was 'very much a man of his times: the sixties was that burgeoning period, it seemed as if the left was going to sweep the world in front of it'.[10] Goulding's reading of Irish republicanism was certainly class-tinged: 'The class that always plays the leading role in any national liberation struggle is the working class, the people of no property, the landless people, the industrial workers in the city, and the very small peasant farmer. These are the people who have traditionally supported the national liberation movements in Ireland all through the centuries. Rich people were never interested in national liberation. They are already liberated.'[11]

Goulding was rightly wary of causing disaffection among the IRA faithful by appearing to favour too dramatic a break from the republican tradition of force. However, the new Chief of Staff did attempt a certain shift away from the emphasis on violence: so much so that, in 1968, the IRA apparently sold some of its weapons to the Free Wales Army (a small group who were soon arrested, with the formerly Irish republican guns being seized by the British police). The IRA's weapons were far from impressive; a prominent member of the organization said in 1966 that any they obtained were 'generally obsolete'.[12] There was less emphasis during the 1960s on military training, and more on a leftist definition of republican struggle: 1967 saw the IRA Army Council alter Sinn Féin's constitution in favour of a socialist republican objective;[13] and, in Cathal Goulding's own words, 'Republicanism stands for the liberation of people. We have been accused of being to the left, but if that means seeking an end to partition, to the exploitation of our people and placing them in the position of masters of their destiny rather than slaves of a capitalist economy, then we are to the left.'[14] To mark the bicentenary of the birth in 1763 of Theobald Wolfe Tone (Patrick Pearse's great hero, celebrated by Irish republicans as their ideological founding father), IRA members helped set up commemorative committees. From these, in 1964, sprang the Wolfe Tone Societies: radical republican discussion groups designed to hold debates across Ireland and 'to foster republicanism by educating the masses in their cultural and political heritage';[15] the Societies had as one of their explicit objectives 'a united Irish republic'.[16] (Intriguingly – given his later importance in republican deliberation over violence, politics and social radicalism – one of those participating in Wolfe Tone Society debates in the 1960s was a youthful Gerry Adams.)

The Wolfe Tone Societies were a key initiative within militant Irish republicanism, and one to which the IRA's enthusiastic participation was essential. Crucial to Cathal Goulding's leftist shift here was the influence upon him of certain key intellectuals, including Roy Johnston. Born in Dublin in 1929 of Protestant background (and educated at Trinity College, Dublin (TCD), Johnston had been involved with the socialist republican Connolly Association in London during 1960–3. Returning to Ireland in 1963, he joined the Wolfe Tone Society in early 1964, impressed Goulding, and came to have considerable influence over the IRA's thinking. A distant relative of that founder of the 1913 Irish Volunteers, Bulmer Hobson, Johnston became a member of the IRA's ruling Army Council and there he advocated a committedly socialist case.[17] Amid the complex mosaic of influences upon him was that of his father, Joseph Johnston (1890–1972). A Fellow of TCD and an Ulster Protestant Liberal Home Ruler, Johnston senior had argued in 1913 that the dangers of Home Rule had been overplayed by its unionist opponents ('the evils ensuing from the acceptance of the Home Rule Bill by Ulster are exaggerated beyond all reasonable limits'),[18] and that one simply would not be justified in fighting a civil war in order to avoid any negative features that Home Rule did possess.

Thus Johnston junior, in part, was continuing in the 1960s his father's Protestant Irish nationalism, and echoing his father's tradition

by looking for Ulster Protestants to join in the Irish national movement. In the admirable spirit of Wolfe Tone, he wanted to unify Irish
Protestant and Catholic. And in his energetic, intelligent radicalism, he
sought to interweave Marxism with what he saw as 'the Enlightenment
republican concept',[19] a notion which he held to be directly hostile to
the Catholic nationalism of romantic Irish republican tradition and its
Fenian-style conspiratorialism. With his TCD education and his TCD
father, Johnston perhaps exemplified what the historian Roy Foster has
referred to as that 'little-noted Irish subculture: Trinity College nationalism'.[20] (Given its Protestant Ascendancy character, Trinity was nicely
described by Irish writer and ex-IRA man Sean O'Faolain as 'that alien
nursery of native causes'.)[21] Certainly, Johnston held that the late 1960s
offered a real possibility of reinventing IRA republicanism along more
radical, non-sectarian lines: 'In the 1968 [Sinn Féin] *ard fheis* [conven-
tion] the general political flavour was positive and forward-looking;
most if not all of the politically progressive motions were carried, and
the "sea-green incorruptible" ones rejected.'[22]

Besides Johnston, another major intellectual influence upon the
IRA's new departure was Anthony Coughlan, a University College,
Cork, graduate who had – like Roy Johnston – been involved in the
Connolly Association in London. Coughlan returned to Ireland to
become a lecturer in social administration at TCD in 1961. He was
co-opted into the Wolfe Tone Societies in 1964 and, though not a
member of the IRA, was one of the major influences on republican
thinking in this period.

The intellectual and personal influences, ignored in most accounts,
are important here. Coughlan was himself greatly influenced by his
Connolly Association mentor and James Connolly biographer, the
historian Desmond Greaves, to whom he credited the 1960s Northern
Irish civil rights initiative: 'there is a good case for regarding Desmond
Greaves as the intellectual progenitor of the civil rights movement of
the 1960s. For it was he, and his Connolly Association, that pioneered
the idea of a civil rights campaign as the way to undermine Ulster
unionism.'[23] Greaves had also had 'quite considerable'[24] influence over
the thinking of Roy Johnston. Johnston had first met the historian
in the late 1940s, and Greaves had stayed with the Johnstons then
and through the 1950s when in Dublin. A guru, therefore, for the two
key intellectuals in the republican leftward shift, Greaves himself was a

leftist republican, energetic both as an activist and an intellectual, and one who held resolutely to Irish republican ambition: 'Of course the only basis for a liberal democracy is a united Ireland.'[25] Greaves's Connolly Association had indeed promoted the idea of a civil rights campaign as the way to undermine Ulster unionism.[26]

And behind both Greaves and Coughlan lay important republican socialist influences from an earlier generation. Both men greatly admired those eminent 1930s IRA socialists, Peadar O'Donnell and George Gilmore (Coughlan becoming a particularly close friend of the latter). Despite the failure of their own interwar argument and project, O'Donnell and Gilmore none the less became role models for the 1960s radical republican venture (Coughlan observing that it was 'hard to impugn the logic' of their doomed 1930s Republican Congress movement).[27] And both Coughlan and Goulding also looked even further back in Irish history for inspiration: to the most famous figure in Ireland's socialist republican tradition (and himself a huge influence on Gilmore and O'Donnell), the 1916 leader James Connolly. As we have seen, Desmond Greaves was one of Connolly's most eulogistic biographers, while Anthony Coughlan also rallied to the 1916 martyr's defence.[28] Thus there were strong personal and ideological connections linking the 1960s IRA to earlier republican socialist thinking: Connolly, O'Donnell, Gilmore, Greaves, Coughlan, Johnston and Goulding provided a line of descent running through the alternative philosophy offered by the twentieth-century Irish republican left.

This point is reinforced by consideration of other figures within this left-republican circle in the late 1960s. One fascinating example is Derry Kelleher, a former IRA man who had been interned in the Curragh in the 1940s alongside Cathal Goulding. (During the 1930s Kelleher and Goulding had shared both IRA membership and membership of the Republican Swimming Club.) Kelleher had parted company with the IRA in the 1940s, eschewing what he saw as its secret-society militarism, and was in the 1950s a member of the Connolly Association. He was also a member of the Dublin Wolfe Tone Society from 1966, a close associate of Roy Johnston, and (along with leading IRA figures like Goulding and Sean Garland) a leading late-1960s Sinn Féin activist. Like Johnston and Coughlan, Kelleher had been profoundly influenced by the thinking of Desmond Greaves; like Coughlan, he stressed the importance of Greaves in generating the civil rights project as an anti-unionist strategy, describing the leftist historian as the 'progenitor of the six counties civil rights struggle 1968–72';[29] and, again like Coughlan, Kelleher greatly admired socialist republican George Gilmore ('that great and wise Protestant republican'), and saw himself in a tradition running back through Greaves, Gilmore, O'Donnell and Connolly to Wolfe Tone's United Irishmen of the late eighteenth century. He saw himself and his Wolfe Tone Society comrades as aiming to unite different religious groups in Ireland in pursuit of Irish independence from England.

Radical republican and civil rights enthusiast, Kelleher saw Ireland's relationship with Britain as a colonial one, from which she should be emancipated through the ending of partition, the ending of the British occupation of the north, and the setting up of a united, independent, thirty-two-county Irish republic. The civil rights movement that he helped create in the 1960s was, in his view, an attempt to reach this goal by peaceful, radical means: 'the six counties of the nation has remained under British occupation since 1603 and remains to be freed of British forces (as was the Free State in 1922) with the re-establishment of the thirty-two county Irish republic proclaimed in arms in 1916 and established by popular suffrage in 1918. The completion of that final emancipation began with the peaceful civil rights campaign in Dungannon in 1968.'[30]

The radical IRA (together with non-IRA republicans like Greaves, Coughlan and Kelleher) played a significant role in generating the civil rights project, and did so self-consciously within a radical republican ideological framework. But their inherited leftist republican philosophy was to set in train events which, tragically, they could not control. For while they were inspired by friends and heroes from the past, the 1960s republican thinkers also gazed forward to new dawns, and the argument expounded through the Wolfe Tone Societies was indeed an ingenious one. They held, traditionally enough for a republican group, that the people of Ireland formed one natural unit, divided only by artificially fostered divisions inimical to all. They held that Ulster unionism, and the loyalty of northern Protestant workers to Northern Ireland, relied on systematic discrimination against northern Catholics: 'The basis of partition in the six counties [of Northern Ireland] is an artificially fostered sectarianism, an anti-Catholic prejudice and bigotry which has become identified with the state system . . . without which the system could not survive and without which there would be no reason for its existence.'[31] The Northern Ireland state was thus considered irreformable, and so to campaign for reform concerning northern discrimination was to campaign for something that the state could not yield without causing its own collapse and the loss of its Protestant working-class support. If they did pursue such reform, working-class Protestants would, it was argued, recognize that they too were exploited by the unionist state that oppressed their Catholic fellow workers; they would thus unite with Catholic workers in a newly forged radical alliance which would simultaneously undermine Irish capitalism and Irish partition alike.

A Northern Irish civil rights campaign was, according to this reading, necessarily anti-unionist; and it was a distinctly republican argument. For the Wolfe Tone Societies represented a mixture of iconoclasm and continuity regarding republican tradition. They clearly held that there was a need for some real republican rethinking. An editorial in the group's newsletter *Tuairisc* from June 1966 stated that one of the obstacles to be overcome was 'the illusion still current in some pockets of the republican movement that a simple-minded armed struggle against the British occupation is alone sufficient to generate sufficient popular support to complete the national revolution'. But this did not involve a complete rejection of the traditional republican recourse to violence. Echoing the 1930s thinking of Gilmore and O'Donnell, the same editorial envisaged 'a movement of a new type' in which

> the role of military activity will consist in defending the gains obtained by political, agitational and economic-organisational means, against physical attack by forces organised to defend British interests, either from without or within. It is not the policy of *Tuairisc* to 'advocate' military activity. We are merely making a statement, based on historical experience, that in order to make such change in the social structure of the nation as is necessary to remove the incubus of foreign domination, it may on occasion be necessary to defend gains made by political means by resort to the arming of the common people.[32]

Anthony Coughlan offered one of the most impressively sophisticated versions of the Wolfe Tone Society argument, and his thesis was indeed ingenious. It was firmly in the tradition of Irish socialist republicanism: 'Our idea is the achievement of an all-Ireland republic – politically and economically in control of its own destiny, the home of a nation of free and educated citizens, in which the exploitation of man by man has been abolished.' He called explicitly for 'a return to Connolly', and considered that 'a revolution' would be needed in order to create the desired republic. For Britain's overall aim with regard to Ireland remained unchanging: 'namely to maintain her domination *over the island as a whole* and to keep the whole country in a weak and dependent position'. The most important part of his analysis concerned the north, where things were 'changing rapidly': 'The iceberg of political life in that part of the nation, seemingly frozen solid for half a century, is beginning to melt and to drift into new and strange waters.' By 1966 unionism was in crisis, divided between reformist and hard-line instincts, and in this situation there were 'many possibilities'; Coughlan set out what he saw as the most benign of the possible trajectories:

> [The] unfreezing of political life in the six counties may release the political energies of the people, and particularly the Catholic people and the Protestant working class, and lead to results which the unionists never bargained for. If things change too much the orange worker may see that he can get by alright without dominating his Catholic neighbour. The two of them may in time join forces in the Labour movement, and where would unionism be then? How can unionism possibly survive when Protestant and Catholic are no longer at one another's throats, when discrimination has been dealt a body-blow?[33]

Republican input into the civil rights movement, and the deeply anti-partitionist ambition behind that input, are frequently ignored or downplayed in readings of the north's descent into violence. But – while it would be quite wrong to overstate their importance in Irish history – the Wolfe Tone Societies are, in fact, vital to any proper understanding of the birth of the Provisional IRA. There was a direct, causal, practical and ideological connection between the 1960s IRA and the civil rights initiative; and it was from the IRA's Wolfe Tone Societies that the Northern Ireland civil rights movement emerged. That movement's careful historian, Bob Purdie, has made clear that

'The initiative of setting up NICRA [the Northern Ireland Civil Rights Association] was very much that of [Roy] Johnston, [Anthony] Coughlan and the Dublin Wolfe Tone Society . . . It was the Dublin Wolfe Tone Society which suggested a civil rights campaign';[34] that 'republicans and communists were centrally involved in the creation of the [civil rights] movement'; that NICRA 'had been founded as a direct result of an initiative taken by a section of the republican movement'; and that 'the involvement of republicans in the setting up of the NICRA cannot be denied'.[35] As the leading figure in the subsequently emerging Provisional republican movement, Gerry Adams, was himself to put it, 'Republicans were actually central to the formation of NICRA'; even more pointedly, the civil rights movement was 'the creation of the republican leadership'.[36]

In August 1966 (in Maghera, County Derry) there was a joint meeting of the Wolfe Tone Societies, at which the idea of a civil rights campaign was proposed. IRA Chief of Staff Cathal Goulding attended, and duly pledged the IRA's support. From this August meeting followed a Belfast gathering later in the year, from which in turn sprang the formation of NICRA. Indeed, when NICRA was set up on 29 January 1967 in Belfast, the thirteen-person committee chosen to run the organization included two Wolfe Tone Society representatives (Fred Heatley and Jack Bennett) as well as the IRA's Liam McMillen. There was, therefore, an intentional and personal link between old-IRA anti-unionism and the creation of the civil rights movement; and it was the agitation of the latter which (with admittedly idealistic intentions) spiralled Ulster into the sectarian violence from which the Provisional IRA emerged.

There are far greater continuities, connections and ironies here than are usually recognized. There was a dramatic irony in Cathal Goulding setting in motion the events that would produce a Provisional movement which wrested the IRA away from his control. There was an appalling irony in an initiative sincerely aimed at doing away with northern sectarianism helping, ultimately, to stimulate that very sectarianism into a more excited condition. The radical republicans' 1930s mentors, O'Donnell and Gilmore, had in their own day hoped that shared class interest might overcome sectarian division in the north; so, too, the 1960s Wolfe Tone Societies thought it possible to achieve unity between workers in the two northern communities through activism and turbulence built around the civil rights question. This proved, in each case, not to be possible – however idealistic or genuine it was in origin or intention. The first stage of the Wolfe Tone Societies' thesis did develop: agitation around civil rights indeed produced turbulence which shook the Northern Ireland state in the 1960s. But the second phase – the conversion of working-class Protestants to a radicalized, neo-nationalist unity with northern Catholics – never became anything like a reality. Far from uniting with their Catholic fellow workers, Protestants in the north (dreadfully and entirely without justification) proved more likely to join paramilitary organizations determined to kill them.

But if the 1960s Dublin leadership was out of touch with northern sectarian realities, the ambitious radicalism of the Wolfe Tone Societies did resonate with a wider political and social zeitgeist. Certainly, the youthful radicals who would emerge as leaders of the next generation of Irish republicanism were greatly influenced by precisely this times-changing, optimistic radical mood. Gerry Adams:

> People did not live their lives in isolation from the changes going on in the world outside. They identified to a greater or lesser extent with the music, the politics, the whole undefined movement of ideas and changes of style. Bob Dylan, the Beatles and the Rolling Stones, long hair and beads, the 'alternative society', music and fashion were all markers put down by a new generation against the complacencies of the previous one, and one of the most important messages to come across was that one *could* change the world.[37]

Danny Morrison: 'people of my age, my generation, we watched the civil rights movement in the States, we watched the Vietnam war and the anti-war protests'.[38]

While it is important to detail the role played by civil rights radicals in helping to generate 1960s turbulence, it would clearly be wrong to blame the civil rights activists or movement for starting the troubles. Yet the new, radical thinking of the 1960s IRA did fail to appreciate the deep, tangled roots of sectarian division (attributing it simply to ruling-class manipulation), or to attribute any autonomy or self-sustaining seriousness to Protestant unionism in the north. In helping to prompt political turbulence in Northern Ireland, the 1960s IRA unleashed a conflict with battle lines different from those they had anticipated, and a struggle that they could not direct. Not for the first time in revolutionary history, Frankensteinian intellectuals had helped create a monster beyond their control.

For the northern chaos which quickly developed in the late 1960s reinforced a sectarianism which many on the republican left had nobly opposed, but which they had simply failed to understand. Indeed, Anthony Coughlan, one of the key intellectuals in the new initiative, unwittingly testified to this failing when on 3 August 1969 he suggested that the civil rights movement's greatest achievement over the preceding year had been the way in which it had 'unified and raised the morale' of the Catholic population in Northern Ireland: 'I use the word Catholic deliberately, for there is no denying that it is the Catholic people of the north whom the orange-unionist machinery of bigotry is mainly directed against. The basic policy of unionism is to stay in power by keeping the Catholics suppressed and by giving Protestant workers the impression that they benefit from that suppression.' While the ostensible intention behind Coughlanite civil rights enthusiasm had been the creation of cross-sectarian unity, its main achievement by the start of August 1969 was thus, in Coughlan's own judgment, the unification and invigoration of one of the north's communal groups through a movement which expressly condemned the politics of the other. That Coughlan's observations here were made at a commemoration for the executed Irish republican hero (and Protestant convert to Catholicism), Roger Casement, merely made this irony more acute. Casement, Coughlan suggested, 'would surely have fully supported' the civil rights movement – a comment no more likely to win northern Protestant support than was the raising of the tricolour during the commemoration or the holding of a Catholic Mass (in Irish) beforehand.[39]

The IRA itself had genuinely hoped to win Ulster Protestants to their cause. As a leading figure in the organization put it in the mid-1960s, 'We want to try to get through to the Protestant working classes. We realise our success there depends on the amount of understanding. If these people understand, I believe they would support us.'[40] Tragically for such aspirations, the civil rights campaign – though intentionally non-sectarian – became associated with the Catholic community as a consequence of its (perfectly reasonable) demands on behalf of Catholics, and because of its challenging attitude towards the unionist government. In their intensification of sectarian division, the civil rights activists showed how, not for the first time in Irish history, a movement defining itself in non- or even anti-sectarian terms could unwittingly deepen intercommunal animosity.

Thus the Goulding turn to the left prompted changes beyond the republican movement which were to help in producing the Provisionals. The nature of the 1960s army itself also contributed to the process, for the IRA began to take a shape that some of its members felt to be deeply inappropriate. Goulding proposed at a 1964 Army Convention that republicans should immerse themselves in social and economic struggles, that they should build an alliance with other radical groups to create a national liberation front and (most alarmingly to traditionalist republican eyes) that they should contest elections and take their seats in the parliaments in Dublin, Belfast and London. These parliaments had long been considered illegitimate in republican thinking, and while his other proposals were accepted, this last suggestion – in effect, to end parliamentary abstentionism – was defeated. But the determination of leading republicans to politicize the movement was unquestionable, Sinn Féin President Tomás Mac Giolla – for example – firmly endorsing the trend: 'Sinn Féin intends to throw the full weight of the organisation into the local government elections in the twenty-six counties this year [1967] and a major effort will be made to gain a greater foothold in local councils.'[41] Statements such as this, together with the broader approach pursued by Goulding, reflected the long-term, ongoing debate within republicanism regarding the relation between politics and violence. Although the emphasis of the then leadership was less military than political, this was a view from which many were to dissent – and the dissenters became the Provisionals.

Yet it was beyond the IRA that perhaps the most significant tremors were being registered. Although it was by republicans that the civil rights idea had been planned and conceived, this should not lead one to see the campaign that actually emerged merely as a republican front, a movement dominated or controlled by republicans. It was not. The Northern Ireland civil rights movement comprised a number of groups, including NICRA, the Campaign for Social Justice in Northern Ireland (CSJNI),[42] the Derry Citizens' Action Committee (DCAC)[43] and the People's Democracy (PD). Admittedly, the last of these epitomized the more radical strain of thinking within the civil rights family, some of which did echo in argument and instinct the ideas of the IRA's favoured Wolfe Tone Societies. The PD was formed at Queen's University, Belfast (QUB), in October 1968, pursuing the goals of one-man-one-vote in local council elections (this provision already existing for elections to the London and Belfast parliaments), fairer electoral boundaries, the allocation of houses on the basis of need, the awarding of jobs on merit, the maintenance of free speech and the repeal of the north's Special Powers Act. It was very much a student movement. That a university should spawn radicalism in the late 1960s is unsurprising: with its sit-ins, marches, pickets and so forth, the PD echoed much that was happening in the militant European student movement elsewhere. That QUB generated civil rights energy in the north had a more locally precise dimension to it, however, as the university was one of the few centres of religiously mixed education in the province.

The key figure in the PD was the able and profoundly anti-unionist Michael Farrell: student activist and politician, leftist zealot and person-ification of the PD phenomenon.[44] Here, too, socialist republican influences were important. Farrell himself was clear in 1966 about his Connollyite vision of Ireland's future: 'Fifty years after Connolly's death his dream of an Irish workers' republic has still to be achieved. Only the united action of working-class people north and south, Catholic and Protestant, in a single Labour and Trade Union movement can achieve Connolly's aim.'[45] And the zeal of other civil rights activists was also fuelled by socialist republican conviction. In her excellent memoir of these years, the boisterous civil rights leader and PD activist Bernadette Devlin demonstrated the profound republican influences (home and school) in her background; she also made clear that she was convinced by the arguments of James Connolly, and that her reading of Irish history relied centrally on socialist thought: 'Since the Treaty of 1921, which freed the south from British rule but severed the north from the rest of the country, the republican target has been a reunited, socialist Ireland ... From [1801] on national feeling grew and throughout the nineteenth century, there was continual struggle, punctuated by famine and emigration, to end British occupation, British imperialism and British capitalism; and this was throughout Ireland as a whole.'[46] The charismatic and influential Derry civil rights activist, Eamonn McCann, also owed a profound debt to socialist thinking and was deeply hostile to the northern state.[47]

And, armed with such ideas, these talented radicals in late 1968 and early 1969 were deliberately trying to provoke the state into overreaction;[48] they sought to destroy tranquillity and generate turbulence in the conviction that they knew the benign way in which such actions would lead future Irish history. The classic example of their radical action occurred at the start of 1969 with what later became known as the Burntollet march. On 1 January, at a comparatively quiescent moment when it seemed that the north's Prime Minister, Terence O'Neill, might just enjoy sufficient space and calm to defuse civil rights tension with effective reform, forty or more PD members began a march from Belfast to Derry. This decision was taken against the advice of NICRA, and it was taken at a delicate moment. In November 1968 O'Neill had introduced a significant reform package which had been sympathetically received by moderate civil rights enthusiasts.[49] In contrast, the PD's more militant spirits dismissed the Prime Minister's reforms. Hence the Burntollet march. The key organizer was the able and fiery Farrell, while another of the marchers (Devlin) has tellingly observed: 'Our function in marching from Belfast to Derry was to break the truce, to relaunch the civil rights movement as a mass movement, and to show people that O'Neill was, in fact, offering them nothing. We knew we wouldn't finish the march without getting molested ... What we really wanted to do was pull the carpet off the floor to show the dirt that was under it, so that we could sweep it up.'[50]

The marchers were indeed duly harassed by loyalists along their route (one eminent Northern Irish civil servant reflecting that the loyalist attackers reacted to the march 'with all the unthinking automatism of Pavlov's dog').[51] For the late sixties had occasioned deep anxiety among many northern Protestants that their state was under attack from its traditional nationalist opponents. On 4 January the marchers were violently attacked at Burntollet Bridge near Derry by a group of loyalists, some of whom were off-duty members of the Ulster Special Constabulary (USC), and against whom the RUC clearly offered (at best) insufficient protection. This brutal episode unsurprisingly strengthened the hostility of many Catholics to the Northern Ireland state. If the police colluded in – or at least did little to prevent – such an assault, then how could they be relied upon to treat all citizens fairly?

The responsibility for the deplorable violence at Burntollet clearly lies with those who delivered it. Loyalist aggression played a major part in creating the post-1960s northern troubles; and while Protestant anxiety can be explained, such explanation in no way provides a justification for the loyalist violence of these years. Yet the wisdom of holding a provocative march with the intention of inflaming Ulster politics at this key moment in early 1969 must surely also be open to question. Could Northern Ireland's descent into sectarian carnage have been avoided had certain key decisions been taken differently during the late 1960s and early 1970s?

Burntollet is one episode open to such counterfactual speculation. Condemnation for the decision to march came even from some of those who had themselves hoped to stimulate turbulence with a view to changing Irish history. The IRA's honoured intellectual, Roy Johnston, was among those who saw the Burntollet march as crucial and disastrous: 'It basically trailed the coat in those Antrim towns and set up the civil rights movement as a perceived nationalist provocation. It was obvious to those of us with experience that the Orange element would react as they did at Burntollet. This could only polarise.'[52] In Johnston's view, the march was 'disastrously counter-productive': 'It helped reduce civil rights to a Catholic ghetto movement, and made it difficult for Protestant trade unionists to rally in support of local government electoral rights ("one-man-one-vote"). After Burntollet, civil rights became a crypto-nationalist issue.'[53] Critical, too, was Connolly Association guru Desmond Greaves: 'The Burntollet march was a disaster. Instead of uniting the people they created a riot.'[54] For this was indeed a delicate moment. In December 1968 Terence O'Neill, appealing for calm and stressing the decisive importance of the coming days and weeks if conflict was to be avoided, had publicly observed that Ulster stood at the crossroads.

There were, of course, those who welcomed the Burntollet development. The first Chief of Staff of the soon to be formed Provisional IRA (Seán MacStiofáin) certainly read this inflammatory intervention as having been decisive and, from his perspective, greatly welcome. O'Neill might have outmanoeuvred the civil rights movement, Mac-Stiofáin claimed, had it not been for 'the courage and foresight of the

People's Democracy members who refused to observe any let-up in the protest campaign ... The PD went ahead and called a long march from Belfast to Derry, over seventy miles ... This daring action by a few dozen young people put new life into the civil rights campaign, and effectively ended O'Neill's chances of political survival.'[55]

One strand, therefore, within the civil rights movement consisted of a family of radicals influenced by socialist republican thought, and convinced that their understanding of the dynamics of Irish history and politics would allow them to predict the consequences of the turbulence they deliberately provoked. It was a dangerous exercise, and the integral involvement of such figures[56] should form at least a part of our picture of Northern Ireland's civil rights experience.

But the civil rights movement comprised, for the most part, people with far less radical views – people for whom the thrust of the campaign was the entirely reasonable demand for fair treatment within a state which had not hitherto provided it. The Northern Irish civil rights activists were – in part – influenced by the US black civil rights movement;[57] and, as Lord Cameron's report on the 1968–9 disturbances in Northern Ireland rightly pointed out, genuine Catholic grievance there was central to explaining the outbreak of late-1960s violence – agitation for civil rights was not purely a cover for ulterior subversion.[58] True, the republicans who first initiated the civil rights project held that one could not reform Northern Ireland without, of necessity, destabilizing and toppling it; but many northern Catholics seem, in the event, to have held that just such a process of reform within the north was, in fact, a possibility. The IRA might have helped to create the civil rights movement, but they did not control or run it once it was established. In this sense, unionist politician Brian Faulkner presented things the wrong way around when suggesting that the IRA had taken over a civil rights movement initially not bearing their ideals;[59] rather, it was the IRA that had helped to initiate a civil rights campaign which grew to encompass many people who did not share the IRA's philosophy.

As we have seen, against the insecure background of a hostile southern Ireland and a large disaffected minority within its own territory, Ulster unionists had built a Northern Ireland which prized and rewarded loyalty, and within which many Catholics experienced discrimination in areas such as employment, housing and electoral

practice. The reason for the civil rights movement gaining momentum among large numbers of people was, quite simply, the Catholic
experience of discrimination within the northern state. After Harold
Wilson's accession to power in 1964, Irish nationalists in the north
had a sympathetic London Prime Minister, and it seemed to many that
reform might shape the agenda. And reform was surely required.

But, despite the reasonable intentions of most of its supporters, the
civil rights movement of the north unintentionally helped to produce
a descent into awful and lasting violence. The attempt to pursue equal
rights for northern Catholics within a UK framework, rather than
stress the need to end partition, was one that failed, strangled by the
more traditional issue of the struggle between unionism and nationalism. As one leading Irish nationalist politician was to put it, 'One of
the features of the civil rights movement that distinguished it from any
earlier anti-unionist organisation in Northern Ireland was the priority
it gave to internal reform in Northern Ireland. The reunification of
Ireland was seen by the organisers of this movement as something that
should be left on one side while this internal reform was being pursued
by non-violent agitation'; yet 'the civil rights movement, through the
bitterness of the reaction it provoked in unionist circles, eventually
sparked off the very kind of sectarian conflict which its organisers had
hoped and planned to avoid'.[60]

For the northern context was a volatile one in which rival conceptions of injustice and threat fuelled sectarian fire. Just as the IRA felt
that the illegitimacy and injustice of the north legitimated their own
military existence, so loyalists for their part considered the republican
and nationalist threat to their state a sufficient justification for carrying out appalling actions. Loyalist fears here during the 1960s were
certainly exaggerated: there *was* no IRA uprising in 1966 or, for that
matter, in the crucial year of 1969. But loyalist fears there were. So in
1966 a new Ulster Volunteer Force (UVF) was founded, with Augustus
'Gusty' Spence as one of its leaders. In May 1966 this Protestant
paramilitary group fatally wounded Matilda Gould and John Scullion
in separate, dreadful incidents in Belfast; in June they killed Peter
Ward. Scullion and Ward were attacked because they were thought to
be IRA men. (The UVF had been keen to kill leading Belfast republican
Leo Martin, who was to become a key member of the Provisionals;
failing to find him on either occasion, they had attacked Scullion and

Ward.) These three UVF killings, occurring as they did several years before the founding of the Provisionals, clearly show as false any suggestion that it was the Provisional IRA that started the troubles. Political violence in the north – in these cases, loyalist violence – clearly predated the Provos' establishment.

Into this combustible mixture was added one final catalytic ingredient: the civil rights movement. The year 1967 was comparatively quiet, but in 1968 the pace and tension of civil rights activity increased. In the spring, NICRA embarked on a series of protest marches, partly inspired by the American black civil rights example: in August a march in Dungannon, County Tyrone, passed off comparatively quietly; on 5 October in Derry things were very different. Ulster marches had a long history as occasions of sectarian conflict, and this Derry demonstration against discrimination in housing and employment fulfilled its volcanic potential. Clashes erupted between demonstrators and the RUC, with the latter deploying batons and water cannon to visibly harsh effect. In the words of one of the main organizers of the march, Eamonn McCann, 'The march was trapped between two cordons of police in Duke Street and batoned into disarray.'[61] State brutality was here evident internationally: 'The attack on the civil-rights marchers by the police on 5 October had been seen by television viewers all around the world. The government and police had tried to brazen it out, blaming the disturbance on the IRA and subversives. But there was no way they could refute the charges of brutality, or wish away the images of uniformed thugs batoning defenceless people.'[62] In Gerry Adams's later analysis, 'The RUC smashed into the relatively small demonstration, exposing the brutal nature of unionist domination and the ruthless denial of basic democratic rights.'[63] Two days of rioting followed. Here, again, police activity during these disturbances contributed to the situation in which many Catholics – not surprisingly – saw the state as unlikely to treat their community or their demands fairly.

Much of the anger on such occasions had a very localized quality (a thread which was to run throughout the history of the ensuing troubles). Derry was particularly charged, being the scene of some of the worst anti-Catholic discimination in the north. It is possible that had such local anger been quickly defused, then the subsequent history of Northern Ireland might have been far less bloody. One authoritative local study of the degeneration into violence has concluded of the early civil rights period: 'It was a Derry campaign and, if the Stormont government had reacted with a few well-placed concessions to local grievances, it might even have been able to implement a "Derry solution".'[64] Tragically, this was not to happen. For the year 1969 was to witness the birth of the bloody troubles and of their most lethal offspring: the Provisional IRA. The vital period was, not for the last time in Northern Ireland, the summer marching season. Days of rioting were occasioned in Belfast and Derry by the Protestant 12 July celebrations, and after this – in Labour Party Home Secretary James Callaghan's words – 'an uneasy peace ensued. In London we were debating whether we should intervene, but hoping and praying that we would not have to.'[65]

The following month saw an escalation in intercommunal violence. On the nights of Saturday 2 and Sunday 3 August 1969, there was considerable violence in Belfast. On the latter night this included rioting on the Protestant Shankill Road, with a van and cars being set alight and a police Land-Rover being damaged by a petrol bomb. The Sunday night also witnessed trouble after midnight in the Crumlin Road area of north Belfast, petrol bombs being thrown from Catholic streets (one setting light to a policeman). Both Catholic and Protestant families were forced out of streets in which they represented a minority. A group of about a hundred loyalists toured part of the Crumlin Road area warning Catholics to 'get out or be burned out'. Protestant families, for their part, were ordered out of the predominantly Catholic Hooker Street, their vacated homes being taken over by Catholics who had themselves been driven out from mainly Protestant streets: 'It was a case of swopping houses', in the words of one Hooker Street resident.[66] Significantly, the anger in Hooker Street seems mainly to have been directed towards the police, who were (not unjustifiably) held to have acted without impartiality in their treatment of the rival Protestant and Catholic crowds during the disturbances.

On 4 August the Northern Irish Prime Minister, James Chichester-Clark[67] (who had replaced O'Neill in May), said he thought the Belfast situation should be left in the hands of the police, and that he would be very reluctant to call in British troops at this stage. But that night, the Crumlin Road area again erupted. Rioters in Catholic Hooker Street and Protestant Disraeli Street were separated by police, who found themselves in a cross-fire of stones and petrol bombs. Things also worsened in the north's second city, as middle ground and compromise receded from view. The Protestant Apprentice Boys' parade in Derry on 12 August – marches again – sparked rioting which spread to Belfast, where thousands (mostly Catholic) were left homeless after the destruction. The Derry violence had begun when Catholic and Protestant crowds exchanged insults, stones and bottles as the Protestant parade passed through the city centre in the afternoon of the 12th. Later, the pattern of police-versus-Catholic violence emerged, with prolonged disturbances in the Bogside area of the city: rioting, street clashes and the burning of buildings met with police baton charges and the use of tear gas in what became known as the battle of the Bogside. The nationalist Stormont MP for the city, John Hume, said that the trouble had been foreseeable, and that he had vainly said as much to the north's Prime Minister. Hume himself was shrewdly aware of the gravity of the moment: 'If the situation is not to deteriorate further with serious risk to human life then the Westminster government must intervene at once and take control.'[68]

Certainly, the police could no longer hope to contain the chaos, and the Northern Irish government asked that British troops be deployed which, on 14 August, they were. This was a crucial moment. As one military commentator put it, 'The week from 12 to 16 August 1969 was a watershed: that week the Army became inextricably involved in Ulster.'[69] Meanwhile, that alternative army – the IRA – were frantically and unsurprisingly searching for weapons in the context of the attacks on their community. Rifles, machine-guns and revolvers (stashed away in dumps in the Republic of Ireland after previous IRA campaigns) were now brought to Belfast. And although the weakness of the IRA that summer was to become central to Provisional – and many other – accounts of the period, the IRA did in fact take as well as lose some life in that fateful month.

Belfast saw further violence overnight during 13–14 August, with attacks by Catholics on police stations in west Belfast, and with clashes in the Crumlin Road area involving Catholics, Protestants and the police. Then, over 14–16 August, there was dramatic and appalling violence in the Falls and Crumlin Road areas. Many Catholic families were ordered out of their homes by Protestants, and there were claims that police (and members of the police reserve, the B Specials) stood by while it happened. Numerous people were killed. The disturbances had already seen the RUC fatally injuring several – in April, Samuel Devenney in Derry; in July, Francis McCloskey in nearby Dungiven; on 2 August, Patrick Corry in Belfast. All three were Catholic. Further tragedies were to follow. On 14 August John Gallagher, also a Catholic, was killed in Armagh in a shooting incident following a civil rights meeting in the city; the gunfire came from the USC (Northern Ireland's part-time Special Constabulary, initially set up in 1920 to combat the IRA). The same day, Protestant Herbert Roy was shot dead in disturbances in the Lower Falls, by the IRA. Over 14–15 August, another four Catholics were killed by the forces of the state during the Belfast turbulence: Hugh McCabe, Samuel McLarnon, Michael Lynch and nine-year-old Patrick Rooney. As one west Belfast-born poet put it, with understandable anger:

> The altar boy was shot dead
> By some trigger-happy cowboy cop.[70]

And the same terrible mid-August period saw fifteen-year-old Gerald McAuley, a junior IRA member, killed by loyalists, and a Protestant man, David Linton, killed by republicans; again, both shootings happened in the capital city.

Different lessons were drawn from these deaths. Many Catholics unsurprisingly saw police killings as evidence of the hostility of the northern state towards their community: not only were the police offering inadequate protection, they were, on occasion, the attackers from whom protection was so urgently required. (On the early morning of 16 August, B Specials apparently went on a rampage in Catholic Ardoyne.) But other people drew an alternative lesson: that the republican violence vindicated the fears and warnings offered during the late 1960s regarding paramilitary subversion within Ulster. On both sides, Catholic and Protestant, the violence reinforced those very perceptions by which it had been generated.

Violence in Catholic Belfast in August 1969 was crucial in the development of Irish republican history. Traditional republican argument held that the northern state was of necessity unjust, that its reason for existence and its structures were alike thoroughly sectarian; traditional republican argument had it that peaceful politics would be ineffective, and that the Northern Irish state could not be reformed, but only removed by force; traditional republican argument stressed the necessity for the IRA as defenders of northern Catholics in a hostile and dangerous environment. In the late 1960s a civil rights movement, most of whose members sought the peaceful reform of the north, had met with loyalist violence; in the late 1960s the IRA had not been concentrating its energy primarily on military issues, and had been unable to offer any kind of meaningful defence against loyalist violence; in the late 1960s traditional republican arguments thus seemed to many to have been conclusively vindicated.

The word 'pogrom' is frequently applied to anti-Catholic violence in August 1969,[71] and although this both exaggerates the scale of the events[72] and rather simplifies the direction of the violence, it does register something of the terrible importance of these summer days for later republicans. The civil rights movement, far from ending sectarian division in the north (as its initial sponsors had anticipated and genuinely sought), had helped to bring about the terrifying localized experiences of Catholics in August 1969; in that month, as leading northern nationalist Maurice Hayes recalls, 'Belfast was indeed an eerie place. Frightening, particularly at night. Isolated Catholic families were burned out or expelled. There was retaliation, with people moving in both directions carrying their pitiful belongings.'[73] Sectarianism had been intensified, and the need for Catholic ghetto defenders now seemed unchallengeable.

So in the immediate circumstances of that summer, the division of opinion within Irish republicanism – between innovators and traditionalists – became more sharply focused. The IRA were back in action, a fact noticed as far away as Dublin: 'Some element of [the] IRA was certainly in action in Belfast during [the] night of 14th August [1969], including some men from Dublin.' Indeed, the energy and ambition of the IRA were what struck the southern state: 'As in [the Derry] Bogside, [the] IRA now seem to be in control of barricade defence in Belfast. Reports indicate that such defence is on an organised, disciplined basis with elements of [the] southern IRA taking an active part ... the IRA sees the time as ripe for the establishment of a united Ireland and they intend fighting to achieve this objective.'[74] If one is to believe such new evidence, from files released only in 2001, the IRA was perhaps slightly better organized in its defensive activities, and more proactive in its ambitions, than is customarily assumed. Immediately after the arrival of British troops in 1969, both radical and traditionalist republicans had certainly begun preparing for military action. One of their most pressing concerns lay within, rather than without, their organization. How was the IRA to be defined: according to traditional, or Gouldingite, preferences? By the end of the year, it was to have split over precisely this question.

On 24 August a secret meeting was held in Belfast by republicans dissatisfied with the IRA's shift towards leftist politics and away from traditional methods and approaches. The gathering had been instigated by veteran IRA man Jimmy Steele, and it reflected irritation at the republican leadership and in particular at its hesitation in arming members. Present at the meeting were some of the figures who became central to the Provisional republican movement: Billy McKee, John Kelly and his brother Billy, Joe Cahill, Leo Martin, Seamus Twomey, Gerry Adams, Daithi O'Connell, Jimmy Drumm. In the view of these people the Belfast IRA commander, Liam McMillen, and his adjutant, Jim Sullivan, had not done the necessary in terms of providing defence during the recent crisis; it was decided that the two men should be removed as soon as possible and that work should also begin on the replacement of Goulding's Dublin leadership with people of more traditional republican views.

The dissidents decided to confront McMillen and Sullivan. On 22 September an armed group (including McKee, Adams and Twomey) burst dramatically into a Belfast meeting of McMillen and his supporters and accused the IRA leader of not defending the Catholic population. A temporary compromise was nervily arrived at, with both factions now to be represented in the northern IRA command structure. Two wings had now emerged, and this situation was to become more sharply defined very soon. Rather ironically, the dissidents – the nucleus of what was to become the Provisional IRA, fiercely committed to a united Ireland – were at this stage, organizationally, seeking a break from Dublin. In Billy McKee's words, 'We realised that the Dublin crowd and the Dublin leadership were nothing other than conmen ... So the northern lads got together and we told them that we wouldn't have any more truck with the south and with the Dublin leadership.'[75]

In October 1969 the IRA Army Council met and voted against maintaining the traditional policy of abstention under any circumstances from the parliaments of Belfast, Dublin and London. In mid-December an Army Convention held in the Republic further reflected the Gouldingites' desire to break with republican orthodoxy. There were two main items on the agenda: first, that the IRA should join a national liberation front in alliance with the radical left; and second, that parliamentary abstentionism should be dropped. The meeting was packed with Goulding supporters. But Army Council member Seán MacStiofáin, a sceptic regarding Goulding's revisionism, was also present, and he took a different view. When the two motions had been passed, an IRA split was effectively sealed.

MacStiofáin and his dissident comrades had already prepared their next moves. Keen to act quickly in the event of a Convention defeat, they had prearranged a meeting place from which they could at once begin to build an alternative IRA, one which would embody traditional republican values. MacStiofáin was eager to tell the Belfast dissidents of the Convention's decisions, so immediately upon his departure from the GAC he went to the northern capital and addressed a meeting of dissenting IRA men who agreed to set up a new organization. On 18 December 1969 this group's core – thirteen dissident delegates from the IRA Convention and thirteen of their supporters – met and elected a twelve-member Provisional IRA Executive, who in turn chose a seven-member Provisional IRA Army Council – with Seán MacStiofáin as its Chief of Staff. A new IRA had been born.

On 28 December, in Dublin, the Provisionals issued their first public statement. In it they devoutly reaffirmed 'the fundamental republican position': 'We declare our allegiance to the thirty-two-county Irish republic, proclaimed at Easter 1916, established by the first Dáil Eireann in 1919, overthrown by force of arms in 1922 and suppressed to this day by the existing British-imposed six-county and twenty-six-county partition states.'[76] Sinn Féin (the political wing of the IRA) experienced their version of the split over 10–11 January 1970 at the party's ard fheis (convention) in Dublin's Intercontinental Hotel; as one of the new Provisionals, Ruairí Ó Brádaigh, observed: 'It was all very, very tense and very highly charged.'[77] Delegates knew of the IRA's December decision, but Provisionals such as MacStiofáin and Ó Brádaigh hoped to swing the Sinn Féin decision the other way from the army's. To no avail. In the crucial 11 January debate on abstention, Sinn Féin President Tomás Mac Giolla and most other party leaders spoke against the traditional parliamentary boycott. As the refusal to recognize the three parliaments was written into the Sinn Féin constitution, a two-thirds majority was required in order to change it; in the event, the motion against abstention was carried, but not by the required margin. Then a delegate proposed that the *ard fheis* endorse the policies of the IRA Army Council – which meant rejecting abstentionism, and which motion did not require the two-thirds majority. Traditionalists like MacStiofáin saw the way things were going: taking about a third of the delegates with him, the Provisionals' Chief of Staff departed, reassembled in a pre-booked hall for another meeting, formed what became Provisional Sinn Féin (PSF) and announced publicly that a Provisional Army Council had been set up to reorganize the IRA.

Why, precisely, had this republican split occurred? Essentially, the schism involved the interweaving of three strands: legitimacy, ideology and militarism. The break came over the issue of parliamentary abstentionism, an emblem of republican alternative legitimacy. The states in Ireland were, in traditional republican thinking, illegitimate: Britain had had no right to partition Ireland, to govern the north or to control (as republicans traditionally saw it) the south. To send representatives to the Belfast, Dublin or London parliaments would legitimize the illegitimate. One should try to *abolish* the northern parliament, not campaign for seats there. Moreover, this tied in with an ideological divergence over politics. The Provisionals were not right-wing nationalists. But they were sceptical about an IRA that wanted to focus its energies on an alliance with the radical left in a national liberation front: such an approach distracted attention from true republican goals and methods. A concentration on Marxism and anti-abstentionism within the old IRA reflected a lack of commitment to what traditionalists saw as the IRA's primary function: its military role. The Provisionals argued that the ending of abstentionism had represented 'the logical outcome of an obsession in recent years with parliamentary politics, with consequent undermining of the basic military role of the IRA'.[78] The maintenance of internal discipline, of training and of a military sharpness had seemed important to dissidents before the August 1969 attacks on northern Catholics; after the events of that month, they seemed essential. The crisis of 1969 demonstrated – to those who formed the Provisionals – that it would be politically and literally fatal to avoid the military duty traditionally cherished by the IRA. This reading has drawn together unlikely allies, including leading republican Danny Morrison ('out of the ashes of August 1969 arose the unbeatable Provisionals')[79] and future Conservative Party politician in Northern Ireland, Brian Mawhinney:

> It can be said that civil war started in Belfast on the 14th [August 1969]. That night extremists of both sides and B-Specials, an auxiliary – largely Protestant – police force, went on a spree of shooting and arson ... The spectacle of Bombay Street, between the Protestant Shankill and Catholic Falls Roads, burning from end to end, signalled the total inability of Stormont to enforce law and order or to protect the citizenry ... In 1969, the Official IRA in the north was advocating political change and eschewing violence. Yet the very violence of August 1969 undermined its authority; out of the ashes of Bombay Street arose the Provisional IRA.[80]

It is clearly not the case that the old IRA were solely, or even primarily, responsible for the outbreak of Northern Ireland's troubles. The roots and responsibilities involved are far too tangled for that, and the ultimate cause of the troubles' emergence lay with the understandable disaffection from the northern state of a large minority of its population. But it is a significant part of the story that a 1960s initiative set in motion by the IRA – one deliberately aimed at undermining Northern Ireland – had prompted the turbulence which ignited the conflict and which unintentionally led to a republican split. For all the intelligence and integrity of its framers, the Goulding strategy had helped, in the end, to intensify sectarianism and to lead the army away from any supposed capacity to defend northern Catholics in the dangerous context thus produced. The politics of the old IRA had led to the generation of a new one; the latter owed the conditions of its birth, as well as the experience of some of its key personnel, to the former.

2

'In a sense I had absorbed an ethos of republicanism while growing up.'

Gerry Adams[81]

Who exactly were the Provisionals? It was the distinctive experience of nationalists in the north that had decisively generated the new IRA. And this was often reflected in the strength of the membership's local roots. Indeed, this is echoed in the case of the most significant member of the Provisional movement's entire history: Gerry Adams. As a later acquaintance (US politician George Mitchell) was to put it, in trans-Atlantic idiom, Adams had been 'raised in the Catholic west side of Belfast'.[82] In Adams's own west-side story, his local area of Belfast – Ballymurphy – was vitally important. Talking of the late 1960s Adams himself acknowledged that 'To a large extent, my political world was Ballymurphy';[83] elsewhere he claims that 'Ballymurphy was a state of mind';[84] and he has commented on having 'loved the city of Belfast, its streets, its hills, its people'.[85]

Within that local world, family connections and experience were crucial in forming the young Provisional. Adams, more than most, bore out a former Provisional's claim that, with the IRA, 'there's an element of the extended family even involved'.[86] On both Adams's father's and his mother's side of the family there were important republican, local connections. As we have seen, his father (also Gerry) and his uncle (Dominic Adams) had both been IRA men. Adams's mother (Annie Adams, née Hannaway) also came from a strongly republican family. Her brother Liam Hannaway had joined the IRA in 1935 when aged seventeen, had been imprisoned in the 1940s and had become an active IRA man again upon his release in 1946. Uncle Liam was involved on the IRA's behalf in the clashes of 1969, and was a senior Provisional during the early 1970s. Some members of Adams's family tree had had Fenian/IRB involvement, while his grandfather (Billy Hannaway) had been a Connollyite republican.

Family connections, and the immediate concerns of his northern setting, helped lead Adams towards the Provisionals in the split – but cautiously. At the January 1970 Sinn Féin *ard fheis*, he had remained in his seat rather than depart with the dissidents. It took him another three months to decide which side to follow: in his Provisional choice he was partly influenced by his uncle Liam's closeness to people such as Jimmy Steele. Most of Adams's family went Provisional rather than Official.

In his intriguing autobiography Adams stresses the importance of Catholic identity in a hostile northern state, saying of the early 1960s: 'Although I was unaware of it at the time, there was a kind of collective Catholic thinking which was conscious that, no matter what status the individual might achieve, Catholics in the north of Ireland were ghettoised, marginalised, treated as inferior.'[87] This is a crucial point. For northern Catholics' experience of a state that they considered neither legitimate nor fair was the foundation upon which Provisionals such as Adams built their politics. A republican family embedded in Ballymurphy's Catholic community helped engender in Gerry Adams a republican sensibility from early on; the immediacy of northern needs was interwoven with the longevity of republican attachment.

For while it is frequently – and not without reason – assumed that the violent loyalist response to civil rights agitation produced the Provisionals, it is also worth noting how many of the Provisionals had prior IRA commitment. Adams himself appears to have joined the Belfast IRA in 1965, aged sixteen. (This was two years before the founding of NICRA, thus dispelling any notion that civil rights experience had led to republican commitment: if anything, in Adams's case, it was the other way round.) And it seems to have been the beginning of an impressive IRA career. Between April/May 1971 and March 1972 Gerry Adams was OC of the Provisionals' 2nd Battalion in Belfast; in the latter year he became Adjutant for the Belfast Brigade as a whole; by the time of his arrest on 19 July 1973 he had become OC of the entire Belfast Brigade. (This was a bloody period: between May 1971 and the start of July 1973 the Belfast IRA was responsible for 211 deaths.)[88]

Adams was released from prison in 1977 and in the same year became an Army Council member, a position which he was to hold for a long time. In 1983 he became President of Sinn Féin, but this – like his formal IRA titles – does not do justice to his long-term influence as one of the ablest members of the Provisional movement, and easily its most significant figure.[89] Adams's local, family, deep-rooted connections reflect the importance to some early Provisionals of a combination of two factors: a military emphasis appropriate to the north, and a striking continuity with the old IRA. This was true in the case of other key figures too. The pre-Provisional, mid-1969 Army Council had, for example, included Seán MacStíofáin, Ruairí Ó Brádaigh and Daithí O'Connell. All three possessed an impressive IRA pedigree and all were to be crucial in the Provisional movement. Seán MacStíofáin (1928–2001) was born in England, and served during 1945–8 in the Royal Air Force before joining the IRA shortly afterwards. In 1953 he was arrested and jailed after an arms raid; in the 1960s he joined the IRA's Army Council, being appointed IRA Director of Intelligence in 1966. He was the Provisionals' Chief of Staff from their 1969 creation until 1972. Less politically oriented than figures like Ó Brádaigh and O'Connell, he had – like them – come through the preceding decades of IRA experience. The latter two had seen their first IRA military action in the 1956–62 campaign. Despite a certain evasiveness over the issue – 'I am not the leader of the IRA nor have I ever claimed to be a leader of that body'[90] – Ó Brádaigh was both a member of the first Provisional Army Council and the President (1970–83) of the organization's political arm, Provisional Sinn Féin. His brother, Sean, was also prominent in Provisional politics.

Another key old IRA man turned Provisional leader, Daithí O'Connell (1938–91), had been born in Cork and had joined the republican movement while a teenager (Sinn Féin in 1955 and subsequently the IRA). As we have seen, his military record included participation in the IRA's January 1957 Brookeborough raid; three years later he was shot and captured by Crown Forces in County Tyrone and sentenced to eight years' imprisonment in Crumlin Road Jail. A member of the Provisionals' first Army Council, he was also the first Vice-President of Provisional Sinn Féin, a post he held until 1983. In the early 1970s O'Connell was one of the key enthusiasts for the Provos' use of the car-bomb. (He was also, apparently, something of a drinker. According to Maria McGuire's bomb-and-tell IRA memoir, *To Take Arms*, O'Connell had joked – in reference to his and McGuire's affair during a European weapons-procuring trip – that 'he wasn't worried by the newspaper reports of how many beds had been used, so long as they didn't discover all the whiskey bottles underneath them'!)[91]

In some contrast, leading Provisional Billy McKee's reputation frequently focuses on his profound Catholic devotion: he attended Mass daily and was widely recognized for sincere piety. (Less generously, he was later described by another IRA man as being 'an arch-Catholic bigot'.)[92] A Belfast man born in the early 1920s, McKee had joined the IRA in 1939. During the Second World War he was imprisoned in Crumlin Road Jail; released in 1946, he reported back for IRA duty. He was interned in the 1950s, spent much of the 1956–62 campaign behind bars and was Belfast OC in the early 1960s – a position he again held with the Provisionals in the following decade.

Like McKee, Joe Cahill was a Belfast man. Born in 1920, he had joined the IRA in the 1930s, and – again like McKee – he had known imprisonment: in his own case in the 1940s, 1950s and the 1960s. In the mid-1960s Cahill had left the IRA in protest at its political and leftward emphasis. But he had returned to the army in 1969 prior to the split. The Provisionals' Belfast Brigade OC in 1971, he – like many – came from a family with republican sympathies. For his defensive IRA role in 1969, Cahill had been helped with the supply of guns by John Joe McGirl (1921–88). A County Leitrim man, McGirl had joined the IRA in 1937, had been interned in the south during the Second World War, had been elected in 1957 as an abstentionist member of the Dublin Dáil, and had been a member of the IRA Army Council which oversaw and executed the 1956–62 campaign. Siding with the Provisionals from 1969 onwards, McGirl remained staunch within the movement, being Sinn Féin Vice-President at his death in 1988.

Seamus Twomey (1919–89) was born in Belfast, had joined the IRA in 1937 and been interned during the Second World War. His father had been an IRA Volunteer in the 1920s, and Seamus himself had been interned in the 1940s. He became Belfast Brigade OC in August 1971 and was Provisional Chief of Staff during 1972–3 and 1975–7. Veteran Belfast man Proinsias Mac Airt (Francis Card, 1922–92) also had a long (pre-Provisional) IRA career: he had joined the Fianna as a boy, been jailed in 1942 for illegal drilling, and interned during the 1956–62 campaign. When Mac Airt died, Gerry Adams's graveside oration declared that the deceased had given 'his entire life to the republican struggle and was a radical in the Connolly tradition'.[93] Another key figure, Seamus (Jimmy) Steele, was born in Belfast in 1907. He joined the IRA in the early 1920s, was first arrested in 1923, and then again in 1924 and in 1935. This last arrest left him in Crumlin Road Jail until 1940. On release he was appointed Adjutant to the IRA's Northern Command Staff, but in December 1940 was once again arrested. Interned during the 1956–62 border campaign, he was during the 1960s sceptical of the leftist politics of the IRA leadership. He sided with the Provisionals at the split, was elected to the new IRA's Executive and held this post until his death in August 1970; he was described by fellow Provisional Billy McKee as 'a master of judgement'.[94]

Some resemblances might be discerned here among the people forming the nucleus of the new IRA: lengthy prior involvement in the IRA, prison experience, family and local connections. It was on such foundations that the proto-Provisionals *initially* built. Their first Army Council comprised Seán MacStiofáin (Chief of Staff), Ruairí Ó Brádaigh, Joe Cahill, Daithi O'Connell, Sean Tracey, Patrick Mulcahy, Leo Martin. (Martin had been born in 1937, and was interned for republican activities during the border campaign.) By September 1971, the Council consisted of MacStiofáin, Ó Brádaigh, Cahill, O'Connell, explosives expert Paddy Ryan, J. B. O'Hagan and Dennis McInerney (the latter two being veterans of 1956–62).

And the point regarding continuity is underlined by the fact that the newly established Provisionals both sought and obtained the blessing of veteran IRA intransigent, Tom Maguire. The last surviving member of the 1921 Second Dáil (in unswerving republican eyes, the last legitimate authority in Ireland), Maguire had resolutely opposed compromise: whether from those who had accepted partial Irish independence in 1921, or from those who had tried to build on it from within the system in the 1930s. Maguire had impeccable republican credentials, being the only surviving signatory to the 1938 document by which the Second Dáil remnant had handed legitimate authority in Ireland to the IRA Army Council. He was a hero of leading Provisional, Ruairí Ó Brádaigh, who admired his 'unswerving fidelity' to the pure Irish republic, celebrated the fact that 'He would not be bought, could not be broken or bent', and set his heroic commitment within the context of a tradition of Irish resistance going back 'over 800 years to the original Anglo-Norman invasion and colonisation of Ireland'.[95]

To Ó Brádaigh's delight, Maguire now rejected the December 1969 shift away from abstentionism by the Goulding leadership. In a statement issued on 4 January 1970, Maguire argued that that IRA Convention had possessed 'neither the right nor the authority' to pass the resolution abandoning the abstentionist policy regarding Stormont, Leinster House (the seat of the Dublin parliament) and Westminster. 'Accordingly, I, as the sole surviving member of the executive of Dáil Éireann, and the sole surviving signatory of the 1938 proclamation, hereby declare that the resolution is illegal.'[96] The flame of legitimacy had been passed on.

If Ó Brádaigh revered Tom Maguire, he was also in thrall to that other legendary republican of revolutionary vintage, Ernie O'Malley ('an extraordinary person by any standards'),[97] whose own military instincts were certainly echoed in one of the Provisionals' early preoccupations: how was the army to be (re)organized? As in previous generations, so also this new IRA modelled its structure on the British Army: brigades containing battalions containing companies. Nine of the eleven IRA company commanders in Belfast had sided with the Provisionals in the split, and as early as the end of January 1970 the army was taking military shape. In Belfast itself there were three battalions, in a brigade which had Billy McKee as its OC and Seamus Twomey as adjutant. By mid-1970 the organization had approximately a thousand members in Ireland as a whole. By no means all of these people were armed guerrilla fighters, but even those working on security, intelligence, safe houses and so forth were an integral part of the armed Provisional movement.

The ruling body of the Provisionals was (as in previous IRA practice) to be a seven-person Army Council, chosen by a twelve-person Army Executive, in turn elected by a General Army Convention or GAC. In theory, Conventions were to be held at least every other year; in practice this did not prove possible. Indeed, between September 1970 – the Provos' first formal GAC – and October 1986 there were no IRA Conventions at all: it was just too difficult against the setting of their campaign to guarantee the safety and freedom from arrest of a large representative body of IRA people. Political organization focused on the army's alter ego, Sinn Féin. The latter was a creature of the former, and overlap of membership was – and long remained – extensive. The Provisional Sinn Féin caretaker executive put together in January 1970, for example, contained IRA Army Council members Ruairí Ó Brádaigh, Seán MacStiofáin and Paddy Mulcahy (with Ó Brádaigh as its chair). Another PSF caretaker executive member, John Joe McGirl, again reflected the organic links between the political and military parts of the Provisional movement.

But if Provo politics were to be communicated, then a newspaper was required, and one of the first tasks to which the organization directed its energy was precisely this. The first issue of the Provisionals' Dublin-based paper, *An Phoblacht*, appeared early in 1970. Edited by Ruairí Ó Brádaigh's brother Sean, this became the movement's main organ in the south during the 1970s.[98] Also relaunched in 1970 was the Belfast-produced *Republican News*. This was to be the Provo paper read most widely in the north. The first issue appeared in June 1970 and the paper was edited (and almost exclusively written) by IRA veteran Jimmy Steele until his death in August 1970, when he was succeeded by Proinsias Mac Airt.[99] (Former Chief of Staff Hugh McAteer was also a member of the initial editorial staff of *Republican News*, another experienced hand offering wisdom for the new venture.)

At the very start of their existence, the Provisionals' 'real problem' – in their Chief of Staff's view – was resources: a lack of equipment and money.[100] So the procurement of money and weapons was a primary focus of attention for the Provos, and their energy was partly directed towards the United States. There had been some early hostility from Irish Americans towards the Northern Irish civil rights movement, the latter evoking unattractive parallels with America's own (black) civil rights initiative.[101] But the Provisionals themselves came to establish important US links. A key contact was George Harrison, a long-term supplier of arms for the IRA with a gun-running career going back to the 1950s. Born in County Mayo in 1915, Harrison had emigrated to the USA in 1938, where he embarked on an interesting combination of leftist and Irish republican enthusiasms. He had not – indeed, still has not – ever been back to Ireland since he emigrated, and the influence upon his thinking of his early Irish years and his youthful IRA involvement was vital in moulding his aggressive republicanism: 'the basis of all my thought was the Irish Republican Army in my very early days, and from a very early stage I was inclined to the left wing of the movement'. Like Ruairí Ó Brádaigh, Harrison revered Tom Maguire. Like Harrison, Maguire was a Mayo man, and the former recalls the latter having made a profound impression upon him when he was about fourteen years old: 'He [Maguire] came into our local company area and I think he had a trench-coat on and he was like a god-like figure to me. In fact, God would have taken second place.'[102] Harrison admired Maguire for being committed to 'an Ireland totally free from all the shackles and tentacles of the monster octopus of British imperialism and its cancerous offsprings of sectarianism and puppet parliaments'.[103]

Republican socialist influences were also significant for the emigrant gun-runner: 'Connolly was a big influence in my life'; as was an admiration for 1930s IRA radicals, Frank Ryan and George Gilmore. With Harrison, as so often with the Provisionals, leftism and militarism were shared enthusiasms; in the USA, Harrison was a trade union activist and a great enthusiast for left-wing causes. Like Tom Maguire, he held compromise to be a significant failing; and, like Ruairí Ó Brádaigh, he celebrated republican violence as part of a centuries-old struggle which was, in essence, unchanging: 'The Brits – they're the problem, and will be. They have been since 1169, and will be until such time as they leave.' Armed with such faith, Harrison was happy to support the Provisionals. They, too, had opposed compromise; and it was they who recognized what he considered the urgent needs of the 1970 situation: 'you had to defend the ghettos . . . the thing to do now is to get weaponry in to the people who are willing to defend the nationalist ghettos'.[104] Daithi O'Connell spoke with Harrison when he visited New York early in 1970, and a supply line was set up. As Harrison later put it, 'I sent thousands of guns to Ireland, and I'd do it again tomorrow. I'm only sorry I didn't send more.'[105]

The nucleus of the gun-running network was the same as with Harrison's previous arms provision. It was a small group which included Harrison's friend Liam Cotter, until the latter's death in 1976. Harrison paid a US contact of Corsican background, George De Meo, who duly procured guns (including what was to become arguably the Provos' favourite weapon, the Armalite); Harrison and his comrades then shipped these to Ireland. Hundreds of light, powerful, collapsible, concealable Armalite rifles found their way to Ireland during the 1970s through this connection. In 1971 the security forces in the north of Ireland captured about 700 weapons, two tons of explosives and 157,000 rounds of ammunition: the bulk of the weapons and ammunition came from the USA.[106]

The Provisionals themselves initially relied very much on those weapons that could be purchased in America (together with those left over from previous campaigns in Ireland), and by early 1972 the plentiful supply of Armalites meant that the new army was well armed and lethal. According to Harrison, the money to pay for this supply of weapons came largely from outside Ireland: 'The main source of money was here [the USA].'[107] Indeed, the establishment of fund-raising ventures in the States was a priority for the newly established Provisionals. The Irish Northern Aid Committee (Noraid) was set up in New York in 1970 to raise funds for the Provisional movement (which it did with great energy, especially in working-class Irish America).[108] The key figure here was Michael Flannery (1902–94) – 'by any standards a remarkable man', in Ruairí Ó Brádaigh's opinion.[109] Born in County Tipperary, Flannery had joined the IRA as a teenager, had fought in the Anglo-Irish War of 1919–21 and (as an anti-Treatyite) in the 1922–3 Civil War. In the 1920s he had emigrated to the USA (where he became a leading member of the US Irish republican organization, Clan na Gael), and it was this IRA veteran who founded and led Noraid. While Harrison maintained a discreet public distance from Flannery's organization – for reasons of clandestine effectiveness – there is no doubt that Noraid helped considerably in sustaining the Provisionals' war. As early as September 1971, two Noraid emissaries visited Ireland to arrange with Joe Cahill, Daithi O'Connell and Seán MacStiofáin for the financing of arms purchases in Europe. So, with Flannery as with Harrison, it was *Irish-born* republicans who were key to the Provisionals' support group in the States.

But some money and support were also available for the new IRA much closer to home. As papers released in 2001 demonstrate, the southern Irish state had in 1969 (in response to the northern crisis) considered four different settings in which cross-border military intervention might be required: 'attacks on the Catholic minority by Protestant extremists with which the Northern Ireland security forces cannot cope'; 'conflict between the Catholic minority and the Northern Ireland security forces on civil rights issues'; 'conflict between republican-nationalist elements . . . and the Northern Ireland security forces'; and 'conflict between Protestant extremists and Northern Ireland security forces not directly involving the minority'. The limitations of the possible were acknowledged: 'were operations in any form to be launched into Northern Ireland we would be exposed to the threat of retaliatory punitive military action by United Kingdom forces on the Republic. Therefore any operations undertaken against Northern Ireland would be militarily unsound'; 'The Defence Forces have no capability to engage successfully in conventional offensive military operations against the security forces in Northern Ireland at unit or higher level.'[110] Nonetheless, on 6 February 1970 the Republic's Minister for Defence (James Gibbons) informed the military Chief of Staff (Sean McKeown) and the Director of Intelligence (Michael Hefferon) that the Dublin government had instructed him to order McKeown 'to prepare and train the Army for incursions into Northern Ireland', if and when such a course was judged necessary.[111]

All of this indicated a theoretical preparedness on the Republic's part to become immersed in the northern crisis. But some southern involvement in the escalating northern violence was also of a more practical nature. Again, files released in Dublin in 2001 show that by the time of the 6 February directive to the Army's Chief of Staff, the Taoiseach (Jack Lynch) and other ministers had 'met delegations from the north. At these meetings urgent demands were made for respirators, weapons and ammunition the provision of which the government agreed.'[112] But on 6 May 1970 Lynch sacked two of his most senior ministers, Charles Haughey, Minister for Finance, and Neil Blaney, Minister for Agriculture and Fisheries, because of their alleged involvement in a plot to import arms in the spring of 1970 for use by northern republicans. On 28 May Haughey and Blaney were arrested and charged with attempting to smuggle arms, and also in the dock were Belfast Provisional John Kelly, Belgian-Irish businessman Albert Luykx and former Irish Army Intelligence officer James Kelly. Charges against Blaney were dismissed in July because of lack of evidence. In October Haughey, Luykx and the two (unrelated) Kellys were acquitted: it was judged that all had acted with appropriate state sanction.

It was not that no importation plot had existed. The Dublin government had decided to make money available to victims of the 1969 attacks on northern Catholics.[113] Some of the money thus provided by the Irish state went for that purpose, but some was directed to fund the purchase of arms for use by the Provisional IRA. The key figure here was Army Intelligence officer, James Kelly. From August 1969 until his retirement on 1 May 1970,[114] Kelly's work had focused on northern affairs. In the wake of the mid-August violence, northern Catholic representatives had come to him looking for weapons for defence. After a visit to Belfast in September, Kelly himself had stressed in Dublin the urgent need for arms. He has maintained that his Minister for Defence (Gibbons) and the Taoiseach were both aware of his actions in attempting to provide support for the proto-Provisionals, and he has accused Lynch's government of 'chicanery and betrayal'[115] in relation to his own subsequent treatment. Himself deeply critical of unionist rule in Northern Ireland, Captain Kelly had worked with Fianna Fáil politicians including Haughey, in liaison with the Provisionals' John Kelly. There is now no doubt that some money did go from the Dublin government to the proto-Provisionals.[116] And this was not just a matter of northern defence: by the time of the 1970 arms importation plot, the Provisionals had committed themselves to a war against Britain.

It is important to stress that the new IRA were generated by northern realities: they would have come into being regardless of southern backing, and the importance of such backing should not be exaggerated. But the new Provisionals were given support from a section of the southern establishment at a time when such strengthening was of some value. That a wing of the Dublin government helped the growth of the proto-Provisionals in 1969–70 reflected an ambivalence about communal violence which contrasted sharply with the Republic's professed state policy and instinct. For the Taoiseach, Jack Lynch, was publicly clear that 'in this island there is no solution to be found to our disagreements by shooting each other'.[117] And he defined the Republic's attitude to the north in less inflammatory terms than those adopted by Haughey and Blaney. Writing in August 1970 to UK Prime Minister Edward Heath, for example, Lynch stressed that he had no desire to coerce Ulster unionists: 'There is no thought in my mind of imposing solutions against the will of sizeable numbers of people.'[118]

3

'We have met violence with violence'

Leading IRA man, Joe Cahill, 1971[119]

What was the thinking, the philosophy of the newly founded Provisional IRA? The issue to start with is defence, and their self-image as necessary defenders: the immediate context for the creation of the Provisionals was one that pointed to a stark need for some kind of Catholic self-protection in the north. And this was deeply, lastingly embedded in their thinking. Seán MacStiofáin observed that northern republicans, after the events of August 1969, 'were determined that they would not be caught defenceless again'.[120] A Belfast Provisional leader, interviewed in February 1971, asserted the IRA's preparedness 'to use force to any extent required to protect the minority in Belfast from attack from any sources – be it the British Army, the RUC or Protestant bigots'.[121] In the fictional-autobiographical version of 1969 offered by one of the Provisional movement's most significant assets, Danny Morrison, 'a new IRA was being built to ensure that nationalists were never left defenceless again'.[122] People in these early days joined the IRA at least partly because their own community was under attack. Even if attacks took place in another part of the north, this was still a communal attack on you: on the Catholic community that you valued, with which you identified and sided – and that you wanted to protect. This was the sectarian reality in the north to which the Provisionals responded. Perhaps rather paradoxically, the IRA tried to distance itself from sectarianism, while acknowledging that it was a sectarian conflict with which it was dealing. A Belfast leader, quoted in early 1971, claimed: 'We will attack Protestants only if they attacked Catholics and we would do this simply because the Catholics would have no one else to defend them.'[123]

But defence was also interwoven, in the IRA's thinking, with an attitudinal shift: towards 'pride in resistance',[124] towards defiance in place of subservience and deference. Provisionals have frequently sketched a picture of a cowed pre-1969 Catholic minority, grudgingly accepting their second-class lot in Northern Ireland. In such portraits, the birth of the Provisionals transformed that situation. For Danny Morrison, 'People were in a hopeless situation until then, and the [Provisional] IRA provided people with hope. Just its existence, just its saying: "We're not having any of this. Come into our areas *again* and try to burn us out and see what happens." And the attitudes changed. It was fundamental.'[125] Morrison again: 'the IRA had been deliberately run down so that when August 1969 came there was little or no defence. There was much burning of homes but it was the burning sense of humiliation felt by nationalists that provided the exponential growth in support for those republicans who declared: "Never Again!"'[126] In the September/October issue of 1970 *Republican News* claimed it was important that Irish people 'realise that British imperialists do not respect, fear or pay much attention to people who beg, grovel or crawl for favours or concessions'. Respect was vital: 'If we do not respect ourselves, we need not expect our British overlords to respect us. If we act like slaves and lick-spittles, we deserve to be treated as such.' Self-respect would come through defiant resistance. In Patrick Magee's Unity Flats part of Belfast there was 'a fierce pride in that area. Everybody felt a part of something . . . absolutely behind the armed struggle.' In this context, 'Generally, it seemed to be [that] the most natural thing to do in the world was [to] become part of the struggle. It never occurred to me not to become involved. The misgivings I would have had would have been in the nature of "Would I be up to it, would I be capable of it, would I have the personal strength?" But once I'd resolved those issues, there was nothing else I could have done.'[127]

And defence was accompanied within the new IRA thinking by retaliatory violence. As one Belfast ex-IRA man said of the early 1970s: 'People were very, very much interested in defence, and very much interested in retaliation as well 'cos people were very, very angry. They really were angry . . . There was a real rage there, amongst young people.'[128] One figure, having been involved in an incident in which four Protestants were fatally shot, observed: 'We had a feeling of victory, a feeling that revenge is sweet.'[129] In the words of the Provisionals' Brooklyn gun-runner, George Harrison (speaking of 1970): 'first, I think, was defence of the ghettos . . . and then to retaliate too.

Defence and retaliation [were] the terms we used to use.'[130] Revenge against the British Army quickly came to be vital: we must hit them because they hit us. Attrition – searches, street clashes, arrests and so on – began to redefine the initially friendly relationship between the Catholic working class and the British Army. The year following mid-1969 saw Catholic Belfast and Derry turn substantially against the soldiers, the latter's harshness helping to intensify and extend that very subversion against which it was supposedly employed. IRA man Pat McGeown,[131] describing his route into the organization, referred to the 1969 'pogroms' and to the subsequent role of the British Army: 'Probably one of the deciding factors would have been constant harassment of British troops at that time on the streets. It generally created an atmosphere of violence and the desire to fight back and not to accept that type of state.'[132]

Tommy Gorman, who joined the IRA in 1970, describes the British Army as having been crucial in strengthening the Provisionals' hand: 'Sometimes the IRA used to come up with some mistake and do something, but then the British Army come out and eclipsed that by doing something even worse ... We were creating this idea that the British state is not your friend ... and at every twist in the road they were compounding what we were saying, they were doing what we were saying, fulfilling all the propaganda ... the British Army, the British government, were our best recruiting agents.'[133]

Hostile reaction to the Army could reinforce other impulses towards republican action. As another ex-IRA Volunteer reflected, on his reasons for joining the struggle:

> I came from a republican family, but it's important to note that there was no hint of zealotry in this republican family. It was a household back in the early sixties where Kevin Barry and Roger Casement hung on the wall ... My father's side of the family were very pro-British: he was a lifetime in the British Army (fought at Arnhem). My mother's side of the family were republican. My parents were separated from when I was a very young age so I grew up in my mother's wing of the family and it *was* a republican family ... So that was one reason [for joining the IRA]. Another reason – and this cannot, *cannot* be overestimated – was, when the troubles did break out, the reaction of the security forces within

the nationalist areas . . . So those are basically the two reasons, and mostly I would say the latter – to strike back at what was going on in those districts.[134]

For others too the role of the British Army in pushing them towards joining the IRA was 'a very, very important factor'[135] or even, in some cases, the decisive one. State repression through military force was, for some, the crucial dynamic behind their involvement. In the words of one early-1970s recruit: 'Why did I become involved in the IRA? It was because of a process of British state repression as clearly distinct from any sort of attachment to republican ideology.'[136] Future Brighton bomber Patrick Magee had an IRA grandfather; but his own arrest and beating-up at the hands of British soldiers also contributed to his joining the IRA: there was 'a sense of anger. Real anger. I felt I just couldn't walk away from this, and I did join up.'[137]

Now there was clearly great advantage for the Provisionals in presenting the British Army in a negative light: 'Within months of coming on to the streets of Belfast and Derry in August 1969 the British Army were increasingly seen by the nationalist people as being defenders of the loyalist state and not in a "peace-keeping" role.'[138] But this does not mean that such judgments lack substance. Nor was it just the Army against whom one was hitting back. Cycles of revenge and hatred involved defending your own community and avenging it upon its more local enemies too – in the chilling words of one north Belfast Provisional, looking over a Protestant area of the city: 'that's my dream for Ireland. I would like to see those Orange [Protestant or loyalist] bastards just wiped out.'[139] Sectarian influences played a vital part in moulding the thinking of the Provisionals.[140] Having a go at the Orange bastards, or at the Brits in revenge for harassment by soldiers, were key and lasting strains in IRA thinking. The Provisionals were indeed fighting back.

But defence and retaliation were interlinked, in Provo thinking, with a committed anti-imperialism. It was, the Provisionals asserted, against 'the forces of British imperialism' that the old IRA had failed to defend Catholics in August 1969.[141] Ireland had been denied her rightful self-determination by an imperialist Britain, and Irish partition embodied this historical crime. British actions in Northern Ireland were held to demonstrate the point. Ruairí Ó Brádaigh observed in mid-1971 that British soldiers' behaviour in Northern Ireland was 'typical of an imperial power. I think that to maintain an imperial grasp, reprehensible methods have to be employed.'[142] It was, at least in part, against imperial forces that the IRA were now aiming to defend their community. Seán MacStiofáin saw things in similar terms. He described the Northern Ireland of 1969 as 'a neglected colony of a decaying imperial power', and observed of the arrival of British troops in the north that 'a colonial power does not send its army to hurry up social reforms'.[143] The Army, in this view, was there to repress, to maintain control.

Thus, significantly, defence and anti-imperialist offence were, from early on, interwoven in the IRA's thinking. In January 1971 Daithi O'Connell claimed that the IRA had 'purified itself', that it would not allow a recurrence of the August 1969 situation when 'defenceless people were attacked by the forces of sectarianism' – and that when the time was opportune the organization would go into action to end, once and for all, the problem of British forces in Northern Ireland.[144] Anti-imperialism also provided a hopeful framework. Just as other British colonies had been freed by force, so, the Provisionals argued, the Irish colony would finally be liberated by similar means. Great encouragement was taken from the recent example of Aden (the 'most humiliating defeat the British Army has suffered in the twentieth century', as the IRA's Belfast paper put it).[145] The use of violence would force the British to talk, just as in other anti-imperialist/anti-colonial struggles. On 25 September 1971 *Republican News* compared the pressure being exerted on the British to reach a settlement with the IRA, with the experience of the USA in being forced to talk to the Viet Cong, and that of the British themselves in being forced to talk to EOKA in Cyprus and to Irgun in the Middle East. In each case, such talking was done only after the power in question had lost many soldiers; in republican eyes, the logic was for Britain to settle early: 'The responsibility for violence and death, for injury and destruction, is yours.' Anti-imperialism offered legitimacy combined with the promise of victory: 'imperialism' had become something of a discredited word by the time of the Provos' formation, and the dismantling of European empires in the postwar period suggested that history was on the side of those whose instincts were anti-colonial.

This interrelation between defence, retaliation and anti-imperialism was embodied in the IRA Army Council's January 1970 decision to adopt a three-stage approach: first, defence; second, a combination of defence and retaliation; third, a sustained offensive engagement with the British in a guerrilla campaign. At this point, they recognized that they were not yet in a position to drive, determine and dictate events. But the emphases on defiant defence, retaliation and an anti-imperialist offensive co-existed in the mind of the new army's ruling council and constituted the essence of Provisional thinking.

For crucial to the new IRA's thought was the rejection of conventional politics as ineffective and effete. Instead they adopted the politics of force. The northern state of the 1960s – in Gerry Adams's evaluation, 'a state based upon the violent suppression of political opposition'[146] – was simply deemed irreformable. The politics of reform, and of peaceful method, were felt to have been tried in vain. As one early-1970s IRA recruit observed, in relation to the civil rights episode: 'There was a clear perception that a very basic demand had been made for simple fair treatment, and [that] it was met with the coercive end of the state rather than anything else.' The issue seemed clear: 'There was an accumulation of evidence to say to me that, really, the six-county area is irreformable: we cannot change it. And the argument that the British, the central government is interested in making possible progressive change is open to serious question.'[147] As leading republican and early-1970s IRA man, Martin McGuinness, put it: 'It was blatantly clear to me that the [people in the] community [from] which I came were effectively being treated as second-class citizens in their own country. The state put in place at the time of partition was a unionist state for a unionist people, and any recognition of Irishness was something to be frowned upon by the authorities . . . Catholics did not have the liberties that other sections of the community had and were effectively being ruthlessly discriminated against by the unionist administration.'[148] The state that discriminated against them was unavoidably, of its very nature, sectarian; it had to be abolished; the only way to do this was through violence; Britain would only respond to force. Violence would be used to make the state ungovernable, and to make it more costly for the British to remain than it would be for them to go. In contrast to their Gouldingite rivals, this IRA gave primacy to military thinking.

Leading IRA figures interviewed in June 1971 claimed, 'We hate to see the loss of anybody's life, but this becomes necessary in certain extreme circumstances. For a long time, various forms of protest against repression in Northern Ireland have been employed by the people but with little effect.'[149] Without violence, it was held that meaningful change would not occur. Danny Morrison's fictional account of this period sets out something of the classic Provisional reading of events: 'A civil rights movement, demanding justice and reforms, had been launched ten months previously. The unionist government and its supporters attacked the movement and in a number of confrontations three nationalists had died at the hands of the RUC. But the repression had only brought more international scrutiny of the abuse of power by the unionist party which had been in government for fifty years.'[150]

Suspicious opposition to conventional politics should not imply, however, that the Provisionals were straightforwardly anti-political. Their violence arose from a political conflict and from sincere political convictions. And even in its comparatively unsophisticated early years, the movement did have political programmes and preferences. Aspects of this were simple and definitional: 'we are NOT British, WE ARE IRISH. We will not willingly accept British rule. England for the English and Ireland for the Irish. Is that unreasonable?'[151] Backing up this insistence on Irish/British mutual exclusivity was an enthusiasm for emphatically non-British cultural politics. A *Republican News* article on the Irish language in May 1971 was entitled 'Learn Irish, speak Irish, be Irish': 'Sinn Féin members have a duty to encourage the use of Irish among themselves and the public at large.' The Provisionals frequently reflected this very strong identification between Irishness and the Irish language. Maria McGuire observed of Seán MacStiofáin – originally John Stephenson – that he 'had a vision of a united Gaelic-speaking Ireland; having taken the trouble to learn Gaelic himself, he no doubt thought that everyone else could and should.'[152] The sceptical Roy Johnston observed of MacStiofáin that 'His English accent and background [were] rendered acceptable in some quarters by doctrinaire insistence on the use of Irish on all possible occasions.'[153]

Some aspects of the Provisionals' politics were more formalized. In 1971 they unveiled Eire Nua (New Ireland), a plan for each of Ireland's four provinces to have its own regional parliament within a federal framework. The creation of Ó Brádaigh and O'Connell, this scheme was intended in part to meet the fears of northern unionists about their being subsumed into an all-Ireland polity: the Ulster parliament would provide them with certain protection of interests and influence. The early 1970s Provisionals thus sought not only 'British withdrawal', but also the reorganization of Irish political structures and society. There would be a four-level arrangement: federal (central) government, provincial government, regional (administrative) government and district (local) government.[154]

More immediately, the Provisionals offered what they considered appropriate political proposals for the end to the northern conflict. On 5 September 1971 they issued 'interim proposals', public acceptance of which by the British would (they believed) 'bring immediate peace'. This five-point plan comprised: first, the 'immediate cessation to the British forces' campaign of violence against the Irish people'; second, the abolition of Belfast's Stormont parliament; third, non-interference in an election to establish a regional parliament for the nine-county Ulster province, 'as a first step towards a new governmental structure for the thirty-two counties'; fourth, the immediate release of all Irish political prisoners; and fifth, a guarantee of compensation 'for all those who suffered as a result of direct and indirect British violence'. A Provisional spokesman said that they had issued this statement 'to demonstrate the genuine concern we feel for the people in Northern Ireland'.[155] Admittedly, that concern might have been obscured from the vision of some people by incidents such as the IRA killing of one-year-old Angela Gallagher two days before the above proposals were issued. (The baby was shot in her pram, during a sniper attack on the British Army in Belfast.) But, as the Provisionals' proposals certainly did indicate, the movement had firm political objectives. In particular, the northern regime at Stormont, synonymous in republican eyes with sectarian discrimination, was a prime political target for the IRA. In his October 1971 presidential address to Sinn Féin's *ard fheis* in Dublin, Ruairí Ó Brádaigh claimed that 'Stormont has grown more and more repressive and has shown [itself] to be incapable of reform . . . The abolition of Stormont has been one of the foundation stones of our policies over the past two years.'[156] The following year, after Stormont had been prorogued by the British, Ó Brádaigh referred to the fall of Stormont as having been 'a prime political objective of our movement'.[157] This clearly made sense for the IRA. A Belfast regime reflecting the wishes of the unionist majority in the north had acted as a kind of insulation against greater British involvement there. It also implied that the key difficulty in Ulster related to differences of opinion between local people. In contrast, the Provisionals wanted the conflict to be seen as one between Ireland and Britain: to remove Stormont would help to clarify that republican reality.

However immediate their strategy on such points, Provisional political thinking was cast in terms of Irish republican tradition and, in particular, it was contextualized within the richness of a tradition validated by contemporary experience. Patrick Magee commented of early-1970s Belfast that there was a 'very, very strong-rooted belief system of republicanism in the communities'.[158] The dynamics that produced the Provos may have been contemporary and urgent, but such immediate events fitted into a longstanding republican framework. In 1970 Ruairí Ó Brádaigh argued that the republican movement maintained 'direct organisational continuity from Fenian times, through the Irish Republican Brotherhood, past 1916 and the First Dáil to the present day'. Drawing explicitly on heroes from the republican Valhalla (Theobald Wolfe Tone, James Fintan Lalor, James Connolly), Ó Brádaigh sought to link his own vision of Irish republicanism to that of revered nationalists from the past: 'a republican today is one who seeks a great deal more than just physical control of the thirty-two counties for the Irish people ... To give depth and meaning to republicanism ... is to see the republican objective as one with political, social, economic and cultural dimensions.'[159]

IRA prisoners seeking books in the 1970s often looked, in particular, for the works of such figures such as Connolly, Fintan Lalor, Pearse and Mellows.[160] One Derry man who joined the Provisionals as a teenager pointed not only to his family connections with IRA men of earlier generations, but also to the way in which – as a child – he was attracted to the writings of republican heroes such as the 1916 rebels.[161]

This identification with the past sometimes had a personal dimension to it, since the validation of republican tradition could also involve the vindication of one's own family and community. Early-1970s IRA Volunteer Marian Price recalls: 'I was born into a very staunch republican family. My father was a republican (had been a member of the IRA in the forties) and my mother's family were very staunchly republican (her sisters and herself were members of Cumann na mBan

[Irish women's Council]) . . . So we always grew up with republican-ism, and with a deep sense of pride in republicanism.'[162] (Price's parents, Albert Price and Chrissie Dolan, had been good friends of Danny Morrison's IRA uncle, Harry White.) Ex-IRA man Tommy McKearney stresses the importance of material, contemporary events in having led him into the IRA, but also points to his personal immersion in republican tradition: 'I was very closely connected to the history and tradition of physical-force republicanism . . . Both my grandfathers had been members of the IRA in the 1920s . . . More-over, I lived among people in the south Tyrone area where there was a strong tradition of physical-force republicanism . . . When I was a youngster going to secondary school in Dungannon, I passed every morning the house where [1916 republican martyr] Tom Clarke had been reared.'[163] Family, locality, tradition.

It is not that the Provisionals were trapped in, or unavoidably mandated by, history or tradition, for the contemporary experiences of northern nationalists were essential to the formation and growth of the new IRA: the reaction to day-to-day events as they unfolded (loyalist attacks, friction with the British Army, the experience of a hostile northern state) injected life and energy into Provisional republicanism. Yet republican history and tradition were certainly not irrelevant to the shape that the Provisionals assumed. True, their first public statement referred powerfully to the failure of republicans to provide defence in 1969; but it also declared an emphatic allegiance to the traditional republic associated with 1916 and 1919.[164] What happened at the end of the 1960s and the beginning of the 1970s was that urgent contemporary circumstances in the north seemed to validate certain traditional republican assumptions. The Provisionals would not have emerged as a vibrant force purely because of republican tradition; but that tradition did help to shape the ideology and rhetoric of the movement that the Provisionals became. Immediate northern need and longstanding republican argument reinforced one another power-fully; continuities as well as discontinuities produced and defined the Provos.

Just as in earlier phases of republican activity, so also with the early Provisionals there was a complex relationship with socialist thought. In 1970 the IRA remained at least rhetorically committed to the ultimate objective of a socialist republic. There was, especially among those of the younger generation, what Danny Morrison has called an 'instinctive affinity with working-class politics',[165] and Morrison himself had been involved in left-wing PD protests. Marian Price's father had been 'a very strong socialist', and in Marian's own view socialism and republicanism were inextricably interwoven: 'I really don't think you can have one without the other.'[166] But, as Price acknowledges, the Provos' relationship with leftism was complex. Looking back at the emerging Provisionals, Seán MacStiofáin himself commented, 'Certainly as revolutionaries we were automatically anti-capitalist. But we refused to have anything to do with any communist organisation in Ireland, on the basis of their ineffectiveness, their reactionary foot-dragging on the national question and their opposition to armed struggle.'[167] Elsewhere, he declared himself to be anti-capitalist, but not Marxist.[168] At times, the Provisionals explicitly declared that their social radicalism sought to avoid the evils of either Cold War system, American or Soviet: 'The republican movement has never looked on the ending of British rule in Ireland as an end in itself, but rather as a means to restore the ownership of Ireland to the people of Ireland. The movement seeks to establish a system free of any exploitation of man by man and which will be truly democratic right down through society.' The Provisionals wanted 'a social system which would transcend both western individualistic capitalism, with its poor and hungry amid plenty, on the right, and eastern Soviet state capitalism (or any of its variations) with its denial of freedom and human rights, on the left'.[169]

Some of the older Provos tended towards a marked conservatism, reflecting in part the significance of that communal Catholicism identified as crucial even by younger Provisionals such as Gerry Adams. (Here again there was some continuity with the pre-split IRA: a leading member of that supposedly radical army had acknowledged ruefully in the mid-1960s that 'the majority of our members are anything but anti-clerical').[170] Catholicism was a formative part of many Provisionals' experience (as Martin McGuinness commented of his own family upbringing: 'We were reared in the nationalist, Catholic tradition, with the greater emphasis being on Catholic');[171] and it was important to the Provisionals in terms of background, culture, language, symbolism, imagery, identity and cohesion.

Indeed, the early Provisional movement demonstrated some strikingly Catholic-influenced conservatism, to accompany and at times compete with its left-leaning declarations. On 9 February 1974 the IRA's Belfast paper, *Republican News*, carried a major article written by a Dublin Sinn Féiner, opposing a bill aiming to provide for limited access to contraception in the Republic of Ireland. Accompanied by a large photograph of a baby, the article argued that this bill should anyway be rejected, but that there were also 'special reasons why republicans more than others' should oppose contraception in the Republic:

> It is essential to the Free State [Republic of Ireland] parties if they and their British masters are to defeat the Provisionals that people in the twenty-six counties, especially the young, are provided with a surfeit of drink, drugs, fags and sex. The politicians won't put it in these words but instinctively they know the conscience of the nation can only be deadened in our present circumstances if it is perverted and degraded by a diet of bread and circuses, by the excesses of drugs, drink and sexuality. It will suit British political strategy if the Free Staters succeed in weakening the fibre of the Irish people. It will also suit the British contraceptive industry if they can help to create and supply an Irish market for their easily produced and highly profitable products.

According to one source, Seán MacStiofáin himself so objected to these easily produced and highly profitable products that he refused to bring any contraceptives from Northern Ireland (where they were more easily available) to the Republic, despite his organization's desire to experiment with them to make acid fuses for bombs: 'He would rather, it seemed, be caught with a Thompson [submachine gun] in his car boot than with a packet of contraceptives in his pocket.'[172]

Not for the first time in Irish republican history, therefore, there existed a tension between publicly declared leftism and intense Catholic conservatism. For some, indeed, Christianity and leftism were extremely unhappy cellmates. One Belfast IRA leader was quoted in February 1971 as stating: 'We could never come to terms with the Goulding IRA which is now Marxist and socialist. We are republicans and our notions of a free Ireland are based on Christian principles and democracy.'[173] And personal differences probably overlaid and reinforced ideological divergence here too; the relaxed, bohemian Cathal Goulding thought the dour MacStiofáin not to be 'the sort of fellow I'd look for after a political meeting to have a drink with'.[174]

Just as rage, hatred and contempt could be expressed towards one's *extra*-communal enemies, so also the Provisionals provided a mechanism for obtaining power and prestige *within* the Catholic community, and for controlling and defining it. Indeed, the Provisionals' battles with their intracommunal opponents were frequently vicious. This was true verbally, with outpourings of bile upon rivals such as the constitutional nationalist party, the Social Democratic and Labour Party (SDLP) – formed in August 1970 by Stormont MPs Gerry Fitt, Paddy Devlin, Austin Currie, John Hume, Paddy O'Hanlon and Ivan Cooper, their aims including 'To promote the cause of Irish unity based on the consent of the majority of people in Northern Ireland'.[175] And there was also some bloody feuding with the Official IRA. Who was to represent and define northern nationalism? Those who believed in radicalized Gouldingite republicanism, those who espoused constitutional nationalist politics – or the Provisionals?

And behind the IRA's various ostensible aims, political ambitions and assumptions there also lay a whole series of less prominent aspects to their thought and motivation. Just as in previous periods of IRA activity, so also with this new IRA the search for meaning, distinctive identity, prestige and power played its part as personal instincts interwove with political projects. Partly, it could be a story of adventure: 'It was an exciting time. I was nineteen, sleeping in ditches, outbuildings or safe houses, always with my clothes on, always armed';[176] 'There was a really exciting aspect to being on the run, living from house to house and travelling about.'[177] Secrecy and the clandestine excitement of conspiracy were part of the appeal, complementing political motivation. And, again with echoes of earlier episodes, the attractions of soldiership played their part. More than one person under Gerry Adams's authority at a 1967 Fianna Eireann camp in Leitrim later joined the British, rather than the Irish Republican, Army: 'For some at least it was the thrill of fighting, rather than fighting for Ireland, which was foremost in their youthful minds.'[178] The attractions of soldiership were such that some who later became IRA men had formerly admired the British Army, had respected the Army when it came to Northern Ireland in the late 1960s, were fascinated by the soldiers in a positive way[179] and had – in some cases – even thought of joining up themselves.[180] And even some who joined the Provisionals acknowledged a prior soldierly appeal independent of republican commitment: 'When the [British] Army first came in and billeted in places like the lower Ormeau Road for a very short period of time, we found it very exciting, and we used to get rides in their jeeps and stuff and it was all very good.'[181]

It would be misleading to present the IRA's politics as too formalized, elaborate or coherent. They emerged out of turbulence and crisis, and were as frequently visceral as intellectual or philosophical in approach. But there *was* a definite IRA politics: defence, defiance, retaliation and anti-imperialism were interwoven in their thinking; force would work, they believed, where conventional politics simply would not, and violent revolution was preferred to an impossible, peaceful reformism; contemporary conditions validated a lengthy republican tradition and orthodoxy; Catholicism as well as socialism informed the organization's thinking and identity; Irish cultural politics complemented formal programmes for Irish self-determination; intra-communal competition with nationalist rivals complemented inter-communal, sectarian and anglophobic instincts; and as with any group, essentially non-political, personal impulses found expression in the alternative army.

In various, varying ways these ideas informed, defined and motivated the new IRA. And in various, varying ways they are again and again evident in the Provisionals' early years, to which we now turn.

4

'It has been said that most revolutions are not caused by
revolutionaries in the first place, but by the stupidity and
brutality of governments. Well, you had that to start with in
the north all right.'

Seán MacStiofáin, first Provisional IRA Chief of Staff[182]

On 29 March 1970 trouble erupted after a republican Easter Rising
commemoration in Derry: a crowd attacked an RUC station and there
were riots, arrests and injuries. In April 1970 the first major confrontations between Catholics and soldiers in Belfast took place, with three
nights of rioting in Ballymurphy. As a result, Sir Ian Freeland – who
had arrived as General Officer Commanding British troops in Northern
Ireland the previous July – announced that petrol bombers risked
being shot. Such friction, in a sense, suited the Provisionals. If the
Catholic community was in violent conflict with an aggressive British
Army, then the organization most sharply hostile to the latter could
reap communal rewards and support. Attrition with the British Army
was vital in producing the atmosphere in which the new IRA grew and
in which their violence gradually became acceptable to people who
would not otherwise have condoned or supported it.

On 27 June marches again inflamed the emerging war. On that day
the Protestant Orange Order provocatively paraded on the edge of
Belfast's Catholic Ardoyne, up Crumlin Road and past Hooker Street.
Three days earlier the Joint Security Committee, meeting at Stormont,
had been divided about whether to ban the coming marches. With
questionable judgment, they had decided not to do so. For it turned
out to be an ill-advised decision to allow Protestants to march in this
way so close to already angry Catholic areas: on the 27th, Catholic and
Protestant crowds gathered and a fight developed in which the IRA
shot dead three Protestants. Further violence erupted later in the day
in another part of the city: the Short Strand area, where a Catholic
ghetto was set vulnerably against Protestant east Belfast. In the after-

noon, an Orange parade had passed the corner of nationalist Seaforde Street and so tensions were already high. Anticipating a dramatic and dangerous evening, the IRA's Tom O'Donnell (Finance Officer on the Belfast Brigade Staff) ordered that arms be lifted from dumps and, along with members of the Catholic Citizens' Defence Committee (one of a plethora of defence groups then springing up), the Provisionals prepared for defence against impending attack.

Around 10 p.m. Billy McKee arrived (having earlier attended Mass), and more weapons were brought in from the Falls Road area in the west of the city. Petrol bombs began to be thrown at the Catholic St Matthew's Church, and a Protestant mob appeared intent on destroying it. McKee and his comrades defended the church in an epic encounter which has subsequently acquired legendary standing in republican memory, and which has been used to testify to the necessity and efficacy of the Provisionals: 'The heroic defence of the Short Strand in June 1970 showed the fruits of all the reorganising and training that had followed August 1969, and that when it came to it the Irish Republican Army could and would defend the oppressed nationalist people.'[183]

During a five-hour gun-battle McKee himself was wounded and one of his fellow defenders, Henry McIlhone, was fatally wounded: 'I told Henry to get behind a tree as a couple of men came forward. I told him [to] fire and he did but I don't think he hit anybody. All I heard was a clomp like a wet log hitting the ground. It was like a big tree falling ... He was hit in the throat ... I was shot in the back and the bullet came up through my neck. There was a lot of blood. So I spun round and got [to] the wall ... I survived. Henry didn't.'[184] (Though subsequently claimed as one of their Volunteers,[185] McIlhone was not, in fact, an IRA man.) In the absence of adequate police or Army protection, the Catholics had defended themselves. They had also inflicted fatal wounds on four Protestants in the encounter.

In the wake of the Short Strand battle, the new Conservative Home Secretary Reginald Maudling visited Northern Ireland, coming to Belfast on 30 June and returning to London the following day. Maudling was apparently appalled by his experience in the north: boarding his plane to leave troubled Belfast, he immediately demanded a large whisky and exclaimed, 'What a bloody awful country!' (The IRA newspaper's response was, yes, but 'Who *made* it "a bloody awful country!"?')[186] The IRA killings were followed by what became known as the Falls curfew, the authorities aiming to obtain the weapons that might make further republican killings possible. An extensive search of Belfast's Lower Falls was undertaken by British troops, beginning on Friday 3 July. Rioting followed; a curfew was imposed, lasting till Sunday; much damage was done to houses during the search and a number of people were killed. This Falls curfew produced ambiguous results. Many weapons were indeed gathered by the Army, the haul including 100 firearms, 100 home-made bombs, 250lb explosives and 21,000 rounds of ammunition. This aspect of the episode understandably pleased the Northern Irish government ('In addition to the very substantial haul of arms and ammunition, information had been discovered which would be of great value to Special Branch').[187] But the Falls curfew was also instrumental in heightening tensions further, and was arguably decisive in terms of worsening relations between the British Army and the Catholic working class. Gerry Adams: 'The Falls Road curfew in July 1970 made popular opposition to the British Army absolute in Belfast ... After that recruitment to the IRA was massive.'[188] From now on, the Army were definitely not going to be seen as defenders of the Catholic community.

This seems much clearer now than it did at the time. In August 1970 the authorities still detected signs of hope for more benign Army–Catholic relations. After a quiet night on 18–19 August, there were noted 'reports of a great improvement in relations between the Army and the local population in Belfast, particularly in the Falls Road', as a result of Army assistance with flood relief following very heavy rain and gales over the preceding weekend.[189] But it was not to be. As was suggested at the Ministry of Defence, the situation by September was 'an inflamed sectarian one, which is being deliberately exploited by the IRA and other extremists'.[190] And the authorities' own actions frequently exacerbated the north's difficulties. Prime Minister Edward Heath[191] had rightly felt in July that year 'that nothing should be done which would suggest any partiality to one section of the community';[192] but events such as the Falls curfew seemed to suggest precisely that. As the Taoiseach, Jack Lynch, rightly observed in a letter to Heath in the immediate aftermath of the curfew, 'arms searches must not only be complete and impartial but must be seen to be so if they are not to be regarded as further repression of the minority'.[193]

Strengthened as they were by such counterproductive British military gestures, the IRA was by October 1970 ready to go on the full offensive and that month began a bombing campaign – mostly aimed at commercial targets. In the following month, leading British Army figure Anthony Farrar-Hockley claimed that the soldiers in Northern Ireland were now facing 'organised terrorism'. He claimed that recent riots, in which soldiers had been injured, had indeed been orchestrated; but he considered that the Army was not confronted by a 'well-oiled machine', and that the terrorists were not particularly 'good' at their trade.[194] Yet further rebel escalation was in store. At the beginning of 1971 the IRA Army Council sanctioned offensive operations against the British Army, and early in that year the IRA started systematically to shoot at British troops in Belfast. In the early hours of 6 February a British soldier, Robert Curtis, was killed by machine-gun fire from the IRA in north Belfast's New Lodge Road. A twenty-year-old member of the Royal Artillery, Gunner Curtis was the first British soldier to be killed in the modern troubles. He had been married for thirteen months and his wife was three months pregnant at the time of his death. At his Newcastle-upon-Tyne home on the day after the killing, the dead soldier's father observed: 'I do not even know what my son died for.'[195] Curtis's killer, IRA man Billy Reid, was himself to be a tragic early victim of the troubles, shot dead by the British Army some months later during a ninety-second exchange of gunfire in Belfast; thirty-two years old, he was married with four children.

From February until August 1971 the IRA became more and more fiercely anti-Army and the tit-for-tat escalation proceeded bloodily. The Army were seen as repressive, as backing the unionists, as saturating republican areas in a partisan and offensive way. Friction, harassment and attrition became daily realities and not for the first time in Irish history a British Army deployed to undermine republican subversion in fact helped to solidify the very subversion that it was supposed to stem. Each side's actions provoked aggressive responses from the other, both the IRA and the Army holding that the other's atrocities demanded a response in kind. And atrocities there certainly were. On 10 March three off-duty Scottish soldiers were shot through the back of the head, by the IRA, in the Ligoniel area of north Belfast. The young members of the Royal Highland Fusiliers – Dougald McCaughey (twenty-three) and brothers Joseph (eighteen) and John (seventeen) McCaig – had been lured to their deaths from a Belfast bar with the promise of a party. Their bodies were discovered on the lonely Old Squires Hill Road by three children.

Soldierly responses were predictable: brutalities such as this triple killing had an intensifying effect on the conflict through the unsurprising response of the British Army itself to such incidents. One young Scottish Catholic working-class member of the Parachute Regiment, then about to go to Northern Ireland, later recalled how this story broke among his comrades:

> 'Anybody heard the news? The IRA bastards have just murdered three young Scots soldiers in Ligoniel, just outside Belfast. They were off duty and drunk. All shot in the back. They never had a chance.' There was no outburst of anger – just silence. I looked at the faces of the older soldiers around me. I read on them the same thing: 'Just wait till we get across.' The IRA didn't know what they'd let themselves in for. Many historians who write about Ulster talk of turning points. For me and everybody at the table, that was the major turning point.[196]

Arriving in Ulster in May 1971, this soldier (Harry McCallion) was to take part in the internment arrests of August 1971 which yet further fuelled the fire of Catholic resentment. The attitudes of such soldiers contextualize the frictional relationship that was to develop – in internment and other forms – during these attritional, escalatory early years of the troubles. If the IRA (who by the spring of 1971 were bombing with energy and intensity) saw themselves as retaliating for the atrocious actions of their opponents, then so too did the soldiers.

Not that there was no humour to these days. Ex-IRA man Tommy Gorman recalls a 1971 Belfast IRA operation which involved the taking over of a house with an old woman in it. One of the Volunteers (a solicitor) was anxious, asking, 'What will I do with the old dear?' He was told to take her to the back of the house, not to let her see his face, not to panic her but just to keep her calm. When the operation was over, Gorman went to the back of the house to find the Volunteer and the woman sitting talking together: she was drinking tea quite happily, while – to prevent his face from being seen – the IRA man had a wicker basket over his head.[197]

On 20 March 1971 Northern Irish Prime Minister James Chichester-

Clark resigned, to be replaced on the 23rd by Brian Faulkner.[198] On the day of his appointment the new man stated: 'Obviously, the kernel of our immediate problems is the law and order situation. Let me say right away that I am convinced that what we need on this front are not new principles, but practical results on the ground in the elimination not only of terrorism and sabotage, but of riots and disorder.'[199] But the old unionist principles were simply not working. At the end of March the IRA's bombing campaign began in earnest, and their war with the Army continued to intensify. At the start of July there was a deliberate and sudden escalation of activity from the IRA in Derry, following extensive rioting there during the early months of the year. Shots were fired at soldiers on 4, 5, 6 and 7 July, and following rioting on the last of these nights, an unarmed man (Seamus Cusack) was fatally shot by the British Army in the early hours of the 8th. Intense rioting ensued, during which the Army shot dead another man (Desmond Beattie). In the intimacy of Derry's Catholic community, personal links – and identification – with these two men were understandably strong. Anger at the Army's fatal shootings produced a flow of recruits to the IRA in the city: those most prepared to attack the Army reaped the benefit from anti-Army anger. As Derry's most famous modern republican, Martin McGuinness, later put it, the Cusack/Beattie killings marked the 'rejection of the British Army and the establishment of the republican base in Derry'.[200]

But one of the most infamous British Army operations was launched the following month, with spectacularly counterproductive consequences. In the face of continuing civil disorder and an intensified IRA campaign of violence, the Northern Irish government applied pressure on London to introduce internment without trial; as Prime Minister Faulkner had himself explained it on the very morning of internment's introduction: 'in a deteriorating security situation with its damaging effects on the economy, and in the absence of any other initiative which might be taken, he had told the Home Secretary of his conclusion that the powers of detention and internment should be invoked'.[201]

Around 4 am on 9 August 1971 Operation Demetrius commenced. During the first twenty-four hours, 342 people were arrested by the Army and police. Fewer than a hundred of them were either Provisional or Official IRA Volunteers. The intelligence on which internment

had been based was insufficiently accurate; key sections of the Provisional leadership (including MacStiofáin, Ó Brádaigh, O'Connell)
were based in the Republic of Ireland anyway; and many republicans
had gone on the run, apparently forewarned of the likelihood of
internment. Of those lifted, 116 were quickly released, while the other
226 were placed either in the *Maidstone* prison ship in Belfast docks or
in Crumlin Road Jail. Subsequently, people were taken to Long Kesh
(near Belfast) or Magilligan (near Derry).

The initial swoops were on republicans[202] (although loyalists were
later interned), and this one-sidedness was one of the features which
enraged Catholics in the north. Such outrage fitted in well with what
the IRA had been saying. At the start of the year, *Republican News* had
warned: 'Imprisonment without trial or charge has been and still is an
occupational hazard for members of the republican movement.' There
was no doubt, the paper claimed, that 'if and when internment does
start', republicans would be the victims. (An indication of republican
perceptions is evident from the fact that this article on internment
was illustrated with a drawing of a man behind barbed wire, with
the caption: 'Name . . . Could be you; Crime . . . None; Reason for
internment . . . Being an Irishman'.)[203] The effect on the Catholic
community was certainly to strengthen resistance to the government,
and to unite the Catholic people in opposition to the authorities. Even
if one is sceptical about Provisional leader Joe Cahill's version – 'the
people's reaction was far beyond anything that I thought could come.
It was 100% opposition to internment and backing for the IRA'[204] – it
remains clear that internment helped to invigorate that which it had
been intended by the authorities to uproot. This was reflected in the
mass hostility at the time: large crowds emerged, barricades went up
in response to the raids, lethal violence broke out. Within a few days
over twenty people were killed and thousands (mostly Catholics) were
left homeless by house-burnings. Any notion that Operation Demetrius
had knocked out the IRA was undermined by a press conference held
in Belfast on 13 August. Journalists were taken in secret to a Ballymurphy school gym where Joe Cahill refuted British Army claims that the
IRA was virtually beaten: 'We have plenty of guns and ammunition,'
he stressed.[205]

Condemnations of internment have been extensive. William Whitelaw (who became the first Secretary of State for Northern Ireland in

1972) observed that 'The introduction of internment was predictably followed by heavy rioting during which twenty-one people were killed in three days. Thereafter internment did nothing to stem the deterioration in the situation. On the contrary, it remained a source of discontent and a spur to more violence.'[206] Military judgments tend to be similar. 'Internment was a political disaster, nor was it particularly effective in military terms';[207] 'The only people in the battalion who knew we were going to lift people that Monday morning, 9 August, were the commanding officer and myself. I personally thought it was a necessary move, but the commanding officer, who was a Catholic, was a very sad man that night. He said, "This is disaster."'[208] Certainly, Prime Minister Heath and Home Secretary Maudling (together with leading soldiers such as the then senior British Army officer in Northern Ireland, Harry Tuzo) had been sceptical about the policy: it was Northern Irish Prime Minister Faulkner who had pressed them into its introduction. But perhaps one should not overstate the simplicity of the issue. Past experience of internment (during 1939–45 and 1956–62) had been positive for the authorities in terms of dealing with the IRA. And British politician James Callaghan honestly acknowledges that 'It is doubtful whether anyone, including myself, foresaw just how violent the Catholic reaction to internment would be. Certainly they could not have foreseen how ineffectual it would prove as an answer to terrorism.'[209] (And it could be pointed out, though it rarely is, that even the initial swoops did net *some* IRA activists.)

There is, however, no doubting that internment confirmed a widespread Catholic rejection of the unionist government and that it thus helped to undermine Stormont rather than strengthen it. During the pre-internment period of 1971 (up to 9 August) the Provisionals killed ten British soldiers; during the remaining months of the year they killed thirty. For many Catholics, internment confirmed what their experiences had up until that point been suggesting. One Belfast woman, explaining why she joined the IRA, referred to having experienced loyalist intimidation, then British Army raids – and then to having witnessed internment: 'I felt I'd no other option but to join after that. That's when it became crystal clear to me that the Brits were here to suppress the Catholic minority, and for no other reason.'[210]

And the problems with the introduction of internment were compounded by subsequent mistreatment of those detained while in custody. Among the methods used on the internees were the 'five techniques': placing a hood over the head; forcing the internee to stand spreadeagled against a wall for long periods; denying regular sleep patterns; providing irregular and limited food and water; and subjecting people to white noise in the form of a constant humming sound. Tommy Gorman, interned in 1971:

> it was bad ... They brought us into the cell, in this place, [and it] had blankets hanging up everywhere and there was eye-holes in the blankets ... you could see the eyes at these holes in the blanket and we walked in [and they said,] 'That's him, that's him' ... we were battered, just battered for three days. There was no subtlety to it. It was just, you were hauled out of bed at two o'clock in the morning and brought in and questioned, battered against the wall, stuff like that. There was no good cop and bad cop, it was just bad cop and worse cop. It was just sheer brutality.[211]

The bad publicity generated by such episodes[212] was registered at the highest level in London, Edward Heath himself stressing on 19 August 'that greater efforts were necessary to counteract the propaganda being mounted against internment, the allegations of Army brutality and so on'.[213]

So Army actions such as internment or the killing of Cusack and Beattie, strengthened republican conviction, as is evident for example in the case of Martin McGuinness, who has offered the dreadful killings of Cusack and Beattie as key reasons for his becoming a republican.[214] The chronology here does not strictly work, for McGuinness – by his own account – had been an IRA officer long before Cusack and Beattie were killed.[215] But the role of the British Army – tragically epitomized by such killings – did indeed play its part in intensifying McGuinness's republican energy and commitment:

> it was plain as daylight that there was an Army in our town, in our country, and that they weren't there to give out flowers. Armies should be fought by armies. So, one night, I piled into a black Austin, me and five mates, and we went to see a Provo across the border. We told him our position and there were several meetings after that. Then we joined. Nothing really happened until Seamus Cusack was killed and internment came soon after. Then the Provos

in Derry were ordered into full-time military action. I gave up my job working in the butcher's shop.[216]

By the latter part of 1971, the accumulation of antagonism between the Army and the IRA (and, as a by-product, between the Army and the wider Catholic community) had led to a kind of war. Naïvely, in a Christmas message issued on 20 December that year, Harry Tuzo (Army GOC in Northern Ireland) appealed to the Catholic community to end violence. Regarding friction between northern Catholics and the Army, he commented: 'I sincerely hope that the friction and ill-feeling that has arisen – magnified a hundredfold by those who seek to divide the community and exacerbate relations with the Army – will not be allowed to cloud judgment or give rise to despair. I say to the Catholics of Northern Ireland: let us see an end to violence. Without the gunmen in your midst you have nothing to fear from the Army; furthermore we are here to protect you from any threat to your security.'

It was unlikely to persuade its intended audience. Leading Nationalist Party figure Eddie McAteer (whose brother Hugh had, of course, been a one-time IRA Chief of Staff), responded: 'As one member of the Catholic community here I am not rushing under General Tuzo's mistletoe.'[217] Yet, even after internment, the Northern Irish authorities hoped that things might be restored to order and political progress made: on 10 August Brian Faulkner had alluded in cabinet to 'the onus which lay with the Northern Ireland government to make progress in the achievement of greater consensus in conducting the business of government once the gunmen had been eliminated and calm restored in the community'.[218]

But these were days of revolutionary expectation on the part of the Provisionals, and of panic for many who feared deepening disorder. Edward Heath felt the need, in the turbulent wake of internment, to reassure Brian Faulker 'that no constitutional change was contemplated';[219] and, as is evident from archives released in 2002, the Dublin authorities were certainly concerned in 1971 that the northern crisis would endanger their own state. They kept a close watch on the actions of the Provos, military and political.[220] And they were alarmed at the prospect of further northern chaos infecting their own polity. A secret paper of 5 July, by the Chief of Staff of the Republic's Defence Forces, identified problems of manpower and material relating to the Forces as due to financial constraints on expenditure, and concluded, 'I am deeply concerned at the low standard of effectivity of the Forces.'[221] Eight days later, the same authoritative source was even more worried: 'There is a distinct probability that at some future date, perhaps sooner than might seem possible at present, British forces would be withdrawn from Northern Ireland, either to meet a crisis elsewhere, or by decision of the British parliament. The vacuum thus created would create a situation of grave peril for the country as a whole.'[222] Following internment, the northern situation was judged more threatening still for the safety of the Republic. A 'Top Secret' document of 23 August set out possible contingencies, and evaluated their implications for the state. Four possibilities were detailed: 'a. The interference with the democratic institutions of this state by subversive elements. b. Incursions into the Republic by organised security forces or partisan elements from Northern Ireland. c. A situation developing in Northern Ireland which might justify incursions into that area by elements of our Forces. d. A situation developing in Northern Ireland following a withdrawal of the British armed forces from that area which might justify incursions by elements of our Forces.' Having outlined and examined each in turn, the paper (by the then Chief of Staff of the Defence Forces) concluded, 'The present strength of the permanent Defence Force is critically inadequate to meet any of the contingencies outlined.'[223]

The northern crisis itself was becoming very bloody. During 1971 nine IRA men and women, and thirty-three Catholic civilians, were killed by the security forces; fifty-six members of the security forces were killed by the IRA. Indeed, by now the northern troubles had a momentum of their own. Often highly localized, the war – once ignited – had become a self-fuelling conflict. Revenge and politics reinforced one another as motivations for killing. And all of this created a certain confidence on the part of the IRA. In January 1972 they declared that 'England is on her knees; Stormont is finished': 'Heath, Maudling, Wilson, Callaghan and company see the six counties slipping from their grip.'[224] Republicans assumed that the conflict would end soon: 1972 was going to be 'The Year of Victory'.[225]

So the birth of the Provisional IRA could be read as a doubly Hobbesian moment. In helping to produce the Provisionals, late-1960s Protestant loyalist attacks on Catholics decisively regenerated a movement in need of reinvigoration. But, as Hobbes scholar Richard Tuck points out, the great philosopher considered people to be 'fundamentally self-protective, and only secondarily aggressive – it is the fear of an attack by a possible enemy which leads us to perform a pre-emptive strike on him'.[226] However exaggerated the fear, and however counterproductive the result, there is no doubt that loyalist action in the late 1960s grew out of a longstanding anxiety regarding the threat posed by Catholic Irish nationalism, and especially by republicans within Northern Ireland. But one might also read the emergence of the Provisionals through Hobbesian lenses from a second angle. Northern Catholics might claim that as, in the late 1960s and early 1970s, the sovereign's representatives were on occasions attacking them, they were quite justified in rebelling. At the very outset of the Provisionals' long life, therefore, Hobbesian reflections point towards pessimistic conclusions: towards a popular reluctance to accept that what people (on various sides) claim as good or right is in fact merely what is or seems to be in their own particular interest; or to the fact that while people typically argue that an opinion (their own) deserves widespread acceptance because it is right, a more probable and painful reality is the persistence of differing and clashing interests. It was to take thirty years for the implications of such logic to generate an apparent end to the war thus begun.

The events described in the above pages are frequently assumed to have had an inevitability about them, as though somehow Irish history or Anglo-Irish relations predetermined an unavoidable growth of carnage in the north. Civil rights leader Michael Farrell, for example, claimed that the Belfast sectarian rioting of the summer of 1969 had an inevitable quality to it. For fifty years, he said, those who ruled the north had sustained a system based on privilege, through the intentional fostering of hatred between the two communities; sectarianism had consequently become such an integral part of the system that the latter's decay inevitably led to a sectarian outburst.[227] But such views are surely misleading. For debatable and avoidable decisions – not least by Farrell himself – were far more responsible for the north's emerging troubles. What if Stormont had been replaced by less partial London government in 1969 (as demanded by John Hume) rather than in 1972, by which time the situation was far less open to remedy? (By late 1968 contingency plans for direct rule had indeed been prepared in London.)[228] What if earlier and more substantial reform had been implemented during the 1960s? What if the Burntollet march had not taken place? What if figures such as the eye-catching Protestant cleric and unionist politician, Ian Paisley, had adopted a less inflammatory approach?[229] What if internment had not been introduced?

And what if the Provisional IRA had themselves acted differently? For just as the actions of the pre-Provisional IRA had helped to produce the sequence of events that spawned the Provisionals, so too the actions of the early Provos helped (along with the actions of others) to produce the conditions within which they could themselves grow and flourish. Timing is crucial here. Republican accounts of the birth of the new IRA stress – and rightly so – the crimes committed against northern Catholics. Loyalist assaults of the 1960s, British Army actions such as the Falls curfew in 1970 or internment in 1971, etched themselves painfully into northern republican memory. But it is also important to examine the chronology closely. The Provisionals themselves were clear that their 'full-scaled offensive against the might of the British Army' had long preceded internment or Bloody Sunday.[230] Indeed, the Army Council's January 1970 decision to pursue a sustained offensive engagement with the British long predated even the Falls curfew. The killings of Cusack and Beattie in Derry in 1971 had been preceded and partly occasioned by a prior, deliberately provocative escalation of anti-Army violence by the IRA (though this in no way detracts from the awfulness of the deaths). For the Provos were revolutionaries, whose desire to engage in a war existed before, and helped to create, the conditions within which it could lastingly be fought.

This is *not* to claim that the Provisional IRA started the troubles, or that they were responsible for the northern conflict: multicausality is more striking than monocausality in these years. Some would seek simple allocation of blame but such an approach is hard to defend. For one thing, the Northern Irish conflict was about the failure of *two* national and state traditions to deal adequately with their respective minorities: the UK had not satisfactorily accommodated or absorbed Catholics in the north of Ireland; for its part, the Irish nationalist tradition and its southern Irish state had never made significant progress in attracting or appealing to northern Protestant opinion.

And the key point to recognize is this: that both the Provisional

IRA and the northern troubles arose out of an interwoven, complex sequence of events, none of which is singly responsible for what followed. Discrimination against Catholics in the north had created a lasting and understandable sense of resentment on the minority's part; but this in itself had not been sufficient cause for the generation of the Provisionals. (Had it been so, then something like the Provisionals would have emerged decades earlier.) It was, rather, a series of interconnected, often avoidable initiatives and activities that produced the Provisional IRA and the northern war of the early 1970s. The old IRA had helped to generate a civil rights campaign expressly anti-unionist in character; this, together with their residual military threat, had unwittingly exacerbated sectarian tension in the north and helped to occasion (unjustifiable) loyalist violence. The civil rights movement had taken on a broad Catholic quality because of northern state structures which were themselves the product of definite choices made by successive unionist governments. Radicals within the civil rights movement had helped to prevent compromise and defusion. Unionist hard-liners such as Ian Paisley and practitioners of loyalist violence had, in their different ways, stimulated the war. When intercommunal clashes occurred, the police were far from impartial. The actions of the British Army at times stimulated precisely that subversion against which they were often clumsily and lethally deployed. Each of these actions made internal sense to their practitioners; each contributed to the emergent war; and between them they led to the birth of the Provisional IRA.

FOUR
THE POLITICS OF VIOLENCE
1972–6

1

'If the Army had persisted in its "low-key" attitude and had
not launched a large-scale operation to arrest hooligans the
day might have passed off without serious incident.'

Lord Widgery's report on Bloody Sunday, 30 January 1972[1]

In the last two weeks of January 1972 the IRA was active in Derry,
with hundreds of shots fired at the security forces, and many nail-
bombs also thrown. After internment, sections of nationalist Derry had
effectively come under IRA control, and the organization clearly had
lethal potential. On 27 January two young RUC men were killed when
the IRA riddled their patrol car with bullets in Derry: Peter Gilgun, a
twenty-six-year-old Catholic from County Fermanagh, was married
with an eight-month-old son; David Montgomery, a twenty-year-old
Belfast Protestant, was due to be married five months later. The SDLP
MP for mid-Derry, Ivan Cooper, condemned the policemen's killing:
'This is a dastardly act.'[2]

But Cooper himself was to be present in Derry a few days later,
on Sunday the 30th, at one of the most awful and lastingly controversial episodes of the entire troubles. Derry had been at the centre of
the civil rights struggle, and many of the injustices suffered by northern Catholics had been sharply evident in that city. By early 1972
there was considerable tension there, with frequent rioting and clashes
between locals and the British Army. The Northern Ireland Civil
Rights Association organized an anti-internment march for the 30th
in the city; and, though processions and parades had been banned in

the north since the previous August, the march went ahead, with several thousand participants starting out in benign mood. The authorities had decided to contain the march (in order to avoid rioting and damage in the commercial part of Derry), by having barricades built by the security forces to prevent the marchers from moving out of the nationalist part of the city and into its centre. Soldiers from the First Battalion, the Parachute Regiment, were among those present that day.

Some kind of clash between soldiers and some of the marchers was expected on 30 January, and the British Army certainly anticipated that there might be IRA attacks on them during the event. Already numerous British soldiers had been killed by IRA snipers or bombers in Derry: these included twenty-three-year-old Ian Curtis, who had been shot by a sniper in November 1971, and Angus Stephens and David Tilbury, killed the previous month when bombs were thrown into their observation post. So on the day of the January march, with prior warning of probable sniping and bomb-attacks against them, the soldiers were tense and anticipatory. And highly aggressive. The Parachute Regiment was hardly the gentlest collection of men, even for an army, and the soldiers were intent on preventing extended assaults.

Most of the marchers did turn when reaching the barricades that the Army had set up to block their route. Some, however, did not, and the soldiers were attacked with stones and other missiles. Tear gas and water cannon were deployed in response and just after 4 p.m. the Army began, as had been planned, to make arrests. In doing so, they entered the nationalist Bogside area of Derry, with truly dreadful consequences. Soldiers claim that they came under fire (though this was, and remains, fiercely disputed by many marchers). There was, however, little ambiguity about the soldiers' own response: that afternoon in Derry they killed thirteen civilians, fatally injuring a fourteenth. The brief, appalling period of violence occasioned mayhem: confusion, shock, people running and screaming and diving for the ground – or falling, having been shot. Those who died were all Catholic, their names lastingly serving as a condemnation of British violence in Ireland: Patrick Doherty, Gerald Donaghy, Jack Duddy, Hugh Gilmore, Michael Kelly, Michael McDaid, Kevin McElhinney, Barney McGuigan, Gerald McKinney, William McKinney, William Nash, James Wray, John Young and John Johnston (who died some months later, on 16 June).

On 1 February the *Derry Journal* observed that the city 'was still reeling' from the shock of Bloody Sunday and noted that 'anger against British troops mounted to a new height'. The following day, over 25,000 people gathered outside St Mary's Church in the Creggan area, to watch the coffins of the thirteen dead being taken from the Derry church; another 2,000 packed the church itself for the Requiem Mass inside. The world's press, and at least twenty film crews, looked on. And they saw devastating personal loss. Gerald McKinney's widow, Ita: 'I remember him going out that day. He picked me up and swished me around and said, "I'll see you at six, doll." I kissed him and told him I loved him.' Jack Duddy's sister, Kay: 'I phoned casualty at Altnagelvin [Hospital] and asked if a Jackie Duddy had been admitted that afternoon. There was a lapse and then the nurse or whoever it was asked who was speaking and I told her I was Jackie Duddy's sister, and she said: "Jackie Duddy was dead on admission." I remember throwing the phone up in the air and standing there, screaming.'[3] Not all observers at the time shared the grief. Some members of the Parachute Regiment who were not in Ulster heard the news of Bloody Sunday on the radio; one recalled:

> Few of us knew anything about the situation in Ulster . . . We were not trained or schooled in subtlety. The Paras had taken out the enemy. They had won the firefight . . . None of us identified with the suffering of the victims or their families . . . Like most of my colleagues, I felt no animosity towards the Catholics of Northern Ireland. What was significant was that the victims of Bloody Sunday were against us. They were but one guise of the enemy that wore a thousand faces. When the news of Bloody Sunday came through, I am ashamed to say we cheered.[4]

Leading Derry republican Martin McGuinness many years later acknowledged that he had, as a twenty-one-year-old, been the second-in-command of the Derry IRA at the time of Bloody Sunday. Himself one of the marchers, he plausibly claims that the Provisionals had decided not to engage the British Army in Derry that day. According to McGuinness, 'Everybody knew that no shots were fired on the British Army and that there were no nail or blast bombs or the like thrown that day.'[5] As far as McGuinness's Provisionals were concerned, this may well be true. But there was, it appears, at least one shot fired at soldiers on Bloody Sunday in Derry: just before four o'clock a single shot came from the Bogside, apparently from a member of the Official IRA (OIRA), as those from whom the Provisionals had split were now known. This (*possibly* the first shot fired on Bloody Sunday)[6] might have confirmed some soldiers' expectation that violence would be directed against them; but it cannot be taken as either explaining all of the soldiers' actions, or as justifying the fatal violence that they deployed that day. For this was an appalling afternoon, with unarmed demonstrators against government policy being shot dead by the Army.

Reaction to Bloody Sunday was, of course, strong. Bernadette Devlin, who had been present, observed, 'It was mass murder by the British Army.' Taoiseach Jack Lynch spoke of the afternoon's incidents as 'unbelievably savage and inhuman'.[7] British Conservative politician William Whitelaw recalled of the immediate aftermath to the tragedy, 'All hell broke loose in the next few days.'[8] Both wings of the IRA, Provisional and Official, intensified their campaigns as a response to the events of the 30th, as support for militant republicanism dramatically grew in the wake of the killings. In the words of one figure who was to gain prominence in the Provisionals, 'Bloody Sunday was a turning point. Whatever lingering chance had existed for change through constitutional means vanished. Recruitment to the IRA rocketed as a result. Events that day probably led more young nationalists to join the Provisionals than any other single action by the British.'[9] For understandable rage among northern Catholics led hundreds to join the Provisionals; indeed, the organization seems to have had more potential recruits than they could easily absorb. Not for the first or last time in Ireland, British military violence, intended to quell subversion, had produced a major boost for subversive republican militants. The seed planted that January in some cases germinated most visibly years later; Raymond McCartney, who was to become famous as a republican hunger-striker in 1980, was a cousin of Jim Wray (one of those killed on Bloody Sunday), and joined the republican movement after what happened on that day.

The events in Derry on 30 January 1972 have frequently been portrayed as a turning-point in the troubles, producing greater support for violence, a hardening of views and a decreased possibility of compromise or calm. But it is important to remember that this was one event in an unfolding drama, rather than a stand-alone episode;

for some it might have been decisive, but even here other events played their part. As one Derry Provisional recalled: 'For a lot of people Bloody Sunday was a defining moment. I was present on Bloody Sunday, but it wasn't the reason I joined the IRA, it was just a culmination after a lot of things. A lot of people after that supported the IRA and empathised with what they were doing, engaging the Army on a regular basis and bombing the town.'[10] Here, as on other occasions, fatal British violence in Ireland far more effectively generated Irish nationalist sympathy than Irish republican violence could itself hope to do.

Outrage extended beyond the north. Irish-American opinion in places such as Boston was horrified and mobilized. Provisional supporters in the United States certainly reaped benefit: Bloody Sunday was, in the words of Michael Flannery, Noraid's 'first big publicity break'.[11] In Ireland itself, the Dublin government announced a national day of mourning and brought its ambassador back from London; in Dublin an irate crowd burned down the British embassy, and British-owned businesses were petrol-bombed. And worse, in a sense, was to come. The UK government set up a tribunal (headed by the Lord Chief Justice, Lord Widgery) to investigate the events leading up to the shootings. This heard evidence from a wide range of people, and Widgery's report was published in April 1972. Its mild rebuke to the soldiers for some of their shooting was seen, not surprisingly, as a wholly inadequate response to the horror. Widgery's conclusions were broadly favourable to the British Army, and largely exonerated the soldiers of wrongdoing on that day (though even he acknowledged that a number of those killed had not been carrying bombs or firearms and that 'None of the deceased or wounded is proved to have been shot whilst handling a firearm or bomb').[12] Widgery did, however, hold that a large number of civilians had been carrying firearms that day, and that the soldiers had come under a significant amount of fire. Indeed, he presented Bloody Sunday as involving British soldiers, for the most part, firing shots at those whom they held to have been attacking them with bombs and guns.

Widgery's report has been widely judged to lack credibility, and close inspection of all the currently available evidence makes it clear why this is so.[13] Certainly, his strong reliance upon soldierly recollection seems, on close inspection, markedly dubious. Widgery's argument was that 'in the majority of cases the soldier gave an explanation which, if true, justified his action', and that 'in general the accounts given by the soldiers of the circumstances in which they fired and the reasons why they did so were, in my opinion, truthful'.[14] But the accounts given by the soldiers to Widgery conflicted seriously with those that they had presented immediately after the events of the day itself. Widgery's crucial dependence on the reliability of the soldiers' accounts as presented to his tribunal therefore looks very questionable. The available evidence suggests that the soldiers fired on unarmed civilians in circumstances in which there was not, in fact, a serious threat from those people to the soldiers' lives.

When the violence of Bloody Sunday was followed by Widgery's report, northern Catholic confidence that the state would treat them fairly was finally shattered. For the report was understandably seen as compounding in April what had been done in January. The *Derry Journal* referred to anger 'in Derry and Ireland generally over what nationwide was considered the whitewashing of the British Army's role in Derry on Bloody Sunday in the Widgery Report',[15] and it is hard not to sympathize. Nationalist confidence in the capacity or preparedness of UK law and authority to protect them, to treat them fairly within Northern Ireland, was severely battered. If people marching to protest against government policy could be killed by the state, when no serious threat to soldiers' lives existed, then (yet again in Irish history) the violence of the state forces provided a powerful argument for popular disaffection from that state itself. In this sense, Bloody Sunday reinforced the fault-lines of the northern conflict, and helped to render meaningful compromise beyond reach. Of course, the context for the march should not be forgotten: British soldiers *had* been attacked and killed in the conflict and did, on that day, come under *some* form of hostility. But the weight of evidence suggests that the killings of Bloody Sunday were utterly unjustified; and their consequences, personally and politically, were dire. It is no surprise that this day has become the focus for lasting and public attention.[16]

For its part, republican judgment has long remained condemnatory, and outraged at what it sees as the cold murder of unarmed victims. Martin McGuinness: 'As far as I am concerned the British Army got away with murder on Bloody Sunday';[17] Gerry Adams: 'My consistent view, from that day, is that this was a premeditated and well-planned attempt to suppress the movement for civil and democratic rights, with clearance at the very top of the British establishment.'[18] But even if one doubts that Bloody Sunday was a preplanned, deliberate massacre sanctioned from the upper reaches of the state, the culpability of the state in this fatal injustice remains, on the balance of evidence, quite clear.

For one thing, the deployment of the aggressive, hard-edged Parachute Regiment for such a predictably tense task as the containment of that march seems profoundly ill-judged. Nor is this merely a view afforded by hindsight. Only a few days before Bloody Sunday the journalist Simon Hoggart reported that British Army units in Northern Ireland *themselves* had made requests to HQ that the Parachute Regiment be kept out of their areas, as they were considered too brutal and rough. One Army officer was quoted as saying, 'The paratroops undid in ten minutes the community relations which it had taken us four weeks to build up.' Hoggart himself observed, 'Undoubtedly the regiment is the one most hated by Catholics in troubled areas where among local people at least it has a reputation for brutality. More strikingly, however, many officers in other regiments in the city [Belfast] are now prepared to voice their own considerable doubts about the paratroops' role.' He quoted one Army officer as saying, 'They are frankly disliked by many officers here, who regard some of their men as little better than thugs in uniform. I have seen them arrive on the scene, thump up a few people who might be doing nothing more than shouting and jeering, and roar off again. They seem to think that they can get away with whatever they like.'[19] That such opinions were prevalent even within the British Army itself in Northern Ireland, and that they were widely disseminated *prior to* Bloody Sunday, raises very painful questions about the decision to deploy the Parachute Regiment on that day. Likely to use extreme force rather than delicacy, the Paras were hardly the most appropriate body for carrying out an arrest operation in such a volatile setting as Derry in January 1972. Moreover, the wisdom of carrying out an arrest operation at all must be open to question. Even Lord Widgery, hardly the sharpest critic of Army actions on that day, observed that 'In the light of events the wisdom of carrying out the arrest operation is debatable.'[20]

If the Provisionals' perception that they were entering the final phase of Ireland's struggle was heightened by Bloody Sunday, then such a view was further reinforced by the prorogation (or discontinuation without dissolution) of Stormont, the hated Belfast regime, in March 1972. On Friday the 24th Prime Minister Edward Heath announced that, in place of the Belfast government, there was now to be direct rule from London (intended as a temporary measure). There would, as of 30 March, be a Secretary of State for Northern Ireland (the first of which was William Whitelaw), who would enjoy executive and legislative powers there. A Northern Ireland Office (NIO) would deal with political, constitutional and security issues.

The Provisionals' public response to this was negative, Sean MacStiofáin rejecting what Heath proposed for the north. The IRA had their own view of what should be done. On 10 March 1972 the Provisionals had announced a seventy-two-hour ceasefire, to begin at midnight, and their statement was made by Chief of Staff MacStiofáin:

> The leadership of the republican movement wishes to state that the following conditions are considered necessary to secure peace in the present conflict between British and Irish forces. 1) The immediate withdrawal of British Army forces from the streets of Northern Ireland coupled with a statement of intent as to the actual evacuation date of HM forces and an acknowledgement of the rights of the Irish people to determine their own future without interference from the British government. 2) The abolition of the Stormont parliament. 3) A total amnesty for all political prisoners in Ireland and England, both tried and untried, and for those on the wanted list. As a gesture of the sincerity of the leadership of the republican movement to secure a just and lasting peace, the Army Council of the IRA has instructed all units to suspend military operations for a period of seventy-two hours beginning at midnight, Friday, March 10, and terminating at midnight, Monday, March 13, 1972.[21]

With the prorogation of Stormont, MacStiofáin stated, the IRA would stick to *all* of the ambitions set out in this plan: 'We will continue our operations until these three points are met.'[22] But, in helping to fulfil one of their ambitions, the end of Stormont did represent a kind of progress, from the Provisionals' perspective. They had wanted to see an end to the regime that they considered illegitimate, and its fall could be read as a direct result of their military campaign against the state. A little over two years after their formation, the Provos had seen Stormont brought down, and victory must seem closer – even imminent – after that. Moreover, the end of Stormont clarified what the IRA held to be the essence of the conflict. For now there was no distraction concerning local unionist opinion and power; it was instead clearly a matter of Britain versus Ireland, an issue rendered starkly clear by direct British rule over the occupied part of the island.

If the fall of the old regime might have brought renewed republican confidence, then the violence that preceded it had caused huge damage. For if the IRA aimed to make the north ungovernable in the early 1970s, then their violence frequently made individual lives unbearable. On Saturday 4 March 1972 a Provisional IRA bomb exploded in the packed Belfast Abercorn Restaurant. Two young women were killed, and 136 men, women and children were reported injured. Some of the injuries were truly horrific. Two Belfast sisters in their early twenties each lost both legs in the explosion; one of them (who was that day apparently shopping for her wedding dress) also lost an arm and an eye. One ambulance man said that the area had been 'awash with blood after the explosion and so were the ambulances. It was the most distressing scene I have ever witnessed. There were bloody, mangled bodies lying everywhere'.[23] In an operating theatre in Belfast's Royal Victoria Hospital, anaesthetist Fred Bereen dealt with the casualties from the explosion, unaware until later that his own daughter was one of the two people who had been killed in the bombing. Twenty-one-year-old Janet Bereen had been having coffee in the Abercorn with her friend Ann Owens, with whom she had been out shopping. They were close to the bomb when it exploded. Both were Catholic.

On 13 March Harold Wilson, leader of the British Labour Party, together with Labour's shadow Northern Ireland Secretary Merlyn Rees, met leading IRA men in Dublin. The latter included Daithi O'Connell (the Adjutant-General) and Joe Cahill, and the episode reflects an often neglected aspect of the IRA's history: that during the long troubles they were *frequently* in contact and discussion with their British opponents. Any suggestion that the organization is, of its essence, non-political or opposed to the very notion of negotiation should be qualified by recognition of this fact.

And politics were implicit too in a significant IRA press conference in Derry on 13 June that year. MacStiofáin, McGuinness, Twomey and O'Connell participated, and the army publicly offered to meet the Secretary of State for Northern Ireland; MacStiofáin told the press conference that the IRA would suspend all military operations for seven days if their invitation to Whitelaw to meet them was accepted within forty-eight hours. The Secretary of State publicly rebuffed the offer, saying that he 'could not respond to ultimatums from terrorists who are causing suffering to innocent civilians in Northern Ireland and shooting British troops'.[24] Despite this, however, the next few weeks were to witness attempts by the British and the IRA to achieve a more peaceful encounter, in a more comfortable setting, than had frequently become the norm on the streets of Belfast and Derry. On Thursday 22 June the Provisionals announced that they would commence a ceasefire from midnight on the following Monday, after Whitelaw had said that the British Army would reciprocate in such a ceasefire situation. The Secretary of State told the Commons, in words that read rather painfully thirty years later, 'I believe it is a starting point to the end of violence. I pray it will be so.'[25]

The IRA ceasefire thus provided the backdrop for secret talks between republicans and the British in London; for on 7 July 1972 an encounter took place at the Chelsea home of William Whitelaw's Minister of State, Paul Channon. Whitelaw himself later rationalized the meeting partly on the grounds that there had been 'a desperate longing on all sides for an end to the senseless violence', and that no opportunity for ending the conflict should be missed. In particular, he felt 'that a refusal to talk would leave the political initiative in the hands of the IRA'.[26] The republican team consisted of IRA men Sean MacStiofáin, Seamus Twomey, Ivor Bell, Daithi O'Connell, Gerry Adams and Martin McGuinness. (The republican team were accompanied by a solicitor, Myles Shevlin.) The British were represented by Secretary of State Whitelaw, Channon, NIO official Philip Woodfield and MI6 man Frank Steele. Most of the talking for the Provisionals was done by MacStiofáin, and most for the British by Whitelaw. The two men's impressions are interesting: MacStiofáin thought Whitelaw 'looked exactly the same as he did on television, smooth, well-fed and fleshy';[27] Whitelaw thought the meeting 'a non-event. The IRA leaders simply made impossible demands which I told them the British government would never concede. They were in fact still in a mood of defiance and determination to carry on until their absurd ultimatums were met.'[28]

MacStiofáin had indeed set out the IRA's demands: first, that the British government should publicly recognize that it was the people of Ireland acting as a unit that should decide the future of Ireland as a unit; second, that the British government should declare its intention to withdraw all British forces from Ireland by 1 January 1975 and that, pending withdrawal, British forces should be withdrawn from sensitive areas; third, that internment must end, with an amnesty being introduced for political prisoners, internees, detainees and wanted persons. For their part, the British considered these demands to be simply unrealistic, to show that the Provisionals had no firm grasp of political reality. Unsurprisingly, the meeting ended without agreement. So too did the IRA's ceasefire when on 9 July, following the breakdown of the truce, a four-hour late-night gun-battle between the Provisionals and the British Army in Belfast left a number of people dead; the IRA said that the Army had broken the truce, the Army that they had first been fired on by the Provisionals. Thus, not for the last time, controversy surrounded the ending of an IRA ceasefire.

But, intriguingly, political discussions did not stop: on 18 July an IRA delegation led by Joe Cahill was flown to England to meet British Labour politicians Wilson and Rees. And the IRA's return to violence did not in any case mean that it was without politics: the 1972 Provisionals were, for example, very hostile to the Republic of Ireland joining the European Economic Community (preferring to avoid the restriction, as they saw it, of Irish sovereignty); in 1974 they declared themselves 'still opposed to the basic philosophy of the Treaty of Rome'.[29] Again, they explicitly advocated in early 1972 the replacement of the southern and northern capitalist states in Ireland with a *socialist*, thirty-two-county, united republic in its place.

But violence was, nonetheless, at the centre of the IRA's politics, and some of that violence still shocks many years later. One of the north's worst ever days of political violence occurred on 21 July 1972: Bloody Friday. The IRA planted over twenty bombs in Belfast city centre, killing nine people and injuring many more. Warnings had been given, but because of the number of bombs and the scale of the operation, these were simply insufficient to avoid awful casualties.

Despite IRA insistence that the aim was never to kill civilians, the bombings came to be seen, even by some IRA members themselves, as a major setback. The appearance of indiscriminate civilian death and injury was a publicity own-goal of horrific proportions. One of the car-bombs had been at Belfast's Oxford Street bus station: badly mutilated bodies were thrown long distances by the blast and one civilian witness recalled, 'suddenly there was a tremendous bang. Smoke was everywhere and I could hear people screaming ... There was a horrible smell and a lot of blood on the pavement.'[30]

On 31 July, three IRA car-bombs exploded without warning in the village of Claudy, ten miles from Derry: nine people died as a result. Local nationalist MP Ivan Cooper likened the atrocity to the one he had witnessed on 30 January: 'This incident can only be equated with what happened on Bloody Sunday. I cannot express words strong enough to condemn the people responsible for this terrible outrage'.[31]

Some horrors were (at that time, at least) more hidden. In December 1972 Jean McConville was abducted by the IRA, never to be seen again. Her life had, even up to this point, been troubled. Initially a Belfast Protestant, she had married a Catholic and converted to Catholicism. Having been intimidated out of a Protestant part of Belfast by loyalists, the Catholic family settled in west Belfast. Jean's husband died, leaving her with ten children, of whom the oldest had suffered brain damage necessitating special care. Jean McConville had become suicidally depressed. Then in 1972 she fell foul of her neighbours by comforting a British soldier who had been shot, and who had pleaded for help outside her house. Towards the end of the year, twelve Provisionals burst into the McConvilles' home, where Jean was having a bath. They dragged her from it and – despite her frantic pleading – abducted her in front of her hysterical children. For years their mother's disappearance was a painful mystery, the IRA denying that they had killed her. But in the 1990s a daughter campaigned to discover the truth about Jean and about others who had disappeared, and whose bodies had likewise never been discovered. Could the remains, at least, be pinpointed, thereby allowing relatives to end their agony through burying and properly grieving for their dead? The IRA, it turned out, had indeed killed Jean McConville, accusing her of having been a British Army informer (a claim members of her family have strongly denied). The organization eventually gave information, apparently locating her remains. But her body was never discovered.[32] For their part, on 29 March 1999, the IRA claimed that it had identified the burial places of nine people (including McConville) whom it had killed during the 1970s and whose bodies had never been found. It gave its reasons for the killings: these people had, it was claimed, been security force agents or informers, or had been guilty of stealing IRA weapons and using them in armed robberies.

Despite these gruesome episodes the high levels of violence in this period were not solely due to IRA activity. In 1972, 497 people were killed in the north's political violence. Of these, the Provisionals killed 235, and other republicans 46. Loyalists killed 121 and the British Army 80.[33] On Bloody Friday itself, the Ulster Defence Association (UDA) – a loyalist paramilitary group founded in 1971, sometimes using the cover-name Ulster Freedom Fighters (UFF) – had shot and killed married twenty-one-year-old Belfast Catholic, Anthony David-son. On occasions, loyalist violence took the form of retaliatory action for IRA violence. Belfast Catholic Frank Corr – a Gaelic Athletic Association official, and father of five – was shot dead on 26 July 1972 by loyalists, apparently in retaliation for Bloody Friday. But while specific acts of vengeful retaliation against Catholics were a part of the loyalist story, it would be misleading to suggest that loyalism was (or is) purely responsive or reactive to IRA actions. As we have seen, the UVF in 1966 had killed people several years before the Provisionals were even formed, just as, many years later, loyalist violence would continue (albeit at lower levels) once the Provisionals' campaign had effectively ended through the 1990s peace process. A key part of the explanation for loyalist violence is indeed a reaction to the perceived threat posed by Irish nationalist advance, and part of that has clearly involved violent retaliation for IRA operations. But it is only a part of the story.

As we have seen, the state also reacted to the IRA armed struggle, on occasions with its own lethal violence. On 14 March 1972 two teenage IRA men, Colm Keenan and Eugene McGillan, were shot dead by soldiers when the Army engaged the IRA in a gun-battle in Derry (though it is a matter of controversy whether the two dead men had been directly involved in the battle). The British Army's actions frequently had negative results, in terms at least of their impact on levels of support for anti-state paramilitarism. On 31 July 1972 over

30,000 members of the security forces were involved in the massive 'Operation Motorman', in which the British Army reoccupied barricaded no-go areas of Derry and Belfast, much to the anger of many Catholic nationalists (Gerry Adams: 'Operation Motorman failed to destroy the IRA; it actually increased recruits').[34] But the IRA did suffer setbacks, during late 1972 and early 1973, when a series of arrests dealt them blows north and south. Chief of Staff MacStiofáin was among those involved, being apprehended in the Republic in November 1972 and sentenced to six months' imprisonment for IRA membership. (Seamus Twomey for much of 1972–1977 was the organization's chief.) For despite the Provisionals' tendency to avoid military operations in the south, they did come into much friction with the authorities there. Substantial cooperation existed between the northern and southern security forces and, as we have seen, Dublin regimes had a record of conflict with those in the IRA tradition.

This was evident again on 28 March 1973 when the Irish navy, tipped off by Britain, arrested the IRA's Joe Cahill off the Irish coast on board the *Claudia*: on the ship were five tons of weapons obtained from Libya. Two months later, Cahill was jailed for three years by Dublin Special Criminal Court for illegally importing arms, and for IRA membership. Found on the boat had been guns, pistols, grenades, anti-tank mines, gelignite and over 24,000 rounds of ammunition. Before being sentenced, Cahill said he was proud to be an IRA man, and told the judge, 'If I am guilty of any crime it is that I did not succeed in getting the contents of the *Claudia* into the hands of the freedom fighters of this country.'[35]

This setback underlined the Provisionals' essentially antagonistic relationship, at this stage, with the authorities in the Republic of Ireland. Some mainstream politicians there had adopted a particularly hostile view. A striking example was Conor Cruise O'Brien, one of the most prominent of Irish intellectuals and from an Irish nationalist background himself. By the mid-1970s O'Brien had taken a strongly anti-IRA line of argument. As Minister for Posts and Telegraphs in the Republic, he amended legislation in 1975 to allow for the explicit prohibition[36] of the Provisionals, whether IRA or Sinn Féin, from the airwaves; and this was duly ordered. 'The principle involved there' – O'Brien himself has argued – 'was the protection of the security of the democratic state against the broadcasting of subversive propaganda by organisations whose function was to work under the orders of the leadership of a private army for revolutionary purposes.'[37] There were, however, those proud of their involvement with just such an army. On 29 January 1973 Martin McGuinness was sentenced, by Dublin's Special Criminal Court, to six months' custody for being an IRA member. McGuinness said that he had been a Derry IRA officer for over two years, and told the court, 'I am a member of the Derry Brigade of Óglaigh na hÉireann [the IRA] and I am very, very proud of it.'[38]

The month before this declaration, in December 1972, an official UK report had been published regarding legal procedures appropriate for dealing with paramilitary violence. The Commission, headed by Lord Diplock, concluded that non-jury trials should be introduced to deal with such cases. Since intimidation prevented many people from giving evidence that they would otherwise give, the Diplock Report argued; a judge, without jury, should try a wide range of paramilitary-related cases. This recommendation was incorporated into the 1973 Emergency Provisions Act, and long remained a source of controversy. Meanwhile, the Provisionals themselves continued in vibrancy and self-belief. In February 1973 they even offered a bold analysis of, and invitation to, the loyalists of the UDA. The Protestant community had been installed, they said, as an imperialist garrison in Ireland, now no longer required by the British; the UDA itself was 'being used by the imperialists, to direct attention, men and material, indeed a whole movement, away from our true enemy, namely British imperialism'. The only way to overthrow the existing corrupt system was through revolution directed against the British. The UDA were invited to join a movement capable of pursuing this revolutionary path – 'such as the movement that the Provos have built' – and 'to abandon the present senseless position, in which you are being used by the British to divide our people'.[39] In similar vein, on 9 November 1974 *Republican News* carried a photograph of loyalist paramilitaries, marching; the photograph bore the caption: 'British or Irish? Make up your minds. You can't be both!'

Even at this stage, some republicans seem to have recognized that the war might not end quickly. Patrick Magee recalls Gerry Adams lecturing in Long Kesh in 1973. Adams asked: '"Does anybody here think this war will be over in two years?" There were no takers for that. "Does anybody think this war'll be over in ten years?" No. "Does anybody think this war's going to be over in twenty years?" Well, we were all getting a bit worried at this stage! . . . He was very much aware that this was a long haul.'[40] Militarily, the Provisionals' thoughts had turned directly to Britain, with their formal sanctioning in early 1973 of the idea of extending the bombing campaign to Britain. This had been discussed earlier, and as we have already seen there were precedents in earlier IRA campaigns. On 8 March IRA bombs in London killed one person (through an explosion at the Old Bailey) and injured 243. In November, eight Belfast people (including nineteen-year-old Gerry Kelly,[41] and sisters Marian and Dolours Price, nineteen and twenty-two years old respectively), were found guilty in regard to these London car-bombs. On 15 November at Winchester Crown Court they all admitted being in the IRA, and were given life sentences. Another of the eight was nineteen-year-old William McLarnon. In 1969 he and his family had been intimidated out of their home, which had subsequently been burned out. Here, however, as IRA man, he was defiant: when his sentence was announced he unrepentantly shouted 'Up the Provisional IRA!'[42]

The rationale behind the IRA's English bombings was clear enough: in republican thinking, England had not only caused the problems in Ireland, but was the agent capable of resolving them through withdrawal. And English opinion, popular as well as governmental, was much less affected by deaths in Ireland than by attacks nearer to home. As Marian Price puts it: 'It doesn't seem to matter if it's Irish people dying'; so if the armed struggle was to succeed then it was necessary to 'bring it to the heart of the British establishment'. Hence symbolic targets such as the Old Bailey: 'the targets were carefully chosen'.[43]

The personal consequences of that IRA violence were frequently terrible, leaving literal and metaphorical scars on many people. But Irish republican activists were not necessarily immune to the suffering of their opponents, although they clearly distinguished between what they saw as the different kinds of soldiership involved on the rival sides: 'then, of course, the death of a British soldier is also sad. Because he's just some kid who doesn't even know why he's in Ulster let alone why he has to die. At least our Volunteers know what they are giving their lives for; that's the difference between the idealist and the cannon fodder of the British government.'[44] The idealists who bombed London in 1973 wanted to be treated as political, rather than criminal, prisoners (whether in England, or through being returned to Ireland where effective political status existed). Marian Price and others went on hunger strike to that end ('There was no way I was going to let them criminalize me'), and was force-fed for over 200 days: 'It was horrifying ... It was *very* scary'; but it intensified her determination. 'When they actually did it, I thought, "Bloody Hell, I'm not letting these bastards off with this." So in many ways it had the opposite effect ... It strengthened my resolve ... It was a case of "They're not going to break *me*." '[45]

Some, at least, in the British establishment astutely recognized the potential danger that such commitment involved for Britain. As Labour Party Home Secretary Roy Jenkins intriguingly put it, the Price sisters:

> were the stuff of which Irish martyrs could be made: two young, slim, dark girls, devout yet dedicated to terrorism. I thought of the violent repercussions when [Terence MacSwiney], lord mayor of Cork, starved himself to death in Brixton Gaol in 1920, and decided that if an alderman, even though also a scholar/poet, could produce such a wave of retaliation, the consequences of the death of these charismatic colleens was incalculable. No one, in Home Office, police or cabinet, was inclined to dispute these forebodings of menace.[46]

On 31 October 1973 other leading Provisional republicans made dramatic news when they escaped from Dublin's Mountjoy Jail – by helicopter. J. B. O'Hagan, Seamus Twomey and Kevin Mallon's jailbreak had been in preparation for five weeks. The actual escape involved the helicopter being hired by someone posing as a film producer; the pilot had then been forced to fly it to the jail, where it landed in an exercise yard. With the prisoners aboard, the helicopter flew off; it set down shortly afterwards in north County Dublin, with the prisoners escaping to safe houses. A grimmer episode occurred a couple of months later, with the (apparently unauthorized) IRA kidnapping of Thomas Niedermayer, businessman and West German consul in Belfast. The managing director of a Belfast branch of electronics firm Grundig, the captive was held in a house in the city and died (possibly from a heart attack) on 30 December, while in IRA custody. Niedermayer had had his legs and his hands tied, to restrain him as he frantically struggled with his guards. His firm received a ransom demand; but this occurred after he was dead, and it is possible that the initial motive for the kidnapping was to try to exchange the German's freedom for that of the republican Price sisters, then prisoners in England. Niedermayer's remains were discovered only in 1980, in west Belfast.

Such occurrences were concurrent with attempts to find a settlement to the political problems that had occasioned them. In March 1973 a White Paper was published outlining constitutional proposals for Northern Ireland; these prefigured, as it happens, much that was later to emerge in the eventual end-of-century settlement in the north: a devolved legislative assembly; all-Ireland institutional cooperation and consultation; and provision regarding human rights. Elections for a northern assembly were indeed held in June 1973; in November agreement was reached to set up a power-sharing executive for Northern Ireland, comprising the Official [Ulster] Unionist Party, the SDLP and the Alliance Party; and in the following month these three parties met with the London and Dublin governments (including the respective Prime Ministers, Edward Heath and Liam Cosgrave) at Sunningdale, Berkshire, to agree the framework within which the new executive would operate. The executive took office in January 1974.

Sunningdale was not without positive aspects for unionists: 'The Irish government fully accepted and solemnly declared that there could be no change in the status of Northern Ireland until a majority of the people of Northern Ireland desired a change in that status. The British government solemnly declared that it was, and would remain, their policy to support the wishes of the majority of the people of Northern Ireland. The present status of Northern Ireland is that it is part of the United Kingdom.'[47] But many of Ulster's unionists were hostile to aspects of what was in some ways a very ambiguous deal (especially, perhaps, the cross-border Council of Ireland), and at the February 1974 general election anti-Sunningdale unionists won eleven of the twelve available seats. There followed a strike by the loyalist Ulster Workers' Council (UWC), which brought down the power-sharing Northern Irish experiment (though there is some doubt over whether Sunningdale would have survived even if there had been no strike, or a strike with a different outcome).[48]

Certainly, participants to the Sunningdale deal had different interpretations of what it involved. Unionists such as former northern Prime Minister Brian Faulkner placed much less importance, for example, than did the nationalist SDLP upon the ill-defined cross-border Council of Ireland. Many unionists certainly saw the deal as potentially dangerous to their continued membership of the UK. But while loyalists and unionists opposed Sunningdale (considering it to have gone too far in a nationalist direction), republicans too were hostile to the 1973 compromise (thinking it not to have gone far enough). The assembly elections that June were not contested by Sinn Féin, and the Provisional movement was sharply critical of its constitutional nationalist rivals, the SDLP, for their more conciliatory, compromising approach. Leading figures in the latter party were vilified. On 15 December 1973 *Republican News* asserted: 'In the past few weeks Gerry Fitt and Co. have sold us all out. For a few paltry pounds a year they have sold out the people of Ireland.' Fitt himself was condemned for having become the right-hand man of Brian Faulkner ('that murderous, selfish, power-hungry liar'), while John Hume ('the fish-selling school teacher from Derry') had 'bartered his birthright for the position of commerce'. Intracommunal conflict has been a less obvious, but no less vicious, aspect of the northern troubles and of the IRA's story within it. For in some ways the battle for dominance within one's own community was the key one: the likelihood of gaining support from members of the opposing community was negligible, and so expansion of one's role depended upon gaining ground at the expense of one's intracommunal rivals.

Thus the Provisionals stressed, in these years, that the constitutional nationalist SDLP would sell out the nationalist cause, would compromise too far, would be insufficiently resolute in pressing the northern nationalist case. In April 1975 an IRA Army Council spokesman was quoted as saying that, since Sunningdale, the SDLP's alliance with people such as Faulkner had 'marked them out as unionists. Their abandonment of their principles and the promises given to the people before the Assembly election puts them beyond the pale of civilised behaviour.'[49] By December of the same year, the Provisionals were referring to their constitutional nationalist rivals as a 'discredited party': 'The SDLP have now emerged on the Northern Ireland political scene as a new unionist party. They have demonstrated their ability to betray their own people, to betray their identity, to deny the just right of freedom of this nation from English domination.'[50] Nationalist victory would come via the more aggressive kind of politics practised by the IRA, who had pledged to make 1974 'the year of liberty', and who believed that it would be 'the year of the freedom fighter'.[51]

The republican freedom fighter has sometimes been portrayed as having enjoyed significant international links,[52] and there is certainly something in this theme. Leading County Derry Marxist republican Brian Keenan cultivated connections in the 1970s with East Germany, Libya, Lebanon and Syria in the attempted furtherance of republican goals.

Back home, the violence continued – and on all sides. On 17 May 1974 UVF bombs exploded in Dublin and Monaghan in the Republic of Ireland, in one of the worst atrocities of the entire troubles: thirty-three people were killed or fatally injured. There have been persistent allegations (strongly denied by the authorities) that British Intelligence might have assisted in the attacks. Certainly, the scale and coordination of the bombings were uncharacteristic of loyalist paramilitaries at the time and there have been lasting suspicions that some assistance might have been given by people with professional expertise. Responsibility *was* clear in the case of John Cunningham, a Catholic civilian killed by the British Army in June 1974 in County Tyrone: he was a man in his twenties, with learning difficulties and a fear of the Army; his tragic killing seems to have had absolutely no justification. And the IRA were killing also. On 22 April of the same year Mohammed Abdul Khalid, an eighteen-year-old civilian, was shot dead by the IRA, his car being hit by around forty bullets, fired at very close range. The Provisionals claimed that he was operating for the SAS; in fact he was a caterer at the Bessbrook Army camp. (The *Irish News* carried the rather lurid headline, 'Another Pakistani Killed by Provos',[53] in an allusion to the June 1973 killing in Derry of Noor Baz Khan – another caterer wrongly described by his killers as doing espionage work for the British.)

But some of the most bloody and most widely publicized IRA killings of these years took place not in Ireland, but in England. On 5 October 1974 five people were killed and over sixty injured by two pub bombings in Guildford, Surrey. The two blasts (in the Horse and Groom, and the Seven Stars) happened in quick succession, in crowded bars on a Saturday night. There was no warning in either case.

Guildford was frequented by British military personnel, being near to Army bases and training camps. One soldier who had been drinking in the Seven Stars observed that, 'Only a cold-blooded swine could have done a thing like this.'[54] Condemnation also came from many other sources, including Gerry Conlon – 'It was a terrible atrocity'.[55] Conlon had more reason than most to reflect on the bombings, since he and three others were in 1975 wrongly convicted of having perpetrated them. Along with Paul Hill, Carole Richardson and Patrick Armstrong, Conlon was sentenced to life in prison. In 1989 the convictions were overturned when the Court of Appeal found that they had been based on confessions that the police had fabricated. Four IRA men (Eddie Butler, Harry Duggan, Joe O'Connell and Brendan Dowd) had long claimed to have been responsible for Guildford, asserting that Hill, Armstrong, Conlon and Richardson were innocent people who had been framed.[56]

The suffering of the Guildford four was appalling, a fact reflected in their compelling memoirs. Hill and Conlon (both, like Armstrong, west Belfast Catholics) have powerfully recreated their experiences, both fall and rise. Hill: 'How do you describe the feeling when a policeman arrests you and accuses you of murder? Part of me thought, "This is so ridiculous. We'll get this cleared up." But another part of me was overwhelmed by the enormity of the accusations. I was frightened . . . The terror comes from knowing that you are powerless, that nothing you say or do will save you.'[57] And eventually, after a decade and a half of wrongful imprisonment, the moment of release – Conlon:

> When they saw us the crowd erupted, it was a roar like a football crowd. There were crash barriers out, and beyond them thousands of heads bobbing up and down, cheering and throwing their arms up. There was a building site opposite and all the workers were waving their hard hats. Passers-by were being caught up in it. I felt the rush of happiness and warmth coming out of the people and I was carried out among them on a surge of joy. I suppose when you die and go to heaven you get a feeling like that.[58]

On 7 November 1974 two people were fatally (and numerous others less seriously) injured by an IRA bomb at a crowded pub, close to the Royal Artillery Training Centre in Woolwich, London. There were pools of blood in the King's Arms after the blast. Again, there had been no warning. Ten days later, the Provisionals' Daithi O'Connell tried to set out the organization's thinking, declaring that 'the consequences of war are not going to be kept solely in Ireland; they are going to be felt on the mainland of Britain. Responsibility rests squarely and clearly with the British government. The whole situation can be changed. The British government have simply to say we are not going to stay in Ireland, we are going to disengage from Ireland. They hold the key, the keys of war.'[59]

A few days later his words were to seem blood-red. On 21 November two Birmingham pubs – the Mulberry Bush and the Tavern in the Town – were blown up within minutes of each other, a vague and effectively useless warning having been given for one of them, and no warning for the other. (A third bomb failed to explode.) Twenty-one people died as a result of the two bombs, and over 150 were injured. A female St John Ambulance member at one of the pubs observed simply, 'It was like a slaughterhouse.'[60]

The Birmingham IRA had begun recruiting in the summer of 1973, and had already been active prior to the November 1974 pub bombs. Lieutenant James Patrick McDade of the Provos' Birmingham Battalion had died on 14 November 1974 in Coventry, blowing himself up while planting a bomb outside the city's telephone exchange. Five Irishmen travelling from Birmingham to McDade's Belfast funeral (Paddy Hill, Gerry Hunter, Richard McIlkenny, Billy Power and Johnny Walker) were detained by the police after the Birmingham bombs; together with a sixth man (Hugh Callaghan) they became collectively known as the Birmingham six. They were from the north of Ireland (all but Walker originating in Ardoyne in Belfast), and in 1975 they were sentenced to life imprisonment for the Birmingham bombs of 21 November. As with Guildford, however, there had been a dreadful miscarriage of justice and the wrong people had been put in prison. A lengthy campaign developed, to establish that the men had not been the bombers. Prominent among the campaigners was Labour Party MP, Chris Mullin, who strenuously protested that an awful injustice had been done to the six; he himself claims to have identified, traced and interviewed those actually responsible for the bombings (four people – two of whom made, and two of whom planted, the fatal bombs).[61] The IRA itself stated in the late 1980s that the Birmingham six had not been responsible for the bombings, and that none of the men were or had been IRA members.[62] The six were eventually freed in 1991, the Appeal Court considering that their convictions were no longer safe and satisfactory: it was judged that neither the confessions nor the forensic, scientific evidence upon which the convictions rested were reliable.

There was, from the IRA's perspective, a certain logic in taking their war to England as they did in the 1970s. Attacks in England gained far more publicity than tended to be the case with actions in Ireland. British bombs were intended to put pressure on London, via popular British opinion, to accede to republican demands. But the horrific nature of the 1974 pub bombings offset intended IRA gains, such was the outrage at their consequences. Indeed, it was eleven years before the Provisionals even admitted that its members were responsible for the Birmingham bombs. But, owing to the wrongful convictions of people for Guildford and Birmingham, the 1970s English bombings have carried an ambiguous legacy. The suffering caused by the bombs has often been partially eclipsed, in popular imagination and memory, by entirely understandable outrage at the lengthy incarceration of people for crimes that they did not carry out. Ironically (given the horror of events in the IRA's late-1974 English campaign), what people first think about when Birmingham or Guildford is mentioned is more likely to be the British mistreatment of Irish people than the lives destroyed by callous bombing.

In a sense, this fits a wider pattern already identified in this book, whereby British state action intended to deal with subversion in fact backfires and generates propaganda own-goals. The trick was performed again when, in November 1974, Judith Ward was wrongly jailed for an IRA bombing that had killed twelve people in a coach carrying British soldiers and their families on the M62 motorway, in the north of England the previous February. She was sentenced to thirty years in prison, for this bombing but also for two other explosions; in none of these instances was she, in fact, guilty. The Provisionals emphasized that she was not one of theirs ('The Irish Republican Army wish to let it be known that Miss Ward was never a member of our organisation and was at no time involved in any actions carried out by our organisation');[63] and eventually, in 1992,

Ward's conviction was quashed. But again, as with Birmingham and Guildford, lengthy imprisonment had been inflicted on the innocent.

2

'During the past year there have been ample indications that Britain is accelerating her plan for total withdrawal from the six counties.'

Republican News, 1976[64]

Some of the most brutal violence of the mid-1970s occurred in the border lands of south Armagh. On 1 September 1975 IRA members (using the cover-name South Armagh Republican Action Force) fatally shot five Protestants in Tullyvallen Orange Hall near Newtownhamilton in south Armagh: a caller to the BBC said the killings were in retaliation for 'the assassinations of fellow Catholics in Belfast'. A survivor of the attack recalled, 'The [Orange Lodge] meeting was over and we were just chatting generally in groups when there was a loud bang at the back door and two masked men rushed in firing with the machine-guns at us.'[65] County Armagh had seen three Catholics killed by a UVF gun-and-bomb attack on 22 August, and two other Catholic civilians shot dead by the same organization two days later; these deaths were apparently intended as revenge for the IRA torture and killing of an ex-RUC reservist nearby, on 15 August.

This tragic antiphony could be heard again in County Armagh at the start of 1976. On 4 January the loyalist UVF fatally shot three Catholic brothers (John, Brian and Anthony Reavey) at their Whitecross home as they sat watching television. On the same day in County Down the UVF also killed three members of the Catholic O'Dowd family. The Reavey and O'Dowd killings were supposedly in retaliation for an INLA no-warning pub-bombing on New Year's Eve, which had killed two Protestants. But the UVF's atrocities were themselves to prompt vengeful violence, when on 5 January the IRA (again using the South Armagh Republican Action Force label) killed ten Protestants at Kingsmills, Whitecross, south Armagh. A minibus carrying twelve workers (eleven Protestants and a Catholic) was stopped and the men questioned about their religion. The Catholic was told to disappear, and the Protestants were systematically shot; twelve republican gunmen were involved, using Armalites and sub-machine-guns. One Protestant escaped, but the other ten died. Some of the weapons used at Kingsmills had apparently also been used at Tullyvallen and in previous IRA operations.

Kingsmills became one of the most noted horrors of the troubles, and reactions were sharp from many sides. Cardinal Conway, the Catholic Primate of Ireland, observed that 'These foul murders stand condemned in the sight of God and man.'[66] The British government announced that the Special Air Service would be sent to south Armagh to address the crisis that could result in such violence (although it seems clear that the SAS had been in the north well before this: according to the Provisionals, the regiment had been deployed in Northern Ireland since 1971;[67] according to at least one former SAS soldier, they had been there even earlier).[68] More personal responses to the Kingsmills killings also emerged. Irish poet Paul Durcan mourned that:

> After this night
> In Armagh
> Just after six
> PM
> Liberty in Ireland
> Is a corpse[69]

While (with more chilling implications) loyalist leader Billy Wright – a man whose paramilitary career was to cost many Catholic lives – claimed that it had been the Kingsmills massacre that had prompted him to pursue the path of loyalist violence: 'I was fifteen when those workmen were pulled out of that bus and shot dead ... I was a Protestant and I realised that they had been murdered simply because they were Protestants. I ... immediately joined the youth wing of the UVF. I felt it was my duty to defend my people and that is what I have been doing ever since.'[70]

The sectarian violence of the mid-1970s was not without precedents, both during and preceding the post-1969 troubles. But the intensity of the gruesome sequence epitomized by Tullyvallen, Kingsmills and the Reavey/O'Dowd killings merits close inspection. It is probably pointless to try to identify who started the cycle, since rival combatants would be able to identify ever earlier grievances on their own side, ultimately taking the sequence so far back into history that it would be hard to attribute to them any part of the cause of the specified events. As already noted, the IRA itself publicly claimed to be above sectarian violence. On 17 January 1976 *Republican News* carried a statement from the Provisionals declaring that 'The Irish Republican Army has never initiated sectarian killings, and sectarianism of any kind is abhorrent to the republican movement and contrary to its philosophy.' Yet even here, there was a hint that republicans had been drawn into retaliatory action: 'If the loyalist elements responsible for over 300 sectarian assassinations in the past four years stop such killing now, then the question of retaliation from whatever source will not arise.' And the mid-seventies undoubtedly did witness IRA immersion in some grubby sectarian killing (as, off the record, republicans will themselves concede). Indeed, given the Provisionals' own explanation of the northern conflict, and of the necessity for their own birth – namely, that Northern Ireland was a sectarian state in which sectarian violence against Catholics had necessitated military defence – sectarian violence by republicans comes as no surprise. In part, this might have been a consequence of two mid-1970s factors: high levels of loyalist violence, simultaneous with a diminished IRA capacity to kill British soldiers (partly owing to a lengthy truce in 1975). The UVF during the three years 1974–6 killed 250 people, compared to a figure of eighty-six for the previous three years. During 1971–3, 211 British soldiers died in the troubles; during 1974–6, only seventy-three.[71]

And if the cycles of violence demonstrate the practical inadequacy of IRA strikes as a means of preventing loyalist killings, then to some it seemed that, at least, the IRA were doing *something*. As one ex-IRA man reflects:

As a functional, practical strategy did the IRA protect Catholics, did they succeed in protecting Catholics, from loyalist attack by its activities in 1974, '75, '76? I would say no. Did they make it worse for Catholics? I would say no. At least they were promoting themselves as somebody who would do something about it . . . The IRA, who were supposed to be defenders, could never actually defend. There was no way to defend against these things. So the only way to appear to be defending, to appear to be active, was to take out other people.[72]

In the eyes of some observers, another dimension to the more markedly localized northern targeting during the mid-1970s was the British government's move towards police primacy in Northern Ireland: emphasis was placed on the RUC for security implementation, rather than on the British Army. The front-line, anti-IRA force thus tended more frequently than before to be the police force, and this – together with the use of the locally recruited Ulster Defence Regiment (UDR) – at times accentuated the Catholic-versus-Protestant, local aspect of the war. Indeed, another former IRA man, Tommy McKearney, considers such a policy to have been significantly responsible for the sectarian blood-shedding of this period, offering:

> Very bitter criticism of the British state in Ireland, that it has used locals to police the situation, with all the problems that that creates . . . [In County Tyrone] we struck at the state. But by '75, '76 – and this is really where I would still feel quite angry with the British state in its policy of Ulsterization – once they had decided to bring the regulars out of the front line and put the RUC and the UDR up front, if we, the IRA, were going to strike at the British state we could not ignore the RUC or the UDR . . . In terms of pure, practical, military position, it's not possible to overlook a substantial section of your enemy, that is there to take you out, because of some theoretical position that the British regular alone is our enemy . . . The people that insisted on the primacy of the UDR and the RUC was not the IRA; it was the British government.[73]

There were numerous factors bringing about the mid-1970s sectarian war in places like County Tyrone, but according to McKearney again:

> 'one of the big ones – and I won't excuse them – is the central powers of the British state . . . I do feel quite strongly about it. Had we had a more conscientious central government . . . And if London doesn't know where Ireland is and what [the] dangers in Ireland

are ... They have [had] their intelligence here for long enough to know the dangers of giving practical power to the RUC/UDR ... if the British don't know the dangers of these type of areas, who does?' For, from the IRA's perspective, the off-duty police officer or UDR soldier could – in their capacity as bin-man, milkman, whatever – accumulate and pass on information and intelligence about the republican community. So there was a kind of military necessity, in their view, to the killing of such off-duty figures. Revenge also could play a part: 'There are never clean, clear lines when things like that happen. Undoubtedly, whenever it became, initially, a military necessity for the IRA, within their terms of reference, to cope with that infiltration, obviously there were people going to settle old scores. That's almost inevitable ... But by and large the IRA had a different objective than purely revenge.'[74]

Of course, the Provisionals were not the only IRA operating in the 1970s. After the split of 1969–70 the Officials maintained both a military presence (as the OIRA, with Cathal Goulding as Chief of Staff) and a political one, as Official Sinn Féin (OSF). Many of the existing IRA in Belfast had stayed with the Officials at the split. But the bulk of new recruits during the years of the early troubles went instead to the Provisionals, who soon became the dominant wing of IRA life. Not that the OIRA were inactive. In response to Bloody Sunday they bombed a military barracks at Aldershot in Hampshire, where the Parachute Regiment had headquarters; this February 1972 attack killed five female workers at the base, a gardener and a Catholic Army priest. Three days later, on 25 February, unionist politician and Stormont minister John Taylor was shot and wounded when the Officials tried to kill him in Armagh. In April members of the Parachute Regiment shot and killed an unarmed Joe McCann, one of the OIRA's leading figures, in Belfast. And the following month, the Officials killed nineteen-year-old William Best in Derry: Best was home on leave from the Royal Irish Rangers, and local opinion was horrified at this killing of one of their own. This publicity disaster played a significant part in prompting the Officials to suspend military operations, which they did on 29 May 1972. The ostensible reason for the shift was the desire to avoid descent into utter sectarian carnage in the north, OSF's paper, *United Irishman*, arguing:

The [Official] IRA has decided to suspend armed military actions. News of the IRA's decision has caused a tremendous impact on the political situation and is regarded by observers as being the possible move that may yet prevent a full outbreak of a sectarian civil war ... The only exception to the general suspension of armed actions is the reservation of the right of self-defence and the right to defend any area under aggressive attack by the British military or by sectarian forces from either side.[75]

And the Official republicans tried to maintain the idea that they could reach out to a Protestant northern working class. As one of the key figures in the 1960s left-republican group around Cathal Goulding was to put it in July 1972, 'We need those million Protestant working people on the workers' side in the Irish revolution ... They are still thinking on bigoted, sectarian lines, but the potential exists for growth of consciousness of the common cause between Catholic and Protestant workers as both are facing a sell-out and betrayal.'[76]

The Officials appear to have had around 800 members in Belfast at the end of 1972, so they were still a serious potential force and they would maintain a shadowy military existence for many years to come. Their weapons were never handed in and they were, on occasions during ensuing years, to be put to lethal use. But the Official republican movement's route would increasingly lead it away from systematic campaigns of violence. It was argued, not without reason, that republican violence would be likely to increase rather than to diminish sectarianism in the north, and that – given the depth of communal division, of sectarian polarization – only very slow change could be made. For their part, the Provisionals also recognized the depth and intensity of communal division. But the Provos argued for revolutionary anti-state violence, believing that the only way to end sectarianism was to end the sectarian northern state in Ireland. To Provisional eyes, the Officials 'never understood how to fight the sectarian unionist state in Ulster'.[77]

In 1973 the Official Army Council committed itself to turning the movement into a Marxist party and a metamorphosis was begun, ultimately reflected through a series of relabellings. OSF became Sinn Féin The Workers' Party, then (in 1982) simply the Workers' Party. As such, the remnants of Official republicanism moved away from traditional republican anti-partitionist politics and down a more directly leftist and electorally inclined path. But Irish republican leftism need not involve an absence of violence, and the Officials found themselves involved in blood-spilling feuds episodically – both with the Provisionals, as in 1975, and with another offshoot, the Irish Republican Socialist Party (IRSP), which emerged in December 1974 as a breakaway group from the Officials (around a hundred of whom in Belfast seem to have shifted to the offspring organization). Founded by Seamus Costello, the IRSP experienced a bitter conflict with its parent organization, a feud that caused numerous scars and numerous funerals. On 6 April 1975 Costello's crew – more specifically, Gerard 'Dr Death' Steenson – shot and very nearly killed prominent Official republican Dessie O'Hagan: 'I was nearly killed . . . [The attack] very nearly killed a fourteen-year-old girl as well . . . who was in the living room . . . We were sitting talking. It was her that saved my life because she heard the van stop . . . she said, "There's a car, Dessie, stopped there." And I had been semi-lying stretched out on a sofa, and I jumped to my feet and then I heard the running footsteps . . . He came in firing. I managed to block the inside door . . . I didn't realize that I was as fast on my feet! . . . It leaves you looking over your shoulder.' The revolutionaries had fallen out viciously: 'There was a deep hatred.'[78]

For alongside the new IRSP was a military wing, the Irish National Liberation Army (INLA). This had Costello as its Chief of Staff, and derived much of its strength precisely from such ex-OIRA people angry at the latter organization's ceasefire stance since 1972. The INLA gained a reputation for a potent mixture of hard-left politics and ruthless violence. As one of its leading members was to put it, 'We were a body of individuals prepared to wage war against the British machine in Ireland.'[79] The political wing, the IRSP, epitomized socialist republicanism of an aggressive kind. Its name echoed James Connolly's Irish Socialist Republican Party and, like their 1916 hero, the IRSP combined militant leftism with violent nationalism. A statement from the newly formed Derry IRSP in December 1974 proclaimed that 'there is a need for a real socialist alternative'.[80] In Bernadette McAliskey – the 1960s civil rights diva, formerly known as Bernadette Devlin – the IRSP had an extremely articulate and intelligent figure (one who did, however, leave the party in 1975); and in former-OIRA man (and former car salesman) Seamus Costello they had a leader of ability, energy, ruthlessness and intelligence, whose brutal death – allegedly at OIRA hands – in Dublin in 1977 brought to an end a life of socialistic and violent republican commitment.

While the OIRA/INLA world of bloody feuding represented fissiparous tendencies at their most dangerous, there were also in the mid-1970s attempts at Northern Irish reconciliation, at engagement through dialogue. One such took place in December 1974 in Smyth's Hotel, Feakle, County Clare, when Provisionals met a group of Protestants (mostly clergymen) for discussions. Held on the initiative of the latter ('the attempt of Protestant churchmen from Northern Ireland to halt the campaign of violence that had then been carried on by the Provisional IRA for nearly five years'),[81] the talks involved Church of Ireland Bishop, Dr Arthur Butler, Jack Weir (Clerk of the Presbyterian General Assembly), Revd Eric Gallagher (former President of the Methodist Church in Ireland), Revds William Arlow and Ralph Baxter (both from the Irish Council of Churches), Revd Harry Morton (General Secretary of the British Council of Churches), Revd Arthur McArthur (of the British Council of Churches) and Stanley Worrall (former headmaster of Methodist College, Belfast); they met leading members of the Provisional movement, including Daithi O'Connell, Seamus Twomey, J. B. O'Hagan and Kevin Mallon. The churchmen appealed on humanitarian grounds for an end to the Provo campaign, and argued that the latter would not succeed; for their part, the Provisionals courteously set out their own aims and justifications for their methods. The Feakle talks broke up when the Provisionals departed prior to the intervention of the Irish police – of whose imminent raid the republicans had been forewarned by their own intelligence people. The talks might have seemed to bear no fruit. But as one of the clerics, Arthur Butler, put it, 'The meeting grew out of a feeling among Churchmen in the north that in the present situation it was up to us to go to extreme lengths to see if we could get peace.'[82]

Some condemned the Feakle churchmen for talking with the IRA (Ian Paisley alliteratively denounced 'those fickle, Feakle clergy who would lead the Protestants of Ulster astray').[83] But on 19 January 1975 one of these men (William Arlow) introduced republicans Jimmy Drumm and Proinsias Mac Airt to British officials James Allan and Michael Oatley. For at the end of 1974 and beginning of 1975, the

British were keen to send signals to the Provos that they were seriously considering the possibility of withdrawal from Northern Ireland. (Incidentally, former Northern Irish Prime Minister Terence O'Neill publicly stated in November 1974: 'I do not believe that the British will be willing to put up the men and money for another five years in Northern Ireland.'[84] So if the IRA did indeed think that Britain was about to leave, they seem to have been in interesting company.) All of this helped to prompt a breathing-space in the violence. In the wake of Feakle, the Provisionals produced an extended truce over Christmas 1974. Military action was suspended by the Army Council from 22 December for eleven days; beginning on 2 January 1975, the ceasefire was extended for a further fourteen days until, on 16 January, it came to an end. The truce had ended because of a lack of British governmental response to the IRA's peace proposals, the Provisionals said.

But, Sinn Féin figures having had secret meetings with NIO civil servants, the Provisionals on 9 February announced in Dublin that from 6 p.m. the following day there would be a suspension of their hostilities. This was to run until September, and during these months British officials met leading Provisionals. By September, the Provisionals concluded that nothing significant was in fact going to come of their dealings with the British. But during the discussions of that year the IRA had been led (or, at least, allowed) to believe that the British were looking for a way out of the north. In fact, it seems that Britain used the 1975 ceasefire to improve intelligence and to try to split the republican movement through drawing some of its members into constitutional politics. Indeed, many republicans later believed the extended 1975 truce to have been a mistake, a low point for the IRA, one at which they perhaps even came close to being beaten. Having been given the impression by their leaders that there was now some movement towards victory, IRA members subsequently found that the British were not, in fact, going to leave; the mid-1970s leadership lost credibility as a result. Partly as a consequence, from the mid-1970s a new and younger, northern-based leadership was to assume increasing control over Provisional republicanism.

3

'We, as Volunteers of the republic, must become servants of
the people.'

'Brownie' (Gerry Adams), 1976[85]

The conspicuously political emphasis of the republican movement
from the mid-1990s onwards has sometimes caused observers, in
contrast, to underplay the degree to which earlier Provisionalism had
a political energy and content to it. But even mid-1970s Provos had
definite, motivating political arguments and passions. On 31 May 1975
Republican News carried a front-page headline, 'Ireland Free – No
EEC!', and argued for an independent Ireland that would negotiate its
own trading relations. There was a referendum in the UK on whether
or not to remain in the then European Economic Community, and the
Provisionals' Belfast paper commanded: 'Say no to the EEC ... Your
vote matters. The Scottish and Welsh nationalists oppose the EEC. So
do the trade unions and the best of the British Labour Party. We
should join with them. Vote no to the new act of union.'[86] Republicans
were keen on a sovereign, independent Irish republic, rather than
dictation – whether from mainland Europe or from Westminster. (And
it is interesting to note that people were encouraged here to vote,
rather belying the point sometimes made that the pre-1980s republican
movement was necessarily anti-political. It was always political when it
thought it expedient and sensible to be so.)

The Provisional movement's political argument was to become
more sophisticated, and more persuasively articulated, owing to the
emergence in the mid-1970s of a new wave of leading voices. One key
figure here was Danny Morrison, who became editor of *Republican
News* in 1975. One of the movement's ablest communicators and
publicists, Morrison's interest in writing had, in fact, long predated his
political activism: he had produced a hand-drawn and handwritten
comic at primary school, composed schoolboy poetry and other pieces,
in 1970 brought out a magazine for a youth club and in 1971 edited a
magazine for the Belfast College of Business Studies. In 1971 he had

begun writing republican material, but the writer had preceded the republican activist. 'I always wanted to become a writer ... I poured any talent I had into publicity, or the other term – that the enemy uses – propaganda.'[87]

Good propaganda it was, too, as *Republican News* became more impressively edited and more professional. Moreover, it gave voice to a markedly evolving political Provisionalism. Key here was another of the northern republican leaders, Gerry Adams. Adams had been arrested in July 1973 in Belfast and during his incarceration (which lasted until February 1977) he wrote a series of articles that helped to define a new Irish republicanism. In mid-1975 Morrison asked Adams to write some pieces for *Republican News* and the first of this important sequence (under the pen-name 'Brownie') appeared on 16 August. The Brownie articles of the mid-1970s set out a more diversified vision of republican politics and potential than had hitherto typified the movement. An important piece on abstentionism provides an example. 'I agree completely with abstentionism from any, all and each of the British established and orientated partitionist assemblies but I also believe that abstentionism can be a much more positive and living weapon,' he argued. Abstention from parliaments helped to block any British-imposed solutions for the north. But there was potential for an 'active abstentionism', which would make more of the strategy and build on existing community activism:

> People's organisations have increased as new contingencies have arisen. Now we have housing committees, street committees, local residents' committees, defence committees, prisoners' aid committees, local policing, playschools, parish committees and credit unions. We have sporting, cultural and Gaelic language organisations busy at grass roots level, people's taxis and co-operative schemes progressing and enlarging. All people organisations, all carrying out necessary functions, all for the welfare of the people, all divorced or easily divorced from the Brit administration, all abstaining or eager to abstain if there was an alternative. And where is that alternative?? All around us, friends! In each and every area, to some degree, people are governing and helping themselves. And the republican movement has the structure and the blueprint to make local government outside the British system not alone feasible but necessary. ACTIVE ABSTENTIONISM.[88]

In Belfast, Adams suggested, big nationalist areas could be organized into alternative community councils. Further Brownie pieces set out a vision of an Irish republicanism that used a variety of means of struggle, and that leaned clearly towards the left. 'What then is our definition of republicanism?' asked a piece from May 1976.

> Active republicanism means hard work, action, example ... It means fighting ... There can be no question of that. The enemy allows us no choice. It is an armed struggle, because the enemy is armed. Because he protects and establishes his vested interests by force of arms ... And what are we fighting for? Who are we fighting for? There is a lot of talk about 'The People' as if they are a thing ... The people are here, the people living all around us at the minute ... We fight for the homeless, for those with large families, for those without families at all. We fight for the people who find it hard to make ends meet, whether they be small farmers being pushed off the land by big ranchers or factory workers being sold out by their Trade Union leaderships. They are our fight and our fight must be based among them ... Their enemy must therefore be our enemy, their needs must be our needs, our republicanism must be their republicanism. People's republicanism. Active republicanism.[89]

These prison pieces by Adams reflect a process that has, more than once, occurred in Irish republican thinking: experience of prison contributing significantly to the evolution of political thought. There was, clearly, time to reflect in a way less easy when engaged in a war beyond jail walls. One met, and discussed politics with, people from other areas. One exchanged ideas, developed bonds of comradeship that might be of significance in post-incarceration politics; and one could pause to consider the movement's potential and its weaknesses.

The IRA of 1976 remained publicly bullish, and consistent in its demands. At the start of the year *Republican News* carried a statement from the IRA's Belfast Brigade leadership, which declared that Britain could either 'release the Irish people from the colonial yoke without bloodshed or she can order her beaten and demoralised army to protect the flag for a few years more'. British defeat was definitely coming: 'Make no mistake about it ... Britain's days in Ireland are numbered; the Irish people recognise it, the world at large recognise it, and the Irish Republican Army certainly recognise it.'[90] Shortly after this, the leadership of the IRA's Belfast Brigade claimed to speak for the entire republican movement in reiterating

the three demands which are a prerequisite for a just and lasting peace in Ireland. 1. A planned, phased and orderly withdrawal from Ireland by the British Army over a negotiated period. 2. Acknowledgement by Britain of the right of [the] whole people of Ireland acting as a unit to determine their own future. 3. The declaration of a general amnesty for all political prisoners. Until these demands are met in full the Irish Republican Army will continue to resist British rule with sustained military pressure.[91]

PART THREE

PRISONS AND POLITICS

1976–88

FIVE

THE PRISON WAR
1976–81

1

'We, the Provisional POWs (Long Kesh) reiterate our utter
and total rejection of the attempts of the British government
to deny political status to our comrades "sentenced" after
today's "offences deadline" ... Any member of the Provisional movement who is "sentenced" for any act carried
out in relation to the movement will never accept the status
of a criminal and in this they will have our support.'

Press release, republican prisoners (Long Kesh), 1 March 1976[1]

Twenty years on from the famous Irish republican hunger strike of
1981, leading Sinn Féin politician Tom Hartley[2] reflects calmly and
intelligently on that awful period. He and I are sitting in an elegant
room in the City Hall in Belfast (with an Irish tricolour leaning up
against the wall), and he thoughtfully contextualizes the hunger strike
within the lengthy struggle between Irish republicans and the British
state:

I suppose I would start with the statement by von Clausewitz: the
strategy of one dictates the strategy of the other. I think you need
to, first of all, look at a number of events that start to focus in
around the time of the hunger strike. You had the struggle in the
early seventies, and it has a lot of strength. And one of the responses
is to intern republicans. But by its nature internment means that
it makes political prisoners of those who are interned ... The
British seek to undermine the whole political ethos of the struggle
and what emerges is the policy of Ulsterization, criminalization and

normalization. A *parallel* strategy of the British is to engage with
the republicans; and this leads to the ceasefire of 1975, which causes
a major upheaval inside the republican movement. So on the one
hand the British are proceeding with their strategy of moving
towards criminalization of the republican struggle via its prisoners;
on the other hand they're engaging with republicans to bring them
to a ceasefire situation. But the outcome of this is something that
the British, I don't think, had foreseen and that is that what
emerges in '75 (because of the tensions created by the strategy) is a
new leadership, a new leadership of the republican movement. The
British then are set to implement their strategy . . . and what then
unfolds is the prison struggle. So this new [republican] leadership
. . . [has] a view of putting in place an ideological framework to the
struggle, that is: we need to build up the party, we need a voice, we
need a voice that is articulate on the demands, and we also need to
be very clear about what [are] the demands and what are the aims
and objectives of the struggle. So that's in its infancy in the period
of 1975–6. And the prison struggle begins, and then the prison
struggle moves towards the point of the blanket protest, the hunger
strikes and 1981.[3]

This valuably provides a context for understanding the republican
prison struggle of the late 1970s. On the one hand, British engagement
with republicans had produced a lengthy truce in 1975, which had
discredited republican leaders and therefore led to their replacement;
the new leadership wanted to move in a more emphatically political
direction. On the other, British attempts to criminalize republican
prisoners had resulted in a jail war that provided the route by which
such redirection could be pursued. There was thus, in Hartley's view,
a fusing, a gelling, of republican responses to two strands of British
policy in the north of Ireland.

As he suggests, the roots of the prison war lay in rival conceptions
of the nature of republican incarceration. In 1972 politically motivated
prisoners in the north had been granted special-category status,
which involved conditions similar to those enjoyed by internees
and which effectively bestowed on them a kind of political status. But
the January 1975 Gardiner Report had recommended the phasing out
of prisoners' special-category status because of the sustenance that it
gave to paramilitary organization, and because it reinforced the para-

militaries' own depiction of themselves as engaged in a legitimate political struggle. On 4 November 1975 Secretary of State for Northern Ireland, Merlyn Rees, warned that special-category status would end for those sentenced for offences committed after 1 March 1976; after the change, such prisoners would be treated as ordinary criminals. (A month later, Rees announced the ending of internment, releasing all remaining detainees.)

So prisoners were now to be criminalized, in an effort to delegitim-ize their struggle, and were to be held in newly built cellular accom-modation near Belfast in Long Kesh: the H-Blocks. The officially titled HMP Maze ('Long Kesh, alias the Maze – depending on whether you're a Brit who has put someone in, or someone who has been put in', as Gerry Adams wryly put it)[4] comprised these H-Blocks and a neighbouring compound and was, in effect, two prisons in one. The compound contained Nissen huts (1970s republican inmates referred to these as the cages; they were huts surrounded by barbed wire); in these were held existing prisoners enjoying (and maintaining) special-category status. The cellular part of the Maze contained the H-Blocks (so-named because of their shape) and here were to be housed prisoners convicted of post-1 March 1976 offences, those to be treated as criminals. The H-Blocks were single-storey (in grim, grey brick) and there were eight of them. Each block comprised four wings, each of which contained twenty-five cells, a dining room, toilet area, exercise yard and hobbies room; the central linking section held classrooms, offices for the warders, a medical treatment room and stores.

```
W              W
I              I
N              N
G              G
    L  I  N  K
W              W
I              I
N              N
G              G
```

The facilities themselves were impressive enough; but the problem lay in the authorities' conceptualization of those who were to be held within them. As far as the former were concerned, these were criminals,

responsible for appalling crimes of violence that were utterly unjustified. In stark contrast, the republicans saw themselves as engaged in a
legitimate political-military campaign to achieve national freedom for
their country in the face of occupation and oppression. IRA prisoners
were still IRA men and women, their prison war a part of their army's
wider struggle against the British state in Ireland. To the IRA, imprisonment in Long Kesh ('Britain's concentration camp', in Gerry
Adams's view)[5] was 'a badge of honour to be worn with dignity'.[6]
Battle-lines thus drawn, the late 1970s and start of the 1980s were to
be dominated by attritional warfare in the jails.

There had already been problems in Long Kesh. In July 1975,
Provisional prisoners there had complained that harassment was
'reaching a totally unacceptable level. Day by day, new, petty restrictive
rules are being brought into force which are fast making life unbearable.' Searches of prisoners and visitors were a highlighted grievance,
and there was some threat of the conflict to come: if the prison
authorities remained dogmatic, then republican prisoners would 'have
no choice but to escalate to other forms of protest'.[7] And this did not
apply to just one prison. In July 1976 republican prisoners in Belfast's
Crumlin Road Jail issued a statement protesting at conditions there:
the cells were 'infested with mice and cockroaches', there had been an
outbreak of scabies, and prisoners were 'subjected to a continuous
barrage of abuse, both verbal and physical, from the prison warders'.
They also offered 'a message to Merlyn Rees. You may think that your
plan for the removal of political status will run smoothly and succeed
but soon these delusions will be shattered. We, the republican prisoners
in Crumlin Road Gaol, state categorically that we will *NEVER* allow
ourselves to be treated as common criminals. Therefore all your
attempts are doomed to failure.'[8] Again, dignity and defiance, rather
than humiliating subservience or deference, were to be the republican
emblems.

Thus when Kieran Nugent, in September 1976, became the first
IRA man sentenced under the criminalizing new order, he refused to
wear prison uniform and was consequently put in a cell without any
clothes at all. He covered himself with a blanket. Prison rules required
inmates to wear clothes when leaving their cell, so Nugent and those
who followed him in refusing uniform were confined to their cells
twenty-four hours each day. The stand-off – the blanket protest – had

begun. (In 1993 prison authorities replaced blankets with duvets, prompting the then incarcerated Danny Morrison to look back and wittily reflect that the blanket protest had a more impressive ring to it than republicans would have achieved 'on the duvet': ' "I did four years on the duvet" wouldn't get you as many free pints as having been a "blanket man"!')[9]

The blanket protest embodied IRA prisoners' refusal to accept criminal status ('How dare they call us criminals?'),[10] and it led the authorities to respond by removing from protesters their access to television, radio, reading material (other than the Bible), writings materials and letters, as well as remission on sentences. And, like the violence outside at the start of the troubles, the prison war of the late 1970s escalated nastily, stage by stage, through gradually intensifying attritional battles. In the spring of 1978 the prisoners began a no-wash protest, in response (they said) to prison warders' brutality. The prisoners were allowed out of their cells, down the corridors, to wash – but were refused a second towel with which to dry themselves (the first being used to cover themselves up). They therefore refused to leave their cells, and the no-wash protest began. It was a far from pleasant experience; 'I wasn't particularly enthusiastic at the prospect of not washing for an indefinite period.'[11] Fights began with prison officers over the emptying of chamber pots from the cells: their contents were thrown through spy-holes and windows, and the warders sometimes threw them back; the openings were then blocked, and so prisoners poured urine through any available cracks and put their excrement on the walls. The 'dirty protest' had begun.

Prison had long been a major feature of IRA experience, and the army had devoted much attention to addressing problems encountered when its members were arrested and interrogated. But now, with the blanket, no-wash and dirty protests, the campaign of the incarcerated republicans took on a new, highly charged significance within the republican struggle, dominating their own publicity and becoming the focus for much of their energy and effort. Yet even these three successive protests were to seem like skirmishes when compared with the H-Block hunger-strike battles of 1980 and 1981. By late 1980 in Long Kesh there were over 1,300 prisoners; over 800 were republicans, of whom more than 300 were on the dirty protest. By this stage the prison conflict had become a vital issue to the IRA: allegations of harassment, brutality and inhuman treatment[12] in the jails intensified republican commitment and sense of injustice at the hands of the state.

Republicans felt that drastic action was required to achieve what they felt to be fair treatment in the prisons, and they had already given serious consideration to a hunger strike as early as mid-1978. Now, in 1980, they decided that no other course of action was open to them. On 10 October the H-Block blanket men issued through their Public Relations Officer a statement which inaugurated one of the most dramatic and terrible episodes in modern Irish history: 'We, the republican prisoners of war in H-Block, Long Kesh, demand as of right political recognition and that we be accorded the status of political prisoners. We claim this right as captured combatants in the continuing struggle for national liberation and self-determination. We refute most strongly the tag of criminal with which the British have attempted to label us and our struggle, and we point to the divisive partitionist institutions of the six counties as the sole criminal aspect of the present struggle.' The statement observed that 'men were put in the H-Blocks and were expected to bow the knee before the British administration and wear their criminal uniform. Attempts to criminalise us were designed to depoliticise the Irish national struggle.' No resolution of the prison situation had been reached, and the British government had remained intransigent. Consequently: 'we wish to make it clear that every channel has now been exhausted and, not wishing to break faith with those from whom we have inherited our principles, we now commit ourselves to a hunger strike'.[13] The strike was to start on 27 October.

Already on 21 October, a statement from the H-Blocks' OC Brendan Hughes[14] set the contemporary prison struggle in republican historical context: 'The repeated prison battles of republicans to gain their rights as POWs have been a focal point through successive liberation struggles of the past three centuries.' The 'horrific ordeal of incarceration in barbarous British dungeons' had been endured; torture and inhumanity had been perpetrated against these republicans 'who proudly bore the standard of Tone, Lalor, Pearse and Connolly, and stood in open defiance of the tyrannical oppressor of our nation'. More immediately, during the past four years all other means of protest in the prison had been exhausted, leaving 'no other alternative but to embark on a hunger strike to secure our just demands for political status'.[15] Hughes, who had been a senior Provisional in Belfast in the early 1970s, was to lead the 1980 hunger strike, which lasted from 27 October until 18 December. He stood down as Maze IRA OC (in favour of Bobby Sands) and was accompanied on his strike by six other H-Block republicans: the IRA's Tom McFeeley, Sean McKenna, Leo Green, Tommy McKearney and Raymond McCartney; and INLA man John Nixon. In republican eyes, these people were fighting a logical and utterly justified prison war: 'These men have been arrested under special powers, interrogated in special centres, convicted in special courts under special rules brought about by special legislation. Are they not special category!!!'[16]

There had, of course, been numerous previous Irish republican hunger strikes: 1920 in Mountjoy Jail; the mass strike of 1923 during the Civil War; and strikes in 1972–3 by Joe Cahill, Ruairí Ó Brádaigh and his brother Sean, and by Sean MacStiofáin.[17] In 1972 also Billy McKee had led a strike in Crumlin Road Jail, effectively for political status. At that time there had been two kinds of prisoner: first, internees, who were segregated according to paramilitary affiliation, housed in Nissen huts at Long Kesh, able to wear their own clothes, organize themselves on military lines and run their own affairs; and, second, prisoners like those on strike in Crumlin Road, who had been convicted of paramilitary-related offences but who were treated as ordinary criminals (wearing prison uniform, not segregated according to paramilitary allegiance, not free to associate). The McKee strike was aimed at achieving the status of the first group for the second also. Initially, the government had taken a hard line; but William Whitelaw – anxious about the turbulence that McKee's possible death might occasion, and also keen on a ceasefire and on talks with the IRA – then opted for the granting of special-category status for the prisoners. Thus Crumlin Road prisoners went to Long Kesh, where they – and those subsequently convicted – could enjoy effective political status. So, while some previous strikes (such as that of 1923) had set a far from promising example, there was a fairly recent precedent that pointed to the potentially effective and practical nature of a hunger strike. Could the status won after McKee's 1972 strike be won back through a similar gesture eight years later?

Rather than some obsessive death-fast, therefore, the 1980 strike was an attempt, albeit a drastic and dangerous one, practically to achieve what republicans considered to be their due treatment in the jails. Specifically, the hunger-strikers pursued five demands: the right to wear their own clothes; the right not to do prison work; free association with fellow prisoners; 50 per cent remission of sentences; and normal visits, parcels, educational and recreational facilities. Clothes – during weekday working hours (7.30 a.m.–5 p.m.), the rules required prisoners to wear prison-issue clothing but during weekends and weekday evenings they were allowed to wear their own clothes: prisoners were now demanding the right to wear their own clothes at all times. Work – the rules required prisoners to 'engage in useful work', consisting of four main types (domestic tasks in kitchens, dining areas and so on; industrial employment in prison workshops; vocational training (a wide range of skills was catered for); and education classes): prisoners now demanded the right to refrain from prison work. Association – the rules allowed that on weekday evenings and throughout weekends the prisoners could associate within each wing, watch television, play indoor games and attend education classes; books and newspapers were allowed: prisoners now demanded the right freely and fully to associate with each other. Remission – prisoners demanded restoration in full of the remission that they had lost while on the prison protest. Recreation – prison rules allowed for the use of gymnasium or playing pitch for about three hours a week in exercise periods, in addition to the normal exercise period of not less than one hour each day in the open air: prisoners now demanded the right to organize their own recreational arrangements.

On 1 December three female republican prisoners in Armagh Jail joined the hunger strike: Mairead Farrell, Mairead Nugent and Mary Doyle. On the 10th, a Northern Ireland Office (NIO) official spoke to the hunger-strikers, attempting to set out what was on offer. But on 15 December another twenty-three Maze prisoners entered the strike, to be joined the following day by another seven H-Block inmates. The strike was hurtling, with increasing speed, towards a crisis. It came on the 18th. One of the strikers (Sean McKenna, serving a twenty-five-year sentence for attempted murder and IRA membership) became critically ill. The leader of the strike, Brendan Hughes, knew there to be some kind of offer available from the British, one that might contain enough for a settlement. Hughes was not supposed to decide on the abandonment of the hunger strike without consultation with the Long Kesh OC (Bobby Sands), who was in contact both with the strikers and with the movement's outside leadership. But on 18 December the authorities moved McKenna to the Royal Victoria Hospital in Belfast, apparently to die, and prevented Sands from seeing the strikers again. In a corner, with his comrade nearing death, with a deal apparently available, and cut off from contact with his fellow republicans outside, Hughes ordered an end to the hunger strike. He and his original fellow strikers had been without food for fifty-three days.

What had, in fact, been on offer? An 18 December NIO document set out the authorities' view of what would happen should the protests end. The prisoners would be given clean cells; within a few days clothing provided by their families would be given to them to wear during recreation, association and visits; as soon as possible, prisoners would be issued with 'civilian-type clothing' for use during the working day; there would be access to parcels and visits, and free association within each wing in the evenings and at weekends; there was also the prospect of remission being restored. 'We do not want any prisoners to die ... If they die, it will be from their own choice. If they choose to live, the conditions available to them meet in a practical and humane way the kind of things they have been asking for. But we shall not let the way we run the prisons be determined by hunger strikes or any other threat.'[18]

Republicans have claimed that on 18 December the strikers were told that their five demands had been conceded, and there remains some confusion still about the precise manner in which the protest came to a close. But with the strikes over in the H-Blocks and (a day later) in Armagh, it soon became clear that the prisoners' demands had not in fact been conceded. Things had initially appeared to be going well. On 9 January 1981 new civilian-type clothes were brought to the Maze: prisoners had decided to wear these for visits. On the 14th the Maze Governor acknowledged that some prisoners had moved into cells containing furniture and bedding and that they 'did not foul or damage their cells or their contents'. More such moves into furnished cells were anticipated, and the Governor added that 'as part of the step by step approach, the position remains that any prisoner who has been allocated to clean furnished cells will on request be supplied with the new official issue civilian clothing'.[19] But there remained here a distinction between what the prisoners thought of as civilian clothing (namely, their own clothes) and the authorities' civilian-type clothing.

Later in the month, the prison authorities at the H-Blocks refused to hand out own clothes to twenty men who had moved from dirty to clean cells, and who had begun to slop out, and this pointed the way towards another crisis. Another stand-off had been reached. On 4 February the republican prisoners of the H-Blocks and Armagh issued a statement: 'having waited patiently for seven weeks for evidence that the British government was prepared to resolve the prison crises, and having given them every available opportunity to do so', the prisoners declared their intention 'of hunger striking once more'. The first hunger strike had ended with the prisoners expecting that their protests could soon begin to be wound down, and that as a first step on this road the blanket men could receive their own clothes. This had not happened: 'the Brits were more intent upon humiliating us once again than on settling the prison crises'. The next hunger strike – 'to the death, if necessary' – would start on 1 March, the fifth anniversary of the withdrawal of political status from republican prisoners. 'We are demanding to be treated as political prisoners which everyone recognises we are.'[20] So the second hunger strike was born of a republican sense of British treachery: 'as in other times in Irish history the British once more reneged'.[21]

Thus a second H-Block hunger strike for political status began, when on 1 March 1981 Bobby Sands refused food. Sands was, through his hunger-strike death, to become one of the leading icons of IRA history, from any period. But it was his ordinariness that gave his extraordinary gesture such power. As Gerry Adams aptly put it, 'Bobby Sands was a very ordinary young man ... If you met Bobby Sands there would be nothing about his demeanour or his appearance that set him apart from the rest of us. Yet this very ordinary young man did a very extraordinary thing.'[22] Sands had been born in Belfast in 1954. During his youth, his family were twice forced to move as a consequence of loyalist harassment. After the second of these displacements – to Twinbrook in the west of the city – a teenage Sands joined the IRA. In October 1972, still only eighteen years old, he was arrested and charged with possession of guns. Early in 1973 he was sentenced to five years' imprisonment, and was put in cage 11 where Gerry Adams was OC.

Here he learned Irish and energetically committed himself to prison life and culture. He was released in April 1976 and returned to Twinbrook, where he engaged both in Sinn Féin organizational work and in IRA activism. He was again arrested, in October 1976, in Dunmurry, Belfast, after an IRA operation: they had bombed the Balmoral Furnishing Company in a hit involving nine IRA Volunteers; Sands had been arrested in a car into which he and two others had jumped after the bombs had exploded. He was sentenced in 1977 (for possession of a gun) and was destined for fourteen years in jail. Thus in late September 1977 he arrived in the H-Blocks, duly refused to wear prison uniform, and went 'on the blanket'. Prison life eclipsed a troubled personal world. Of his 1972 capture, Sands had observed: 'I was going with a girl before I got lifted and was going to get married. She was pregnant, I got married in gaol on remand';[23] his arrest in 1976 ruined the marriage. His wife did not share Sands's zeal for the republican cause. Pregnant again at the time of this second arrest, she shortly afterwards had a premature delivery and lost the baby, blaming the loss on the trauma of her husband's arrest and the subsequent destructive British Army raid on their house.

By contrast, his prison life had clear direction to it. Sands had left school at fifteen (to become an apprentice coach-builder) but – like many republican prisoners – he developed his reading while politically incarcerated. During his first period inside, he had read Irish and international revolutionaries: James Connolly, Patrick Pearse, Liam Mellows, Frantz Fanon, Che Guevara. By March 1981 he was being described by one comrade as 'mad about poetry',[24] and was himself to write in this medium.[25] In the H-Blocks in 1979 Sands had read some work by the Irish nationalist writer Ethna Carbery, and had written her a note hoping that she might write them something for their H-Block campaign; she had, in fact, died in 1902.[26] So the image of the prisoner–scholar should not be overplayed, but Sands was certainly an enthusiastic reader (among his favourite novels, Leon Uris's roman-ticized Irish saga, *Trinity*);[27] he became a writer (under the pen-name 'Marcella', after a sister) of articles for the republican press; and he had a clear, resolute sense of his political ambitions and purpose. 'I am

a political prisoner,' he wrote in his diary on 1 March 1981; 'I am a
political prisoner because I am a casualty of a perennial war that is
being fought between the oppressed Irish people and an alien, oppressive, unwanted regime that refuses to withdraw from our land.'[28] The
very nature of this hunger-strike diary – written secretly on toilet paper
and hidden, for the most part, within Sands's own body – reflects the
extremity of the prison conflict within which he was about to become
central.

The IRA authorities outside the jail were far from keen on the idea
of a hunger strike, the momentum for which came very much from
the prisoners themselves. Leaders outside thought such a strike might
be an unwinnable battle, that the British government might not be
moved by such a gesture and that – were this the case – the
implications for morale within the movement might be dire. But
the prisoners' enthusiasm for the hunger-strike strategy – as they saw
it, their last resort – forced the hand of the IRA outside.

So on 1 March Bobby Sands refused food. He was to be followed
by numerous other republicans, nine of whom – like Sands himself –
would die as a consequence. Francis Hughes joined the strike on the
15th. Originally a member of the OIRA, Hughes had left that organization after its 1972 ceasefire and had set up an independent unit in his
native south Derry. This unit had then been accepted into the Provisional IRA. A cousin of fellow hunger-striker Thomas McElwee,
Hughes had been born in 1956 in Bellaghy, into a deeply republican
family. He had joined the Fianna Eireann as a boy; and his republicanism had been intensified when, aged seventeen, he and another boy
were badly beaten by British soldiers in an impromptu interrogation:
'he would get his own back on the people who did it, and their
friends,' he said.[29] Captured in 1978, he now resolutely faced the fast:
'I don't mind dying, as long as it is not in vain, or stupid.'[30]

Raymond McCreesh from south Armagh, who had been captured
as an IRA teenager in 1976; the INLA's Patsy O'Hara, from Derry city:
both had been born in 1957, and both joined the strike on 22 March.
Joe McDonnell from west Belfast, interned in the early 1970s and
then arrested in October 1976 along with Sands, following the IRA's
bombing of the Balmoral Furnishing Company: he replaced Sands
on hunger strike on 9 May 1981. The sequence was to continue,
with names that would rise from comparative obscurity to republican

legend. As strikers died, their comrades stepped forward to replace them on the fast. There was no shortage of would-be hunger-strikers among the republican prisoners.

On 22 May Kieran Doherty joined the strike, to replace Raymond McCreesh. Doherty had been born in Belfast in 1955, had joined the movement in 1971 and experienced internment, release and subsequent rearrest. Charged on the latter occasion with possession of firearms and explosives, and with commandeering a car, he was in January 1978 sentenced to twenty-two years in prison. He had immediately joined the H-Block blanket protest. Other brave figures were to follow. On 23 May the INLA's Kevin Lynch joined the strike to replace Patsy O'Hara; six days later Martin Hurson, from Cappagh, County Tyrone, started to fast. On 8 June Thomas McElwee joined the strike, as did the INLA's Mickey Devine on the 22nd.

But the hunger strike was transformed by an unforeseen development, with the death on 5 March 1981 of Frank Maguire.[31] The independent Westminster MP for Fermanagh/South Tyrone passed away as a result of a heart attack and the consequent by-election for the seat thus vacated presented a possibility for transforming Sands's strike. Maguire – himself a former IRA internee – had been a supporter of the prisoners' demand for political status. But what if Bobby Sands himself were to be elected to the House of Commons? Could the British government really maintain, in such an eventuality, that the IRA were criminals rather than a political force? Could Prime Minister Margaret Thatcher[32] let a Westminster MP starve himself to death? Gerry Adams was among those endorsing the idea that Sands should stand in the post-Maguire by-election, but it was undoubtedly a risky strategy. What if Sands lost? Thatcher and her colleagues would have made much of such a defeat, and the 9 April by-election and its outcome were tense, against the background of Sands's day-by-day fast.

Sands won, narrowly defeating the UUP candidate Harry West. Nationalists in the constituency had voted for him – 30,492 of them – and republican exhilaration knew no bounds. Fellow IRA prisoner Laurence McKeown[33] later recalled, 'We were ecstatic about the victory. We thought it would greatly improve Bobby's chances of living, that the Brits would not want one of their own MPs to die on hunger strike.'[34] The by-election outcome was indeed a politically weighty one.

As Gerry Adams was to argue of Sands's election, 'His victory exposed the lie that the hunger strikers – and by extension the IRA and the whole republican movement – had no popular support.'[35] Of course, support for Sands in 1981 should not imply necessary endorsement of his IRA politics. As Marian Price rightly says, 'A lot of people would have voted for Bobby Sands who certainly wouldn't have agreed with Bobby Sands's politics. But they would have voted for him, not because they were republican, but because they didn't want the man to die, and also because they respected him, that he was prepared to die for what he believed in.'[36] Even the IRA's flinty hunger-strike adversary, Margaret Thatcher, has observed that 'It was possible to admire the courage of Sands and the other hunger-strikers who died, but not to sympathise with their murderous cause. We had done everything in our power to persuade them to give up their fast.'[37]

Despite this famous victory, therefore, the hunger-strike stand-off continued. Fatally. For on 5 May 1981, on his sixty-sixth day without food, Bobby Sands died. At his Belfast funeral on 7 May, a 100,100 people walked silently behind the coffin. Sands was buried in Milltown cemetery in the west of the city, and his election agent, Owen Carron, gave the graveside oration: 'It is hard to describe the sadness and sorrow in our hearts today as we stand at the grave of Volunteer Bobby Sands, cruelly murdered by the British government in the H-Block of Long Kesh.'[38] There was huge media interest in the death of Bobby Sands, MP, and massive international publicity. Then, on 12 May, Sands's comrade Frankie Hughes also perished, on the fifty-ninth day of his strike. In the view of American sympathizers, Hughes had been 'murdered by the British government'; 'Frankie Hughes gave his life and proved his love. The light he kindled will never burn out.'[39] On the 21st of that month, both Raymond McCreesh and Patsy O'Hara passed away. They had been without food for sixty-one days. For all their organizational energy, the republican movement was witnessing a series of deaths that offered ever decreasing power to shock, to move, to have a political impact.

And the republicans were indeed well organized. A National H-Block/Armagh Committee pushed the prisoners' case with zeal and publicity-awareness. The prisoners communicated among themselves, and with the outside, via an elaborate and ingenious set of communications, or 'comms'. Written on improvised (toilet or cigarette) paper, wrapped in cling film and secreted in the body (anus, mouth, under foreskin), these 'comms' or notes were smuggled via visits, family or friends bringing and taking communications (again, hiding them on their own bodies). But they were being smuggled against a drawn-out sequence of tragedies. Joe McDonnell died on 8 July, his poignant story coming to an end after sixty-one days without food. Fellow hunger-striker Laurence McKeown: 'Joe McDonnell, who was married with kids, refused to wear the uniform even for visits so he didn't see his family for four years. He gets to see them when he's dying. In the meantime his children are four years older.'[40] And, contrary to much casual assumption, these were not people destined through long-term inclination for martyrdom. As another of McDonnell's republican comrades recalls, 'There was nobody loved life as much as Joe Mc-Donnell, and lived life to the full as Joe McDonnell ... If somebody had put a thousand people in front of me, Joe was the last one I'd pick to go on hunger strike.'[41]

These were essentially ordinary men, whose zealous conception of their struggle and their circumstances led them to extremity. Leading republican and one-time IRA bomber Gerry Kelly later reflected of the hunger-strike period: 'A large number of prisoners were prepared to die slowly and painfully for us. What the British should take note of is that they were not supermen or women. They were ordinary men and women from the republican community. They were ordinary men and women pushed into extraordinary circumstances, who rose to the challenge and went beyond it.'[42] And memories of that committed struggle can still arouse anger. As one ex-IRA man recalled, 'I knew Joe McDonnell all my life 'cos he came from the lower Falls [in Belfast], where I come from myself ... Every time I think of those hunger-strikers I go into a rage, I really do. I remember how dark those days were. I remember how awful it must have been for them.'[43]

At the time of the strike itself, there was an emotional intensity of commitment that helped to sustain the gesture, and a strong sense that the sacrifices of those who had died should not prove to have been made for nothing. Martin Hurson died on 13 July 1981, Kevin Lynch on 1 August, and Kieran Doherty the following day. Like Sands, though with much less fame, Doherty had become elected to parliament: in June, while on hunger strike, he had won a seat in the Dublin Dáil for Cavan/Monaghan in the Republic of Ireland's general election.

Thomas McElwee died on 8 August, Mickey Devine later in the month, after sixty days without food. McElwee typified the defiant Provoism that was a key part of the hunger strike, and of the organization as a whole; he had once spent fourteen days in the prison punishment block because he refused to call a prison warder 'sir'.

Defiant or not, the strikers were failing to move the British government sufficiently to meet their demands. There *was* contact between the two sides, and republicans knew what was on offer. On 29 July Gerry Adams met with six of the hunger-strikers in order to outline what he knew to be available from the British should the strike be brought to an end: a package that fell short of the full demands, but one that indicated substantial movement – the abolition of prison uniforms, with prisoners to wear their own clothes; the unofficial segregation of prisoners; free association at weekends and for part of each day; the granting of the strikers' demands concerning parcels and visits. But the prisoners rejected this set of offers, and persevered for their full demands. There was to be no compromise this time around.

But, with the diminishing impact of each death and the apparent preparedness of the authorities to allow the grim sequence to go on and on, the brave strike came unavoidably to an end. The pressure on strikers' families had been appalling and – not surprisingly – some of them came to decide that the hunger strike should end. On 31 July 1981 Paddy Quinn (who had joined the strike on 15 June) received medical treatment on the instruction of his relatives, and ended his fast after forty-seven days. On 20 August Pat McGeown's family agreed to medical intervention to save his life on his forty-second day without food. On 4 September Matt Devlin's family agreed to medical intervention to save his life on the fifty-second day of his strike; two days later Laurence McKeown's family agreed to medical intervention to save him on his seventieth day. The strike was effectively collapsing. Thus, on 30 September, the H-Block prisoners issued a statement: 'We, protesting republican prisoners in H-Blocks, being faced with the reality of sustained family intervention, are forced by this circumstance over which we have little control at the moment to end the hunger strike.'[44] On 3 October, with figures such as Pat Sheehan[45] and Jackie McMullan[46] still refusing food, the Long Kesh hunger strike ended.

It did so without the prisoners securing their aims, although on 6 October the Secretary of State for Northern Ireland, James Prior, made significant concessions to their position in regard to clothing, remission, association and visits. But the broader significance of the hunger strike of 1981 stretched far beyond such specifics, and it has rightly been seen as a crucial and telling episode in Provisional republican history; in Sinn Féiner Tom Hartley's view, 'The hunger strike *is* a watershed.'[47] For one thing, it clarified the deficiencies of a reading of republican activity that treated it as if it was merely apolitical crime. To recognize something as political need not bestow upon it a sense of legitimacy or justness. But there is no doubt that the episode demonstrated forcibly the political nature of the Provisional movement. Republicans themselves presented the 1981 strike not merely as a battle for the five demands, but as 'the ultimate reaction to the H-Blocks themselves, the end product of a carefully manipulated legal system which was drafted to replace the internationally embarrassing system of internment without trial introduced in August 1971'.[48] Brendan Hughes, leader of the 1980 hunger strike, later argued with reference to the prison protests that 'What took place between 1976 and 1981 was a war. The British government tried to defeat the republican struggle through a policy of degradation, isolation, beatings and criminalisation. They did not succeed.'[49] In Tom Hartley's opinion, what was begun in 1976 was completed in 1981: 'from the minute Kieran Nugent refused to wear the prison uniform, Britain's policy of criminalization was defeated. Instead, Britain was criminalized in the eyes of the world';[50] 'Criminalization, the very strategy of the British, is broken by the election of Bobby Sands. Basically, you can't talk of someone being a criminal and then 30,000 people going out to vote for them, I think.'[51]

As has been noted, in the IRA's view the British were responsible for the hunger strike, and the prisoners held that the government had 'legally murdered' Bobby Sands.[52] Republicans were also deeply hostile to the role of Dublin, including 'the collaborationist role of Fianna Fáil leader Charles Haughey throughout the present hunger-strike crisis'.[53] And they were sharply critical in this period of their northern constitutional rivals: in February 1980 *An Phoblacht/Republican News* referred to 'the nauseating sight of the SDLP crawling in the corridors of Stormont, desperately seeking what minor "devolved" crumbs of comfort they can find around the table of direct-ruler [then Northern Ireland Secretary of State, Humphrey] Atkins and Orange

King Paisley'.[54] Of course, these were partisan perspectives, and there were other viewpoints. Margaret Thatcher herself stressed that while the issue fought over in the hunger strike must have seemed unimportant to many onlookers, 'both the IRA and the government understood that it was not. The IRA and the prisoners were determined to gain control of the prison and had a well-thought-out strategy of doing this by whittling away at the prison regime.' The Provisionals wanted to establish 'that their crimes were "political", thus giving the perpetrators a kind of respectability, even nobility. This we could not allow.'[55] To British political eyes, the way to express nationalist political opinion was through the vote, through argument – and not through divisive violence such as that practised by the IRA.

But that the hunger strike showed the political dimension to the prison conflict is surely beyond dispute. The second point is that it emphatically extended the republican struggle in terms of depth and range of support. Protests in Britain in support of the hunger-strikers were noted by republicans in Ireland.[56] And broader international sympathy was mobilized in a way embarrassing to Margaret Thatcher's government. Energetically produced publicity abroad told tales of 'un autre crime du colonialisme Britannique'[57] and of those 'murdered by the British'.[58] There had been activity in Holland dating from the first hunger strike: 'A[n] H-Block committee was formed in Amsterdam recently based on the six [sic] demands of the prisoners . . . To date, over 300 letters have been [sent] to organisations and prominent individuals in Holland, asking them to support the prisoners['] demands . . . On the 3rd November a picket was held in front of the British consulate in Amsterdam, and about thirty-five people turned up to picket in the freezing cold.'[59] In the United States the 1981 strike 'galvanised large sections of Irish-America in a way that no armed IRA campaign could ever achieve'.[60]

But the main significance in terms of popular opinion was the intensification of nationalist feeling within and beyond republican ranks in Ireland itself. Martin McGuinness: 'Not since the declaration in arms of the Irish republic on the steps of Dublin's GPO in 1916 has any event in modern Irish history stirred the minds and hearts of the Irish people to such an extent as the hunger strike of 1981.'[61] Too much should not, perhaps, be made of republican electoral success in 1981 (the republican seats in the Dáil won in June 1981, for example, quickly reverted in the February 1982 election back to their previous tenants). But Bobby Sands's election did demonstrate that people who would not customarily be IRA supporters might be engaged on behalf of an IRA man's cause in certain circumstances. While the army had not initially been keen on the idea of a hunger strike, making 'strenuous efforts' to prevent one, they came to recognize that, in the event, the strike had 'obviously increased support for the republican cause'.[62] Indeed, the 1981 hunger strike came to be seen by republicans as having been absolutely central to revitalizing their movement. Brendan McFarlane – OC of the H-Block republicans during the strike – looked back a decade later and argued that 'In the wider political arena the [1981] hunger strike reshaped the nature of the liberation struggle. Traditional strictures were shed as the republican movement found a new political vibrancy, demolishing the British myth that we had little or no support, and moving forward with the people into a new era of struggle.'[63] The hunger strike came to be seen as having shown what could be done if republican politics extended into more broadly based campaigns, Sands's election being the key moment here. As one of Sinn Féin's most gifted publicists of the period, Danny Morrison, reflected, the subsequent reorientation of the republican movement around politics probably would have been impossible 'had it not been for the fortuitous death of Frank Maguire and the election of Bobby Sands, because the movement was totally suspicious of politics, because politics equals compromise'.[64]

But if the 1981 strike, and Sands's electoral success within it, are to be seen as crucial in the eventual development of northern republican-ism in a more fully political direction, then some qualifications and ironies should be noted. First, while republicans recognized that their dead hunger-strikers had politicized for them a section of Irish people, they certainly did not – at the time – draw the lesson that politics rather than violence offered the way forward. Despite much latter-day assumption about the inevitability of post-1981 republicanism moving in a Sinn Féinish, electoral direction, the prisoners at the time in fact drew, if anything, the opposite lesson. Close reading of the archival evidence undermines the (now popular) view that the 1981 experience pointed unambiguously towards the rewards which electoral politics and more conventional political methods offered. In the statement that actually ended the strike, it was observed: 'One of the primary lessons

to emerge from this phase of our protest is that the nationalist minority
in Northern Ireland are politically inconsequential and impotent in the
context of the six-county statelet. That point is very important.' Rather
than their electoral success implying the efficacy of politics, the exact
reverse was suggested by the prisoners: 'Despite the electoral successes
and the inherent implications, despite the 100,000 mourners who
attended Bobby Sands' funeral, despite the massive and unprecedented
display of community support, the British government adhered strictly
to the precept that "might is right" and actively set about hammering
home the lesson that nothing has really changed since the fall of
Stormont.' If republican political success during 1981 did help push
the movement towards a less violent form of struggle, and towards a
rapprochement with constitutional nationalists in the rest of the island,
then it did not seem like this to the prisoners themselves at the end
of their protest:

> nationalist pacifism in the Northern Ireland context is energy-
> wasting, futile and unproductive in that it is a permanent guarantee
> of second-class citizenship and subservience to an alien and foreign
> government ... We believe that the partitionist Dublin bloc of
> Fianna Fáil, Fine Gael [the second main political party in the
> Republic of Ireland] and Labour are accessories to the legalised
> murder of ten true and committed Irishmen who died heroically in
> the long tradition of republican resistance to British imperialism
> and oppression in Ireland. These ten republicans had more moral
> fibre and sincerity than the entire membership of the three parties
> mentioned.[65]

Moreover, scepticism regarding electoral politics is richly evident in
other contemporary sources too. A debate among H-Block prisoners
in the early 1980s acknowledged the 'many inherent dangers in
participation in elections', noted the damage to Sinn Féin electoral
chances should there be an eve-of-election IRA operation, and
observed that Sinn Féin, as a political party, was at that time 'very
weak'.[66]

And it would be wrong anyway to see 1981 as *beginning* a process
of republican politicization: it would be more accurately understood as
an unintended *accelerator* of a process already favoured by the leaders
of the movement. Sinn Féin's Tom Hartley: the hunger-strikers

'accelerated in us the advancement of political strategies, electoralism – which probably was on the cards'.[67] Before 1981, the republican leadership had been trying to move in a political direction; indeed, one of the ironies of the hunger strike was that republican opposition outside the jail to the prisoners' intended strike was partly based on the objection that such a strike would divert time, energy and attention away from the process of politicization which republican leaders wanted to pursue – and which the hunger strike in the end reinforced.

But could this painful episode have been avoided? What if the first hunger strike had been quietly resolved, as seemed possible at the end of 1980 and the start of 1981? One of the 1980 strikers, Tommy McKearney, certainly feels this to have been a possibility ('It could have been sorted out)';[68] one of his movement's leaders, Gerry Adams, agrees: 'There was a deal which had the capacity to resolve the issues at the core of the prison protests';[69] and republican prisoners in the early 1980s certainly read the second hunger strike as having arisen from British failure to live up to the promises that had ended the first – the proposals of December 1980, had they been implemented, representing 'a workable and just solution'.[70] It is sometimes suggested that the hunger strike emerged from a deep-rooted Irish instinct.[71] But its real explanation lay primarily in the politics of the present: in the specifics of the prison war of 1976–81. As such, it is possible that a compromise in 1980 which dealt with prisoners' practical demands might indeed have averted the second, fatal strike.

This might have been preferable for Margaret Thatcher's government, for whom the 1981 strike was something of a Pyrrhic victory. Yes, the hunger strike had ended without the prisoners' demands being conceded. But the intensification of nationalist feeling and sympathy was a high price to pay, and a revivified republican movement was to emerge after the 1981 battle. Mrs Thatcher herself emerged from this episode as a republican hate-figure of Cromwellian proportions ('that unctuous, self-righteous fucker', 'the biggest bastard we have ever known', in Danny Morrison's evocative phrasing).[72] But she too had helped, unwittingly, to inject life into the Irish republican struggle. The 1981 hunger strike might be seen as another instance of stern British policy rebounding to the advantage of militant Irish republicans. As with internment in 1971 or Bloody Sunday in 1972, the IRA now enjoyed a larger reservoir of potential recruits than would have been

the case but for probably ill-advised and avoidable choices made by
the British government. And such reflections are all the more pressing
when one considers the violence during and consequent upon the
hunger strike. The long fast dramatically polarized society in Northern
Ireland, as each taut day exacerbated difference and hostility between
communal opponents. Graffiti on loyalist walls during Sands's strike
apparently included 'Don't be vague, starve a taig [Catholic].'[73] The
satirical *An Phobcrapt/Murderers' News* was to carry in its spoof events
column a listing for a performance by 'Special Guest Star: Bobby Sands
and The Skeletons'.[74]

For their own part, republican prisoners certainly wanted revenge
for the close-proximity deaths of their comrades. Anthony McIntyre,
then an IRA prisoner: 'There was disappointment that the IRA
response to the hunger-strike deaths wasn't what it should have been
. . . We felt that the IRA could have been slaughtering these people in
twenties and thirties; we were expecting Warrenpoints[75] and hoping
for Warrenpoints, 'cos the people were dying in the jails.'[76] Tommy
McKearney: 'The IRA lost a lot of prestige and confidence through the
second hunger strike when, particularly, it found itself incapable of
responding militarily to the death of Bobby Sands.'[77]

But if the IRA were not killing as many as some were hoping for,
they were still bloodily active. Vengeful violence had accompanied the
long prison protest, as reflected in the words of the first blanket man,
Kieran Nugent: 'I remember Governor Myles [sic]. He said, "We are
going to break you." He stood there shouting at me. Gave me a slap in
the face and then he stood back and watched the other warders beat
me up. When he was shot on December 20th 1978, that was a great
morale booster.'[78] Republicans presented the hunger-strikers as victims;
but other victims also suffered at the IRA's own hands. Prison officers
('legitimate targets', in the IRA's view)[79] were killed during the prison
war; and so (on 7 April 1981) was the sad figure of Joanne Mathers.
A twenty-nine-year-old woman, married with a young son, Mathers
had taken a part-time job as a census collector in order to supplement
family income. The IRA opposed the census and urged nationalists not
to take part in it; on 7 April they shot Joanne Mathers in the head
while she was collecting census forms in Derry. (The IRA initially
denied responsibility,[80] but it later transpired that they were in fact
the killers.) And republican prisoners themselves, of course, also had

violent pasts. Brendan McFarlane, who had replaced Sands as OC in Long Kesh in anticipation of the second strike, had been involved in a bloody gun-and-bomb attack in August 1975 on the Bayardo Bar in Aberdeen Street in the Protestant Shankill Road area of Belfast. The bar was allegedly frequented by UVF people, but the attack left dead five Protestants none of whom had paramilitary connections. (Again, the IRA had initially denied any involvement in the Bayardo attack; but, again, it later transpired to have been, indeed, an IRA operation.) And violence past and present was to be complemented by the violence that the hunger strike stored up for the future, as young people – understandably moved by the sight of the dying hunger-strikers – resolved to take the responsive path that the IRA's military politics offered.

Thus 1981 was political and politicizing, avoidable and appallingly violent. But perhaps its most abiding images are of human sadness. From opponents or victims of the IRA, there was – not surprisingly – little sympathy for the strikers. But, just as the suffering of IRA victims should not be forgotten, so too there were human stories around the strikers. 'There was a terrible sadness about their plight that could be appreciated even by those who deplored their affiliations,' observed northern poet, Seamus Heaney.[81] For his part, Brendan McFarlane looked back with much sadness: '1981 was probably the worst year of my life. Despite the political gains, the loss of that year is always with me.'[82] Danny Morrison: 'We'll never get over it. We never will.'[83] For while it is true that, in Tom Hartley's words, 'When you're in struggle, you get on with it',[84] it is also true that – for the prisoners – the endurance or observation of protracted deaths was extraordinarily painful. Sadness, comradeship, commitment, courage and a refusal to be cowed all came together in these days of exaltation during the prison war. 'Camaraderie. You were never as close [as] you were on the blanket';[85] 'I do not believe I will ever again experience the depth of comradeship and closeness to other men that I did during my time in the H-Blocks';[86] 'I don't expect in my life to live those heights again, the hunger strike and the years prior to it: the depths of anger you would have felt, or hatred ... or the exhilaration at Bobby's election, or the feelings of love or comradeship';[87] ' "When this is all over, we'll remember only the good bits." That's what we used to tell each other during the blanket and I suppose in a way it's true.'[88]

IRA prisoners in England, even, during these years felt bound into the comradeship of a broader battle, and were strengthened as a consequence: the political prisoner 'feels a strong bond of comradeship with his fellow POWs, and he feels strongly linked to the struggle for national liberation in Ireland. This is always a great source of strength to the political prisoner. He knows that any suffering he may endure is for a noble objective and that he is not an individual who can be isolated and forgotten, but part of a great movement.'[89]

One other feature of these prison days that screams out from the sources is its profoundly religious, Catholic quality. A Sinn Féin leaflet from Christmas 1977 in support of the prison protest carried a drawing of Christ on the cross, with the caption 'He too was a prisoner of conscience'; next to this image was an H-Block blanket man.[90] The notion of identifying IRA prisoners with Christ perhaps reached its peak when Father Denis Faul attempted to persuade Bobby Sands to desist from his hunger strike, with Sands in response invoking Christ's words from John 15:13, 'Greater love hath no man than that he lay down his life for his friends.' But it was not just the strikers themselves who saw their gesture in Christ-like terms. One Catholic priest reflected that the strikers 'were almost akin to Christ-like ... You could argue that Christ didn't have to die on the cross, he could have created a miracle, but for the good of his people he saw through to the supreme sacrifice of death. I think each individual man attempted that.'[91]

In November 1980 republican blanket man Sam Millar wrote from H-Block 5 to Pope John Paul II ('Dear Holy Father, I hope this small note finds you well and in good health'), on toilet paper ('Please excuse the paper it is written on'), to ask for papal intervention on behalf of the hunger-strikers.

> I am writing this note not to tell you about our conditions but to beg you to save the lives of my comrades who have been forced to hunger-strike by the British government ... The Irish people have suffered to[o] long for their political and religious belief ... Irish history is filled with the blood that Irish men and women have spilled for the nation and the Catholic Church, and now that the Irish nation need the Church we hear naught but a deadly silence. Why?? ... What must the Irish do to get the Church to help? ... By the time you get this it may be too late to save my comrades.

You must speak out now, loudly; behind closed doors is no use.
My comrades will die if you don't.[92]

Bobby Sands's own diary for 3 March 1981 noted that 'The boys are
now saying the rosary twice every day',[93] while his replacement as OC
(Brendan McFarlane) had once studied for the Catholic priesthood
and now, in jail, diligently read the Bible.

Such Catholic religiosity should not be taken to mean that the IRA
prisoners existed cosily with the Church authorities. As in previous
eras,[94] Irish republicans could be Catholic Christians while critical of
the political stance of their Church and there was sharp hostility over
the latter's role during the hunger strike. Republican Gerard Hodgins
later accused Father Faul of having 'demonstrated his desire to destroy
the IRA in 1981 by his treacherous about-turn in relation to the hunger
strike'. Criticizing Faul for attempting to persuade strikers' families to
intervene in the strike, Hodgins observed: 'Nobody likes a turn-coat,
even if he is a priest.'[95] Other republicans also criticized the Church.
Tom Holland, speaking of the summer of 1981: 'In the latter days of
July the Catholic Church began to actively intervene in the protest by
creating dissent and doubt among the families of the hunger-strikers
and encouraging them to prevent their loved ones from dying. This
manipulation caused much anger and frustration in our ranks.'[96]

In this, as in much else, there are unavoidable echoes between 1981
and 1916. Icon-generating, quasi-religious martyrdom, the republican
reaping of benefits from technical defeat, the Pyrrhic nature of the
British victory and the intensification of Irish nationalist sentiment all
point to such a comparison. So, too, does another similarity between
the two epic republican moments. For in each case republican politics
were energized and mobilized, fuelled with recruits and with a sense of
the possibility of victory; in each case a combination of republican
violence and republican politics was used in the hope of translating the
high-ground of sacrifice into ultimate practical victory with the establishment of the free republic. And, in each case, such millenarian hopes
were to prove, ultimately, unfounded. Post-1916, the IRA fought
impressively for the republic in a war which ended in the compromise
of 1921 – a compromise which its political wing, Sinn Féin, endorsed
as the best result then available. Post-1981, the IRA fought tenaciously
for British withdrawal in a conflict which ended with a compromise –

one that its own political wing, Sinn Féin, was to present as the best available option in the circumstances.

2

'Only through armed struggle will we be listened to, only through the struggle waged by the Irish Republican Army can we win national freedom and end division and sectarianism in Ireland.'

IRA Easter statement, 1981[97]

On 21 July 1976 the British Ambassador to the Republic of Ireland, Christopher Ewart-Biggs, was killed by the IRA in Dublin in an operation which prompted political shock and personal pain. The Republic's Taoiseach, Liam Cosgrave, suggested that 'The atrocity fills all Irish people with a sense of shame';[98] Ewart-Biggs's wife poignantly recalled: 'I hadn't even said goodbye to him.'[99]

The Provisionals were about to embark on an explicitly 'long war', and in order to sustain such a struggle it was considered necessary to reorganize the army. Late 1976 and early 1977 (when Roy Mason was Secretary of State for Northern Ireland) were difficult periods for the Provisional movement: Volunteers were being imprisoned in large numbers and military momentum was stalling. In November 1976 it was agreed to establish a new IRA structure that transferred power over much of the IRA's military campaign from the southern leadership into the hands of northerners. Given that the fire-centre of republican military struggle was the north, this made considerable sense. A Northern Command (covering the six Northern Irish counties as well as Louth, Cavan, Monaghan, Leitrim and Donegal) was set up to oversee all offensive operations in the north. This body was largely autonomous of the Army Council and, by the end of 1976, military control in the IRA was almost fully in the hands of northerners.

To the IRA, Ireland was now divided into Northern and Southern Commands: the former drove the struggle, while the latter provided material and back-up. Too much should not be read into the formal positions within the IRA – informal status often transcended official title, when it came to influence within the movement – but there was now a clearly coherent command structure. The General Army Convention was the supreme authority; this elected an Army Executive, which in turn selected a seven-person Army Council, the Council then appointing a Chief of Staff (who need not be an Army Council member); a GHQ Staff complemented the above, and below GHQ there was now a bifurcation into the eleven-county Northern and twenty-one-county Southern Commands. At local level, IRA units operated with considerable autonomy in practice. So, while the Army Council might meet at least once a month, retaining control of overall strategy and tactics, the day-to-day war was fought and determined very much at local level.

The late 1970s also saw the IRA reorganize in other ways for their emergent 'long war' of attrition with the British state. Their brigade/battalion/company structure was to be largely replaced with a cellular structure instead. Each cell comprised a three- or four-person unit that specialized in particular activities (such as sniping, bombing, gathering information). People in one cell were intended not to know the identity of members of other cells, thereby providing more protection against the damaging possibilities after arrest. Now, there was to be far less chance of crucial intelligence being gained by the state through interrogation of an IRA member. The idea of changing to the cellular structure apparently emerged from within the jails and, although the new order was never uniformly implemented throughout the IRA, great success was to be claimed on behalf of its effectiveness: 'Last year [1979] was one of resounding republican success when the IRA's cellular reorganisation was operationally vindicated, particularly through devastating use of remote-control bombs.'[100]

Also emerging from within the jails was the IRA's *Green Book*, a manual apparently begun in 1974, completed in 1978 and produced in 1979, containing the army's aims and objectives and focusing heavily on security. Thus, along with the IRA's standing orders and lectures on Irish history, the *Green Book* also instructed members in practical terms about how to resist interrogation (a long-term preoccupation of the IRA, for obvious reasons). Standard for some time for use by IRA Volunteers, the *Green Book* embodied IRA philosophical orthodoxy, affirming the republican belief that the IRA was 'the direct representative of the 1918 Dáil Éireann parliament, and that as such they are the legal and lawful government of the Irish Republic ... The Irish Republican Army, as the legal representatives of the Irish people, are morally justified in carrying out a campaign of resistance against foreign occupation forces and domestic collaborators.'[101] It further argued that 'The moral position of the Irish Republican Army, its right to engage in warfare, is based on: (a) the right to resist foreign aggression; (b) the right to revolt against tyranny and oppression; and (c) the direct lineal succession with the Provisional Government of 1916, the First Dáil of 1919 and the Second Dáil of 1921.'[102]

For, in the IRA's view, there was a direct line of succession from the 1916 rebels to the Provisional IRA. The sequence of events detailed earlier in this book provided the justificatory narrative for Provisional theology: the 1919 Dáil had inherited the legitimacy of the 1916 rebels and had been succeeded in its turn by the 1921 Second Dáil; when the majority of that body favoured the 1921 Treaty with Britain, its rejectionist minority became – in republican eyes – the legitimate authority in Ireland; when a remnant of that 1921 Dáil refused to back de Valera's Fianna Fáil, this remnant had then come to embody legitimate Irish government, an authority which it passed to the IRA in 1938; the sole survivor of that 1921 remnant (Tom Maguire) had endorsed the Provos at their foundation – and so, in republican thinking, there was a direct chain of legitimacy linking 1916, 1919, 1921, 1938 and the post-1969 Provisionals.

Despite this, however, the energy and momentum of the movement in the modern period were provided primarily by the day-to-day northern experience of Catholics: there may have been an elaborate political theology, but (as, indeed, with other kinds of theology) it would only have continued meaning for people if it somehow related to lived daily experience. IRA members and sympathizers endorsed the alternative legitimacy thesis expounded above, not because they were inexplicable zealots, but rather because the state's structures and activities in the north seemed hostile to their interests in a practical way. An IRA statement of 2 October 1979 argued that, while the roots of the troubles did indeed lie in history, their recent source was to be found 'in the social and economic deprivation suffered by the nationalist people [of the north of Ireland]'; responsibility for that deprivation lay with the Stormont and Westminster governments; peaceful efforts to deal with deprivation having been met by state force, people had been forced to turn instead to their own deployment of force: 'we believe that force is by far the only [sic] means of removing the evil of the British presence in Ireland. Their interference has divided the people and caused untold hardship . . . we believe that our prospects for victory are supported by the examples of other colonial struggles, by our continued existence given the duration of the repression, and by the widespread support which we know we command and which our operations prove.'[103] Thus, for all their celebration of former heroes, and their stress on the continuity of the struggle through the generations, it was recent and contemporary social injustice that was most prominent in the IRA's analysis.

In this sense, the IRA were – again, contrary to much popular assumption – practical rather than mystical, and determined by daily realities rather than by addiction to an ahistorical philosophy. Their military strategy certainly had a practical logic to it, the aim being to sustain a war of attrition that would raise the cost of remaining in Northern Ireland (the human, financial, economic, political, inter-national costs) to a level at which the London government would think it preferable instead to withdraw. This was to become a long-term part of the Provos' long war, remaining key to their thinking well into the 1980s. Republicans were to note in September 1980 the London government's statement that compensation payments of around £400 million had arisen from Northern Irish bombings to date, and that much of this was due to the IRA's commercial bombing campaign, 'one aim of which is, precisely, to raise the Brits' cost of occupation'.[104] Scorning those Irish politicians who worked by means of Westminster constitutionalism, the Provisionals argued the necessity of violence: 'Only when Irish people turned to arms was the hope of real success raised.'[105]

But, as ever, it was not a case of violence alone. The Provisionals, it is true, were keen to distance themselves from full-blooded Marxism during the late 1970s. In 1979 they issued a statement declaring that 'our enemies have now resorted to the "red scare" to which they believe our supporters at home and in America will be particularly susceptible. We place on record that the Irish Republican Army is not a Marxist organisation . . . our aim is the establishment of a democratic socialist republic based on the 1916 Proclamation. Our republican socialism is a radical native brand taken from Tone, Lalor, Connolly and Mellows.'[106] Regarding Sinn Féin, Gerry Adams argued that 'there is no Marxist influence within Sinn Féin, it simply isn't a Marxist organisation. I know of no one in Sinn Féin who is a Marxist or who would be influenced by Marxism . . . It's a straight socialist republican or radical republican organisation.'[107]

Yet, as Adams's words here indicate, there was a strong socialist strain within republican thinking at this stage. In a letter from Long Kesh written in January 1977, Adams identified himself firmly as a 'republican socialist', and set out the colonial analysis which under-pinned his and his movement's politics: 'the problem in Ireland is a problem for all Ireland and can only be resolved in an all-Ireland context. It will not be resolved within a twenty-six-county straitjacket or a six-county fascist statelet. Both these statelets are dependent on Britain, the north as an undisguised British colony, and the south as a neo-colony.' In the margin of this epistle, Adams observed that ' "Long windedness" is one of my many vices!!!!!'[108] In fact, the above-quoted passage concisely communicated the essence of contemporary republi-can thinking. For there was a definite working-class flavour to the republican movement and its political thought at this time. That political thought involved a combination of socialist politics and violent aggression.

In March 1977 another key republican, R. G. McAuley, also referred in prison writings to republicans' colonial analysis, and again reflected a leftist agenda: 'The republican movement regards British colonial presence in Ireland with its gross exploitation of the Irish people and Irish resources, not only as illegal but as the basis for most of our economic and social problems today.' In their war against Britain, therefore, republicans had attacked all 'supports' or 'foundation stones' for the British presence; as part of this they had assaulted 'the economic basis of Britain's stranglehold' through the destruction of business premises and factories. Such violence was the only way forward, and was far preferable to constitutional Irish nationalists' political approach: 'Irish history is littered with the corpses of Irish politicians who genuinely believed that political processes set up by the English would achieve justice and freedom for the Irish nation. There can be no doubt that these politicians, O'Connell, Parnell etc., succeeded to some extent in "reforming" the established system; however, any alterations made had only any real benefit for the middle class and none at all for the vast majority of Irish people who continued to live in poverty.' Northern Ireland could not be reformed: 'The six counties is a politically contrived and manipulated "state" designed specifically to allow the permanent domination of one section of the community over the other. Any reforms which it is forced to accept are only cosmetic in nature and in essence not worth the paper they are written on ... The republican movement will not settle for anything less than British withdrawal.'[109]

And they sought to maintain pressure through violence in order to produce just such a result. Ten years after they had killed their first British soldier of the modern troubles, the IRA issued a statement appealing to the British people: according to this statement the IRA wanted peace, and 'the war in Ireland could be ended very quickly if the British government acknowledged the democratic right of the Irish nation to self-determination, and announced a British withdrawal from Ireland and an amnesty for all political prisoners'. The IRA appealed to the British people 'to put pressure on their government to withdraw from Ireland and no other young British soldiers need die in a war which the British government will lose in the end'.[110]

In June 1977 the annual Bodenstown speech at Wolfe Tone's grave was delivered by longstanding republican Jimmy Drumm. Written by Gerry Adams and Danny Morrison, this proved to be a key articulation of the broadening republican vision for coming years of struggle. The gun was not enough.

> We find that a successful war of liberation cannot be fought exclusively on the backs of the oppressed in the six counties, nor around the physical presence of the British Army. Hatred and resentment of this Army cannot sustain the war, and the isolation of socialist republicans around the armed struggle is dangerous and has produced, at least in some circles, the reformist notion that 'Ulster' is the issue, which can be somehow resolved without the mobilizaton of the working-class in the twenty-six counties. We need a positive tie-in with the mass of the Irish people ... The forging of strong links between the republican movement and the workers of Ireland and radical trade unionists will create an irrepressible mass movement ...

The broadening-out of struggle would not involve a dilution of republican aims: 'we are not prepared to even discuss any watering down of our demands. We can see no future in participating in a restructured Stormont, even with power-sharing and a bill of rights. Nor certainly we will never accept the legitimacy of the Free State [Republic of Ireland]. A fascist state designed to cater for the privileged capitalist sycophants. No! To even contemplate acceptance of either of these partitionist states would be a betrayal of all that Tone preached and died for.'[111]

And the violent campaign continued. On 21 May 1977 the Provisionals' *Republican News* carried the headline, 'SAS Captain Executed'. The IRA's First Battalion in south Armagh was quoted as saying: 'Captain Robert Laurence Nairac was an SAS man and had been operating in the South Armagh area for some time. We arrested him on Saturday night [14 May 1977] and executed him after interrogation in which he admitted he was in an SAS unit.' Robert Nairac was not, in fact, a member of the SAS, but rather a Grenadier Guardsman, who had been educated at Ampleforth (interestingly, the English Catholic public school at which IRA legend Ernie O'Malley had chosen to have his own sons educated) and then at Lincoln College, Oxford. He had spent most of what turned out to be the last four years of his life in Ulster, as an intelligence gatherer for the Army. He had been taken from the car park of the Three Steps Inn, Drumintee, south Armagh (where he had gone, intentionally under cover); was tortured by brutal beating in a vain attempt to make him divulge information; and was then shot dead in a field across the border in County Louth. Nairac's body was never found. Possibly it was buried somewhere near Belfast, possibly in the Republic of Ireland; much currency has also been given to the gruesome suggestion that it was, in fact, destroyed by being put by republicans through a meat-mincer.[112] County Armagh IRA man Liam Townson was among those found guilty in relation to the killing. Nairac himself was posthumously awarded the George Cross, for courage and heroism in danger. Something of a loner in life, he was remembered in death by his closest friend from Oxford as 'a romantic, an enthusiast, simple-hearted, brave'.[113]

The Provos aimed also at more elevated targets. In August 1977 Queen Elizabeth II visited Ulster during her silver jubilee, and the IRA attempted to kill her with a bomb when she visited a university at Coleraine. (The bomb went off after she had left.) In May 1981 the Provos again attempted, without success, to kill the woman they referred to as 'Queen Elizabrit',[114] this time in the Shetland Islands. But targets were frequently hit, and sometimes with shocking consequences. On 17 February 1978 twelve Protestants were killed when the IRA bombed the La Mon House restaurant at Gransha, near Comber in County Down. Petrol had been attached in containers to the bombs, thereby producing a far worse blaze: the remains of victims were so badly burned that identification was very difficult. One policeman observed, 'The bodies are just a charred mess. I've never seen such a horrible sight. There are no human features left on any of them.'[115]

The previous February, Jeffrey Agate, manager of the Derry Du Pont factory, was shot dead by the Provisionals. IRA leader Seamus Twomey argued: 'All British industrialists are targets. They are exploiting the Irish working class'; all those 'directly connected with British imperialism are definite targets'. And *Republican News* – under the headline, 'Panic Hits Local Capitalists as IRA Attacks Grass-Roots Imperialism' – asserted of attacks on members of the business class such as Mr Agate: 'The revolutionary Irish Republican Army is out to break the backs of these bulwarks of British imperialism.'[116] So these were emphatically years of IRA violence as well as republican prison victimhood.

And the IRA were not the only republicans waging war against the British. In March 1979 the INLA killed Conservative Party politician and close friend of Margaret Thatcher, Airey Neave, with a car-bomb in London. A Colditz escapee during the Second World War – 'the first Britisher to make a home run from Colditz', as one of his fellow POWs put it[117] – and a firm anti-Nazi, Neave had had a secret service career and was Conservative spokesman on Northern Ireland; he was also a strong right-wing opponent of Irish republican paramilitarism. The bomb that killed him had been fitted to his car near his flat, and exploded as Neave was driving out of the MPs' car park in the Palace of Westminster.[118] The stunning event won prominence for the republican socialist paramilitaries. As one of their then leaders later put it, 'The killing of Neave put the INLA on the map and made people realise the organisation was very serious about its war with Britain.'[119]

Later in the year, the IRA were to trump even this dramatic strike. On 27 August two IRA operations demanded worldwide attention as, in the words of the newly merged[120] *An Phoblacht/Republican News*, the 'IRA make Britain pay: Mountbatten executed – 18 British soldiers die'.[121] Louis Mountbatten, Earl Mountbatten of Burma, had been the last Viceroy of India. On the morning of the 27th his boat was blown up a short distance from shore at Mullaghmore, County Sligo, in the Republic of Ireland, by the IRA. Mountbatten was killed (along with his fourteen-year-old grandson and another teenage boy; a fourth person was fatally injured); he had taken holidays in Ireland for years, and had long been considered by the IRA as a possible target. He and his companions were comparatively soft victims, and the killing of the seventy-nine-year-old Earl carried with it great anti-royal, anti-establishment prestige. (Ironically, the IRA here killed one of the most skilled decolonizers within the British elite, since Mountbatten had managed British disengagement from India in a spirit of greater goodwill than most would have ensured.) He had been a military leader of some swagger, not least during the Second World War. And he was the cousin of the Queen of England (the Queen's eldest son writing in his diary after the killing, 'Life will *never* be the same now that he has gone').[122]

The IRA's own description of their spectacular operation described Mountbatten's killing as

> a discriminate operation to bring to the attention of the English people the continuing occupation of our country ... The British Army acknowledge that after ten years of war it cannot defeat us but yet the British government continue with the oppression of our people and the torture of our comrades in the H-Blocks. Well, for this we will tear out their sentimental, imperialist heart. The death of Mountbatten and the tributes paid to him will be seen in sharp contrast to the apathy of the British government and the English people to the deaths of over three hundred British soldiers, and the deaths of Irish men, women and children at the hands of their forces.[123]

As if to underline the point, the IRA on the same day as the Mountbatten killing also caused the deaths of eighteen British soldiers near Warrenpoint in County Down. The operation was cleverly conceived, and involved two explosions. Numerous soldiers were killed in the first, which was triggered by two IRA men across the border in the Republic of Ireland as a British Army vehicle passed the tower of Narrow Water Castle. Then, post-explosion, more British soldiers arrived as back-up and – as the IRA had anticipated – they took cover in an old gatehouse nearby. The IRA had left another bomb to target these soldiers and this – again, detonated by remote control from the Republic – brought the death toll to eighteen. The IRA (more specifically, their south Armagh Brigade, in whose area the Mountbatten bomb had also been constructed) had known that soldiers would race to the scene of an explosion such as the first; they had correctly guessed where such troops would seek cover; and they had secured a dramatic hit as a result, inflicting on the Army its heaviest single-operation losses of the troubles. One of the two IRA men who detonated the Warrenpoint bombs, Brendan Burns, was himself to be killed when in February 1988 a bomb on which he was working prematurely exploded. And the human cost, even to those British soldiers who survived Warrenpoint, could be enormous: 'On the physical side I'm now very restricted. My hands shake . . . and I haven't got any control over it . . . Before, I was physically very active. What I miss now is with the kids, not being able to participate in the stuff I know I would enjoy.'[124]

After Warrenpoint, in October 1979, Maurice Oldfield – the former head of Britain's Secret Intelligence Service, MI6 – was appointed British chief security coordinator for Northern Ireland, with the mission to plug gaps and sort out problems between the different arms of the intelligence community in the north. This move demonstrated a recognition that the intelligence war – grubby and clandestine as it necessarily was – carried great significance for the outcome of the troubles. So, too, did the publicity, or propaganda, war. And here too – though less bloodily than on 27 August – the British suffered a setback with the publication of the Bennett Report. A committee had been set up by the Northern Ireland authorities to investigate allegations of ill-treatment during police interrogation, and its report of March 1979 stated embarrassingly that medical evidence indeed showed injuries to have been sustained during police detention – injuries that were not self-inflicted. The far from republican *Belfast Telegraph* itself observed, 'By any standards, the Bennett Committee Report is a deeply disturbing document, whose repercussions will be felt throughout the Northern Ireland community for years to come . . .

In broad terms, it found the allegations of police ill-treatment proven, though it does not attempt to quantify the problem. Hardly any aspect of the system for dealing with suspects, from interrogation to the processing of complaints, escapes criticism.'[125] Claims frequently made in *An Phoblacht/Republican News* might be given overly stark or exaggerated prominence, but they were not without some basis.

Such findings as those of Judge Bennett related to one of the key aspects of the IRA's campaign, namely the leverage upon London that could be gained by means of international opinion. One of the costs that the IRA hoped to raise for the British was that of internationally embarrassing stories emerging from their role in the north. Another international dimension to the IRA's struggle was its need to gain material support. Here, again, the USA was important in providing much sustenance. (Though it should also be noted that the authorities there were actively hostile to the IRA, and were expressly keen to combat the Provisionals.)[126] And the IRA could – as earlier in its history – take backing from a range of apparently divergent international sources. If it was accepted from sympathetic US sources, then it was also drawn from powers opposed to the USA (Libya being a major example).

In other ways too the IRA sought to internationalize their struggle. They targeted British forces abroad, an IRA spokesman in February 1980 outlining the thinking behind attacks on such targets in mainland Europe. The IRA intended to harass soldiers 'the way they've been harassing and killing nationalist people', and to keep Ireland on their minds even while they were stationed elsewhere,

> so that it haunts them and they do something about not wanting to go back. Overseas attacks also have a prestige value and internationalise the war in Ireland. The British government has been successful in suppressing news about the struggle in the North . . . But we have kept Ireland in the world headlines, our struggle is kept in the news and sooner or later an expression of discontentment, probably from the English people rather than from the Army, will snowball and the British government's ability and will to stay, which we are sapping, will completely snap.[127]

Nor were soldiers the only targets. In March 1979 the British Ambassador to the Hague, Richard Sykes, was shot and killed by the

Provisionals. For the IRA's hope remained that violent pressure would eventually achieve the desired change of attitude in London. The transfer of power in 1979 from Labour to the Conservatives had made little difference to them here, though they did keep an eye on the nuances of British politics. Republicans, for example, noted anti-partitionist statements made early in 1980 by British Labour politician Tony Benn, and identified him as a possible future British Prime Minister; they also, however, commented that he had been 'an unobjecting member of the Labour cabinet during [Roy] Mason's tyrannical term as Northern direct-ruler', adding that he 'normally keeps quiet on Ireland'.[128] This is a view endorsed by Benn's biographer – 'Benn had little to say about Northern Ireland' – who points out that the Labour politician had himself come close to being an unintended victim of IRA bombings in England during the 1970s.[129] Irish republicans also noted Labour politician Denis Healey's less sympathetic attitude. Observing that Healey was 'strongly tipped as the next British Labour Prime Minister', *An Phoblacht/Republican News* commented on his scepticism about whether a united Ireland represented a solution to the problem.[130]

So it was through their own struggle forcing the issue, rather than through instinctive sympathy from British politicians, that the Provisionals anticipated progress being made. The British Labour Party's refusal to support Irish republican demands led to its being condemned as imperialistic and colonialist in approach,[131] just as fierce criticism was levelled at the Irish traitors south of the border. Even Fianna Fáil, the supposedly more republican of the two main southern parties, was considered a collaborator with Britain. At the June 1980 Wolfe Tone commemoration at Bodenstown in County Kildare, Derry Sinn Féiner Martha McClelland delivered the republican oration and claimed: 'we are the only organisation in Ireland that can march to this great man's grave with our heads in the air and pride in our hearts – we who have kept faith. When Fianna Fáil creep into this cemetery, they abuse what Wolfe Tone – the revolutionary soldier, the separatist – stood for most clearly. Opportunism draws them here, not real honour of Tone, for Tone can be truly honoured only by carrying on his struggle in the most effective way possible: through force of arms.'[132]

At the previous year's commemoration, a more famous republican had delivered the words. On Sunday 17 June 1979 Gerry Adams, then Sinn Féin Vice-President, spoke at the graveside of the founding father of Irish republicanism and strongly condemned Irish as well as British governments: 'Fianna Fáil promises everything and delivers nothing except more sell-outs on national, social, cultural and economic issues.' Adams declared confidence in the military outcome of the republican struggle – 'The IRA has shown its ability to sustain a protracted and hard-hitting campaign. That the British face military defeat is inevitable and obvious' – but stressed that the republican vision involved more than just violence: 'We are not, and never have been, merely a "Brits-out" movement'; 'As republicans we stand with the have-nots against the haves. We stand with the underprivileged, the young, the unemployed, the workers – the people of no property'; 'We are opposed to big business, to multi-nationalism . . . We stand opposed to all forms and all manifestations of imperialism and capitalism. We stand for an Ireland free, united, socialist and Gaelic.'[133]

And republicans would pursue this through a variety of means. In particular now, elections might be considered a legitimate way of mobilizing and expressing republican opinion. The IRA's public stance regarding constitutional politics was, in its own words of 1981, 'quite simple and clear cut . . . Outside of a thirty-two-county sovereign, independent democracy the IRA will have no involvement in what is loosely called constitutional politics.' But there was, the organization argued, a need to enable the Irish people to seize political and economic control of their own destinies: 'Whether this can be assisted by an intervention in the electoral process should be the basis for discussion within republican circles. What should not be the basis for discussion is whether this intervention means a run-down of the armed struggle. It patently does not.'[134] Thus the militant republican movement was coming to espouse a combination of violent and of more conventional political argument. In the wake of the 1981 hunger strike, this approach was given famous expression by Sinn Féin's Danny Morrison. On 31 October of that year, at the party's *ard fheis* (convention) in Dublin, Morrison sought to reassure people that the development of electoral politics by Sinn Féin need not mean the dilution of republican commitment to more forceful methods; violence could complement politics: 'Who here really believes we can win the war through the ballot box? But will anyone here object if, with a ballot paper in this hand, and an Armalite in this hand, we take power in Ireland?'[135] A republican intellectual as fascinated by Mahler as by Machiavelli, Morrison had in fact thought of the now celebrated phraseology 'about ten seconds' before he spoke: 'I wanted to reassure people that it *was* possible to support the waging of an armed struggle and simultaneously take part in electoral politics – even though deep down I knew there were contradictions. I knew there was a ceiling to how far you could go.'[136]

A statement as famous – and as frequently misquoted! – as Morrison's was to follow shortly afterwards from his prime-ministerial opponent: 'I take the view that Northern Ireland is part of the United Kingdom. It is accepted that it is part of the union. It will remain so unless they [the people of Northern Ireland] wish to the contrary ... Northern Ireland is part of the United Kingdom – as much as my constituency is.'[137]

By the time these remarks were made (10 November 1981), the IRA were in a stronger position than they had enjoyed at Margaret Thatcher's 1979 accession to power. On Saturday 14 November 1981 Revd Robert Bradford, unionist MP for south Belfast since 1974 and a former Methodist minister, was killed by the republican army. Bradford had taken an anti-ecumenical stance in religion and had been very strongly opposed to political ecumenism also, as embodied in the Sunningdale Agreement. He had been very outspoken against the Provisionals, especially regarding their fund-raising activities, into which he had delved. Bradford had been the target of previous attacks, and an IRA spokesman justified his killing by describing him as 'one of the ultra-reactionary loyalists who was vitriolic in his sectarian and racist outbursts against nationalism in any form. Such people are responsible to a considerable degree for motivating the series of purely sectarian attacks on ordinary nationalists, and while they do not personally pull the trigger they provide the ideological framework for the UDA and UVF gunmen who do the murdering.'[138] The elegiac memoir written by Bradford's widow certainly reflected the MP's deep hostility towards the IRA; but also, more gently, it recorded her personal loss: 'The following Saturday was an horrific day for me as I relived every moment of the previous one. I stood alone in the cemetery, weeping silently, trying to understand.' Among the tributes to Bradford following his death was one carrying the same biblical verse (John 15:13) that Bobby Sands had himself deployed: 'Greater love hath no man than that he lay down his life for his friends.'[139]

SIX

POLITICIZATION AND THE CYCLE OF VIOLENCE
1981–8

1

'People are asking us, "How do you describe prison?" The
one that I came up with was that it's like school, only you
don't go home when the bell rings. If you can imagine that
type of cloistering . . . you have to develop a different way of
thinking, a much more open way of thinking, to deal with
people.'

Declan Moen, on republican imprisonment[1]

At the start of the 1980s the Provisionals were emerging as a movement
combining a campaign of attritional violence with a more committedly
political profile. The Sinn Féin *ard fheis* of 1981 decided that, while
abstention would remain in place for the Dublin and London parliaments, and for any Stormont assembly, the party would put up
candidates in the north's local elections and would take take any seats
thus won. They first contested district council elections in 1985,
winning 12 per cent of first-preference votes. And even by 1982, the
Sinn Féin party's importance was clear to former IRA hunger-striker
Raymond McCartney, because 'the armed struggle in fact needed a
sound political machine geared to use itself as another weapon to
help rid us of foreign imperialism north and south of our falsely
divided country'.[2] Earlier in the year an IRA spokesperson had
admitted that the organization had recently experienced 'a number of
problems, logistical problems or problems with materials and supplies',[3] although the campaign continued – with bloody effect. Indeed,
for some within the movement, there had developed a certain

immunity to the ghastliness: 'I had become hardened to death ...
Death had become my way of life, my everyday mission, my business,
my reason for being.'[4]

For those inside the jails, however, the struggle had its own
distinctive dimensions. People such as Raymond McCartney himself
found their lives defined by long-term incarceration: imprisoned during 1977–94 in the H-Blocks, on hunger strike for fifty-three days in
1980, OC H-Blocks during 1989–91, McCartney exemplified committed republican prison struggle. The culture of the jails remained one of
dynamism and of activist energy, and IRA prisoners saw themselves
very much still involved in and connected with the war being pros-
ecuted by their comrades outside. As during earlier periods of IRA
imprisonment, they had their own command structures in the jails;
they remained part of the IRA; and, just as legal battles formed a part
of republican struggle,[5] so too the experience of those whom the legal
system had placed in jail continued to lie at the heart of IRA politics.

Republican prisoners frequently displayed impressive autodidactic
commitment. The post-hunger-strike years also saw many pursue
formal programmes of study, including Open University degrees. OU
courses on politics, sociology and third-world studies combined republican enthusiasms with self-improvement, and a way of loosening the
shackles and of gaining some degree of autonomy. Patrick Magee (who
began to study in jail in 1989, after four years inside, and who was to
pursue undergraduate and postgraduate courses while there) recalled
tellingly: 'Partly, I began to study in order to push the walls back, to
gain a semblance of self-determination in what was an extremely
controlled environment.'[6]

In the 1980s H-Blocks themselves, strong commitment to the
culture of debate complemented educational zeal. As Sean Murray
(H-Blocks 1981–7) put it, 'we had to use our time to the best possible
advantage and one of the best ways to do that was to educate and
politicise ourselves'.[7] In the 1970s IRA prisoners had shunned prison
educational facilities, fearing that involvement with them might
dilute political commitment; in the H-Blocks in the 1980s, by contrast, prisoners availed themselves of the opportunities provided by the
prison authorities, as a complement to their own autodidactic work.

It was not that there had been no political discussion and education
among pre-1981 IRA prisoners: in the 1970s cages there had been Irish

language classes and lectures on republicanism, as well as wide-ranging reading. In jail 'you've got that space to analyse'; 'even in '73, '74 in jail there was political debate going'.[8] In Gerry Kelly's phrase, the prisoners were 'educating for revolution'.[9] Again, during the blanket protest, there had been an intensity of political discussion. Laurence McKeown: 'The blanket protest was, I think, one of the biggest periods of education in my life, even though you had no access to books and literature: discussing . . . thinking of your own opinion, reflecting on it, challenging or being challenged';[10] Anthony McIntyre: 'We had always tried to prompt discussion during the blanket protest . . . We used to call our corner "Commie Corner" in our wing on the blanket because we always used to debate the issues.'[11] So there was nothing new in itself about discussion and reading by IRA prisoners. Just as in the 1920s, when literary republicans such as Peadar O'Donnell and Ernie O'Malley had read and discussed while incarcerated, so too the Provisionals made good, thoughtful use of their time in jail, using it to read, to reflect and to debate.

But after the 1981 hunger strike the scale and coordination of such endeavours in the H-Blocks changed, with access again to books for the first time in years. As noted earlier, during the late 1970s prison protest those politically zealous prisoners had gone without books, newspapers and magazines; when, in years after the strike, that situation changed and books were again allowed in the H-Blocks, there was an energetic enthusiasm for reading. Among those whose work was read and whose ideas had a major influence on republican prisoners was Paulo Freire (1921–97). Professor at the Pontifical Catholic University of São Paulo, Freire celebratedly argued against what he called 'the banking concept of education', in which teachers know everything, think, talk and teach, while students know nothing, listen meekly and are taught.[12] This idea was not entirely new. It is possible to find examples, from much earlier, of people arguing that the teacher should be seen as colleague and fellow learner rather than all-wise imparter of truth.[13] But Freire had an infectious zeal for the interweaving of action and reflection (praxis), and for what he saw as an exciting new kind of education: 'Through dialogue, the teacher-of-the-students and the students-of-the-teacher cease to exist and a new term emerges: teacher-student with students-teachers. The teacher is no longer merely the-one-who-teaches, but one who is himself taught in dialogue with the students, who in turn while being taught also teach. They become jointly responsible for a process in which all grow.'[14]

IRA prisoners came to embrace some of these ideas, and republicans in the jails were keen, in particular, to move away from the hierarchical notions of knowing teacher and passive students. Freire thus reinforced and helped to focus republican prisoners' approach to learning, to discussion, to education. Laurence McKeown first came across Freire's writing in 1982, and recalls: 'It was absolutely brilliant: you were reading it and it was as if things were clicking in your head, these switches, things that you had been doing in a disorganized fashion . . . It wasn't that somebody lifted up a Paulo Freire book and [had] some major revelation . . . We got Freire at the right time: we'd already been doing this journey during the blanket protest and now Freire put words on it and what it was we were thinking.'[15] People would discuss Freire's ideas, which pointed towards a more communal approach to daily existence, towards egalitarianism rather than militaristic hierarchy. The H-Blocks of the 1980s saw republican prisoners set up what were in effect wing communes, as the notion of the group came to dominate their thinking.

Thus Freire's ideas not only related to the prisoners' engaged and active approach to education, but had an impact also on the way they daily lived. Collectivization and collective self-regulation began to compete with a formal chain of command. There would still be specific IRA work that required formal command structures and so on. But, in Laurence McKeown's words, 'Most of the rest of the time in jail is just like people living in a community: they should be able to work out their own thing without being told.'[16]

The openness and egalitarianism of the IRA jail experience should not, of course, be naïvely painted. There is certainly some evidence to suggest that prison debates were, to some extent, constrained by leadership concerns at the dangers of heterodoxy: 'It got to the point where we were getting papers in on a Sunday [with] pages, complete pages, taken out – not by the screws but by our own, the [IRA] staff of the jail; papers coming in censored'; there was 'open debate within certain parameters – very, very tight parameters'.[17] But the excitement generated by books such as Freire's did reflect and contribute towards a culture within the H-Blocks of eagerness and hunger for ideas and learning. As Jackie McMullan has put it, 'Freire argues that education

1. British soldiers in Dublin during the 1916 Easter Rising

2. Irish Republican
leader Michael Collins
(1890–1922), seated
second from the left

3. IRA leader
Ernie O'Malley
(1897–1957)

4. Civil rights demonstrators at a police cordon, Derry, November 1968

5. Bloody Sunday, Derry, 30 January 1972

6. The aftermath
of the IRA explosion
at the Bayardo Bar,
Belfast, August 1975

7. IRA hunger-striker
Bobby Sands (1954–81)

8. The Grand Hotel, Brighton, following the IRA's 1984 bomb during
the Conservative Party Conference

9. The Cenotaph, Enniskillen, with the community centre devastated by the IRA bomb of November 1987

10. Funeral of the Harte brothers, IRA men shot by the SAS in August 1988 in County Tyrone

11. IRA Easter Statement, Crossmaglen, South Armagh, 1996

12. Belfast graffiti, 1996

13. *Left*. Martin McGuinness, Derry, 1996

14. *Below*. Gerry Adams, after voting at the local polling station in Andersonstown, Belfast, 1997

15. *Bottom, left*. Patrick Magee, 2002. Magee was imprisoned for his part in the 1984 Brighton bombing

16. *Bottom, right*. Danny Morrison, 2002

in its true sense should be a revolutionary force ... I felt exhilarated on first reading Freire'.[18]

Thus reading and studying in jail involved self-improvement overlaid with political commitment: 'Certainly,' says Patrick Magee, 'there was an element of personal development in education in jail. You worked to be able to articulate better your political perspective, and I saw education as a means to an end.'[19] In the H-Blocks, one of the most striking features of IRA experience in the troubles is the specific educational endeavour that grew after the 1981 hunger strike. Part of this was centred on the impressive library that they built up during the decade in the Blocks. In the pre-1976 cages, republican prisoners had enjoyed good conditions in terms of access to reading matter; then during the 1976–81 Maze protests, as we have seen, their non-acquiescence under the regime led to their being denied reading material except the Bible (a copy of which was in every cell). Once – gradually, after the hunger strike – books were again allowed in, prisoners keenly built up a library of their own, in addition to the official jail library, which was also used. Prisoners during the 1980s came to be paid a few pounds a week each for their 'work' (cleaning cells, cleaning toilets, mopping the landings and so on), and some of that money went to pay communally for tobacco, some for chocolate, crisps and lemonade to enjoy during the twice-weekly video 'party', and some towards forming an effective book fund. Books were suggested and ordered – paperbacks mostly, the spines of hardback books being seen by the authorities as a possible smuggling route into the jail. There developed a mixture of formal lending procedures and of people just taking a book out and being relied on to put it back again: 'after five years of being starved of any literature or stimulation whatsoever, we were into it big time ... I would have been reading three books a week, and I was a slow reader. I know people who were reading a book every day. We were just eating it up ... We had a conscious programme of organizing, developing ourselves ... The commitment was a hundred per cent. Everyone was involved in it, everyone had an appetite for it – and we had the time.'[20]

At first, prisoners were not allowed by the authorities simply to get any books they wanted; there were different stages to the building up of reading materials, with greater freedom to acquire a wider range of books gradually emerging. But by the mid to late 1980s, prisoners were allowed practically anything. The collection (which was briefly housed in Belfast's Linen Hall Library after the closure of the Maze) was impressively broad and serious in range. The occasional lighter title (such as Nick Hornby's Arsenalesque memoir *Fever Pitch*) stood out from the general trend towards politics, history, literature and international affairs. These were politically minded prisoners, and their reading showed as much. Patrick Magee, transferred to the H-Blocks in August 1996, was struck by 'how overly earnest much of the material was, particularly all those texts about historical materialism'.[21]

The collection was indeed very left-wing, its shelves packed with volumes such as Chris Harman's *How Marxism Works*, Progress Publishers' books such as Dmitri Klementyez and Tamara Vassilyeva's *What is Socialism?*, and many works by legendary Marxist thinkers and leaders: Lenin (*Imperialism, the Highest Stage of Capitalism*; *The State and Revolution*; *What is to be Done?*; *Marxism on the State*; *On Socialist Democracy*); Trotsky (*The History of the Russian Revolution*; *Fascism, Stalinism and the United Front*; *My Life: An Attempt at an Autobiography*); Marx and Engels (*Selected Works in One Volume*; *Manifesto of the Communist Party*; Marx's *The Civil War in France*); Enver Hoxha's *Laying the Foundations of the New Albania*; Mao's *Four Essays on Philosophy*. For IRA prisoners in the 1980s H-Blocks were profoundly influenced by left-wing thought. Laurence McKeown: 'the dominant ideology among republican prisoners in the H-Blocks in the 1980s was that of a revolutionary, left-wing, socialist, Marxist orientation';[22] Jackie McMullan: 'That's what we were into. That was people's inclination, to read that type of literature.'[23]

But while books about Castro and Cuba, and volumes by Marx and Lenin, preoccupied the incarcerated soldiers, their comrades on the outside were less committedly leftist in defining the republican struggle according to Marxist orientation. Indeed, some republicans considered it appropriate that the hard-left material should *not* influence the wider movement too much. As one fellow prisoner commented, on Marxist material, to Anthony McIntyre in jail, ' "You know, there really is a place in the movement for all this." I said, "Where is it?" He said, "Here".'[24] Thus, for some, it seemed a good idea that Marxism itself be imprisoned, and this should caution against exaggerating the Marxianization of the IRA during the 1980s. 'A lot of people in the movement outside were traditional republicans. A lot of them had joined the republican movement just as a response to events: '69, internment, Bloody Sunday, whatever it was';[25] 'The bulk of that leftism [as exemplified in the H-Blocks books] was contained and confined to the prison'.[26] So Marxism had its appeal, but also its limitations as far as the republican movement was concerned. Leftist politics offered an appealing theoretical, analytical framework through which prisoners could view the world in these years. As Danny Morrison put it, 'Marxist-Leninism provided a matrix which they fitted into perfectly. It explained the world. It was very fundamentalist, very pure. There was a theoretical basis to it. You could analyse sociology from that point of view, philosophy, literature . . . it was all there, it fitted. And there was a rush at it . . . People in the jail were far more advanced than the people on the outside.'[27]

It was not that there was no leftist tinge to the wider republican movement in these years, for some of the arguments used inside the prison could be heard outside as well. Writing from H-Block 4 in January 1983, Gerard Hodgins asserted that 'The republican doctrine encompasses several facets, one of which is socialism. We stand for a unified, socialist Ireland . . . Socialism is a doctrine for the advance of the working class, and it is in this noble class that the republican movement has its foundations.'[28] Outside, Martin McGuinness, delivering the annual Wolfe Tone oration in 1986, proclaimed: 'We are a socialist republican movement, a movement that supports the use of armed struggle in the six counties and the establishment of a socialist republic in the thirty-two counties of Ireland.'[29] While drawing on 1970s leftist roots, the 1980s marked a high point of IRA left-wing sympathy. The hard-left volumes that enriched the prisoners' reflections in the 1980s H-Blocks were very much of that time and place.

If the prisoners read left-leaning critiques of capitalism (such as Philip Armstrong, Andrew Glyn and John Harrison's *Capitalism since World War Two*), then they also focused much attention on those other struggles, internationally, with which they identified their own war. Again, this had roots in the earlier period of imprisonment (Jackie McMullan: 'I remember during the blanket protest getting stuff smuggled from the cages dealing with those struggles, with Cuba, with Vietnam').[30] But, again, it reached a crescendo in the H-Blocks in the 1980s. The prisoners collected books such as Thomas Kiernan's biography of Yasser Arafat, Karl Grossman's *Nicaragua: America's New*

Vietnam, Liisa North's *Bitter Grounds: Roots of Revolt in El Salvador*, Helena Cobban's *The Palestinian Liberation Organisation*, Mary Benson's *Nelson Mandela* and Winnie Mandela's *Part of My Soul*; speeches by Nicaragua's Sandinista leaders; Alex Callinicos's Marxist *South Africa between Reform and Revolution*, Phil Marshall's *Intifada* and Graham Usher's *Palestine in Crisis*. The IRA were self-conscious revolutionaries, identifying with revolutions and attempted revolutions elsewhere.[31]

And, of course, they were decidedly anti-colonial in their thinking. Their shelves housed many copies of the writings of Frantz Fanon, who had influenced key republicans (including Bobby Sands) since the 1970s. It was in that decade that Tom Hartley introduced Danny Morrison to Fanon and, for Hartley himself, this author of classic anti-colonial literature made sense of behaviour in a situation such as the north of Ireland: Fanon 'looked at the psychology of the oppressed, and how they worked through the pain of colonialism'.[32] Indeed, close reading of Fanon clearly demonstrates why republicans might want multiple copies of *The Wretched of the Earth* on their H-Block shelves:

> National liberation, national renaissance, the restoration of nationhood to the people, commonwealth: whatever may be the headings used or the new formulas introduced, decolonisation is always a violent phenomenon ... In decolonisation, there is therefore the need of a complete calling in question of the colonial situation. If we wish to describe it precisely, we might find it in the well-known words: "The last shall be first and the first last." Decolonisation is the putting into practice of this sentence ... For if the last shall be first, this will only come to pass after a murderous and decisive struggle between the two protagonists. That affirmed intention to place the last at the head of things, and to make them climb at a pace (too quickly, some say) the well-known steps which characterise an organised society, can only triumph if we use all means to turn the scale, including, of course, that of violence.[33]

National freedom, national rebirth, decolonization through necessary violence – all of this suited and reinforced IRA thinking on Ireland. For Fanon argued, in relation to decolonization, that 'The native who decides to put the programme into practice, and to become its moving force, is ready for violence at all times. From birth it is clear to him that this narrow world, strewn with prohibitions, can only be called in question by absolute violence.'[34] Fanon's attitude towards this violence was far from simple. For him, it had to be seen as a response to the violence of the colonist; and it is not difficult to hear the echoes in IRA thinking, of a Fanonist argument that the violence of the colonized can only be understood within the context of the colonizer's own prior violent actions.

More directly, the prisoners read material that offered an explicit linking of colonial experience elsewhere to the Irish situation. Raymond Crotty's *Ireland in Crisis* is an example, a book that 'tries to explain why for so long so many of us have been denied a livelihood in Ireland ... the failure of the Irish to get a livelihood in their own country is part of a much larger problem. It is part of the heritage of capitalist colonialism; or of the vast, spreading and worsening poverty of all the countries of the Third World which, like Ireland, are former colonies of the capitalist system.'[35]

Committed as they were to Irish cultural and historical awareness, during the blanket protest many IRA prisoners had learned Irish; for one thing, the prison officers could not understand what you were saying if you spoke it. Later, there were *Gaeltacht* wings in the H-Blocks (the first being set up in the mid-1990s), wings in which prisoners spoke Irish and where republican Declan Moen spent two years in the 1990s:

> the best wings I've ever been on ... Those wings were crucial. They were brilliant. They have, to me, generated a whole new level of dynamism and activism within the republican movement. Those people who have come out are Irish language activists to the core, a lot of them, and they are also political activists to the core. What I find really interesting about [the] Irish language is that when you speak it in an Irish environment twenty-four hours a day – non-English environment – it creates little, subtle personality changes. I noticed that people who would have been reasonably boisterous on an ordinary wing, and a little bit more cynical – their personality changed slightly, because the concepts in Irish are completely different. It's very difficult to lose your temper in Irish because the concepts don't exist, the words don't exist for it ... Irish language became a massive motivating factor for people's lives; there is

nobody who was on those wings who didn't enjoy them tremen-
dously and say they are the best times I've ever had in jail.[36]

So the Irish language not only had a practical value for IRA
prisoners as a means of secret communication, but a political value
too. 'Learning and speaking the Irish language ... had significance for
a number of reasons, some practical and some political. It was a means
through which to communicate to comrades; to exclude enemies; to
relieve boredom and stimulate the mind; and ultimately, through
which to express identity. It was therefore a political and subversive
pursuit.'[37]

Much energy was also devoted to absorption in Irish historical and
political reading. Just as Bobby Sands's socialism had sturdy Irish
intellectual roots (Sands noting in his diary for 9 March 1981 his great
admiration for two Irish republican heroes of the left: 'I always keep
thinking of James Connolly ... Connolly has always been the man that
I look up to. I always have tremendous feeling for Liam Mellows as
well'),[38] so too the post-1981 prisoners soaked themselves in such
material. The 1916 rebel leader Connolly was a general favourite:
Labour in Irish History; a well thumbed, extensively annotated copy of
Peter Berresford Ellis's 1970s edition of Connolly's selected writings;
and numerous treatments of the great leader – Andy Johnston, James
Larragy and Edward McWilliams's *Connolly: A Marxist Analysis*; David
Howell's *A Lost Left*; Sean Cronin's *Young Connolly*; Bernard Ransom's
Connolly's Marxism; and Desmond Greaves's classic biography.

But there was a wider range of historical works too: F. S. L. Lyons's
Ireland Since the Famine and his *Culture and Anarchy in Ireland*; John
A. Murphy's *Ireland in the Twentieth Century*; Gearóid Ó Tuathaigh's
Ireland before the Famine; A. T. Q. Stewart's *The Narrow Ground*; Clare
O'Halloran's *Partition and the Limits of Irish Nationalism*; and Ronan
Fanning's *Independent Ireland*. And republican writers were also con-
spicuous in the IRA's H-Blocks reading. John Mitchel's *Jail Journal*
accompanied a well thumbed copy of Ernie O'Malley's IRA memoir,
On Another Man's Wound, and work by Peadar O'Donnell and Sean
O'Faolain. Not that the prisoners were merely wallowing in mystical
pasts: 'It's not looking to gain inspiration or glory from these great
defeats in the past. It's only about learning from the mistakes of the
past so that there are great victories in the future ... It was always

geared towards "what do we take out of this now?" '[39] Practical, present-centred and political.

What about religion? Ex-prisoners now tend to play down the significance on their 1980s H-Block shelves of the very many Bibles – this was, after all, the one book that the authorities had always given out. 'It wasn't because they read the Bible ... There was a Bible in every cell. A Bible with very thin paper. We used to use the Bible paper for rolling cigarettes, for writing notes.'[40] In contrast to the earlier protest period, the later 1980s H-Block prisoners were something of an 'irreligious bunch'; by the 1990s, 'Nobody gave a hoot about the Bible.'[41] They did seem to give a hoot about wider political issues, though, amassing texts on British politics (including at least one biography of Margaret Thatcher, Hugo Young's *One of Us*), theories of justice and of nationalism and (unsurprisingly, perhaps) of guerrilla warfare.

Of course, having books on the shelf does not mean that everybody read them, and – as suggested – there were differences of emphasis between imprisoned IRA members and those still at large. But in reflecting a major commitment to reading, debating and learning (and in demonstrating a strongly left-wing, anti-colonial focus for their politics), these books do form an evocative part of the story of the IRA – albeit one firmly rooted in that enclosed time and space.

2

'The Irish Republican Army cannot be beaten because it is a people's army, recruited from an oppressed people who will fight until that oppression ceases. The armed struggle is the cutting edge of the campaign to remove British forces and achieve a united Ireland.'

IRA spokesperson, early 1984[42]

On 11 November 1982 three unarmed IRA men, Sean Burns, Gervaise McKerr and Eugene Toman, were shot dead by the RUC near Lurgan in County Armagh. On the 24th Martin McCauley was wounded and Michael Tighe killed near Craigavon, again by the RUC. On 12 December two INLA men, Seamus Grew and Roddy Carroll, were shot dead by the RUC near Armagh. The RUC shooting of these seven men prompted the appointment, on 24 May 1984, of John Stalker (Deputy Chief Constable of the Greater Manchester Police) to investigate allegations regarding a state policy of shoot-to-kill. Had people been deliberately killed when they might instead have been arrested? Stalker himself was in no doubt about the seriousness of what he was investigating:

> In May 1984 I was asked to undertake an investigation in Northern Ireland that very soon pointed towards possible offences of murder and conspiracy to pervert the course of justice, these offences committed by members of the proud Royal Ulster Constabulary . . . It cannot be disputed that in a five-week period in the mid-winter of 1982 six men were shot dead by a specialist squad of police officers in Northern Ireland. The circumstances of those shootings pointed to a police inclination, if not a policy, to shoot suspects dead without warning rather than to arrest them.[43]

John Stalker's inquiry was seriously obstructed by the RUC. In June 1986 he was replaced as head of the inquiry, amid allegations that he had associated with criminals – allegations later shown to be false. Stalker himself felt that the RUC had indeed shot dead unarmed men and then lied about the circumstances; though he also concluded that there existed no formal policy of killing suspects in preference to arresting them. Decisively, however, for the credibility of the state, Stalker claimed that he had been taken off the inquiry because of the turbulence that his findings would have created.

Again, therefore, serious doubts had arisen both about the state's use of lethal force and about its unpreparedness to investigate possible abuses in a thorough and open manner. The state, in Weberian manner, identified itself as holding a monopoly over legitimate force. But what if a democratic state used force in arbitrary and extra-legal ways, killing members of its population in dubious circumstances, and then refusing adequately to investigate those circumstances? Could the distinction between legal force and illegal paramilitarism remain crisp after such episodes? Amnesty International hinted that it could not, expressing profound disquiet about the shoot-to-kill controversy (though it should be noted that the body also criticized the IRA and other paramilitary groups for violent actions that they had carried out):

> A series of killings by the security forces in 1982 gave rise to serious allegations of an official policy of planned killings of suspected members of armed opposition groups. Subsequent killings in the next decade increased suspicions that such a policy existed. Amnesty International remains unconvinced by government statements that the policy does or did not exist because such statements are not substantiated by evidence of an official will to investigate fully and impartially each incident, to make the facts publicly known, to bring the perpetrators to justice or to bring legislation concerning such matters into line with international standards.[44]

The murkier aspect of state activities against Northern Irish paramilitaries has, quite properly, prompted much attention.[45] But while dubious British activities could sustain disaffection among Irish republicans, it was also necessary for the movement to pursue positive politics if it was to maintain the necessary momentum. In particular, republicans had to compete against those within their own community who possessed a very different brand of politics. During the IRA's military campaign, the constitutional nationalist SDLP repeatedly outpolled Sinn Féin: in the 1982 Northern Ireland Assembly election, the SDLP gained 118,891 first-preference votes, Sinn Féin only 64,191; in the 1983 UK general election, the SDLP obtained 137,012 votes, Sinn Féin 102,701; in the 1984 European Parliament election, the SDLP's John Hume gathered 151,399 first-preference votes, while Sinn Féin's Danny Morrison obtained 91,476; in the 1985 district council elections, Hume's party managed 113,967 first-preference votes, Sinn Féin 75,686; the 1987 UK general election saw the SDLP get 154,087 votes, with Sinn Féin winning 83,389.[46] Thus Sinn Féin's vote, while sizeable, was consistently smaller than that of its constitutional nationalist rivals. The SDLP leader, John Hume, argued for a very different kind of Irish nationalism from the aggressive brand marketed by the IRA and Sinn Féin, and relations between the two parties of northern nationalism were far from harmonious during most of the 1980s. In November

1988 Hume addressed his party's annual conference in Belfast with
some very critical words concerning the Provisional movement:

> The Irish people are defined by them, if we judge by their actions
> and their contempt for the views and opinions of other Irish
> people, as themselves alone. They are more Irish than the rest of
> us, they believe. They are the pure master race of Irish. They are
> the keepers of the holy grail of the nation. That deep-seated
> attitude, married to their method, has all the hallmarks of undiluted
> fascism. They have also the other hallmarks of the fascist – the
> scapegoat – the Brits are to blame for everything, even their own
> atrocities. They know better than the rest of us. They know so
> much better that they take onto themselves the right, without
> consultation with anyone, to dispense death and destruction.[47]

Some of the harshest criticism of the Provisionals came, here as on
many other occasions, not from outside but from *within* their own
Catholic nationalist community.

John Hume might not have moved all that far from traditional
nationalist assumptions,[48] but during the 1980s his less aggressive
version of Irish nationalism seemed to be making some progress. The
1983–4 New Ireland Forum had been set up to allow Ireland's
constitutional nationalist parties north and south (the SDLP, Fianna
Fáil, Fine Gael and the Irish Labour Party) to meet in an effort to
produce an agreed stance on the north. The Forum report of May
1984 reflected nationalist preference for a united Ireland, but also
offered two other possibilities: a federal or confederal arrangement,
and joint authority between London and Dublin over the north. Both
republicans and Margaret Thatcher dismissed the report. Danny Morrison: 'The report is toothless and wishy-washy. Nowhere does it relate
to the present British violence and realities of life in the north.'[49]
Margaret Thatcher: 'The unified Ireland was one solution – that is
out. A second solution was a confederation of the two states – that
is out. A third solution was joint authority – that is out.'[50]

Despite this, further movement in the direction favoured by John
Hume occurred in 1985 with the Anglo-Irish Agreement. On 15
November, in Hillsborough, County Down, UK Prime Minister Margaret Thatcher and Republic of Ireland Taoiseach Garret FitzGerald
co-signed an accord that was profoundly to alter the framework

within which the IRA were to operate in subsequent years. The Agreement affirmed that Northern Ireland's status would not be altered without the consent of the majority there (and recognized 'that the present wish of a majority of the people of Northern Ireland is for no change in the status of Northern Ireland').[51] It set up an intergovernmental conference (by means of which London and Dublin would address a wide range of matters in relation to the north), and it pledged the two governments to work on issues of security, human rights, communal identities and reconciliation; and it reflected their shared preference for some kind of devolved political arrangement in the north.

The Republic of Ireland was now to have an ongoing, consultative role in the affairs of Northern Ireland, and could genuinely claim to represent northern minority interests. As Richard Needham, a long-serving British politician in the north was to put it, by the mid-1980s 'the British government had long since realised that defeating the IRA was impossible without the wholehearted commitment of the south and unless and until the Republic could be drawn into taking some responsibility for what was happening in the north'.[52]

This focuses attention on one of Margaret Thatcher's key aims in relation to the 1985 Agreement: namely, security. Yes, Mrs Thatcher had something of a personal sympathy for Ulster unionism (partly emergent from her original Methodism);[53] yes, there was a sense that the (probably exaggerated) threat of Sinn Féin dominance in the north necessitated the strengthening of the SDLP. But it was the 'need for Irish help on security'[54] that primarily appealed to the Prime Minister, and in particular her hope that an Anglo-Irish deal might weaken the IRA by strengthening cooperation with the Republic over security issues, in particular along the border between north and south. Both Dublin and London had become anxious about the threat that a post-hunger-strike Sinn Féin posed. As Garret FitzGerald himself put it, 'If Sinn Féin's electoral support in Northern Ireland were to exceed that of the SDLP, the situation there could get out of control and threaten the whole island, for in those circumstances the IRA might seek a violent confrontation with the unionists and try to follow this by an attempt to destabilise the Republic.'[55] Whether or not this fear was justified by Sinn Féin's electoral performance in practice, it shaped joint governmental policy: something must be done to strengthen the

SDLP, to show that constitutional (rather than violent) nationalism was the way to achieve progress and results.

If these were the co-signatories' reflections, what of the contemporary responses of the main intended victim of the Agreement, the Provisional republican movement? Sinn Féin President Gerry Adams told a Belfast press conference days after the signing of the Hillsborough deal that it had been 'designed to isolate and defeat republicans'.[56] In its Easter statement of 1986, the leadership of the republican movement claimed that the fundamental intent of the Anglo-Irish Agreement was clear: 'to maintain Ireland as it is, divided by partition, class and creed, and to smash republicanism which seeks to end division by removing the root cause of that division – direct and indirect British rule and domination'.[57] But the fuller republican response, even at the time, was more subtle than is often recognized. In an interview published in *An Phoblacht/Republican News* the month after the Agreement, Gerry Adams outlined Sinn Féin's essentially dual attitude towards the deal:

> The Hillsborough Agreement consists of two major elements. Firstly, it institutionalises the British presence and pledges Dublin's formal recognition of the six-county state, partition, the loyalist veto [the principle that a majority in the north was needed before Irish unity might come about] and the British connection. Sinn Féin, quite rightly, is opposed to this. No Irish nationalist or republican could support it. Secondly, it contains a promise of concessions to improve the quality of life for nationalists in the six counties. Sinn Féin correctly sees these concessions – if they come and if they have any real substance – as being the result of the steadfastness of a section of the nationalist people, allied to their support for Sinn Féin ... Dublin and London readily admit that their Agreement is partly aimed at isolating Sinn Féin by introducing concessions and creating a political climate. The equation is therefore a simple one: support for Sinn Féin equals concessions from the British.[58]

The evolving tension between these two responses – rejecting partitionism, but welcoming concessions as a result of republican action – was to define the ambiguous nature of republican politics during subsequent years.

Moreover, republican hostility towards the Agreement was tempered by the fact that Ulster's unionists so hated the Hillsborough deal.[59] In the zero-sum world of northern politics, your opponent's hostility towards a given development might be seen as suggesting that the development had within it some benefit for yourself. And unionists were certainly horrified, their sense of betrayal at what the Agreement entailed intensified because they had been left out of its production, not even consulted. Indeed, unionist reaction was worse than Margaret Thatcher appears to have anticipated,[60] the air becoming 'thick with bitter cries, as baffled thousands dream they are betrayed, stripped of the comfort of safe loyalties, their ancient friends considered enemies'.[61] Sinn Féin's Tom Hartley: 'After eighty-one you had the rise of Sinn Féin, and the Dublin government moved to convince the British government that they needed to give the SDLP a helping hand. And it was one of the main objectives of the Anglo-Irish Agreement. And in a sense they took their eye off the unionist ball. They were so focused on defeating republicans that they didn't quite notice the unionists.'[62]

Moreover, the Agreement did not depend upon local support in Northern Ireland for its sustenance (one of its great strengths, according to some observers);[63] as long as the two governments wanted to uphold the deal, then the deal would be upheld. In this, the Agreement differed from initiatives such as James Prior's devolutionary 1982–6 Northern Ireland Assembly.[64] Indeed, when unionist hostility to the 1985 Hillsborough accord was effectively faced down by the London government, it seemed to contain greater potential still for Irish republicans. As one senior Sinn Féiner later observed: 'We saw the coming together of Dublin and London, and this proved London could be shifted. The fact that Britain moved unilaterally was pivotal. They hit the unionists a kick in the balls, saying to them, "We've tried to work with you but that failed." That didn't go unrecorded in republicanism.'[65]

The 1985 Anglo-Irish Agreement both reflected and reinforced a growing harmony between London and Dublin in terms of dealing with Northern Ireland. Hillsborough formally changed the dynamic between the two governments, with Dublin now having a structural role within the running of the north of Ireland. And it was within this context that 1980s Provisional politics developed and matured. In the early 1980s

Sinn Féin proudly located itself as 'a political organisation dedicated to a democratic socialist republic for Ireland based on the Proclamation announced in Dublin at the commencement of the Easter 1916 Rising'.[66] In the summer of 1983 the party's President was Ruairí Ó Brádaigh, its Vice-Presidents Daithi O'Connell and Gerry Adams. But at the *ard fheis*, or convention, in November Ó Brádaigh was replaced as President by Adams, as power within the republican movement was ever more firmly grasped by the northerners. In his presidential address at the *ard fheis*, Adams denied speculation that his election reflected a northern takeover or dominance within Sinn Féin. He also offered reassurance on the questions of abstentionism and violence, both of which had been crucial in the birth of the Provisional movement: 'we are an abstentionist party; it is not my intention to advocate a change in this situation . . . I would like to elaborate on Sinn Féin's attitude to armed struggle. Armed struggle is a necessary and morally correct form of resistance in the six counties against a government whose presence is rejected by the vast majority of Irish people.'[67]

Armed struggle and political campaigning were to be welded together, it seemed. As we have noted, Sinn Féin had contested the 1982 Northern Ireland Assembly election, and although it was heavily outpolled by the SDLP it had none the less attracted over 60,000 first-preference votes. This was certainly a far larger body of concentrated support than appeared to exist in the Republic. Elections there saw Sinn Féin win only tiny percentages of the first-preference vote (1.9 per cent in 1987; 1.2 per cent in 1989; 1.6 per cent in 1992).[68]

What of the party's relationship with the army? In the 1970s Sinn Féin had been very much secondary to the IRA, with the movement's military figures in the ascendancy. At the end of 1977 leading Provo Seamus Twomey had been arrested by the gardai (the police); when searching the Dun Laoghaire flat in which he had been staying, the police found an IRA GHQ Staff report which included the telling passage: 'Sinn Féin should come under [Irish Republican] Army organisers at all levels. Sinn Féin should employ full-time organisers in big republican areas. Sinn Féin should be radicalised (under army direction) and should agitate about social and economic issues which attack the welfare of the people.'[69] During the 1980s, the relative strengths of Sinn Féin and the army were to alter, with the party gaining increasing emphasis. For the party and the army were closely interwoven. Not only had Provisional Sinn Féin been created by the IRA, not only did it share the same republican aims and arguments, but it often had overlapping personnel. IRA members or former IRA members formed a significant part of the Sinn Féin membership. Just as Bobby Sands had been both IRA man and Sinn Féiner in his brief period of Belfast liberty during the mid-1970s, so too IRA man Tony McBride (killed by the British Army in December 1984 in an IRA operation in County Fermanagh) had been active in Sinn Féin while an active IRA Volunteer; likewise, IRA man Martin McCaughey (killed by the SAS in October 1990) had been a Sinn Féin councillor on Dungannon District Council while an IRA Volunteer.[70]

The IRA and Sinn Féin, then, were two parts of the same integrated movement. And the strengthening during the 1980s of the party's electoral and other activities did not mean that republicans were eschewing the violent struggle. Far from it. In June 1984 Martin McGuinness (whose own curriculum vitae combined IRA and Sinn Féin careers) stressed that it was 'the combination of the Armalite and the ballot box' that would achieve freedom, but made it clear which was the weightier of the two:

> The Irish Republican Army offers the only resolution to the present situation. It is their disciplined, well-directed war against British forces that will eventually bring Britain to withdraw. We know that elections, while important in that they show public support, will not achieve a British withdrawal. If Sinn Féin were to win every election it contested, it would still not get an agreement on British withdrawal … We recognise that only disciplined revolutionary armed struggle by the IRA will end British rule.[71]

Thus violence was still to play its part. In the words of leading republican Danny Morrison, 'It isn't a question of driving the British Army into the sea. It's a question of breaking the political will of the British government to remain.'[72]

Sinn Féin politics were hard-hitting too and, apparently, uncompromising. Gerry Adams set out his view lucidly enough in November 1984: 'There can be no such thing as an Irish nationalist accepting the loyalist veto and partition. You cannot claim to be an Irish nationalist if you consent to an internal six-county settlement and if you are willing to negotiate the state of Irish society with a foreign government.'[73]

Moreover, those who opposed the greater emphasis on Sinn Féinish politics within the republican movement were given little space for dissidence. Ivor Bell (veteran Belfast republican, and at one time very close to Adams himself) was expelled in 1985 from the IRA for opposing the diversion of funds from the army to Sinn Féin's electoral work, and for opposing the dual ballot box/Armalite strategy.

In 1987, Sinn Féin set out their thinking in a discussion paper founded on republican fundamentals: 'The island of Ireland, throughout history, has been universally regarded as one unit ... The Irish people have never relinquished their claim to the right to self-determination. What has been in contest is the right of the Irish people, as a whole, to self-determination and their freedom to exercise that right.' The way forward required British movement: 'The ending of partition, a British disengagement from Ireland and the restoration to the Irish people of the right to exercise self-sovereignty, independence and national self-determination remain the only solution to the British colonial conflict in Ireland.' Republicans wanted peace, but only on terms they considered just: 'Sinn Féin seeks to create conditions which will lead to a permanent cessation of hostilities, an end to our long war and the development of a peaceful, united and independent Irish society. Such objectives will only be achieved when a British government adopts a strategy for decolonisation.'[74] And the party built up a repertoire of arguments and activities, expanding its political range. Gerry Adams's election leaflet for the 1987 UK general election asserted that 'There is only one party in this election committed to Irish national self-determination'; but it also stressed Sinn Féin's record and commitment across a wide range of issues including housing, employment and the Irish language.[75]

Yet the IRA remained the sharpest cutting instrument that republicans possessed, and their violence and activities continued incessantly during the 1980s. On 7 December 1983 Edgar Graham – a Queen's University, Belfast, law lecturer and an Ulster Unionist Party politician – was shot dead by the IRA at the university. On the scene were university colleagues David Trimble and Dermot Nesbitt (themselves to become prominent UUP politicians); the death notice for the dead man described him as the 'dearly loved son of Norman and Anna and brother of Anne'.[76] For their part, the IRA declared: 'Today's execution of Edgar Graham by the IRA should be a salutary lesson to those loyalists who stand full-square behind the laws and forces of the repression of the nationalist people.'[77] Later in the month London was shaken, in the run-up to Christmas, when six people died as a consequence of an IRA bomb outside Harrods' famous department store. In February 1985 an IRA mortar bomb attack on Newry RUC station killed nine officers including Chief Inspector Alex Donaldson – brother of Sam Donaldson (whom the IRA had killed in August 1970) and cousin of a man who was to become a prominent Ulster Unionist Party politician: Jeffrey Donaldson.

As we have seen, republicans could be victims too. The security forces often acted in ways that fell short of proper human-rights standards.[78] And more lethal experiences were intended for republicans by their loyalist opponents. In March 1984 Gerry Adams was shot and wounded by the UFF in Belfast (with republicans claiming that British intelligence had known in advance of the attempt). Then on 14 September 1986 the IRA killed John Bingham in north Belfast. A leading UVF man in Belfast, Bingham was considered by republicans to be organizationally responsible for a recent series of loyalist attacks in north Belfast.[79] In its statement following the killing, the IRA distinguished such murders from sectarian attacks on Protestants in general: 'We repeat our consistently held policy position regarding sectarian warfare: at no time will we involve ourselves in the execution of ordinary Protestants but at all times we reserve the right to take armed action against those who attempt to terrorise or intimidate our people into accepting British/unionist rule in the six counties.'[80] But again, the Bingham killing did not stop loyalist violence; indeed, it prompted a UVF revenge killing two days later.[81]

When loyalists killed three people in a Belfast bar on 15 May 1988, the Provisionals issued this statement: 'While we will not allow our-selves to become involved in sectarian attacks, we do reserve the right to execute those responsible for either organising these attacks or actively carrying them out.'[82] The following month the IRA killed UVF man Robert Seymour in east Belfast. In a statement claiming responsi-bility for the killing, the IRA repeated that it retained the right to kill 'those who are involved in carrying out or organising attacks against our community'[83] Again, revenge rather than quiescence was the result, IRA man Brendan Davidson being killed in retaliation by the UVF in Belfast in July.

If war with loyalists represented one military front for the IRA during the 1980s, then the key war in their eyes remained the one against England. This was to be spectacularly, and bloodily, evident in October 1984 with an attack on the Conservative Party Conference in Brighton. Before the 1981 hunger strike had ended, the IRA had decided to try to kill Margaret Thatcher. On 15 September 1984 IRA man Patrick Magee (and a colleague) planted a Semtex bomb in the Grand Hotel, Brighton, setting it on a long-delay timer to explode the following month during the Conservatives' Conference. On 12 October at 2.54 am it did so, with awful personal effect. Five people were killed and over thirty injured ('a night of devastation which I shall never forget');[84] but the Conservative Party Conference continued. Just as the IRA were committedly fighting for their pursuit of democratic politics as they understood it, so too Mrs Thatcher and her Party determinedly battled on in defence of *their* conception of democracy.

Patrick Magee was caught and was to serve fourteen years in prison for his part in the Brighton bombing. Magee's own later view was that, after Brighton, 'I think there was a recognition that we weren't going to go away . . . We had to get that message across. If they thought they could continue to contain the struggle or perhaps in some long term defeat it then of course they were going to go in for that. So the British establishment *had* to understand that we were there for the long haul and we weren't going to go away.'[85] Magee's bomb had been intended to kill most of the British cabinet, together with other leading Conservatives. An IRA spokesperson subsequently outlined the organization's thinking in stark terms: 'Our objective . . . is to wear down their political resolve . . . Britain clearly, after fifteen years, cannot defeat us, so her occupation of Ireland is going to keep on costing her dearly until she quits. They would have said "we lost Airey Neave, Lord Mountbatten, Margaret Thatcher etc. – is it worth it?" '[86] Magee himself was later to argue that this bombing decisively pushed the British government towards negotiations with the IRA, and ultimately towards the 1990s peace process itself; the Brighton bomb gave the IRA 'more political leverage': 'After Brighton, anything was possible and the British for the first time began to look very differently at us.'[87]

The IRA were certainly ready to fight on, and they were well armed to do so. During 1985 and 1986 numerous shipments had landed safely in Ireland, bringing arms and explosives from Libya to the IRA. The army's Libyan connections had long roots. As we have already seen, in 1973 Joe Cahill had been arrested on board the *Claudia* (off the Waterford coast) with five tons of weapons supplied by the Libyan government. Cahill had subsequently maintained amicable relations with the Libyans and by 1984 the link was certainly active once again. The successful mid-1980s shipments from the eccentric and talented Libyan President, Colonel Gaddafi (deeply hostile at that time to the UK), included rifles, machine-guns and the Czech-made odourless explosive, Semtex. By the time the *Eksund* was captured (by the French authorities in late 1987, with a large body of arms on board), the Libyan connection had already provided the IRA with the means of continuing its war. Much of the material already landed had been hidden in bunkers in the Republic of Ireland, greatly transforming the military capacity of the IRA. Setbacks such as the 1984 capture of the *Marita Ann* (off the Kerry coast), and the consequent loss of the IRA-destined American arms on board, were offset by the Libyan link.

In August 1985 there was a refocusing of the targets against which IRA weapons were to be used, with the announcement that anyone involved in building or maintenance work for the security forces would be considered a legitimate target. Having warned builders and contractors to desist from any building or refurbishing work for the RUC or the British Army, the IRA declared itself 'in a position to take effective action if builders do not henceforth desist from playing an active role in support of the Crown Forces'; such people were 'assisting the British in reinforcing their illegal and immoral presence'. Failure to desist would result in 'extreme action' being taken.[88] But while the IRA killed these people, in republican eyes it was *Britain* that was ultimately responsible for any loss of life in the conflict: while Britain wrongly occupied part of Ireland, the IRA would have to fight them. This vital part of republican argument had very deep roots. At Sinn Féin's late-1985 *ard fheis*, Gerry Adams was joined on the platform by veteran republican Dan Gleeson. Born in County Tipperary in 1902, Gleeson had fought in the IRA during the Anglo-Irish War, and in republican thinking emphasized 'the unbroken chain which links earlier phases of the republican struggle to today's struggle for freedom'. Gleeson told *ard fheis* delegates that 'while there is a British presence in our country there will never be peace ... And while they hold guns to the throats of Irish people, there will always be an IRA to fight them.'[89]

Increasingly, however, fighting with weapons was being accompanied by the Provisional movement's electoral, political campaign also. And here the Libyan arms helped, ironically, to strengthen the republican emphasis on politics. Those in the leadership who wanted to move in a more decidedly political direction had hitherto been open to the charge of playing down the armed struggle, as a consequence. Armed with Gaddafi's guns, however, they could confidently proclaim that the war would continue, with electoralism complementing rather than eclipsing physical-force republicanism. With the arms dumps full of weapons, who could charge that the republican movement was moving away from the armed struggle? But if you were going to win seats, would it not be practical and beneficial to sit in them? The tradition of abstention from illegitimate parliaments (whether in Dublin, London or Belfast) while Britain occupied Irish territory was one long cherished by many republicans, as already noted. It had been one of the issues involved in the split from which the Provisionals themselves had emerged. But the changed possibilities of the 1980s led some Provisional politicians to think that modification of republican attitudes here was necessary.

On 14 October 1986 the IRA issued a statement declaring that there had recently been held the first General Army Convention for sixteen years. The gathering had comprised members of the Army Council, and representatives of the Executive, GHQ Staff and departments, Northern and Southern Command Staffs, brigades, battalions and units. The GAC reaffirmed commitment to, and confidence in, the armed struggle. But it also, by more than the necessary two-thirds majority, passed two innovative key resolutions. The first 'removed the ban on Volunteers discussing or advocating the taking of parliamentary seats', while the second 'removed the ban on supporting successful republican candidates who take their seats in Leinster House [seat of the Dublin parliament]'.[90] Republican abstentionism was gone, at least as far as the Dáil was concerned.

Public backing for the new departure came from republicans with sound credentials. 1970s London bomber Gerry Kelly, then in Amsterdam Jail,[91] observed before the Sinn Féin *ard fheis* that was to consider the question, that he was enthusiastic about the ending of abstention. There was, he said, no party then in Leinster House to challenge 'pro-British' policies, and nobody demanding that Fianna Fáil live up to its traditional irredentist rhetoric: 'Abstentionism by Sinn Féin helps the other parties to misrepresent republicanism and go unchallenged ... The republican movement should be in there, challenging them daily.' In the view of this key figure in the IRA's history, both the military struggle and the ending of abstentionism were essential parts of the struggle.[92] 'It is as important' – Kelly argued, in regard to Leinster House abstentionism – 'for Sinn Féin to set aside this anachronism as it has been for Óglaigh na hÉireann [the IRA] to replace old weapons with more modern ones throughout our long struggle.'[93]

The IRA's GAC having given its approval, at the 1986 *ard fheis* Sinn Féin duly approved the ending of abstentionism with regard to Leinster House, by the necessary two-thirds majority. The careful choreography continued, with the IRA publicly approving of Sinn Féin's decision in a statement issued on 5 November 1986. Credible voices were again heard publicly, Brendan McFarlane offering public support from Maastricht Prison later in the month: 'The end of abstentionism is a great step forward.'[94]

Not all republicans thought so. Veteran Dan Gleeson, who had shared a platform with Adams at the 1985 *ard fheis*, opposed the dropping of abstentionism and refused to repeat his platform appearance in 1986. Tom Maguire, whose blessing had been given at the foundation of the Provisionals themselves, had in October 1986 issued a statement in which he spoke as the sole survivor of the Second Dáil Executive Council, and indeed of the Second Dáil itself: 'I do not recognise the legitimacy of any Army Council styling itself the Council of the Irish Republican Army which lends support to any person or organisation styling itself Sinn Féin and prepared to enter the partition parliament of Leinster House.'[95] In his view the Provisionals had now broken faith, and he came to support a new breakaway movement led by Ruairí Ó Brádaigh: Republican Sinn Féin (RSF). When the latter sprouted a military wing (the Continuity IRA [CIRA]), Maguire recognized *them* rather than the now discredited Provisionals as the legitimate inheritors of the republican flame – a flame that he had helped pass on to the IRA in 1938: 'I hereby declare that the Continuity

Executive and the Continuity Army Council are the lawful Executive and Army Council respectively of the Irish Republican Army, and that the governmental authority, delegated in the Proclamation of 1938, now resides in the Continuity Army Council.'[96] Adams had sent people to try to get Maguire's backing for the ending of abstentionism, but the old intransigent had refused.

In contrast to Maguire and Ó Brádaigh, the Provisionals themselves saw their dropping of abstentionism as clearing the road for their progress along another route forward in the republican struggle. At the Sinn Féin *ard fheis* debate on 2 November 1986, the party's National Organizer, Pat Doherty, proposed the resolution which called for an end to Leinster House abstentionism. Doherty advocated 'armed struggle in the six counties in pursuance of British withdrawal, and political struggle throughout the whole thirty-two counties in pursuance of the Republic'. In part, Sinn Féin's move was merely a recognition of certain political realities; as Doherty himself put it, '95% of the people [in the Republic of Ireland] accept Leinster House as being their government'.[97] This point was amplified by Gerry Adams: 'what persuaded Sinn Féin in the end to contest and take seats in Leinster House was that they recognised the reality of the situation in the twenty-six counties; the vast majority of people there, cynical though they may be about their politicians, accept their institutions. Partition has had that effect.'[98] Tom Hartley later put the issue very clearly:

> I think there was a recognition at some point that, in fact, partition had created two very distinct political realities: that the political conditions of the north were not to be found in the political conditions of the south. Partition had acted differently in these two states. And so therefore it was no use republicans, in a way, creating a strategy which was essentially aimed at the north and thinking that it would work in the south ... Whether we liked it or not Leinster House, the Dáil, is an *Irish* institution, it's not a British institution. It might have been an outcome of British strategy or policy, but it certainly wasn't a British institution.[99]

Clearly, the 1986 break with abstention was not presented as indicating that republican violence would cease. Indeed, for years yet the orthodoxy remained that the politics of elections and of violence were necessarily complementary. As late as 1993 an IRA member was proclaiming defiantly: 'It's the gun and the fuckin' ballot box and that's the way it's goin' to stay till Britain leaves. There's no way the nationalist community will be without an army again.'[100] The gloomy, practical echo of such sentiments could be heard repeatedly at funerals – almost literally, in the case of Peter Nesbitt, an RUC reserve constable blown up by the IRA in March 1987 in Belfast. Shortly before his burial an IRA bomb injured four police officers at the gates of the cemetery where the funeral was to take place; the IRA said that the attack was in retaliation for RUC brutality at republican funerals. In April 1987, Lord Maurice and Lady Cecily Gibson were killed by an IRA bomb in County Armagh, as they drove home from holiday. Gibson was one of Northern Ireland's most senior judges, having become a High Court judge in 1968 and a Lord Justice in 1975. He had enraged many republicans with, for example, his acquittal of three RUC men who had been accused of murdering IRA man Eugene Toman in 1982. In republican eyes, Gibson was 'thoroughly representative of the north's colonial judiciary: a unionist, bigoted and biased against nationalists, who constantly used the law to prop up British rule in the six counties'.[101]

Earlier in April 1987 IRA man Laurence Marley was shot and killed by the UVF at his north Belfast home, the loyalists stressing that their victim 'had served long prison sentences for IRA activities including blackmail, possession of arms and explosives. Upon his release he became reinvolved with the organisation and this reinvolvement cost him his life.'[102] A few weeks later, the IRA killed UVF man William Marchant in Belfast, claiming that he had been involved in Marley's killing. Another political blood-cycle was to develop the following month. On 8 May the SAS ambushed an IRA operation at Loughgall, County Armagh, inflicting serious loss on the organization's East Tyrone Brigade. The authorities had gleaned information (apparently through a listening device in premises used by a republican) that an attack was to be made on the RUC station in the village. So when the IRA team of eight men arrived with a bomb in a digger, they were entering a fatal ambush. The bomb exploded, and the SAS then shot and shot and shot, firing from all sides and killing all eight IRA men (as well as a Catholic civilian who happened to be nearby). It was a serious blow to the IRA to lose these active men in such a way: Jim

Lynagh, Patrick Kelly, Declan Arthurs, Tony Gormley, Eugene Kelly, Seamus Donnelly, Padraig McKearney and Gerard O'Callaghan.

Patrick Kelly was the IRA's East Tyrone Brigade commander. Jim Lynagh, too, was experienced. Born in Monaghan in 1956, he had joined the Provisionals as a teenager and had combined long-term IRA activism with a Sinn Féin political career (he had been elected to Monaghan Urban District Council in 1979 as a Sinn Féin councillor) and with political radicalism (during his 1970s imprisonment he had studied and become a keen admirer of Mao Tse-tung). In the early 1980s he had been one of the IRA's most active figures. Like Lynagh, O'Callaghan and Gormley had both joined the IRA as teenagers. In Gormley's case, it was the 1981 hunger strike that had proved galvanic. He had been profoundly moved by the death in that terrible sequence of Martin Hurson, who had lived nearby in County Tyrone. Shortly after Hurson died, Gormley joined the IRA, who could hit back at the British for their condemnation of Hurson to a painful death. Gormley, Arthurs, Donnelly and Kelly had been close friends, and they had died young (at twenty-four, twenty-one, nineteen and twenty-five respectively). Friends, locality, loss, revenge, youth.

And possibly betrayal. The information on which the SAS ambush was based had not come from an informer; but it seems that one of the IRA men killed at Loughgall was indeed a long-time Special Branch source. Among the Special Forces Tony Gormley was apparently known as the 'Banker', owing to the large sums that he was reputed to have been paid for supplying information to the Special Branch.[103] Indeed, controversy surrounded Loughgall. Had the British taken a prior decision to kill rather than even to attempt any arrest? The SAS gave no warning before opening fire. And, although the IRA clearly aimed to kill police officers in their attack, questions were rightly raised about whether the state should adopt such a ruthless, lethal approach even towards armed IRA men. Could the state successfully maintain that its (legal) actions were distinguishable from those of its (illegal) paramilitary opponents if its own soldiers ambushed and brutally killed paramilitaries as they did at Loughgall? (In May 2001 the European Court of Human Rights decided that the British government had violated the human rights of the IRA men killed at Loughgall by not conducting a proper investigation afterwards into their deaths.)

And Ulster's antiphonal chanting went on, with the killing on 12

June by the IRA of Joe McIlwaine, a twenty-year-old member of the Ulster Defence Regiment (UDR), and the apparently retaliatory loyalist killing of Michael Power in August. Power, a married Catholic man with three children, was shot on his way to Mass in south Belfast. A few months later the IRA itself killed people attending a religious ceremony, in one of the most famous incidents of the northern troubles. On Sunday 8 November 1987, in the pretty County Ferman-agh town of Enniskillen, people gathered for a dignified Remembrance Sunday service at the war memorial. An IRA bomb exploded, bringing down the wall of a community hall, and under the rubble eleven Protestants were crushed to death. One of them was twenty-year-old nurse Marie Wilson, whose father recalled the moments as he and his daughter lay buried in the rubble after the bomb had gone off: 'I asked Marie four or five times was she all right, and all the time holding my hand she assured me yes but each time and in between she screamed. I couldn't understand why on the one hand she was telling me that she was all right and on the other hand she screamed as dozens of other people were screaming and I knew something had to be wrong. I couldn't understand it and when I asked her for what was the last time, Marie, are you all right? she said, Daddy, I love you very much.'[104] They were the last words she spoke to her father.

The following day, the IRA issued a statement – 'We deeply regret what occurred' – claiming that their bomb had been aimed at Crown Forces and that it had not been intended to go off during the Remembrance service itself.[105] But, contrary to the Provisionals' initial argument that their device had been radio-controlled and set off by the British Army's countermeasures, in fact the bomb had been not radio-controlled but rather detonated by a pre-set timer.[106] In truth, the bomb had been intended for soldiers and police during their pre-ceremony activities, but had gone off at the wrong time. Yet IRA suggestions that they had not planned for the bomb to go off when it did, or with the horrific consequences that it caused, could hardly be expected to offset the deep and widespread revulsion felt at such an appalling event. Killing Protestant civilians at a religious service was a disastrous own-goal for an organization claiming to be fighting a non-sectarian war against military opponents, and republicans struggled to respond. Gerry Adams: 'In my view the IRA are freedom fighters. They made a terrible mistake at Enniskillen. They must not repeat that

mistake.'[107] The IRA's embarrassment over Enniskillen was deepened
by the contrast popularly drawn between their own actions and the
extraordinarily humane and forgiving attitude subsequently shown by
Marie Wilson's Methodist father, Gordon. But his humanity could not
hide his utter devastation at having lost his precious daughter: 'She
was, I suppose, the "apple of my eye" . . . It is hard to believe, after so
many days and weeks, and now years, of shock, suffering and loss, that
Marie has gone. Somehow, her presence still permeates the house.
There are some days when you still expect her to fling open the back
door, to burst into the room and exclaim, "I'm back again! I'm here!
What's for tea?" But she isn't here, and my wife Joan and I have tea
on our own.'[108]

Early in 1988 a republican setback of a different kind occurred
when three IRA members were killed – again, in controversial circumstances – by the SAS. This time it happened not in Ireland, but on
British Gibraltar, where a large number of British Army personnel
were resident. An IRA unit intended to car-bomb the band and guard
of the Royal Anglian Regiment there, but on 6 March three of the
team – Danny McCann, Sean Savage and Mairead Farrell – were shot
and killed by the SAS. (Apparently, a fourth member of the IRA's
Gibraltar team escaped.)

The IRA's opponents were jubilant; but here again controversy
surrounded British shootings of Irish republicans. The three were
unarmed when shot; there was no bomb in their car; and their
explosive was not found until some days after the shooting and then
in a car park in Spain. Shoot-to-kill allegations again haunted the
British state in its war with the IRA. For important questions were
asked: if they were unarmed, then why had the IRA members not been
arrested rather than shot dead? This was a point raised in an April
1988 Thames Television documentary (*Death on the Rock*), which
questioned the government's version of the killings; and while the
September 1988 inquest into the killings found that they had been
lawful, the 1989 independent Windlesham/Rampton report on the
Death on the Rock programme substantially vindicated its makers.[109]
The four SAS soldiers who shot the IRA team had apparently been
told that the republicans were to detonate their bomb by remote
control (in fact they planned to use a timer) and that the IRA unit
would be armed (which they were not).

Yet whatever succour might have been given to republicans by the government's embarrassment over shoot-to-kill allegations, the fact remained that they had again lost experienced Volunteers to SAS violence. In Mairead Farrell they had lost a significant Volunteer. Born in Belfast in 1957, she was raised in Andersonstown and had family connections both to the IRA and RIC in former generations.[110] Farrell herself joined the IRA as a teenager and had been sentenced in 1976 to fourteen years' imprisonment for possession of explosives and for IRA membership. She became OC women prisoners in Armagh jail, was one of the leaders of the Armagh 1980 dirty protest and a hunger-striker in that year also. She was released from prison in October 1986 and returned to IRA life. Farrell – an intelligent and charismatic figure – became something of a feminist icon, held to exemplify a questioning of masculine power, heroism and orthodoxy[111] (though this picture is somewhat modified if one believes the memoir of a former lover who recalls her declaring, 'I like a man with muscles' and 'you've got such gorgeous muscles').[112] Yet even in death, violence was to follow her. On 16 March Farrell, McCann and Savage were being buried in west Belfast's Milltown cemetery, when loyalist Michael 'Flint' Stone dramatically attacked mourners with grenades and guns, killing three and wounding many more. Though later claiming that he had wanted to kill prominent republicans, he in fact killed two civilians and one inconspicuous IRA man, Kevin Brady. At the latter's funeral on 19 March, the cycle of killing continued. Two British soldiers (David Howes and Derek Wood) unintentionally drove amidst the mourners on their way to Milltown, who initially feared another Stone-like attack. The two corporals were dragged from their car, beaten and then taken off by the IRA and shot dead in a ghastly fifteen-minute episode. A number of people were imprisoned for their part in the corporals' killing, including Terence 'Cleaky' Clarke (a bodyguard for Gerry Adams in the 1990s, and the dedicatee of one of Adams's books),[113] who had been chief steward at the Brady funeral.

This awful sequence of interwoven deaths – the killing of Farrell, McCann and Savage; the Michael Stone attack at their funeral; and the corporals' deaths in turn at the funeral of one of Stone's victims – seemed to embody a crescendo of retaliatory violence. True, more people had been killed the previous year (106 in 1987, 105 in 1988),[114] but the rapid sequence, the appalling drama, and the fact that the

Stone attack and the corporals' deaths were filmed, all made this one of the most strikingly memorable and shocking periods of the northern conflict. And that bloody year offered yet more examples of the horrors of the war. Between the Stone Milltown attack and the corporals' fate, the IRA had killed a young Protestant civilian, Gillian Johnston, in County Fermanagh. They had, they said, intended to kill someone else, and 'deeply regretted and apologised for the killing'; 'members of the ASU [Active Service Unit] involved believed they had properly identi-fied a car which contained a UDR soldier'.[115]

The Provisionals did, however, intend to kill those whom they bombed in June 1988. On the 15th of that month British soldiers took part in an annual sponsored charity fun run through Lisburn. A bomb under a van carrying some of those who had participated killed six soldiers. Condemnation came from many people, including Secretary of State for Northern Ireland, Tom King: 'What words can describe people who set out to commit such an appalling outrage at an event whose purpose is to help the less fortunate in our society – the elderly, the severely disabled, and handicapped children?'[116] Eight more soldiers were killed in August that year when the IRA again bombed a bus carrying troops, this time near Ballygawley in County Tyrone as soldiers returned to barracks after a short holiday. The bomb contained two hundred pounds of Semtex. One eyewitness stated, 'There were bodies strewn all over the road, and others were caught inside the bus and under it. There were people running around stunned, screaming and bleeding, and shouting for someone to come to their aid.'[117] At the end of the same month, in a County Tyrone ambush, the SAS killed three IRA men (brothers Gerard and Martin Harte, and Brian Mullin): to republican eyes, 'three young men in the front line of the struggle for a free and peaceful Ireland'.[118] For while the IRA's violence is rightly recognized as having caused much death and trauma, it need hardly be repeated that they were not the only practitioners of killing. As one hostile observer of the SAS has argued, 'The history of the SAS in Ireland since 1969 is not merely one of intelligence gathering. It is a history of torture, kidnapping, unjustifiable killing and murder.'[119]

But some of the most devastating blows against the IRA in these days were self-inflicted. On 31 August 1988 an IRA booby-trap intended to kill members of the security forces in Derry killed, instead, two local Catholics (Sean Dalton and Sheila Lewis). The IRA had kidnapped the young occupant of a flat in the city, booby-trapping his Creggan home in the hope that investigating British soldiers from a search party would trigger the device. But Dalton, a neighbour, noted the absence of the flat's occupant and (after persistent knocking at the door had produced no response) entered it by a window, intending to check that all was well. He then opened the front door where Lewis, likewise keen to check the well-being of their neighbour, was waiting. The IRA bomb, attached to the door, was accidentally triggered and both Dalton and Lewis died. The IRA's Derry Brigade offered a self-exculpatory statement: 'This operation was designed to inflict casualties on members of the British Army search squad who were in the area this morning. Although the operation was carefully planned it went tragically wrong.' Derry republican Martin McGuinness also commented on the episode, attempting to place ultimate blame for the tragedy on Britain rather than on the republican bomb-planters: 'The tragedy of this war is that IRA Volunteers, British forces and, sadly, also civilians will continue to suffer and die as long as Britain refuses to accept its fundamental responsibility for what is happening in our country.' He added, however, that, 'While the freedom struggle goes on the IRA has a responsibility to ensure as much as humanly possible that civilians are not endangered.'[120]

The 'good neighbours' bomb had killed a sixty-year-old daily-Mass-going woman; and a fifty-five-year-old father of six whose own wife had recently died. The IRA claimed that the booby-trapped flat had been observed by their members on a twenty-four-hour basis to ensure that nobody except the security forces went near it, but that, in the words of a statement, 'A Volunteer whose responsibility it was to monitor the flat left his position for a period of twenty-five minutes. This error in judgement meant that the flat was not under observation and in that period two neighbours tragically tried to gain access.'[121]

On Wednesday 23 November of the same year an IRA bomb at an RUC station in Benburb, County Tyrone, killed another two Catholic civilians, who had been driving past the station as the bomb exploded. Barney Lavery (sixty-seven) and his granddaughter Emma Donnelly (thirteen) were killed instantly. At their funeral the Auxiliary Bishop of Armagh, James Lennon (himself an old schoolfriend of Barney Lavery), told mourners that he wished he could meet face to face with the bombers and planners behind the Benburb attack: 'I would like you to

stand where I am standing and see the grief that's eating into a widow
and a family, and the grief that's eating into the father and mother of
a thirteen-year-old girl taken away on the threshold of life. I would
like you to be here to see the result of hopes and dreams that are
shattered.'[122] Inseparable in life, grandfather and granddaughter were
buried side by side.

Thus the late 1980s offered problems for the IRA. They were losing
members (twenty-six dying violently during 1987–8); they were unintentionally killing civilians (twenty-seven during 1987–8)[123] and losing
the publicity war as a result; they were losing material (as with the
January 1988 arms find at Five Fingers Strand, near Malin in County
Donegal – five machine-guns, 100 rifles, 100 pounds of explosives,
50,000 rounds of ammunition);[124] many of their operations were not
coming to fruition, owing variously to the role of informers, bad luck,
loss of nerve, incompetence and security force activity; and they and
their sympathizers were partly marginalized from the media by a
broadcasting ban which had been introduced by the British authorities
in October 1988. Republicans also complained bitterly about the
censorship of their views in the Republic of Ireland, through govern-
ment-imposed restrictions on media coverage there.[125] Even a comparatively sympathetic observer of the republican movement felt able to
write: 'Today, in mid-1987, it seems most unlikely that unabated
warfare will produce positive results from a republican standpoint.
Instead, there is a strong possibility that both Sinn Féin and the IRA
will lose more than they will gain by continuing indefinitely on their
present course ... Non-violent republicanism may be the most advantageous shape to give to the next phase of the longest war.'[126]

The Provisionals had, in particular, come to recognize the problems
that their killing of civilians caused them. A spokesperson for the
organization's GHQ Staff was quoted early in 1989 as saying that there
was 'a greater realisation than ever of the need for the IRA to avoid
civilian casualties'. 1988 had seen problems: 'Unfortunately, through a
combination of tragic circumstances, many civilians died in operations
which dented the confidence of some of our supporters.'[127] Sharp-
sighted republicans could see that their war was failing to make the
progress they desired. But was there an alternative route forward that
Irish republicans could credibly follow?

PART FOUR

PEACE?

1988–2002

SEVEN
TALKING AND KILLING
1988–94

1

'The IRA strategy is very clear. At some point in the future, due to the pressure of the continuing and sustained armed struggle, the will of the British government to remain in this country will be broken. That is the objective of the armed struggle ... we can state confidently today that there will be no ceasefire and no truces until Britain declares its intent to withdraw and leave our people in peace.'

IRA spokesperson, 1989[1]

The Northern Ireland conflict has involved sharp and brutal antagonisms not only between the two political communities in the north, but also, as already indicated, within each of them. To the Provisional republican movement, constitutional nationalist rivals in the SDLP represented for a long time a deeply unwelcome force. Indeed, the IRA had actually attacked SDLP leader John Hume and his family; and there had been considerable and bitter rivalry between the two wings of northern nationalism for much of the period since the Provisionals had been set up. Hume frequently criticized Provisional violence and politics, and he had long sought to persuade the IRA to end their campaign. An aborted, fruitless meeting to that effect had been held in 1985, but the increasingly productive relationship between the north's two leading nationalist politicians – Hume and the Sinn Féin leader Gerry Adams – was to have enormous significance for the politics of Northern Ireland in the 1990s.

In January 1988 the two men met to discuss their respective analyses of the Northern Irish problem. During the previous couple of years, Father Alec Reid (a Tipperary-born Redemptorist priest from west Belfast's Clonard monastery) had helped to set this up, suggesting both to the SDLP and to Fianna Fáil that there should be talks with republicans, to try to persuade the latter to change their violent approach. Long resident in Belfast, Reid had in the 1970s helped to mediate in republican feuds, and he was a trusted figure of integrity who now argued the case for intranationalist dialogue. Crucially, Reid had Adams's trust: evidence of the decisive importance of personal, individual relationships in the evolution of recent Irish politics. During 1988 (though apparently beginning in late 1987),[2] representatives of the two rival northern nationalist parties met, with some of their most talented figures involved in the dialogue – for Sinn Féin, Gerry Adams, Tom Hartley, Danny Morrison and Mitchel McLaughlin; for the SDLP, John Hume, Seamus Mallon, Sean Farren and Austin Currie. Papers were exchanged, and for much of the year the talking continued. When it ended, in September 1988, it did so without agreement. But Hume and Adams remained in private contact, genuine trust having been established between them; and although the two parties' talks had not produced a common approach, both sides seemed keen to continue some such form of contact.

Both parties agreed that the Irish people had a right to self-determination. But they differed on how to exercise that right, given clear Ulster unionist hostility to Irish unity. To Sinn Féin, the British, an imperialist force in the conflict, were pursuing their control over Irish territory for self-interested reasons. To the SDLP, the British had by now become effectively neutral on the question of Irish unity; according to this reading, the problem was less that of British interests than of the divisions among the Irish people themselves. John Hume's repeated argument was that the real obstacle to Irish unity and separation from Britain was simply that many people in Ireland did not want it: *pace* the IRA, the central problem was not with Britain at all.

During 1989 Hume and Adams met four times, usually in rooms made available by Alec Reid in the monastery. The two nationalist leaders thus continued to consolidate considerable trust and engagement, a development that was to be of great significance. Hume retained his strong hostility to the use of violence, and his belief that the IRA could indeed be persuaded to end its armed campaign. His willingness to engage with republicans was courageous and risky, and he was frequently condemned for his overtures towards those whom many preferred to leave outside the tent of acceptability and of respectable politics.

True, throughout 1988 Sinn Féin argued not only that Britain's six-county occupation denied the Irish people their right to self-determination, but also that the oppressed northern nationalists had the right to use force to end their oppression. Yet the republicans' very engagement in talks with constitutional nationalists itself indicated an awareness on their part, first, that they themselves had not been able (force or not) to achieve their goal of Irish unity and, second, that some form of broader nationalist alliance or liaison appealed to them. There were seeds here which would later flourish with Sinn Féin's support in the 1990s for the idea that nationalists, working together in a broad alliance, might represent a stronger and more effective force than if they continued as rival bickering groups. A united family might prevail. So, even in 1988, Gerry Adams was stressing the 'urgent need to build an all-Ireland movement which would be open to everyone committed to the principle and objective of Irish national self-determination'.[3]

Details of the intranationalist talks which began in 1988 were fed to the British and Irish governments by Hume himself. So while the Hume–Adams talks were secret from the public, they were no secret in London and Dublin. Indeed, prior to the 1988 Sinn Féin/SDLP engagement, Hume had told Fianna Fáil leader Charles Haughey that he was going to meet Adams, with Haughey approving. For his part, Haughey had his own adviser, Martin Mansergh,[4] meet Sinn Féin. Fianna Fáil, like the SDLP, stressed the unacceptability of violence, arguing that republican violence divided nationalists from one another in the north, divided them north from south and divided opinion in the USA.

All of this was to play a part in evolving Irish nationalist debate. At this stage, in the late 1980s, the IRA were not ready to end their violence. Republicans held still that the north was an unfair place (Gerry Adams: 'Three years later it is clear it [the 1985 Anglo-Irish Agreement] has failed to deliver any of the promised improvements for the nationalist community'),[5] and that it remained irreformable. In his presidential address to Sinn Féin's January 1989 *ard fheis*, Adams himself again spelt out the party's stance: 'The history of Ireland and of British colonial involvement throughout the world tells us that the British government rarely listens to the force of argument. It understands only the argument of force. This is one of the reasons why armed struggle is a fact of life, and death, in the six counties.' Republican violence was 'not merely a defensive reaction by an oppressed people. It sets the political agenda.'[6]

Violence was to the fore on 30 July 1990, when Conservative MP Ian Gow was killed by the IRA in England. He had been a close friend of Margaret Thatcher, having advised her on Irish policy, and had been a longstanding unionist sympathizer and outspoken critic of the Provisionals. Gow's death prompted understandable rage and 'deep personal grief'[7] among his friends and political colleagues: 'My first reaction was of sheer overwhelming anger that an old friend, a wonderful husband and father, a courageous and warm-hearted person had been murdered by the IRA.'[8] Personally horrific, this violence was – in the IRA's view – politically necessary. A month earlier a spokesperson for the Provisionals' GHQ Staff had observed that 'The cost of this war on the British at every level should not be underestimated. Our tactics will ensure there is no respite. Besides the high financial cost of maintaining their presence and guarding a vast array of potential targets, this war does and will continue to play havoc with their nerves and their lifestyles.'[9] Some targets could hardly be guarded. On 24 October 1990 the IRA took over a Derry house and deployed what some were to call the human bomb: Patsy Gillespie was forced (his family being held hostage) to drive a car loaded with a bomb to a British Army checkpoint, where it exploded killing five soldiers as well as Gillespie himself. On the same day another proxy bomb outside Newry killed a soldier; yet another attack occurred at Omagh, but the main bomb did not explode – on this occasion a man had been strapped into the driving seat while his wife and child were held hostage.

Clearly, republicans also suffered. On 12 February 1989 Belfast solicitor Pat Finucane was killed by loyalists in north Belfast. Two days later, John Davey – a Sinn Féin councillor – was shot and killed by loyalists on his way home from a council meeting. On 9 October 1990 IRA men Dessie Grew and Martin McCaughey (from the Provisionals' Tyrone Brigade) were shot dead by the SAS, just outside Loughgall in

County Armagh. Grew's INLA brother, Seamus, had been killed by the RUC in 1982; McCaughey was intending shortly to marry. The Pat Finucane killing began a long argument (and ultimately an inquiry) concerning alleged collusion by the security forces in his death. Two of the people involved in the targeting and killing of the lawyer were security force agents, prompting the important question: why did the security forces not prevent the killing from taking place? Republicans unsurprisingly felt that such episodes reinforced their claim that the state in the north was one in which the most lethal of injustices could be carried out by the authorities without redress.

But behind the dreadful killings such as that of Pat Finucane were other developments; in some of them fuses were burning – for once – towards peace. In 1990 the British government embarked on an initiative to woo Irish republicans away from violence. They rightly recognized that it would be difficult to imagine a straightforward military defeat of the IRA, and so began to approach the matter rather more subtly. In October that year a British representative (Michael Oatley, with MI6 experience) met with Sinn Féin's Martin Mc-Guinness, at the prompting of the British themselves. British intelligence sources had suggested to the government that some, at least, of the republican leaders might want an end to the armed conflict; Secretary of State Peter Brooke had thus blessed the use of secret back-channel contacts with republicans. A long and significant sequence now commenced.

As Sinn Féin themselves pointed out in 1994, there was nothing new about contacts between republicans and the British: 'A line of communication has existed between Sinn Féin and the British government for over twenty years. It has not been in constant use. It has been used in an intensive way during such periods as the bi-lateral truce of 1974–75 and the Long Kesh hunger strikes of 1980 and 1981. It was reactivated by the British government in mid-1990, leading to a period of protracted contact and dialogue between Sinn Féin and the British government.'[10] The dialogue involved a chain which also drew in former Catholic priest Denis Bradley as well as an MI5 officer known as 'Fred'. It ran, fitfully, from October 1990 until November 1993.

In the latter month it became known that the back-channel contacts had occurred, and the British tried to defuse embarrassment by claiming that in February 1993 they had received a message (passed on

orally) from Martin McGuinness saying that the conflict was over, but
that republicans needed the advice of the British on how to bring it to
a close. Republicans strongly denied that such a message had been
sent, and what appears to have occurred is this. The British had indeed
received a message, but one put together by the intermediaries between
republicans and the government, rather than directly by the republicans themselves. The contested message was actually drafted by the
three-person Derry Catholic link (including Bradley), and then passed
on to 'Fred', who appears further to have amended the wording before
the finalized message reached the British authorities. So a message had
indeed been sent (as the British claimed), but (as republicans themselves had rightly pointed out) it had not originated with the IRA.
In one sense, both sides had been right. The message purported to
represent what republicans actually thought, rather than what they
would be prepared at that stage to say. The aim had been to push
things forward – which it emphatically managed to do.

   More generally, in publishing their own record of the republican-
British contacts of the early 1990s, Sinn Féin pointed out that the
British had not always been utterly reliable about such matters: 'In
public comments repeated many times British ministers, including
Prime Minister John Major, have said that they would not negotiate
with Irish republicans. That representatives of the British government
have done so, and with approval at the highest level of government, is
clear from this record.'[11] Certainly, the government's credibility was
rather undermined by the less than reliable way in which they dealt
with disclosures of the early-1990s dialogue with Irish republicans;
even the resolutely anti-republican Ian Paisley acknowledged that
people had more faith in his adversaries' accounts of such meetings
than in those offered by his government: 'people believe now that the
IRA version of their undercover talks with Britain has more truth in it
than the Northern Ireland Office's . . . something that is very repugnant
to me, but it's become a reality, that people have more faith in the
statements of the IRA than they have in the statements of the British
government'.[12]

   For its part, the British government under Conservative leader
John Major[13] made Northern Ireland something of a priority. He had
replaced Margaret Thatcher as party leader and Prime Minister in
1990, and was to develop not only a sustained interest in the north,

but also a good relationship with Fianna Fáil's Albert Reynolds (who became Taoiseach in 1992). Major's early 1990s were a period during which signals were being sent. On 9 November 1990 Secretary of State Peter Brooke (in a speech that was sent to the Provisionals in advance) argued that 'the British government has no selfish strategic or economic interest in Northern Ireland',[14] a declaration as upsetting to unionists as it was intriguing to republicans. For this appeared to contradict the IRA's view of British motivation in Ireland, undermining the argument that the continued British presence was due to colonial and self-interested policy on London's part. True, Britain might never be truly neutral in the Irish conflict; but that did not mean that the British necessarily remained in the north because of self-interest or advantage.

So when the IRA declared a Christmas ceasefire at the end of 1990, the gesture formed part of a wider culture of contact, gesture and cautious engagement. The Provisionals' New Year message for 1991 clearly outlined their thinking, in relation to war and peace. The organization existed 'in response to a part of Ireland, and its people, being held by military force against the will of the vast majority of the Irish nation'. Prescription followed neatly from description: 'The challenge to the NIO [Northern Ireland Office] and Downing Street is to face up to the inevitability of Irish unity rather than trying to revitalise a dying colonial rule.'[15]

For, accompanying the music of violence, there were now other – more irenic – themes to be heard in the republican symphony: less obvious perhaps, but increasingly audible. Speaking at the end of January 1991, Sinn Féin President Gerry Adams remained loyal to aggressive republican orthodoxy, but hinted that change might still be possible. There was no doubting his public commitment to the legitimacy of force: 'where you have an occupation force, Sinn Féin believes, whether it be here or South Africa, that people have the right to engage in armed resistance. That is our political opinion.' But there was, he said, a way to end the violence: 'The Sinn Féin position is that, when you have the conditions for conflict, how you end the conflict is to change the conditions.' Adams felt that the conditions for Irish peace could indeed be created, and that inclusive talks would prove the way forward: 'the leaders of unionism know in their heart of hearts that, when there is a settlement thrashed out here, they are going to be sitting down with the rest of us. They know that and what is happening is that they are being pulled slowly, tortuously slowly, kicking and squealing, into that. The nineties is the decade in which peace can be agreed and we can start building a future.'[16]

In August 1991 Adams launched an initiative calling for talks aimed at a political settlement. On the 20th of that month he revealed that he had written to the Irish and British governments, and to political and Church leaders, to say that he was prepared to participate in discussions in pursuit of a solution to the northern troubles. He had written, he said, 'with a view to seeking open-ended discussions on the conflict in the north and the development of a peace process capable of achieving the political conditions necessary for an end to violence . . . We [Sinn Féin] believe that peace can be achieved, we are prepared to take political risks, we are prepared to give and take, we are committed to establishing a peace process.'[17]

During 1991 and 1992 the Provisionals were briefed (indirectly, by the British) on British government policy, and were given advance notice of key speeches. One such major British overture was played in December 1992 in Coleraine when Patrick Mayhew, the then Secretary of State for Northern Ireland, argued that while Northern Irish majority preference for membership of the UK would continue to be respected, 'there is also the aspiration to a united Ireland, an aspiration that is no less legitimate'. Indeed, 'Provided it is advocated constitutionally, there can be no proper reason for excluding any political objective from discussion. Certainly not the objective of an Ireland united through broad agreement fairly and freely achieved.' Were the Provisionals to eschew violence, Mayhew continued, then British attitudes and responses to the northern situation would be looked at afresh. This was a dramatic speech. Here was a British Secretary of State declaring the equal legitimacy of the unionist and republican aspirations, offering the prospect of post-ceasefire flexibility of response from London (and even finding benign words to say about IRA heroes such as Ernie O'Malley).[18] The republican response to Mayhew's Coleraine speech was publicly hostile (*An Phoblacht/Republican News* carried the headline 'Mayhew Blocks Path to Peace');[19] but there was much in it of import for the republican movement (as reflected in some unionist anger at Mayhew's words – DUP leader Ian Paisley held that Mayhew's 'whole speech, in tone and content, is weighed heavily in favour of republicanism. It is outrageous. No wonder he had neither the will nor zeal to put down the IRA. That is why they are having a field day.')[20]

If the British were sending out signals, then the following year also saw further development of intranationalist dialogue. In April 1993 John Hume and Gerry Adams engaged in substantial talks together (which became publicly known when, in April, Adams was seen going into Hume's Derry house), and these resulted in important statements in April and September. The first of these firmly endorsed the crucial nationalist view that the Irish people as a whole possessed the right to national self-determination – a central theme in the evolving peace process of the 1990s; the second set of agreed points was forwarded to Dublin. An IRA statement released in that city on 3 October welcomed the Hume–Adams initiative: 'We are informed of the broad principles which will be for consideration by the London and Dublin governments ... if the political will exists or can be created, it [the Hume–Adams initiative] could provide the basis for peace.'[21]

On 15 December 1993 the London and Dublin governments offered their own joint initiative, with the dually sponsored Downing Street Declaration. Launched by the respective premiers, Major and Reynolds, the Declaration attempted to square the Northern Irish circle, deploying commas to powerful effect, with successive phrases intended to placate competing nationalist and unionist audiences: 'The British government agree that it is for the people of the island of Ireland alone, by agreement between the two parts respectively, to exercise their right of self-determination on the basis of consent, freely and concurrently given, north and south, to bring about a united Ireland, if that is their wish.' John Major pledged himself to 'uphold the democratic wish of the greater number of the people of Northern Ireland on the issue of whether they prefer to support the union or a sovereign united Ireland'. Albert Reynolds acknowledged that 'it would be wrong to attempt to impose a united Ireland, in the absence of the freely given consent of the majority of the people of Northern Ireland'; thus 'the democratic right of self-determination by the people of Ireland as a whole must be achieved and exercised with and subject to the agreement and consent of a majority of the people of Northern Ireland'.[22] So the language of Irish self-determination was firmly established in formal British-Irish politics, but with the vital qualification that it should be exercised with respect for majority (effectively, unionist) opinion in the north.

The Downing Street Declaration, with its attempt to build a consensual set of relationships both in Northern Ireland and between Ireland and Britain, won support from many quarters. In the view of SDLP leader John Hume, the Declaration undermined by the IRA's insistence on the use of republican violence:

> it goes through the ... traditional reasons given by the IRA. It makes very clear that the British government have no selfish or strategic interest or economic interest in Ireland ... And the second major reason given for the use of physical force is that they [the British] are preventing the people of Ireland from exercising the right to self-determination and the Declaration is very clear on that because, as I have often argued, it's *people* that have rights, not *territory*. And unfortunately, but it is a fact, the people of this island are divided on how to exercise that right.[23]

But the December 1993 Declaration had aimed to draw aggressive political players into constitutional politics, and Irish republican responses were hesitant and sceptical. Prisoners in the H-Blocks held discussions on the Declaration in December and January, and expressed an 'initial disappointment' with it:

> What is wrong with the Downing Street Declaration is that it ignores why partition has failed to bring peace, justice or stability to the people of this island (unionist and nationalist). It ignores Britain's responsibility and role. Instead, we are asked to recognise as some great concession to the principle of national self-determination the British government position that should a majority in favour of Irish unity emerge in the north then Britain would not stand in its way. As if Britain could but do anything else! But this will never happen.

Northern Ireland had been 'artificially created to perpetuate a unionist majority', and there remained 'no incentive to unionists to change their attitudes'. Yet the prisoners' response was tellingly complicated by a more positive strain of thinking: 'we should continue to urge Britain to join the ranks of the peace-makers ... and to persuade unionists to consider visualising an accommodation with the rest of the people of Ireland and within Ireland. For our part we recognise that there could be no durable peace without unionist consent to new political structures.' The prisoners were not, therefore, counselling withdrawal from the process, in part because of a confidence in their own importance to that process: the British could not risk pushing republicans too hard because 'There can be no viable peace process which does not include the republican movement.'[24]

Republican leaders were not convinced of British intentions – 'From the beginning the Major government has been devious and mischievous in its approach to the Irish peace initiative'[25] – Gerry Adams issuing a statement in January 1994 to the effect that 'The London government also demands an IRA surrender, as a precondition to dialogue with Sinn Féin.'[26] But – though Sinn Féin were formally unimpressed by the Downing Street Declaration – they remained involved in the broad peace process. And there were certainly some soothing developments for Irish republicans. In January 1994 the Republic of Ireland's broadcasting ban on Sinn Féin was lifted; and later in the same month came another indication of the thaw towards militant republicanism, with the granting by President Bill Clinton of a short-term visa for Gerry Adams to visit the USA. The British government had opposed such a move, hoping to prevent Adams making it to the States (he had been refused a visa as recently as late-1993). But in early 1994 he enjoyed his first American jaunt. Fifteen years earlier, he had denounced big business, multinationalism and capitalism; now, he made a good impression with respectable America and became something of a celebrity. Soft-spoken and articulate, he defied the assumptions of those who had expected political militancy to be manifested in unsophisticated rage. As the influential Irish-American journalist Niall O'Dowd[27] recalled, Adams did well on his first visit: 'He was a huge success. He made a tremendous impact.'[28] Irish republicans were being listened to, and were apparently enjoying an opportunity to talk.

2

'Sinn Féin is convinced that partition and Britain's continued
presence are the core issues creating conflict and division.
They are the political barriers to peace and political progress.'

Gerry Adams, addressing the Sinn Féin *ard fheis*
in February 1992[29]

But talking did not preclude killing. The IRA continued to represent
an aggressive form of Irish nationalism, as was evident during the
early 1990s, which witnessed various kinds of political violence. On
17 September 1990, in Margaret Thatcher's constituency of Finchley in
London, the IRA shot a British soldier as he emerged from a recruiting
office. In their statement on this shooting, the Provisionals commented: 'We take this opportunity to remind the Thatcher regime that
they have it in their power to grant peace to Ireland and to end their
futile conflict with our people.'[30] On 7 February the next year an IRA
mortar attack on Downing Street, which had initially been conceived
with Thatcher herself as its target, came close to hitting her successor
as Conservative Prime Minister, John Major. In the wake of this close-
to-home attack, a spokesperson for the IRA's GHQ Staff suggested that
'Like any colonialists, the members of the British establishment do not
want the result of their occupation landing at their front or back
doorstep . . . Are the members of the British cabinet prepared to give
their lives to hold on to a colony? They should understand the cost
will be great while Britain remains in Ireland.' The answer lay in
moving towards 'the only possible lasting solution', namely British
disengagement from Ireland: 'History has proved in many, many
colonial struggles that once the colonial power leaves, true peace and
democracy can flourish.'[31]

While some IRA violence was aimed clearly at the British, in other
instances it took a different form. Intracommunal punishment attacks
occupied much of the Provisionals' energy, as those Catholics in the
north deemed to be engaged in antisocial action (such as repeated
house robberies, car thefts or joy-riding) were brutally policed with,

for example, beatings or kneecappings (shooting victims through the knees), or other punishment shootings. These were extremely numerous, republicans apparently carrying out 1,228 punishment shootings between 1973 and 1997, and a further 755 beatings during 1982–97.[32] Clearly, there was a problem in some republican areas with petty (and with not so petty) crime, and the hostility of those areas towards the RUC meant that there was something of a vacuum in terms of policing. Equally clearly, the practice of kneecapping was ineffective in terms of deterrence – with consistently high levels of offence and reoffence of those crimes or activities for which people were being punished in this way. Moreover, it seems clear that in some cases people's real crime was to have defied the IRA. Intracommunal vendettas and power struggles played their part in these gruesome IRA policing methods. (Even a comparatively sympathetic observer of Irish republicans such as Kevin Kelley was forced to acknowledge that 'kneecapping is, in general, neither a humane nor a foolproof practice').[33] The IRA's social war included conflict with alleged drug dealers. On 4 and 5 October 1991 there occurred in Belfast a series of IRA operations in which individuals and premises allegedly involved in the drugs trade were served notice to end their activities. The Provisionals issued a statement shortly after bombing a Belfast city-centre bar, allegedly linked to the drugs trade:

> The bombing of Monaghan's Bar and the shooting of four men in the west Belfast area on Friday night were carried out by our Volunteers following a long-term and in-depth investigation into the supply and use of a range of drugs including ecstasy, acid and cannabis, which has been escalating over recent months. [The four men] were all shot and have been ordered to leave Ireland for supplying drugs and organising so-called 'raves'. A further twenty individuals have been ordered to leave Belfast or face military action because of their direct involvement in the drugs trade.[34]

Part of the Provos' concern about policing lay in the fact that the RUC tried to recruit informers from among petty criminals in Catholic areas. And certainly, the intelligence battle between state and anti-state rebels was a vital one.[35]

The war continued to take its painful toll on republicans themselves: once again, public attention to the suffering of the IRA's victims should not blind us to the suffering that republicans themselves endured. On the morning of 3 June 1991 three IRA men – Peter Ryan, Tony Doris and Lawrence McNally – were killed in an SAS ambush in the County Tyrone village of Coagh. The DUP's Ian Paisley responded enthusiastically, 'The Army has once again demonstrated its ability to take out of circulation the IRA murdering thugs who are carrying out a campaign of blood in our province.'[36] Yet violence was increasingly combined with a demand that some form of settlement be hammered out. The IRA's New Year statement for 1992 contained a defiant demand for an end to the conflict: 'Our ability to diversify and to strike effectively and hard has driven home the message that Britain is fast running out of options and must soon face the inevitable by taking the steps necessary to resolve this conflict and grant peace and stability to the people of Ireland.' Britain knew, the statement continued, that the IRA could continue and intensify their struggle, and that the organization could not be contained or defeated. 'We for our part genuinely desire peace; the British have it in their power to grant peace.'[37]

That the IRA had the capacity to carry on their attritional war was again evident on Friday 17 January 1992: seven Protestants were killed when an IRA landmine blew up the van in which they were travelling near Teebane Crossroads in County Tyrone. The seven (an eighth victim also subsequently died) were workmen who had been engaged in construction work at a security base in Omagh. The IRA's Tyrone Brigade claimed responsibility for the attack on what *An Phoblacht/ Republican News* referred to as 'collaborators'. The IRA's own statement set out their rationale clearly enough:

> the IRA reiterates its long-standing call to those who continue to provide services or materials to the forces of occupation to desist immediately. Since 1985 the IRA has adopted a policy of taking military action aimed at ending Britain's cynical use of non-military personnel for the servicing and maintenance of British Crown Forces' bases and installations . . . For our part we in the IRA will not tolerate a situation where military personnel are freed from essential services and maintenance tasks and then deployed where they can carry out wholesale repression within our community.[38]

Condemnation of the Teebane killings was widespread and emphatic. UK Prime Minister John Major said that the killers were 'odious, contemptible and cowardly and would never change government policy'. Northern Ireland Secretary of State Peter Brooke observed: 'The IRA will not succeed by the means they are using. A democratic society cannot give in to the bullet and the bomb.' The SDLP's Denis Haughey stated, 'This was an appalling crime – and to what purpose? This bloody slaughter must cease.'[39] But Sinn Féin President Gerry Adams struck a different note, claiming that the IRA's killing of the construction workers at Teebane was 'a horrific reminder of the failure of British policy in Ireland'.[40]

On 5 February 1992 loyalists of the UFF exacted revenge for the Teebane killings when they shot dead five Catholics in a crowded betting shop on Belfast's lower Ormeau Road. The UFF declared that the lower Ormeau was 'one of the IRA's most active areas'; 'Remember Teebane,' they warned. The IRA had killed Protestants; the UFF had killed Catholics. So the cyclical tragedy seemed to have life in it yet. After the Ormeau Road killings, the cousin of one of the dead men stood staring at the door of the bookmakers where the atrocity had occurred, and said: 'I just don't know what to say but I know one thing – this is the best thing that's happened for the Provos in this area in years. This is the best recruitment campaign they could wish for.'[41] For while the conflict in the north was more than *just* a cyclical feud between Protestant and Catholic paramilitaries, that had indeed become one strain to the war. Whatever its intention, violence by loyalists or by republicans tended – in practice – often to stimulate rather than stifle further killing by the other side.

On the relationship between the organization's recent operations in Britain and the forthcoming UK general election, a representative of the Provisionals' GHQ Staff commented in early 1992: 'each IRA operation, particularly if it takes place within England, has the effect of focusing the establishment's attention on their war in Ireland, which they would otherwise ignore. On this level then, it is fair to comment that operations around major political events do carry the added bonus of forcing the Irish war onto the British political agenda.'[42]

The 9 April 1992 UK general election saw Gerry Adams lose his seat as west Belfast MP, a deeply demoralizing moment for Irish republicans in terms of their capacity to determine that British political agenda. True, Sinn Féin obtained 10 per cent of the Northern Ireland vote; but the loss of their only seat (to the SDLP's Joe Hendron) was a blow, just as John Hume's easy victory in Foyle over Martin McGuinness (26,710 votes compared with 9,149) demonstrated the length of the road faced by militant republicans if they wanted to claim genuine nationalist pre-eminence in the north.[43] Indeed, would Adams's defeat mean that the Provisionals would move away from politics and go back more unambiguously towards a physical-force approach? Danny Morrison hoped not: 'There may now be a big temptation, because of frustration and alienation, for many republicans to abandon even their limited faith in politics and place all their trust in armed struggle. That emotional reaction should be resisted. It is no guarantee of success. It is to go in the wrong direction.'[44]

The day after the general election saw an operation that might have seemed to confirm Morrison's fears, when the IRA bombed London's Baltic Exchange, killing three people, and leading to a massive insurance pay-out. To target the City of London in this way was to attack a key part of the UK economy, and attracted more attention – internationally, as well as in London itself – than did the killing of people in the north of Ireland – as the IRA well knew. Since, to republican eyes, the conflict was between Britain and Ireland, it made more sense to apply pressure where the (British) political decisions would ultimately be made. Members of the security forces were proving more difficult to kill as they became more adept at their anti-IRA role, and this too reinforced the IRA logic of English bombs: during the 1970s, 583 soldiers and police officers had been killed in the troubles; during the 1980s, 341.[45]

In May 1992 it was announced that MI5 were taking over the primary role against the IRA's war in Britain. But that war continued, with *An Phoblacht/Republican News* gloating on 10 December that 'The IRA's bombing campaign in England is turning Britain's capital city into an armed fortress. Specialist heavily-armed squads have been mounting road blocks, stopping and searching traffic and causing major delays and disruption in the London area for the past two weeks.' The Provisionals' New Year message for 1993 sounded ever-confident. They claimed that British attempts to persuade republicans that their struggle was at a dead end, had failed. And the organization had their own message for British ears: 'we will, by our continued efforts, sooner or later, convince them that there is but one solution and that solution is based upon British disengagement.'[46] At Easter, the IRA leadership lamented British and unionist attempts 'to copper-fasten partition and set the unionist veto in bronze, thus conferring on a national minority the power to block the desires of the overwhelming majority of our people'.[47]

And so the bombs continued to be heard. On 24 April 1993 another devastating explosion in central London saw one person killed, many others injured and millions of pounds' worth of damage done. In its statement relating to this bomb at the Bishopsgate NatWest tower the IRA said, 'The leadership of the IRA repeats its call for the British establishment to seize the opportunity and to take the steps needed for ending its futile and costly war in Ireland. We again emphasise that they should pursue the path of peace or resign themselves to the path of war.'[48] The IRA also sought to apply financial pressure upon the British government indirectly. In a statement sent to foreign-owned financial institutions in the City of London, the organization noted that Bishopsgate had been the second attack of its kind in a year, and warned that 'no one should be misled into underestimating the seriousness of the IRA's intention to mount future planned attacks in the political and financial heart of the British state': 'In the context of present political realities, further attacks on the City of London and elsewhere are inevitable. This we feel we are bound to convey to you directly, to allow you to make fully informed decisions.'[49] On 3 February 1994 *An Phoblacht/Republican News* trumpeted that 'IRA bombs once again exploded in London last week ... Over a million pounds of trade was lost over a three-day period when incendiary bombs began to detonate at various locations in central London.'

Loved lives were also destroyed. On Saturday 20 March 1993 Jonathan Ball (aged three) was killed and twelve-year-old Tim Parry was fatally injured by IRA bombs in the northern English town of Warrington. Tim's parents, Colin and Wendy Parry, the following day broke down outside the hospital where their dying son was being treated. The boy's father agonizingly spoke: 'I have got a son who is not going to live, a good-looking twelve-year-old boy pulled apart ... and for what? I just feel empty.'[50] Tim Parry's injuries had indeed been horrific: most of his face had been blown away and his skull had been fractured. He died on Thursday 25 March. In a statement issued on the day after the bombing, the IRA said that it had indeed planted the Warrington bombs. But the Provisionals said that 'Responsibility for

the tragic and deeply regrettable death and injuries caused in Warrington yesterday lies squarely at the door of those in the British authorities
who deliberately failed to act on precise and adequate warnings.'[51] Yet,
in an interview with the *Irish News*, an IRA spokesperson acknowledged that the Warrington episode 'did not serve the interests of the
IRA'.[52]

Popular and understandable revulsion at the Warrington tragedy
did not alter Irish republican aspirations. A representative of the IRA's
General Headquarters Staff was reported in October of the same year
as reiterating republican orthodoxy: 'The obstacle to peace in Ireland
is the British presence and the partition of Ireland.' The IRA and their
supporters had 'a vested interest' in seeking a just, lasting peace but
the British had responded negatively: 'The British government attitude
seems set to condemn us all to continued conflict.'[53] So there was
much continuity in republican thinking. As Gerry Adams observed,
'Simplistically put, the republican objective remains as it always was.
Sinn Féin has not ceased to be a republican party. We want to see an
Irish republic.'[54] Or, as leading Sinn Féiner Mitchel McLaughlin put it,
'Everyone knows that attempts in the past at internal solutions have
always failed. There can be no internal solution.'[55]

Despite this, republicans were now engaged in a long political
strategy of which peace negotiations formed a significant part. They
wanted inclusive dialogue leading to the ending of the stalemated
conflict. Speaking in early April 1993, an IRA spokesperson argued
that resolution of the Northern Irish conflict required 'dialogue which
is both inclusive and without preconditions'. The IRA were prepared
to demonstrate the leadership and courage necessary 'to bring such a
dialogue to a fruitful conclusion. Those who have the power to resolve
this conflict will find republicans are people they can do business
with.'[56]

Yet while London and the republicans had by this stage been in
lengthy contact, there remained the central problem of how unionists
and loyalists in the north were to fit into any prospective settlement
process. And the early 1990s witnessed not a diminution but an
intensifying of intercommunal violence in Ulster. *An Phoblacht/Repub-
lican News* referred on 9 September 1993 to the loyalist murder of
Catholics by 'sectarian death squads, armed by the British government',
but loyalism seemed to have sturdy enough local roots to produce

lasting obstacles to republican aspiration. At times, the IRA became drawn into the brutal interparamilitary cycle. On Monday 11 January 1993 the Tyrone Brigade had killed alleged UVF organizer Matthew John Boyd, from Dungannon, County Tyrone. A Provisional statement on the killing said: 'Boyd had a long involvement in the UVF dating back to the 1970s ... his increasingly crucial role in UVF sectarian murders became clear and IRA intelligence had him under surveillance along with several other UVF personnel.' The IRA 'will not get involved in a sectarian campaign but, as on Monday afternoon, we will execute those involved in sectarian killings'.[57]

Yet sectarian killing is precisely what seemed to be going on, and the bloody nature of that conflict was made horrifically evident later in 1993 with one of the most notorious of all IRA operations. On Saturday 23 October an IRA bomb exploded around lunchtime on the Protestant Shankill Road in Belfast. The bombing occurred in a fish shop owned by the Frizzells, the ostensible target being a UDA meeting mistakenly thought by the IRA to have been taking place above the shop. In particular, the IRA had hoped to kill Johnny 'Mad Dog' Adair of the UFF. The bombers, dressed in white overalls and posing as fish-delivery men, left a box containing the device at the fish shop. The time was 1.15 p.m., and the Shankill Road was predictably packed with Saturday shoppers. The bomb exploded prematurely, killing one of the bombers (IRA man Thomas Begley) and nine Protestants, in scenes of appalling horror. One paramedic later recalled: 'There was one lady lying in the road with head injuries and half her arm was blown off. She later died. But the worst part for me was when we unearthed the body of a young girl. I will never forget seeing that face staring up out of the rubble.'[58]

Nearly sixty people were injured in the Shankill bombing, and of the nine Protestants killed (four women, three men, two girls), none were paramilitaries. IRA protestations that they were a non-sectarian organization sounded empty and unpersuasive in such circumstances. Particularly to the bereaved. Among the victims were George and Gillian Williamson. They had just moved house, were out shopping for curtain material for their new home, and died instantly in the blast. The day after the bomb, their twenty-three-year-old son Ian sat, his face wet with tears and his arm around his older sister Michelle. 'I had to go to the morgue,' Ian said, 'and identify my Mum and Dad. I will never forget that. I will never forget their faces.' Michelle, her voice frequently breaking down, spoke out in rage: 'I am angry. I am bitter. I will never forgive them for this. Never. I want to see Gerry Adams face-to-face. I want to tell him that the people who did this to my Mammy and Daddy are nothing but scum. I want to tell him they are evil bastards.'[59] Three days later, on the day of their parents' funeral, Ian and Michelle offered a plea for there to be no retaliation for their mother's and father's killing.

Another of the shoppers on the Shankill Road that Saturday had been Mrs Gina Murray. She had been with her thirteen-year-old daughter Leanne, who had gone into the fish shop and was killed by the IRA bomb: 'Leanne had just left me to go in to the fish shop. Suddenly there was this huge bang. We ran screaming for Leanne. We couldn't find her. No one had seen her. There were people lying in the street covered in blood. My little girl was underneath all that rubble. We started clawing at it with our bare hands. I was screaming her name but it was no use. My little daughter was dead.'[60]

IRA man and Shankill-bomber Thomas Begley was twenty-three, from Ardoyne in Belfast. He died just seconds after planting the bomb, while his fellow bomber, Sean Kelly, was injured and later jailed. The UDA office upstairs had actually been empty, the loyalist organization having stopped using that building some weeks earlier. Gerry Adams, speaking on 24 October, said of the Shankill bomb: 'It was wrong. It cannot be excused.'[61] The IRA themselves claimed that they believed a meeting of the UDA Inner Council to have been in progress in the building.

In the weeks preceding the Shankill bombing a number of Catholics had been killed by the UDA/UFF. Thus that bomb was itself a response to loyalist violence. It was followed by more. On 25 October Sean Fox (Catholic, a retired grocer in his seventies) was shot dead by the UVF, who claimed that he was a republican. The killing – involving a number of gunshot wounds to the head – took place at Fox's Glengormley home, just north of Belfast. The UVF said that attacks like this would continue, and that there would be no let-up after the Shankill bomb.

Indeed, the IRA's Shankill gesture had provoked the UFF into swift retaliation. On 26 October more blood followed threats when the UFF killed two Catholic men in west Belfast: Mark Rodgers (twenty-eight, and married with children aged six and two) and Jim Cameron (fifty-four, and married with children of twenty, seventeen and eleven). On Saturday the 30th, in the village of Greysteel in County Derry, a UFF gun attack killed seven people: about two hundred had been in the lounge of the Rising Sun Bar waiting for a special Hallowe'en night country-and-western dance to start; two hooded gunmen (armed with a machine-gun and a rifle) entered the bar, one said 'Trick or Treat', and then the killing started. The dead were six Catholics and one Protestant; eleven others were wounded. The UFF observed of these killings, 'This is the continuation of our threats against the nationalist electorate that they would pay a heavy price for last Saturday's slaughter of nine Protestants.'[62] In the month before the IRA's Shankill bombing, loyalists killed three people; in the month after the bomb, thirteen.[63]

Could an end be seen to all of this? In early 1994 the IRA was certainly declaring itself positively minded towards the evolving Irish peace process: 'We are prepared to be flexible in exploring the potential for peace. All concerned should leave no stone unturned.'[64] That spring, the Provisionals announced that they would suspend offensive military actions for three days in April, and they presented the gesture as reflecting their positive and flexible attitude towards the search for peace.[65] In its Easter message, the IRA leadership claimed that it was the responsibility of all involved to overcome the obstacles on the road to peace, but that this responsibility fell 'particularly' on the British government.[66]

Republicans came to talk in terms of a new strategy, TUAS; originally taken by some to mean Totally Unarmed Strategy, it later transpired that the letters referred to the Tactical Use of Armed Struggle. TUAS – set out in a document circulated in the summer of 1994 – involved republicans aiming to build an Irish nationalist consensus or alliance with international dimensions, the peace process thus necessitating combined effort between Sinn Féin, the SDLP, Dublin and Irish America. The republican goal was said not to have changed, a 'united 32-county democratic socialist republic'. But republicans on their own lacked the power to achieve this objective. The TUAS argument was that, with a broader nationalist consensus, a momentum-generating alliance, it might be possible to move the struggle forward. The major Irish nationalist parties were thought to have much that was shared in terms of their preferred direction, and such a moment – it was felt – should be seized. This had implications, clearly, for the use of violence: the alliances envisaged here could be built and sustained only if the IRA were at least to stall their war. But the Provisionals would still be fighting on, in a different way: 'It is vital that activists realise the struggle is not over. Another front has opened up and we should have the confidence and put in the effort to succeed on that front.'[67] But if republican violence was to be replaced by republican politics, then the latter path would have to appeal as one that could offer progress: 'there is an onus on those who proclaim that the armed struggle is counter-productive to advance a credible alternative'.[68]

EIGHT

CESSATIONS OF VIOLENCE
1994–2002

1

'The IRA is a very political organization, and it made political decisions on the basis of what . . . it felt it could prosecute, not on what it felt its community was absorbing. Because the IRA is a very stubborn organization as well . . . It would go against public opinion, and did on many occasions in the past (even republican grassroots opinion), if it thought that there was an achievable objective.'

Danny Morrison, 2000[1]

On Wednesday 31 August 1994 the IRA issued a potentially epoch-making statement: 'Recognising the potential of the current situation and in order to enhance the democratic peace process and underline our definitive commitment to its success the leadership of Óglaigh na hÉireann have decided that as of midnight, Wednesday, 31 August, there will be a complete cessation of military operations. All our units have been instructed accordingly.' This was an 'historic crossroads': the IRA reiterated their commitment to republican objectives, but argued that new times had been reached: 'Our struggle has seen many gains and advances made by nationalists and for the democratic position. We believe that an opportunity to create a just and lasting settlement has been created. We are therefore entering into a new situation in a spirit of determination and confidence: determined that the injustices which created the conflict will be removed and confident in the strength and justice of our struggle to achieve this.'[2]

Immediate responses to the cessation varied greatly. The northern

nationalist paper, the *Irish News*, carried a front-page headline proclaiming, 'A New Era', with the subheading 'Time to build a peaceful
future for all': 'The IRA ceasefire is not the end of something, it is the
beginning. From today the future of Ireland is in the hands of its
people – nationalist and unionist, Catholic and Protestant. We must
seize the day and build for peace. By announcing a complete cessation
of military operations, the IRA has taken the gun out of Irish
republican politics and passed the initiative to political leaders, of
all parties, to move things forward.' This was, the paper asserted, an
'historic time'.[3] The *Guardian* sensed 'The Promise of Peace', claiming
that an 'historic resolution of Northern Ireland's bloody troubles' had
begun to emerge with the ceasefire announcement.[4] The *Belfast Telegraph* front page declared that 'After 3,168 deaths and twenty-five years
of terror, the IRA says . . . It's Over.'[5]

Dublin's *Irish Times* cautiously captured the northern mood with
its front-page declaration, 'Northern Ireland Hopeful and Uncertain as
the IRA Ends Campaign of Violence'. The paper argued: 'There must
be a welcome. And there must be caution. It may not yet be the day
to hang out the flags and colours to mark a full and final peace. But
with the IRA ceasefire since midnight, it becomes possible to hope that
such a happy condition is now within measurable reach.'[6] And distinguished *Independent* journalist David McKittrick wisely observed that
'this is not an IRA surrender. The organisation has the guns, the
expertise and the recruits to go on killing: it has not been militarily
defeated. Rather, it has allowed itself to be persuaded that in the
circumstances of today it stands a better chance of furthering its aims
through politics rather than through violence.'[7]

Many Catholic areas of Belfast were jubilant, the IRA cessation
being seen as a sign of victory (a sense mirrored by some loyalist
anxiety that the ceasefire had been achieved through a secret deal,
through British concessions to the IRA). London itself adopted a
cautious approach. The IRA's announcement was said not to go far
enough. Was the IRA cessation permanent? The clock would not start
ticking for Sinn Féin's entry into political negotiations, so the argument
ran, until the Provisionals clarified that their campaign had ended for
ever.

In contrast, republicans urged fast forward movement. *An
Phoblacht/Republican News* carried a front-page headline proclaiming,

'Seize the Moment for Peace'.[8] And Gerry Adams gave Sinn Féin's response to the cessation: 'The search for peace has reached a decisive moment. I salute the IRA's bold and courageous decision.' The new opportunity had to be seized, 'fundamental political and constitutional change' introduced: 'The unionist veto must be ended. Partition and the six-county state have failed. We must move beyond these failures.'[9] And movement did come. In September 1994 the UK's broadcasting ban on Sinn Féin (which had prevented the voices of Provisionals or their enthusiasts being heard on the media) was lifted. On 13 October, a loyalist ceasefire was announced. The Combined Loyalist Military Command (CLMC) declared that loyalist paramilitaries would cease operational hostilities, confident that the union with Britain had been secured. People were to be killed in subsequent years by loyalist paramilitaries; but the levels of killing were henceforth to be significantly lower.

Republican guns were, likewise, to be quieter – though far, it should be said, from silent. On 10 November a postal worker (Frank Kerr) was killed by south Armagh IRA Volunteers in Newry, during a post office robbery in which £131,000 was stolen. (Apparently, this IRA robbery was very much a local operation, not officially sanctioned by the army's leadership. When the IRA admitted that its members had indeed killed Kerr, they stated: 'Those carrying out the robbery were acting on instructions but the so-called operation had not been sanctioned by the IRA leadership.')[10] Yet there remained a sense of momentum. On 30 November a joint statement from Gerry Adams and John Hume declared: 'We have met to assess the peace process. It is clear to us that the unprecedented opportunity which has been created by the Irish peace initiative, the IRA announcement of 31 August and the loyalist response to this, to peacefully and democratically resolve the causes of conflict, should be addressed energetically by all sides ... A unique opportunity to put the past behind has now been created. It is essential that everyone responds to this new situation.'[11]

In its submission to the British government presented at talks in Belfast on 9 December 1994, Sinn Féin welcomed the resumption of discussions between government and party ('dialogue offers us the best hope of moving forward'), and argued that 'British sovereignty over the six counties, as with all of Ireland before partition, is self-evidently the inherent cause of political instability and conflict.'[12] It was a traditional-sounding argument; but the context within which it was made was decisively new. For in his presidential address to the Sinn Féin *ard fheis* on 25 February the next year, Gerry Adams set out the layered vision republicans held of the peace process: 'We want to see an end to partition. This is our primary objective at this time. Our strategy between now and the ending of partition should be based upon the widely-accepted view that there can be no internal solution, that there has to be fundamental change and that during a transitional phase there must be maximum democracy. There has also to be equality of treatment and parity of esteem.'[13] For new republicans, the ultimate goal of Irish unity was to be interwoven with the pursuit (within Northern Ireland) of an equality agenda.

It was not that republicans had suddenly changed their political minds about their overall reading of Irish political history. In its 1995 Easter message, the IRA leadership reaffirmed their view that the conflict of the preceding twenty-five years had stemmed 'directly from British policy and from the unionist intransigence which the British military and political presence' sustained. But they also reflected the newer strand in their argument, stating that their 1994 ceasefire had been 'aimed at enhancing the climate for inclusive negotiations which would, given the political will on all sides, lead to a just and lasting resolution of this conflict'.[14] For the political dimensions of the north were altered now. In February 1995 documents set out the framework envisaged by Dublin and London for the new arrangements: a northern assembly would be complemented by structures for north–south coop-eration in Ireland. But for peace to work, weaponry had to be dealt with – one way or another. On 7 March Secretary of State for Northern Ireland Patrick Mayhew set out in a speech in Washington three stages for republicans to follow with regard to the decommissioning of their weapons, in order to allow Sinn Féin to enter political talks: there had to be 'a willingness in principle to disarm progressively', practical agreement on the method of doing so, and – as a confidence-building gesture – a tangible beginning to that decommissioning process.[15] The IRA seemed unimpressed. On 1 September a spokesman said that there was 'absolutely no question of any IRA decommissioning, either through the back door or the front door'.[16]

On 29 September a Provisional statement angrily referred to the

British government's demand for a handover of weapons as a precondition for talks, what it called a 'new and unreasonable demand for a handing over of IRA weapons. The entire decommissioning issue is a deliberate distraction and stalling tactic by a British government acting in bad faith.'[17] To republican eyes, the demand for prior decommissioning seemed to amount to a demand for the IRA to admit effective defeat or surrender. In order to try to deal with the decommissioning question, a Commission had been set up, headed by American politician George Mitchell, and in January 1996 the Mitchell Commission reported its findings. Mitchell and his two colleagues on the arms decommissioning team, former Finnish Prime Minister Harri Holkeri and former Chief of Canadian Defence Forces John de Chastelain, suggested that arms be decommissioned alongside – rather than before or after – talks. They also laid down six principles to which political parties should affirm full commitment: first, that political issues be resolved through democratic, exclusively peaceful means; second, that total disarmament of all paramilitary organizations should be achieved; third, that such disarmament be verified by an independent commission; fourth, that parties renounce for themselves and others the use or threat of force to try to influence the outcome of negotiations; fifth, that parties would abide by any agreement reached through negotiations and would use only democratic, peaceful means in trying to alter any part of it to which they objected; sixth, that parties urge the cessation of punishment attacks, and take effective steps to prevent such attacks from occurring.

But the IRA had by this stage reached the view that John Major's government had spent the months since the Provisionals' cessation announcement in prevarication rather than honest commitment to moving the peace process forward. On 9 February 1996 this view resulted in the return of blood-spilling bombs. At 5.30 p.m. on that day the IRA issued a statement announcing 'with great reluctance' the end, from 6 p.m. that evening, of their cessation of military operations. It was the fault of the British: 'Instead of embracing the peace process, the British government acted in bad faith, with Mr Major and the unionist leaders squandering this opportunity to resolve the conflict.'[18] At 7.01 p.m. a bomb exploded near London's Canary Wharf, killing two and injuring many more. Prime Minister John Major called the Canary Wharf bomb 'an appalling outrage', a view echoed by Labour leader Tony Blair who called it a 'sickening outrage'.[19] Those who had been sceptical regarding the IRA's ceasefire felt vindicated. Ian Paisley junior stated that 'the ceasefire was a tactical move by the IRA to achieve by political means what twenty-five years of terrorism had failed to achieve ... If ever there was a lesson on the dangers of cavorting with terrorism then the peace process and the Canary Wharf bomb is such.'[20]

Preparations for this attack had been made, at the latest, in the latter part of 1995; the bomb itself was made in early 1996 by the south Armagh IRA. In mid-February an IRA GHQ Staff spokesperson elaborated the organization's view. The IRA had delivered their 1994 cessation 'on a clear, unambiguous and shared understanding that inclusive negotiations would rapidly commence to bring about political agreement and a peace settlement'. But John Major had reneged on such commitments, introducing preconditions and betraying the peace process in order to keep himself in power (through procuring unionist support). Instead of negotiations there had been 'a year and a half of stalling, prevarication and provocation'. 'British and unionist intransigence' had thus far thwarted the peace process.[21] Gerry Adams, three days after the Canary Wharf bomb, offered similar thoughts. During the IRA ceasefire, he argued,

> the British government and the unionists erected one obstacle after another to frustrate every attempt to sit down around the negotiating table. Inclusive negotiations, without preconditions or vetos, [are] the key to advancing the peace process to a peace settlement. This was the commitment given by the two governments, publicly and repeatedly in the run-up to the IRA cessation. This was the context in which the IRA in August 1994 made their historic announcement. Since that time there has not been one word of real negotiations.

But, significantly, the Sinn Féin President also reaffirmed his party's commitment to the process of peace: 'we are firmly committed to democratic and peaceful means of resolving political issues and to the objective of an equitable and lasting agreement ... Sinn Féin also remains committed to the total disarmament of all armed groups and to the removal, forever, of all guns, republican, loyalist and British, from the political equation in Ireland. Sinn Féin's commitment to our peace strategy and to a lasting peace based on democratic negotiations remains absolute.'[22]

Gerry Adams and John Hume met the IRA on 28 February 1996; in Adams's words, 'John Hume and I spelt out our view of the current situation and of the need to restore the peace process.'[23] But by then more blood had been spilled. On 18 February IRA Volunteer Edward O'Brien had died when a device he was carrying exploded in central London (the twenty-one-year-old Irishman, who had joined the IRA in 1992, was on a bus when the premature explosion occurred). Now, ten days after O'Brien's young death, the British and Irish governments jointly tried to inject life into the now bloodstained peace process: 10 June was set as a date on which all-party talks would commence; elections to a negotiating forum would be held in May. The results of the latter reflected the spread of opinion within as well as between northern unionism and nationalism: the four top parties were the UUP (24 per cent of the vote, 30 seats), the SDLP (21 per cent, 21 seats), the DUP (19 per cent, 24 seats) – and Sinn Féin (15.5 per cent, 17 seats). Sinn Féin's vote here was impressive in comparison with their preceding election performances in the north: in the 1992 UK general election they had obtained 10 per cent of the vote; in the 1993 district council elections, 12 per cent; in the 1994 European parliament elections, 10 per cent.

But pressure remained on the IRA to renew their ceasefire before their political self, Sinn Féin, could enter talks. The republican party was seen by many as being a different *kind* of party from others in Northern Ireland, because of its links to aggressive paramilitary politics. Speaking on 1 June 1996, Secretary of State Patrick Mayhew said, 'People cannot, in a democracy, be expected to sit down and negotiate the future of their democracy with people who are inextricably linked with people who have used weapons in the past for identical political motives and refuse to even contemplate giving them up in the course of those negotiations.'[24] Such fears were reinforced six days later when garda Jerry McCabe was shot dead by the IRA during a robbery in Adare, County Limerick. The Provisionals at first denied responsibility – 'None of our Volunteers or units were in any way involved in this morning's incident at Adare. There was absolutely no IRA involvement'[25] – but later admitted that its Volunteers had indeed been responsible.

And the IRA's continuing violence was accompanied by a continuity of rhetoric. Some things were apparently ruled out in Provisional thinking. Of a return to Stormont the IRA's Easter statement of 1996 commented: 'That is never going to happen. Partition in Ireland was founded and sustained on injustice and a denial of democracy. It has failed and failed utterly.'[26] So, too, did an IRA bomb planted under London's Hammersmith Bridge a few weeks later. The substantial device was placed there on 26 April, and while the detonators apparently exploded, they failed to ignite the Semtex and therefore to set off the bomb. But two months later the Provisionals had more success with a massive explosion in central Manchester. The bomb of 15 June caused huge damage and formed part of the IRA's argument regarding the direction – and, in their view, the corruption – of the peace process. In their statement claiming responsibility for the Manchester bomb, the organization claimed, 'The British government has spent the last twenty-two months since August 1994 trying to force the surrender of IRA weapons and the defeat of the republican struggle.'[27] The Manchester bomb contained over a ton of explosives (mixed, again, by the south Armagh IRA), and more than three hundred people required treatment in its wake – some for dreadful injuries. And the psychological effects on the victims were devastating too: 'I don't think I will ever get over it'; 'He's in shock, shaking all the time and crying – in a really bad way'; 'I'm on tranquillisers – a nervous wreck'.[28]

When the 10 June Stormont talks began, between the north's political parties, Sinn Féin were excluded from the process. The talks chairman was George Mitchell, all talks participants being asked to sign up to the six Mitchell principles set out earlier in the year. But the IRA themselves objected to too close a focus upon military questions. In July 1996 a member of their GHQ Staff was quoted as saying that the key to genuine peace lay with the British and the unionists looking for a political settlement rather than dealing with the conflict from the sole perspective of security: 'Let them honestly address the problem as a political one and not as a security one.'[29] Their 1997 New Year statement declared the IRA to be 'unified, confident and steadfast in our commitment to succeed';[30] and the pages of *An Phoblacht/Republican News* certainly suggested that, from a republican point of view, the peace process was far from over. An editorial of 9 January observed: 'Republicans stand ready to embrace change and to re-create in new and better circumstances the opportunity to transform the political life of our country. 1997 may have begun gloomily but with determination it can be the year when hope is reborn.' (The republican movement's newspaper also occasionally managed lighter touches, early in 1997 offering the 'First joke of the year [in reference to loyalist marches]. Have you heard about the new Orange calendar? It's marked January, February, March, March, March, March, March . . .')[31]

Much within the Provisionals' analysis remained constant: 'While British military occupation persists the Irish people are denied their right to national self-determination and sovereignty. Faced with this reality we remain committed to bringing the British government's undemocratic rule of the occupied part of our country to an end, once and for all.' But the message also reflected, even in its denunciations of British policy, the IRA's continuing engagement with the possibility of peace: The unprecedented opportunity for the establishment of a meaningful peace process presented by our initiative in August 1994 stands as both testimony to our belief that a resolution to the conflict here demands a process built upon inclusive negotiations and proof of our willingness to facilitate such.' The IRA were prepared to face their responsibilities 'in facilitating a process aimed at securing a lasting resolution' to the conflict.[32]

But the conflict had far from claimed its last victim. On 12 February 1997 Stephen Restorick, a twenty-three-year-old British soldier, was shot dead by the IRA just outside Bessbrook, County Armagh, at a checkpoint. Gerry Adams described Restorick's killing as 'tragic': 'the event re-emphasises the need for all of us to redouble our efforts to rebuild the peace process'.[33] When Restorick's mother was informed of her son's death, 'Everything stopped. I just kept saying, "It's not true, it's not true, it's not true. I don't believe it." He couldn't possibly be dead.'[34]

The broader political context for Irish republican violence, or otherwise, was then transformed when in May 1997 the British Labour Party won a landslide general election victory. Mo Mowlam became Secretary of State for Northern Ireland; and while not everything the new Prime Minister, Tony Blair, said was to republicans' liking, the unassailable Labour government warmed up the peace process considerably. And Blair stressed, in Belfast very early in his premiership, that he wanted republicans involved: 'I want the talks process to include Sinn Féin. The opportunity is still there to be taken, if there is an unequivocal IRA ceasefire.'[35]

And republicans' own electoral success in the general election had added to the Provisionals' confidence in the political process: Gerry Adams and Martin McGuinness both won seats. Politics seemed even more fruitful when the Republic of Ireland's general election the following month saw Sinn Féin winning their first Leinster House seat for decades (Caoimhghín O Caoláin topping the poll in Cavan/Monaghan to become a Teachta Dála (TD, member of the Dáil)). Irish republicans were understandably excited by all this. On 12 June an *An Phoblacht/Republican News* front page proclaimed, 'One TD and Two MPs', with a full-page picture of O Caoláin being carried aloft on the shoulders of Adams and McGuinness. The same issue's editorial exuded confidence: 'The stunning victory of Sinn Féin in Cavan/Monaghan represents the biggest breakthrough for the party in the twenty-six counties for decades. No one should underestimate the importance of this achievement. Sinn Féin has truly arrived as a strong political force with its entry to Leinster House and this is not only because of the Cavan/Monaghan victory. The party's vote increased significantly across all fourteen constituencies contested.' 1997 had been 'Sinn Féin's year': 'With dramatic victories in Mid-Ulster and West Belfast and now Cavan/Monaghan, Sinn Féin is on the rise . . . Now with the Sinn Féin mandate massively increased and a momentum for change built up it is time to organise our renewed political strength towards achieving our goals.'

This mood of republican political confidence was further reflected when Caoimhghín O Caoláin gave his opening speech as a Sinn Féin TD in the Dublin Dáil: 'I represent an all-Ireland party that enjoys a significant mandate in both parts of our divided island, and I welcome the presence here today of my colleagues Gerry Adams, MP for West Belfast, and Martin McGuinness, MP for Mid-Ulster. I look forward to the day when I will join them and all the others elected by the Irish people as a whole in a national parliament for the thirty-two counties.'[36] Clearly, though, with 2.4 per cent of the votes cast in the election, Sinn Féin was still a very minor player in Republic of Ireland politics (although even this represented a marked improvement on the party's 1.6 per cent of the votes in the 1992 general election). Moreover, as long as IRA violence continued, there remained a ceiling on the political heights to which republicans were likely to rise electorally. On 16 June 1997 in Lurgan, County Armagh, two RUC men, John Graham and David Johnston, were shot dead by the IRA's North Armagh Brigade – the first members of the RUC to be killed by the IRA since the latter's February 1996 resumption of war. Yet the pressure on republicans to opt decisively for talking rather than for killing was soon to produce results: on Saturday 19 July 1997 the IRA announced a ceasefire. This second cessation was, arguably, a more telling fault-line than the first. The change of government in London had helped produce a different context, one offering new possibilities.

> On August 31 1994 the leadership of Óglaigh na hÉireann (Irish Republican Army) announced their complete cessation of military operations as our contribution to the search for lasting peace. After seventeen months of cessation in which the British government and the unionists blocked any possibility of real or inclusive negotiations, we reluctantly abandoned the cessation. The IRA is committed to ending British rule in Ireland. It is the root cause of division and conflict in our country. We want a permanent peace and therefore we are prepared to enhance the search for a democratic peace settlement through real and inclusive negotiations. So having assessed the current political situation, the leadership of Óglaigh na hÉireann are announcing a complete cessation of military operations. From mid-day Sunday 20 July 1997, we have ordered the unequivocal restoration of the ceasefire of August 1994. All IRA units have been instructed accordingly.[37]

To republicans, the new circumstances offered challenge and opportunity. An editorial in *An Phoblacht/Republican News* observed: 'The renewed IRA cessation has challenged everyone to play their part in the reconstruction of the peace process. For republicans the challenge is to enter a new phase of struggle with the same resourcefulness and determination that they have shown in all previous phases.'[38] Sinn Féin's Martin McGuinness made pacific noises, on behalf of his party: 'We are totally committed to peaceful and democratic means of resolving political problems and we will endeavour to build confidence into the search for agreement through our unremitting efforts to promote dialogue.'[39]

Thus in September 1997 Sinn Féin endorsed the Mitchell principles and entered formal political talks at Stormont in Belfast. This of itself implied that the Provisional movement was prepared to compromise. As the party's leading figure himself observed, 'Negotiations are negotiations, you can't go in and dictate them and have a "take it or leave it" position. So we have to go in and listen. We will put our position and will obviously look at all sorts of suggestions, ideas and proposals put by others. We will consider all of that in the round as part of how you get a democratic peace settlement.'[40] And there were some high-profile opportunities for putting the case. No longer were republicans in a ghetto, as was evident from the meeting in October between Tony Blair and Adams in Belfast (the first meeting between a UK Prime Minister and the Sinn Féin leadership since Lloyd George had met Arthur Griffith and Michael Collins in 1921).

But not all Irish republicans were impressed. In early October an IRA General Army Convention in County Donegal saw a split in the movement. At the GAC the IRA's Quartermaster General denounced the army leadership and called for an end to the IRA ceasefire. Backed by another member of the IRA Executive, he failed to get sufficient support and the orthodox, pro-ceasefire line won the day. The following week saw the dissenting Executive duo resign from the body, after which they formed what later became known as the Real IRA (RIRA). The RIRA were to cause some appallingly bloody violence. But loyalist paramilitaries were active too. On 27 April 1997 Robert Hamill, a Catholic, was fatally attacked in Portadown by loyalists who beat him unconscious; he died on 8 May, his pregnant girlfriend at his hospital bedside. On the 12th a sixty-one-year-old Catholic, Sean Brown, was killed by the Loyalist Volunteer Force (LVF); Seamus Heaney knew the Browns, and was to record Sean's dreadful death.[41] On 1 June RUC officer Gregory Taylor was kicked to death by loyalists as he left a pub in County Antrim: there had been much anger among loyalists because of the rerouting or proscribing of Orange marches and parades, and the police had come to be seen by some loyalists as treacherous to their own cause. Indeed, there was awful variety to loyalist victims. The following year's tense marching season (focusing sharply on the stand-off at Drumcree, where Orangemen resented the banning of one of their march routes) saw loyalist arsonists firebomb a County

Antrim house where a Catholic family lived. The attack, in the early morning of 12 July 1998, left Richard, Mark and Jason Quinn dead: the boys were aged ten, nine and eight, their dreadful 'tiny coffin' destiny movingly captured by northern poet Tom Paulin, as yet more deaths entered the literary record.[42]

Against such tragedy, moves towards peace seemed simultaneously helpless and more urgent. On 12 January 1998, London and Dublin had offered their joint 'Propositions on Heads of Agreement'. These outlined a Northern Irish Assembly; modification both of the Republic of Ireland constitutional claim to the north and also of British legislation concerning Ulster's place in the UK; a north–south ministerial council; and also an intergovernmental council comprising representatives from Irish and British assemblies. The IRA rejected the Propositions. In a statement issued on Wednesday 21 January, the Provos stated: 'The leadership of Óglaigh na hÉireann do not regard the "Propositions on Heads of Agreement" document as a basis for a lasting peace settlement. It is a pro-unionist document and has created a crisis in the peace process.'[43]

The ensuing weeks and months resounded with such negative noises. Yet, with Prime Minister Blair himself supervising the latter stages of the party talks, there apparently emerged, on 10 April, the elusive miracle: a seemingly genuine Northern Irish agreement. The 'Agreement Reached in the Multi-Party Negotiations' – the Belfast Agreement, or Good Friday Agreement – was presented by its participant-creators as offering 'a truly historic opportunity for a new beginning' in Northern Ireland. Commitment was made to 'partnership, equality and mutual respect as the basis of relationships within Northern Ireland, between north and south, and between these islands [of Ireland and Britain]'. Constitutional issues were addressed; efforts were made to balance unionist concern regarding majority northern consent to any change with nationalist belief in Irish self-determination. The British and Irish governments would:

i) recognise the legitimacy of whatever choice is freely exercised
by a majority of the people of Northern Ireland with regard to
its status, whether they prefer to continue to support the
union with Great Britain or a sovereign united Ireland;

ii) recognise that it is for the people of the island of Ireland
    alone, by agreement between the two parts respectively and
    without external impediment, to exercise their right of self-
    determination on the basis of consent, freely and concurrently
    given, north and south, to bring about a united Ireland, if that
    is their wish, accepting that this right must be achieved and
    exercised with and subject to the agreement and consent of a
    majority of the people of Northern Ireland;

iii) acknowledge that while a substantial section of the people in
    Northern Ireland share the legitimate wish of a majority of the
    people of the island of Ireland for a united Ireland, the present
    wish of a majority of the people of Northern Ireland, freely
    exercised and legitimate, is to maintain the union and,
    accordingly, that Northern Ireland's status as part of the
    United Kingdom reflects and relies upon that wish; and that it
    would be wrong to make any change in the status of Northern
    Ireland save with the consent of a majority of its people.

The Agreement provided for the setting up of a Northern Irish
Assembly, and an Executive with a First, a Deputy First and other
ministers. There was to be a north–south dimension to the new order,
with a 'North/South Ministerial Council' bringing together 'those with
executive responsibilities in Northern Ireland and the Irish government, to develop consultation, co-operation and action within the
island of Ireland ... on matters of mutual interest within the com-
petence of the administrations, north and south'. This would be
balanced by an east–west dimension, with the setting up of a 'British-
Irish Council', 'to promote the harmonious and mutually beneficial
development of the totality of relationships among the peoples of
these islands'. Commitments were made regarding human rights and
equality within the north; regarding progress towards the decommissioning of paramilitary weapons; and to the pursuit of 'a new beginning to policing in Northern Ireland with a police service capable
of attracting and sustaining support from the community as a whole'
(an independent Commission being established to further this).
Accelerated release of paramilitary prisoners was also included in the
deal.[44]

The Belfast Agreement was sold to different people on very different
terms. Republicans saw it as transitional to a united Ireland, unionist

supporters as a barrier precisely *against* such a development. The IRA's attitude at the time of the Agreement's emergence was a complex one. Much remained constant in their thinking, their 1998 Easter message declaring: 'We will carefully study the outcome of the talks process against its potential to move us towards our primary objective, a thirty-two-county, democratic, socialist republic. We will judge it against its potential to deliver a just and durable peace to our country.'[45]

But what emerged on 10 April was not what the IRA had fought their long war to achieve. Even cautious endorsement on their part involved considerable compromise. In a responsive statement, the IRA said:

> The leadership of Óglaigh na hÉireann have considered carefully the Good Friday document. It remains our position that a durable peace settlement demands the end of British rule in Ireland and the exercise of the right of the people of Ireland to national self-determination. Viewed against our republican objectives or any democratic analysis, this document clearly falls short of presenting a solid basis for a lasting settlement. In our view the two imminent referenda [on the Agreement, north and south] do not constitute the exercise of national self-determination . . . However, the Good Friday document does mark a significant development.[46]

This was classic end-of-century Provisional prose: careful, avoiding the closure of a political route but retaining a sense that more – much more – was yet required. For republicans to back the deal and to retain their supporters' enthusiasm, it was necessary to present the Good Friday compromise as a step on the road forward rather than as a final destination. According to such a view, the Irish border would be broken down stage by stage, and one stage had just been reached: in the Good Friday Agreement, Adams said, 'The UUP had been moved much further than they had intended.'[47]

So republican responses were guarded, with Sinn Féin initially delaying its verdict on the Agreement before deciding to work for a 'Yes' vote in the referendums on the deal. Martin McGuinness (who had emerged as a skilled negotiator in the build-up to the Agreement, and who had apparently once said exasperatedly to Secretary of State

Mo Mowlam, 'I do wish you would stop calling me a bastard'),[48] commented, 'The Agreement is not a peace settlement. Nor indeed does it purport to be one. Rather, it is an important staging post of the peace process which can, like others before it in recent years, create the conditions for further movement in that direction.'[49] Adams expanded on the republican position:

> There is no big secret about republican strategy, just as there is no big secret about British government and unionist strategy. They want to maintain the union and we want to end it in order to secure our objective – Irish reunification and independence. We are Irish republicans. We want an end to partition, an end to conflict and division ... The reality is that the Good Friday Agreement is not a peace settlement. It does not claim to be. However, it is a basis for advancement. It is transitional. It is an accommodation. It heralds a change in the status quo. It is a transitional stage towards a democratic peace settlement. And it could become a transitional stage towards reunification.[50]

Speaking on 24 January 1999, the Sinn Féin President said that the Belfast Agreement 'represents what is possible at this time; not the preferred option of any of the participants – certainly not Sinn Féin's. That is the political reality. The Good Friday Agreement is the essential compromise for this phase of the peace process.'[51]

IRA members were briefed to the effect that this deal was better than had been expected; they were also told that the northern Assembly established by the Agreement represented a transitional arrangement on the way to a united Ireland. Confidence was expressed that demographic change would soon enough produce a nationalist Northern Irish majority in favour of Irish unification. Unionist opinion was profoundly divided. Yes, David Trimble and his supporters within the UUP had been crucial to the securing and endorsing of the deal. But other unionists were hostile and angry. Robert McCartney, leader of the small UK/Unionist Party, had interpreted the peace process as one that involved governmental appeasement of the IRA. Rewards had been given for violence, in an anti-democratic attempt to buy off the paramilitaries, and the Good Friday deal was more of the same: 'The Belfast Agreement was, and is, a disaster for the pro-union people and for democracy,' McCartney said.[52]

Tony Blair was crucial to the securing of the unionist support that the Belfast Agreement *did* attract. He had, after all, helped to shift his party's policy on Northern Ireland away from a commitment to Irish unity and towards a respect for northern consent: 'The important thing is not that the government takes up the role of pushing people in one direction or another, but that they allow the wishes of those in Northern Ireland to be paramount.'[53] And when, on 22 May 1998, referendums were held north and south in Ireland on the Agreement, Blair made public pledges and pleas on its behalf, in particular trying to reassure nervous unionist opinion:

> I believe the Agreement can work because it is just and it is based on principle. The principle of consent is clear – there can be no change in the status of Northern Ireland without the express consent of the people here . . . There can be no accelerated prisoner releases unless the organisations and individuals concerned have clearly given up violence for good – and there is no amnesty in any event. Representatives of parties intimately linked to paramilitary groups can only be in a future Northern Ireland government if it is clear that there will be no more violence and the threat of violence has gone. That doesn't just mean decommissioning but all bombings, killings, beatings, and an end to targeting, recruiting and all the structures of terrorism.[54]

In the event, turnout in the Agreement referendum was high in Northern Ireland (81 per cent) and so was the popular backing for the deal: 71 per cent voted 'Yes', 29 per cent said 'No'. In the Republic (admittedly, with a much lower turnout) the margin was even clearer, with a 'Yes' vote of 94 per cent.

Sinn Féin leaders enthused over the emphatic Irish 'Yes' vote, Adams presenting the result as a good thing, but, once again, as only the beginning (a view echoed by the *An Phoblacht/Republican News* front-page headline: 'Yes Vote Was For Real Change').[55] Nationalist Ireland, south and north, had overwhelmingly backed the Agreement (despite the fact that it entrenched the unionist consent principle in the north, and partially dissolved the Republic's constitutional claim over Northern Ireland). Ulster Protestants were more ambivalent, being evenly divided about whether the 1998 deal was in their interests.

The range of political opinion was again reflected when elections took place in June 1998, to the newly created northern Assembly. The 108 seats went to the UUP (28), the SDLP (24), the DUP (20), Sinn Féin (18), the cross-community Alliance Party (6), the UK/Unionist Party (5), Independent Unionists (3), the Progressive Unionist Party (PUP) (2) and the Women's Coalition (2). Sinn Féin had again polled well, winning 18 per cent of first-preference votes (compared to the SDLP's 22 per cent, the UUP's 21 per cent, the DUP's 18 per cent, the Alliance's 6.5 per cent and others at 14.5 per cent), and republicans noted this keenly: 'The votes cast today for Sinn Féin in the election to the transitional Assembly in the six counties will ensure that a strong, committed team of activists will take their seats. They will be voices for change in the Assembly, the Executive and in the all-Ireland Ministerial Council. This is an historic election from which republican-ism will emerge closer to our goal of a free Ireland'.[56]

Looking back on the Assembly election a week later, indeed, *An Phoblacht/Republican News* seemed triumphant: 'Sinn Féin's Spec-tacular Rise Continues,' the paper proclaimed; 'For the record, in last week's Assembly election Sinn Féin registered its highest vote since it began in 1981 to contest elections on a systematic basis.'[57] On 1 July 1998 Northern Irish politics took another major step, with the newly elected Assembly holding its first meeting at Castle Buildings, Stor-mont, Belfast. Secretary of State for Northern Ireland Mo Mowlam argued at the end of the year that 'Northern Ireland has a lot to celebrate. 1998 has been a year of achievement, topped by the Good Friday Agreement and the resounding Yes vote in the May referen-dum. People in Northern Ireland should rightly feel proud of themselves and their politicians for what they have accomplished together.'[58]

2

'Even conflicts that appear to be intractable can eventually
be brought to an end.'
Gerry Adams, 1995[59]

Why had the IRA engaged with this peace process? The Good Friday
Agreement fell strikingly short of what they had long set out as their
objective, and there is no question that their 1990s peace process
strategy involved a truly dramatic shift on their part – in terms of
activities as well as goals. And the IRA's new preparedness to endorse
the kind of world created by the 1998 deal represents one of the major
foundational shifts (probably *the* major change) in Northern Irish
realities in modern times. So why *did* the Provisionals opt for a
cessation of their campaign of violence against the British state,
accepting terms far less to their taste than those for which they had
fought, year after year?

One set of possible reasons involves international developments and
dimensions. The late-1980s collapse of Soviet communism is one such
factor. As we have seen, the IRA, especially during the 1980s, had
exhibited some enthusiasm for hard-left politics. But now it might
seem that the Moscow-published communist material that many had
read in the H-Blocks had led them down a blocked path. Republicans
have been lucidly articulate on this point. The 1989–90 crisis of world
communism certainly changed the world for left-leaning prisoners:
'I think that did have an impact and did lead to a reappraisal. And I
suppose there are still people who are trying to make sense of it, who
haven't come to terms with it yet.'[60] Patrick Magee: 'I would hazard
that events in Eastern Europe during the course of 1989 impacted
profoundly, and apart from the odd hopelessly unreconstructable
Marxist, that a savage dose of *realpolitik* left its mark.'[61] Anthony
McIntyre: 'With the closing down of the Marxist regimes throughout the world, there was a need for republicans to think about the
space that was open to them.'[62] Indeed, the international crisis of
Marxism apparently prompted some of the more cynical republicans

to comment that there were now only two places in the world where there was communism: 'fucking Albania and Cell 26!'[63] Writing in August 1990, Danny Morrison observed, 'If there is one thing last year in Eastern Europe should have taught us it was the bankruptcy of dogmatism, of communism, which couldn't put food on the table. The lesson has certainly helped me rethink my politics and taught me to be more pragmatic and realistic in terms of our own struggle. If we all lower our demands and our expectations a peg or two we might find more agreement.'[64]

In contrast to their 1970s confidence in absolute revolutionary possibility, therefore, or their 1980s absorption in hard-left writings, the post-1989 setting left the IRA with far less room for leftist conviction. And other world-political shifts may also have made their mark on IRA thinking, certainly within the jails. There seemed to be significant movement towards political change in other arenas of struggle with which Irish republicans had identified (in the Middle East, in South Africa with Nelson Mandela's emblematic release, as well as with the apparent international victory of consumerism and capitalism over communism). There had been, in Morrison's words, a 'world reorientation which had an effect on the prisoners', with the collapse of communism in particular having 'a devastating effect'.[65]

Some have also pointed to the wider context of the Soviet collapse, with the ending of the long Cold War. It has been argued that the USA was less likely to interfere in Northern Irish politics contrary to UK wishes, as long as the UK was a necessary ally against the Soviet empire; that need gone, the USA could become actively involved in ways more to Irish republican than to British official taste.[66] Crucial here was Bill Clinton, and his keen involvement in the northern peace process. Republicans have been clear that Clinton was (in Tom Hartley's words) 'an important factor'[67] in political movement towards Good Friday: here was someone involved sympathetically, who was more powerful than the British, who might act against British preferences (as with the 1994 Adams visa) and who might serve as a kind of guarantor of fair dealing, an international referee with muscle. Clinton's preparedness to open doors to militant republicans made a difference ('He did open up a lot of roads, and he gave visas [to republicans] . . . The Irish situation is not in a ghetto any more, and he did help to open up that').[68] Indeed, some have made stronger claims for the significance of Clinton's actions. Niall O'Dowd:

> Clinton did a remarkable thing. He overturned 220 years of a policy of non-intervention in Ireland by American governments. And the fact that he took that step, I think, had a profound impact. I think republicanism understood some time ago that they were essentially ghettoized, that they were caught in the situation where despite their best efforts they were banned from media in Ireland, and they essentially were unable to reach outside the confines of their base support. And they understood that they had to somehow try and internationalize the issue of Northern Ireland, try and bring a different focus on it. And I think Clinton destroyed any attempt to ghettoize them ... I think the fact that he gave the visa to Gerry Adams was probably more significant than any other intervention that he made in this conflict, because it immediately created a whole international dimension to Irish republicanism ... Irish republicanism desperately needed an outside force ... desperately needed someone to break through the kind of barriers that had been erected against them for almost thirty years ... Clinton provided that impetus ... all the parties in Northern Ireland were locked inside this box and were reacting against each other and ... only an outside force could change that dynamic inside the box, and ... the Americans provided that. I think they created a counterweight to the British in a way that was impossible otherwise.[69]

The European Union also provided a changing context within which Irish republicans had to make their decisions. In late 1994 Sinn Féin argued that 'The emerging political and economic imperatives both within Ireland and within the broader context of greater European political union support the logic of Irish unity.'[70] Could the evolving European setting make republicans confident that history was pushing in their direction, and that argument, negotiation and discussion – rather than violence – might indeed be able to bring about their desired goal? Again, one important trend during the late 1980s and the 1990s was the increasingly integrated relationship of London and Dublin in their approach towards Northern Ireland. Here too the EU played a part, the ongoing relationship there between civil servants and politicians from the two member states helping to build trust and a new framework within which the UK and the Republic could address an old problem.

Certainly, there is evidence to suggest that the combined roles of London, Dublin and Washington helped convince the republican movement that a postwar politics might work for them. Gerry Adams: 'If anyone is waiting for any brand of unionism to do a decent deal with any brand of nationalism or republicanism, then they will have a very long wait indeed. That is why it needed the intervention and the focused attention and presence of Mr Blair and Mr Ahern [Fianna Fáil Taoiseach] to get the Good Friday Agreement. That is why we have a Good Friday Agreement. Because the British Prime Minister and the Taoiseach were involved, as well as President Clinton.'[71]

Yet, despite all this, it would be wrong to exaggerate the role played by external developments in bringing about the IRA's 1990s evolution. Some leading figures in the republican movement play down the significance of the death of communism (Tom Hartley: 'I never remember sitting down with any republicans and people saying, "Oh, what does this mean to our struggle?" [Question: 'Not at all?'] Not at all').[72] And it should be remembered both that 1980s republican enthusiasm for hard-left politics was more prevalent in the jails than it was outside, and that it was *outside* that the key decisions were taken. Again, one would have to qualify arguments suggesting that the end of the US-Soviet Cold War was crucial. For one thing, the post-Second World War relationship between the USA and the UK was of such a power imbalance that the USA could, at any stage it desired, have disagreed decisively on a matter such as Northern Ireland, with the UK in no position to object effectively. There had certainly been many issues on which the UK was bypassed by the USA during the 1940s–80s,[73] and this suggests that British wishes were perhaps less vital to the USA during this period than some have implied.

The reason for President Clinton's active involvement in the politics of the north of Ireland is more likely to be found in the complexities of his own political trajectory and interests – such as his response to a new kind of Irish-American lobbying, or his desire to be associated with international success stories in conflict resolution – than in the macropolitics of interstate power relations. Moreover, previous US presidents had been involved in Northern Irish politics to a degree that observers often forget.[74] The 1998 Belfast Agreement completed a process begun during the era of Margaret Thatcher and Ronald Reagan (committed Cold War warriors, in fact) with the 1985 Anglo-Irish Agreement, an Agreement that the Reagan administration had helped to produce. So the roots of the changes in Northern Ireland clearly preceded the end of the Cold War. And again, while EU trends might suggest an historical tendency towards unity, this has not involved the removal of the state as an important unit of power in modern Europe.[75] Battles over state boundaries and sovereignty and power remain to be fought, despite the rhetoric of a new Europe or the onset of the Euro currency.

For if one is to find the proper explanation for the IRA's remarkable shift from war to peace at the end of the twentieth century, it is to internal rather than external forces that one must primarily look. Three (internally layered) factors are crucial.

First, the IRA recognized by the start of the 1990s that there existed a military stalemate between themselves and the British state. Put bluntly, their war of attrition had not had the intended effect of breaking British will to remain in Northern Ireland. This had been acknowledged, it seems, by the 1980s: 'Our aim is to create such psychological damage to the Brits that they'll withdraw. Sick of the expense, the hassle, the coffins coming back to England. But we know we can't defeat them in a military sense, no more than they can beat us. So there's a kind of stalemate'.[76] Indeed, as early as 1986 Gerry Adams had recognized the reality of 'a situation of deadlock in which Óglaigh na hÉireann [the IRA] were able to block the imposition of a British solution but were unable to force the British to withdraw'.[77] By 1990 the sharp-sighted had certainly acknowledged the stalemate situation:[78] while the IRA could not be simply defeated militarily (a point publicly stated, for example, by Secretary of State Peter Brooke),[79] nor could they win as had been anticipated in earlier years of the struggle. The IRA could go on fighting; but so too could the British state, and so too could Ulster loyalists. The state had shown itself capable of developing a wide range of anti-IRA strategies: the intelligence war had involved agents and informers and the penetration of the IRA in ways that did limit its capacity. By the mid-1980s the capacity of the security forces to constrain Provisional activity through surveillance, arrests and so on was more impressive than it had been in the 1970s.[80]

Moreover, the continuation of IRA violence was not going to better the bargaining position that republicans possessed. The longer the IRA's campaign had continued without breaking the will of the British, arguably the *less* effective a weapon it had become. Indeed, the idea that attritional violence would have a cumulatively ever weightier effect, that in time its force would become irresistible, is possibly the opposite of the truth. For the longer the war went on without the state yielding ground, the less unbearable it seemed for the state to fight on. It was less that the ballot box and Armalite were necessarily incompatible, than that the latter was no longer gaining any ground.

Might the IRA's violence have become, indeed, something of a hindrance to republican advance? Certainly, Sinn Féin's capacity to gain more substantial electoral support during the post-1994 period suggests that there might have been a ceiling on popular endorsement while car-bombs were going off. Again, might the British preparedness to grant what republicans demanded be *more* rather than less likely once the war had ended? Britain could perhaps more easily move towards disengagement from Ireland through long-term, peaceful dialogue than humiliatingly under pressure of IRA violence. As early as 1988 John Hume had written powerfully to Gerry Adams to the effect that the IRA's violence was doing more harm than good, that one could not sustain the view that the cause of all the violence was simply Britain's presence in Ireland, that people – rather than territory – were what had to be united, and that the Provisionals' strategy and methods had 'actually become more sacred than their cause'.[81]

Much of this was clear to the intelligent republican leadership (and it is intriguing to note that Gerry Adams has been described by one former British Secretary of State, Peter Mandelson, as a man of 'superior intelligence',[82] while Martin McGuinness has been presented even by popular novelist Jack Higgins as 'a clever man. Too damned clever').[83] From the late 1980s such men worked towards the broadening of republican politics in ways that might make something out of the stalemate situation. In 1989 a leading Belfast IRA figure referred to Martin McGuinness and others talking about 'bringing the armed struggle to a conclusion'.[84] If they were not going to win in the way initially expected, then perhaps it made sense to take a pragmatic decision, to obtain the best terms possible, to compromise in a situation in which all sides moved ground. As Danny Morrison made clear, 'Republicans now are fed up glorifying past defeats and are determined to show something substantial for the sacrifices. I can't see it being resolved until ... everybody agrees to come down a few rungs ... The point is that people's pride and self-respect and all their past and present sacrifices and all the unrealised aspirations have a certain value and meaning and have to be taken on board. People would have to feel that a settlement was just and that their opponents were making compromises also';[85] Martin McGuinness: 'The IRA stopped because people put a political analysis to them which in their judgment was a project worthy of support.'[86]

This brings us to the *second* key point about the IRA's changed direction: the bargaining position that existed for 1990s republicans contained both definite rewards and results, and the prospect that these might be significantly improved upon through engagement with a peace process. There was the prospect of ending political ghettoiz-ation (with White House invitations replacing broadcasting bans); of gaining places for republicans in government; of seeing reform in the north on questions such as policing, with the consequent establish-ment of good terms for Catholics within a reinvented north; of procuring prisoner release;[87] of significantly increasing the number of people voting for Sinn Féin (in the south as well as the north: as early as 1984 Gerry Adams had admitted that the prospect of holding the balance of power in the Dublin Dáil was a 'tempting option').[88] If more people would talk to you, listen to you, vote for you and include you in the creation of a new society once violence was eclipsed, then the eclipsing of violence could be seen to have definite rewards. Where in the past London, Dublin, the SDLP and Washing-ton had been combined in ways from which the Provisionals were excluded, might it now be possible for republicans to work with Dublin, Washington and the SDLP in ways disadvantageous to the British? To end the violence would end the pariah status which stood in the way of such a development, and which thus blocked forward progress. Tom Hartley: 'Sinn Féin, SDLP, Dublin and North America: so there is in fact a new alliance in place which, in a sense, weakens

British strategy and allows republicans to begin to see the potential of that new alliance to create political forces which really have a greater impact than the armed conflict.' Momentum was crucial in determining republican engagement with the peace process: 'Our sense of it was: how do you keep moving a struggle forward?'[89]

The 1990s offered not the revolutionary change that the Provisionals had traditionally sought. But it did offer the prospect of a stronger, far less isolated Sinn Féin and of greater equality and power for republicans in the north. For what was visibly on offer could be improved upon through hard and able bargaining, and through the leverage of threatened force. Republicans rightly recognized that this was to be a lengthy game, as complex perhaps as chess but requiring more muscle on occasions. Thus politics was to be endorsed and its rewards accepted; but at times the threat or use of force was also deployed to achieve greater leverage. For republicans sought not only to pursue the long-term goal of Irish unity, but also to maintain forward movement and to obtain concessions in more immediate, short-term struggles. In the words of one Sinn Féin politician (long after the 1998 Agreement), the peace process was 'a constant process of negotiation', ever evolving.[90]

If demographics were held to offer that future northern nationalist majority required to vote the north into a united Ireland, then in the nearer future republicans had to apply whatever pressure they could on the British to change their traditional stance: as Gerry Adams has said, 'the task of democratic opinion in Ireland and Britain and further afield – and this includes the USA – is to get a change of British policy from upholding partition and the union to a policy of ending partition and the union in consultation with the people of this island'.[91] And republicans were confident that such forward motion was possible – that history was moving inevitably, inexorably, in the right direction – their confidence making them more likely to innovate and to engage with the peace process. An *An Phoblacht/ Republican News* front-page article from 27 October 1994 proclaimed 'The tide of history is with Irish nationalists.' Irish unity seemed inevitable. In its submission to the British government presented at talks in Belfast on 9 December 1994, Sinn Féin asserted: 'We believe that the wish of the majority of the Irish people is for Irish unity. We believe that an adherence to democratic principles makes Irish unity inevitable.'⁹² Armed with such a reinforcingly teleological reading of history, no wonder that republicans were confident. Danny Morrison could argue in 1997 that, 'Throughout the north nationalists have a drive and a confidence which is palpable';⁹³ Tom Hartley observed the 'amazing [post-Agreement] confidence of the Irish nationalist community in the north';⁹⁴ while Gerry Adams felt able to claim that early-twenty-first-century Belfast had become 'the most republican city' in Ireland.⁹⁵

There was confidence too in republican political ability to maximize the available benefits. It was felt that, while 1970s republicans had lacked a range of political skills and projects to complement their violence, the new republicanism had a wider repertoire. Speaking in Dublin in February 1984, Gerry Adams had reflected that the 1975 IRA truce had been a mistake: 'Once the IRA was removed from the scene, and because there were no other manifestations of the struggle, it meant that the British were able to confuse republicans.'⁹⁶ The 1990s republican movement was determined that the absence of an IRA military campaign would not mean that there were 'no other manifestations of the struggle': now there was a more rounded movement, and it was one that believed that the British could be moved. In March 1995 the Sinn Féin leader commented, 'My one-sentence description of the British establishment position is that they have no bottom line. They can be moved as far as the political influence or power that can be harnessed for a democratic solution; they will move as far as that can push them.'⁹⁷

And there was a sense that republicans would out-perform and outmanoeuvre unionists in a lengthy process of political engagement; that – when faced with an IRA peace strategy – Ulster unionists would be confused, divided and demoralized. The republican movement would present itself as the key initiator and mover of the peace process, and by comparison make unionists look resistant to positive change. Just as Gerry Adams had suggested after the 1985 Anglo-Irish Agreement that the reason for any concessions being made to nationalists was simply republican pressure, so too in the 1990s peace process republicans would present themselves as the crucial player ('Sinn Féin is the driving force in the Irish peace process';⁹⁸ Sinn Féin had played a 'crucial and pivotal role in laying the foundation for the peace process').⁹⁹ Thus whether the peace process succeeded or failed,

republicans could gain comparative advantage over unionists. If the
process worked, then it would yield certain, and expanding, rewards
for republicans; if it failed, then unionists could be presented as the
boulder against which a decent attempt at peace-making had stum-
bled; and unionists would have been left divided in any case. (Some
encouragement could be found for those republicans who had held
such a view. A listing of parties eligible to compete electorally in
Northern Ireland in 2001 included the Democratic Unionist Party,
the Liberal Unionist Party, the Northern Ireland Unionist Party, the
Progressive Unionist Party, the Ulster Unionist Party, the United
Kingdom Unionist Party and the United Unionist Assembly Party,[100]
and the relations between (at times, within) some of these groups had
involved stark hostility.)

And the *third* point: militant republicans recognized some of the
realities about the broader politics and economics of the north that
had earlier been eclipsed from their vision. Yes, unionists might be
clumsy and divided when responding to political change. But they
were not, *pace* early-troubles Provisional thinking, a problem that
was simply going to dissolve. In May 1991 Danny Morrison candidly
referred to 'the lack of republican understanding of the unionist/
Protestant people',[101] and another of republicanism's most intelligent
figures, Tom Hartley has offered similarly crisp comment upon the
former republican approach to their unionist neighbours: 'In a way
we made them a non-people. We just said: you can't move the
unionists until you move the Brits. So we didn't even see them as
part of the problem, never mind as being part of the solution.'[102] But
this began to change, with republicans such as Morrison observing
that a more nuanced approach was required: 'When you're engaged
in a struggle, you fight with basics in mind. It's a united Ireland or
nothing; the unionists are basically tools of British imperialism; they
don't know what they're doing; they'll come into a united Ireland like
sheep once you break the will of the British. That was a very simplistic
view of unionism.' Indeed, Morrison recalls a debate among republican prisoners in the H-Blocks in which he and a fellow republican
played devil's advocate by presenting the unionist case: 'The funny
thing about it is that afterwards everybody was saying, "We think that
your argument was better than the republican argument!"' Morrison

himself certainly had no difficulty in recognizing how unionists *should* construct their case: 'It's so easy to do, once you pick up their arguments and present them as a human rights issue ... "Don't be talking about Northern Ireland being [artificial]; every country was made artificially, all nations are artificial. It's been seventy years: Israel has a right to exist – we're living longer than them [i.e. Northern Ireland has existed longer than Israel, and should likewise have a right to exist]. Okay, you didn't get civil rights but we're sorry, we want to have a new start." '[103]

So, just as some unionists during the 1990s developed a more flexible attitude towards republicans,[104] so too there had emerged a different attitude among some Irish republicans towards their northern opponents. For unionists were not going to disappear, or suddenly to lose their horror at the thought of being expelled from the UK, the state of their choice; as the ever-quotable Ian Paisley colourfully put it in 2002, 'Gerry Adams can grow his beard until he is Rip Van Winkle but we will be saying no to the destruction of the union.'[105] So there was a recognition that compromise, discussion and dealing would need to be done, and done seriously: 'When the time for talking does come and everybody's talking, republicans will have to address themselves to *realpolitik* – to the crucial issue of the unionists, their identity, their rights, their security, their fears and the institutions they would be prepared to support. That is a huge subject and, obviously, one for negotiation.'[106]

And other broad realities had also begun to impinge more firmly on republican thinking. One concerned economics. Northern Ireland, far from being an economically advantageous colony, was a financial drain of serious proportions upon Britain. This had implications for republican analysis of Britain's role in the north, but also for the prospects of a post-British dispensation. Put simply: where would the money come from were Britain actually to give the IRA what they wanted and withdraw from Northern Ireland? As early as the mid-1980s the more perceptive in the movement had realized some of these key economic truths. In September 1985, one republican produced a thoughtful piece on the subject, 'Why Does Britain Remain in Control of the Six Counties?' The author went some way to acknowledging the economic implications of British withdrawal:

The bulk of the debate about the viability or non-viability of
the six-county economy surrounds the British subsidy (subvention)
to the six counties ... In the six counties the statelet is *not* able to
raise sufficient revenue through taxation to pay for its expenditure, but instead of borrowing the shortfall, instead the British
exchequer supplies it in the form of an interest-free loan which
does not have to be repaid – that is the subvention – the economic
subsidy of the six-county administration ... If this subsidy ceased
it is wrong to believe that the economy would cease to exist – its
level of activity and value would certainly drop and living standards would also fall but an economy would still exist at a lower
level than present – it would probably step back to closer to third-
world levels though probably a 'better-off' third-world type of
level.[107]

Such reflections did not at this stage lead too far into heterodox
argument, for the author maintained that partition itself, as a form of
neo-colonialism, had suited British economic interests. But the acknowledgment that British economic support prevented the north of
Ireland from descending into third-world conditions – even 'better-
off' ones – did set a fuse burning: if a lengthy transitional phase was
required before a united Ireland could come about, then this might
have implications for republican preparedness to compromise, and to
agree to (what they would see as) an interim northern arrangement.

So, just as the birth of the Provisional IRA at the end of the 1960s
and their growth to prominence in the early 1970s had been products
not of one but of many interconnected forces, the same was true of
the organization's shift from war to something like peace during the
1990s and beyond. As already noted, this shift was arguably *the* major
historical change in Ireland in the end-of-century period: it was not
inevitable, or irreversible or simple – as is evident from the serious
splits that did occur in republican ranks. But the sea-change in
Provisional republicanism was a world-significant event and requires
careful, detailed explanation. International dimensions played some
part – the collapse of communism and the end of the Cold War; the
changes in the political struggles with which the Provos had identified;
the changing role of Washington, Dublin and London; the evolving
EU context. But internal forces were the vital ones: republicans
acknowledged the existence of a triangular – republican-British-

loyalist – stalemate; their own violence was going neither to win the war, nor to improve upon a bargaining position that offered both definite results and the prospect of increasing rewards achieved through political process; whether the peace process succeeded or fell, republicans sensed that they could gain relative advantage over their unionist competitors; and the lengthy struggle had awoken republicans to key political and economic realities that necessitated a modulated pursuit of their traditional goals. The war was effectively over.

3

'They've tried to sell a defeat as a victory.'

Marian Price, on Sinn Féin and the Good Friday Agreement[108]

But not every republican was persuaded. Three clear groups of dissenters, or dissidents, might be identified, people who sharply disagreed with Provisional orthodoxy about the evolving peace process. In 1986, founding-Provo Ruairí Ó Brádaigh had left the movement in protest at what he felt to be the heretical shift indicated by the Provisionals' abandonment of parliamentary abstentionism in the south of Ireland. Ó Brádaigh felt that an internal northern – and therefore partitionist – arrangement was implicit in the Provisionals' shift towards electoral preocccupation. And he was deeply hostile to it: 'I have opposed the republican policy since 1981 ... I am against the way republicanism has been moving since 1986, and before that, to the 1921 partitionists who created the problem. I am part of a tradition of dissenters who feel that philosophy was lost then, and if Sinn Féin gets sucked into the constitutional line, who else is there to speak up?'[109] In 1969–70 Ó Brádaigh had broken with Cathal Goulding's more political IRA to protect and preserve this republican purism; now he was breaking from the Provisionals in similar spirit. (For his own part, Goulding now watched with bleak wit: 'We were right too soon, Gerry Adams is right too late and Ruairí Ó Brádaigh will never be fucking right.')[110]

The Provisionals' 1970s gun-supplier, George Harrison, shared Ó Brádaigh's views, like him seeing the Provos' new 1986 departure as a betrayal. He aligned himself with Ó Brádaigh's Republican Sinn Féin, and as the 1990s peace process progressed he became yet more convinced that the 1994 IRA ceasefire was a sell-out, a surrender, and that republican engagement with the peace process was 'a total and a complete departure from the traditions of the past ... It's a betrayal.' The Belfast Agreement of 1998 was 'a total and a complete compromise, just the same as the compromise in '22 ... Traditional republicans didn't fight and lay down their lives for a reformed Stormont, nor for a puppet government in Leinster House. They fought for a free and independent Irish socialist republic and a thirty-two-county government.' Why had republican leaders taken this new approach? Harrison was scathing of Adams and McGuinness: 'Once they come in out of the cold, and experience the good life and not the rain and the cold, then they don't want to go out there again.' A new generation would carry on the traditional fight now betrayed by the Provisional movement: 'As long as the Brits are there ... there will be young fellows who will prepare for another go ... That day will come as sure as tomorrow's sun will come ... There will be another phase of clandestine armed struggle to get the Brits out.'[111] The Continuity IRA – RSF's armed alter ego – had a small member-ship (apparently in the region of thirty to fifty in mid-1998), but showed itself capable of repeated violence. In July 1996 a CIRA bomb blew up a hotel just outside Enniskillen in County Fermanagh, and numerous other bombing and shooting incidents took place in Belfast and elsewhere.

As already mentioned, a second group of dissenters had emerged in autumn 1997 with the disillusioned Provisional Quartermaster General departing from the organization to found what became known as the Real IRA. County Louth in the Irish Republic was a key base for the new group, whose political wing was the 32-County Sovereignty Committee (or Movement). This political wing was led by Michael McKevitt and his partner Bernadette Sands-McKevitt (a sister of Bobby Sands): they aimed to uphold an uncompromising and uncompromised Irish republicanism, and to oppose anything emerg-ing from the 1997 party talks that should fall short of Irish unity and independence. Sands-McKevitt was emphatic that her brother's famous hunger-strike death was being betrayed by his Provisional comrades: 'Bobby did not die for cross-border bodies with executive powers. He did not die for nationalists to be equal British citizens within the Northern Ireland state.'[112] In early 1998 she was hostile alike to British involvement in Ireland and to republicans' peace strategy and political talks: 'We don't need a foreign government interfering in our affairs. We are quite capable of deciding our own destiny, but we have been prevented from doing that . . . I believe the talks are a farce. There are those prepared to compromise, and that is totally wrong, totally unacceptable.'[113]

Active also in the 32-County Sovereignty Movement was Marian Price, famous for her 1970s London bombing and for her subsequent force-feeding while on courageous hunger strike in jail. Price left the Provisional movement in 1998 owing to differences over the peace process strategy, and became sharply critical of Sinn Féin: 'As far as republicanism goes, I wouldn't consider Sinn Féin of today [2002] being republicans.' She came under great pressure from former comrades for dissenting from their peace process orthodoxy: 'A member of the Provisionals visited my home to tell me that the fact that I was expressing views that were critical of Sinn Féin, was not tolerable, and that I should better keep my mouth shut.'[114] But she staunchly refused, and remained extremely critical of mainstream republican post-Good Friday politics: if they were happy to settle for what 1998 offered, then why had the war been fought?

> To suggest that a war was fought for what they have today, it diminishes anybody who partook in that war, anybody who died for it, and went out there and sacrificed their lives and their liberty. It diminishes all that to suggest that this is what it was fought for. In 1974 the Sunningdale Agreement was a much stronger agreement, and offered much more to republicans and nationalists, than the Good Friday Agreement and it was rejected outright by the republican movement. And there was a war fought for thirty years after that. After having rejected Sunningdale, to accept the Good Friday Agreement and suggest that that was what the war [was for], it's criminal, downright criminal, for them to suggest that . . . And when [the SDLP's] Seamus Mallon said that the Good Friday Agreement was Sunningdale for slow learners, he hit the nail on the head. It wasn't: it was Sunningdale for retards.[115]

Thus there were people with distinguished republican credentials, people such as the articulate and trenchant Marian Price, who now took issue with Provisional politics.

But while Price was arguing forcefully with words, there were other anti-Provisional republicans who used violence to make their case. A Real IRA bomb in Omagh, County Tyrone, on 15 August 1998 killed twenty-nine people (thirty-one if one includes two unborn babies). Many others were appallingly mutilated. This awful carnage among civilians produced shock, and intensified resolve on the part of some. George Mitchell: 'My most fervent prayer is that history will record that the troubles ended in Omagh on the sunny afternoon of Saturday, August 15, 1998. There, a murderous explosion laid bare for all to see the brutality, the senselessness, the utter insanity of political violence in Northern Ireland.'[116] Sinn Féin chairperson Mitchel McLaughlin observed, 'All of us must change. All of us, Irish republicans, members of the British and Irish governments, unionists and nationalists, have a duty to ensure that such terrible actions never again occur.'[117] Gerry Adams was clear in referring to the republican bombers: 'We are saying they should stop and stop now.'[118] Under enormous pressure, not least from Provisional republicans, after Omagh the RIRA declared a suspension and then a cessation of its operations. But despite the revulsion that their Omagh bomb had created, they continued to recruit and to train. They had acquired weapons (some brought by their former-Provo Quartermaster, some acquired from Eastern Europe) and by late 2000 were thought to have between a hundred and two hundred members. They maintained a periodically violent presence (for example, exploding a bomb on 4 March 2001 outside the BBC Television Centre in Shepherd's Bush in London).

A third group within republican ranks (dissenters rather than dissidents) disagreed with the Provisionals' peace strategy while being simultaneously explicit that they wanted no continuation of, or return to, physical-force campaigns. Despite their clear opposition to violence, such people were convinced that the Provisional shift of the 1990s represented a sell-out, an unappealing compromise of republican principle. In this view, the Good Friday Agreement is seen as having strengthened rather than weakened partition; GFA is (only half-jokingly) said by such people to stand for 'Got Fuck All'. And, so the argument runs – echoing the words of Marian Price – if the Provisional leadership is indeed happy with the compromise that 1998 offered, then why was such a long war endured on the principle of fighting for something so different? 1970s IRA leader Brendan Hughes acknowledges that the military conflict has come to an end, but is deeply unhappy about mainstream republican participation in current politics: 'I basically strongly agree that the war in Ireland with the British is over. I believe that the military struggle is over but I totally disagree with the Good Friday Agreement ... Sinn Féin people have now become part of the occupation forces in the north of Ireland. I disagree with that. I disagree with the whole concept of administering British rule in Ireland, which I believe Sinn Féin is now doing.'[119] Another former Provisional, Tommy Gorman, also laments the Provisionals' attitude during the peace process: 'all these humiliating climb-downs are being painted as just tactical change, and victories'.[120]

Similar in outlook is another ex-Provisional, Anthony McIntyre. As a prisoner in Long Kesh in 1990, he had looked back critically at the Greaves/Coughlan/Johnston thinking that had influenced republicans in the 1960s: their notion 'that the Orange state could be progressively democratised' had influenced republican leaders of that period 'with disastrous consequences'.[121] Similarly, McIntyre came to argue that republicans were wrong to endorse a 1990s peace process strategy that rested upon the notion of reforming Northern Ireland, of working phase by phase; the adoption of this strategy meant that republicanism had effectively died, being eclipsed by constitutional nationalism – albeit one fronted by Sinn Féin. On the supposed advances made by republicans through the 1990s peace process strategy, McIntyre asks: 'If it is progress, then why could we not have had it in 1974? Why could we not have [avoided] the long war and [gone] for a strategy similar to this? Why did so many people have to die to bring us back round to accepting what we rejected in 1974, and called everybody else bastards for accepting?'[122]

For there is among this group of disaffected republican dissenters too a feeling that their own painful struggle has been betrayed by the compromises of modern-day Provisionalism. Asked in 1999 whether he felt any satisfaction at the way the struggle had turned out, Brendan Hughes replied emphatically: 'No. I do not feel any satisfaction whatsoever. All the questions raised in the course of this struggle have not been answered and the republican struggle has not been concluded.' In such a view, the long war now looked futile: its commitments had been abandoned, while the eventual outcome could have been achieved without years of pain – 'the things that we cherished such as a thirty-two-county democratic socialist republic are no longer mentioned . . . what we have now we could have had at any time in the last twenty-five years'.[123]

From a mainstream republican view, the disobedience implicit in such views compounded the heterodoxy of the opinions held. In some cases, this proved fatal. On Friday 13 October 2000 Joseph O'Connor, a leading member of the Belfast Real IRA, was shot dead in Bally-murphy, west Belfast. No group claimed responsibility. Indeed, the Provisional IRA denied that they had carried out the killing. A state-ment issued on the 17th of the month declared of O'Connor that 'the IRA wishes to state that it was not involved in his death. The IRA leadership extends its condolences to the O'Connor family.'[124]

But it was alleged by the man's family, and by others locally, that it was in fact Provisionals who had killed him. Joseph O'Connor had been deeply opposed to the compromises involved in the Good Friday Agreement and to the Provisional movement's peace strategy; the Real IRA had been recruiting heavily in Ballymurphy around that time; and, it was believed, the Provisionals had in truth killed this rebel. The operation drew criticism. Marian Price, of the 32-County Sovereignty Movement, delivered a fierce funeral oration for O'Connor in which she attacked the Provisionals for his killing: 'contrary to the deliberate misinformation being peddled by the Provisional movement and aided by RUC sources, those responsible for this foul murder have been clearly identified. Shame! Shame on you!' In Price's view, the Provos were now so committed to upholding the administration of British rule in Ireland against people such as O'Connor that they would even be prepared to kill them: 'They are now reduced to an armed militia of the British state.'[125] Anthony McIntyre and Tommy Gorman (emphatically not RIRA supporters) publicly stated their belief that it was the Provos who had killed O'Connor. In a flinty statement published in the *Irish News* on 17 October, they stated their own 'stringent opposition to the Real IRA' but denounced O'Connor's killing and blamed it unambiguously on the Provisionals: 'there is no room for doubt. We state publicly that it is our unshakeable belief that the Provisional IRA carried out this assassination.' McIntyre and

Gorman's analysis of the episode reflected the doubts of other republicans regarding the Provisional movement's peace process strategy. In their view, modern-day Provisionals were defending an unacceptable compromise, just as pro-Treatyites had done in the 1920s: 'What difference is there between the Free State murder of Rory O'Connor in defence of the 1922 British treaty and the murder of Joseph O'Connor in defence of the 1998 British treaty?' These accusations aroused Provisional fury, with McIntyre's home in Ballymurphy being picketed by Sinn Féiners. Republican unity had, for the most part, held; but such episodes showed that there were indeed dissenters among those who had fought the republican war against the British.

O'Connor's killing was condemned also by the indefatigable George Harrison in New York: 'The murder of Joseph O'Connor was to me a real murder most foul,' he observed, likening it to killings by the Free State in the 1920s Civil War: 'This is going down the road of '22 again.'[126] The Real IRA man had been 'murdered by revisionists', his killers simply rendering a service to their masters in Westminster, Stormont and Leinster House, and in doing so adding their names 'to the turncoats and traitors of the past'.[127]

Dissenters could rightly claim that the IRA's war had not been fought with a view to obtaining what the Good Friday Agreement offered, and they clearly had a right to ask whether the suffering they had endured and inflicted could be justified in pursuit of what the Provisional movement eventually seemed to have settled for. But another case could surely be made. Given that Provisional expectation of victory had proved – in the end – to be mistaken, and that a stalemate existed, was there not a case for engagement, for obtaining the best available terms and using them to build forward movement? Put another way, did those republicans who objected to the 1990s settlement have any alternative to offer that had any likelihood of producing the measure of popular cross-community endorsement that the Belfast Agreement had done? The IRA had not won the desired victory. But nor had it been militarily beaten. And while it could be argued that the 1998 deal was closer to traditional British aims than to those of the Provos, dissent from republican orthodoxy would only gain momentum if it could be shown that there was a feasible alternative strategy, another way of moving closer to traditional republican goals than that offered by a vibrant Sinn Féin.

For, during the 1990s and even beyond, the Provisionals saw themselves very much as moving forward: 1998 was in their view not the end point, but a stage on a longer journey. And – as the Joseph O'Connor killing showed – the IRA had not disappeared. Ceasefire politics in fact involved considerable violence. During the first cessation, by the end of 1995, the IRA had (under the title Direct Action Against Drugs) killed six alleged drug-dealers, and such activities continued long after this, including the IRA/DAAD killing of alleged drug-dealer Brendan Campbell, in Belfast in February 1998. In the same month the IRA also killed the loyalist Robert Dougan, and so while the war against the British state had effectively come to an end, the violence had not fully done so. An IRA statement of 31 March 1999 claimed that 'IRA guns are silent';[128] they were certainly less frequently noisy, but silent they were not. That July saw the killing of Charles Bennett in Belfast: he had been blindfolded and his hands tied behind his back, then shot at close range with a sawn-off shotgun; September 2000 saw the killing in County Derry of alleged drug-dealer Patrick Quinn.

It would have been a naïve observer who expected the IRA's violence simply to fizzle out immediately. For one thing, there were ongoing loyalist killings, such as that of solicitor Rosemary Nelson in March 1999. Thirty years of war were not going to end abruptly, suddenly and cleanly. Moreover, much paramilitary violence had, throughout the troubles, taken an intra- rather than intercommunal form. The war with the British state might be over; but tensions within the Catholic community (from which people like Brendan Campbell, Charles Bennett and Patrick Quinn themselves came) were to remain. The post-1994 ceasefire period, in fact, saw a dramatic rise in punishment attacks by the IRA within their own community. In 1993 (the year before the first IRA ceasefire) there were thirty-one paramilitary republican shootings or other assaults; in 1994 this figure rose to eighty-six, in 1995 it reached 141; and in 1996 it totalled 175.[129] For the period 1988–2000 as a whole, there were 756 republican assaults and 479 shootings.[130] Some of these could involve shocking brutality, as with the case of west Belfast teenager Martin Doherty in 1996: he was nailed by republicans to a wooden fence with metal spikes through his knees and elbows.[131]

Beatings, shootings and expulsions were directed against people judged to have been involved in repeated crime, in drug-dealing, or sometimes in defiant conflict with republicans. Andrew Kearney was killed by the IRA in July 1998 in Belfast. There had previously occurred a fight between Kearney and a leading Belfast Provisional, and this appears to have been the direct cause of the IRA's attack on the man. On that day, eight Provisionals came to the tower block where Kearney lived with his girlfriend and their baby; they chloroformed him, shot him in the legs (severing an artery), tore out the telephone wire to prevent them calling for help, and blocked the lifts so that his girl-friend – holding the baby – had to run down the stairs to call for an ambulance. Andrew Kearney bled to death. His mother, Maureen Kearney, was broken by the incident, and died the following year.

Paramilitary punishment attacks in the north of Ireland occur in loyalist as well as republican areas, so the root of the phenomenon is not simply that of Irish nationalist disaffection from a British state and from its supposedly illegitimate police force. But, while incidents such as Andrew Kearney's death appear to have arisen primarily from personal clashes, it remains the case that the problems of policing in Northern Ireland provide the context for explaining IRA punishment culture. In February 1999 Sinn Féin's Martin McGuinness argued: 'Punishment beatings exist for two main reasons: the absence of an adequate policing service and the rising levels of antisocial behaviour and petty crime. The RUC is not a normal policing service. It has no credibility in nationalist areas.'[132] The IRA has claimed that, in the absence of a locally acceptable police force, they themselves had to step into the gap.

Policing certainly constituted one of the key features of the 1998 peace agreement, which had looked for a new start to policing and for a new force supported by both sections of the community. The Commission consequently appointed to investigate the matter (a body chaired by former Conservative Party Chairman, Chris Patten) reported in September 1999. Its report rightly noted that 'the issue of policing is at the heart of many of the problems that politicians have been unable to resolve in Northern Ireland', recognizing that 'real community policing is impossible if the composition of the police service bears little relationship to the composition of the community as a whole'. In Northern Ireland this had long been the case, with an RUC which many Catholics were reluctant to join and which was thus overwhelmingly Protestant in membership. (Catholics comprised less than 10 per cent of the police but more than 40 per cent of the population.) Rightly, it was acknowledged that a police force in a starkly divided society was unlikely to be effective if its members were drawn so overwhelmingly from one side only. The Patten Commission recommended therefore that Catholics and Protestants be recruited in equal numbers for a ten-year period, and that the culture of the police be altered in order to try to attract Catholics into the force: a name change was recommended, along with a new badge and symbols 'which are entirely free from any association with either the British or Irish states'.[133]

The problem with policing should not, of course, be overemphasized. The Patten Report recognized that approval rating for the RUC ran at over 80 per cent for Protestants in the north, and approached 50 per cent for Catholics; so it was a force not uniformly condemned by the northern Catholic population. Nor should the RUC be equated with paramilitary groups in terms of the number of people whom it killed: during the troubles, the RUC was responsible for 1.4 per cent of deaths, the IRA for 48.5 per cent.[134] But that policing is a major problem within the north is unquestionable: for the state to be seen to be equitable, both main communities in Northern Ireland would need to feel that this crucial arm of the state was one with which they were comfortable in terms of ethos, identity and composition. In Northern Ireland that has simply not been the case.

The Patten Report met with much unionist rage, and yet it fell short too of what Irish republicans would have preferred. Indeed, the battle over the implementation of Patten was one of a series of conflicts in the post-Agreement period in which the Provisional movement played a key part. Politics were to be a continuation of war by other means, and the (non-)implementation of the Belfast Agreement was to be riddled with crises – a climax-driven soap opera of compelling seriousness. Much did happen. Paramilitary prisoners were released. This had long been an important strand of republican argument. In November 1997 Gerry Adams had stated in Belfast stated the republican view that 'There cannot be any settlement while there are prisoners in prison. We have been clear about this from day one. The release of prisoners has to be part of any settlement ... We want to see the release of all prisoners.'[135] Under the terms of the 1998 deal, IRA prisoners had been released from the Maze by July 2000 – 'free from this prison camp, proud republicans, unbowed and unbroken', as their OC Jim McVeigh put it at their confetti-and-champagne release.[136]

Pat Sheehan was released in October 1998, nine years into a twenty-four-year sentence: 'Even those who do not support Sinn Féin still give prisoners a warm welcome.'[137] Séanna Walsh, in jail for most of the 1970s and 1980s and one of the first prisoners released under the terms of the Belfast Agreement: 'In the community here in nationalist Belfast, one in six are ex-prisoners. I know I have friends here I can talk to about the problems. There are support networks for prisoners and their families.' Having spent twenty-one of his previous twenty-five years in prison, Walsh was unsurprisingly enthusiastic about liberty: 'when you're in jail you get a half-hour, maybe an hour-long visit a week. You can sit down, have a cup of tea, have a talk, give the kids a cuddle. And that is the high point of your week. Now I can do that maybe ten, fifteen times in any one day – call relatives, go for a coffee, meet for a pint. It's just wonderful.'[138] (Predictably, the prisoner-release process angered many in the unionist community.)

And broad political structures were also changing. At midnight on 2 December 1999 direct rule over Northern Ireland from London finally came to an end, with a devolved government coming into effective operation at Stormont: power-sharing between unionists, nationalists and republicans was now, at last, in place. But the operation of the Assembly and the Executive was to stall in the coming days, over another key issue featured in the Good Friday Agreement. Decommissioning. If the republicans' war was indeed to be replaced by politics, then would the IRA, the republican army, put its weapons beyond use, having no further need for them in these new times? The Belfast Agreement had recognized the crucial significance of decommissioning, and had involved all participants in reaffirming 'their commitment to the total disarmament of all paramilitary organisations'.[139] But the decommissioning question already had a long history, before 1998. In an October 1993 radio interview Northern Ireland Secretary of State Patrick Mayhew had said that the IRA would have to make its guns and explosives available to demonstrate that its violence was over. In the same year Gerry Adams had been warned by Fianna Fáil President Albert Reynolds that illegal arms and equipment would have to be dealt with. At the end of 1993 both British and Irish politicians made it publicly clear that IRA handover of weapons was expected as part of the process,[140] a point reiterated in the Dáil in June 1994 by the Republic's Minister for Foreign Affairs, Dick Spring. Even by early January that year, the issue of decommissioning had clearly already been raised with Gerry Adams, who responded negatively to what he called this question of 'how the IRA can hand over its weapons'.[141]

So after the IRA's August 1994 ceasefire, it was not for the first time that decommissioning was raised. This in itself does not mean, of course, that it was necessarily a legitimate demand, though it was one that seemed to resonate with popular opinion. An opinion poll in the north of Ireland in the immediate aftermath of the IRA's 1994 cessation found that 72 per cent of people thought that the IRA should hand over all of its weapons and explosives before Sinn Féin should be allowed into discussions to determine Northern Ireland's future (92 per cent of Protestants favoured such a prior handover; 46 per cent of Catholics supported, and 37 per cent opposed it).[142] Republicans felt, however, that decommissioning should happen at the end of negotiations rather than at the start.

Could a compromise be reached? In mid-July 1995 SDLP leader John Hume said that he thought the Provos would get rid of weapons if republicans were included in political talks. The British had taken a different line, with Mayhew's Washington speech of March 1995 requiring as its third point a tangible start to IRA decommissioning prior to Sinn Féin participation in the talks – a position to which Prime Minister John Major stuck at a 28 November 1995 Downing Street press conference. Question: 'Prime Minister, where do we stand on Washington 3 – is it an absolute precondition for Sinn Féin's entry into all-party talks that the IRA makes a first physical hand-over of weapons?' Major: 'Yes, we have not changed our position on Washington 3.'[143]

Republicans initially appeared unyielding. An IRA representative was quoted in March 1996 as stating: 'There will be no decommissioning either through the front or the back doors. This is an unrealistic and unrealisable demand which simply won't be met. The IRA will under no circumstances leave nationalist areas defenceless this side of a final settlement.'[144] With ongoing loyalist attacks, this was a perhaps understandable position. (Ironically, loyalist and republican paramilitaries were to have common views in regard to the decommissioning

issue: on the prospect of whether there should be prior decommissioning to allow paramilitary-related parties to enter talks in 1997, George
Mitchell observed: 'Although the IRA and the loyalist paramilitaries
had fought on opposite sides throughout the troubles, they were united
in their opposition to prior decommissioning.')[145]

By April 1997 John Major had shifted ground, suggesting the need
for some decommissioning to occur *during* talks. But even by the time
his successor supervised the April 1998 conclusion of the Good Friday
Agreement, there had been no practical movement on the question.
Indeed, UUP leader David Trimble supported the 1998 Agreement
partly because of an explicit statement from Tony Blair that, in the
British government's view, 'the effect of the decommissioning section
of the Agreement ... is that the process of decommissioning should
start straight away'.[146] This was not, it seemed, how the IRA saw it.
For in April 1998 a post-Good Friday Agreement IRA statement was
emphatic: 'Let us make it clear that there will be no decommissioning
by the IRA.'[147] Later in the year *An Phoblacht/Republican News* reiterated the republican view:

> The issue of decommissioning has once again been pushed to the
> top of the political agenda ... unionist political opponents of the
> Good Friday Agreement are using the issue in a completely spuri-
> ous way in an attempt to wreck the Agreement. By insisting that
> the IRA hand over weapons before Sinn Féin can take seats in an
> Executive and in the All-Ireland Council, they are deliberately
> pushing the Agreement into crisis. They are quite aware that
> nowhere in the Agreement is there such a precondition to Sinn
> Féin taking seats, nor is decommissioning something that Sinn Féin
> can deliver. In that sense, it is a dead-end issue. It can only be read
> as a wrecking tactic.[148]

Republicans were anxious that neither unionists nor the British
were honouring their side of the bargain reached in April 1998. In
October Martin McGuinness accused David Trimble of seeming
unprepared 'to honour the commitments given on Good Friday',
and argued that the unionist leader sought instead a renegotiation of
the Belfast deal (especially in regard to the decommissioning of paramilitary weapons).[149] McGuinness held that the relinquishing of weapons
seemed too much like a demand for surrender, stating that military

defeat 'is not on offer from the IRA'.[150] In July 1999 Danny Morrison, former Sinn Féin Director of Publicity, said that many IRA personnel 'view decommissioning as a unionist demand for surrender'.[151] And there remained a violent threat to republican areas, against which IRA weapons were claimed as a defence.[152]

Unionists, whether pro- or anti-Agreement, took a very different view. Decommissioning was, in David Trimble's words, 'a test of whether the paramilitaries were committed to peaceful means'.[153] The incorporation of Sinn Féin into the institutions of Northern Irish government without the IRA having given up their weapons represented, in anti-Agreement unionist Robert McCartney's view, a deviation from proper democratic practice: 'No democratic institution worthy of the name can exist if it contains the political representatives of an unlawfully armed organisation which is committed to bringing about change by either the use or threat of acts of terrorism.' The issue of decommissioning paramilitary weaponry was, from such a perspective, of vital significance: 'The requirement for all paramilitary groups to decommission their weaponry as a prerequisite for their political wings taking part in government is not a precondition imposed by other parties, it is a fundamental demand of democracy itself.'[154]

Tension rose again when in 1999 in Florida a large-scale gun-running plot was uncovered by the FBI, involving – it appeared – the Provisional IRA buying arms in the USA. Yet by the end of the year the IRA had confirmed that it would enter discussions with the Independent International Commission on Decommissioning (IICD), set up by the British and Irish governments in 1997. In a statement released on 5 December 1999, the IRA confirmed that a meeting had been held between an IRA representative and the IICD head, distinguished Canadian General John de Chastelain: 'In line with our commitment of 17 November to appoint a representative to enter into discussions with John de Chastelain and the IICD it is anticipated that further discussions will take place.'[155] And at the end of November, the Ulster Unionists had approved the establishment of the new Northern Irish Executive, but had set a February deadline for IRA decommissioning to begin; when this was not met, the infant northern government was suspended by Northern Ireland Secretary of State, Peter Mandelson – much to the annoyance of the IRA: 'The British Secretary of State

has reintroduced the unionist veto by suspending the political institutions'.[156] In David Trimble's contrasting view, unionists had moved
first – agreeing to go into government with Sinn Féin in anticipation
of decommissioning – and republicans had simply not reciprocated:
'We took the risks, we made the effort, they did not'.[157] On 15 January
2000, Trimble had made clear that, in his view, responsibility for
progress lay with the IRA: 'The future depends entirely on what they
do, not on what they or Sinn Féin say, and the ball is firmly in their
court on the decommissioning issue'.[158]

But the new institutions were soon breathing again, facilitated by a
scheme in which former Finnish President Martti Ahtisaari and ANC
politician Cyril Ramaphosa were to act as independent arms inspectors,
with the job of regularly inspecting a number of sealed IRA arms
dumps, and of reporting back to the IICD to confirm that the weapons
contained in them had remained out of use. The IRA had reiterated
in February 2000 that they remained 'totally committed to the peace
process, that the IRA wants a permanent peace, that the declaration
and maintenance of the cessation, which is now entering its fifth year,
is evidence of that, that the IRA's guns are silent and that there is no
threat to the peace process from the IRA.'[159] On Saturday 6 May 2000
the Provisionals issued an important statement:

> The political responsibility for advancing the current situation rests
> with the two governments, especially the British government, and
> the leadership of the political parties. The full implementation, on
> a progressive and irreversible basis, by the two governments,
> especially the British government, of what they have agreed will
> provide a political context, in an enduring political process, with
> the potential to remove the causes of conflict and in which Irish
> republicans and unionists can, as equals, pursue our respective
> political objectives peacefully. In that new context the IRA leader-
> ship will initiate a process that will completely and verifiably put
> IRA arms beyond use. We will do it in such a way as to avoid risk
> to the public and misappropriation by others and ensure maximum
> public confidence. We will resume contact with the Independent
> International Commission on Decommissioning and enter into
> further discussions with the Commission on the basis of the IRA
> leadership's commitment to resolving the issue of arms. We look
> to the two governments, and especially the British government, to

fulfil their commitments under the Good Friday Agreement and the Joint Statement.[160]

That Joint Statement, by the British and Irish governments on 5 May, saw both London and Dublin committing themselves to the full implementation of the Belfast Agreement by June 2001. They set about restoring the Assembly and Executive in a letter the following day to party leaders and laid out their proposals regarding movement on rights and equality, security, policing and prisoner releases.

Then, in June, the Provisionals announced that they had re-established contact with the IICD, and – significantly – that a number of their arms dumps had indeed been inspected: 'We now wish to confirm that we have re-established contact with the IICD, and that a number of arms dumps have been examined by the two agreed third parties [Ramaphosa and Ahtisaari]. These dumps contained a substantial amount of material including weapons, explosives and other equipment.'[161] On 25 October a Provisional statement declared that 'the IRA leadership has decided that the re-inspection of a number of arms dumps will be repeated to confirm that our weapons remain secure'. They continued, 'The IRA are doing our best to enhance the peace process. This is not our responsibility alone. Others also must play their part. The political responsibility for advancing the current situation and making progress rests with the two governments, especially the British government.'[162] The IRA soon announced that dumps had duly been reinspected (a claim confirmed by the inspectors themselves at the start of November, who reported that the weapons in the dumps remained out of action).

In early December 2000 an IRA statement reaffirmed the organization's 'commitment to the resolution of the issue of arms': 'We remain prepared to initiate a process which would completely and verifiably put IRA arms beyond use.' But such a development 'cannot and will not happen on terms dictated by the British government or the unionists'.[163] It was important to the IRA that the British government deal, to republicans' satisfaction, with questions such as the implementation of the Patten Report on policing, or the process of demilitarization of British structures in the north. To the Provisionals, IRA decommissioning was part of a wider fulfilment of everyone's duties and obligations under the Good Friday Agreement. And there remained a persistent republican sense that the British were not implementing their part of the 1998 deal. Early in 2001 an *An Phoblacht/Republican News* front-page headline, accompanying a picture of Prime Minister Tony Blair, proclaimed, 'It's Simple, Tony: Uphold the Agreement You Signed'.[164]

But the process of engagement continued. On 8 March 2001 the IRA leadership re-established contact with the IICD, and the IRA's representative went on to hold numerous meetings with them. At the end of May it was confirmed by Ahtisaari and Ramaphosa that a third inspection of IRA arms dumps had taken place, and that these had not been interfered with and had remained secure. But in June it was confirmed by the IICD that no actual IRA decommissioning had occurred, and so on 1 July David Trimble resigned as Northern Ireland's First Minister. So the dance proceeded. On 8 August the IRA publicly stated that it had 'agreed a scheme with the IICD which will put IRA arms completely and verifiably beyond use';[165] this gesture was not, however, enough to satisfy the UUP or the British government, and the latter therefore suspended the institutions set up under the Belfast Agreement; as a consequence, the IRA in their turn withdrew their arms offer, saying in a statement of 14 August: 'We are withdrawing our proposal.'[166]

How could this stand-off be ended? Could international events jolt things forward? This had happened in the past: in February 2000 in Belfast, Sathyandranath Maharaj – who had been an ANC militant – had a secret meeting with leading IRA figures, which had helped to push them towards compromise on the arms question and led towards agreement on the inspection of arms dumps. Now during 2001, international events of a very different kind helped to facilitate further republican movement over arms, as two unexpected developments tarnished somewhat the IRA's image in the United States. First, three Irish republicans (James Monaghan, Martin McCauley, Niall Connolly) were arrested in the Colombian capital, Bogota, on Saturday 11 August. They had arrived in Colombia in June, and had spent several weeks in part of the country controlled by guerrillas of the left-wing rebel group, the Revolutionary Armed Forces of Colombia (FARC).

Alleged links between the three men and this Marxist anti-government organization were embarrassing for the republican movement in Ireland. FARC had for decades been violent opponents of the

Colombian state, their activities including guerrilla war against the authorities, bombings, killings, hijackings, kidnappings; and they represented a very serious threat to state stability. Some FARC money came from payments made to them by drug-traffickers, and so the three Irishmen were associated in the public mind with a well-armed Marxist guerrilla group that was partly funded by drug money – and that had been at war with a state backed by the USA. For the United States cooperated very closely with the Colombian authorities, whose army was backed financially by a Washington that considered FARC – and Colombian drugs production – to be a serious problem in – effectively – its own back yard. If the IRA were to be linked in the American mind with such forces, then their image would be potentially tarnished. Sinn Féin raise large amounts of money in the USA, republicans having tried for years to build there a reputation of respectability and to forge links with corporate America.

So the IRA was keen to deny allegations that it was in league with FARC: 'We wish to make it clear that the Army Council sent no one to Colombia to train or to engage in any military cooperation with any group.'[167] Monaghan, McCauley and Connolly had entered Colombia using false passports, and it was alleged that they had been training FARC members. All three had Irish republican connections (McCauley had been a comparatively prominent Sinn Féiner; Monaghan had been well known in the party too, and had been imprisoned for his role in republican violence; Sinn Féin initially denied, but later admitted, that Niall Connolly had been their representative in Cuba). The Provisional republican movement had previously registered some hostility towards the role of the USA in Colombia,[168] but that was far less prominent than this very public embarrassment. The British had for years been drawing to American attention the IRA's sympathy for forces (Marxist and other) that were internationally opposed to US interests, with a view to strengthening Washington's anti-IRA position.[169] After the FARC 2001 episode, US politicians might not quite share the response of those loyalist graffiti-writers who daubed Belfast walls with the slogan 'FARC Off Gerry Kelly' (a reference to the leading Sinn Féin politician); but Colombia was certainly unhelpful to the new republicans' cause.

This was as nothing, however, to the events of 11 September 2001, when attacks on the USA famously destroyed New York's World Trade

Towers, along with thousands of lives in that city and elsewhere. Of all the repercussions of this appalling tragedy, the impact on the IRA might rightly be seen as comparatively minor. But 11 September did generate a far more horrifying and urgent conception of anti-state violence than had largely existed in the USA until then, and those with Irish paramilitary backgrounds and links were to suffer colder winds as a result. Irish republicans were quick to condemn the attacks on New York and Washington. An *An Phoblacht/Republican News* editorial observed, 'No matter who was to blame, it was utterly reprehensible and must be condemned. The deliberate killing of civilians is always wrong, no matter whether it is governments, armed political groups or individuals who carry it out.'[170] The IRA themselves referred to the 'deplorable attacks in New York, Washington and Pennsylvania' and simultaneously stated: 'as an earnest of our willingness to resolve the issue of arms, the IRA leadership wish to confirm that our representative will intensify the engagement with the IICD'.[171]

The causal link between 11 September and the subsequent path taken by the IRA towards the actual decommissioning of arms should not be overplayed. As has been noted, the army had already moved a long way before September 2001, and it is arguable that some form of decommissioning would have occurred anyway. But there was, after those attacks on America, a measure of pressure from American sources for the IRA to decommission; and in the period after 11 September and the Colombian episode, the US State Department called for the IRA 'to just totally dissociate itself from any terrorist activity'.[172]

If Colombia and 11 September made the USA less friendly towards an Irish republican movement that refused to break with violence, then this might explain – in part – the acceleration of the decommissioning process. For on Monday 22 October 2001, in Conway Mill off the Falls Road in Belfast, Gerry Adams gave an historically significant speech. The peace process, he said, was in crisis because the British government had not honoured its commitments, and because unionists had been obstructive of necessary change. But republicans wanted to save the 1998 Agreement and the peace process:

> Sinn Féin's commitment to the process is absolute. The initiatives we have taken, the initiatives we have encouraged others to take,

including the IRA, have contributed decisively to the peace process
... Many republicans are angry at the unrelenting focus on silent
IRA weapons. This is in marked contrast to the attitude to loyalist
weapons and bombs in daily use, and the remilitarisation by the
British Army of republican heartlands in the north. The issue of all
arms must be resolved. But not just IRA weapons – British weapons
as well.

Adams and McGuinness had 'put to the IRA the view that if it
could make a groundbreaking move on the arms issue ... this could
save the peace process from collapse and transform the situation'.
But 'if the IRA takes yet another initiative on the arms issue then
the British government needs to build upon the dynamic created by
that'.[173] An IRA statement was duly issued on 23 October: 'The IRA is
committed to our republican objectives, and to the establishment of a
united Ireland based on justice, equality and freedom ... The political
process is now on the point of collapse. Such a collapse would certainly
and eventually put the overall peace process in jeopardy. There is a
responsibility upon everyone seriously committed to a just peace to do
our best to avoid this. Therefore in order to save the peace process we
have implemented the scheme agreed with the IICD in August.'[174] The
IICD for their part confirmed that they had witnessed the IRA putting
a quantity of material (including arms, ammunition and explosives)
beyond use. As the head of the IICD, John de Chastelain, emphatically put it to UUP leader David Trimble that same day, 'We are all
satisfied that the process renders the materials permanently unusable
or unavailable'; David Trimble: 'You are quite satisfied with that?';
John de Chastelain: 'Yes, we would not have said so otherwise.'[175]
When, in April 2002, the IICD verified that a second act of IRA
decommissioning had taken place ('an event in which the IRA leadership has put a varied and substantial quantity of ammunition, arms
and explosive material beyond use'),[176] it seemed that genuine progress
had been made towards the solution of this major problem.[177]

Decommissioning unquestionably reflected issues central to the
northern conflict in Ireland, and central also to its attempted resolution. Contrary to some casual speculation, decommissioning *was* a very
important issue. For unionists and the British government, the relinquishing or destroying of weapons would demonstrate a necessarily

unambiguous commitment to peaceful rather than violent politics on the part of the IRA. And there was much popular support for such a move. Asked in 1998, 'Could you tell me how you feel about ... decommissioning of paramilitary weapons?', 88 per cent of northern Catholics and 95 per cent of northern Protestants said that they supported or strongly supported such a development.[178] Why, then, did it take so long for the IRA to make the moves that it eventually did? Six main reasons can be identified. First, the handing over or destruction of weapons risked giving the appearance (or marking the reality) of surrender, of humiliating defeat. As has been seen, the notion that the IRA could not be beaten went deep into the organization's self-image. Second, decommissioning was a demand publicly and repeatedly made by the IRA's enemies, the unionists and the British government, and for republicans to make such a gesture at the behest of these forces came dangerously close to that very deference that the Provisionals had emerged to defy. Third, to decommission seemed to suggest that paramilitary violence in the future (even, perhaps, in the past) represented an illegitimate way of pursuing one's goals – and many Provisionals simply did not think this to be the case. If a significant number of people doubted the rightness of such symbolism, then further schism – a nightmare for the leadership – might result. Fourth, amid ongoing sporadic loyalist violence, some felt that weapons were required for possible defence of Catholic areas. Fifth, the handing over or the destruction of weapons would diminish the power of republican leverage: with guns and bombs, there existed the threat of a renewed war, and this gave extra weight to republican argument when dealing with the governments and the unionists. At the very least, if decommissioning *were* to occur, then republicans might feel it wise to postpone the move for as long as possible, in order to extract maximum concession, maximum advantage from the strength that the threat of violence offered. Sixth, a refusal to decommission IRA weapons generated and sustained rancour and division within Ulster unionism: in the traditionally zero-sum game of Ulster politics, disadvantage for one's opponent might be judged to offer benefit for oneself.

In light of such considerations one can see why republicans delayed so long in decommissioning, just as one can understand why their opponents felt such a move to be required as a mark of genuine transformation into peaceful political activity. Decommissioning was never going to be a one-off event but – like the peace process as a whole – a lengthy, much negotiated process. Yet, even before the international events of 2001, the IRA had moved considerably on the arms question and, in a sense, such movement merely followed the logic of the Provisionals' engagement with politics and compromise. If elections and government offered expanded possibilities for Irish republicans, then – ultimately – the gun would be as much a hindrance as a blessing. Even after its initiation of a decommissioning process in 2001 and 2002, the IRA possessed the capacity to return to war if it so wished. But it appeared not to have the desire to do so. In part, such reluctance might be explained by the political momentum evident in the 2001 UK general election. On 7 June the voters gave Sinn Féin an extra two seats in Westminster from which to abstain: the party now had four seats, their nationalist rivals (the SDLP) only three. The long peace process had proved an ironic one. It had begun in 1985 with an Anglo-Irish Agreement intended to strengthen the SDLP at republicans' expense; it had now produced this strikingly different outcome.

CONCLUSION

1

'As we enter 2001 we reaffirm our commitment to the achievement of our objectives, and the creation of a national democracy through a united, independent and free Ireland.'

IRA's New Year message for 2001[1]

Stereotypes have dominated much popular understanding of the Provisional IRA. Recently, it has been strongly argued that popular fiction concerning the troubles has unhelpfully relied on negative images of Irish republicans;[2] and stereotypes – negative as well as positive – have also flourished in cinematic representations of republican Ireland. At times Irish republicans in film have been depicted as unredeemed psychopaths, as with Sean Bean's vengeful character in *Patriot Games* (1992; a film that presented Irish republicans in such a negative light that *An Phoblacht/Republican News* referred to it as 'pro-British propaganda under the guise of an action movie').[3] At other times, an equally implausible caricature has presented the Irish republican as unblemished hero, a trend exemplified in Alan Pakula's *The Devil's Own* (1997). Here, Brad Pitt plays Belfast IRA man Frankie McGuire as a justified, romantic, beautiful hero drawn in stark contrast to the film's vicious, untrustworthy, devious Brits. Pitt's Frankie McGuire is, in the words of one recent commentator, 'probably the screen's most attractive IRA man ever'.[4] A challenger for that title might, however, be found in James Mason's gentle IRA leader, Johnny, in Carol Reed's 1947 film *Odd Man Out*. For if Bean and Pitt typify, respectively, the cinema's villainous and heroic stereotypes of the Irish republican, then here we find a third persistent caricature: the IRA man as semi-detached wanderer, as dilemma-ridden, tortured and solitary individual, in a tale told in essentially apolitical terms.

These three images (the justified, political hero-warrior; the evil psychopath; the lost, lonely wanderer) have between them accounted for most cinematic treatments of the IRA persona. The attraction is not difficult to explain, for there is something here for most people in any imagined audience. Those who hate the IRA can see them as psychopaths; those who love them can see them as heroes; and those who do not really want to get involved can think that they are all James Mason. But each of these evocations of the IRA is clearly a distortion. The organization cannot satisfactorily be explained according to any of them, unless one believes in caricatured heroes and villains of implausible simplicity; in an inexplicable and spontaneous outburst of mass psychopathology in the north of Ireland; or in the possibility of one of the world's most durable rebel organizations thriving on doubt-ridden loners.

This book has been written in the belief that, whether one supports the IRA or not, it is important to understand what they have done, why and with what consequences – and to do so in terms of serious, detailed explanation rather than simple stereotype. In particular, I have sought to present very many examples of what the IRA themselves have thought and said. For the Provisional IRA has sustained an evolving and strongly articulated argument to accompany its violent thirty-year career. And this argument has been repeatedly and loudly made; the reference of one observer in 1971 to the Provisionals' 'avoidance of publicity'[5] is hardly one that could be sustained three decades later! Contrary to some popular opinion, the IRA is in fact utterly comprehensible: their actions can be systematically explained, and their arguments clearly set out and analysed.

They began primarily in response to defensive need, to urgent danger. In the face of the late-1960s crisis in the north of Ireland, so the Provisional argument goes, there was an overriding need for a defence force to protect vulnerable Catholic communities from sectarian attack. This has remained a central part of the IRA's self-image throughout the troubles, and of wider republican perception of the organization. As late as 1997 leading Sinn Féiner Francie Molloy referred to the IRA as 'the defenders of our people for the last twenty-five or thirty years'.[6] In 1969 the oppressed communities required muscular defence, and the IRA provided it. Tied in with this in the IRA argument is a second point: the attacks of the late 1960s upon Catholic communities were part of longstanding unfair treatment of those people within a state that had been of its nature hostile to its Catholic inhabitants.

If defence is the first foundation stone of the IRA argument, then the unfairness of the northern state is the second. Just as with much Catholic Irish experience within the pre-1922 United Kingdom, so too there was a problem with northern Catholic treatment and experience after partition. Gerry Adams: 'In 1922, the six northeastern counties of Ireland were partitioned from the rest of the island by the British government, against the will of the Irish people and under threat of war. This partition resulted in the creation of a sectarian state in which nationalists have always been treated as second-class citizens.'[7] Systemic, collective grievance provided the well from which Provisional republicanism was able to draw, and the IRA relentlessly made their point that loyalty was impossible to a state built in such a way as to exclude them; and lack of allegiance to the state had brought unfair treatment, discrimination, exclusion. In Provisional eyes, partition had set up a state that denied Irish democracy: 'People talk about fighting for a united Ireland, but really that was always just a means to political ends: ... to extend democracy as much as you can, and [to get] political strength and the strength of your communities.'[8]

For the day-to-day denial of northern nationalist democratic rights was held to arise from a broader, third point: that the very existence of Northern Ireland involved a denial of Irish self-determination, and thus the sustenance of an illegitimate state. As Sinn Féin put it in 1992: 'British rule in Ireland lacks democratic legitimacy either domestically or internationally ... Peace, to be both achievable and sustainable, must have as its foundation democracy, of which national self-determination is the cornerstone.'[9] Ireland, naturally, should be united: 'Ireland is historically, culturally and geographically one single unit.'[10] Its 1920s partition was therefore wrong, artificial and in conflict with majority nationalist opinion on the island. An IRA GHQ spokesperson neatly articulated that key part of IRA thinking in 1990: 'We demand the basic right of every nation to national self-determination. The denial of that right by armed might will always legitimise and give rise to armed struggle in pursuit of that right.'[11] A Sinn Féin statement of late 1993 identified movement towards peace with movement towards self-determination: 'Sinn Féin believes that the route to peace in Ireland is to be found in the exercise of the right to self-determination, without impediment of any kind, by the Irish people as a whole.'[12] And the party argued again in late 1994 that the settlement to the Northern Ireland conflict 'should be based on the fundamental right of the Irish people to national self-determination'.[13]

And it was emphatically *national* self-determination for which the IRA were fighting. Indeed, as in 1920, the IRA identified itself in a vanguardist way with the nation. They stressed, as for example in their *Green Book*, the longstanding nature of Irish nationhood: 'The nationhood of all Ireland has been an accepted fact for more than 1500 years and has been recognised internationally as a fact.'[14] To the IRA, self-determination was easily defined in an Irish setting: the nation, the island and the state should have the same boundary, with national sovereignty residing in the people who lived there. In their own view, the IRA were the legitimate army of a nation that had been denied proper self-determination. The troubles were thus a 'conflict between the British government and the Irish people'.[15] The denial of self-determination had, predictably, brought conflict and appalling consequences:

> The border partitioning Ireland was contrived by a British government so as to ensure an artificially constructed unionist majority. The partitioned area had no basis in geography or history. The foremost consequence of partition was that it institutionalised sectarianism . . . Partition affects every aspect of Irish society. In the north it has created a failed political entity marred by economic apartheid, political repression and religious intolerance. In the south the political division resulting from partition has stunted normal political, economic and social development. Both states are in a deep and permanent crisis.[16]

Thus the IRA's argument had deep historical roots. Republicans were no more trapped by the past than other political players, but they did express an argument with historical (at times, teleological) dimensions: 'For the past 800 years the British ruling class have attempted to smash down the resistance of the Irish people. Campaign after campaign, decade after decade, century after century, armies of resistance have fought and despite temporary setbacks, slavery and famine, penal laws and murder, the will of the Irish people in their desire to cast off the chains of foreign occupation continue[s] an unremitting and relentless war against enemy occupation';[17] Patrick Magee: 'The contemporary republican movement, by which I mean primarily the Provisional IRA and Sinn Féin, claims a common lineage stretching back to [Theobald Wolfe] Tone and beyond to embrace the long history of resistance to oppression under the English crown.'[18] The Provos made use of history where they could, to strengthen their case. March 15, 1984 saw *An Phoblacht/Republican News* link the life and death of one martyred IRA hero with contemporary republican struggle: 'Tomás MacCurtain, the first republican lord mayor of Cork, was born ... on March 20 1884, a century ago this week. He was murdered by the RIC thirty-six years later ... The cause for which MacCurtain laboured and died is today, the centenary of his birth, the very same cause for which republicans continue to work and die.'

If past struggles helped to legitimate those of the present, then past iniquity on the part of republicans' enemies pointed in the same direction. The discriminatory record of unionist rule in Northern Ireland – 'seventy-five years of unionist misrule and its accompanying suppression of democracy', as the IRA put it early in 1998[19] – was held to delegitimize Ulster unionism and British rule in Ireland alike; the unacceptability in republican areas of the RUC meant that the IRA could present themselves as the effective police in local areas; the historical sense of suffering and of losing out legitimated resistance to an order so unfair as to produce such experience. And one did not have to be an IRA sympathizer to recognize the depth of the northern Catholic sense of past suffering: as Marianne Elliott, the leading historian of Catholic Ulster, has herself put it, 'It is important to recognise that Ulster Catholics have been on the losing side for most of the past four centuries'.[20]

As we have seen, responsibility for conflict lay, in IRA opinion, with the British, the oppressors. Martin McGuinness has said: 'The British portray republicans as the cause of the conflict. The British are dishonest. We are not the cause of this conflict; we are the victims of it. We are the product of decades of British tyranny and misrule.'[21] Whoever killed in the troubles, the ultimate responsibility lay with

Britain, the ultimate victimhood with the nationalist people of Ireland. There was a moralization of politics here which, again, delegitimized republicans' opponents. RUC and British Army misdeeds long featured prominently in IRA argument and propaganda: republicans were the resisters and the victims. Since all deaths were, ultimately, Britain's fault, the responsibility for sorting the conflict out, for ending it, was primarily Britain's also.

Defence and the dual unacceptability of the north – its unfairness and its illegitimacy – were compounded in IRA thinking by a fourth point: that the north was considered irreformable. This was the lesson that the Provos drew from the 1960s civil rights episode, and from attempts during ensuing years at an essentially internal Northern Irish solution. The state, in their view, had to be removed rather than reformed. Constitutional-style politics – gradualist and reformist, and epitomized for nationalists during the troubles by the SDLP – were eschewed in favour of a more aggressive form of Irish nationalism. Constitutional politics would prove ineffective, and had missed the central point that the state must be destroyed rather than changed. And if more moderate nationalists had missed the point about the aims – undoing the British connection – then they were also wrong about the means: for Provo politics were centrally defined by the necessity for political violence.

Force was essential to the achievement of republican goals. 'At one time that was all we *could* do, that was the only avenue open to us, was to engage in armed struggle'; and armed struggle was 'basically about reversing a denial of rights to the nationalist people,' says Patrick Magee.[22] Other avenues had been closed down, and Britain – ultimately – only listened to force. Violence was, in this republican view, considered inevitable. As one Sinn Féiner put it in 1993: 'They [the British] came by force of arms many hundreds of years ago. They maintain their presence by force of arms and they'll have to be removed by force of arms.'[23] Late in 1994 Sinn Féin argued: 'the existence of injustice, allied to the absence of any real prospect of redress, made political violence inevitable'.[24] Magee again: 'I believe that the IRA actions over the last thirty years were justified . . . There was simply no other way'; 'Every generation of republicans has had to turn to violence.'[25] More peaceful politics were deemed not to have worked, and so it seemed logical, indeed necessary, to use force to achieve political progress. Constitutionalism was held to be corrupting, distracting, compromising. If the British connection was to go (and this was axiomatic to republicans, centuries of British involvement in Ireland having produced 'suffering, grief, death and division'),[26] then violence was necessary. Gerry Adams argued in 1986 that armed action in the north was 'a necessary form of struggle'; violence was 'of primary importance because it provides a vital cutting edge. Without it the issue of Ireland would not even be an issue.'[27]

IRA muscle offered much: defence, and a culture of resistance. Fifteen years into the Provisionals' existence, Martin McGuinness gave pithy expression to such thinking: 'Without the IRA we are on our knees. Without the IRA we are slaves. For fifteen years this generation of republicans have been off their knees. We will never be slaves again.'[28] But that IRA muscle also had a Clausewitzean quality, applying pressure upon Britain to disengage from Ireland by making the war more painful than would be the concession of republican demands. Force offered, it was thought, ever increasing leverage over London. Attritional pressure would gradually wear down the public and politicians until they decided that it was no longer worth the cost to remain in the north of Ireland. And violence by the IRA offered republicans an effective veto over forms of settlement that they found disagreeable: as long as the Provisionals could maintain their war, then any internal northern settlement could be said not to be working, and the army could thereby prevent the peaceful functioning of an internal, reformist, Northern Irish settlement. The IRA were aware of their military limitations, but also of their weight. As an Army Council spokesperson put it in the 1980s: 'We can't be beaten; there is no question of us winning in the sense of driving the British Army into the sea. But we always maintain the capacity to bring the situation to a crisis at some stage'.[29]

It was initially thought that the British would snap early on; they did not, and a long war ensued. But throughout, it was held that ultimately the British would indeed be forced to leave. So the use of force was emphatically political. Even in its most violent phases, the IRA was fighting a politically motivated war. Whether one abhors or celebrates IRA actions, it remains true that they have had a primarily political root – without which they are not properly explicable: 'Military action is an extension of political action therefore the military campaign being waged by the IRA is in effect a political campaign. People with no political concepts have no place in the army, because the actions of the army are directed towards a political objective that is the real meaning of the present military campaign.'[30]

Thus the IRA's argument was not always subtle or nuanced, but the questions to which it related (legitimacy, government, independence, sovereignty, territory, force and order) were all crucial to the state and to politics. Violence, and the belief in the necessity and primary efficacy of force, were what centrally defined IRA politics; once it came to be thought, at the end of the 1990s, that more conventional politics in fact offered superior rewards, then the IRA began to cease to exist. During the troubles, however, the IRA argument centred on political violence, violence carried out with dedication and resilience. Their arsenal was diverse, including Semtex, Russian RPG-7 rockets and Kalashnikov rifles, Chinese Simarol rifles, Armalites and M60 machine-guns. As we have seen, funding included American contributions; and, in Ireland, it was obtained from protection, bank and post office robberies, republican clubs, local collections, kidnappings. Consider-able money could thus be gathered: IRA revenue in 1987 appears to have been in the region of £7 million. Numbers are difficult to agree on. In the late 1970s the British Army thought the IRA to have had around 500 full-time members; in the mid-1980s the Provisionals probably had between 200 and 300 active Volunteers. But these varied in role: in 1988 it was claimed that the IRA had 'no more than thirty experienced gunmen and bombers, with perhaps twenty apprentices and up to 500 Volunteers who can be called upon to support their operations'.[31]

Thus the IRA's military argument had some threat behind it. The argument was also backed up by a broader ideological conviction that they were fighting a war which reflected the direction of world history. For the Provisionals saw their conflict with Britain as part of a wider process of decolonization. British colonialism and imperialism in Ireland were to be challenged just as Britain and other colonial/imperial powers were – in the republican view, rightly – being fought elsewhere in the world. As *Republican News* put it in 1975, 'It is the stated intention of the republican movement to destroy the colonial and neo-colonial states in Ireland.'[32] The IRA held it as axiomatic that Ireland was an English colony, their *Green Book* confidently asserting: 'In the six counties we still have naked, undisguised colonialism effected by British politicians and enforced by British troops and judiciary, while the manifestations of imperialist domination in all of Ireland remain and are increasingly more obvious.'[33] Republican writings repeatedly affirmed this view, that the struggle against Britain was an anti-colonial and anti-imperial one.[34]

If anti-imperial and anti-colonial, then republicans were victims of historical oppression, were legitimated, and were hopeful of victory in a late twentieth century that had witnessed the crumbling of the British and other empires. Anti-colonial struggles, and their theorists, became celebrated by the IRA. Just as Che Guevara and Frantz Fanon remain alluring for many others and the focus still of much debate well beyond Ireland,[35] so too they held an appeal for the Provisionals.[36] (*An Phoblacht/Republican News* referred to Che's writings and speeches as containing 'some of the clearest revolutionary thinking this century').[37] Indeed, revolutionary struggles for liberation throughout the world were seen as echoing and reinforcing the IRA's own campaign for Irish freedom. Irish Catholics in the north had, according to the Provos, experienced oppression similar to appalling suffering elsewhere: Northern Ireland under pre-troubles Stormont 'was a police state similar to South Africa's apartheid system';[38] 'Within the six counties, a divisive, violent and sectarian system of apartheid has held sway since partition';[39] the north was 'a six-county fascist statelet'.[40]

If what they were opposing was likened to fascism, then what they endorsed was often informed from the left. Indeed, socialism played a longstanding, if protean, role in IRA thought. The Provisionals frequently celebrated the socialist republican martyr of the Easter Rising, James Connolly,[41] and they explicitly identified their own project with his Marxist-inspired version of republicanism:

Connolly's life's work had become centred on the need to combine the two currents of revolutionary thought in Ireland, the national and the social. He saw that both were two sides of the same coin and that they were not antagonistic but complementary . . . Today's Sinn Féin is the only organised political party which currently upholds Connolly's teachings. The party's ultimate objective is the establishment of a thirty-two-county democratic, socialist republic.

True to Connolly, Sinn Féin links the struggle for socialism to the
fight against British imperialism.[42]

In one of a series of articles written in prison during 1979 and
1980, Bobby Sands argued: 'Only radical socialist thought – that
promoted by Connolly, Tone, Lalor, Mellows, and others, the peren-
nially pure republicanism that holds the answers – must be put into
practice and must be taught, preached and spread both in and out of
the movement.'[43] Gerry Adams likewise breathed socialist air. Speaking
in Dublin on 12 August 1993, he said of Sinn Féin: 'Our long-term
goal is for a thirty-two-county, democratic, socialist republic based
upon the 1916 Proclamation.'[44]

Provisional republicans have, indeed, often argued that they wanted
a socialist Ireland in line with the 1916 Easter Proclamation,[45] and
Adams himself was heavily influenced by Connolly.[46] Indeed, the Sinn
Féin leader has repeatedly emphasized that socialism forms part of the
new world sought by Irish republicans: 'You cannot be a socialist and
not be a republican';[47] 'The true socialist will be an active supporter
of the right of the Irish nation to self-determination';[48] 'If you want
to talk about socialism in the Irish context, you cannot divorce the
socialist aspiration from the aspiration of national independence. This
is the big lesson of the Connolly experience. In order to bring about a
socialist society, you must have real national independence.'[49]

Socialism of a revolutionary kind offered, and reflected, a belief in
millenarian change, in the creation of a new and golden era. After all,
the Provisional movement had been born in a late-1960s/early 1970s
world characterized by a faith in radical possibility, in revolutionary
change and re-creation. And other forms of change were also desired,
and other cultural influences evident. Irish cultural distinctiveness was
embodied in and furthered by a zeal for the Irish language: a Gaelic
dimension remained a key part of the Provos' preferred Ireland. And
the overwhelming majority of Provisionals came from Catholic backgrounds, as was evident in particular in some of the arguments offered
during the 1970s. Yet, though clearly influenced by their Catholicism,
the IRA themselves repeatedly declared that they were a non-sectarian
army. Sectarianism was presented as characteristic of loyalists, of
unionists and the British state; it would, indeed, only be removed by

the destruction of British rule in Ireland – which the Provos themselves would bring about.

Republicans had, in fact, long proclaimed themselves non-sectarian. The IRA statement ending the 1956–62 border campaign had stated that 'the movement takes its stand against any attempt to foment sectarian strife which is alien to the spirit of Irish republicanism'.[50] And, for their part, the Provisionals' self-image was decidedly that of a non-sectarian organization, operating in a sectarian world of others' creation.[51] The Provisionals have certainly not enjoyed a cosy relationship with the authorities of the Catholic Church (Gerry Adams: 'It is my contention as a lay member of the Catholic Church, that the hierarchy of that Church have been found somewhat lacking in their contribution and in their attitudes to the resolution of the situation in which we find ourselves').[52] And republican attacks on the local (mainly Protestant) security forces have been, in the IRA's view, not attacks on the Protestant community but rather attacks on the forces of the British state in Ireland. (It should also perhaps be noted that, while the IRA claims, for example, to have attacked the RUC on the grounds that it was the repressive arm of the British colonial state, for their own part, RUC officers during the conflict tended to see themselves in a depoliticized way, as ordinary people, normal human beings just doing their daily job.[53] Via such starkly different perceptions was the conflict born and sustained.)

Sectarianism, the IRA claim, originates with and is practised by their opponents. 'Who started sectarianism?' asked *Republican News* on 19 May 1973, answering: 'The English murderers who invaded Ireland, massacred the native population who were Catholic and established a Protestant Ascendancy based on the Penal Laws and backed by all the forces of the British Empire.' The catechism continued: 'Who maintained sectarianism?' Answer: 'First the English and Scottish landlords and later the Protestant working class and planters, through the Orange Order, by discrimination, corruption and terrorism.' Then, 'Who is maintaining it now?' 'Protestant ultra-right-wing politicians and the Orange fascist organisations who have long outlived their usefulness to the British. They are the Frankenstein [sic] the British are faced with now.'

Analysis of unionists – Frankensteinian monsters or not – formed the final part of the republican argument. Unionists were held to be Irish people holding to a deluded notion that their interests would be better served by the union with Britain than by involvement in a united independent Ireland. They were a minority of the Irish nation, and had no right to a veto over the destiny and indeed the unity of that nation. To sustain the unionist veto was to maintain an undemocratic situation. Gerry Adams, interviewed in September 1988, put it lucidly: 'We would argue that it is undemocratic to give the loyalists some sort of veto over national sovereignty . . . They are an artificial majority.'[54] (And, to republican eyes, an ugly one, Adams himself being clear about 'the neo-fascist nature of loyalism'.)[55]

To the republican movement, as we have seen, unionists and loyalists were a residue of British colonialism in Ireland. Gerry Adams: 'The British must recognise that unionism is the child of the British connection which is afraid of being orphaned and must be brought round to the point where it realises that its natural family is the Irish one.'[56] The basic conflict was one between Ireland and Britain, with the unionists painfully caught between the two. Tom Hartley: 'I see Irish history in terms of two major political forces: the British state or British imperialism, and Irish nationalism in all its different forms and shapes.' The unionists and Britain? 'It's a relationship of the colonial to the mother country. There is a dependency each has on [the other], and yet I think in the colonial there's always the sense that some day the senior partner is going to pull the plug.' Unionists were the problem: 'In essence, nobody knows what to do with the unionists.'[57]

Republicans stressed publicly that they did not want to drive Ulster's unionists physically from Ireland. Gerry Adams argued early in 1994 that 'the republican demand for British withdrawal is not aimed at them. It is directed solely at the British government's control in Ireland.'[58] Nor was it about religion: loyalism had 'nothing to do with the Protestant religion', in Adams's view.[59] Rather, the question was one of the Protestant population of the north coming *politically* to terms with a necessarily new Ireland. In his presidential address to the 1994 Sinn Féin *ard fheis*, Adams addressed the question of unionism and loyalism thus: 'Loyalism is part of the British way of life in Ireland. It, like unionism, is a child of the British connection.' Its extremists would find themselves redundant once that connection was severed 'and when the Protestant section of our community can shake off the shackles of unionism'. Once emancipated from their unionism, Protestants could be proud of the Irishness they shared with Irish nationalists: 'Protestants need to be encouraged to recognise that they share a common history with their Catholic fellow countrymen and women in the common territory of Ireland. They need to be encouraged to look at the traditions of which we can be proud, and in this regard, where else need we look but to the long tradition of Protestant participation in the democratic struggle of the Irish people for self-government?'[60]

Unionists and loyalists were a function of British rule in Ireland; that gone, they would change their nature. And republicans offered at least a rhetorical welcome and embrace: 'Ireland is moving towards Irish unity. The historical tide cannot be wished back. But as I have indicated previously, and reiterate now, republicans do not want unionists to be politically drowned in a sea of nationalism. We, in the original spirit of [Theobald Wolfe] Tone, want them to be accommodated, to be included – to belong. We do not want them to be strangers in their own land, in our own land. Our Ireland is a shared Ireland, an inclusive Ireland.'[61]

Irish republicanism is often presented as rooted in ancient pasts[62] – at times as though it exists fixedly, as if unchanging through time. And republicans have sometimes themselves given the impression of an unbroken, unchanging struggle over centuries against the same enemy. A document of May 1979, apparently produced in prison, argued: 'From 1169 there has been a history of militant separatism in Ireland. This separatist cause, basically a desire to be rid of the English invader, developed under men like Tone, Davis, Lawlor [Lalor] and Mitchell [Mitchel] into a philosophy now recognisable and readily identifiable as that of Irish republicanism.' The republican movement had been 'fighting the British for hundreds of years now'.[63]

But the IRA's argument was not a static one: socialist thinking was less dominant at the start and end of the troubles than it had been in the middle phase; the precise mechanism of force – short war, long war and so on – changed as circumstances suggested that it must. In important ways republican politics have not been unchanging. As Tom Hartley rightly says of Sinn Féin:

> What people I think don't realise about us is that really we've always been a party of change ... We changed our attitude towards elections. We changed our attitude towards Leinster House ... "No return to Stormont" – now we're in the building ... People ... often see us as a very centralised, fixed entity but in fact we have been consistently able to bring our constituency into new political spaces ... Republicans don't have a static view of politics. This generation knows that you're in there, you're ducking and weaving, you're shaping. Some days you win, some days you lose, but all the time you're in there shaping the agenda.[64]

Nor has the republican movement been monolithic: divergence over strategy and belief have been evident, just as with any other political player.

Yet, despite this, there has been a traceable, coherent IRA argument which can be set out crisply and lucidly. Defence had been urgently required. The northern state had proved doubly undemocratic, being both unfair towards Catholics and illegitimate in its very existence: this British denial of Irish self-determination was the root of the conflict. The north was irreformable; and force was necessary in order to destroy it. Such political violence fitted a wider pattern of legitimate decolonization. It had a frequently socialistic dimension, as well as Gaelic and, at times, Catholic inflections – though republicans stressed their non-sectarian aim and self-image. It was unionists who were primarily sectarian, and unionists who must shed their colonial skin to accommodate themselves to a new Ireland.

2

'I make no apologies whatsoever for this party.'

Gerry Adams on Sinn Féin, 2002[65]

What are we to make of these arguments? Predictably, no simple answer, no easy judgment, emerges from serious scrutiny of the IRA's case. *First*, defence. Clearly, there was a need for Catholic self-protection in the late 1960s (and beyond). Catholic communities did (and do) come under attack, and the state was not providing anything like adequate protection. The impulse towards communal self-defence made sense. Yet the Provisionals' defensive record has, in practice, been a poor one. Gerry Adams has argued that by 1972 the Provisional IRA had 'created a defensive force of unprecedented effectiveness'.[66] But this is a view difficult to reconcile with the evidence. Despite such courageous episodes as the June 1970 battle of St Matthew's in Belfast (when republicans had defended their Short Strand area against loyalist attack), it remains hard to sustain the argument that the IRA were effective defenders of the northern Catholic community in this early period at all. During the first three years of the Provisionals' existence (from 18 December 1969 to 17 December 1972), 171 Catholic civilians were killed by loyalists or the security forces.[67] Hailed recently as 'a classic example of the traditional role of the IRA in Belfast defending Catholic areas against hostile Protestant attacks',[68] the battle of St Matthew's was thus, in fact, far from paradigmatic for these years.

Indeed, it is sadly more plausible to argue that, during the troubles as a whole, IRA violence made more rather than less likely the prospect of Catholics suffering violence. Much IRA violence, of course, itself caused death and injury among northern Catholics: sometimes deliberately, as with Catholic RUC officers, or those within the Catholic community targeted for death or punishment attacks; and sometimes inadvertently. And, while it is vital to stress that loyalist violence was not simply a response to IRA violence – indeed, as noted, loyalist violence predated the foundation of the Provisionals – it is undeniable that IRA actions did often prompt direct loyalist reprisal.[69] IRA violence was more a case of taking *some* action, of hitting back, than a practical means of preventing violence against northern Catholics. During the post-1960s troubles the Provisional IRA were not, in fact, able to defend northern Catholics from attack.[70]

Second, what of the north's unfairness towards its Catholic inhabitants? The deplorable practice of anti-Catholic discrimination in Northern Ireland has rightly been recorded and analysed repeatedly.[71] And while there remains much disagreement about its extent and causes, there seems virtually no doubt that serious discrimination occurred, especially in the areas of employment, housing and electoral practice. As shrewd republicans have themselves acknowledged, these injustices were not of the same order as those in, for example, South Africa; nor were they the direct cause of the emergence of the Provisional IRA – had they been so, then something like the Provos would have emerged much earlier. But discrimination did produce genuine and lasting grievances and, as we have seen, it did contribute to that escalatory turbulence during the late 1960s that was to produce the new IRA.

Discrimination along confessional lines in modern Ireland was not, of course, the sole preserve of Protestant unionists: communities on both sides, north and south, at times discriminated, believing it necessary and natural as a way of protecting their own community interests. But in Northern Ireland during the years 1921–72 formal state power, and informal economic power, were so weighted in favour of the unionist rather than the nationalist community that the over-whelming bias of discriminatory practice worked against northern Catholics. At times indignation, perhaps unsurprisingly, has led to some simplification and exaggeration. Thus 1960s civil rights leader, Michael Farrell, quite rightly highlighting the fact of discrimination, at times blurred his reading of the evidence. (Even the justly infamous quotation from unionist politician Basil Brooke, used by Farrell to demonstrate discriminatory attitudes among unionists, contains some ambiguity, for it begins with the words, 'There were a great number of Protestants and Orangemen who employed Roman Catholics.')[72] And it is often overlooked how, even before the Provisionals were born, some key changes had been initiated. By the time of Terence O'Neill's resignation as Prime Minister of Northern Ireland in 1969, the vital civil rights demand for one-man-one-vote in local government elec-tions had been conceded.

So some qualifications can be offered: structural disadvantage (in jobs, for example) arose not solely because of discrimination; nor was the level of disadvantage unique in western societies; and, as in many other countries, some structural inequalities are far from easily remedied – as any resident of the United States or Britain might testify, in relation to racial disadvantage. But the central fact remains that Northern Ireland during the 1921–72 period was structurally biased towards unionists and against nationalists; 'legislation and administra-tive action made the unionist hold on public life almost absolute'.[73] Moreover, unequal opportunities for employment persisted through the troubles; 'the striking difference in rate of unemployment between Protestants and Catholics, and the smaller differences in circumstances of employment and standard of living, cannot be explained on the assumption that members of the two groups who are comparable in all relevant ways are competing on equal terms'.[74]

Discrimination set in train the sequence of events (civil rights protests; loyalist response; state action, and so on) that produced the crisis from which the Provos emerged; and at the same time the day-to-day experience of a state substantially built against their interests provided northern Catholics with a culture of grievance that helped to strengthen the IRA in many nationalist minds.

Third, what of Northern Ireland's illegitimacy? To the IRA, the issue has traditionally been quite simple: Irish national self-determination was a matter for the Irish people as a whole; early in the twentieth century they had expressed a majority nationalist opinion, but this had been overruled by Britain with the creation of a partitioned Ireland. The ultimate remedy, therefore, was to end partition. In defence of this one could certainly point to the strength of the Irish nation as embodied in the nationalist preference of most of the island's inhabitants. As one leading scholar of nationality has observed, 'nations exist when their members recognise one another as compatriots, and believe that they share characteristics of the relevant kind'.[75] This clearly validates an Irish nationalist identity and an Irish nationalist nation.

But what of those on the island who do not share that self-image, who consider their interests – their economic, cultural, political, religious, symbolic interests – to be better suited to and better protected within the UK? If northern nationalists, understandably, resented being in a state to which they felt no loyalty, and one constructed by people with a different identity from their own, could Ulster's unionists not make a similar case against forced inclusion in a separatist, united Ireland? For while the principle of self-determination is an important and respected one, its problem is that those areas in which it is most urgently invoked, like Ireland, are precisely those in which there is no easy agreement about the identity of the self that will do the determining. Should one island automatically mean one nation? Much international assumption suggests so, but the matter is far from simple. Would Irish nationalists, for example, deny the possibility of an independent Scottish nation on the ground that Scotland is on the same island as England and Wales? Ulster unionists themselves present a view of the self-determination issue starkly at variance with that of the Provos. UUP politician Jeffrey Donaldson:

> Unionists would see partition as a legitimate and democratic recognition of the fact that in the north-east of the island of Ireland they were in a majority; and that there is no justifiable argument to say that the frame of reference for self-determination is the island of Ireland; [that] there are many examples throughout the world where self-determination is exercised by a people; and that geographical boundaries are not the primary point in terms of reference for the exercise of self-determination; and that unionists saw themselves as a distinct and unique people, or belonging to a wider nation: the British nation is a diverse, multi-cultural, multi-ethnic nation, of which the Protestants or unionists in Northern Ireland see themselves as a distinct entity, but within a wider entity. And the frame of reference for unionists for self-determination is Northern Ireland, but within the United Kingdom. So you've got this fundamental clash of philosophies between unionism and republicanism, republicans seeing the island of Ireland and the geographical limits of the island as the unit of self-determination, and putting forward this spurious argument that ergo all of the people who live on the island of Ireland belong to one nation, the Irish nation; and the unionist viewpoint, which is that the geographical limits are not necessarily the frame of reference, and that in fact it is perfectly legitimate for people living on part of the island to have the right to self-determination and to determine that they wish to remain part of the United Kingdom.[76]

Given the patchwork pattern of Ulster residence, it seems implausible to assume that there will exist a neatly accepted unit for self-determination in the region. To allow for unionist self-determination in the six counties understandably prompted nationalists there to protest at unfair treatment; but to expel unionists from the UK on similar grounds of simple head-counting self-determination would surely risk the same problem in reverse. One does not have to espouse the theory that there are two nations in Ireland to notice that unionists in Ulster do not fit neatly or willingly into the Irish nation as imagined and preferred by modern Irish nationalists. The IRA has stressed that partition originated with British policy; but it is also true that the partitioning of Ireland was a response to deep division among people in Ireland about whether or not to belong to the United Kingdom. If nationalist objections to British rule are to be respected, then unionists might claim that their preferences also deserve serious recognition. And the most sustained scholarly consideration has tended not to endorse the view that there exists in Ireland an essentially simple one-nation situation.[77] The IRA have presented their case as embodying a defence of true democracy; but Ulster's unionists have keenly stressed that their democratic wishes should not be crushed by expulsion from the state of their choice.[78] Arguably, the accommodation of such competing claims in ways other than simple victory for one or other self-determining majority might offer the best answer to this painful question.

Part of the problem for the IRA has been the division of opinion in Ireland – among nationalists, as well as between nationalism and unionism; and there have been those (like John Hume of the SDLP) who have persistently asserted that it is such division on the island, rather than any British colonial self-interest, that constitutes the real challenge for those pursuing Irish unity. Yet the IRA could certainly point to a longstanding historical problem in Ireland, of a nationalism that the British state could not accommodate or contain.[79] And the contested legitimacy of Northern Ireland has not been one easily settled by recourse, either, to the living. True, opinion within the north has consistently shown a clear majority preferring membership of the UK to removal from it. But republicans could fairly argue that this was hardly surprising, given that the state had been created with a deliberate (and, in their view, artificially created) unionist majority. So the rival sides in the Irish conflict disagreed on whether the north was a legitimate unit within which to seek majority preference.

Anyway, even in the north there was a persistently committed minority of nationalists who supported the IRA: they might represent a minority of the minority in this smaller part of Ireland, but any reading of the IRA that ignores this committed popular support will be unable to explain the organization at all effectively. (Though it is equally true that, if one is to take seriously the views of the Irish republican electorate in the north, which one must, then one must also respect the validity of those in the north – persistently the clear majority – who did not vote for Sinn Féin.) And even if one looked to British opinion, the picture was complex, and far from reassuring perhaps for Ulster unionists. Irish republicans have frequently noted signs of English-based sympathy for their cause (as when *An Phoblacht/ Republican News* noted a 'massive London demonstration' on 6 February 1986: 'Thousands of people marched through central London on Sunday, February 2, to commemorate the 14th anniversary of Derry's Bloody Sunday and to demand a British withdrawal from Ireland'; or when they highlighted intellectuals' support for British withdrawal from the north).[80] They drew comfort from any evidence suggesting that British popular opinion favoured withdrawal from Northern Ireland.[81]

Yet British opinion polls could offer ambiguous evidence. On 21 August 2001 the *Guardian* newspaper published results of a poll in Britain showing that 41 per cent of people felt that Northern Ireland should become part of a united Ireland, and that only 26 per cent felt that it should remain part of the UK. The newspaper made much of these results. Under a front-page headline 'Surge in Support for Irish Unity', it declared that this was a 'verdict to strike a chill through Ulster unionism'; its editorial pronounced it 'heartbreaking news to unionists' and claimed that the poll results confirmed what had for years been only a 'sneaking suspicion', 'that Britons are pretty fed up with Northern Ireland and would rather be shot of the whole place'. Unsurprisingly, republicans picked up on these findings.[82] But there was perhaps little new in the *Guardian* story, and its August 2001 figures were probably far less significant than the paper itself suggested. For, interestingly, opinion polls had long shown that a majority of British people favoured any option other than continued union between Northern Ireland and Great Britain. Indeed, previous polls had frequently shown a greater disinclination than did this one on the part of British people to support continued union.[83] Moreover, it very much depends on what question one asks. That put by the *Guardian* in August 2001 was a rather stark one: 'Do you think that Northern Ireland should be a part of the UK or a united Ireland?' Previously, when the only options offered were the status quo or Irish unity, the majority of British people had indeed tended to go for Irish unity. But if a more nuanced and wider range of choices was offered, then the British people were consistently much less likely to opt for a united

Ireland as their preferred solution, frequently favouring instead a Northern Ireland independent both of Britain and of the Republic of Ireland.

There is no question that a significant proportion of British public opinion long favoured the withdrawal of British troops from Northern Ireland. But this opinion did not, unfortunately for the IRA, reflect any sustained or committed interest, on the part of most British people, in the Northern Irish conflict itself. Indifference and incomprehension were more common than commitment to unionist or to nationalist goals, and the north of Ireland rarely featured prominently in British general election campaigns or party priorities.

What, then, of Irish opinion as a whole? Irish republicans could certainly point to an overall Irish nationalist majority on the Irish island. But most of the population in the south (and certainly most of its politicians) have tended to exhibit at most a low-level aspiration to Irish unity, indifference towards the issue, or even anxiety about the prospect.[84] Republic of Ireland opinion has shifted here: in 1984 Irish unity was the preferred solution for 72 per cent of people in the south; by 1991 this figure had dropped to 41 per cent. On the rather more vague question of whether Irish unity is something to be hoped for as an ultimate aspiration, majorities of people in the Republic have responded positively: indeed, in 1991 82 per cent said they aspired to ultimate Irish unity. So rhetorical and long-term aspiration certainly exists; but practical commitment to the achievement of Irish unity is far from a priority for most voters in the Republic of Ireland.

The question of Northern Ireland's legitimacy is not, therefore, neatly resolved by recourse to popular opinion in the competing arenas within which a head-count might be taken. And the legitimacy issue raises questions also regarding responsibility for the northern conflict. As already noted, the IRA has long maintained that ultimate responsibility for the war, and for creating the conditions to end it, lie with Britain. Certainly, it would be wrong to write British responsibility out of the story, to present Britain as a neutral arbiter between two parties to a conflict in which the British are not involved. Equally, one could reasonably suggest that a British political desire to insulate itself from the problems of the north during 1921–72 perpetuated the problems and injustices that lay behind the troubles. But British responsibility in a simple imperial-villain sense is harder to sustain.

For one thing, the idea that an expensive, politically turbulent and internationally embarrassing area would be held on to because London had an advantage in doing so is one that is hard to accept. Veteran republican and one-time IRA Chief of Staff Sean MacBride in his latter years disputed the idea that the British would withdraw from the north, if asked to do so by Ulster unionists.[85] But it is hard to see why they would not. British politicians have been quick to recognize the financial drain that Northern Ireland has represented.[86] Given such obvious drawbacks for the UK in retaining Northern Ireland, it is unconvincing to argue that the British state has simply and sustainedly sought colonial control over the place for its own advantage. In any case, there is nothing simple about the state: it is a far from unitary actor, and its various wings – governments, parliaments, Army, police force, judiciary, civil service, media – have not only changed their attitudes over time, but have often come into conflict with one another (as when the courts do not act as the police would wish; when the judiciary sentences members of the security forces; when the government takes a broadcasting-related decision with which the state broadcasting corporation, the BBC, disagrees; when there is a divergence of policy between different sections of the civil service, and so on). The notion that the UK or British state has had a single, continuous, simple interest in Northern Ireland seems, on these grounds alone, unpersuasive.

That the British state is central to the Northern Irish conflict is clear. Equally clear, however, is that London has consistently tried to provide a context – largely inadequate, to republican eyes – in which the various problems in the north might be alleviated. The approach has shown much consistency – as regards devolution, the all-Ireland dimension, ending the violence, recognition of the northern consent principle, attempted reforms – and has involved the state in trying to deal, simultaneously, with political violence and security and with the economic, constitutional and social dimensions to Northern Ireland as well.[87] As Patrick Mayhew, then Secretary of State for Northern Ireland, said in 1993, 'The division which exists within the community (together with grievances which exist ... in the social, the economic and constitutional fields), has led to intercommunal violence and terrorism and it is the elimination of terrorism – from whatever quarter – that is the government's overriding objective. But the government believes that the underlying causes have to be addressed at the same time.'[88]

Republicans have rightly pointed out that the conflict in the north has deep roots, many of them tangled in British policy- and decision-making. But recognition that the origins of the war are deep should lead also to acknowledgment that they are complex, involving culpability not on one side alone. To some degree, the northern war was self-fuelling once begun: grievance and countergrievance made compromise more difficult, and violence more cyclically intense. But in sustaining the conflict the Provisionals themselves clearly played a deliberate and self-proclaimed long-war role; and as this book has shown, Irish republicans and nationalists, north and south, each played some part in the emergence of the crisis and conflict that raged after 1969. Nor were they alone – British, unionist, loyalist and international actors, too, all played their various parts.

What of the *fourth* part of the republican argument, the irreformability of Northern Ireland? It is easy to understand why many in the northern nationalist community came to this conclusion. The state had treated them differently, the civil rights movement had been met by much Protestant hostility, and there was deep unionist reluctance to grant too much movement in the direction of reasonable nationalist demands for better treatment. Moreover, while it might be pointed out that the eventual 1990s deal involved substantial reform of a Northern Ireland that remained foreseeably intact, the IRA might counter that such an outcome would not have emerged without their campaign of violence.

Certainly, if it is conceded that the north *was* after all reformable, then a central plank in the IRA's ideological foundation looks, at best, shaky. For here we are into the crucial issue of the legacy and achievements – in the IRA's view, the necessity – of political violence. In the post-Belfast Agreement context, the IRA seems to have settled for a (transitional, in their view) reformed northern state. They maintain that the north was only reformed even thus far because of their violence, and there is no doubt that their long war did make attention to the north more urgent, and the bargaining position of republicans themselves much stronger. The IRA sharpened awareness of the problem in the north, though arguably their violence also made more difficult the attainment of the trust and goodwill necessary to the eventual compromise needed to address that problem. Some scholars certainly consider IRA violence to have been effective. Referring to the Irish revolution as well as to post-1960s politics, Robert White argues: 'Irish republicans have good reason to perceive that their violence is effective.'[89] Yet the broad shape of the eventual settlement – power-sharing, an Irish dimension, recognition of the consent principle for unionists – was known decades before the Good Friday Agreement. Indeed, it was sponsored by the British government in the early 1970s. Clearly, the IRA cannot solely be blamed for sustaining the war for decades beyond the point (Sunningdale, for instance) at which such compromise was earlier available; other players too – Ulster's unionists and loyalists, the British government itself – were less compromising, inclusive and accommodating at that stage than they (in many cases) later became.

But it is hard to resist the conclusion that what was done in the 1990s might have been possible in the 1970s had there been – on all sides, it should be stressed – a greater willingness to replace a naïve hope of clear victory with the acceptance of the necessity for compromise. In that sense, it is less true that IRA violence was necessary for the achievement of reform than that it was one of numerous factors that delayed it.

For reform of the north was not what the IRA were fighting for. As many of their statements have made clear, they were fighting to end British rule in Ireland (an objective to which they still proclaim dedication). Here, their argument does seem to have run into some serious problems. Yes, the IRA could apply Clausewitzean pressure on the British: give us what we want, or we will make life more painful for you than if you were to do so. But loyalist paramilitaries could apply a version of the same pressure in the opposite direction: if you do give the IRA what they want, and threaten to withdraw from Northern Ireland, then we will make life considerably more painful for you than it would be if you were to give us what we demand, the maintenance of the union. Thus London feared what might now perhaps be referred to as a post-Yugoslavian situation, should they withdraw from the north of Ireland, and their anxiety may not have been misplaced.[90]

As noted, recognition of this triangular stalemate (republicans-London-loyalists) was the true origin of the Northern Irish peace process. The IRA had hoped to wear down the British population and government, to bomb the government to a point at which attrition had the desired outcome: withdrawal from the north. Unable to persuade unionists to stop being unionists, however, the IRA could not remove the main reason for British retention of the north within the UK: that they saw no way of leaving without far worse carnage ensuing should they do so. And the full Clausewitzean argument had serious implications for the 1990s IRA. General Clausewitz had argued that war was a rational political instrument which could be used for national ends. But he had asserted not only that effective war must be more painful for one's opponent than would be their granting of one's demands, but also that the war must threaten to be a lengthy one in which any change must be a change for the worse as far as one's enemy is concerned. The IRA had certainly shown that their war could be a long one. But changes in the long war had not involved such a worsening for the British that London felt compelled to yield. Indeed, it could be argued that the longer the war went on without British will breaking, the less oppressive was the IRA threat.[91]

IRA violence certainly prevented the imposition of a solution from which they were excluded, and it gave republicans greater leverage in the negotiation of the final deal arrived at in 1998 – one which included republicans in government, prisoner releases, significant reform to the state and the hope of its ultimate dissolution. The IRA themselves held, and hold, to the view that its violence was historically inevitable, necessary. There are, of course, alternative views. Even in the early 1970s, for example, it was noted by many observers that the violent coercion of Ulster's unionists into a united Ireland might be less possible – or even desirable – than the Provisionals themselves supposed, and that a more consensual approach would be better for Ireland.[92] And such views were frequently articulated by Irish nationalists themselves, recently released archives indeed showing them to have been current before the troubles even erupted. In November 1968, over a year before the foundation of the Provisionals, one of Taoiseach Jack Lynch's ablest advisers, T. K. Whitaker,[93] penned a prescient *Note on North-South Policy*, which deserves lengthy consideration.

Whitaker, who had earlier been instrumental in leading the Republic of Ireland away from its Sinn Féinish economic protectionism, here challenged other features of traditional republican thinking. Force had rightly been abandoned by the Republic, he observed, as a way of undoing partition 'because (1) the use of force to overcome northern unionists would accentuate rather than remove basic differences and (2) it would not be militarily possible in any event'. The only option was 'a policy of seeking unity in Ireland by agreement in Ireland between Irishmen. Of its nature this is a long-term policy, requiring patience, understanding and forbearance and resolute resistance to emotionalism and opportunism. It is none the less patriotic for that.' Whitaker based his own patriotic view on a cold reading of the complex realities of partition: 'The British are not blameless, as far as the origins of partition are concerned, but neither are they wholly to blame. Nobody can read the history of the past century in these islands without some understanding of the deep, complex and powerful forces which went into the making of partition. It is much too naïve to believe that Britain simply imposed it on Ireland.'

Crucial here was an acknowledgment of the problem that Ulster unionists represented for Irish irredentists; in particular, their economic concerns were thought to merit attention. Unionists were conscious of the economic advantages of being in the UK; indeed, Whitaker argued that any shift towards Irish unity would be disastrous unless Britain continued for some time to provide a subvention to the north:

> all we can expect from the British is a benevolent neutrality – that no British interest will be interposed to prevent the reunification of Ireland when Irishmen, north and south, have reached agreement. This, of itself, will be cold comfort if we cannot, in addition, achieve a good 'marriage settlement', in the form of a tapering-off over a long period of present British subsidisation of Northern Ireland. Otherwise, we in the south will be imposing on ourselves a formidable burden which many of our own citizens, however strong their desire for Irish unity, may find intolerable. We cannot lay certain social ills in the north at the door of partition without acknowledging (at least in private) that conditions for the Catholics in Northern Ireland would be far worse if partition were abolished overnight.

Whitaker was clear about what he saw as the counterproductive nature of political violence in pursuit of Irish unity: 'The most forceful argument in favour of the patient good-neighbour policy aimed at ultimate "agreement in Ireland between Irishmen" is that no other policy has any prospect of success. Force will get us nowhere; it will only strengthen the fears, antagonisms and divisions that keep north and south apart.'[94]

Here, before they even existed, was an assault on ideas central to the Provisional IRA's philosophy: according to Whitaker, force would divide rather than unite; agreement between Irish people was the only basis for unity; the origins and undoing of Irish partition were complex questions, and could not be placed solely at Britain's door; economic realities must modify the south's approach towards prospective Irish unity; long-term, patient patriotism would be more effective than emotional opportunism. Much of this offered pre-echoes of the events of the thirty years that divide these reflections from the 1998 Belfast Agreement: it is no coincidence that all of these arguments are embodied in that latter deal and in the peace process which produced it, for thirty years of violence had, for many people, reinforced what Whitaker here had argued a generation earlier.

This is *not* to suggest that if only the Provisionals had not acted as they did then all would have been well. But it is striking and poignant to see an Irish patriot setting out so clearly, and so long ago, some of the key realities with which British and Irish politicians, Sinn Féin among them, would wrestle after the thirty years' war in the north.

Similarly, it is interesting to reflect how long other key components of the 1990s political consensus were present before the conflict really got under way. UK Home Secretary Reginald Maudling issued a statement in August 1970 which argued two points that were to be of crucial importance to the 1990s peace process: first, the 'use of violence on the streets will do no good to anyone. Indeed it will only bring widespread suffering'; second, British governments had 'made it clear that Northern Ireland will not cease to be part of the United Kingdom without the consent of the people of Northern Ireland'.[95]

Once a more inclusive politics seemed available, and a stalemate was recognized for what it was, the Provisional movement coura-geously shifted ground on key aspects of what it had previously believed and done. It had argued that force alone would bring Irish unity; in the new times of the later 1990s, it held that demography and politics might do so instead.[96] The Provisionals had said they would not go into a partitionist Stormont, but later did so; that they would never accept the consent principle (according to which, Northern Ireland would only cease to be a part of the UK if a majority of Northern Irish people so wished), but again changed tack. This was not a case simply of republicans admitting they had been wrong: the other key players had shifted ground also. The 'importance of maintaining good relations with the government of the Republic of Ireland' was recognized in Whitehall before the Provisionals even existed.[97] The British Ambassador to the Republic of Ireland, Andrew Gilchrist, set out – again, prior to the Provisionals' birth – one of the crucial dimensions of the political arrangement that was profoundly to affect IRA momentum. The Dublin government, Gilchrist argued in September 1969, 'shied away from the prospect of assuming full responsibility for Ulster as this would raise economic and social problems which southern Ireland was incapable of mastering'. They did, however, want 'to have some degree of participation in the solution of Ulster's constitutional problems and in her subsequent development . . . It would be in our interest, as well as that of southern Ireland, to explore means by which the Dublin government could be associated with the creation of new arrangements for Ulster which would be acceptable to all the people living there.'[98] Yet it took many years for the implications of these reflections to define British policy in the way that yielded such results in the 1990s.

But even allowing for changed contexts, the extent of the republicans' movement in the 1990s is truly impressive. In 1986 Gerry Adams argued that Leinster House (the seat of the Dublin parliament) was 'the preserve, by and large, of unprincipled careerists jockeying for the Ministerial Mercedes', and that the northern SDLP performed the role of an 'Uncle Tom'.[99] By the 1990s Adams's party was trying to build a nationalist alliance and consensus with these players. Force alone had proved not to be the appropriate way of moving forward.

It must be recognized, however – and has been amply shown in this book – that force was always part of a broader ideological argument on the Provisionals' part: they were fighting a war of decolonization. Careful assessment of this strand of the IRA's argument is unlikely to produce clear-cut answers. There is certainly much evidence in favour of a colonial reading of the north's relationship with Britain, and some commentators have given strong backing to this view.[100] Indeed, it is impossible to understand the IRA without considering the degree to which British colonialism and empire have impacted on Ireland. There were unquestionably colonial elements to British rule in Ireland during the period of the union (1801–1922): in some ways Ireland was seen as an integral part of the UK; in others as a place apart – indeed, somewhat akin to a colony. The British empire was one profoundly coloured by a Protestant self-image, and it therefore faced a lasting, potential problem in a Catholic Irish majority. And before the union there had, again, been much that could be read as colonial in the relationship between the two neighbouring islands (though scholarly debate rages over how accurate the term 'colony' actually is, when applied to Ireland in that period).[101]

Certainly, the Provisionals themselves have existed during a period of British imperial decline. Between Indian independence in 1947 and the handover in 1997 of Hong Kong to the Chinese, the British empire died. It was not only in the aftermath of the Second World War that it showed cracks. But it was in the wake of that conflict that the map began strikingly and emphatically to change colour, as Britain gradually lost its empire: Transjordan (1946), Pakistan (1947), India (1947), Burma (1948), Ceylon (1948), Palestine (1948), Libya (1951), Ethiopia (1952), Sudan (1956), Malaya (1957), Ghana (1957), Cyprus (1960), Nigeria (1960), Cameroun (1960), Somalia (1960), Sierra Leone (1961), Tanganyika (1961), Uganda (1962), Kenya (1963), Malta (1964), Zambia (1964), Malawi (1964), Gambia (1965), Aden (1967), Swaziland (1968), Tonga (1970). No wonder the Provisionals thought they were in tune with historical development in this respect! The empire *was* in retreat ('The number of people under British rule in the two decades after 1945 was reduced from 700 million people to five million, of which three million were concentrated in Hong Kong'),[102] and the force of various nationalisms had been one factor in helping to produce this world-changing outcome.

But while anti-colonial nationalisms and their sometime violence played a part in the end of the British empire, the process was clearly far more complex than that alone. The combination of forces behind the imperial collapse included the economic fact that Britain could no longer afford the cost of empire; the shifting of attention away from empire towards the necessity of a postwar Anglo-American alliance; and the eclipse of British international influence by the two superpowers after the Second World War. Moreover, the impact of nationalist sentiment was not necessarily a straightforward question of rebellion followed by imperial withdrawal. The dissolution of much of the British empire involved, in fact, not disengagement after violence, but rather disengagement to *avoid* the emergence of a crisis of management, to *prevent* violence. And in any case, as already established, Ireland's relationship to the British empire was far from simple. Irish people experienced British colonialism as the colonized – but frequently also as the colonizer. Huge numbers of Irish people (Catholic and nationalist as well as Protestant and unionist) were involved in the building, settlement, maintenance, administration and defence of the British empire, and many Irish people were great supporters of the British imperial project;[103] 'After 1800, the Irish of all descriptions entered enthusiastically into the business of Empire';[104] far more Irish people have served militarily in defence of the British empire than have fought in the IRA against it.[105] Ireland has had its resister-rebels – the Provisional IRA being a conspicuous and resilient example – but to assume that this was the only Irish response to empire or to the British connection is to deny existence to very large numbers of Irish people throughout modern history. Even many Irish nationalists have seen Irish patriotism, and substantial Irish autonomy, as compatible with some form of British connection.

It is not that there has been a negligible colonial dimension to Irish history and politics, but rather that overly neat readings of the British-Irish relationship within this framework risk obscuring the complexities and ambiguities of actual Irish experience through the centuries. The idea that English colonial expansion proceeded first through an Irish colony and then on to the west and America (that Ireland was, in effect, England's prototypical colony) is now treated sceptically by scholars.[106] Again, as has been pointed out, 'Unlike the populations of other colonies in the Atlantic world, the population of Ireland by the late-seventeenth century resolutely resisted simple categorisation into colonised and coloniser. Religion, not national origins or even date of arrival, was to be the great divide'.[107]

Later, there were indeed discernible colonial aspects to eighteenth-century Ireland; but these were offset by other dimensions, less easily fitted into a colonial pattern. Yet again, Ireland's colonial experience of England was complicated by its unique proximity to the imperial power, and this meant that intermingling of populations and cultures was far more pronounced than in other British colonies, and that Irish experience was far more closely interwoven with British than was colonially typical. There was not, for example, colonial representation in the London parliament, but Ireland (and, since partition, Northern Ireland) *was* represented there. Indeed, the most sustained analysis yet of the application to Ireland of imperial and colonial models has left its author largely unpersuaded of their relevance,[108] and it might be argued that a European framework is rather more appropriate for modern Ireland than is a third-worldist colonial/post-colonial one.[109] Irish experience thus seems more aptly described as quasi-colonial or semi-colonial than as colonial or simply colonized. There has been a hybridity and ambiguity to Irish experience which too rigid a colonial framework tends to obscure and distort; Ireland appears, in the end, 'certainly not a typical imperial possession'.[110]

The IRA have, however, identified powerfully with other revolutionary – often anti-colonial – campaigns elsewhere in the world. There have frequently been mutual echoes back and forward between the Irish and other cases of political or national conflict. But even here a couple of qualifications might be offered. First, it seems clear that one – perhaps the – key appeal of international links for the IRA has been the practical and logical one of gaining support, whether material or symbolic. The IRA throughout its history has engaged in alliances with a range of forces ideologically incompatible with one another – as, in truth, do formal states themselves – in accordance with their perceived practical needs. Similarly, the Provisionals have obtained backing from, for example, supporters in the USA and also – at the same time – from the USA's dedicated opponent during the 1980s, Libya. Functional considerations – where will arms, money, support come from? – have often outweighed ideological ones.

Second, a related concern has been to establish links with struggles of oppressed against oppressor, to link the IRA with legitimate wars of liberation. Here, there have been some complicating factors to the IRA's experience. Supposedly similar struggles – that of South African blacks, for instance – have sometimes involved markedly different political situations and extremely different degrees of oppression from the Northern Irish one. It is true that Northern Ireland during 1921–72 was an unbalanced polity and one that treated Catholics unfairly; it is simply not true to say that there was a body of laws segregating people in the way that apartheid legislation did in South Africa. Indeed, any serious comparison of Northern Ireland and South Africa would demonstrate that profound differences are at least as evident as similarities, in terms, for example, of constitutional arrangements or of the degree of economic disparity between conflicting groups. To call Northern Ireland an apartheid state along South African lines has a clear propagandist value, but little historical justification.

Similarly, while one must respect republican endorsement of anti-tyrannical struggles elsewhere, the suggestion that Northern Ireland has been a fascist state again stretches the evidence beyond plausibility. Certainly, any comparison of Stormont unionism with Nazi Germany is profoundly exaggerated: the Nazi goal of 'killing every Jewish man, woman and child that they could round up or capture'[111] simply has no parallel in Northern Ireland's history. In fact, it was the IRA which had an alliance with the Nazis, while Britain – including some who famously became victims of republican violence – fought against them. While the IRA were colluding with Hitler, Lord Mountbatten and Airey Neave had been fighting against him (as, indeed, had future unionist Prime Ministers, Terence O'Neill and James Chichester-Clark).

Neave (whose committed anti-Nazism had extended beyond the Second World War) was killed by the INLA, although he had also apparently been an IRA target. His career, and those of fellow wartime prisoners, had involved intriguing pre-echoes of some Irish republican themes. Like IRA prisoners, Colditz inmates had engaged in reading and education and had attended classes; like IRA prisoners, Neave had smuggled things out of jail in cellophane, inserted into his rectum; like IRA prisoners, those in Colditz experienced rectal examinations.[112] Indeed, articulate Irish republican ex-prisoner Declan Moen fascinatingly cited Neave's fellow British prisoner in Colditz, Patrick Reid, when explaining what Irish republican imprisonment was like:

I remember a fantastic quote from a guy called [Patrick] Reid. He's written a number of books on Colditz, and he was the main trickster within Colditz; he organized Airey Neave's escape. And he said, in Colditz, what you had was five per cent of the prisoners who did everything, all the time, twenty-four hours a day, they existed to escape. They were the schemers, the people who were involved in making uniforms and bribing guards, who were looking for opportunities; the chancers. You had ninety per cent of the jail who were sound, did you no harm, you asked them to do something, watch that screw, get his routine – they would do it. You had five per cent who were absolute scum. They would do everything in their power to undermine everything you were trying to achieve. I think that holds true for most communities. And then your battle is to decide which has more influence, which extreme, which five per cent is going to call the shots, carry the day.[113]

That the north of Ireland witnessed nothing of Nazi proportions does not mean that Northern Ireland was not unfair towards its Catholic population. It should also be stressed that the attempt to describe the IRA themselves as fascist[114] is itself analytically unpersuasive. But, equally, claims that Irish republicans have always been on the progressive side in life's struggles[115] sit awkwardly with episodes such as the IRA's involvement with the Nazis, or with the Provisionals' newspaper's endorsement of anti-contraception stances in the 1970s. And even in terms of their chosen thinkers there has been a tendency at times, perhaps, towards an exaggerated identification. One must respect the degree to which republican prisoners found value in Paulo Freire; but Freire was clearly not thinking of settings such as Northern Ireland when writing his classic *Pedagogy of the Oppressed*, with its references to illiterate populations, to the masses with no food, clothes or shoes, to the millions who 'died of hunger'.[116]

Yet radical ideas, and specifically socialist ones, have formed a key part of IRA thinking, and analysis of this strand is important to any understanding of the Provisional movement's evolution. The IRA's adherence to socialistic aims has varied in intensity according to time and place, but it has remained evident in their argument and has reflected a working-class dimension to their support, constituency and recruit-base.[117] Economically poorer areas – those that have experienced social deprivation, high unemployment and comparative poverty – have traditionally been more productive than others of Sinn Féin support. But what of the Provisional socialist argument itself? In parts, it has echoed previous republican thinking. True, Provisional claims here have not always been the most accurate: Bobby Sands depicted

Theobald Wolfe Tone and James Fintan Lalor as radical socialists, which they were not; and the Provisional IRA have frequently demanded a socialist Ireland in line with the 1916 Proclamation, while the truth is that there was nothing necessarily socialist about that Proclamation. Yet there have been striking resonances between earlier republicans' combination of republicanism and socialism and that of the Provisionals in the modern period.

It has not been a case of identical argument, but rather of family resemblances. Compare, for example, the 1980s Gerry Adams with 1930s IRA and Republican Congress leader Peadar O'Donnell. Both were intelligent exponents of socialist republicanism, and both craftily preferred not to label their movement as such. O'Donnell held that, in order to be a true republican, you had to espouse the kind of class-struggling, anti-capitalist politics that he himself practised. So, while he preferred to avoid the term 'socialist republicanism', his view was that all genuine republicanism was effectively socialist.[118] The Gerry Adams of 1986, also prefering that his movement should not define itself as 'socialist republican', nonetheless was himself – like O'Donnell – a socialist republican figure. But Adams's reasoning was rather different. Whatever he may have thought about public labels, O'Donnell defined republicanism as necessarily socialistic (anti-capitalist, class-struggling, socially revolutionary) in practice, and he thus defined out of the republican movement those who rejected this view. Adams, by contrast, wanted to avoid the movement styling itself 'socialist republican' precisely because he did *not* want to exclude non-socialist republicans: he recognized and, indeed, welcomed into the family those republicans who were *not* socialist.[119]

Just as socialism has long remained part of the Provisional movement's argument, so, too, it has continued to proclaim that its overwhelmingly Catholic composition need not make it a sectarian political force. There are scholars who hold that IRA violence does not arise from sectarian motivation,[120] and this claim is frequently made by republicans themselves. It is reinforced by observations from experienced commentators such as Tim Pat Coogan: 'It is official IRA policy (broken only very rarely and in exceptional circumstances . . .) that a Protestant is not a target for his religion.'[121]

Yet perhaps the picture is slightly greyer than such arguments would suggest. First, as the Provisionals themselves say, they emerged from a context of sectarian conflict. The historically entrenched experience has been that in modern Ireland confessional background and political allegiance have been deeply interwoven. Yes, the IRA have been fighting not a self-consciously religious war of Catholic against Protestant, but rather a war of national liberation from colonial enslavement. But experience, in Irish history, does not define itself as *either* religious *or* national. Rather, different definitions have overlaid one another. So the Provisionals have been fighting a war between Irish nationalism and British imperialism; but the Irish nationalist tradition, and the state that it produced after 1922, were deeply coloured by the religious experience, grievance and thinking of one denomination – the Catholic Church. And the British state, and British empire, were both coloured profoundly by the Protestant self-image. It is historically implausible simply to remove these religious dimensions and suppose that one can adequately account for or describe the evolution of Irish and British histories, or nations, without them.

So attempts to suggest that the conflict in the north has been *either* sectarian and visceral on the one hand *or* ethno-national, rational-instrumental, tactical and strategic on the other[122] possibly miss the point here; close inspection of the conflict clearly suggests that it has involved not one or the other, but both. That a target made strategic sense, or could be identified according to the rationale or the objectives of national and political violence, need not mean that there was no visceral dimension to the act of violence against that target, nor that one's national goals had not been formed and defined – in part – under the influence of specific denominational beliefs and cultures. This book has repeatedly shown that the IRA were indeed a political force, engaged in a war as rational as that of any other group that considers violence necessary to its ends; it has also shown repeatedly that Catholic thinking has informed the culture of IRA members in ways that have influenced the organization's imagery, argument and activity. It is possible for a movement to have a rational, political, national quality and for this to co-exist and be interlayered with emotional, religious, sectarian themes and influences. Indeed, the only serious definition of such a movement as the Provisionals is one that will recognize the possibility of such a complex and layered reality.

Indeed, it is easy to find voluminous evidence from those who have been in the IRA that specifically Catholic nationalism has played a – to some of them, lamentable – role in Irish republicanism. Thus former IRA man Tommy McKearney (himself clearly committed to a secular form of republican politics) has referred to 'the often baleful influence' of Catholic nationalism within Irish republicanism.[123] Ex-IRA man Sean Garland – a veteran of the army's famous 1957 Brookeborough raid and subsequently a Gouldingite republican – has observed that 'Nationalism has played a very destructive role . . . in Irish politics, and I think that the alliance of religion and nationalism is a deadly combination'; the Provisionals were, in his view, a product of Catholic nationalism, whose actions have exacerbated sectarian divisions: 'the division is much deeper in Northern Ireland than ever it has been because the Provisionals, through their activities, have deepened this division; and then you have had Protestant terror gangs on their side deepening it as well . . . it is, I think, impossible to ignore the effect and influence that religion has had, and does have, on the situation in Northern Ireland.'[124] Another man who took the Official rather than the Provisional path was Dessie O'Hagan: 'The concept of republican-ism, as I understand it, has four distinct characteristics. It is in my view democratic, internationalist, secular and socialist . . . A Roman Catholic nationalist ethic in fact became the driving force behind Provisionalism.'[125] Clearly, those – such as Garland or O'Hagan – who early on broke with the Provos might be expected to suggest that the Provisionals took a wrong turn on this issue: but their evidence should not casually be dismissed purely for that reason.

Another key point concerns the effects of IRA violence on sectarian division. For even if the organization has intended to avoid sectarian warfare – and it seems fair to acknowledge, for example, that the IRA could easily have carried out far more simply sectarian killings than it has done – that does not mean that its campaign has not had a divisive effect in some respects. The post-1960s violence in Northern Ireland – for which the IRA was significantly, but not solely, responsible – greatly deepened the political and personal divisions and lack of trust between the two communities there. The Provisional IRA certainly did not create Northern Irish sectarianism. But their violence, along with that of other agents of violence in the conflict, unquestionably intensified it, producing bloody grievances and hatreds that will take longer to die out than the violent conflict itself.

The final chain in the IRA argument concerned Ulster's unionists, who – in a sense – represented the most significant problem for republican politics. How, in short, do republicans in Ireland persuade unionists effectively to cease being unionists, and instead to build a new, shared, independent Irish politics and culture together? Neither force of argument nor the argument of IRA force has worked here, since unionist resolve to oppose a united Ireland has remained strong throughout the troubles. Part of the problem has been that those features of Irish nationalist and republican culture which understandably gave those ideological traditions meaning and cohesion during the twentieth century – the aspiration towards independence from Britain; the grievances born of Irish Catholic experience; an enthusiasm for Gaelic culture – have overwhelmingly repelled rather than attracted Ulster unionists. To claim northern Protestants as part of the Irish nation, while simultaneously defining true Irishness in terms with which they do not identify, is unlikely to prove effective.

For their part, the IRA have tended to argue that, once Britain decides to withdraw from the north, then unionists will see reason and simply accommodate themselves to a post-union fate. But, as noted, probably the main reason for Britain *not* considering withdrawal to be a practical possibility is the very fact of mass unionist objection to being expelled from the state of their preference. And it is worth noting that most scholarly observers have found that it is the self-generating resilience of unionist belief (rather than any artificial, propped-up quality) that is striking on close inspection.[126] Unrepentant republican purists like George Harrison might dismiss unionism merely as a 'Brit creation',[127] and other republicans might reasonably seek to end what they see as unionist dominance in northern politics. But the notion that unionism will simply dissolve is unpersuasive.

As recorded earlier in this book, brothers and RUC officers Sam and Alex Donaldson were killed by the IRA respectively in August 1970 and February 1985. But their cousin, unionist politician Jeffrey Donaldson, responded by intensifying his unionist resolve rather than by allowing it to flag:

> I would be honest with you and say that a big part of the motivation for me in becoming actively involved in politics was the deep sense of injustice that I felt had been perpetrated against my people, and specifically against my family, and I wanted to do

something about that. And it's why at the age of eighteen I did two things: I joined the Ulster Defence Regiment part-time and I joined the Ulster Unionist Party, because I wanted to pursue – through involvement with the forces of the state and the forces of law and order – the IRA and to oppose their campaign. But I also wanted to be involved politically in opposing that campaign as well.[128]

For it is clear that unionist resolve to remain in the UK has not, in practice, been weakened by the IRA's long war. As Ian Paisley has said, 'The unionists are not aspiring for anything: they've already got their aspirations, they're in the union, and they mean to maintain the union.'[129]

Certainly, some Ulster loyalists have shown a persistent preparedness to use awful violence in order to maintain their place in the UK. As one UVF man put it, 'The Provisionals will have to accept the fact that the Protestant people of Northern Ireland will not give up their Protestant liberties.'[130] And if one is, in fairness, to study what the IRA have said about unionists, then one should examine also the other side of that political coin. Archbishop Robin Eames (from 1986 onwards, Church of Ireland Primate of All Ireland) readily and rightly acknowledged the horrific nature of violence perpetrated by loyalist paramilitaries,[131] and he also acknowledged that the IRA's own actions were far from simply mindless. So this was no narrow observer. But the Protestant Archbishop tellingly also identified one of the key problems inherent in the long IRA campaign: 'To argue that its violence is a consequence of injustices perpetrated on the community it claims to defend seems to ignore the real injustice the IRA inflicts on its victims.'[132] For republicans to say that the unionist community is misguided about its identity, that it will have to accommodate itself to political defeat, and that in the meantime its sons and daughters will have to die at the IRA's hands as a consequence of their beliefs and actions, is to condemn a community to immense suffering.

As noted, republican approaches towards unionism have evolved significantly, and perhaps the days of the starkest conflict in the north of Ireland are nearing an end. Perhaps, rather than seeing an incompatibility between Britishness and Irishness, a more layered sense of identity will emerge as a flexible possibility. Intelligent observers have made this point eloquently and forcibly ('Irish, or British, or both').[133]

If such a view – perhaps through the courageous intermediation of figures like John Hume – has also rendered republican thinking more flexible, then all in Ireland and Britain might be the beneficiaries, especially if similar flexibility is shown by the republicans' opponents.

There is, therefore, much of weight and seriousness in the IRA's argument; but much also that might lead one not quite to share their sense of political certainty and brutal clarity. In some ways, indeed, it might even be argued that the IRA have themselves contributed to a certain distancing from some of the goals that they have so committedly professed. They wanted to end sectarianism, but their violence helped to ossify and to bloodstain sectarian division in the north; they wanted to unite Ireland, north and south, but made Irish unity seem less appealing still to Ulster Protestants (and even less of a priority to many in the south of Ireland); they aimed to prevent violence against northern Catholics but, directly and indirectly, were instrumental in such violence occurring. It could also be argued that they have achieved much: a sustained culture of resistance that will not allow the former second-class status to return; an increasing sense of the unappealing nature – for Britain itself – of the union; and in the ultimate late-1990s settlement, substantial reform of the north itself, with the prospect of working still to unite the island in the end. As noted, the war seems to have ended, as one might perhaps have predicted, in compromise – and for their part in that compromise, the Provisionals have probably received less recognition than they deserve – rather than in clear victory for either side. The Provisional IRA sought revolution, national and socialist; in 1998 they effectively settled for much less. One leading British historian has persuasively presented English eighteenth- and nineteenth-century history as 'a story of quasi-revolutionary change accomplished by non-revolutionary means'.[134] In the very different context of late-twentieth-century Ireland, the IRA ultimately agreed to non-revolutionary change accomplished after years of revolutionary means.

As we have seen, there are those who feel the war to have been justified by its eventual outcome, others who protest that the compromise of the 1990s could have been achieved much earlier and much less painfully without the Provisionals' long war. But the most persuasive analysis of the IRA will concentrate less on whether their war was justified than in careful explanation of why it happened. It does seem hard to believe that a war that was fought to prevent any internal compromise short of Irish independence could be considered necessary to the achievement of just such a result. But, on the other hand, it is unhistorical to blame solely the IRA for the continuation of the conflict for so long. To say 'if only the IRA had not acted as they did, then all would have been well', is to remove one player's input from history while leaving that of all the others in place, a process that would distort the dynamics of political and historical interaction. For the IRA to have stopped earlier would probably have required others to have adopted different perspectives also – effectively, for all players to have eschewed the pursuit of victory and to have opted for compromise – and such IRA action would have been the outcome, rather than the sole cause, of those better relations that might have yielded earlier, more fruitful agreement.

As far as violence is concerned, two arguments, sometimes blurred, need to be distinguished here. It is possible to hold, first, that the IRA's violence was not carried out in pursuit of what was achieved in 1998, and that it was not necessary for the achievement of such partial compromise; while rejecting a second argument: that the IRA were the sole villains of the northern conflict, and that if only they had seen sense earlier then all could have been sorted out decades ago. The first of these arguments seems, to me, utterly persuasive on the evidence; the second seems much less so.

For while one might question the IRA's ruthless certainties and lament the human damage caused by their equally ruthless acts, it seems important for the historical record to recognize that the Provisionals were as rational as any other political players tend to be. (One can agree with Patrick Magee that the IRA were guerrillas rather than gangsters, without thinking that the guerrillas were necessarily right.)[135] It is sometimes implied that the IRA are somehow a disturbedly irrational group, one whose thinking defies the kind of logic characteristic of other people.[136] This seems to me a profoundly mistaken notion. My own sense, on the basis of the extensive research conducted for this book, is that the IRA act with just that mixture of the rational and the visceral that one commonly finds throughout human history, and with a combination of interwoven motives much as one would find in other political organizations.

Of course, the IRA's story is one determined by forces unique to their time and place: but that is also true of all other human history. And there are certainly many echoes of IRA thought and action to be found in other periods and other countries. Yes, the IRA has been schismatic: the Provisionals emerged from a split, and they have themselves seen numerous groups break away from them in subsequent years. But to see this tendency as a distinctively Irish republican habit would be to overplay it. It is, in fact, far from uncommon for organizations to experience schism in which (as in the IRA) people break away as heretics from the mainstream movement, but do so in defence of what they perceive to be an orthodoxy betrayed by the group that they are leaving.[137] Yes, the Provisional IRA at times adopted a fierce leftism which now appears overly rigid, dogmatic and naïve. But, again, such an inclination was far from uncommon in postwar Europe, and indeed characterized some of the most outstanding and influential of modern intellectuals.[138] Yet again, observers have often thrown their hands up despairingly when considering the modern troubles in the north of Ireland, regarding the conflict as an atavistic spectacle of brutal political competition and associated vengeful killing campaigns. But again, are these things really so rare? The literature of other countries would suggest that they are not.[139]

This is not to suggest that the northern troubles, or the IRA themselves, can be explained according to some generalized template or theory. One can understand the IRA only in terms of the time- and place-specific evolution of the Irish conflict itself, and attention to detailed chronology and experience has been at the centre of this present book. My point is merely that it would be quite wrong to imagine that the IRA inhabit a world beyond rationality or political explanation. They do not. They have held political beliefs that arose from their observation of a profound political conflict of interest; they have held political aims, to which their violence was persistently directed; they have evolved strategic objectives and analyses which have sometimes proved unjustified (as in their belief that attritional warfare would break the will of the British state), but that have been no more prone to miscalculation than have many other strategic analyses.

Of course, there have been other motives that have overlaid such rational arguments: the IRA are human beings and do not, any more than others, act out of pure, cold reason unaffected by emotion or other motivational forces. There has been a Fanonist rage, a hitting back at those who have hit their own people. There has been the appeal of excitement – 'We didn't really think of killing or being killed; in later years you might think about it but at the time it was all a high. There was a feeling of great exhilaration after an operation. We'd go back and wait for the news to hear the damage we'd done'[140] – and of comradeship – 'Now I felt I was one of the boys.'[141] Salaries and wages have accrued to some IRA Volunteers[142] and, more rewardingly, from IRA membership, considerable prestige and status and power within some communities.

These features are part of the story. But they cannot in themselves explain the IRA: in order to do that, I have had to treat seriously the political context that produced the Provisionals, and the political aims that sustained and ultimately motivated them. Anger, excitement, thirst for adventure, comradeship and prestige could, and did, coexist with a desire to free Ireland from British rule, to achieve better treatment and more power for their community, and to pursue goals seen in socialistic and democratic terms.

3

'The killing of Jonathan and Tim was wrong. It should not have happened and there is a responsibility on all of us to bring about a peace process.'

Martin McGuinness, speaking in 2001 about the IRA killing in 1993 of Jonathan Ball and Tim Parry in Warrington[143]

But the voices of the victims still deafen. And the IRA were responsible for more deaths in the northern troubles than any other group. In causing 1,778 deaths, the Provisionals killed 48.5 per cent of those lost in the troubles (compared with the UVF, 14.8 per cent; the UDA/UFF, 11.3 per cent; the British Army, 6.5 per cent; the SAS, 1.7 per cent; the RUC, 1.4 per cent). The Provisional IRA were thus by far the most lethal agent in the conflict. True, the IRA themselves suffered 293 dead. But while they presented themselves as embodying victimhood, as representatives of a community oppressed by sectarianism, by

TROUBLES DEATHS 1966–2001

	Number killed by the IRA	Total number killed
1966	0	3
1967	0	0
1968	0	0
1969	2	19
1970	18	29
1971	86	180
1972	235	497
1973	125	263
1974	130	304
1975	94	267
1976	138	307
1977	68	116
1978	60	88
1979	91	125
1980	45	86
1981	70	118
1982	52	112
1983	50	87
1984	45	71
1985	44	59
1986	37	66
1987	58	106
1988	66	105
1989	53	81
1990	50	84
1991	45	102
1992	34	91
1993	36	90
1994	19	69
1995	7	9
1996	8	22
1997	3	22
1998	4	57
1999	1	7
2000	4	19
2001	0	4
Total	1,778	3,665

colonialism, by the state, an alternative case could surely also be made. For in terms of the most extreme instance of oppression – that of taking life through violence – the IRA were easily the most active agent in the late-twentieth-century conflict in Ireland. And who *were* the IRA's victims? Not uncommonly for late-twentieth-century wars, civilians featured prominently. Indeed, civilians formed the largest single category of IRA victims (642), followed by the British forces (456), the RUC/RUCR (273), the UDR/RIR (182), republicans (162), loyalists (28), prison service (23), others (12).[144]

Overall, in terms of religion, 43 per cent of those killed in the conflict were Catholic, 30 per cent Protestant, 9 per cent not known and 18 per cent not from Northern Ireland; and in terms of region: 'there are parts of Northern Ireland which have only been marginally touched by the conflict. Within Belfast, the intensity of violence has been skewed towards the north and west of the city.'[145] There has certainly been marked regional variation in terms of the concentration of IRA activity. In south Armagh the degree of local sympathy, the comparative lack of a Protestant community and the proximity to the border with the south have all placed the Provisionals in a very strong position, uncommon elsewhere in the north. Since the early days of the troubles, south Armagh has been an area in which the IRA had a strength and effective space for operations which made the security forces' job incredibly difficult (much British Army movement in the area of necessity being effected by helicopter because of the high risk involved in travelling overland in such an IRA-strong area). By December 1993 fifty-eight British soldiers had been killed in the troubles within five miles of Crossmaglen village.[146]

There was variation also according to period. As the table on the previous page shows, during the years 1972–6 the IRA killed 722 people – an average of 144 per year, and 41 per cent of their total killings during 1969–2001. In the entire 1977–2001 period, they never again killed over a hundred people in a year. So there was a comparatively early peak to their lethal operations, and the implications of this for their long attritional war were perhaps significant. If London could endure the comparatively high levels of IRA killing typical of 1972–6 without withdrawing from the north, would the much lower average of deaths inflicted during subsequent decades really be likely to force Britain to yield what the Provisionals wanted?

By 1998 'one in seven of the population of Northern Ireland reported being a victim of violence; one in five had a family member killed or injured; and one in four had been caught up in an explosion'; since 1972, more than 18,000 people have been charged with terrorist offences.[147] So how are we to describe the conflict in which so many have participated and from which so many have suffered? The term 'guerrilla war' perhaps suits the IRA's campaign best, carrying as it does the dual implication of the seriousness of war, and the irregularity and small-scale aspect of the paramilitaries' struggle.[148] It also avoids too obvious a value-judgment, being a more neutral and less presumptuous label than, for example, 'terrorism'.[149] Of the three main categories identified in Charles Townshend's *Political Violence in Ireland* (still the outstanding general treatment of that theme in Irish history) – namely, 'the spontaneous collective violence (or social violence) which may have no explicit political intention but has political implications; systematic covert intimidation or terrorism; and organised open insurrection'[150] – none seems quite to fit. The Provisionals have at times (rather misleadingly) implied that they fit the third definition; their actions have at times overlapped with the first; and the second of Townshend's three categories is probably the closest to the historical reality. Yet none of the three quite seems to capture in full a campaign that has been characterized by often overt acts falling somewhere between intimidation and sustained military conflict or engagement; a campaign fought with skill and determination; and one comprising operations that have constituted a lengthy and ultimately inconclusive guerrilla war in the north of Ireland.

4

'I actually don't feel any guilt ... I did do a fair bit of damage myself. I felt I did the right thing ... If you turned the clock back I would do exactly the same thing that I did. I don't feel any guilt at all. They really were – the Army, the police, the government, back in those days – they were the aggressors here. They started this thing.'

Ex-IRA man, interviewed in 2001[151]

In December 2000 Patrick Magee (face to face with the daughter of Anthony Berry, whom his IRA Brighton bomb had killed sixteen years earlier), balanced his conviction that the war had been necessary with a sense of the loss thus incurred. 'Brighton, from our perspective, was a justified act. Your father was a part of the political elite, Tory government etc. In that sense, there's that cruel word, cruel expression: he was a legitimate target. Meeting you, though, I'm reminded of the fact that he was also a human being and that he was your father and that he was your daughter's grandfather, and that's all loss.'[152] For while the cost of IRA violence (like that carried out by other players) has often been appalling in terms of its human consequences, the pain is something that many former IRA members do recognize. Even Tommy McKearney's bravely candid comment, 'We did not understand the actual, brutal damage that we were doing to the Protestant community by killing UDR and RUC men',[153] of itself demonstrates a sense – now – of what was done to families, to relationships, to precious human intimacy. In the IRA's eyes, the war was directed against the forces of the state and it was justified; but there is also a recognition that private loss exists behind the uniformed victims: 'There's a profound sadness ... At an intellectual level I can stand over it. But the fact that you've caused hurt and pain to people, you have to live with that ... But it had to be done, and you were in a position to do it.'[154] The IRA themselves issued an apology in July 2002, to those whom they referred to as 'non-combatants' – civilians whom they had felled or injured, but whom they had not been intending to target: 'we offer our sincere apologies and condolences to their families'.[155]

A sense of the pain inflicted does not mean that former IRA members regret their violent actions. Marian Price, looking back: 'I wouldn't change my life at all. I don't regret anything and I wouldn't change anything.'[156] Séanna Walsh, who spent many years in jail, regrets being 'caught red-handed three times. And of course I regret all the things I missed – my brothers' and sisters' weddings, my wee girls' birthdays. And I missed the whole punk-rock thing. But I don't regret my actions ... in 1972, in Belfast, it was bedlam. Anyone who cared about anything was involved in some way. It was the situation I was in and as a young man living in nationalist Belfast, I would say I had no choice.'[157]

I myself was born in Belfast in December 1963 (by chance, in the same hospital as Gerry Adams). My mother was from that city, and although I grew up in England there was a certain Irish dimension to my upbringing, as holidays and relatives alike gave an Irish tinge to an essentially English childhood. But, unlike Mr Adams's family, my mother's were Irish Protestants. So, despite having lived most of my adult life in the north of Ireland, I am in a sense doubly outside the community about which I have written in this book. My accent is an English one; and, while my friends in Ireland are drawn from across a spectrum of nationalist, unionist and other backgrounds, my Irish *family* connections lie with Protestant rather than Catholic Ireland. Some readers may feel that someone from outside the Provisionals' community cannot understand their politics, their philosophy, their argument. But I hope that this is not the case. I have tried in this book to look seriously and in all its complex detail at an organization that most people – supporters and critics alike – have tended to approach with fairly simple assumptions and with less than rigorous analysis. The picture painted in these pages is not, I think, a simple one: in different lights, differing kinds of relief seem most prominent and unavoidably striking.

From their own perspective, Irish republicans are understand-ably proud of the IRA. As Gerry Adams has said, 'The strength and character of any guerrilla army is to be found in the calibre of the men and women who make it up. And the calibre of IRA Volunteers is extraordinary.'[158] I have amassed here a vast amount of evidence,

Conclusion

particularly what the Provisionals have *themselves* said – about their aims, their motivations, their analyses and their experiences. Some will consider it inappropriate to have taken the IRA's views so seriously. But it seems to me that the only proper way of responding to the northern conflict is to look closely and respectfully – but not uncritically – at this very serious revolutionary movement and to try to understand it just as one would any other important historical or political phenomenon. Republican Patrick Magee has recently expressed the desire 'just to be understood, to get a chance to explain'.[159] As this concluding chapter has demonstrated, I myself am – in the end – not really persuaded by the IRA's argument that their violence was necessary or beneficial. But nor am I satisfied with a depiction of the IRA which casually or myopically condemns them.

Notes and References

PREFACE

1. *Ballymena Guardian* 14 Oct. 1976.
2. See, for example, the excellent work of P. Hart, *The IRA and Its Enemies: Violence and Community in Cork 1916–1923* (Oxford: Oxford University Press, 1998), or of M. Hopkinson, *Green Against Green: The Irish Civil War* (Dublin: Gill and Macmillan, 1988).
3. Outstanding examples include: R. F. Foster, *Modern Ireland 1600–1972* (London: Allen Lane, 1988); C. Townshend, *Political Violence in Ireland: Government and Resistance since 1848* (Oxford: Oxford University Press, 1984; 1st edn 1983); D. G. Boyce, *Nationalism in Ireland* (London: Routledge, 1995; 1st edn. 1982); T. Garvin, *Nationalist Revolutionaries in Ireland 1858–1928* (Oxford: Oxford University Press, 1987); A. Jackson, *Ireland 1798–1998: Politics and War* (Oxford: Blackwell, 1999).
4. There have been excellent studies of partial aspects of the Provisionals' history, but none has been a full exploration. H. Patterson, *The Politics of Illusion: A Political History of the IRA* (London: Serif, 1997; 1st edn 1989) is a fine book, but one which deals really with the relationship between republican thought and socialism; likewise, M. L. R. Smith's *Fighting for Ireland? The Military Strategy of the Irish Republican Movement* (London: Routledge, 1997; 1st edn 1995) is an excellent treatment of military strategic thinking rather than a full study of the movement in wider political, social, motivational terms. Again, the impressive work of McIntyre, Harnden and O'Doherty is, in each case, specific to region, period or thematic emphasis in ways that distinguish it from the current project (A. McIntyre, 'Modern Irish Republicanism: The Product of British State Strategies', *Irish Political Studies* 10 (1995); T. Harnden, *'Bandit Country': The IRA and South Armagh* (London: Hodder and Stoughton, 1999); M. O'Doherty, *The Trouble with Guns: Republican Strategy and the Provisional IRA* (Belfast: Blackstaff Press, 1998)). Ed

Moloney's compelling book, *A Secret History of the IRA* (London: Allen Lane, 2002), is primarily a treatment of Gerry Adams rather than a full study of the IRA.

5. Tom Hartley, interviewed by the author, Belfast, 24 Oct. 2001.

ONE: THE IRISH REVOLUTION 1916–23

1. M. Collins, *The Path to Freedom* (Cork: Mercier, 1968; 1st edn 1922), p. 60. Michael Collins (1890–1922): born County Cork; in London, joined the Irish Republican Brotherhood (IRB); in Dublin, fought in the 1916 Rising; post-1916, leading Sinn Féiner, IRB man and Irish Volunteer; during the 1919–21 War of Independence, Dáil Minister of Home Affairs then Minister of Finance, and Volunteer Director of Organization and Intelligence; negotiated the 1921 Anglo-Irish Treaty, and was killed in the Civil War which followed it.

2. W. B. Yeats, 'Easter 1916' in *Yeats's Poems* (Dublin: Gill and Macmillan, 1989), pp. 287–9.

3. 'We declare our allegiance to the thirty-two-county Irish republic, proclaimed at Easter 1916' (*IN* 29 Dec. 1969).

4. R. Doyle, *A Star Called Henry* (London: Jonathan Cape, 1999). For other literary echoes of 1916 see (for examples among very many): L. O'Flaherty, *Insurrection* (Dublin: Wolfhound, 1993; 1st edn 1950); J. Hewitt, 'Nineteen Sixteen, Or the Terrible Beauty' in F. Ormsby (ed.), *The Collected Poems of John Hewitt* (Belfast: Blackstaff Press, 1991), p. 204; B. Tóibín, *The Rising* (Dublin: New Island Books, 2001).

5. J. Stephens, *The Insurrection in Dublin* (Gerrards Cross: Colin Smythe, 1992; 1st edn 1916), p. 53.

6. Mary Louisa Hamilton Norway, in K. Jeffery (ed.), *The Sinn Féin Rebellion as They Saw It* (Dublin: Irish Academic Press, 1999), p. 39.

7. O'Malley to Childers, 26 Nov.–1 Dec. 1923 in R. English and C. O'Malley (eds), *Prisoners: The Civil War Letters of Ernie O'Malley* (Dublin: Poolbeg, 1991), pp. 72–3. Ernie O'Malley (1897–1957): born County Mayo; educated by the Christian Brothers and at University College, Dublin; joined the Irish Volunteers in the wake of the Easter Rising; 1921 Commandant General, IRA's Second Southern Division; leading anti-Treaty republican in the 1922–3 Irish Civil War; travelled widely after the revolution and wrote classic autobiographical accounts of his IRA adventures: *On Another Man's Wound* (Dublin: Anvil, 1979; 1st edn 1936); *The Singing Flame* (Dublin: Anvil, 1978). For a study of

his dramatic life, see R. English, *Ernie O'Malley: IRA Intellectual* (Oxford: Oxford University Press, 1998).

8. Tom Maguire, quoted in U. MacEoin (ed.), *Survivors* (Dublin: Argenta, 1987; 1st edn 1980), p. 278. Tom Maguire (1892–1993): 1920 OC IRA South Mayo Brigade; 1921 General OC, IRA Second Western Division; 1931 Vice-President of Sinn Féin.

9. T. Barry, *Guerilla Days in Ireland* (Dublin: Anvil, 1989; 1st edn 1949), p. 2. Tom Barry (1897–1980): born County Cork; British soldier turned IRA leader; OC West Cork Brigade Flying Column during the War of Independence; anti-Treaty republican during the Civil War.

10. L. Deasy, *Towards Ireland Free: The West Cork Brigade in the War of Independence 1917–21* (Cork: Mercier, 1977), p. 5.

11. 'Proclamation of the Republic', reprinted in R. F. Foster, *Modern Ireland 1600–1972* (London: Allen Lane, 1988), pp. 597–8.

12. G. Adams, *Who Fears to Speak . . .? The Story of Belfast and the 1916 Rising* (Belfast: Beyond the Pale, 2001; 1st edn 1991), p. 46.

13. During the rebellion, 450 people were killed, 2,614 wounded and nine declared missing (M. Foy and B. Barton, *The Easter Rising* (Stroud: Sutton, 1999), pp. 210–11).

14. Roger Casement (1864–1916): born County Dublin; worked in the British colonial service; highlighted the often exploitative treatment of indigenous people under imperial rule; Irish nationalist, who sought German aid for an Irish rising against Britain; German support disappointed him, and on his arrival in Ireland in 1916 he wanted to postpone the rebellion; arrested, he was tried for treason and hanged. Controversy surrounding his alleged homosexual activities long outlived him.

15. Sean Clancy, quoted in *Guardian* 24 Oct. 1998.

16. 'Report of the Royal Commission on the Rebellion in Ireland 1916' in *The Irish Uprising, 1914–21: Papers from the British Parliamentary Archive* (London: Stationery Office, 2000), p. 82.

17. Patrick Pearse, quoted in M. Caulfield, *The Easter Rebellion* (London: Frederick Muller, 1964), p. 359.

18. P. H. Pearse, 'The Sovereign People' (1916) in *Political Writings and Speeches* (Dublin: Phoenix, n.d.), p. 333.

19. P. H. Pearse, 'The Separatist Idea' (1916) in *Political Writings and Speeches*, p. 283.

20. The views of the actual Irish people, including Pearse's heroes, had been far more complex than his brilliant pamphlets suggested. For rich historical treatment of the four heroes themselves, see M. Elliott, *Wolfe Tone: Prophet of Irish Independence* (New Haven: Yale University Press, 1989); T. Bartlett, *Theobald Wolfe Tone* (Dundalk: Dundalgan Press,

1997); D. N. Buckley, *James Fintan Lalor: Radical* (Cork: Cork University Press, 1990); R. Davis, *The Young Ireland Movement* (Dublin: Gill and Macmillan, 1987).

21. C. Townshend, *Ireland: The Twentieth Century* (London: Arnold, 1999), pp. 26–7.

22. Marx to Engels, 14 Dec. 1867; Engels to Marx, 19 Dec. 1867 in K. Marx and F. Engels, *Ireland and the Irish Question* (London: Lawrence and Wishart, 1971), p. 159.

23. R. F. Foster, *The Irish Story: Telling Tales and Making it up in Ireland* (London: Allen Lane, 2001), p. 34.

24. P. O'Donnell, *The Knife* (Dublin: Irish Humanities Centre, 1980; 1st edn 1930), p. 93. Peadar O'Donnell (1893–1986): born County Donegal; schoolteacher, trade union organizer, IRA socialist and novelist; fought in the 1919–21 War of Independence; anti-Treatyite in the Civil War; leading IRA socialist after the 1916–23 revolution, and central figure in the breakaway Republican Congress of the 1930s.

25. George Gilmore (1898–1985): born County Dublin, of Protestant family background; IRA man in the War of Independence and, as an anti-Treatyite, in the Civil War; socialist republican of some influence in the post-revolutionary IRA; leading figure in the 1930s Republican Congress movement.

26. G. Gilmore, *The Relevance of James Connolly in Ireland Today* (Dublin: Fodhla, n.d.), pp. 3–4.

27. John Redmond, quoted in D. Fitzpatrick, *Politics and Irish Life 1913–1921: Provincial Experience of War and Revolution* (Cork: Cork University Press, 1998; 1st edn 1977), p. 97.

28. F. O'Donoghue, 'Easter Week, 1916' in G. A. Hayes-McCoy (ed.), *The Irish at War* (Cork: Mercier, 1964), pp. 94–5.

29. P. O'Donnell, *Monkeys in the Superstructure: Reminiscences of Peadar O'Donnell* (Galway: Salmon Publishing, 1986), p. 28.

30. Sean Clancy, quoted in *Guardian* 24 Oct. 1998.

31. Among the many treatments, see: A. Morgan, *James Connolly: A Political Biography* (Manchester: Manchester University Press, 1988); J. L. Hyland, *James Connolly* (Dundalk: Dundalgan Press, 1997); D. Howell, *A Lost Left: Three Studies in Socialism and Nationalism* (Manchester: Manchester University Press, 1986); W. K. Anderson, *James Connolly and the Irish Left* (Blackrock: Irish Academic Press, 1994).

32. C. D. Greaves, *1916 as History: The Myth of the Blood Sacrifice* (Dublin: Fulcrum Press, 1991), p. 24.

33. C. D. Greaves, *The Life and Times of James Connolly* (London: Lawrence and Wishart, 1972; 1st edn 1961), p. 431.

34. J. Connolly, 'Labour in Irish History' (1910) in *Collected Works: vol. 1* (Dublin: New Books Publications, 1987), p. 183.

35. D. Breen, *My Fight for Irish Freedom* (Dublin: Anvil, 1989; 1st edn 1924), p. 32.

36. Richard Mulcahy (1886–1971): born Waterford; CBS-educated IRB man and Irish Volunteer; 1916 rebel; 1918 Chief of Staff of the Volunteers; pro-Treatyite in the Civil War, and a prominent Irish politician after it.

37. 'Interned Rebels: Classification', 1916 Rising Internees, NAD 16627/ 1918.

38. *AP/RN* 28 Mar. 1991.

39. Although formally entitled the Irish Volunteers/Óglaigh na hÉireann until 1922, the Volunteers during 1919 came to use the title Irish Republican Army. This name had been used earlier (in connection with the 1916 rebels and even, it appears, on at least one occasion by nineteenth-century Fenians), and the Irish title – Óglaigh na hÉireann, which long remained that used by the IRA – had been the name in Irish of the Volunteers founded in 1913.

40. Cathal Brugha (1874–1922): Dubliner; Gaelic Leaguer and Irish Volunteer; 1916 rebel; 1917 Volunteer Chief of Staff; leading figure in the IRA during War of Independence; killed, fighting as an anti-Treatyite republican, in the Civil War.

41. R. E. Childers, 'Law and Order in Ireland', *Studies* 8 (1919), p. 601.

42. D. Macardle, *The Irish Republic: A Documented Chronicle of the Anglo-Irish Conflict and the Partitioning of Ireland, with a Detailed Account of the Period 1916–1923* (London: Corgi, 1968; 1st edn 1937), p. 251.

43. Breen, *My Fight*, p. 31.

44. Eamon de Valera (1882–1975): born New York; raised in County Limerick; mathematics teacher; Gaelic Leaguer and 1916 rebel; 1917 President of Sinn Féin and Irish Volunteers; 1919 President of the Dáil; anti-Treatyite during Civil War; 1926 founded Fianna Fáil; Irish Prime Minister 1932–48, 1951–4, 1957–9.

45. R. Mulcahy, *Richard Mulcahy (1886–1971): A Family Memoir* (Dublin: Aurelian Press, 1999), p. 104.

46. Brilliantly depicted for County Cork in the work of Peter Hart: *The IRA and Its Enemies: Violence and Community in Cork 1916–1923* (Oxford: Oxford University Press, 1998).

47. O'Malley, *On Another Man's Wound*, p. 326. Compare the scholarly view of Charles Townshend that the British response to the IRA campaign was 'brutal, and in many ways counter-productive' (C. Townshend, *The British Campaign in Ireland, 1919–1921: The Development of Political and Military Policies* (Oxford: Oxford University Press, 1975), p. 206).

48. M. Brennan, *The War in Clare 1911–1921: Personal Memoirs of the Irish War of Independence* (Dublin: Four Courts Press, 1980), pp. 80–1.

49. D. Macardle, *Tragedies of Kerry 1922–1923* (Dublin: Irish Freedom Press, 1988; 1st edn 1924), p. 5.

50. *Rebel Heart*, shown on BBC television in 2001: written by Ronan Bennett, directed by John Strickland.

51. The couple was Tomás Malone and Peig Hogan; see T. Malone, *Alias Sean Forde: The Story of Commandant Tomás Malone, Vice OC East Limerick Flying Column, Irish Republican Army* (Dublin: Danesfort, 2000), p. 63.

52. M. A. Doherty, 'Kevin Barry and the Anglo-Irish Propaganda War', *Irish Historical Studies* 32, 126 (2000).

53. T. R. Dwyer, *Tans, Terror and Troubles: Kerry's Real Fighting Story 1913–23* (Cork: Mercier, 2001), pp. 209, 221–3, 225–7.

54. P. Béaslaí, *Michael Collins and the Making of a New Ireland: vol. 2* (Dublin: Phoenix, 1926), p. 23.

55. Pat Doherty, quoted in J. A. McLaughlin, *Carrowmenagh: History of a Donegal Village and Townland* (Browne: Letterkenny, 2001), pp. 30–1.

56. On the British IRA during these years, see P. Hart, '"Operations Abroad": The IRA in Britain, 1919–23', *English Historical Review* 115, 460 (2000).

57. E. M. Brady, *Ireland's Secret Service in England* (Dublin: Talbot Press, n.d.), p. 44.

58. T. G. McMahon (ed.), *Pádraig Ó Fathaigh's War of Independence: Recollections of a Galway Gaelic Leaguer* (Cork: Cork University Press, 2000), p. 84.

59. Fitzpatrick, *Politics and Irish Life*, p. 6.

60. Summary of Police Reports, 1 July 1920, PROL CO 904/141.

61. Summary of Police Reports, 1 Aug. 1920, PROL CO 904/142.

62. See, for example, Summary of Police Reports, 10 July 1920, PROL CO 904/141; Summary of Police Reports, 1 Aug. 1920, PROL CO 904/142.

63. M. Tanner, *Ireland's Holy Wars: The Struggle for a Nation's Soul, 1500–2000* (New Haven: Yale University Press, 2001), p. 287.

64. Some felt that the police had been allowed to lose their hold even before the IRA's campaign, and that their problems thus had deeper roots. In one RIC man's recollection, 'The police, disheartened and discouraged by persistent neglect and contempt of their warnings, had lost their hold of information, and so the Easter week of 1916 came upon a government uninformed, and unprepared to meet the outbreak' (S. Ball (ed.), *A Policeman's Ireland: Recollections of Samuel Waters, RIC* (Cork: Cork University Press, 1999), p. 89).

65. C. Markievicz, *Prison Letters of Countess Markievicz* (London: Virago, 1987; 1st edn 1934), p. 241.

66. T. Barry, *The Reality of the Anglo-Irish War 1920–21 in West Cork: Refutations, Corrections and Comments on Liam Deasy's 'Towards Ireland Free'* (Tralee: Anvil, 1974), p. 17.

67. Breen, *My Fight*, p. 30.

68. *IT* 26 Oct. 1917.

69. C. von Clausewitz, *On War* (Harmondsworth: Penguin, 1968; 1st edn 1832), p. 104.

70. Mulcahy, *Richard Mulcahy*, p. 69.

71. *An t-Óglách* 15 Aug. 1918, 30 Sept. 1918, 15 Dec. 1919.

72. O'Malley to Lynch, 9 Jan. 1923 in English and O'Malley (eds), *Prisoners*, p. 25.

73. Breen, *My Fight*, p. 174.

74. Tom Maguire, quoted in MacEoin (ed.), *Survivors*, p. 278.

75. Liam Lynch, quoted in M. Ryan, *Liam Lynch: The Real Chief* (Dublin: Mercier, 1986), p. 9.

76. Collins, *Path to Freedom*, p. 98.

77. O'Malley, *Singing Flame*, p. 279.

78. Among the many examples, see F. Gallagher, *Days of Fear* (London: John Murray, 1928), pp. 13, 35–6, 57, 60–1, 75, 110.

79. See, for example, Brennan, *War in Clare*, p. 81.

80. M. Chavasse, *Terence MacSwiney* (Dublin: Clonmore and Reynolds, 1961), p. 170.

81. Gallagher, *Days of Fear*, p. 67.

82. M. Hopkinson (ed.), *Frank Henderson's Easter Rising: Recollections of a Dublin Volunteer* (Cork: Cork University Press, 1998), pp. 58, 61.

83. IRA Field HQ, 3rd Southern Division to Adjutant General, 2 Oct. 1922, Twomey Papers, ADUCD P69/94 (41).

84. Barry, *Guerilla Days*, pp. 208–9.

85. E. O'Malley, *Raids and Rallies* (Dublin: Anvil, 1982), p. 65.

86. P. Hart, 'The Social Structure of the Irish Republican Army, 1916–1923', *Historical Journal* 42, 1 (1999); J. Augusteijn, *From Public Defiance to Guerrilla Warfare: The Experience of Ordinary Volunteers in the Irish War of Independence 1916–1921* (Blackrock: Irish Academic Press, 1996), p. 360.

87. For a stimulating statement of this thesis, see T. Garvin, *Nationalist Revolutionaries in Ireland 1858–1928* (Oxford: Oxford University Press, 1987).

88. Ernie O'Malley manuscript, 'Sean Connolly', Ernie O'Malley Papers in the possession of Cormac O'Malley.

89. On Clare and Cork respectively, see the excellent treatments of Fitz-patrick, *Politics and Irish Life* and Hart, *The IRA and Its Enemies*.

90. Oscar Wilde, *An Ideal Husband* in *Complete Works of Oscar Wilde: vol. 2* (London: Heron Books, 1966), p. 181.

91. F. O'Connor, *The Big Fellow* (Dublin: Poolbeg, 1991; 1st edn 1937), p. 155.

92. M. Laffan, *The Resurrection of Ireland: The Sinn Féin Party, 1916–1923* (Cambridge: Cambridge University Press, 1999), p. 350.

93. See, for example, T. P. Coogan, *Michael Collins: A Biography* (London: Hutchinson, 1990), or Neil Jordan's 1996 film, *Michael Collins*.

94. Collins, *Path to Freedom*, p. 13.

95. Arthur Griffith, quoted in Macardle, *Irish Republic*, pp. 556–7.

96. B. O'Connor, *With Michael Collins in the Fight for Irish Independence* (London: Peter Davies, 1929), p. 180.

97. Béaslaí, *Collins and the Making of a New Ireland: vol. 2*, pp. 310–11.

98. *IT* 6 Dec. 1921.

99. Austin Stack, quoted in Macardle, *Irish Republic*, p. 558.

100. *Private Sessions of Second Dáil*, 17 Dec. 1921 (Dublin: Dáil Éireann), p. 245.

101. M. Farry, *The Aftermath of Revolution: Sligo 1921–23* (Dublin: UCD Press, 2000), p. 44.

102. M. Gallagher (ed.), *Irish Elections 1922–44: Results and Analysis* (Limerick: PSAI Press, 1993), pp. 2, 15.

103. O'Malley, *Singing Flame*, p. 25.

104. O. Coogan, *Politics and War in Meath 1913–23* (Dublin: Folens, 1983), p. 269.

105. O'Malley, *Singing Flame*, p. 94.

106. Provisional government statement, quoted in *IT* 28 June 1922.

107. P. Béaslaí, *Michael Collins and the Making of a New Ireland: vol. 1* (Dublin: Phoenix, 1926), p. 78.

108. English and O'Malley (eds), *Prisoners*, p. 132.

109. F. O'Connor, *An Only Child* (Belfast: Blackstaff Press, 1993; 1st edn 1961), p. 263.

110. P. O'Donnell, *The Gates Flew Open* (London: Jonathan Cape, 1932).

111. D. Morrison, *Then the Walls Came Down: A Prison Journal* (Cork: Mercier Press, 1999), p. 234.

112. O'Donnell, *Gates Flew Open*, p. 30.

113. Aiken to all Volunteers on hunger strike, 5 Nov. 1923, Ernie O'Malley Papers, ADUCD P17a/43.

114. O'Donnell, *Gates Flew Open*, pp. 46–7.

115. Unionist prime ministers of Northern Ireland were: James Craig,

1921–40; J. M. Andrews 1940–3; Basil Brooke 1943–63; Terence O'Neill 1963–9; James Chichester-Clark 1969–71; Brian Faulkner 1971–2.

116. The population numbers for the six-county area which became Northern Ireland were as follows: 1911 – 430,161 Catholics, 820,370 all other religions (a category composed overwhelmingly, but not exclusively, of Protestants); 1926 – Catholics 420,428, all other religions 836,133; 1937 – Catholics 428,290, all other religions 851,455 (PRONI CAB 3A/92).

117. *IT* 4 Nov. 1922.

118. Sectarian and political violence left over 100 dead in Belfast in 1921, and around 300 in Northern Ireland the following year (D. Fitzpatrick, *The Two Irelands 1912–1939* (Oxford: Oxford University Press, 1998), pp. 118–19).

119. Collins, *Path to Freedom*, p. 79.

120. B. Behan, *Confessions of an Irish Rebel* (London: Arrow Books, 1991; 1st edn 1965), p. 39.

121. T. Hennessey, *A History of Northern Ireland 1920–1996* (Dublin: Gill and Macmillan, 1997), p. 11.

122. See, for example, Summary of Police Reports, 10 July 1920, PROL CO 904/141.

123. G. B. Kenna, *Facts and Figures of the Belfast Pogrom 1920–1922* (Dublin: O'Connell Publishing Company, 1922), p. 159.

124. Summary of Police Reports, 2 July 1920, PROL CO 904/141.

125. Summary of Police Reports, 22 Aug. 1920, PROL CO 904/142.

126. *IN* 25 Mar. 1922.

127. *IN* 20 May 1922.

128. D. Kleinrichert, *Republican Internment and the Prison Ship Argenta 1922* (Dublin: Irish Academic Press, 2001), pp. 10, 250–1.

129. J. Lynch, *A Tale of Three Cities: Comparative Studies in Working-Class Life* (Basingstoke: Macmillan, 1998), p. 1.

TWO: NEW STATES 1923–63

1. Seachranaidhe [as F. Ryan], *Easter Week and After* (Dublin: National Publicity Committee, 1928), pp. 11, 15. Frank Ryan (1902–44): born County Limerick; IRA man in War of Independence and, as an anti-Treatyite, in the Civil War; post-revolutionary IRA man and socialist; in 1936 led a contingent to fight against fascism in Spain; in 1938 captured and, in 1940, handed to the Germans, with whom he shared a Second World War anti-British interest; died in Dresden.

2. *Irish People* 21 Mar. 1936.

3. *Constitution of Óglaigh na h-Éireann (IRA) as Amended by General Army Convention 14–15 Nov. 1925*, Blythe Papers, ADUCD P24/165 (10). GAC delegates were representative of the army as a whole; the GAC elected a twelve-member Army Executive; this in turn appointed a seven-person Army Council, which was the real central authority within the IRA.

4. Frank Edwards, quoted in U. MacEoin (ed.), *Survivors* (Dublin: Argenta, 1987; 1st edn 1980), p. 5.

5. Gannon statement, NAD 999/951.

6. R. Briscoe, *For the Life of Me* (London: Longmans, 1959), p. 224.

7. B. Hanley, *The IRA, 1926–1936* (Dublin: Four Courts Press, 2002), p. 11.

8. O. Wilde, *An Ideal Husband* in *Complete Works of Oscar Wilde* (London: Heron Books, 1966), p. 176.

9. MacBride to McGarrity, 19 Oct. 1933, McGarrity Papers, NLI 17456.

10. Army Council Despatch No. 223, to Secretary, Clan na Gael, 13 Feb. 1933, Twomey Papers, ADUCD P69/185 (88).

11. Army Council Despatch No. 222, to Secretary, Clan na Gael, 13 Feb. 1933, Twomey Papers, ADUCD P69/185 (90)–(91).

12. S. O'Callaghan, *The Easter Lily: The Story of the IRA* (London: Allan Wingate, 1956), p. 9.

13. Army Council Despatch No. 220, to Secretary, Clan na Gael, 13 Feb. 1933, Twomey Papers, ADUCD P69/185 (95)–(96).

14. Sheila Humphreys, interviewed by the author, Dublin, 26 Feb. 1987.

15. It is a point of some debate both whether the term 'revolution' should be applied to 1916–23 and (if so) precisely what the term should be taken to mean. For varying views, see: M. Hopkinson, *Green against Green: The Irish Civil War* (Dublin: Gill and Macmillan, 1988), p. 272; D. Fitzpatrick, *Politics and Irish Life 1913–1921: Provincial Experience of War and Revolution* (Cork: Cork University Press, 1988; 1st edn 1977), p. 192; D. Fitzpatrick, *The Two Irelands 1912–1939* (Oxford: Oxford University Press, 1998), pp. 3–4; and the Introduction by M. Cronin and J. M. Regan to their co-edited volume, *Ireland: The Politics of Independence, 1922–49* (Basingstoke: Macmillan, 2000), p. 1.

16. G. Gilmore, *Labour and the Republican Movement* (Dublin: Repsol, 1977; 1st edn 1966), p. 11.

17. G. Gilmore, *The Irish Republican Congress* (Cork: Cork Workers' Club, 1978), p. 3.

18. Saor Eire, *Constitution and Rules Adopted by First National Congress Held in Dublin 26 and 27 Sept. 1931*, Files of the Dept of the Taoiseach, NAD S5864A.

19. Peadar O'Donnell, quoted in Gilmore, *Irish Republican Congress*, p. 52.
20. Athlone Manifesto (8 Apr. 1934), quoted in *Republican Congress* 5 May 1934.
21. MacSwiney to Brugha, 23 Jan. 1935, Brugha Papers, ADUCD P15/8.
22. Desmond FitzGerald, quoted in J. M. Regan, *The Irish Counter-Revolution 1921–1936: Treatyite Politics and Settlement in Independent Ireland* (Dublin: Gill and Macmillan, 1999), p. 280. See also J. Hogan, *Could Ireland Become Communist? The Facts of the Case* (Dublin: Cahill, n.d.).
23. Sean Nolan, interviewed by the author, Dublin, 3 Feb. 1988.
24. For full discussion of the interwar Irish republican left, see R. English, *Radicals and the Republic: Socialist Republicanism in the Irish Free State 1925–1937* (Oxford: Oxford University Press, 1994).
25. H. Patterson, *The Politics of Illusion: A Political History of the IRA* (London: Serif, 1997; 1st edn 1989), p. 80.
26. Minutes of 17 Mar. 1934 IRA GAC, MacEntee Papers, ADUCD P67/525.
27. Army Council Despatch No. 203, to Secretary, Clan na Gael, 8 Nov. 1932, Twomey Papers, ADUCD P69/185 (153).
28. Army Council Despatch No. 225, to Secretary, Clan na Gael, 13 Feb. 1933, Twomey Papers, ADUCD P69/185 (37).
29. Minutes of 17 Mar. 1934 IRA GAC, MacEntee Papers, ADUCD P67/525.
30. Ibid.
31. See the absorbing account in J. O'Neill, *Blood-Dark Track: A Family History* (London: Granta, 2000), specifically pp. 280, 292.
32. M. Kennedy, *Division and Consensus: The Politics of Cross-Border Relations in Ireland 1925–1969* (Dublin: Institute of Public Administration, 2000), p. 70.
33. 'IRA During the War' (RUC document), PRONI CAB 3A/78B.
34. Proceedings of Court of Inquiry into Raid on Magazine Fort, 23 Dec. 1939 (witness: Captain Joseph Curran), MacEntee Papers, ADUCD P67/531.
35. Stephen Hayes, quoted in T. P. Coogan, *The IRA* (London: Harper-Collins, 1987; 1st edn 1970), p. 201.
36. Special Communiqué issued by the IRA Army Council, 10 Sept. 1941, PROL DO 130/23.
37. Stephen Hayes, quoted in R. J. Quinn, *A Rebel Voice: A History of Belfast Republicanism 1925–1972* (Belfast: Belfast Cultural and Local History Group, 1999), p. 83.
38. Special Communiqué issued by the IRA Army Council, 10 Sept. 1941, PROL DO 130/23.

39. Ibid.
40. N. Browne, *Against the Tide* (Dublin: Gill and Macmillan, 1986), p. 89.
41. *RN* 20 Sept. 1975.
42. See, for example, *Northern Whig* 21 Sept. 1945.
43. D. Kelleher, *Buried Alive in Ireland: A Story of a Twentieth-Century Inquisition* (Greystones: Justice Books, 2001), p. 25.
44. Óglaigh na hÉireann (IRA), Special Manifesto (1942), MacEntee Papers, ADUCD P67/540 (20).
45. On White's career, see U. MacEoin, *Harry* (Dublin: Argenta, 1986; 1st edn 1985).
46. IRA Army Council to the People of Ireland (Oct. 1938), Files of the Dept of the Taoiseach, NAD S11564A.
47. The Second Dáil had been elected in 1921; in October 1922 those Deputies who opposed the 1921 Treaty had formed an alternative government, since they considered those who had endorsed the Treaty to have forfeited membership of the legitimate Dáil; the group approached now, in 1938, by the IRA was that small circle who had also refused to recognize the legitimacy of de Valera's regime in southern Ireland, and who had maintained the claim that they themselves were the true government of Ireland. At its close in 1938, the Executive Council of the Second Dáil comprised Seán Ó Ceallaigh (Sceilg), Count Plunkett, Cathal Ó Murchadha, Mary MacSwiney, Brian Ó hUiginn, W. F. P. Stockley and Tom Maguire.
48. *Wolfe Tone Weekly* 17 Dec. 1938.
49. The sequence of IRA Chiefs of Staff had run: Frank Aiken 1923–5, Andy Cooney 1925–6, Moss Twomey 1926–36, Sean MacBride 1936, Tom Barry 1937, Michael Fitzpatrick 1937–8, Sean Russell 1938–.
50. Quoted in Coogan, *The IRA*, pp. 165–7.
51. B. Behan, *Borstal Boy* (London: Arrow Books, 1990; 1st edn 1958), p. 1.
52. Samuel Hoare, speaking on 24 July 1939, *House of Commons Official Report*, 350/1049–50.
53. Russell to McGarrity, 21 Sept. 1938, McGarrity Papers, NLI 17485.
54. Coogan, *The IRA*, p. 157.
55. F. McGarry, *Irish Politics and the Spanish Civil War* (Cork: Cork University Press, 1999); R. A. Stradling, *The Irish and the Spanish Civil War 1936–1939* (Manchester: Mandolin, 1999); M. Cronin, *The Blue-shirts and Irish Politics* (Dublin: Four Courts Press, 1997).
56. Ryan to Kerney, 6 Nov. 1941, Files of the Dept. of Foreign Affairs, NAD A20/4.
57. *War News* 16 Nov. 1940.
58. *War News* 22 Mar. 1940.

59. *War News* 29 Aug. 1940.
60. 'IRA in Germany', Bryan Papers, ADUCD P71/30 (12).
61. Dessie O'Hagan, interviewed by the author, Belfast, 5 Mar. 2002. Dessie O'Hagan: born in Belfast, 1934; joined the Fianna Eireann in 1947 and the IRA in 1949 (lying about his age in order to become a member); a student at the London School of Economics, 1962–5 (where he was taught by, among others, Ernest Gellner and Michael Oakeshott); 1966 returned to Belfast; founder-member of civil rights movement, 1967; joined IRA and Sinn Féin again in 1969, siding with Cathal Goulding; became a leading figure in the Workers' Party.
62. Patterson, *Politics of Illusion*, p. 94.
63. Eileen O'Neill, quoted in O'Neill, *Blood-Dark Track*, p. 160.
64. The impact of southern developments on northern unionist thinking is well documented in D. Kennedy, *The Widening Gulf: Northern Attitudes to the Independent Irish State, 1919–49* (Belfast: Blackstaff Press, 1988).
65. For pre-partition sectarianism in Ireland see S. Paseta, *Before the Revolution: Nationalism, Social Change and Ireland's Catholic Elite, 1879–1922* (Cork: Cork University Press, 1999); P. Maume, *The Long Gestation: Irish Nationalist Life 1891–1918* (Dublin: Gill and Macmillan, 1999); and T. Hennessey, *Dividing Ireland: World War One and Partition* (London: Routledge, 1998).
66. D. J. Smith and G. Chambers, *Inequality in Northern Ireland* (Oxford: Oxford University Press, 1991), p. 368.
67. On this most heated of topics, see the measured and wise judgment of J. Whyte, *Interpreting Northern Ireland* (Oxford: Oxford University Press, 1990), pp. 64, 168.
68. P. Buckland, *The Factory of Grievances: Devolved Government in Northern Ireland, 1921–39* (Dublin: Gill and Macmillan, 1979).
69. Charlie McGlade, quoted in Quinn, *Rebel Voice*, p. 17.
70. 'IRA During the War' (RUC document), PRONI CAB 3A/78B.
71. P. Devlin: *Straight Left: An Autobiography* (Belfast: Blackstaff Press, 1993), pp. 26, 28–9.
72. 'IRA During the War' (RUC document), PRONI CAB 3A/78B.
73. Broadcast of 30 Aug. 1942, B. Barrington (ed.), *The Wartime Broadcasts of Francis Stuart 1942–1944* (Dublin: Lilliput, 2000), p. 83.
74. *IN* 3 Sept. 1942.
75. Joe Cahill, in J. McVeigh, *Executed: Tom Williams and the IRA* (Belfast: Beyond the Pale, 1999), p. xix.
76. *IN* 16 Jan. 1943.
77. B. Lynn, *Holding the Ground: The Nationalist Party in Northern Ireland, 1945–72* (Aldershot: Ashgate, 1997).

78. F. L. Green, *Odd Man Out* (Harmondsworth: Penguin, 1948; 1st edn 1945), pp. 41, 57, 74, 255.
79. *IN* 27 Feb. 1962.
80. *IN* 28 Nov. 1955.
81. IRA proclamation of Dec. 1956, quoted in J. B. Bell, *The Secret Army: The IRA 1916–1979* (Swords: Poolbeg, 1989; 1st edn 1970), p. 291.
82. *IN* 12 Dec. 1956.
83. *IN* 13 Dec. 1956.
84. Dessie O'Hagan, interviewed by the author, Belfast, 5 Mar. 2002.
85. Conclusions of a Meeting of the Cabinet held at Stormont Castle, 19 Dec. 1956, PRONI CAB 4/1028/15.
86. *IN* 13 Nov. 1961.
87. *IN* 27 Feb. 1962.
88. S. Heaney, 'The Border Campaign' in *Electric Light* (London: Faber and Faber, 2001), p. 18.
89. D. Morrison, 'The Union: A Republican Perspective' in R. Hanna (ed.), *The Union: Essays on Ireland and the British Connection* (Newtownards: Colourpoint, 2001), p. 89.
90. D. P. Barritt and C. F. Carter, *The Northern Ireland Problem: A Study in Group Relations* (Oxford: Oxford University Press, 1972; 1st edn 1962), pp. 1–2 (Introduction: Dec. 1961).
91. Sean Lemass (1899–1971): born in County Dublin; Irish Volunteer and 1916 rebel; Tánaiste (Deputy Prime Minister), 1945; 1959–66 Taoiseach.
92. S. O'Faoláin, *De Valera* (Harmondsworth: Penguin, 1939), p. 117.
93. Terence O'Neill (1914–90): born County Antrim; educated at Eton; fought in the Irish Guards during the Second World War; Prime Minister of Northern Ireland 1963–9.
94. Transcript of an interview with the Prime Minister of Northern Ireland, Telefís Eireann, 18 Feb. 1965, Files of the Dept of Defence, NAD S613.
95. It has been suggested that this ambiguity in Lemass's approach to the north be explained in the following terms. First, Lemass was arguing for reintegration of the Republic of Ireland into the UK economy; if he rejected altogether Irish nationalism's hard line on the north, then he would lose a bargaining counter with London, where his pragmatism would be more highly valued if reminders existed of less harmonious Irish possibilities. Second, Lemass decisively broke with southern Irish economic protectionism, and told those hostile to such a change that the jettisoning of protectionism and allowing free trade formed part of a process of reuniting Ireland. Third, having thrown out Sinn Féinish economics, his Irish nationalist ideological base might have been

altogether undermined if he had had to admit that, in addition to revolutionary economics, revolutionary assumptions about Irish unity were also unpersuasive. See the valuable article by H. Patterson, 'Sean Lemass and the Ulster Question, 1959–65', *Journal of Contemporary History* 34, 1 (Jan. 1999).

96. MacEntee to Lynch, 6 Nov. 1969, Lynch Papers, NAD 2001/8/5.

THREE: THE BIRTH OF THE PROVISIONAL IRA 1963–72

1. Tommy McKearney, interviewed by the author, Belfast, 20 Sept. 2000. McKearney was born in Lurgan in 1952 and brought up in Moy, County Tyrone. He joined the Provisional IRA in late 1971.
2. P. Taylor, *Provos: The IRA and Sinn Féin* (London: Bloomsbury, 1997), pp. 6, 28, 37; E. Collins, *Killing Rage* (London: Granta, 1997), p. 37; F. O Connor, *In Search of a State: Catholics in Northern Ireland* (Belfast: Blackstaff Press, 1993), p. 114.
3. M. McGuire, *To Take Arms: A Year in the Provisional IRA* (London: Quartet, 1973), p. 21. Maria McGuire's own IRA career was an unconventional one: from the middle-class Dublin suburbs and a non-republican family, she joined the Provisionals in July 1971 and remained in the organization for a year, before defecting and subsequently publishing a memoir in which she told (among other things) of her affair with leading Provisional, Daithi O'Connell.
4. Eoghan Harris, *Sunday Times* 3 Jan. 1999.
5. *IT* 9 July 1971.
6. *DT* 13 Jan. 1970.
7. *IP* 24 May 1971.
8. Papers Relating to a Meeting of the Cabinet held at Stormont Castle, 25 July 1966, PRONI CAB 4/1336.
9. Precise figures are difficult to establish. Some sources state that the Belfast IRA grew from 24 members in 1962 to around 120 by 1969 (H. Patterson, *The Politics of Illusion: A Political History of the IRA* (London, Serif, 1997; 1st edn 1989), p. 108); others have the 1969 Belfast IRA possessing approximately 80 full-time, and 200 auxiliary members (R. J. Quinn, *A Rebel Voice: A History of Belfast Republicanism 1925–1972* (Belfast: Belfast Cultural and Local History Group, 1999), p. 141). It is worth noting Gerry Adams's observation that republicans in Belfast in 1966 were actually 'enjoying a rise in local support' (G. Adams, *The Politics of Irish Freedom* (Dingle: Brandon, 1986), p. 6). Overall IRA membership appears to have risen from 657 in 1962 to 1,039 in 1966

(P. Dixon, *Northern Ireland: The Politics of War and Peace* (Basingstoke: Palgrave, 2001), p. 75).

10. Dessie O'Hagan, interviewed by the author, Belfast, 5 Mar. 2002.

11. Cathal Goulding, speaking in Dublin on 19 Aug. 1970, quoted in G. Foley, *Ireland in Rebellion* (New York: Pathfinder Press, 1971), p. 22.

12. *BT* 17 Feb. 1966.

13. R. Dunphy, 'The Contradictory Politics of the Official Republican Movement, 1969–1992' in R. Deutsch (ed.), *Les Républicanismes Irlandais* (Rennes: Presses Universitaires de Rennes, 1997), p. 121.

14. *IN* 2 Nov. 1970.

15. Fred Heatley, Wolfe Tone Society member, in *Fortnight* 22 Mar. 1974.

16. Constitution of Wolfe Tone Societies, quoted in P. Walsh, *Irish Republicanism and Socialism: The Politics of the Republican Movement 1905 to 1994* (Belfast: Athol Books, 1994), p. 50.

17. For an example of Johnston's socialist thinking, see *United Irishman* May 1968.

18. J. Johnston, *Civil War in Ulster: Its Objects and Probable Results* (Dublin: UCD Press, 1999; 1st edn 1913), p. 5.

19. Correspondence from Roy Johnston, 16 May 2001.

20. Foster, *The Irish Story: Telling Tales and Making it up in Ireland* (London: Allen Lane, 2001), p. 48.

21. S. O'Faolain, *The Irish* (West Drayton: Penguin, 1947), p. 91.

22. Roy Johnston, manuscript (2001) dealing with Sinn Féin Ard Comhairle (National Executive) Minutes, copy in the author's possession.

23. A. Coughlan, *C. Desmond Greaves, 1913–1988: An Obituary Essay* (Dublin: Irish Labour History Society, 1991; 1st edn 1990), p. 8.

24. Correspondence from Roy Johnston, 16 May 2001.

25. C. D. Greaves, *Reminiscences of the Connolly Association* (London: Connolly Association, 1978), p. 34.

26. S. Redmond, *Desmond Greaves and the Origins of the Civil Rights Movement in Northern Ireland* (London: Connolly Publications, 2000).

27. Anthony Coughlan, interviewed by the author, Dublin, 5 Feb. 1988.

28. C. D. Greaves, *The Life and Times of James Connolly* (London: Lawrence and Wishart, 1972; 1st edn 1961); Coughlan, *Greaves*, p. 20.

29. D. Kelleher, *Irish Republicanism: The Authentic Perspective* (Greystones: Justice Books, 2001), p. iii; cf. D. Kelleher, *An Open Letter to Ian Paisley: Demythologising History* (Greystones: Justice Books, n.d.), p. 13, and D. Kelleher, *Buried Alive in Ireland: A Story of a Twentieth-Century Inquisition* (Greystones: Justice Books, 2001), p. vii.

30. Kelleher, *Irish Republicanism*, pp. 160, 168.

31. Constitution of Wolfe Tone Societies, quoted in Patterson, *Politics of Illusion*, p. 101.

32. *Tuairisc* (no. 6) June 1966.

33. A. Coughlan, 'Our Ideas', *Tuairisc* (no. 7) 31 Aug. 1966.

34. B. Purdie, *Politics in the Streets: The Origins of the Civil Rights Movement in Northern Ireland* (Belfast: Blackstaff Press, 1990), pp. 130, 132.

35. B. Purdie, 'Was the Civil Rights Movement a Republican/Communist Conspiracy?', *Irish Political Studies* 3 (1988), pp. 33, 34, 36.

36. Adams, *Politics of Irish Freedom*, pp. 12, 17.

37. Ibid., p. 10.

38. Danny Morrison, interviewed by the author, Belfast, 26 May 2000. Danny Morrison: born in Belfast in 1953, editor of *Republican News* 1975–9 and of *An Phoblacht/Republican News* 1979–82; writer and, for years, a leading Sinn Féin politician.

39. *IN* 4 Aug. 1969.

40. *BT* 16 Feb. 1966.

41. *United Irishman* Jan. 1967.

42. CSJNI: founded in Dungannon in January 1964 by Conn and Patricia McCluskey; a small group of Catholic professional people producing well documented publicity regarding civil rights abuses.

43. DCAC: formed in Derry in October 1968; a comparatively moderate group comprising members from the Catholic professional and business classes.

44. For a thoughtful treatment of the PD, see P. Arthur, *The People's Democracy 1968–1973* (Belfast: Blackstaff Press, 1974).

45. Michael Farrell, quoted in Purdie, *Politics in the Streets*, p. 230.

46. B. Devlin, *The Price of My Soul* (London: Pan, 1969), pp. 13, 55, 88.

47. E. McCann, *War and an Irish Town* (London: Pluto Press, 1993; 1st edn 1974), pp. 59, 62, 95.

48. N. Ó Dochartaigh, *From Civil Rights to Armalites: Derry and the Birth of the Irish Troubles* (Cork: Cork University Press, 1997), pp. xvii–xviii.

49. On 22 November 1968 the government announced that local authorities would publish a scheme for the allocation of houses; that an Ombudsman was to be appointed to investigate grievances in central governmental administration; that the business vote in local government elections was to be abolished and that comprehensive reform of local government was to follow; that the Special Powers Act was to be reviewed; and that Londonderry City Council was to be suspended. The following year, further reforms were announced: the setting up of a central housing authority; the establishment of a Ministry of Community Relations and of an independent Community Relations Commission;

the appointment of a local government commissioner for complaints; universal suffrage in local elections; and the introduction of a bill to curb incitement to hatred. 1960s reform in Northern Ireland might be judged to have occurred too late, or to have been insufficiently dramatic; but reform there unquestionably was and it would be unhistorical to ignore it.

50. Devlin, *Price*, p. 120.
51. K. Bloomfield, *Stormont in Crisis: A Memoir* (Belfast: Blackstaff Press, 1994), p. 102.
52. Correspondence from Roy Johnston, 16 May 2001.
53. Roy Johnston, manuscript (2001) dealing with Sinn Féin Ard Comhairle Minutes, copy in the author's possession.
54. Greaves, *Reminiscences*, p. 33.
55. S. MacStiofáin, *Memoirs of a Revolutionary* (Edinburgh: Gordon Cremonesi, 1975), p. 116.
56. For example, Michael Farrell and Kevin Boyle (both PD members) were elected to the NICRA Executive in February 1969.
57. B. Dooley, *Black and Green: The Fight for Civil Rights in Northern Ireland and Black America* (London: Pluto Press, 1998), p. 4.
58. *Disturbances in Northern Ireland: Report of the Commission Appointed by the Governor of Northern Ireland* (Belfast: HMSO, 1969), p. 63.
59. B. Faulkner, *Memoirs of a Statesman* (London: Weidenfeld and Nicolson, 1978), p. 47.
60. G. FitzGerald, *Towards a New Ireland* (Dublin: Torc, 1973; 1st edn 1972), pp. 122–3.
61. McCann, *War and an Irish Town*, p. 83.
62. P. Doherty and P. Hegarty, *Paddy Bogside* (Cork: Mercier, 2001), p. 72.
63. Gerry Adams, in M. Farrell (ed.), *Twenty Years On* (Dingle: Brandon, 1988), p. 47.
64. Ó Dochartaigh, *From Civil Rights*, p. 26.
65. J. Callaghan, *A House Divided: The Dilemma of Northern Ireland* (London: William Collins, 1973), p. 15.
66. *IN* 4 Aug. 1969.
67. James Chichester-Clark (born 1923): Eton-educated Prime Minister of Northern Ireland, 1969–71; had fought, and been wounded, in the British Army during the Second World War. See C. Scoular, *James Chichester-Clark: Prime Minister of Northern Ireland* (Killyleagh: Clive Scoular, 2000).
68. *IN* 13 Aug. 1969.
69. M. Dewar, *The British Army in Northern Ireland* (London: Arms and Armour Press, 1985), p. 33.

70. P. Fiacc, 'Elegy for a "Fenian Get"' in *Ruined Pages: Selected Poems* (Belfast: Blackstaff Press, 1994), p. 112.

71. See, among the many examples, R. W. White, *Provisional Irish Republicans: An Oral and Interpretive History* (Westport: Greenwood Press, 1993), p. 64; D. De Bréadún, *The Far Side of Revenge: Making Peace in Northern Ireland* (Cork: Collins, 2001), p. 2; Adams, *Politics of Irish Freedom*, pp. 31, 42, 150; J. B. Bell, *The IRA 1968–2000: Analysis of a Secret Army* (London: Frank Cass, 2000), pp. 50, 169.

72. Literally, a pogrom is an organized massacre. Awful though the events of mid-August undoubtedly were, they were simply not on that scale.

73. *Irish Independent* 10 Jan. 2000.

74. Summary of Northern Ireland Situation, 31 Aug. 1969, Military Intelligence File 4, NAD. Other sources confirm that southern republicans were active in the north in August 1969; see, for example, J. O'Neill, *Blood-Dark Track: A Family History* (London: Granta, 2000), pp. 234–5.

75. Billy McKee, quoted in P. Taylor, *Provos: The IRA and Sinn Féin* (London: Bloomsbury, 1977), p. 61.

76. *IN* 29 Dec. 1969.

77. Ruairí Ó Brádaigh, quoted in Quinn, *Rebel Voice*, pp. 152–3.

78. *IN* 29 Dec. 1969.

79. Danny Morrison, speaking on 9 Nov. 1986, quoted in *AP/RN* 13 Nov. 1986.

80. B. Mawhinney and R. Wells, *Conflict and Christianity in Northern Ireland* (Berkhamsted: Lion, 1975), pp. 46, 109.

81. G. Adams, *Before the Dawn: An Autobiography* (London: Heinemann, 1996), p. 73.

82. G. J. Mitchell, *Making Peace* (London: William Heinemann, 1999), p. 111. George Mitchell: born 1933; lawyer and US Democratic Senator; chair of peace talks which produced the 1998 Belfast Agreement.

83. Adams, *Before the Dawn*, p. 122.

84. G. Adams, *An Irish Journal* (Dingle: Brandon, 2001), p. 195.

85. Adams, *Politics of Irish Freedom*, p. 3. This strong attachment to locality is striking among many Provisionals, including the highly influential Danny Morrison: 'I think I would find it extremely hard to live anywhere but Belfast, or, more precisely, west Belfast' (D. Morrison, *Then the Walls Came Down: A Prison Journal* (Cork: Mercier, 1999), p. 66).

86. Tommy McKearney, interviewed by the author, Belfast, 20 Sept. 2000.

87. Adams, *Before the Dawn*, p. 44.

88. Figures from M. Sutton, *Bear in Mind These Dead: An Index of Deaths from the Conflict in Ireland 1969–1993* (Belfast: Beyond the Pale, 1994), pp. 5–47.

89. For fine treatments of Adams's life and politics (and IRA involvement), see D. Sharrock and M. Devenport, *Man of War, Man of Peace: The Unauthorised Biography of Gerry Adams* (London: Pan, 1998; 1st edn 1997); Moloney, *Secret History*.

90. Ruairí Ó Brádaigh, speaking on 29 Aug. 1971, quoted in *IN* 30 Aug. 1971.

91. M. McGuire, *To Take Arms: A Year in the Provisional IRA* (London: Quartet, 1973), p. 54.

92. Tommy Gorman, quoted in J. Stevenson, *'We Wrecked the Place': Contemplating an End to the Northern Irish Troubles* (New York: Free Press, 1996), p. 54. Tommy Gorman: born Belfast 1945; joined IRA 1970; interned 1971, escaped 1972, interned 1973–5; on the blanket protest 1978–81; imprisoned again 1981–6.

93. *IN* 11 Jan. 1992.

94. Billy McKee, quoted in Quinn, *Rebel Voice*, p. 138.

95. R. Ó Brádaigh, *Dílseacht: The Story of Comdt. General Tom Maguire and the Second (All-Ireland) Dáil* (Dublin: Irish Freedom Press, 1997), pp. 1, 3, 54.

96. *IP* 5 Jan. 1970.

97. *Saoirse* Nov. 1991.

98. *An Phoblacht*: in the summer of 1972 Coleman Moynihan succeeded Sean Ó Brádaigh as editor; Moynihan was arrested in November 1972 and Eamonn Mac Thomais replaced him; in July 1973 Mac Thomais was arrested, charged with IRA membership and (in August 1973) sentenced to fifteen months' imprisonment – he was succeeded as *AP* editor by Deasun Breathnach; after completing his sentence, in July 1974, Mac Thomais again became editor, briefly; subsequently, the position was held by Gerry Danaher (1974–5); Gerry O'Hare (1975–7); Deasun Breathnach (1977–9).

99. *Republican News*: editors after Steele were Proinsias Mac Airt (1970–2); Leo Martin, assisted by Henry Kane (1973–4); Sean McCaughey (1974–5); Danny Morrison (1975–9).

100. MacStiofáin, *Memoirs*, p. 138.

101. N. Ó Dochartaigh, ' "Sure, It's Hard to Keep up with the Splits Here": Irish-American Responses to the Outbreak of Conflict in Northern Ireland 1968–1974', *Irish Political Studies* 10 (1995), p. 140.

102. George Harrison, interviewed by the author, New York, 30 Oct. 2000.

103. George Harrison, quoted in Ó Brádaigh, *Dílseacht*, p. 84.

104. George Harrison, interviewed by the author, New York, 30 Oct. 2000.

105. George Harrison, quoted in Institute for the Study of Terrorism, *IRA, INLA: Foreign Support and International Connections* (London: Institute for the Study of Terrorism, 1988), p. 57.

106. D. Barzilay, *The British Army in Ulster: vol. 1* (Belfast: Century Services, 1973), p. 131.
107. George Harrison, interviewed by the author, New York, 30 Oct. 2000.
108. R. Byron, *Irish America* (Oxford: Oxford University Press, 1999), pp. 257–8.
109. Ruairí Ó Brádaigh, in D. O'Reilly (ed.), *Accepting the Challenge: The Memoirs of Michael Flannery* (Dublin: Irish Freedom Press, 2001), p. iv.
110. Interim Report of Planning Board on Northern Ireland Operations (1969), Military Intelligence Files, NAD.
111. Ministerial Directive to Chief of Staff, 6 Feb. 1970, Military Intelligence Files, NAD; Brief for Ceann Fóirne, 9 June 1970, ibid.
112. Ministerial Directive to Chief of Staff, 6 Feb. 1970, Military Intelligence Files, NAD.
113. Cabinet Minutes, 16 Aug. 1969, NAD 2000/9/2.
114. Captain James Joseph Kelly: enlisted in the Defence Forces as a Private, Feb. 1949; awarded cadetship, May 1949; commissioned 2nd Lieutenant, May 1951; Lieutenant, May 1953; Captain, Oct. 1960.
115. J. Kelly, *The Thimbleriggers: The Dublin Arms Trials of 1970* (Dublin: James Kelly, 1999), p. viii.
116. See the fine treatment in J. O'Brien, *The Arms Trial* (Dublin: Gill and Macmillan, 2000), and also in Patterson, *Politics of Illusion*.
117. 'All Irish Traditions', address on RTÉ, 11 July 1970, copy in Military Intelligence File: NICRA, NAD.
118. Lynch to Heath, 11 Aug. 1970, PROL PREM 15/101.
119. Speaking on 21 Aug. 1971, quoted in *IN* 23 Aug. 1971.
120. MacStiofáin, *Memoirs*, p. 123.
121. *IP* 5 Feb. 1971.
122. D. Morrison, *West Belfast* (Cork: Mercier, 1989), p. 114.
123. *IP* 6 Feb. 1971.
124. P. Magee, *Gangsters or Guerrillas? Representations of Irish Republicans in 'Troubles Fiction'* (Belfast: Beyond the Pale, 2001), p. 41.
125. Danny Morrison, interviewed by the author, Belfast, 26 May 2000.
126. *AP/RN* 25 Sept. 1997.
127. Patrick Magee, interviewed by the author, Belfast, 5 Mar. 2002. Patrick Magee: born Belfast, 1951; family moved to England when he was four; he returned to Belfast when nineteen (briefly) and when twenty (for good); joined IRA aged twenty-one; interned 1973–5; jailed 1985–99 for his role in the 1984 Brighton bombing of the British Conservative Party Conference.
128. Ex-IRA man, interviewed by the author, Belfast, 31 Oct. 2001.

129. Ballymacarrett Research Group, *Lagan Enclave: A History of Conflict in the Short Strand 1886–1997* (Belfast: BRG, 1997), p. 60.
130. George Harrison, interviewed by the author, New York, 30 Oct. 2000.
131. Pat McGeown was born in 1956; joined the IRA's youth wing (Fianna Eireann) aged thirteen; was involved as a teenager in Belfast bombings; and was repeatedly imprisoned and interned; he died aged forty.
132. Pat McGeown, quoted in L. Clarke, *Broadening the Battlefield: The H-Blocks and the Rise of Sinn Féin* (Dublin: Gill and Macmillan, 1987), p. 16.
133. Tommy Gorman, interviewed by the author, Belfast, 2 May 2001.
134. Ex-IRA man, interviewed by the author, Belfast, 31 Oct. 2001.
135. Tommy McKearney, interviewed by the author, Belfast, 20 Sept. 2000.
136. Anthony McIntyre, interviewed by the author, Belfast, 23 Aug. 2000. McIntyre was born in Belfast in 1957; grew up in the working-class Catholic lower Ormeau Road area of Belfast; joined the IRA in 1973; and was jailed 1974–5 and 1976–92.
137. Patrick Magee, quoted in *Guardian* 10 Dec. 2001.
138. *AP/RN* 28 June 1980.
139. Quoted in O Connor, *In Search of a State*, p. 140; see also the important points made in S. O'Callaghan, *The Informer* (London: Bantam, 1998), pp. 54, 76, 81.
140. Collins, *Killing Rage*, pp. 30, 32, 36–7.
141. *IN* 29 Dec. 1969.
142. *Times* 4 June 1971.
143. MacStiofáin, *Memoirs*, pp. 115, 123.
144. *BT* 4 Jan. 1971.
145. *RN* 1 Sept. 1973.
146. Adams, *Before the Dawn*, p. 51.
147. Tommy McKearney, interviewed by the author, Belfast, 20 Sept. 2000.
148. Martin McGuinness (speaking on 10 Sept. 2001), quoted in *Corrymeela Connections* 3, 2 (2001), p. 8. Martin McGuinness: born in Derry in 1950; joined the IRA in 1970 and became a leading figure in the organization in his home city and beyond; late 1970s became IRA Chief of Staff; elected Westminster MP, 1997; Northern Ireland Minister for Education from 1999; in the latter post, committed to abolishing Northern Ireland's eleven-plus examination (though his own experience proves that failure in that examination need not preclude a powerful career). For biographical detail, see L. Clarke and K. Johnston, *Martin McGuinness: From Guns to Government* (Edinburgh: Mainstream, 2001).
149. *IP* 2 June 1971.
150. Morrison, *West Belfast*, p. 103.

151. *RN* 28 July 1972.
152. McGuire, *To Take Arms*, p. 65.
153. Roy Johnston, manuscript (2001) dealing with Sinn Féin Ard Comhairle Minutes, copy in the author's possession.
154. 'Peace with Justice' (1972, reprinted 1974), copy in McLaughlin Papers, PRONI D2879/6/1A.
155. *IN* 6 Sept. 1971.
156. *RN* 30 Oct. 1971.
157. *RN* 3 Nov. 1972.
158. Patrick Magee, interviewed by the author, Belfast, 5 Mar. 2002.
159. R. Ó Brádaigh, *What is Irish Republicanism?* (1970), LHLPC, Sinn Féin (Provisional) Box 1.
160. *RN* 15 Nov. 1975.
161. S. O'Doherty, *The Volunteer: A Former IRA Man's True Story* (London: Fount, 1993), pp. 12, 16–17, 27–37.
162. Marian Price, interviewed by the author, Belfast, 28 Feb. 2002. Marian Price: born in Belfast, 1954; grew up in Andersonstown; joined the IRA aged seventeen.
163. Tommy McKearney, interviewed by the author, Belfast, 20 Sept. 2000.
164. Provisional IRA statement of 28 Dec. 1969, quoted in *IN* 29 Dec. 1969. One of the sharpest recent commentators on republican politics, Anthony McIntyre, has rightly stressed the role of contemporary urgency and circumstance in producing the Provisionals. But it is important also to note the other side of this coin. McIntyre quotes part of the above statement to support his view that the Provisionals resulted from 'a dynamic different from that of traditional republicanism', and that 1916 and all that possessed little relevance for them in their early days (A. McIntyre, 'Modern Irish Republicanism and the Belfast Agreement: Chickens Coming Home to Roost, or Turkeys Celebrating Christmas?' in R. Wilford (ed.), *Aspects of the Belfast Agreement* (Oxford: Oxford University Press, 2001), pp. 210–12). But this same IRA statement does explicitly, loyally and centrally refer to the importance of Easter 1916, and it seems a more rounded interpretation to accept that both traditional republican thinking *and* immediate exigency played their part in producing the Provisionals.
165. Danny Morrison, interviewed by the author, Belfast, 26 May 2000.
166. Marian Price, interviewed by the author, Belfast, 28 Feb. 2002.
167. MacStiofáin, *Memoirs*, p. 135.
168. 'I just want a fair, square deal, and rights for everybody. And you won't get that under a capitalist system. I'm anticapitalist' (Seán MacStiofáin, quoted in White, *Provisional Irish Republicans*, p. 35).

169. 'Peace with Justice' (1972, reprinted 1974), copy in McLaughlin Papers, PRONI D2879/6/1A.

170. *BT* 15 Feb. 1966.

171. Martin McGuinness, quoted in Clarke and Johnston, *McGuinness*, p. 15.

172. McGuire, *To Take Arms*, p. 66.

173. *IP* 6 Feb. 1971.

174. Cathal Goulding, quoted in P. Bishop and E. Mallie, *The Provisional IRA* (London: Corgi, 1988; 1st edn 1987), p. 86.

175. Constitution of the SDLP, quoted in I. McAllister, *The Northern Ireland Social Democratic and Labour Party: Political Opposition in a Divided Society* (London: Macmillan, 1977), p. 168.

176. O'Callaghan, *Informer*, p. 69. O'Callaghan became disillusioned with the IRA ('I knew that I had devoted five years of my life to something that was evil ... I realised that joining the Provisional IRA had been the biggest mistake of my life' (ibid., p. 85)), and became a valuable informant for the police in the Republic of Ireland: 'by June 1985 I was OC of the IRA's Southern Command, a member of GHQ staff, a member of Sinn Féin's National Executive and a local councillor – as well as being a high-level informer for the Irish police' (ibid., p. 214).

177. Martin McGuinness, quoted in Clarke and Johnston, *McGuinness*, p. 47.

178. Sharrock and Devenport, *Man of War, Man of Peace*, p. 42.

179. Taylor, *Provos*, pp. 57–8.

180. Collins, *Killing Rage*, p. 41.

181. Anthony McIntyre, interviewed by the author, Belfast, 23 Aug. 2000.

182. MacStiofáin, *Memoirs*, p. 115.

183. *AP/RN* 28 June 1980.

184. Billy McKee, quoted in Taylor, *Provos*, p. 77.

185. See, for example, '2001 Republican Roll of Honour' in *AP/RN* Diary for 2001.

186. *AP* Jan. 1972.

187. Conclusions of a Meeting of the Cabinet held at Stormont Castle, 7 July 1970, PRONI CAB 4/1532/15.

188. Adams, *Politics of Irish Freedom*, p. 55.

189. Report on Period 9 am 18 Aug. [1970] to 9 am 19 Aug. [1970], PROL PREM 15/101.

190. Ministry of Defence, Chiefs of Staff Committee, Memorandum 61, 11 Sept. 1970, PROL DEFE 5/186.

191. Edward Heath: born 1916; Conservative Party leader 1965–75; UK Prime Minister 1970–4.

192. Note of the Prime Minister's Meeting with the Prime Minister of Northern Ireland, 17 July 1970, PROL PREM 15/101.

193. Lynch to Heath, 7 July 1970, PROL PREM 15/100.

194. *IN* 3 Nov. 1970.

195. *BT* 8 Feb. 1971.

196. H. McCallion, *Killing Zone* (London: Bloomsbury, 1995), p. 30.

197. Tommy Gorman, interviewed by the author, Belfast, 2 May 2001.

198. Brian Faulkner (1921–77): born in County Down, but educated in County Dublin; Northern Irish Minister of Home Affairs (1959), Minister of Commerce (1963) and Prime Minister (1971–2); 1973–4, backed the Sunningdale power-sharing/Irish dimension deal and became head of the brief administration thus established.

199. *BT* 23 Mar. 1971.

200. Martin McGuinness, quoted in Bishop and Mallie, *Provisional IRA*, p. 183.

201. Conclusions of a Meeting of the Cabinet held at Stormont Castle, 9 Aug. 1971, PRONI CAB 4/1607/14.

202. Faulkner maintained that internment 'applied to anyone, regardless of political or religious affiliation, about whom there was information to justify detention; at present he was advised there was no case to justify the detention of Protestants' (Conclusions of a Meeting of the Cabinet held at Stormont Castle, 17 Aug. 1971, PRONI CAB 4/1609/17).

203. *RN* Dec. 1970/Jan. 1971.

204. Joe Cahill, quoted in Quinn, *Rebel Voice*, p. 175.

205. *IN* 14 Aug. 1971.

206. W. Whitelaw, *The Whitelaw Memoirs* (London: Aurum Press, 1989), p. 78.

207. Dewar, *British Army*, p. 54.

208. Captain, 2 Royal Green Jackets, quoted in M. Arthur, *Northern Ireland Soldiers Talking* (London: Sidgwick and Jackson, 1987), p. 56.

209. Callaghan, *House Divided*, p. 168.

210. Quoted in E. Fairweather, R. McDonough and M. McFadyean, *Only the Rivers Run Free: Northern Ireland – The Women's War* (London: Pluto Press, 1984), pp. 234–6.

211. Tommy Gorman, interviewed by the author, Belfast, 2 May 2001.

212. For other evidence of brutality towards internees, see J. Holland, *Too Long a Sacrifice: Life and Death in Northern Ireland Since 1969* (New York: Dodd, Mead and Co., 1981), ch. 3; J. McGuffin, *Internment* (Tralee: Anvil, 1973), pp. 119–27.

213. Note of a Meeting held at Chequers, 19 Aug. 1971, PRONI CAB 4/1607/19.

214. Martin McGuinness, quoted in *Corrymeela Connections* 3, 2 (2001), p. 8; K. Toolis, *Rebel Hearts: Journeys within the IRA's Soul* (London: Picador, 1995), p. 304.

215. Martin McGuinness, quoted in *IT* 30 Jan. 1973.
216. Martin McGuinness, quoted in *Observer* 6 Feb. 2000.
217. *IN* 21 Dec. 1971.
218. Conclusions of a Meeting of the Cabinet held at Stormont Castle, 10 Aug. 1971, PRONI CAB 4/1608/19.
219. Note of a Meeting held at Chequers, 19 Aug. 1971, PRONI CAB 4/1607/19.
220. See the files of cuttings, 'Republican Movement (Provisional Council)', Defence Forces Files, NAD G2/C/1866 and 'Sinn Féin – Brady Group', Defence Forces Files, NAD C/1888A.
221. P. Delaney, 'Effectivity of the Defence Forces', 5 July 1971, Defence Forces Files, NAD SCS 18/1.
222. P. Delaney, 'Military Commitments and Requirements', 13 July 1971, Defence Forces Files, NAD SCS 18/1.
223. T. O'Carroll, 'Contingencies August 1971: Military Considerations', 23 Aug. 1971, Defence Forces Files, NAD SCS 18/15.
224. *AP* Jan. 1972.
225. *RN* 2 Jan. 1972.
226. R. Tuck, *The Rights of War and Peace: Political Thought and the International Order from Grotius to Kant* (Oxford: Oxford University Press, 1999), p. 130.
227. *IN* 6 Aug. 1969.
228. One recent study (devoted to answering the central question of why London did not act sooner during the crisis which erupted in the 1960s) has concluded 'that there was a real chance that earlier intervention by the [London] government might have prevented the rise of the Provisional IRA without provoking an unmanageable Protestant backlash' (P. Rose, *How the Troubles Came to Northern Ireland* (Basingstoke: Palgrave, 2001; 1st edn 2000), p. xvi).
229. S. Bruce, *God Save Ulster! The Religion and Politics of Paisleyism* (Oxford: Oxford University Press, 1989; 1st edn 1986).
230. New Year Message from the IRA's Belfast Brigade, quoted in *RN* 3 Jan. 1976.

FOUR: THE POLITICS OF VIOLENCE 1972–6

1. *Bloody Sunday, 1972: Lord Widgery's Report of Events in Londonderry, Northern Ireland, on 30 January 1972* (London: Stationery Office, 2001; 1st edn 1972), p. 98.
2. *IN* 28 Jan. 1972.

3. Ita McKinney and Kay Duddy, quoted in E. McCann, M. Shiels and B. Hannigan, *Bloody Sunday in Derry: What Really Happened* (Dingle: Brandon, 1992), pp. 24, 132.

4. M. Asher, *Shoot to Kill: A Soldier's Journey through Violence* (London: Viking, 1990), p. 65.

5. Martin McGuinness, quoted in *Independent* 24 Jan. 2002.

6. On this shot, see *Sunday Times* Magazine 26 Jan. 1992. Others argue that it was the British soldiers who fired the first shots on Bloody Sunday (D. Mullan (ed.), *Eyewitness Bloody Sunday* (Dublin: Wolfhound, 1997), p. 85).

7. *IN* 31 Jan. 1972.

8. W. Whitelaw, *The Whitelaw Memoirs* (London: Anrum Press, 1989), p. 79.

9. P. Magee, *Gangsters or Guerrillas? Representations of Irish Republicans in 'Troubles Fiction'* (Belfast: Beyond the Pale, 2001), p. 65.

10. Eamonn MacDermott, quoted in K. Bean and M. Hayes (eds), *Republican Voices* (Monaghan: Seesyu Press, 2001), p. 41.

11. D. O'Reilly (ed.), *Accepting the Challenge: The Memoirs of Michael Flannery* (Dublin Irish Freedom Press, 2001), p. 143.

12. *Bloody Sunday, 1972*, p. 99.

13. See, for example, the persuasive arguments offered in D. P. J. Walsh, *Bloody Sunday and the Rule of Law in Northern Ireland* (Basingstoke: Macmillan, 2000).

14. *Bloody Sunday, 1972*, pp. 94, 96.

15. *DJ* 21 Apr. 1972.

16. Note, for example, two well publicized films shown on television early in 2002, thirty years after the event: *Sunday* (written by Jimmy McGovern and directed by Charles McDougall) and Granada/Hell's Kitchen's *Bloody Sunday*.

17. Martin McGuinness, speaking on 30 Apr. 2001, quoted in *Guardian* 1 May 2001.

18. G. Adams, *An Irish Journal* (Dingle: Brandon, 2001), p. 89.

19. *IN* 26 Jan. 1972.

20. *Bloody Sunday, 1972*, p. 32.

21. *IN* 11 Mar. 1972.

22. Sean MacStiofáin, quoted in *IN* 25 Mar. 1972.

23. *IN* 6 Mar. 1972.

24. *IN* 14 June 1972.

25. William Whitelaw, quoted in *IN* 23 June 1972.

26. Whitelaw, *Whitelaw Memoirs*, pp. 99–100.

27. S. MacStiofáin, *Memoirs of a Revolutionary* (Edinburgh: Gordon Cremonesi, 1975), p. 281.

28. Whitelaw, *Whitelaw Memoirs*, p. 100.

29. Sinn Féin, *Eire Nua is Local Democracy* (Dublin: Elo Press, 1974), p. 6.

30. *BT* 22 July 1972.

31. *BT* 31 July 1972.

32. S. McKendry, *Disappeared: The Search for Jean McConville* (Dublin: Blackwater, 2000); Moloney, *Secret History*, pp. 122–5.

33. Figures taken from the excellent volume, D. McKittrick, S. Kelters, B. Feeney and C. Thornton, *Lost Lives: The Stories of the Men, Women and Children Who Died as a Result of the Northern Ireland Troubles* (Edinburgh: Mainstream, 2001; 1st edn 1999), p. 1495.

34. G. Adams, *Before the Dawn: an Autobiography* (London: Heinemann, 1996), p. 210.

35. *IN* 22 May 1973.

36. Broadcasting by the IRA had long been prohibited in practice in the Republic, but the relevant legislation did not explicitly name them. After O'Brien's amending legislation, this ambiguity was removed.

37. C. C. O'Brien, *Memoir: My Life and Themes* (Dublin: Poolbeg, 1998), p. 356.

38. Martin McGuinness, quoted in *IT* 30 Jan. 1973.

39. *RN* 16 Feb. 1973.

40. Patrick Magee, interviewed by the author, Belfast, 5 Mar. 2002. Some context is important here. In Magee's view, Adams was:

> warning that unless we developed politically, that is, that we secured the political strength and means to counter our enemies, then we were inevitably faced with the long-war course. That or defeat. I would argue that in fact the long war endured for so long because the republican movement's best attempts to negotiate for peace were continually thwarted by the machinations of the British and Irish political establishments. There have been many missed opportunities when peace could have been furthered, for example, the truce in 1972, and again in 1974–75 (correspondence from Patrick Magee, 13 May 2002).

41. Gerry Kelly: born Belfast 1953; joined the republican movement in 1970; married, 1973, while on remand in Brixton prison; 1983, one of the main organizers of a republican escape from the Maze Prison; captured Amsterdam, 1986; released from prison, 1989; 1990–3, involved in secret contacts with British representatives; 1990s, a prominent Sinn Féin politician.

42. *IT* 16 Nov. 1973.

43. Marian Price, interviewed by the author, Belfast, 28 Feb. 2002.

44. Dolours and Marian Price, Brixton Prison, 17 Mar. 1974, in *Prison Writings of the Price Sisters*, p. 13, copy in LHLPC.
45. Marian Price, interviewed by the author, Belfast, 28 Feb. 2002.
46. R. Jenkins, *A Life at the Centre* (London: Macmillan, 1991), p. 378. The Price sisters eventually came off their strike, and were moved to jail in Northern Ireland in 1975.
47. Sunningdale Agreement, reprinted in M. Elliott (ed.), *The Long Road to Peace in Northern Ireland* (Liverpool: Liverpool University Press, 2002), p. 189.
48. See the perceptive essay by Gordon Gillespie: 'The Sunningdale Agreement: Lost Opportunity or an Agreement Too Far?', *Irish Political Studies* 13 (1998).
49. *RN* 30 Apr. 1975.
50. *RN* 6 Dec. 1975.
51. *RN* 22 Dec. 1973.
52. For example, 'the Provisionals have forged links with the revolutionary left in France, West Germany, Italy, Holland, Spain, Austria and Belgium, benefiting from the work of solidarity committees and laying the groundwork for informal links with terrorist groups in those countries' (M. Tugwell, 'Politics and Propaganda of the Provisional IRA' in P. Wilkinson (ed.), *British Perspectives on Terrorism* (London: George Allen and Unwin, 1981), p. 23).
53. *IN* 23 Apr. 1974.
54. *IT* 7 Oct. 1974.
55. G. Conlon, *Proved Innocent* (Harmondsworth: Penguin, 1993; 1st edn 1990), p. 58.
56. *AP/RN* 1 Mar. 1980.
57. P. Hill and R. Bennett, *Stolen Years: Before and After Guildford* (London: Doubleday, 1990), p. 56.
58. Conlon, *Proved Innocent*, pp. 3–4.
59. *IT* 18 Nov. 1974.
60. *IT* 22 Nov. 1974.
61. See his important book, C. Mullin, *Error of Judgement: The Truth about the Birmingham Bombings* (Dublin: Poolbeg, 1990; 1st edn 1986).
62. See, for example, *AP/RN* 24 Aug. 1989.
63. *RN* 2 Nov. 1974.
64. *RN* 7 Feb. 1976.
65. *BT* 2 Sept. 1975.
66. *BT* 6 Jan. 1976.
67. *RN* 10 Jan. 1976.
68. H. McCallion, *Killing Zone* (London: Bloomsbury, 1995), p. 159.

69. P. Durcan, 'The Minibus Massacre: The Eve of the Epiphany' in *The Selected Paul Durcan* (Belfast: Blackstaff Press, 1985; 1st edn 1982), p. 94.
70. Billy Wright, quoted in T. Harnden, *'Bandit Country': The IRA and South Armagh* (London: Hodder and Stoughton, 1999), p. 140.
71. McKittrick et al., *Lost Lives*, pp. 1494–5.
72. Anthony McIntyre, interviewed by the author, Belfast, 23 Aug. 2000.
73. Tommy McKearney, interviewed by the author, Belfast, 20 Sept. 2000.
74. Tommy McKearney, interviewed by the author, Belfast, 20 Sept. 2000.
75. *United Irishman* June 1972.
76. T. MacGiolla, *Where We Stand: The Republican Position* (Dublin: Workers' Party of Ireland, 2000; 1st edn 1972), p. 30.
77. *RN* 23 June 1973.
78. Dessie O'Hagan, interviewed by the author, Belfast, 5 Mar. 2002.
79. INLA member, quoted in J. Holland and H. McDonald, *INLA: Deadly Divisions* (Dublin: Torc, 1994), p. 33.
80. *IN* 14 Dec. 1974.
81. E. Gallagher and S. Worrall, *Christians in Ulster* (Oxford: Oxford University Press, 1982), p. 1.
82. *IN* 13 Dec. 1974.
83. Quoted in Gallagher and Worrall, *Christians in Ulster*, p. 101.
84. *IT* 9 Nov. 1974.
85. *RN* 1 May 1976.
86. *RN* 7 June 1975.
87. Danny Morrison, interviewed by the author, Belfast, 23 Jan. 2002.
88. *RN* 18 Oct. 1975
89. *RN* 1 May 1976.
90. *RN* 3 Jan. 1976
91. *RN* 13 Mar. 1976.

FIVE: THE PRISON WAR 1976–81

1. Copy in LHLPC.
2. Tom Hartley: born in Belfast 1945; joined the republican movement in the late 1960s; eminent Sinn Féiner during the 1990s.
3. Tom Hartley, interviewed by the author, Belfast, 24 Oct. 2001; cf. C. von Clausewitz, *On War* (Harmondsworth: Penguin, 1968; 1st edn 1832), pp. 103–4.
4. *RN* 16 Aug. 1975.
5. G. Adams, *Cage Eleven* (Dingle: Brandon, 1990), p. 10.

6. L. McKeown, *Out of Time: Irish Republican Prisoners Long Kesh 1972–2000* (Belfast: Beyond the Pale, 2001), p. xiii.

7. Press Release, Sentenced Republican Prisoners (Provisional), Long Kesh, 18 July 1975, LHLPC.

8. Statement on behalf of republican prisoners (remand) in Crumlin Road Jail, 28 July 1976, LHLPC.

9. D. Morrison, *Then the Walls Came Down: A Prison Journal* (Cork: Mercier, 1999), p. 316.

10. 'From H-5 Block Long Kesh to the Citizens of the USA, from the Irish Republican Prisoners of War Presently Engaged in Struggle on the Blanket Protest in the H-Blocks of Long Kesh Concentration Camp', LHLPC, H-Block/Hunger Strike Box 3.

11. Republican prisoner Brendan 'Bik' McFarlane, quoted in B. Campbell, L. McKeown and F. O'Hagan (eds), *Nor Meekly Serve My Time: The H-Block Struggle 1976–1981* (Belfast: Beyond the Pale, 1994), p. 38.

12. See, for example, the claim that 'brutality and petty harassment have continued to be perpetrated against the 360 H-Block blanket men by the sadistic and sectarian warders' (*AP/RN* 16 Feb. 1980).

13. Statement by PRO, blanket men, H-Blocks, 10 Oct. 1980, LHLPC.

14. Brendan 'The Dark' Hughes: born in Belfast, 1948; from a strongly republican family in the Lower Falls (his father had been interned in Crumlin Road in the 1940s); jailed for fourteen years in 1974 on arms/explosives charges; went on the blanket 1978; OC Long Kesh cages 1977–8; OC H-Blocks 1978–80; released 1986; nicknamed 'The Dark' by British Army on account of his swarthy appearance.

15. Statement to *ard fheis*, 21 Oct. 1980, Brendan Hughes, LHLPC.

16. *Hunger Strike to the Death*, issued by the Ulster Executive of Sinn Féin, 1980, LHLPC, H-Block/Hunger Strike Box 1.

17. Other republican hunger strikes had included those by the 1973 London car-bombers; by Michael Gaughan (who refused food in 1974, was force-fed, and died of pneumonia); by Frank Stagg, who died in 1976 after sixty-two days without food; and by Portlaoise prisoners in 1977.

18. What Will Happen When the Protests End (NIO), 18 Dec. 1980, LHLPC, H-Block/Hunger Strike Box 1.

19. The Maze Protest: Statement by the Governor, 14 Jan. 1981, LHLPC, H-Block/Hunger Strike Box 1.

20. Statement by PRO H-Blocks 3, 4, 5, 6 and PRO Women Political Prisoners, Armagh Jail, 4 Feb. 1981, LHLPC, H-Block/Hunger Strike Box 1.

21. British Renege on Hunger Strike Commitments, issued by National H-

Block/Armagh Committee, Dublin, 1981, LHLPC, H-Block/Hunger Strike Box 1.

22. G. Adams, *An Irish Journal* (Dingle: Brandon, 2001), p. 142.
23. Bobby Sands, quoted in D. Beresford, *Ten Men Dead: The Story of the 1981 Irish Hunger Strike* (London: Grafton, 1987), p. 55.
24. Brendan McFarlane, quoted in ibid., p. 99.
25. Including a poem about a legendary IRA leader of a former generation, 'Tom Barry' (B. Sands, *Prison Poems* (Dublin: Sinn Féin, 1981), p. 77).
26. Ethna Carbery (pseudonym of Anna MacManus, 1866–1902): poet and short story writer; born Ballymena, County Antrim; co-founder in 1896 of *Shan Van Vocht* – a literary Irish nationalist magazine; author, *The Four Winds of Ireland* (1902).
27. L. Uris, *Trinity* (London: Corgi, 1977; 1st edn 1976).
28. B. Sands, *The Diary of Bobby Sands* (Dublin: Sinn Féin, 1981), p. 7.
29. T. Collins, *The Irish Hunger Strike* (Dublin: White Island Book Company, 1986), p. 149.
30. Francis Hughes (8 May 1981), quoted in Beresford, *Ten Men Dead*, p. 167.
31. Frank Maguire (1929–81): County Galway-born publican in Lisnaskea, County Fermanagh, where he had moved as a teenager; IRA man, interned 1957–8; late 1960s, prominent in civil rights movement; 1974, elected MP.
32. Margaret Thatcher: born 1925; leader of the British Conservative Party, 1975–90; UK Prime Minister, 1979–90.
33. Laurence McKeown: born 1956, Randalstown, County Antrim; 1973, joined IRA; 1976, arrested; 1977, sentenced; received four life sentences for causing a series of bomb explosions, and a fifth for the attempted killing of a police officer; released 1992; author, *Out of Time*.
34. Ibid., p. 78.
35. G. Adams, *The Politics of Irish Freedom* (Dingle: Brandon, 1986), p. 80.
36. Marian Price, interviewed by the author, Belfast, 28 Feb. 2002.
37. M. Thatcher, *The Downing Street Years* (London: HarperCollins, 1993), p. 391.
38. Quoted in J. M. Feehan, *Bobby Sands and the Tragedy of Northern Ireland* (Cork: Mercier, 1983), p. 19.
39. Irish Northern Aid (Irish Prisoners of War Committee), *Frankie Hughes 1956–1981*, LHLPC, H-Block/Hunger Strike Box 3.
40. Laurence McKeown, interviewed by the author, Belfast, 21 Jan. 2002.
41. Tommy Gorman, interviewed by the author, Belfast, 2 May 2001.
42. Gerry Kelly, quoted in *AP/RN* 18 May 1995.

43. Ex-IRA man, interviewed by the author, Belfast, 31 Oct. 2001.
44. Statement from republican POWs, H-Blocks, 30 Sept. 1981 (LHLPC, H-Block/Hunger Strike Box 5). The draft version of this statement from 29 September uses the phrase 'suspend the hunger strike' rather than 'end the hunger strike' (Statement from republican POWs in H-Block, 29 Sept. 1981, LHLPC).
45. Pat Sheehan: Belfast republican; arrested 1978; charged in connection with a Belfast bombing; 1979, sentenced to fifteen years; on hunger strike 10 August until 3 October 1981.
46. Jackie McMullan: born in Belfast 1956, grew up in Andersonstown; imprisoned 1976–92; on hunger strike 17 August until 3 October 1981.
47. Tom Hartley, interviewed by the author, Belfast, 24 Oct. 2001.
48. *The Significance of the Hunger Strike*, leaflet issued by the Belfast H-Block/Armagh Committee, 1981, LHLPC, H-Block/Hunger Strike Box 1.
49. Brendan Hughes, speaking on 27 May 1990, *AP/RN* 31 May 1990.
50. Tom Hartley, speaking on 23 Sept. 2001, *AP/RN* 27 Sept. 2001.
51. Tom Hartley, interviewed by the author, Belfast, 24 Oct. 2001.
52. Statement from republican POWs in H-Block, 29 Sept. 1981, LHLPC.
53. *AP/RN* 13 June 1981.
54. *AP/RN* 2 Feb. 1980.
55. Thatcher, *Downing Street Years*, pp. 389–90.
56. *AP/RN* 30 May 1981.
57. Comité de Défense des Prisonniers Politiques Irlandais (Paris), leaflet entitled *Francis Hugues est mort*, 1981, LHLPC, H-Block/Hunger Strike Box 5.
58. Irish Northern Aid (New York), leaflet entitled *Murdered by the British*, 1981, LHLPC, H-Block/Hunger Strike Box 5.
59. Letter of 7 Nov. 1980 from H-Block Committee, Amsterdam, LHLPC, H-Block/Hunger Strike Box 3.
60. N. O'Dowd, 'The Awakening: Irish-America's Key Role in the Irish Peace Process' in M. Elliott (ed.), *The Long Road to Peace in Northern Ireland* (Liverpool, Liverpool University Press, 2002), p. 67.
61. Speaking on 17 May 1987, *AP/RN* 28 May 1987.
62. IRA spokesman, quoted in *AP/RN* 5 Sept. 1981.
63. *AP/RN* 2 May 1991.
64. Danny Morrison, interviewed by the author, Belfast, 26 May 2000.
65. Statement from republican POWs in H-Block, 29 Sept. 1981, LHLPC.
66. Sinn Féin Cumann 'B' Wing H3: report concerning debate held on elections in Ireland in the future, LHLPC.
67. Tom Hartley, interviewed by the author, Belfast, 24 Oct. 2001.

68. Tommy McKearney, interviewed by the author, Belfast, 20 Sept. 2000.
69. Adams, *Irish Journal*, p. 8.
70. Statement from republican POWs, H-Blocks, 30 Sept. 1981, LHLPC, H-Block/Hunger Strike Box 5.
71. Padraig O'Malley's valuable book on the period, for example, presents Sands's fast as being 'in the ancient tradition of the heroic quest, embedded in the hidden recesses of the Celtic consciousness' (P. O'Malley, *Biting at the Grave: The Irish Hunger Strikes and the Politics of Despair* (Belfast: Blackstaff Press, 1990), p. 61).
72. Morrison, *Walls Came Down*, pp. 120–1.
73. J. Conroy, *War as a Way of Life: A Belfast Diary* (London: Heinemann, 1988), p. 154.
74. *An Phobcrapt/Murderers' News* (1989).
75. Warrenpoint was an IRA operation in 1979 in which eighteen British soldiers were killed.
76. Anthony McIntyre, interviewed by the author, Belfast, 23 Aug. 2000.
77. Tommy McKearney, interviewed by the author, Belfast, 20 Sept. 2000.
78. Kieran Nugent, quoted in T. P. Coogan, *On the Blanket: The H-Block Story* (Dublin: Ward River Press, 1980), p. 81. In fact, Albert Miles, Deputy Governor of the Maze, was shot on 26 Nov. 1978 (in Belfast, in front of his wife and son).
79. *RN* 20 Mar. 1976.
80. *AP/RN* 11 Apr. 1981.
81. S. Heaney, *The Redress of Poetry: Oxford Lectures* (London: Faber and Faber, 1995), p. 187.
82. *AP/RN* 1 Feb. 2001.
83. *AP/RN* 26 Sept. 1996.
84. Tom Hartley, interviewed by the author, Belfast, 24 Oct. 2001.
85. Tommy Gorman, interviewed by the author, Belfast, 2 May 2001.
86. McKeown, *Out of Time*, p. 193.
87. Laurence McKeown, interviewed by the author, Belfast, 21 Jan. 2002.
88. Felim O'Hagan, quoted in Campbell, McKeown and O'Hagan (eds), *Nor Meekly*, p. 71.
89. R. McLaughlin, *Inside an English Jail* (Dublin: Borderline, 1987), p. 29. Raymond McLaughlin (1951–85): born Buncrana, County Donegal; IRA Volunteer; imprisoned 1974–83.
90. *Prisoners of War*, leaflet produced by Clonard Martyrs Sinn Féin Cumann, Christmas 1977, LHLPC, H-Block/Hunger Strike Box 1.
91. Father Matt Wallace, quoted in O'Malley, *Biting at the Grave*, p. 109.
92. Millar to Pope John Paul II, 30 Nov. 1980, LHLPC.
93. Sands, *Diary*, p. 12.

94. See J. Whyte, *Church and State in Modern Ireland 1923–1979* (Dublin: Gill and Macmillan, 1984; 1st edn 1971).
95. Hodgins to *Sunday World*, 25 Jan. 1983, LHLPC.
96. Tom Holland, quoted in Campbell, McKeown and O'Hagan (eds), *Nor Meekly*, p. 237.
97. *AP/RN* 25 Apr. 1981.
98. *IN* 22 July 1976.
99. J. Ewart-Biggs, *Pay, Pack and Follow: Memoirs* (London: Weidenfeld and Nicolson, 1984), p. 220.
100. *AP/RN* 5 Jan. 1980.
101. Quoted in T. P. Coogan, *The IRA* (London: HarperCollins, 1987; 1st edn 1970), pp. 679–80.
102. Quoted in ibid., p. 685.
103. *AP/RN* 6 Oct. 1979.
104. *AP/RN* 20 Sept. 1980.
105. *AP/RN* 24 May 1980.
106. *AP/RN* 3 Nov. 1979.
107. *AP/RN* 3 Nov. 1979.
108. Adams to Arnlis [Danny Morrison], 5 Jan. 1977, LHLPC.
109. Piece by R. G. McAuley, Long Kesh, 14 Mar. 1977, LHLPC.
110. *AP/RN* 14 Feb. 1981.
111. *RN* 18 June 1977.
112. J. Parker, *Death of a Hero: Captain Robert Nairac, GC, and the Undercover War in Northern Ireland* (London: Metro, 1999), pp. 253–4; S. McKendry, *Disappeared: The Search for Jean McConville* (Dublin: Blackwater, 2000), p. 71.
113. Quoted in Parker, *Death of a Hero*, p. 9.
114. *AP/RN* 16 May 1981.
115. *BT* 18 Feb. 1978.
116. *RN* 19 Feb. 1977.
117. P. R. Reid, *The Colditz Story* (London: Cassell, 2001; 1st edn 1952), p. 147.
118. P. Routledge, *Public Servant, Secret Agent: The Elusive Life and Violent Death of Airey Neave* (London: Fourth Estate, 2002), pp. 7, 355.
119. *Sunday Life* 10 Mar. 2002.
120. In the autumn of 1978 it was decided that the southern *An Phoblacht* and the northern *Republican News* would amalgamate as *An Phoblacht/ Republican News*. In January 1979 the new paper appeared, *Republican News* having effectively absorbed *An Phoblacht*. The early editors of *AP/ RN* were Danny Morrison (1979–82), Mick Timothy (1982–5) and Rita O'Hare (1985–90).

121. *AP/RN* 1 Sept. 1979.

122. B. Pimlott, *The Queen: A Biography of Elizabeth II* (London: Harper-Collins, 1996), p. 471.

123. *AP/RN* 1 Sept. 1979.

124. Lance Corporal, 2 Para (a Warrenpoint survivor), quoted in M. Arthur, *Northern Ireland Soldiers Talking* (London: Sidgwick and Jackson, 1987), p. 138.

125. *BT* 16 Mar. 1979.

126. See the valuable treatment in J. Holland, *The American Connection: US Guns, Money and Influence in Northern Ireland* (Boulder: Roberts Rinehart, 1999; 1st edn 1987).

127. *AP/RN* 23 Feb. 1980.

128. *AP/RN* 26 Jan. 1980.

129. J. Adams, *Tony Benn: A Biography* (London: Macmillan, 1992), p. 361. Benn's socialist arguments at the end of the 1970s certainly did not focus on Northern Ireland: see T. Benn, *Arguments for Socialism* (Harmondsworth: Penguin, 1980; 1st edn 1979).

130. *AP/RN* 5 Apr. 1980.

131. *AP/RN* 4 Oct. 1980.

132. *AP/RN* 28 June 1980.

133. Gerry Adams, quoted in *AP/RN* 23 June 1979.

134. IRA spokesman, quoted in *AP/RN* 5 Sept. 1981.

135. *AP/RN* 5 Nov. 1981.

136. Danny Morrison, interviewed by the author, Belfast, 26 May 2000.

137. Margaret Thatcher, *Parliamentary Debates* (sixth series, vol. 12), pp. 238–9.

138. IRA spokesman, quoted in *AP/RN* 19 Nov. 1981.

139. N. Bradford, *A Sword Bathed in Heaven* (Basingstoke: Pickering, 1984), pp. 155–6.

SIX: POLITICIZATION AND THE CYCLE OF VIOLENCE 1981–8

1. Declan Moen, interviewed by the author, Belfast, 27 Sept. 2000. Moen was born in Monaghan in 1969, and imprisoned 1989–97.

2. McCartney to editor, *AP/RN*, 23 Nov. 1982, LHLPC; McCartney was at this time in H-Block 2, Long Kesh, and was PRO republican prisoners.

3. IRA spokesperson, quoted in *AP/RN* 1 Apr. 1982.

4. E. Collins, *Killing Rage* (London: Granta, 1997), pp. 187, 192.

5. K. McEvoy, 'Law, Struggle and Political Transformation in Northern Ireland', *Journal of Law and Society* 27, 4 (2000).

6. Correspondence from Patrick Magee, 9 Oct. 2000.
7. Sean Murray, quoted in L. McKeown, *Out of Time: Irish Republican Prisoners Long Kesh 1972–2000* (Belfast: Beyond the Pale, 2001), p. 138.
8. Patrick Magee, interviewed by the author, Belfast, 5 Mar. 2002.
9. Gerry Kelly, quoted in McKeown, *Out of Time*, p. 41.
10. Laurence McKeown, interviewed by the author, Belfast, 21 Jan. 2002.
11. Anthony McIntyre, interviewed by the author, Belfast, 23 Aug. 2000.
12. P. Freire, *Pedagogy of the Oppressed* (Harmondsworth: Penguin, 1996; 1st edn 1970), p. 54.
13. See, for example, B. Truscot, *Red Brick University* (Harmondsworth: Penguin, 1951; 1st edn 1943), p. 191.
14. Freire, *Pedagogy*, p. 61.
15. Laurence McKeown, interviewed by the author, Belfast, 21 Jan. 2002.
16. Laurence McKeown, interviewed by the author, Belfast, 21 Jan. 2002.
17. Tommy Gorman, interviewed by the author, Belfast, 2 May 2001.
18. Jackie McMullan, quoted in McKeown, *Out of Time*, p. 130.
19. Patrick Magee, interviewed by the author, Belfast, 5 Mar. 2002.
20. Jackie McMullan, interviewed by the author, Belfast, 27 Sept. 2000.
21. Correspondence from Patrick Magee, 9 Oct. 2000.
22. McKeown, *Out of Time*, p. 144.
23. Jackie McMullan, interviewed by the author, Belfast, 27 Sept. 2000.
24. Anthony McIntyre, interviewed by the author, Belfast, 23 Aug. 2000.
25. Jackie McMullan, interviewed by the author, Belfast, 27 Sept. 2000.
26. Tommy McKearney, interviewed by the author, Belfast, 20 Sept. 2000.
27. Danny Morrison, interviewed by the author, Belfast, 26 May 2000.
28. Hodgins to the editor, *IN*, 30 Jan. 1983, LHLPC.
29. M. McGuinness, *Bodenstown '86* (London, Wolfe Tone Society, n.d.), p. 10.
30. Jackie McMullan, interviewed by the author, Belfast, 27 Sept. 2000.
31. For details of the IRA's links with, and support from, international players, see Institute for the Study of Terrorism, *IRA, INLA: Foreign Support and International Connections* (London: Institute for the Study of Terrorism, 1988); connections included links with Palestinian groups – see pp. 65–71, and cf. R. Gilmour, *Dead Ground: Infiltrating the IRA* (London: Little, Brown, 1998), p. 4.
32. Tom Hartley, interviewed by the author, Belfast, 24 Oct. 2001.
33. F. Fanon, *The Wretched of the Earth* (Harmondsworth: Penguin, 1967; 1st edn 1961), pp. 27–8.
34. Ibid., p. 29.
35. R. Crotty, *Ireland in Crisis: A Study in Capitalist Undevelopment* (Dingle: Brandon, 1986), p. v.

36. Declan Moen, interviewed by the author, Belfast, 27 Sept. 2000.
37. McKeown, *Out of Time*, pp. 68–9.
38. B. Sands, *The Diary of Bobby Sands* (Dublin: Sinn Féin, 1981), p. 23.
39. Declan Moen, interviewed by the author, Belfast, 27 Sept. 2000.
40. Jackie McMullan, interviewed by the author, Belfast, 27 Sept. 2000.
41. Declan Moen, interviewed by the author, Belfast, 27 Sept. 2000.
42. IRA spokesperson, quoted in *AP/RN* 5 Jan. 1984.
43. J. Stalker, *Stalker* (London: Harrap, 1988), pp. 9, 253.
44. Amnesty International, *Political Killings in Northern Ireland* (London: Amnesty International, 1994), p. 6.
45. See, for example, P. Foot, *Who Framed Colin Wallace?* (London: Macmillan, 1989).
46. S. Elliott and W. D. Flackes, *Northern Ireland: A Political Directory 1968–1993* (Belfast: Blackstaff Press, 1994), pp. 389, 393, 396–7, 401.
47. *IN* 28 Nov. 1988.
48. See the thoughtful analysis offered by Michael Cunningham: 'The Political Language of John Hume', *Irish Political Studies* 12 (1997).
49. *AP/RN* 3 May 1984.
50. *BT* 20 Nov. 1984.
51. T. Hadden and K. Boyle, *The Anglo-Irish Agreement: Commentary, Text and Official Review* (London: Sweet and Maxwell, 1989), p. 18.
52. R. Needham, *Battling for Peace* (Belfast: Blackstaff Press, 1998), p. 37. Richard Needham: born 1942; Conservative politician; 1983–4, parliamentary private secretary to James Prior (Secretary of State for Northern Ireland); 1985–92, minister, NIO.
53. M. Thatcher, *The Downing Street Years* (London: HarperCollins, 1993), p. 385; M. Thatcher, *The Path to Power* (New York: HarperCollins, 1995), p. 327.
54. Thatcher, *Downing Street Years*, p. 396.
55. G. FitzGerald, *All in a Life: An Autobiography* (Dublin: Gill and Macmillan, 1992; 1st edn 1991), pp. 496–7.
56. Speaking on 18 Nov. 1985, *AP/RN* 21 Nov. 1985.
57. *AP/RN* 3 Apr. 1986.
58. Gerry Adams interview, *AP/RN* 12 Dec. 1985.
59. For impressive treatment of unionist responses, see F. Cochrane, *Unionist Politics and the Politics of Unionism since the Anglo-Irish Agreement* (Cork: Cork University Press, 1997).
60. Thatcher, *Downing Street Years*, p. 403; cf. FitzGerald, *All in a Life*, p. 569. Some of her colleagues seem to have anticipated unionist disaffection: see, for example, N. Lawson, *The View from No. 11: Memoirs of a Tory Radical* (London: Bantam, 1992), p. 670.

61. J. Hewitt, 'The Anglo-Irish Accord' in F. Ormsby (ed.), *The Collected Poems of John Hewitt* (Belfast ; Blackstaff Press, 1991), p. 537.

62. Tom Hartley, interviewed by the author, Belfast, 24 Oct. 2001.

63. Cochrane, *Unionist Politics*, p. 22.

64. On the Northern Ireland Assembly, see C. O'Leary, S. Elliott and R. Wilford, *The Northern Ireland Assembly 1982–1986: A Constitutional Experiment* (London: Hurst, 1988).

65. Quoted in D. McKittrick and D. McVea, *Making Sense of the Troubles* (Belfast: Blackstaff Press, 2000), pp. 167–8.

66. Sinn Féin leaflet: *What is Sinn Féin?* (1983), LHLPC, Sinn Féin (Provisional) Box 1.

67. *AP/RN* 17 Nov. 1983.

68. R. Sinnott, *Irish Voters Decide: Voting Behaviour in Elections and Referendums since 1918* (Manchester: Manchester University Press, 1995), p. 302.

69. Quoted in L. Clarke, *Broadening the Battlefield: The H-Blocks and the Rise of Sinn Féin* (Dublin: Gill and Macmillan, 1987), p. 253.

70. For the intimacy and overlap between the IRA and Sinn Féin, see (for example) P. Taylor, *Provos: The IRA and Sinn Féin* (London: Bloomsbury, 1997), p. 272; S. O'Callaghan, *The Informer* (London: Bantam, 1998), pp. 40, 49, 129, 141, 183, 188, 193, 214; F. Burton, *The Politics of Legitimacy: Struggles in a Belfast Community* (London: Routledge and Kegan Paul, 1978), p. 79; B. Feeney, *Sinn Féin: A Hundred Turbulent Years* (Dublin: O'Brien, 2002), pp. 189–90, 198, 208–9, 269, 295–6, 303.

71. Speaking in Derry, 24 June 1984, *AP/RN* 28 June 1984.

72. Danny Morrison, quoted in R. W. White, *Provisional Irish Republicans: An Oral and Interpretive History* (Westport: Greenwood Press, 1993), p. 173.

73. *AP/RN* 22 Nov. 1984.

74. Sinn Féin, *A Scenario for Peace: A Discussion Paper* (Dublin: Sinn Féin, n.d.), pp. 2, 5.

75. Gerry Adams's Election Leaflet, Westminster Election (1987), LHLPC, Sinn Féin (Provisional) Box 2.

76. *BT* 8 Dec. 1983.

77. IRA statement, quoted in *AP/RN* 8 Dec. 1983.

78. On alleged ill-treatment by the RUC, see – for example – 'Statement from Sinn Féin Elected Representative, Martin McGuinness' (13 Sept. 1984), LHLPC, Sinn Féin (Provisional) Box 2.

79. Bingham had, in fact, been central to the UVF's recent campaign of killings in Belfast: J. Cusack and H. McDonald, *UVF* (Dublin: Poolbeg, 2000; 1st edn 1997), p. 244.

80. *AP/RN* 18 Sept. 1986.
81. Cusack and McDonald, *UVF*, p. 245.
82. *AP/RN* 19 May 1988.
83. *AP/RN* 16 June 1988.
84. Lawson, *View from No. 11*, p. 307.
85. Patrick Magee, interviewed by the author, Belfast, 5 Mar. 2002.
86. *AP/RN* 18 Oct. 1984.
87. Patrick Magee, quoted in *Guardian* 28 Aug. 2000.
88. *AP/RN* 15 Aug. 1985.
89. *AP/RN* 7 Nov. 1985.
90. *AP/RN* 16 Oct. 1986.
91. Kelly and Brendan McFarlane had been among republican prisoners escaping from the Maze Prison in September 1983; they had been arrested in Holland in January 1986.
92. *AP/RN* 16 Oct. 1986.
93. *AP/RN* 30 Oct. 1986.
94. Speaking on 24 Nov. 1986, *AP/RN* 4 Dec. 1986.
95. Tom Maguire, quoted in R. Ó Brádaigh, *Dílseacht: The Story of Comdt General Tom Maguire and the Second (All-Ireland) Dáil* (Dublin: Irish Freedom Press, 1997), pp. 48–9.
96. Tom Maguire, quoted in ibid., p. 66.
97. *AP/RN* 6 Nov. 1986.
98. *AP/RN* 27 Nov. 1986.
99. Tom Hartley, interviewed by the author, Belfast, 24 Oct. 2001.
100. Quoted in B. O'Brien, *The Long War: The IRA and Sinn Féin 1985 to Today* (Dublin: O'Brien Press, 1993), p. 162.
101. *AP/RN* 30 Apr. 1987.
102. Quoted in S. Bruce, *The Red Hand: Protestant Paramilitaries in Northern Ireland* (Oxford: Oxford University Press, 1992), pp. 113–14.
103. H. McCallion, *Killing Zone* (London: Bloomsbury, 1995), pp. 240–1. It has been suggested that Lynagh's group *may* have thought of breaking away from the IRA (Moloney, *Secret History*, p. 315).
104. Gordon Wilson, quoted in B. Rowan, *Behind the Lines: The Story of the IRA and Loyalist Ceasefires* (Belfast: Blackstaff Press, 1995), p. 10.
105. *AP/RN* 12 Nov. 1987.
106. D. McDaniel, *Enniskillen: The Remembrance Sunday Bombing* (Dublin: Wolfhound, 1997), p. 195.
107. *AP/RN* 19 Nov. 1987.
108. G. Wilson, *Marie: A Story from Enniskillen* (London: Marshall Pickering, 1990), p. 2.
109. R. Bolton, *Death on the Rock and Other Stories* (London: Allen, 1990).

Lord Windlesham was a Conservative politician, Richard Rampton a lawyer specializing in libel. Their inquiry focused on the making and screening of *Death on the Rock*, and especially on its possible impact on the subsequent inquest.

110. N. Eckert, *Fatal Encounter: The Story of the Gibraltar Killings* (Dublin: Poolbeg, 1999), p. 15.
111. B. Aretxaga, *Shattering Silence: Women, Nationalism and Political Subjectivity in Northern Ireland* (Princeton: Princeton University Press, 1997), pp. 168–9.
112. S. Graham, *Violent Delights* (London: Blake, 1997), pp. 40, 51.
113. 'Cleaky 1947–2000' in G. Adams, *An Irish Journal* (Dingle: Brandon, 2001).
114. D. McKittrick, S. Kelters, B. Feeney and C. Thornton, *Lost Lives: The Stories of the Men, Women and Children Who Died as a Result of the Northern Ireland Troubles* (Edinburgh: Mainstream, 2001; 1st edn 1999), p. 1494.
115. *AP/RN* 24 Mar. 1988.
116. *BT* 16 June 1988.
117. *BT* 20 Aug. 1988.
118. *AP/RN* 1 Sept. 1988.
119. R. Murray, *The SAS in Ireland* (Cork: Mercier, 1990), p. 30.
120. *AP/RN* 1 Sept. 1988.
121. *IN* 2 Sept. 1988.
122. *IN* 26 Nov. 1988.
123. McKittrick et al., *Lost Lives*, pp. 1059–1155.
124. *DJ* 29 Jan. 1988.
125. *AP/RN* 26 July 1980.
126. K. J. Kelley, *The Longest War: Northern Ireland and the IRA* (London: Zed Books, 1988; 1st edn 1982), pp. 376–7.
127. *AP/RN* 26 Jan. 1989.

SEVEN: TALKING AND KILLING 1988–94

1. *AP/RN* 17 Aug. 1989.
2. S. Farren and R. F. Mulvihill, *Paths to a Settlement in Northern Ireland* (Gerrards Cross: Colin Smythe, 2000), p. 141. A leading SDLP figure, Sean Farren was himself involved in these SDLP–Sinn Féin talks.
3. G. Adams, *A Pathway to Peace* (Cork: Mercier, 1988), p. 77.
4. Martin Mansergh: Fianna Fáil adviser on the north of Ireland; member of the Irish delegation that negotiated the 1998 Belfast Agreement.

5. Speaking on 13 Nov. 1988, quoted in *IN* 14 Nov. 1988.
6. *AP/RN* 2 Feb. 1989.
7. M. Thatcher, *The Downing Street Years* (London: HarperCollins, 1993), p. 414.
8. K. Baker, *The Turbulent Years: My Life in Politics* (London: Faber and Faber, 1993), p. 365.
9. *AP/RN* 28 June 1990.
10. Sinn Féin, *Setting the Record Straight: A Record of Communications Between Sinn Féin and the British Government October 1990–November 1993* (1994), p. 3 (copy in LHLPC). Adams had apparently had communication with the British as early as 1986–7 (Moloney, *Secret History*, p. 247).
11. Sinn Féin, *Setting the Record*, p. 2.
12. Ian Paisley, interviewed by the author, Belfast, 21 Feb. 1994.
13. John Major: born 1943; Conservative UK Prime Minister 1990–7.
14. *IN* 10 Nov. 1990.
15. *AP/RN* 3 Jan. 1991.
16. Gerry Adams, quoted in *IN* 1 Feb. 1991.
17. Gerry Adams, quoted in *IN* 21 Aug. 1991.
18. P. Mayhew, 'Culture and Identity', speech delivered in Coleraine, 16 Dec. 1992, pp. 6, 8, 15.
19. *AP/RN* 17 Dec. 1992.
20. *BT* 17 Dec. 1992.
21. *IN* 4 Oct. 1993.
22. Downing Street Declaration, 15 Dec. 1993, reproduced in M. Cox, A. Guelke and F. Stephen (eds), *A Farewell to Arms? From 'Long War' to Long Peace in Northern Ireland* (Manchester: Manchester University Press, 2000), p. 328.
23. John Hume, speaking on BBC Radio Ulster, 'Inside Politics', 29 Jan. 1994.
24. H-Block Prisoners' Response [to 1993 Downing Street Declaration], 21 Feb. 1994, LHLPC.
25. G. Adams, *An Irish Voice: The Quest for Peace* (Dingle: Mount Eagle, 1997), p. 36.
26. *IN* 14 Jan. 1994.
27. Niall O'Dowd: Irish-born founder of the influential *Irish Voice* newspaper; UCD graduate who, in 1979, emigrated to the USA.
28. Niall O'Dowd, interviewed by the author, New York, 2 Nov. 2000.
29. *AP/RN* 27 Feb. 1992.
30. *AP/RN* 20 Sept. 1990.
31. *AP/RN* 14 Feb. 1991.

32. M. Fay, M. Morrissey and M. Smyth, *Northern Ireland's Troubles: The Human Costs* (London: Pluto Press, 1999), p. 195.

33. K. J. Kelley, *The Longest War: Northern Ireland and the IRA* (London: Zed Books, 1988; 1st edn 1982), p. 291.

34. *AP/RN* 10 Oct. 1991.

35. There are now a number of autobiographical accounts by state agents and informers, including S. O'Callaghan, *The Informer* (London: Bantam, 1998) and M. McGartland, *Fifty Dead Men Walking* (London: Blake, 1998; 1st edn 1997).

36. *BT* 3 June 1991.

37. *AP/RN* 2 Jan. 1992.

38. *AP/RN* 23 Jan. 1992.

39. *IN* 18 Jan. 1992.

40. *IN* 20 Jan. 1992.

41. *IN* 6 Feb. 1992.

42. *AP/RN* 12 Mar. 1992.

43. S. Elliott and W. D. Flackes, *Northern Ireland: A Political Directory 1968–1993* (Belfast: Blackstaff Press, 1994), pp. 408–9.

44. D. Morrison, *Then the Walls Came Down: A Prison Journal* (Cork: Mercier, 1999), p. 290.

45. Figures compiled from D. McKittrick *et al.*, *Lost Lives: The Stories of the Men, Women and Children Who Died as a Result of the Northern Ireland Troubles* (Edinburgh: Mainstream, 2001; 1st edn 1999), p. 1494.

46. *AP/RN* 31 Dec. 1992.

47. *AP/RN* 8 Apr. 1993.

48. *AP/RN* 29 Apr. 1993.

49. *AP/RN* 8 July 1993.

50. *IN* 22 Mar. 1993.

51. *AP/RN* 25 Mar. 1993.

52. *IN* 25 Mar. 1993.

53. *AP/RN* 14 Oct. 1993.

54. Gerry Adams, in *AP/RN* 7 Oct. 1993.

55. Mitchel McLaughlin, speaking on 29 Oct. 1993, quoted in *AP/RN* 4 Nov. 1993.

56. *AP/RN* 15 Apr. 1993.

57. *AP/RN* 14 Jan. 1993. The IRA used their victim's loyalist connections to justify also their killing (on 18 August 1994) of Dublin criminal Martin 'The General' Cahill. In a statement claiming responsibility for the killing of Cahill (with whom they had had long-term friction), the Provisionals said that they had been forced to act because of his involvement with, and assistance to, loyalists: 'The IRA reserves the right

to execute those who finance or otherwise assist loyalist killer gangs'
(IRA statement, quoted in *AP/RN* 25 Aug. 1994). On Cahill's murky
glamour, see P. Williams, *The General: Godfather of Crime* (Dublin:
O'Brien Press, 1998; 1st edn 1995).

58. Quoted in D. McKittrick and D. McVea, *Making Sense of the Troubles*
(Belfast: Blackstaff Press, 2000), p. 192.

59. *IN* 25 Oct. 1993.

60. Gina Murray, quoted in E. Mallie and D. McKittrick, *The Fight for
Peace: The Secret Story behind the Irish Peace Process* (London: Heinemann, 1996), p. 195.

61. *IN* 25 Oct. 1993.

62. *IN* 1 Nov. 1993.

63. Figures compiled from McKittrick *et al.*, *Lost Lives*, pp. 1326–37.

64. *AP/RN* 16 Mar. 1994.

65. *AP/RN* 31 Mar. 1994.

66. *AP/RN* 31 Mar. 1994.

67. TUAS, reprinted in Cox, Guelke and Stephen (eds), *Farewell to Arms?*,
pp. 333–5.

68. Sinn Féin, *Towards a Lasting Peace in Ireland* (Dublin: Sinn Féin, 1992),
p. 11.

EIGHT: CESSATIONS OF VIOLENCE 1994–2002

1. Danny Morrison, interviewed by the author, Belfast, 26 May 2000.

2. IRA statement, 31 Aug. 1994, in *AP/RN* 1 Sept. 1994.

3. *IN* 1 Sept. 1994.

4. *Guardian* 1 Sept. 1994.

5. *BT* 31 Aug. 1994.

6. *IT* 1 Sept. 1994.

7. *Independent* 1 Sept. 1994.

8. *AP/RN* 1 Sept. 1994.

9. Gerry Adams, quoted in *AP/RN* 1 Sept. 1994.

10. *IN* 21 Nov. 1994.

11. *AP/RN* 1 Dec. 1994.

12. *AP/RN* 15 Dec. 1994.

13. *AP/RN* 2 Mar. 1995.

14. *AP/RN* 13 Apr. 1995.

15. *IT* 8 Mar. 1995.

16. *IT* 2 Sept. 1995.

17. *AP/RN* 5 Oct. 1995.

18. *AP/RN* 15 Feb. 1996.
19. *IT* 10 Feb. 1996.
20. *BT* 13 Feb. 1996.
21. *AP/RN* 15 Feb. 1996.
22. *Guardian* 12 Feb. 1996.
23. G. Adams, *An Irish Voice: The Quest for Peace* (Dingle: Mount Eagle, 1997), p. 208.
24. *BT* 1 June 1996.
25. *AP/RN* 13 June 1996.
26. *AP/RN* 4 Apr. 1996.
27. *AP/RN* 20 June 1996.
28. *Guardian* 4 July 1996.
29. *AP/RN* 4 July 1996.
30. *AP/RN* 9 Jan. 1997.
31. *AP/RN* 9 Jan. 1997.
32. *AP/RN* 27 Mar. 1997.
33. Gerry Adams, quoted in *AP/RN* 20 Feb. 1997.
34. R. Restorick, *Death of a Soldier: A Mother's Search for Peace in Northern Ireland* (Belfast: Blackstaff Press, 2000), pp. 3–4.
35. *IN* 17 May 1997.
36. *AP/RN* 26 June 1997.
37. IRA statement 19 July 1997, *AP/RN* 24 July 1997.
38. *AP/RN* 24 July 1997.
39. *IN* 21 July 1997. It should also be noted that eminent Sinn Féiners could retain influence within the IRA also. Both McGuinness and Adams were apparently members of the IRA Army Council which, in 1995, decided to end the first IRA ceasefire – the decision which led to the 1996 Canary Wharf bomb. They were still both members of that body in mid-2001.
40. Gerry Adams, quoted in D. De Bréadún, *The Far Side of Revenge: Making Peace in Northern Ireland* (Cork: Collins, 2001), p. 60.
41. S. Heaney, 'Sonnets from Hellas' in *Electric Light* (London: Faber and Faber, 2001), p. 41
42. T. Paulin, 'The Quinn Brothers' in *The Wind Dog* (London: Faber and Faber, 1999), p. 7.
43. *AP/RN* 22 Jan. 1998.
44. 'Agreement Reached in the Multi-Party Negotiations' (1998), quotations at pp. 1, 3–4, 23, 31, 48. For a rigorous analysis of the Agreement from a political-science perspective, see B. O'Leary, 'The Nature of the Agreement', *Fordham International Law Journal* 22, 4 (1999).
45. *AP/RN* 9 Apr. 1998.

46. *AP/RN* 30 Apr. 1998.
47. Adams, *An Irish Journal*, p. 58.
48. J. Langdon, *Mo Mowlam* (London: Little, Brown, 2000), p. 281. For her part, Mowlam thought McGuinness and Adams 'two very serious, committed human beings' (M. Mowlam, *Momentum: The Struggle for Peace, Politics and the People* (London: Hodder and Stoughton, 2002), p. 123).
49. *IT* 29 Oct. 1998.
50. *AP/RN* 6 Aug. 1998.
51. *AP/RN* 28 Jan. 1999.
52. R. McCartney, *Reflections on Liberty, Democracy and the Union* (Dublin: Maunsel, 2001), p. 181. For another ably crafted version of this peace-process-as-appeasement thesis, see J. M. Skelly, 'Appeasement in Our Time: Conor Cruise O'Brien and the Peace Process in Northern Ireland', *Irish Studies in International Affairs* 10 (1999).
53. Tony Blair, quoted in J. Rentoul, *Tony Blair* (London: Little, Brown, 1995), p. 409.
54. *IN* 22 May 1998.
55. *AP/RN* 28 May 1998.
56. *AP/RN* 25 June 1998.
57. *AP/RN* 2 July 1998.
58. *Guardian* 31 Dec. 1998.
59. G. Adams, *Free Ireland: Towards a Lasting Peace* (Dingle: Brandon, 1995; 1st edn 1986), p. 191.
60. Jackie McMullan, interviewed by the author, Belfast, 27 Sept. 2000.
61. Correspondence from Patrick Magee, 9 Oct. 2000.
62. Anthony McIntyre, interviewed by the author, Belfast, 23 Aug. 2000.
63. Recollection of Anthony McIntyre, interviewed by the author, Belfast, 23 Aug. 2000. In each H-Block wing, Cell 26 was a big, double cell.
64. D. Morrison, *Then the Walls Came Down: A Prison Journal* (Cork: Mercier, 1999), p. 91.
65. Danny Morrison, interviewed by the author, Belfast, 26 May 2000.
66. See the valuable article by M. Cox, 'Bringing in the "International": The IRA Ceasefire and the End of the Cold War', *International Affairs* 73, 4 (1997).
67. Tom Hartley, interviewed by the author, Belfast, 24 Oct. 2001.
68. George Harrison, interviewed by the author, New York, 30 Oct. 2000.
69. Niall O'Dowd, interviewed by the author, New York, 2 Nov. 2000.
70. *AP/RN* 15 Dec. 1994.
71. Adams, *Irish Journal*, pp. 82–3.
72. Tom Hartley, interviewed by the author, Belfast, 24 Oct. 2001.

73. P. Arthur, *Special Relationships: Britain, Ireland and the Northern Ireland Problem* (Belfast: Blackstaff Press, 2000), pp. 120–1.

74. On this, see J. Dumbrell, 'The United States and the Northern Irish Conflict 1969–94: From Indifference to Intervention', *Irish Studies in International Affairs* 6 (1995); and A. Guelke, 'The United States, Irish Americans and the Northern Ireland Peace Process', *International Affairs* 72, 3 (1996).

75. E. Meehan, 'Member States and the European Union' in R. English and C. Townshend (eds), *The State: Historical and Political Dimensions* (London: Routledge, 1999).

76. IRA figure quoted in T. P. Coogan, *The IRA* (London: HarperCollins, 1987; 1st edn 1970), p. 604.

77. G. Adams, *The Politics of Irish Freedom* (Dingle: Brandon, 1986), p. 58.

78. Morrison, *Walls Came Down*, p. 71.

79. See his November 1989 statement of this point, reprinted in D. Bloomfield, *Political Dialogue in Northern Ireland: The Brooke Initiative, 1989–92* (Basingstoke: Macmillan, 1998), p. 16.

80. A valuable source for gauging the extent of security force success in this area is the record of leading RUC surveillance operative Ian Phoenix: J. Holland and S. Phoenix, *Phoenix: Policing the Shadows* (London: Coronet, 1997; 1st edn 1996).

81. Hume to Adams, 17 Mar. 1988, quoted in P. Arthur, 'The Anglo-Irish Joint Declaration: Towards a Lasting Peace?', *Government and Opposition* 29, 2 (1994), p. 225.

82. P. Mandelson, 'The GQ Column', *GQ* 151 (2002), p. 57.

83. J. Higgins, *Confessional* (London: Pan, 1986; 1st edn 1985), p. 46.

84. Quoted in Holland and Phoenix, *Phoenix*, p. 295.

85. Morrison, *Walls Came Down*, pp. 96–7, 235.

86. Martin McGuinness, quoted in *Observer* 6 Feb. 2000.

87. Prisoner release was an important question for republicans in the 1990s, as before. But the influence of this issue, or of prisoners themselves, for the peace process is sometimes overstated. 'The movement outside ... had a high regard for prisoners and prison struggle. But in terms of policy, in terms of strategy, the people outside were the people who decided' (Jackie McMullan, interviewed by the author, Belfast, 27 Sept. 2000). Prisoners were less in touch with the resources and conditions of the movement than were the people outside, so it was the people on the outside who made the choices: 'We were consulted on the ceasefire and we didn't see the reason for it whatsoever: things aren't great, could be a lot better, but why are you calling a ceasefire now? What has changed to make a ceasefire so promising or such a radical

option? Because ... we were not in possession of all the facts. And you can't trust the judgment of somebody who hasn't got all the facts to hand. We never wanted that role' (Declan Moen, interviewed by the author, Belfast, 27 Sept. 2000).

88. Gerry Adams, quoted in B. O'Brien, *The Long War: The IRA and Sinn Féin 1985 to Today* (Dublin: O'Brien Press, 1993), p. 123.

89. Tom Hartley, interviewed by the author, Belfast, 24 Oct. 2001.

90. Barry McElduff, in *DJ* 7 Dec. 2001.

91. Adams, *Irish Journal*, p. 22.

92. *AP/RN* 15 Dec. 1994.

93. *AP/RN* 25 Sept. 1997.

94. Tom Hartley, interviewed by the author, Belfast, 24 Oct. 2001.

95. G. Adams, *Who Fears to Speak...?: The Story of Belfast and the 1916 Rising* (Belfast: Beyond the Pale, 2001; 1st edn 1991), p. viii.

96. *AP/RN* 1 Mar. 1984.

97. Gerry Adams, quoted in B. Rowan, *Behind the Lines: The Story of the IRA and Loyalist Ceasefires* (Belfast: Blackstaff Press, 1995), pp. 48–9.

98. Sinn Féin election leaflet (Alex Maskey, south Belfast), June 2001 UK general election.

99. Gerry Adams, speaking on 25 Feb. 1995, quoted in *AP/RN* 2 Mar. 1995.

100. *BT* 8 May 2001.

101. Morrison, *Walls Came Down*, p. 195.

102. Tom Hartley, interviewed by the author, Belfast, 24 Oct. 2001.

103. Danny Morrison, interviewed by the author, Belfast, 26 May 2000.

104. See, for example, the arguments of UUP leader David Trimble, for an inclusive, pluralistic, liberal unionism. Trimble publicly acknowledges the great changes that have taken place in Irish republican politics during the peace process period, changes that have opened up possibilities for cooperative engagement between unionists and republicans (D. Trimble, *To Raise Up a New Northern Ireland: Articles and Speeches 1998–2000* (Belfast: Belfast Press, 2001)).

105. *IT* 18 Feb. 2002.

106. Morrison, *Walls Came Down*, p. 236.

107. P. Nash, 'Why Does Britain Remain in Control of the Six Counties?', 9 Sept. 1985, LHLPC.

108. Marian Price, interviewed by the author, Belfast, 28 Feb. 2002.

109. *BT* 29 Mar. 1996.

110. Cathal Goulding, speaking in 1990, quoted in *Observer* 3 Jan. 1999.

111. George Harrison, interviewed by the author, New York, 30 Oct. 2000.

112. Bernadette Sands-McKevitt, quoted in T. Hennessey, *The Northern*

Ireland Peace Process: Ending the Troubles? (Dublin: Gill and Macmillan, 2000), p. 112.

113. *Guardian* 10 Mar. 1998.
114. Marian Price, quoted in *The Blanket* 1, 1 (2002), pp. 4, 10.
115. Marian Price, interviewed by the author, Belfast, 28 Feb. 2002.
116. G. J. Mitchell, *Making Peace* (London: William Heinemann, 1999), p. 184.
117. *BT* 2 Sept. 1998.
118. *AP/RN* 20 Aug. 1998.
119. Brendan Hughes interview, *The Blanket* (Dec. 2000).
120. Tommy Gorman, interviewed by the author, Belfast, 2 May 2001.
121. *AP/RN* 13 Sept. 1990.
122. Anthony McIntyre, interviewed by the author, Belfast, 23 Aug. 2000.
123. Brendan Hughes, quoted in *Fourthwrite: The Journal of the Irish Republican Writers' Group* 1 (2000), pp. 6–7.
124. *AP/RN* 19 Oct. 2000.
125. Marian Price, 'Funeral Oration at the Burial of Joe O'Connor', 18 Oct. 2000, Belfast, Milltown Cemetery, copy in LHLPC.
126. George Harrison, interviewed by the author, New York, 30 Oct. 2000.
127. George Harrison, 'In Memoriam Joseph O'Connor', copy in the author's possession.
128. *AP/RN* 1 Apr. 1999.
129. RUC, *The Chief Constable's Report 1997–98*, p. 101.
130. M. Morrissey and M. Smyth, *Northern Ireland after the Good Friday Agreement: Victims, Grievance and Blame* (London: Pluto Press, 2002), p. 74.
131. *BT* 28 Mar. 1996.
132. *IT* 8 Feb. 1999.
133. Independent Commission on Policing for Northern Ireland, *A New Beginning: Policing in Northern Ireland* (1999), pp. 2, 9, 13, 83, 99. On policing more generally, see B. O'Leary and J. McGarry, *Policing Northern Ireland: Proposals for a New Start* (Belfast: Blackstaff Press, 1999); G. Ellison and J. Smyth, *The Crowned Harp: Policing Northern Ireland* (London: Pluto Press, 2000); J. D. Brewer and K. Magee, *Inside the RUC: Routine Policing in a Divided Society* (Oxford: Oxford University Press, 1991).
134. D. McKittrick *et al.*, *Lost Lives: The Stories of the Men, Women and Children Who Died as a Result of the Northern Ireland Troubles* (Edinburgh: Mainstream, 2001; 1st edn 1999), p. 1502.
135. *IN* 1 Dec. 1997.
136. C. Ryder, *Inside the Maze: The Untold Story of the Northern Ireland Prison Service* (London: Methuen, 2000), pp. 342–3.

137. *Guardian* 17 Nov. 1998.
138. *IT* 4 Nov. 1998.
139. 'Agreement Reached in the Multi-Party Negotiations', p. 45.
140. For a good treatment of the decommissioning issue, see C. Hauswedell and K. Brown, *Burying the Hatchet: The Decommissioning of Paramilitary Arms in Northern Ireland* (Derry: Incore, 2002).
141. *IN* 8 Jan. 1994.
142. Data Section, *Irish Political Studies* 10 (1995), p. 309.
143. *IT* 29 Nov. 1995.
144. *AP/RN* 7 Mar. 1996.
145. Mitchell, *Making Peace*, p. 108.
146. Tony Blair, quoted in Trimble, *To Raise Up*, p. 36.
147. *AP/RN* 30 Apr. 1998.
148. *AP/RN* 24 Sept. 1998.
149. *IT* 29 Oct. 1998.
150. *AP/RN* 4 Mar. 1999.
151. *BT* 28 July 1999.
152. Loyalist attacks on Catholics in the north continued to occur at an appalling rate, as was repeatedly and understandably noted by *An Phoblacht/Republican News*; see, for example, *AP/RN* 16 Aug., 23 Aug., 30 Aug., 6 Sept., 13 Sept., 29 Nov., 6 Dec. 2001.
153. Trimble, *To Raise Up*, p. 33.
154. McCartney, *Reflections*, pp. 167, 171.
155. *AP/RN* 9 Dec. 1999.
156. *AP/RN* 17 Feb. 2000.
157. David Trimble, quoted in *IT* 2 Feb. 2000.
158. David Trimble, quoted in *Sunday Independent* 16 Jan. 2000.
159. *IT* 2 Feb. 2000.
160. *AP/RN* 11 May 2000.
161. *AP/RN* 29 June 2000.
162. *AP/RN* 26 Oct. 2000.
163. *IN* 6 Dec. 2000.
164. *AP/RN* 18 Jan. 2001.
165. *AP/RN* 9 Aug. 2001.
166. *AP/RN* 16 Aug. 2001.
167. *AP/RN* 20 Sept. 2001.
168. See, for example, *AP/RN* 30 July 1998.
169. K. McElrath, *Unsafe Haven: The United States, the IRA and Political Prisoners* (London: Pluto Press, 2000), pp. 118–19.
170. *AP/RN* 13 Sept. 2001.
171. *AP/RN* 20 Sept. 2001.

172. *BT* 28 Sept. 2001.
173. G. Adams, 'Looking to the Future', Belfast speech, 22 Oct. 2001, pp. 4, 8–9, 15, copy in LHLPC.
174. *AP/RN* 25 Oct. 2001.
175. *IT* 27 Oct. 2001.
176. IICD Report, quoted in *IN* 9 Apr. 2002.
177. Though, not surprisingly, reports that the IRA were still buying weapons led some to doubt the sincerity of republican intentions on this question of decommissioning; see, for example, *Sunday Telegraph* 21 Apr. 2002.
178. B. C. Hayes and I. McAllister, 'Sowing Dragon's Teeth: Public Support for Political Violence and Paramilitarism in Northern Ireland', *Political Studies* 49, 5 (2001), p. 917.

CONCLUSION

1. *AP/RN* 11 Jan. 2001.
2. P. Magee, *Gangsters or Guerrillas? Representations of Irish Republicans in 'Troubles Fiction'* (Belfast: Beyond the Pale, 2001).
3. *AP/RN* 18 June 1992. Though it should, perhaps, be pointed out that in both the film and the novel upon which it was based this psychopathic character belongs not to the IRA, but to an offshoot republican group (T. Clancy, *Patriot Games* (New York: Berkley, 1988; 1st edn 1987), p. 18).
4. M. McLoone, *Irish Film: The Emergence of a Contemporary Cinema* (London: British Film Institute, 2000), p. 66.
5. J. Pilgrim, 'The Provisionals', *Fortnight* 19 Feb. 1971, p. 8.
6. *IN* 2 Apr. 1997.
7. G. Adams, 'To Cherish a Just and Lasting Peace', *Fordham International Law Journal* 22, 4 (1999), p. 1180.
8. Patrick Magee, interviewed by the author, Belfast, 5 Mar. 2002.
9. Sinn Féin, *Towards a Lasting Peace in Ireland* (Dublin: Sinn Féin, 1992), pp. 1, 9.
10. G. Adams, *The Politics of Irish Freedom* (Dingle: Brandon, 1986), p. 88.
11. *AP/RN* 28 June 1990.
12. *AP/RN* 4 Nov. 1993.
13. *AP/RN* 15 Dec. 1994.
14. *Green Book*, quoted in T. P. Coogan, *The IRA* (London: HarperCollins, 1987; 1st edn 1970), p. 683.
15. IRA Easter message 1997, *AP/RN* 27 Mar. 1997.
16. *AP/RN* 8 Dec. 1994.

17. *Green Book*, quoted in B. O'Brien, *The Long War: The IRA and Sinn Féin 1985 to Today* (Dublin: O'Brien Press, 1993), p. 289.

18. Magee, *Gangsters or Guerrillas?*, pp. 10–11.

19. IRA New Year Message, *AP/RN* 8 Jan. 1998.

20. M. Elliott, *The Catholics of Ulster: A History* (Harmondsworth: Allen Lane, 2000), p. xxxviii.

21. Martin McGuinness, 'Inter-Party Talks', 1993 Sinn Féin *ard fheis*, LHLPC, Sinn Féin (Provisional) Box 2.

22. Patrick Magee, interviewed by the author, Belfast, 5 Mar. 2002.

23. Pat Cox, quoted in O'Brien, *Long War*, p. 59.

24. *AP/RN* 8 Dec. 1994.

25. Patrick Magee, quoted in *Guardian* 28 Aug. 2000.

26. G. Adams, *An Irish Journal* (Dingle: Brandon, 2001), p. 33.

27. Adams, *Politics of Irish Freedom*, p. 64.

28. Speaking in Derry, 24 June 1984, *AP/RN* 28 June 1984.

29. Quoted in Coogan, *The IRA*, p. 650.

30. *Green Book*, quoted in O'Brien, *Long War*, p. 291.

31. J. Adams, R. Morgan and A. Bambridge, *Ambush: The War Between the SAS and the IRA* (London: Pan, 1988), p. 29.

32. *RN* 23 Aug. 1975.

33. *Green Book*, quoted in O'Brien, *Long War*, p. 87.

34. Adams, *Politics of Irish Freedom*, pp. 3, 14, 30, 39, 69, 79, 86, 96–7, 106, 114, 126, 128–9, 131, 135, 143, 156.

35. See, for example, J. L. Anderson, *Che Guevara: A Revolutionary Life* (London: Bantam, 1997); D. Macey, *Frantz Fanon: A Life* (London: Granta, 2000); A. C. Alessandrini (ed.), *Frantz Fanon: Critical Perspectives* (London: Routledge, 1999).

36. Adams, *Politics of Irish Freedom*, p. 58; G. Adams, *Before the Dawn: An Autobiography* (London, Heinemann, 1996), p. 115.

37. *AP/RN* 7 Jan. 1988.

38. Adams, *Politics of Irish Freedom*, p. 5; cf. also pp. 18, 27–8.

39. Adams, *Irish Journal*, p. 188.

40. Adams to Arnlis (Morrison), 5 Jan. 1977, LHLPC.

41. See, from the very many examples, *AP/RN* 1 July 1993.

42. *AP/RN* 26 Aug. 1993.

43. B. Sands, 'The Socialist Republic', *AP/RN* 17 Dec. 1981.

44. *AP/RN* 19 Aug. 1993.

45. See, for example, Magee, *Gangsters or Guerrillas?*, p. 11.

46. Adams, *Politics of Irish Freedom*, pp. 1, 6–7, 14, 37–8, 70, 88, 90, 122, 128–36, 149, 155–6.

47. Ibid., p. 132.

48. G. Adams, *A Pathway to Peace* (Cork: Mercier, 1988), p. 79.
49. G. Adams, *Free Ireland: Towards a Lasting Peace* (Dingle: Brandon, 1995; 1st edn 1986), p. 126.
50. *IN* 27 Feb. 1962.
51. Magee, *Gangsters or Guerrillas?*, p. 222.
52. G. Adams, *Cage Eleven* (Dingle: Brandon, 1990), p. 101. And see the hostility of leading Catholic clergy towards the IRA's violent campaign, epitomized perhaps by C. B. Daly's *Violence in Ireland and Christian Conscience* (Dublin: Veritas, 1973).
53. J. D. Brewer and K. Magee, *Inside the RUC: Routine Policing in a Divided Society* (Oxford: Oxford University Press, 1991), p. 150.
54. B. Fletcher, 'Interview with Sinn Féin President Gerry Adams', *Monthly Review* 41, 1 (1989), p. 20.
55. Gerry Adams interview, *AP/RN* 12 Dec. 1985.
56. Gerry Adams, in *AP/RN* 7 Oct. 1993.
57. Tom Hartley, interviewed by the author, Belfast, 24 Oct. 2001.
58. *AP/RN* 3 Mar. 1994.
59. G. Adams, *Who Fears to Speak . . .? The Story of Belfast and the 1916 Rising* (Belfast: Beyond the Pale, 2001; 1st edn 1991), p. 29.
60. *AP/RN* 3 Mar. 1994.
61. Gerry Adams, speech in Dublin on the 86th anniversary of the Easter Rising (2002), copy in LHLPC.
62. Even impressively knowledgeable observers have sometimes played up the supposedly ancient dimensions to republicanism: 'The true cultural and psychological origins of republican strategic thinking stretch back to the outer reaches of Irish history, and even to mythic prehistory' (M. L. R. Smith, *Fighting for Ireland? The Miliary Strategy of the Irish Republican Movement* (London: Routledge, 1997; 1st edn 1995), p. 6); 'The most import[ant] special factor in Ireland has been the impact of the perceived history of a struggle that traces IRA organisational origins to 1858, the republican movement to 1798 and Irish resistance to the twelfth century' (J. B. Bell, *The IRA 1968–2000: Analysis of a Secret Army* (London: Frank Cass, 2000), p. 320); 'It [the hunger strike] is an ancient weapon in Ireland . . . even more ancient than the cause in the name of which it was wielded at the end of 1980' (D. Beresford, *Ten Men Dead: The Story of the 1981 Irish Hunger Strike* (London: Grafton, 1987), p. 14).
63. 'The H-Blocks: The Protest in Perspective', May 1979, LHLPC.
64. Tom Hartley, interviewed by the author, Belfast, 24 Oct. 2001. Clearly, republican presence at Stormont after the 1998 Belfast Agreement involved engagement with a very different kind of politics from that

embodied in the pre-1972 Stormont regime: republicans had changed, but so had Stormont.

65. *IT* 1 Apr. 2002.
66. Adams, *Politics of Irish Freedom*, p. 53.
67. Data compiled from M. Sutton, *Bear in Mind These Dead: An Index of Deaths from the Conflict in Ireland 1969–1993* (Belfast: Beyond the Pale, 1994), pp. 2–38.
68. Ballymacarrett Research Group, *Lagan Enclave: A History of Conflict in the Short Strand 1886–1997* (Belfast, BRG, 1997), p. 60.
69. Malachi O'Doherty is lucid on this point: 'The fact is that the Provisionals articulated not defence but defiance, and the cost of that defiance was increased casualties among the Catholic working classes . . . The reality is that loyalist violence against Catholics increased as IRA violence against the police and Army and commerce increased, that there was something more like a symbiotic relationship between loyalists and republicans than is implied by a simple vision of one as a restraint on the other' (M. O'Doherty, *The Trouble with Guns: Republican Strategy and the Provisional IRA* (Belfast: Blackstaff Press, 1998), p. 73). Cf. Charles Townshend's judgment: 'In fact the defenders [the IRA] brought down more trouble on the people they claimed to be protecting' (C. Townshend, *Ireland: The Twentieth Century* (London: Arnold, 1999), p. 208).
70. M. Fay, M. Morrissey and M. Smyth, *Northern Ireland's Troubles: The Human Costs* (London: Pluto Press, 1999), p. 178.
71. From a vast literature, see: *Disturbances in Northern Ireland: Report of the Commission Appointed by the Governor of Northern Ireland* (Belfast: HMSO, 1969), pp. 55–64; D. J. Smith and G. Chambers, *Inequality in Northern Ireland* (Oxford: Oxford University Press, 1991); P. A. Compton, 'Employment Differentials in Northern Ireland and Job Discrimination: A Critique' in P. J. Roche and B. Barton (eds), *The Northern Ireland Question: Myth and Reality* (Aldershot: Avebury, 1991); P. Devlin, *Straight Left: An Autobiography* (Belfast: Blackstaff Press, 1993); P. Devlin, *Yes We Have No Bananas: Outdoor Relief in Belfast 1920–39* (Belfast: Blackstaff Press, 1981); B. O'Leary and J. McGarry, *Explaining Northern Ireland: Broken Images* (Oxford: Blackwell, 1995), pp. 205–6, 283–5.
72. Basil Brooke, speaking on 12 July 1933, quoted in M. Farrell, *Northern Ireland: The Orange State* (London: Pluto Press, 1980; 1st edn 1976), p. 90.
73. P. Buckland, *A History of Northern Ireland* (Dublin: Gill and Macmillan, 1981), p. 63.

74. Smith and Chambers, *Inequality in Northern Ireland*, p. 234.

75. D. Miller, *On Nationality* (Oxford: Oxford University Press, 1995), p. 22.

76. Jeffrey Donaldson, interviewed by the author, Lisburn, 19 Apr. 2002. Jeffrey Donaldson: born 1962, Kilkeel, County Down; UUP MP for Lagan Valley since 1997.

77. After exhaustive scrutiny of competing frameworks, Michael Gallagher has suggested the appropriateness of a ' "three-nations" (or "two nations and part of another nation") perspective, identifying an Irish nation, an Ulster Protestant nation and a part of the British nation' (M. Gallagher, 'How Many Nations Are There in Ireland?', *Ethnic and Racial Studies* 18, 4 (1995), p. 715).

78. From the countless examples of unionists presenting their case in terms of democracy, see J. Hunter, *Unionism: A Brief History of the Ulster Unionist Council* (Belfast: UUP, 1993), which also draws attention to those unionist politicians (in unionist view, themselves principled democrats) killed by the IRA, pp. 4–5, 19, 27.

79. Though it might be noted that Provisional readings of history have often been unpersuasive in detail, when set against close scholarly appraisal. Compare, for example, Gerry Adams's claim that the eighteenth-century United Irishmen aimed 'to create a secular society' with the contextualized picture painted by the historian Ian McBride (Adams, *Before the Dawn*, p. 73; cf. I. R. McBride, *Scripture Politics: Ulster Presbyterians and Irish Radicalism in the Late Eighteenth Century* (Oxford: Oxford University Press, 1998)).

80. See, for example, the piece on British historian A. J. P. Taylor in *AP/RN* 13 Sept. 1990.

81. See, for example, reference to a MORI poll conducted in Britain and reported on Channel 4 television, which suggested that 61 per cent of people favoured withdrawal within four years (*AP/RN* 24 Oct. 1991).

82. *AP/RN* 23 Aug. 2001.

83. Unless stated otherwise, material concerning opinion polls in Britain and the Republic of Ireland is drawn from: B. C. Hayes and I. McAllister, 'British and Irish Public Opinion towards the Northern Ireland Problem', *Irish Political Studies* 11 (1996).

84. T. Garvin, 'The North and the Rest: The Politics of the Republic of Ireland' in C. Townshend (ed.), *Consensus in Ireland: Approaches and Recessions* (Oxford: Oxford University Press, 1988); D. G. Boyce, ' "Can Anyone Here Imagine . . .?": Southern Irish Political Parties and the Northern Ireland Problem' in Roche and Barton (eds), *Northern Ireland Question*; G. FitzGerald, *All in a Life: An Autobiography* (Dublin: Gill and Macmillan, 1992; 1st edn 1991), p. 259.

85. S. MacBride (ed.), *Ireland's Right to Sovereignty, Independence and Unity is Inalienable and Indefeasible* (Dublin: Hyland, n.d.), p. 4.
86. G. Howe, *Conflict of Loyalty* (London: Macmillan, 1994), p. 412.
87. M. Cunningham, *British Government Policy in Northern Ireland 1969–89: Its Nature and Execution* (Manchester: Manchester University Press, 1991); M. Cunningham, *British Government Policy in Northern Ireland 1969–2000* (Manchester: Manchester University Press, 2001).
88. Patrick Mayhew, lecture at Queen's University, Belfast, 22 Nov. 1993.
89. R. W. White, *Provisional Irish Republicans: An Oral and Interpretive History* (Westport: Greenwood Press, 1993), p. 172.
90. From the many studies that address this point, see, for example, S. Bruce, *The Red Hand: Protestant Paramilitaries in Northern Ireland* (Oxford: Oxford University Press, 1992), p. 290; J. Cusack and H. McDonald, *UVF* (Dublin: Poolbeg, 2000; 1st edn 1997), pp. 1–3.
91. C. von Clausewitz, *On War* (Harmondsworth: Penguin, 1968; 1st edn 1832), pp. 104, 119, 121; see also the valuable discussion of IRA strategy contained in Smith, *Fighting for Ireland?*
92. G. FitzGerald, *Towards a New Ireland* (Dublin: Torc, 1973; 1st edn 1972); C. C. O'Brien, *States of Ireland* (St Albans: Panther, 1974; 1st edn 1972), p. 314.
93. Whitaker had played a leading role in the Republic's northern policy since the mid-1960s, when he had set up the Lemass/O'Neill meetings.
94. T. K. Whitaker, *A Note on North–South Policy*, 11 Nov. 1968, Lynch Papers, NAD 2001/8/1.
95. Statement by Home Secretary Reginald Maudling issued 10 Aug. 1970, PROL PREM 15/101.
96. Though whether demography is likely to yield such a result seems far from clear: see P. A. Compton, 'Why There May Not Be a Catholic Majority', *Parliamentary Brief* 5, 6 (1998).
97. Minutes of Meeting held in Conference Room A, Cabinet Office, Whitehall, 22 Aug. 1969, PROL CAB 130/422.
98. Minutes of Meeting held in Conference Room A, Cabinet Office, 18 Sept. 1969, PROL CAB 130/422.
99. Adams, *Politics of Irish Freedom*, pp. 38, 111.
100. D. Miller (ed.), *Rethinking Northern Ireland: Culture, Ideology and Colonialism* (London: Longman, 1998); Bell, *IRA 1968–2000*, p. 87.
101. R. Eccleshall, 'Anglican Political Thought in the Century after the Revolution of 1688' in D. G. Boyce, R. Eccleshall and V. Geoghegan (eds), *Political Thought in Ireland since the Seventeenth Century* (London: Routledge, 1993); cf. S. J. Connolly, *Religion, Law and Power: The Making of Protestant Ireland 1660–1760* (Oxford: Oxford University Press, 1992).

102. W. R. Louis, 'The Dissolution of the British Empire' in J. M. Brown and W. R. Louis (eds), *The Twentieth Century* (Oxford History of the British Empire, vol. 4) (Oxford: Oxford University Press, 1999), p. 330.

103. D. H. Akenson, *The Irish Diaspora: A Primer* (Belfast: Institute of Irish Studies, 1993), p. 142; J. H. Ohlmeyer, '"Civilizinge of those Rude Partes": Colonisation within Britain and Ireland, 1580s–1640s' in N. Canny (ed.), *The Origins of Empire: British Overseas Enterprise to the Close of the Seventeenth Century* (Oxford History of the British Empire, vol. 1) (Oxford: Oxford University Press, 1998), p. 146.

104. T. Bartlett, '"This Famous Island Set in a Virginian Sea": Ireland in the British Empire, 1690–1801' in P. J. Marshall (ed.), *The Eighteenth Century* (Oxford History of the British Empire, vol. 2) (Oxford: Oxford University Press, 1998), p. 273.

105. Akenson, *Irish Diaspora*, p. 144.

106. D. Armitage, *The Ideological Origins of the British Empire* (Cambridge: Cambridge University Press, 2000), pp. 24–5.

107. Bartlett in Marshall (ed.), *Eighteenth Century*, pp. 253–4.

108. S. Howe, *Ireland and Empire: Colonial Legacies in Irish History and Culture* (Oxford: Oxford University Press, 2000).

109. Ibid., p. 4; N. Whyte, *Science, Colonialism and Ireland* (Cork: Cork University Press, 1999), p. 190; L. Kennedy, 'Modern Ireland: Post-Colonial Society or Post-Colonial Pretensions?', *Irish Review* 13 (1992–3).

110. D. G. Boyce, *Decolonisation and the British Empire, 1775–1997* (Basingstoke: Macmillan, 1999), p. 304.

111. M. Burleigh, *The Third Reich: A New History* (London: Macmillan, 2000), p. 571.

112. P. Routledge, *Public Servant, Secret Agent: The Elusive Life and Violent Death of Airey Neave* (London: Fourth Estate, 2002), pp. 2, 74, 79, 81, 83, 94, 161–89, 309.

113. Declan Moen, interviewed by the author, Belfast, 27 Sept. 2000.

114. See, for example, R. Needham, *Battling for Peace* (Belfast: Blackstaff Press, 1998), p. 319. Republicans themselves, of course, strongly denied any such accusation: Gerard Hodgins stated in January 1983 that republicans were 'opposed to fascism as it is merely an off-shoot of capitalism, and thus inimical to working-class progress' (Hodgins to the editor, *IN*, 30 Jan. 1983, LHLPC).

115. 'Irish republicanism has always been at the forefront of progressive forces in Ireland' (Magee, *Gangsters or Guerrillas?*, p. 10).

116. P. Freire, *Pedagogy of the Oppressed* (Harmondsworth: Penguin, 1996; 1st edn 1970), pp. 39, 91.

117. K. Boyle, T. Hadden and P. Hillyard, *Ten Years On in Northern Ireland: The Legal Control of Political Violence* (London: Cobden Trust, 1980), p. 19.

118. R. English, *Radicals and the Republic: Socialist Republicanism in the Irish Free State 1925–1937* (Oxford, Oxford University Press, 1994), pp. 54, 216–37.

119. Adams, *Politics of Irish Freedom*, p. 132.

120. White, *Provisional Irish Republicans*, p. 90.

121. Coogan, *The IRA*, p. 475.

122. B. O'Duffy, 'Violence in Northern Ireland 1969–1994: Sectarian or Ethno-National?', *Ethnic and Racial Studies* 18, 4 (1995).

123. T. McKearney, 'Republicanism Should Be Neither Catholic or Nationalist', *The Other View* 1 (2000), p. 10.

124. Sean Garland, interviewed by the author, Dublin, 24 Feb. 1987. Garland had been one of Cathal Goulding's key supporters within the 1960s IRA.

125. D. O'Hagan, 'The Concept of Republicanism' in N. Porter (ed.), *The Republican Ideal: Current Perspectives* (Belfast: Blackstaff Press, 1998), pp. 85, 90.

126. J. Whyte, *Interpreting Northern Ireland* (Oxford: Oxford University Press, 1990), p. 125.

127. George Harrison, interviewed by the author, New York, 30 Oct. 2000.

128. Jeffrey Donaldson, interviewed by the author, Lisburn, 19 Apr. 2002.

129. Ian Paisley, interviewed by the author, Belfast, 21 Feb. 1994.

130. Quoted in P. Taylor, *Loyalists* (London: Bloomsbury, 1999), p. 123.

131. It should also be noted that mainstream Ulster unionist politicians have forthrightly condemned loyalist paramilitary violence; the UUP's Jeffrey Donaldson: 'I on many occasions have stuck my neck out and condemned, unequivocally, loyalist violence from whatever quarter it has come' (Jeffrey Donaldson, interviewed by the author, Lisburn, 19 Apr. 2002).

132. R. Eames, *Chains to be Broken: A Personal Reflection on Northern Ireland and Its People* (Belfast: Blackstaff Press, 1993; 1st edn 1992), pp. 16–17, 160.

133. D. Kiberd, *Irish Classics* (London: Granta, 2000), p. 632.

134. D. Eastwood, *Government and Community in the English Provinces, 1700–1870* (Basingstoke: Macmillan, 1997), p. 5.

135. Magee, *Gangsters or Guerrillas?*

136. Thus John Bowyer Bell, one of the most experienced observers of the IRA, effectively presents IRA violence as emerging from an essentially non-rational source, recently describing the republican world as 'a matter of faith and perception and a dream', arguing that 'the ideology

of the Provisional IRA is not about logic or reason or the correlation of forces, not about political structures or British capacity, not a matter of analysis, not a display of ideas but about the perception assured by the dream' (Bell, *IRA 1968–2000*, pp. xiii, 62).

137. Of the very many available examples, see the excellent recent treatment of one: E. Cameron, *Waldenses: Rejections of Holy Church in Medieval Europe* (Oxford: Blackwell, 2000).

138. See, for example, Sunil Khilnani's fine treatment of the postwar French left: *Arguing Revolution: The Intellectual Left in Postwar France* (New Haven: Yale University Press, 1993).

139. Again, many examples suggest themselves; from among them, see Michael Gilsenan's compelling *Lords of the Lebanese Marches: Violence and Narrative in an Arab Society* (London: I. B. Tauris, 1996).

140. IRA member, quoted in T. Harnden, *'Bandit Country': The IRA and South Armagh* (London: Hodder and Stoughton, 1999), p. 47.

141. E. Collins, *Killing Rage* (London: Granta, 1997), p. 96.

142. Coogan, *The IRA*, pp. 604, 698; Harnden, *'Bandit Country'*, p. 47.

143. *IT* 17 Dec. 2001.

144. Figures here, including table, compiled from D. McKittrick *et al.*, *Lost Lives: The Stories of the Men, Women and Children Who Died as a Result of the Northern Ireland Troubles* (Edinburgh: Mainstream, 2001; 1st edn 1999), pp. 1495, 1499, 1502, 1504. The various compilations of statistics on troubles' deaths can vary, usually to limited effect. To offset the potential bias contained in any one source, I have drawn material from a number of reliable books, the notes indicating specific sources. The main volumes used have been McKittrick *et al.*, *Lost Lives*; M. Sutton, *Bear in Mind These Dead: An Index of Deaths from the Conflict in Ireland 1969–1993* (Belfast: Beyond the Pale, 1994); M. Fay, M. Morrissey and M. Smyth, *Northern Ireland's Troubles: The Human Costs* (London: Pluto Press, 1999).

145. Fay et al., *Human Costs*, pp. 145, 164.

146. D. MacDonald, *The Chosen Few: Exploding Myths in South Armagh* (Cork: Mercier, 2000), pp. 35, 282. See also the compelling account in Harnden, *'Bandit Country'*.

147. B. C. Hayes and I. McAllister, 'Sowing Dragon's Teeth: Public Support for Political Violence and Paramilitarism in Northern Ireland', *Political Studies* 49, 5 (2001), pp. 901, 903.

148. 'Guerrilla war . . . An irregular war carried on by small bodies of men acting independently' (*Shorter Oxford English Dictionary: vol. 1* (Oxford: Oxford University Press, 1980; 1st edn 1933), p. 900).

149. The terms 'terrorism' and 'terrorist' are frequently used by observers in

relation to the IRA, and a plausible case could be made for so doing. But I have eschewed the term in this book for two reasons. First, it is a label so reeking in condemnation that its analytical and explanatory usefulness seems to me to have diminished. Second, the fairest definitions of the word – such as 'an organized system of intimidation, esp. for political ends' (*Chambers 20th Century Dictionary* (Edinburgh: Chambers, 1983), p. 1335) – could neatly fit some state actions in the war as well, and this again blunts the term's use for analysis. To call the IRA a 'guerrilla force' distinguishes them from the British Army, which is clearly not such a force. To call the IRA 'terrorists' risks opening up an antiphonal sequence of largely pointless name-calling.

150. C. Townshend, *Political Violence in Ireland: Government and Resistance Since 1848* (Oxford: Oxford University Press, 1984; 1st edn 1983), pp. 407–8.
151. Ex-IRA man, interviewed by the author, Belfast, 31 Oct. 2001.
152. Patrick Magee, in 'Facing the Enemy', BBC 2001.
153. Tommy McKearney, interviewed by the author, Belfast, 20 Sept. 2000.
154. Patrick Magee, interviewed by the author, Belfast, 5 Mar. 2002.
155. IRA statement of 16 July 2002, quoted in *IN* 17 July 2002.
156. Marian Price, interviewed by the author, Belfast, 28 Feb. 2002.
157. *IT* 4 Nov. 1998.
158. G. Adams, speech in Dublin, 13 Apr. 2002, p. 3, copy in LHLPC.
159. Patrick Magee, interviewed by the author, Belfast, 5 Mar. 2002.

Bibliography

MANUSCRIPTS, ARCHIVES

Archives Department, University College, Dublin – Ernest Blythe Papers, Caithlin Brugha Papers, Daniel Bryan Papers, Sheila Humphreys Papers, Sean MacEntee Papers, Richard Mulcahy Papers, Ernie O'Malley Papers, Moss Twomey Papers.

Linen Hall Library Political Collection, Belfast – H-Block/Hunger Strike Boxes, Peace Process Boxes, Sinn Féin (Provisional) Boxes, Miscellaneous Archives.

National Archives, Dublin – Cabinet Minutes, Jack Lynch Papers, Military Intelligence Files, Files of the Department of Defence, Files of the Department of the Taoiseach, Files of the Department of Foreign Affairs.

National Library of Ireland, Dublin – Michael Collins Papers, Frank Gallagher Papers, Ernie O'Malley Papers, Joseph McGarrity Papers.

Papers in Private Possession – Papers in the possession of Roy Johnston, Papers in the possession of Cormac O'Malley.

Public Record Office, London – Records of the Cabinet Office, Colonial Office, Ministry of Defence, Dominions Office, Prime Minister's Office.

Public Record Office, Northern Ireland – Cabinet Files, McLaughlin Papers.

NEWSPAPERS

An Phoblacht, An Phoblacht/Republican News, An t-Óglách, Ballymena Guardian, Belfast Telegraph, Daily Telegraph, Derry Journal, Guardian, Independent, Irish Independent, Irish News, Irish People, Irish Press, Irish Times, Irish Voice,

Northern Whig, Observer, Republican Congress, Republican News, Saoirse, Sunday Business Post, Sunday Independent, Sunday Life, Sunday Telegraph, Sunday Times, Sunday Tribune, Times, Tuairisc, United Irishman, War News, Wolfe Tone Weekly.

BOOKS, ARTICLES AND OTHER WRITTEN MATERIAL

Adams, G., *Falls Memories* (Dingle: Brandon, 1983; 1st edn 1982).
—— *The Politics of Irish Freedom* (Dingle: Brandon, 1986).
—— *A Pathway to Peace* (Cork: Mercier, 1988).
—— *Cage Eleven* (Dingle: Brandon, 1990).
—— *Free Ireland: Towards a Lasting Peace* (Dingle: Brandon, 1995; 1st edn 1986).
—— *Before the Dawn: An Autobiography* (London: Heinemann, 1996).
—— *An Irish Voice: The Quest for Peace* (Dingle: Mount Eagle, 1997).
—— *Who Fears to Speak...? The Story of Belfast and the 1916 Rising* (Belfast: Beyond the Pale, 2001; 1st edn 1991).
—— *An Irish Journal* (Dingle: Brandon, 2001).
—— 'To Cherish a Just and Lasting Peace', *Fordham International Law Journal* 22, 4 (1999).
Adams, J., *Tony Benn: A Biography* (London: Macmillan, 1992).
Adams, J., Morgan, R., and Bambridge, A., *Ambush: The War between the SAS and the IRA* (London: Pan, 1988).
Akenson, D. H., *The Irish Diaspora: A Primer* (Belfast: Institute of Irish Studies, 1993).
—— *Conor: A Biography of Conor Cruise O'Brien* (*vol. 1, Narrative; vol. 2, Anthology*) (Montreal: McGill–Queen's University Press, 1994).
Alessandrini, A. C. (ed.), *Frantz Fanon: Critical Perspectives* (London: Routledge, 1999).
Alexander, Y., and O'Day, A. (eds), *Ireland's Terrorist Dilemma* (Dordrecht: Martinus Nijhoff, 1986).
Allen, G., *The Garda Siochana: Policing Independent Ireland 1922–82* (Dublin: Gill and Macmillan, 1999).
Amnesty International, *Political Killings in Northern Ireland* (London: Amnesty International, 1994).
Anderson, D., *14 May Days: The Inside Story of the Loyalist Strike of 1974* (Dublin: Gill and Macmillan, 1994).
Anderson, J. L., *Che Guevara: A Revolutionary Life* (London: Bantam, 1997).
Anderson, M., and Bort, E. (eds), *The Irish Border: History, Politics, Culture* (Liverpool: Liverpool University Press, 1999).

Anderson, W. K., *James Connolly and the Irish Left* (Blackrock: Irish Academic Press, 1994).

Andrews, C. S., *Dublin Made Me: An Autobiography* (Cork: Mercier, 1979).

—— *Man of No Property: An Autobiography* (*vol. 2*) (Cork: Mercier, 1982).

Aretxaga, B., *Shattering Silence: Women, Nationalism and Political Subjectivity in Northern Ireland* (Princeton: Princeton University Press, 1997).

Armitage, D., *The Ideological Origins of the British Empire* (Cambridge: Cambridge University Press, 2000).

Arthur, M., *Northern Ireland Soldiers Talking* (London: Sidgwick and Jackson, 1987).

Arthur, P., *The People's Democracy 1968–1973* (Belfast: Blackstaff Press, 1974).

—— 'The Anglo-Irish Joint Declaration: Towards a Lasting Peace?', *Government and Opposition* 29, 2 (1994).

—— *Special Relationships: Britain, Ireland and the Northern Ireland Problem* (Belfast: Blackstaff Press, 2000).

Asher, M., *Shoot to Kill: A Soldier's Journey through Violence* (London: Viking, 1990).

Augusteijn, J., *From Public Defiance to Guerrilla Warfare: The Experience of Ordinary Volunteers in the Irish War of Independence 1916–1921* (Blackrock: Irish Academic Press, 1996).

Baker, K., *The Turbulent Years: My Life in Politics* (London: Faber and Faber, 1993).

Ball, S. (ed.), *A Policeman's Ireland: Recollections of Samuel Waters, RIC* (Cork: Cork University Press, 1999).

Ballymacarrett Research Group, *Lagan Enclave: A History of Conflict in the Short Strand 1886–1997* (Belfast: BRG, 1997).

Bardon, J., *A History of Ulster* (Belfast: Blackstaff Press, 1992).

Barnard, T., *Cromwellian Ireland: English Government and Reform in Ireland 1649–1660* (Oxford: Oxford University Press, 2000; 1st edn 1975).

Barrington, B. (ed.), *The Wartime Broadcasts of Francis Stuart 1942–1944* (Dublin: Lilliput, 2000).

Barritt, D. P., and Carter, C. F., *The Northern Ireland Problem: A Study in Group Relations* (Oxford: Oxford University Press, 1972: 1st edn 1962).

Barry, T., *The Reality of the Anglo-Irish War 1920–21 in West Cork: Refutations, Corrections and Comments on Liam Deasy's 'Towards Ireland Free'* (Tralee: Anvil, 1974).

—— *Guerilla Days in Ireland* (Dublin: Anvil, 1989; 1st edn 1949).

Bartlett, T., *Theobald Wolfe Tone* (Dundalk: Dundalgan Press, 1997).

Barzilay, D., *The British Army in Ulster* (Belfast: Century Services, 4 vols, 1973, 1975, 1978, 1981).

Bean, K., *The New Departure: Recent Developments in Irish Republican Ideology and Strategy* (Liverpool: Institute of Irish Studies, 1994).

—— and Hayes, M. (eds), *Republican Voices* (Monaghan: Seesyu Press, 2001).

Béaslaí, P., *Michael Collins and the Making of a New Ireland* (Dublin: Phoenix, 1926, 2 vols).

—— *Michael Collins, Soldier and Statesman* (Dublin: Talbot Press, 1937).

Behan, B., *Borstal Boy* (London: Arrow Books, 1990; 1st edn 1958).

—— *Confessions of an Irish Rebel* (London: Arrow Books, 1991; 1st edn 1965).

Bell, J. B., *The Secret Army: The IRA 1916–1979* (Swords: Poolbeg, 1989; 1st edn 1970).

—— *IRA Tactics and Targets* (Swords: Poolbeg, 1990).

—— *The Gun in Politics: An Analysis of Irish Political Conflict, 1916–1986* (New Brunswick: Transaction Publishers, 1991; 1st edn 1987).

—— *The Irish Troubles: A Generation of Violence, 1967–1992* (Dublin: Gill and Macmillan, 1993).

—— *Back to the Future: The Protestants and a United Ireland* (Dublin: Poolbeg, 1996).

—— *The IRA 1968–2000: Analysis of a Secret Army* (London: Frank Cass, 2000).

Benn, T., *Arguments for Socialism* (Harmondsworth: Penguin, 1980; 1st edn 1979).

Beresford, D., *Ten Men Dead: The Story of the 1981 Irish Hunger Strike* (London: Grafton, 1987).

Bew, P., *Ideology and the Irish Question: Ulster Unionism and Irish Nationalism 1912–1916* (Oxford: Oxford University Press, 1994).

—— *John Redmond* (Dundalk: Dundalgan Press, 1996).

—— Gibbon, P., and Patterson, H., *Northern Ireland 1921–1994: Political Forces and Social Classes* (London: Serif, 1995).

—— Patterson, H., and Teague, P., *Between War and Peace: The Political Future of Northern Ireland* (London: Lawrence and Wishart, 1997).

—— and Gillespie, G., *Northern Ireland: A Chronology of the Troubles 1968–1999* (Dublin: Gill and Macmillan, 1999).

Bishop, P., and Mallie, E., *The Provisional IRA* (London: Corgi, 1988; 1st edn 1987).

Blake, J. W., *Northern Ireland in the Second World War* (Belfast: Blackstaff Press, 2000; 1st edn 1956).

Bloody Sunday, 1972: Lord Widgery's Report of Events in Londonderry, Northern Ireland, on 30 January 1972 (London: Stationery Office, 2001; 1st edn 1972).

Bloomfield, D., *Political Dialogue in Northern Ireland: The Brooke Initiative, 1989–92* (Basingstoke: Macmillan, 1998).

Bloomfield, K., *Stormont in Crisis: A Memoir* (Belfast: Blackstaff Press, 1994).

—— *We Will Remember Them: Report of the Northern Ireland Victims Commissioner, Sir Kenneth Bloomfield* (Belfast: Stationery Office, 1998).

Boland, K., *'We Won't Stand (Idly) By'* (Dublin: Kelly Kane, n.d.).

Bolton, R., *Death on the Rock and Other Stories* (London: Allen, 1990).

Boulton, D., *The UVF 1966–73: An Anatomy of Loyalist Rebellion* (Dublin: Torc, 1973).

Bourke, J. (ed.), *The Misfit Soldier: Edward Casey's War Story 1914–1918* (Cork: Cork University Press, 1999).

Bowden, T., 'Bloody Sunday – A Reappraisal', *European Studies Review* 2, 1 (1972).

Bowman, J., *De Valera and the Ulster Question, 1917–1973* (Oxford: Oxford University Press, 1982).

Boyce, D. G., *The Irish Question and British Politics 1868–1986* (Basingstoke: Macmillan, 1988).

—— *The Sure Confusing Drum: Ireland and the First World War* (Swansea: University College of Swansea, 1993).

—— *Nationalism in Ireland* (London: Routledge, 1995; 1st edn 1982).

—— *Decolonisation and the British Empire, 1775–1997* (Basingstoke: Macmillan, 1999).

—— (ed.), *The Revolution in Ireland, 1879–1923* (Basingstoke: Macmillan, 1988).

—— Eccleshall, R., and Geoghegan, V. (eds), *Political Thought in Ireland since the Seventeenth Century* (London: Routledge, 1993).

Boyd, A., *Jack White: First Commander Irish Citizen Army* (Belfast: Donaldson Archives, 2001).

—— *Republicanism and Loyalty in Ireland* (Belfast: Donaldson Archives, 2001).

Boyle, K., and Hadden, T., *Ireland: A Positive Proposal* (Harmondsworth: Penguin, 1985).

—— and Hadden, T., *Northern Ireland: The Choice* (Harmondsworth: Penguin, 1994).

—— and Hadden, T., *The Anglo-Irish Agreement: Commentary, Text and Official Review* (London: Sweet and Maxwell, 1989).

—— Hadden, T., and Hillyard, P., *Ten Years On in Northern Ireland: The Legal Control of Political Violence* (London: Cobden Trust, 1980).

Bradford, N., *A Sword Bathed in Heaven* (Basingstoke: Pickering, 1984).

Bradley, A., *Requiem for a Spy: The Killing of Robert Nairac* (Cork: Mercier, 1993).

Brady, C., *Guardians of the Peace* (Dublin: Gill and Macmillan, 1974).

Brady, E. M., *Ireland's Secret Service in England* (Dublin: Talbot Press, n.d.).

Breen, D., *My Fight for Irish Freedom* (Dublin: Anvil, 1989; 1st edn 1924).

Brennan, M., *The War in Clare 1911–1921: Personal Memoirs of the Irish War of Independence* (Dublin: Four Courts Press, 1980).

Brennan-Whitmore, W. J., *With the Irish in Frongoch* (Dublin: Talbot Press, 1917).

Brewer, J. D., and Magee, K., *Inside the RUC: Routine Policing in a Divided Society* (Oxford: Oxford University Press, 1991).

Briscoe, R., *For the Life of Me* (London: Longmans, 1959).

Brown, J. M., and Louis, W. R. (eds), *The Twentieth Century* (Oxford History of the British Empire, vol. 4) (Oxford: Oxford University Press, 1999).

Browne, N., *Against the Tide* (Dublin: Gill and Macmillan, 1986).

Bruce, S., *God Save Ulster! The Religion and Politics of Paisleyism* (Oxford: Oxford University Press, 1989; 1st edn 1986).

—— *The Red Hand: Protestant Paramilitaries in Northern Ireland* (Oxford: Oxford University Press, 1992).

—— *The Edge of the Union: The Ulster Loyalist Political Vision* (Oxford: Oxford University Press, 1994).

—— 'Victim Selection in Ethnic Conflict: Motives and Attitudes in Irish Republicanism', *Terrorism and Political Violence* 9, 1 (1997).

Bryan, D., *Orange Parades: The Politics of Ritual, Tradition and Control* (London: Pluto Press, 2000).

Buckland, P., *The Factory of Grievances: Devolved Government in Northern Ireland, 1921–39* (Dublin: Gill and Macmillan, 1979).

—— *James Craig, Lord Craigavon* (Dublin: Gill and Macmillan, 1980).

—— *A History of Northern Ireland* (Dublin: Gill and Macmillan, 1981).

Buckley, D. N., *James Fintan Lalor: Radical* (Cork: Cork University Press, 1990).

Burleigh, M., *The Third Reich: A New History* (London: Macmillan, 2000).

Burton, F., *The Politics of Legitimacy: Struggles in a Belfast Community* (London: Routledge and Kegan Paul, 1978).

Butler, E., *Butler's Flying Column* (London: Leo Cooper, 1971).

Byrne, P., *Memories of the Republican Congress* (London: Connolly Association, n.d.).

—— *The Irish Republican Congress Revisited* (London: Connolly Publications, 1994).

Byron, R., *Irish America* (Oxford: Oxford University Press, 1999).

Callaghan, J., *A House Divided: The Dilemma of Northern Ireland* (London: William Collins, 1973).

Cameron, E., *Waldenses: Rejections of Holy Church in Medieval Europe* (Oxford: Blackwell, 2000).

Campbell, B., McKeown, L., and O'Hagan, F. (eds), *Nor Meekly Serve My Time: The H-Block Struggle 1976–1981* (Belfast: Beyond the Pale, 1994).

Campbell, C., *Emergency Law in Ireland 1918–1925* (Oxford: Oxford University Press, 1994).

Cannadine, D., *Class in Britain* (New Haven: Yale University Press, 1998).

—— *Ornamentalism: How the British Saw Their Empire* (London: Allen Lane, 2001).

Canny, N. (ed.), *The Origins of Empire: British Overseas Enterprise to the Close of the Seventeenth Century* (Oxford History of the British Empire, vol. 1) (Oxford: Oxford University Press, 1998).

Carey, T., *Mountjoy: The Story of a Prison* (Cork: Collins, 2000).

Caulfield, M., *The Easter Rebellion* (London: Frederick Muller, 1964).

Chavasse, M., *Terence MacSwiney* (Dublin: Clonmore and Reynolds, 1961).

Childers, R. E., 'Law and Order in Ireland', *Studies* 8 (1919).

Clancy, T., *Patriot Games* (New York: Berkley, 1988; 1st edn 1987).

Clark, D. J., *Irish Blood: Northern Ireland and the American Conscience* (Port Washington: Kennikat Press, 1977).

Clarke, L., *Broadening the Battlefield: The H-Blocks and the Rise of Sinn Féin* (Dublin: Gill and Macmillan, 1987).

—— and Johnston, K., *Martin McGuinness: From Guns to Government* (Edinburgh: Mainstream, 2001).

Clausewitz, C. von, *On War* (Harmondsworth: Penguin, 1968; 1st edn 1832).

Cochrane, F., 'The Isolation of Northern Ireland', *Political Studies* 43, 3 (1995).

—— *Unionist Politics and the Politics of Unionism since the Anglo-Irish Agreement* (Cork: Cork University Press, 1997).

Coldrey, B., *Faith and Fatherland: The Christian Brothers and the Development of Irish Nationalism, 1838–1921* (Dublin: Gill and Macmillan, 1988).

Collins, E., *Killing Rage* (London: Granta, 1997).

Collins, M., *The Path to Freedom* (Cork: Mercier, 1968; 1st edn 1922).

Collins, T., *The Irish Hunger Strike* (Dublin: White Island Book Company, 1986).

Comerford, J. J., *My Kilkenny IRA Days 1916–22* (Kilkenny: privately published, 1980; 1st edn 1978).

Comerford, M., *The First Dáil: January 21st 1919* (Dublin: Joe Clarke, 1969).

Comerford, R. V., *The Fenians in Context: Irish Politics and Society 1848–82* (Dublin: Wolfhound, 1998; 1st edn 1985).

Compton, P. A., 'Why There May Not Be a Catholic Majority', *Parliamentary Brief* 5, 6 (1998).

Conlon, G., *Proved Innocent* (Harmondsworth: Penguin, 1993; 1st edn 1990).

Connolly, J., *Collected Works* (Dublin: New Books, 2 vols, 1987, 1988).

Connolly, S. J., *Religion, Law and Power: The Making of Protestant Ireland 1660–1760* (Oxford: Oxford University Press, 1992).

Conroy, J., *War as a Way of Life: A Belfast Diary* (London: Heinemann, 1988).

Coogan, O., *Politics and War in Meath 1913–23* (Dublin: Folens, 1983).

Coogan, T. P., *On the Blanket: The H-Block Story* (Dublin: Ward River Press, 1980).

—— *The IRA* (London: HarperCollins, 1987; 1st edn 1970).

—— *Michael Collins: A Biography* (London: Hutchinson, 1990).

—— *De Valera: Long Fellow, Long Shadow* (London: Hutchinson, 1993).

Costello, F. J., *Enduring the Most: The Life and Death of Terence MacSwiney* (Dingle: Brandon, 1995).

Coughlan, A., *C. Desmond Greaves, 1913–1988: An Obituary Essay* (Dublin: Irish Labour History Society, 1991; 1st edn 1990).

Cox, M., 'Bringing in the "International": The IRA Ceasefire and the End of the Cold War', *International Affairs* 73, 4 (1997).

—— ' "Cinderella at the Ball": Explaining the End of the War in Northern Ireland', *Millennium* 27, 2 (1998).

—— Guelke, A., and Stephen, F. (eds), *A Farewell to Arms? From 'Long War' to Long Peace in Northern Ireland* (Manchester: Manchester University Press, 2000).

Cronin, M., *The Blueshirts and Irish Politics* (Dublin: Four Courts Press, 1997).

—— and Regan, J. M. (eds), *Ireland: The Politics of Independence, 1922–49* (Basingstoke: Macmillan, 2000).

Cronin, S., *Frank Ryan: The Search for the Republic* (Dublin: Repsol, 1980).

—— *Irish Nationalism: A History of its Roots and Ideology* (Dublin: Academy Press, 1980).

Cunningham, M., *British Government Policy in Northern Ireland 1969–89: Its Nature and Execution* (Manchester: Manchester University Press, 1991).

—— 'The Political Language of John Hume', *Irish Political Studies* 12 (1997).

—— *British Government Policy in Northern Ireland 1969–2000* (Manchester: Manchester University Press, 2001).

Curtin, N. J., *The United Irishmen: Popular Politics in Ulster and Dublin 1791–1798* (Oxford: Oxford University Press, 1994).

Cusack, J., and McDonald, H., *UVF* (Dublin: Poolbeg, 2000; 1st edn 1997).

Dalton, C., *With the Dublin Brigade (1917–1921)* (London: Peter Davies, 1929).

Daly, C. B., *Violence in Ireland and Christian Conscience* (Dublin: Veritas, 1973).

—— *Peace: The Work of Justice* (Dublin: Veritas, 1980; 1st edn 1979).

Darby, J., *Scorpions in a Bottle: Conflicting Cultures in Northern Ireland* (London: MRG, 1997).

Darwin, J. G., 'The Fear of Falling: British Politics and Imperial Decline Since 1900', *Transactions of the Royal Historical Society* 5th Series, 36 (1986).

Davis, R., *Revolutionary Imperialist: William Smith O'Brien* (Dublin: Lilliput, 1998).

Deane, S., *Reading in the Dark* (London: Jonathan Cape, 1996).

Deasy, L., *Towards Ireland Free: The West Cork Brigade in the War of Independence, 1917–1921* (Cork: Mercier, 1977).

—— *Brother Against Brother* (Cork: Mercier, 1982).

De Bréadún, D., *The Far Side of Revenge: Making Peace in Northern Ireland* (Cork: Collins, 2001).

Deutsch, R. (ed.), *Les Républicanismes Irlandais* (Rennes: Presses Universitaires de Rennes, 1997).

Devlin, B., *The Price of My Soul* (London: Pan, 1969).

Devlin, P., *Yes We Have No Bananas: Outdoor Relief in Belfast 1920–39* (Belfast: Blackstaff Press, 1981).

—— *Straight Left: An Autobiography* (Belfast: Blackstaff Press, 1993).

Dewar, M., *The British Army in Northern Ireland* (London: Arms and Armour Press, 1985).

Dillon, M., and Lehane, D., *Political Murder in Northern Ireland* (Harmondsworth: Penguin, 1973).

Disturbances in Northern Ireland: Report of the Commission Appointed by the Governor of Northern Ireland (Belfast: HMSO, 1969).

Dixon, P., 'Internationalisation and Unionist Isolation: A Response to Feargal Cochrane', *Political Studies* 43, 3 (1995).

—— *Northern Ireland: The Politics of War and Peace* (Basingstoke: Palgrave, 2001).

Doherty, M. A., 'Kevin Barry and the Anglo-Irish Propaganda War', *Irish Historical Studies* 32, 126 (2000).

Doherty, P., and Hegarty, P., *Paddy Bogside* (Cork: Mercier, 2001).

Dooley, B., *Black and Green: The Fight for Civil Rights in Northern Ireland and Black America* (London: Pluto Press, 1998).

Doyle, C., *People at War* (Dublin: Teoranta, 1975).

Doyle, R., *A Star Called Henry* (London: Jonathan Cape, 1999).

Drower, G., *John Hume: Peacemaker* (London: Victor Gollancz, 1995).

Dumbrell, J., 'The United States and the Northern Irish Conflict 1969–94: From Indifference to Intervention', *Irish Studies in International Affairs* 6 (1995).

Dunne, D., *The Birmingham Six* (Dublin: Birmingham Six Committee, 1988).

Dunphy, R., *The Making of Fianna Fáil Power in Ireland 1923–1948* (Oxford: Oxford University Press, 1995).

Durcan, P., *The Selected Paul Durcan* (Belfast: Blackstaff Press, 1985; 1st edn 1982).

Dwyer, T. R., *Tans, Terror and Troubles: Kerry's Real Fighting Story 1913–23* (Cork: Mercier, 2001).

Eames, R., *Chains to be Broken: A Personal Reflection on Northern Ireland and Its People* (Belfast: Blackstaff Press, 1993; 1st edn 1992).

Eckert, N., *Fatal Encounter: The Story of the Gibraltar Killings* (Dublin: Poolbeg, 1999).

Edwards, R. D., *Patrick Pearse: The Triumph of Failure* (Swords: Poolbeg, 1990; 1st edn 1977).

—— *James Connolly* (Dublin: Gill and Macmillan, 1981).

Egan, B., and McCormack, V., *Burntollet* (London: LRS Publishers, 1969).

Elborn, G., *Francis Stuart: A Life* (Dublin: Raven Arts Press, 1990).

Elliott, M., *Wolfe Tone: Prophet of Irish Independence* (New Haven: Yale University Press, 1989).

—— *The Catholics of Ulster: A History* (Harmondsworth: Allen Lane, 2000).

—— (ed.), *The Long Road to Peace in Northern Ireland* (Liverpool: Liverpool University Press, 2002).

Elliott, S., and Flackes, W. D., *Northern Ireland: A Political Directory 1968–1993* (Belfast: Blackstaff Press, 1994).

Ellison, G., and Smyth, J., *The Crowned Harp: Policing Northern Ireland* (London: Pluto Press, 2000).

English, R., *Radicals and the Republic: Socialist Republicanism in the Irish Free State 1925–1937* (Oxford: Oxford University Press, 1994).

—— 'Reflections on Republican Socialism in Ireland: Marxian Roots and Irish Historical Dynamics', *History of Political Thought* 17, 4 (1996).

—— *Ernie O'Malley: IRA Intellectual* (Oxford: Oxford University Press, 1998).

—— and O'Malley, C. (eds), *Prisoners: The Civil War Letters of Ernie O'Malley* (Dublin: Poolbeg, 1991).

—— and Townshend, C. (eds), *The State: Historical and Political Dimensions* (London: Routledge, 1999).

Evans, G., and O'Leary, B., 'Frameworked Futures: Intransigence and Flexibility in the Northern Ireland Elections of May 30 1996', *Irish Political Studies* 12 (1997).

Ewart-Biggs, J., *Pay, Pack and Follow: Memoirs* (London: Weidenfeld and Nicolson, 1984).

Fairweather, E., McDonough, R., and McFadyean, M., *Only the Rivers Run Free: Northern Ireland – The Women's War* (London: Pluto Press, 1984).

Fanon, F., *The Wretched of the Earth* (Harmondsworth: Penguin, 1967; 1st edn 1961).

Farrell, M., *Northern Ireland: The Orange State* (London: Pluto Press, 1980; 1st edn 1976).

—— (ed.), *Twenty Years On* (Dingle: Brandon, 1988).

Farren, S., and Mulvihill, R. F., *Paths to a Settlement in Northern Ireland* (Gerrards Cross: Colin Smythe, 2000).

Farry, M., *The Aftermath of Revolution: Sligo 1921–23* (Dublin: UCD Press, 2000).

Faulkner, B., *Memoirs of a Statesman* (London: Weidenfeld and Nicolson, 1978).

Fay, M., Morrissey, M., and Smyth, M., *Northern Ireland's Troubles: The Human Costs* (London: Pluto Press, 1999).

Feehan, J. M., *Bobby Sands and the Tragedy of Northern Ireland* (Cork: Mercier, 1983).

Feeney, B., *Sinn Féin: A Hundred Turbulent Years* (Dublin: O'Brien, 2002).

Fiacc, P., *Ruined Pages: Selected Poems* (Belfast: Blackstaff Press, 1994).

Fisk, R., *In Time of War: Ireland, Ulster and the Price of Neutrality 1939–45* (London: Paladin, 1985; 1st edn 1983).

FitzGerald, D., *Memoirs of Desmond FitzGerald, 1913–1916* (London: Routledge and Kegan Paul, 1968).

FitzGerald, G., *Towards a New Ireland* (Dublin: Torc, 1973; 1st edn 1972).

—— *All in a Life: An Autobiography* (Dublin: Gill and Macmillan, 1992; 1st edn 1991).

Fitzpatrick, D., 'The Logic of Collective Sacrifice: Ireland and the British Army 1914–1918', *Historical Journal* 38, 4 (1995).

—— *Politics and Irish Life 1913–1921: Provincial Experience of War and Revolution* (Cork: Cork University Press, 1998; 1st edn 1977).

—— *The Two Irelands 1912–1939* (Oxford: Oxford University Press, 1998).

—— (ed.), *Ireland and the First World War* (Mullingar: Lilliput, 1988).

—— (ed.), *Revolution? Ireland 1917–1923* (Dublin: TCD, 1990).

Foley, C., *Legion of the Rearguard: The IRA and the Modern Irish State* (London: Pluto Press, 1992).

Foley, G., *Ireland in Rebellion* (New York: Pathfinder Press, 1971).

Foot, P., *Who Framed Colin Wallace?* (London: Macmillan, 1989).

Foster, R. F., *Modern Ireland 1600–1972* (London: Allen Lane, 1988).

—— *Paddy and Mr Punch: Connections in Irish and English History* (London: Allen Lane, 1993).

—— *W. B. Yeats: A Life. 1: The Apprentice Mage* (Oxford: Oxford University Press, 1997).

—— *The Irish Story: Telling Tales and Making it up in Ireland* (London: Allen Lane, 2001).

Foy, M., and Barton, B., *The Easter Rising* (Stroud: Sutton, 1999).

Freire, P., *Pedagogy of the Oppressed* (Harmondsworth: Penguin, 1996; 1st edn 1970).

Freyer, G., *Peadar O'Donnell* (Lewisburg: Bucknell University Press, 1973).

Gaffikin, F., and Morrissey, M., *Northern Ireland: The Thatcher Years* (London: Zed Books, 1990).

Gallagher, E., and Worrall, S., *Christians in Ulster 1968–1980* (Oxford: Oxford University Press, 1982).

Gallagher, F., *Days of Fear* (London: John Murray, 1928).

Gallagher, M., 'Do Ulster Unionists Have a Right to Self-Determination?', *Irish Political Studies* 5 (1990).

—— 'How Many Nations are There in Ireland?', *Ethnic and Racial Studies* 18, 4 (1995).

—— (ed.), *Irish Elections 1922–44: Results and Analysis* (Limerick, PSAI Press, 1993).

—— and Sinnott, R. (eds), *How Ireland Voted: 1989* (Galway: Centre for the Study of Irish Elections, 1990).

—— and Laver, M. (eds), *How Ireland Voted 1992* (Dublin: Folens, 1993).

Garvin, T., *Nationalist Revolutionaries in Ireland 1858–1928* (Oxford: Oxford University Press, 1987).

—— *1922: The Birth of Irish Democracy* (Dublin: Gill and Macmillan, 1996).

Gellner, E., *Nations and Nationalism* (Oxford: Basil Blackwell, 1983).

George, A. (ed.), *Western State Terrorism* (Cambridge: Polity, 1991).

Gillespie, G., 'The Sunningdale Agreement: Lost Opportunity or an Agreement Too Far?', *Irish Political Studies* 13 (1998).

Gilligan, O. (ed.), *The Birmingham Six: An Appalling Vista* (Dublin: LiterÉire Publishers, 1990).

Gilmore, G., *The Relevance of James Connolly in Ireland Today* (Dublin: Fodhla Printing Co., n.d.).

—— *Labour and the Republican Movement* (Dublin: Repsol, 1977; 1st edn 1966).

—— *The Irish Republican Congress* (Cork: Cork Workers' Club, 1978).

Gilmour, R., *Dead Ground: Infiltrating the IRA* (London: Little, Brown, 1998).

Gilsenan, M., *Lords of the Lebanese Marches: Violence and Narrative in an Arab Society* (London: I. B. Tauris, 1996).

Gonzalez, A. G., *Peadar O'Donnell: A Reader's Guide* (Chester Springs: Dufour, 1997).

Gordon, D., *The O'Neill Years: Unionist Politics, 1963–1969* (Belfast: Athol Books, 1989).

Graham, S., *Violent Delights* (London: Blake, 1997).

Greaves, C. D., *Liam Mellows and the Irish Revolution* (London: Lawrence and Wishart, 1971).

—— *The Life and Times of James Connolly* (London: Lawrence and Wishart, 1972; 1st edn 1961).

—— *Reminiscences of the Connolly Association* (London: Connolly Association, 1978).

—— *1916 as History: The Myth of the Blood Sacrifice* (Dublin: Fulcrum Press, 1991).

Green, F. L., *Odd Man Out* (Harmondsworth: Penguin, 1948; 1st edn 1945).

Greenfeld, L., *Nationalism: Five Roads to Modernity* (Cambridge: Harvard University Press, 1992).

Guelke, A., *Northern Ireland: The International Perspective* (Dublin: Gill and Macmillan, 1988).

—— 'The United States, Irish Americans and the Northern Ireland Peace Process', *International Affairs* 72, 3 (1996).

—— *The Age of Terrorism and the International Political System* (London: I. B. Tauris, 1998; 1st edn 1995).

Hamill, D., *Pig in the Middle: The Army in Northern Ireland 1969–1984* (London: Methuen, 1985).

Hanley, B., *The IRA, 1926–1936* (Dublin: Four Courts Press, 2002).

Hanna, R. (ed.), *The Union: Essays on Ireland and the British Connection* (Newtownards: Colourpoint, 2001).

Harkness, D., *Northern Ireland Since 1920* (Dublin: Helicon, 1983).

—— *Ireland in the Twentieth Century: Divided Island* (Basingstoke: Macmillan, 1996).

Harnden, T., *'Bandit Country': The IRA and South Armagh* (London: Hodder and Stoughton, 1999).

Hart, P., 'The Geography of Revolution in Ireland 1917–1923', *Past and Present* 155 (1997).

—— *The IRA and Its Enemies: Violence and Community in Cork 1916–1923* (Oxford: Oxford University Press, 1998).

—— 'The Social Structure of the Irish Republican Army, 1916–1923', *Historical Journal* 42, 1 (1999).

—— '"Operations Abroad": The IRA in Britain, 1919–23', *English Historical Review* 115, 460 (2000).

Harvey, C. J. (ed.), *Human Rights, Equality and Democratic Renewal in Northern Ireland* (Oxford: Hart, 2001).

Hauswedell, C., and Brown, K., *Burying the Hatchet: The Decommissioning of Paramilitary Arms in Northern Ireland* (Derry: Incore, 2002).

Hayes, B. C., and McAllister, I., 'British and Irish Public Opinion towards the Northern Ireland Problem', *Irish Political Studies* 11 (1996).

—— and McAllister, I., 'Sowing Dragon's Teeth: Public Support for Political Violence and Paramilitarism in Northern Ireland', *Political Studies* 49, 5 (2001).

Hayes, M., *Minority Verdict: Experiences of a Catholic Public Servant* (Belfast: Blackstaff Press, 1995).

Hayes, P. (ed.), *Themes in Modern European History, 1890–1945* (London: Routledge, 1992).

Hayes, S., 'My Strange Story', *The Bell* 17, 4 (1951).

Hayes-McCoy, G. A. (ed.), *The Irish at War* (Cork: Mercier, 1964).

Heaney, S., *New Selected Poems 1966–1987* (London: Faber and Faber, 1990).

—— *The Redress of Poetry: Oxford Lectures* (London: Faber and Faber, 1995).

—— *Electric Light* (London: Faber and Faber, 2001).

Heath, E., *The Course of My Life: My Autobiography* (London: Coronet, 1999).

Hegarty, P., *Peadar O'Donnell* (Cork: Mercier, 1999).

Hennessey, T., *A History of Northern Ireland 1920–1996* (Dublin: Gill and Macmillan, 1997).

—— *Dividing Ireland: World War One and Partition* (London: Routledge, 1998).

—— *The Northern Ireland Peace Process: Ending the Troubles?* (Dublin: Gill and Macmillan, 2000).

—— and Wilson, R., *With All Due Respect: Pluralism and Parity of Esteem* (Belfast: Democratic Dialogue, 1997).

Hepburn, A. C., 'The IRA in Historical Perspective', *L'Irlande Politique et Sociale* 1, 1 (1985).

Heskin, K., *Northern Ireland: A Psychological Perspective* (Dublin: Gill and Macmillan, 1980).

Hewitt, C., 'Catholic Grievances and Violence in Northern Ireland', *British Journal of Sociology* 36, 1 (1985).

Hezlet, A., *The 'B' Specials: A History of the Ulster Special Constabulary* (Belfast: Mourne River Press, 1997; 1st edn 1972).

Higgins, J., *Confessional* (London: Pan, 1986; 1st edn 1985).

Hill, P., and Bennett, R., *Stolen Years: Before and After Guildford* (London: Doubleday, 1990).

Hobsbawm, E. J., *Nations and Nationalism since 1780: Programme, Myth, Reality* (Cambridge: Cambridge University Press, 1990).

—— *Age of Extremes: The Short Twentieth Century 1914–1991* (Harmondsworth: Penguin, 1994).

Hogan, G., and Walker, C., *Political Violence and the Law in Ireland* (Manchester: Manchester University Press, 1989).

Hogan, J., *Could Ireland Become Communist? The Facts of the Case* (Dublin: Cahill, n.d.).

Holland, J., *Too Long a Sacrifice: Life and Death in Northern Ireland Since 1969* (New York: Dodd, Mead and Co., 1981).

—— *The American Connection: US Guns, Money and Influence in Northern Ireland* (Boulder: Roberts Rinehart, 1999; 1st edn 1987).

—— and McDonald, H., *INLA: Deadly Divisions* (Dublin: Torc, 1994).

—— and Phoenix, S., *Phoenix: Policing the Shadows* (London: Coronet, 1997; 1st edn 1996).

Hopkinson, M., *Green Against Green: The Irish Civil War* (Dublin: Gill and Macmillan, 1988).

—— (ed.), *Frank Henderson's Easter Rising: Recollections of a Dublin Volunteer* (Cork: Cork University Press, 1998).

Howe, G., *Conflict of Loyalty* (London: Macmillan, 1994).

Howe, S., *Ireland and Empire: Colonial Legacies in Irish History and Culture* (Oxford: Oxford University Press, 2000).

Howell, D., *A Lost Left: Three Studies in Socialism and Nationalism* (Manchester: Manchester University Press, 1986).

Hunter, J., *Unionism: A Brief History of the Ulster Unionist Council* (Belfast: UUP, 1993).

Hutchinson, J., *The Dynamics of Cultural Nationalism: The Gaelic Revival and the Creation of the Irish Nation State* (London: Allen and Unwin, 1987).

Hyland, J. L., *James Connolly* (Dundalk: Dundalgan Press, 1997).

Inglis, B., *Roger Casement* (Belfast: Blackstaff Press, 1993; 1st edn 1973).

Institute for the Study of Terrorism, *IRA, INLA: Foreign Support and International Connections* (London: Institute for the Study of Terrorism, 1988).

Irvine, M., *Northern Ireland: Faith and Faction* (London: Routledge, 1991).

Jackson, A., *Sir Edward Carson* (Dundalk: Dundalgan Press, 1993).

—— *Ireland 1798–1998: Politics and War* (Oxford: Blackwell, 1999).

James, S., *The Atlantic Celts: Ancient People or Modern Invention?* (London: British Museum Press, 1999).

Jarman, N., *Displaying Faith: Orange, Green and Trade Union Banners in Northern Ireland* (Belfast: Institute of Irish Studies, 1999).

Jeffery, K., 'Irish Culture and the Great War', *Bullán* 1, 2 (1994).

—— *Ireland and the Great War* (Cambridge: Cambridge University Press, 2000).

—— (ed.), *'An Irish Empire'? Aspects of Ireland and the British Empire* (Manchester: Manchester University Press, 1996).

—— (ed.), *The Sinn Féin Rebellion as They Saw It* (Dublin: Irish Academic Press, 1999).

—— and Bartlett, T. (eds), *A Military History of Ireland* (Cambridge: Cambridge University Press, 1996).

Jenkins, R., *A Life at the Centre* (London: Macmillan, 1991).

Johnston, J., *Civil War in Ulster: Its Objects and Probable Results* (Dublin: UCD Press, 1999; 1st edn 1913).

Jordan, A. J., *Major John MacBride 1865–1916* (Westport: Westport Historical Society, 1991).

Jordan, N., *Sunrise with Sea Monster* (London: Vintage, 1996; 1st edn 1994).

Kee, R., *The Green Flag: A History of Irish Nationalism* (Harmondsworth: Penguin, 2000; 1st edn 1972).

Keena, C., *Gerry Adams: A Biography* (Cork: Mercier, 1990).

Kelleher, D., *Buried Alive in Ireland: A Story of a Twentieth-Century Inquisition* (Greystones: Justice Books, 2001).

—— *Irish Republicanism: The Authentic Perspective* (Greystones: Justice Books, 2001).

—— *An Open Letter to Ian Paisley: Demythologising History* (Greystones: Justice Books, n.d.).

Kelley, K. J., *The Longest War: Northern Ireland and the IRA* (London: Zed Books, 1988; 1st edn 1982).

Kelly, J., *Orders for the Captain?* (Dublin: James Kelly, 1971).

—— *The Genesis of Revolution* (Dublin: Kelly Kane, 1976).

—— *The Thimbleriggers: The Dublin Arms Trial of 1970* (Dublin: James Kelly, 1999).

Kenna, G. B., *Facts and Figures of the Belfast Pogrom 1920–1922* (Dublin: O'Connell Publishing Company, 1922).

Kennedy, D., *The Widening Gulf: Northern Attitudes to the Independent Irish State, 1919–49* (Belfast: Blackstaff Press, 1988).

Kennedy, L., *The Modern Industrialisation of Ireland 1940–1988* (Dublin: Economic and Social History Society of Ireland, 1989).

—— 'Modern Ireland: Post-colonial Society or Post-colonial Pretensions?', *Irish Review* 13 (1992–3).

Kennedy, M., *Division and Consensus: The Politics of Cross-border Relations in Ireland 1925–1969* (Dublin: Institute of Public Administration, 2000).

Keogh, D., *Twentieth-Century Ireland: Nation and State* (Dublin: Gill and Macmillan, 1994).

Khilnani, S., *Arguing Revolution: The Intellectual Left in Postwar France* (New Haven: Yale University Press, 1993).

Kiberd, D., *Irish Classics* (London: Granta, 2000).

Kitson, F., *Low-intensity Operations* (London: Faber and Faber, 1971).

Kleinrichert, D., *Republican Internment and the Prison Ship Argenta 1922* (Dublin: Irish Academic Press, 2001).

Kostick, C., *Revolution in Ireland: Popular Militancy 1917 to 1923* (London: Pluto Press, 1996).

Kotsonouris, M., *Retreat from Revolution: The Dáil Courts, 1920–24* (Blackrock: Irish Academic Press, 1994).

Laffan, M., *The Partition of Ireland 1911–25* (Dundalk: Dundalgan Press, 1983).

—— *The Resurrection of Ireland: The Sinn Féin Party, 1916–1923* (Cambridge: Cambridge University Press, 1999).

Langdon, J., *Mo Mowlam* (London: Little, Brown, 2000).

Lavelle, P., *James O'Mara: A Staunch Sinn Féiner 1873–1948* (Dublin: Clonmore and Reynolds, 1961).

Lawson, N., *The View from No. 11: Memoirs of a Tory Radical* (London: Bantam, 1992).

Lee, J. J., *Ireland 1912–1985: Politics and Society* (Cambridge: Cambridge University Press, 1989).

Lloyd, D., *Anomalous States: Irish Writing and the Post-colonial Moment* (Dublin: Lilliput Press, 1993).

Lodge, J. (ed.), *Terrorism: A Challenge to the State* (Oxford: Martin Robertson, 1981).

Lynch, J., *A Tale of Three Cities: Comparative Studies in Working-Class Life* (Basingstoke: Macmillan, 1998).

Lynn, B., *Holding the Ground: The Nationalist Party in Northern Ireland, 1945–72* (Aldershot: Ashgate, 1997).

McAllister, I., *The Northern Ireland Social Democratic and Labour Party: Political Opposition in a Divided Society* (London: Macmillan, 1977).

Macardle, D., *The Irish Republic: A Documented Chronicle of the Anglo-Irish Conflict and the Partitioning of Ireland, with a Detailed Account of the Period 1916–1923* (London: Corgi, 1968; 1st edn 1937).

—— *Tragedies of Kerry 1922–1923* (Dublin: Irish Freedom Press, 1988; 1st edn 1924).

McArdle, P., *The Secret War: An Account of the Sinister Activities along the Border Involving Gardai, RUC, British Army and the SAS* (Cork: Mercier, 1984).

McBride, I. R., *Scripture Politics: Ulster Presbyterians and Irish Radicalism in the Late Eighteenth Century* (Oxford: Oxford University Press, 1998).

—— (ed.), *History and Memory in Modern Ireland* (Cambridge: Cambridge University Press, 2001).

MacBride, S. (ed.), *Ireland's Right to Sovereignty, Independence and Unity is Inalienable and Indefeasible* (Dublin: Hyland, n.d.).

McCallion, H., *Killing Zone* (London: Bloomsbury, 1995).

McCann, E., *War and an Irish Town* (London: Pluto Press, 1993; 1st edn 1974).

—— Shiels, M., and Hannigan, B., *Bloody Sunday in Derry: What Really Happened* (Dingle: Brandon, 1992).

McCann, J., *Ampleforth Abbey and College: A Short History* (York: Ampleforth Abbey, 1953; 1st edn 1936).

McCartney, R., *Reflections on Liberty, Democracy and the Union* (Dublin: Maunsel, 2001).

McClean, R., *The Road to Bloody Sunday* (Dublin: Ward River Press, 1983).

McDaniel, D., *Enniskillen: The Remembrance Sunday Bombing* (Dublin: Wolfhound, 1997).

MacDermott, E., *Clann na Poblachta* (Cork: Cork University Press, 1998).

MacDonald, D., *The Chosen Few: Exploding Myths in South Armagh* (Cork: Mercier, 2000).

McDonald, H., *Trimble* (London: Bloomsbury, 2000).

McElrath, K., *Unsafe Haven: The United States, the IRA and Political Prisoners* (London: Pluto Press, 2000).

McElroy, G., *The Catholic Church and the Northern Ireland Crisis, 1968–1986* (Dublin: Gill and Macmillan, 1991).

MacEoin, U. *Harry* (Dublin: Argenta, 1986; 1st edn 1985).

—— (ed.), *Survivors* (Dublin: Argenta, 1987; 1st edn 1980).

McEvoy, K., 'Law, Struggle and Political Transformation in Northern Ireland', *Journal of Law and Society* 27, 4 (2000).

McGarry, F., *Irish Politics and the Spanish Civil War* (Cork: Cork University Press, 1999).

McGartland, M., *Fifty Dead Men Walking* (London: Blake, 1998; 1st edn 1997).

MacGiolla, T., *Where We Stand: The Republican Position* (Dublin: Workers' Party of Ireland 2000; 1st edn 1972).

McGuffin, J., *Internment* (Tralee: Anvil Press, 1973).

McGuinness, M., *Bodenstown '86* (London: Wolfe Tone Society, n.d.).

McGuire, M., *To Take Arms: A Year in the Provisional IRA* (London: Quartet, 1973).

McInerney, M., *Peadar O'Donnell: Irish Social Rebel* (Dublin: O'Brien Press, 1974).

McIntyre, A., 'Modern Irish Republicanism: The Product of British State Strategies', *Irish Political Studies* 10 (1995).

MacIntyre, T., *Through the Bridewell Gate: A Diary of the Dublin Arms Trial* (London: Faber and Faber, 1971).

McIntyre, W. D., *British Decolonisation, 1946–1997: When, Why and How Did the British Empire Fall?* (Basingstoke: Macmillan, 1998).

McKendry, S., *Disappeared: The Search for Jean McConville* (Dublin: Blackwater, 2000).

McKenzie, F. A., *The Irish Rebellion: What Happened – and Why* (London: C. Arthur Pearson, 1916).

McKeown, L., *Out of Time: Irish Republican Prisoners Long Kesh 1972–2000* (Belfast: Beyond the Pale, 2001).

McKittrick, D., Kelters, S., Feeney, B., and Thornton, C., *Lost Lives: The Stories of the Men, Women and Children Who Died as a Result of the Northern Ireland Troubles* (Edinburgh: Mainstream, 2001; 1st edn 1999).

—— and McVea, D., *Making Sense of the Troubles* (Belfast: Blackstaff Press, 2000).

McLaughlin, J., *Re-Imagining the Nation-State: The Contested Terrains of Nation-Building* (London: Pluto Press, 2001).

McLaughlin, J. A., *Carrowmenagh: History of a Donegal Village and Townland* (Browne: Letterkenny, 2001).

McLaughlin, R., *Inside an English Jail* (Dublin: Borderline Publications, 1987).

McLoone, M., *Irish Film: The Emergence of a Contemporary Cinema* (London: British Film Institute, 2000).

McMahon, D., '"A Worthy Monument to a Great Man": Piaras Béaslaí's Life of Michael Collins', *Bullán* 2, 2 (1996).

McMahon, T. G. (ed.), *Pádraig Ó Fathaigh's War of Independence: Recollections of a Galway Gaelic Leaguer* (Cork: Cork University Press, 2000).

MacStiofáin, S., *Memoirs of a Revolutionary* (Edinburgh: Gordon Cremonesi, 1975).

McVeigh, J., *Executed: Tom Williams and the IRA* (Belfast: Beyond the Pale, 1999).

Macey, D., *Frantz Fanon: A Life* (London: Granta, 2000).

Magee, P., *Gangsters or Guerrillas? Representations of Irish Republicans in 'Troubles Fiction'* (Belfast: Beyond the Pale, 2001).

Maher, J., *The Flying Column: West Kilkenny 1916–21* (Dublin: Geography Publications, 1987).

Mallie, E., and McKittrick, D., *The Fight for Peace: The Secret Story behind the Irish Peace Process* (London: Heinemann, 1996).

Malone, T., *Alias Sean Forde: The Story of Commandant Tomás Malone, Vice OC East Limerick Flying Column, Irish Republican Army* (Dublin: Danesfort, 2000).

Mandle, W. F., *The Gaelic Athletic Association and Irish Nationalist Politics 1884–1924* (London: Christopher Helm, 1987).

Mansergh, M. (ed.), *The Spirit of the Nation: The Speeches and Statements of Charles J. Haughey (1957–1986)* (Cork: Mercier, 1986).

Markievicz, C., *Prison Letters of Countess Markievicz* (London: Virago, 1987; 1st edn 1934).

Marsh, M., and Mitchell, P. (eds), *How Ireland Voted in 1997* (Boulder: Westview, 1999).

Marshall, P. J. (ed.), *The Eighteenth Century* (Oxford History of the British Empire, vol. 2) (Oxford: Oxford University Press, 1998).

Marx, K., and Engels, F., *Ireland and the Irish Question* (London: Lawrence and Wishart, 1971).

Maume, P., *The Long Gestation: Irish Nationalist Life 1891–1918* (Dublin: Gill and Macmillan, 1999).

Mawhinney, B., and Wells, R., *Conflict and Christianity in Northern Ireland* (Berkhamsted: Lion, 1975).

Meehan, E., ' "Britain's Irish Question: Britain's European Question?" British-Irish Relations in the Context of European Union and the Belfast Agreement', *Review of International Studies* 26 (2000).

Megahey, A., *The Irish Protestant Churches in the Twentieth Century* (Basingstoke: Macmillan, 2000).

Miller, D. [David Leslie], *On Nationality* (Oxford: Oxford University Press, 1995).

Miller, D. (ed.), *Rethinking Northern Ireland: Culture, Ideology and Colonialism* (London: Longman, 1998).

Mitchell, A., *Revolutionary Government in Ireland: Dáil Éireann, 1919–22* (Dublin: Gill and Macmillan, 1995).

Mitchell, G. J., *Making Peace* (London: William Heinemann, 1999).

Moloney, E., *A Secret History of the IRA* (London: Allen Lane, 2002).

Moody, T. W. (ed.), *The Fenian Movement* (Cork: Mercier, 1978; 1st edn 1968).

Morgan, A., *James Connolly: A Political Biography* (Manchester: Manchester University Press, 1988).

—— *Harold Wilson* (London: Pluto Press, 1992).

Morgan, M., 'Post-war Social Change and the Catholic Community in Northern Ireland', *Studies* 77, 308 (1988).

Morrison, D., *West Belfast* (Cork: Mercier, 1989).

—— *Ireland: The Censored Subject* (Belfast: Sinn Féin, 1989).

—— *Then the Walls Came Down: A Prison Journal* (Cork: Mercier, 1999).

Morrissey, M., and Smyth, M., *Northern Ireland after the Good Friday Agreement: Victims, Grievance and Blame* (London: Pluto Press, 2002).

Mowlam, M., *Momentum: The Struggle for Peace, Politics and the People* (London: Hodder and Stoughton, 2002).

Mulcahy, R., *Richard Mulcahy (1886–1971): A Family Memoir* (Dublin: Aurelian Press, 1999).

Mulholland, M., *Northern Ireland at the Crossroads: Ulster Unionism in the O'Neill Years 1960–9* (Basingstoke: Macmillan, 2000).

—— *The Longest War: Northern Ireland's Troubled History* (Oxford: Oxford University Press, 2002).

Mullan, D. (ed.), *Eyewitness Bloody Sunday* (Dublin: Wolfhound, 1997).

Mullin, C., *Error of Judgement: The Truth about the Birmingham Bombings* (Dublin: Poolbeg, 1990; 1st edn 1986).

Munck, R., Rolston, B., and Moore, G., *Belfast in the Thirties: An Oral History* (Belfast: Blackstaff Press, 1987).

Murphy, B. P., *Patrick Pearse and the Lost Republican Ideal* (Dublin: James Duffy, 1991).

Murphy, J. A., *Ireland in the Twentieth Century* (Dublin: Gill and Macmillan, 1975).

Murphy, S., '"I Don't Support the IRA, But . . .": Semantic and Psychological Ambivalence', *Studies* 82, 327 (1993).

Murphy, Y., Leonard, A., Gillespie, G., and Brown, K. (eds), *Troubled Images: Posters and Images of the Northern Ireland Conflict from the Linen Hall Library, Belfast* (Belfast: Linen Hall Library, 2001).

Murray, R., *The SAS in Ireland* (Cork: Mercier, 1990).

Needham, R., *Battling for Peace* (Belfast: Blackstaff Press, 1998).

Newsinger, J., 'Thatcher, Northern Ireland and The Downing Street Years', *Irish Studies Review* 7 (1994).

Ní Dhonnchadha, M., and Dorgan, T. (eds), *Revising the Rising* (Derry: Field Day, 1991).

Ó Brádaigh, R., *Dílseacht: The Story of Comdt General Tom Maguire and the Second (All-Ireland) Dáil* (Dublin: Irish Freedom Press, 1997).

O'Brien, B., *The Long War: The IRA and Sinn Féin 1985 to Today* (Dublin: O'Brien Press, 1993).

O'Brien, C. C., *States of Ireland* (St Albans: Panther, 1974; 1st edn 1972).

—— *Passion and Cunning: Essays on Nationalism, Terrorism and Revolution* (New York: Simon and Schuster, 1988).

—— *Memoir: My Life and Themes* (Dublin: Poolbeg, 1998).

O'Brien, J., *The Arms Trial* (Dublin: Gill and Macmillan, 2000).

O'Callaghan, S., *The Easter Lily: The Story of the IRA* (London: Allan Wingate, 1956).

O'Callaghan, S., *The Informer* (London: Bantam, 1998).

O'Casey, S., *Three Plays* (London: Pan, 1980).

O'Connor, B., *With Michael Collins in the Fight for Irish Independence* (London: Peter Davies, 1929).

O Connor, F., *In Search of a State: Catholics in Northern Ireland* (Belfast: Blackstaff Press, 1993).

O'Connor, F., *My Father's Son* (London: Pan, 1971; 1st edn 1968).

—— *The Big Fellow* (Dublin: Poolbeg, 1991; 1st edn 1937).

—— *An Only Child* (Belfast: Blackstaff Press, 1993; 1st edn 1961).

Ó Dochartaigh, N., ' "Sure, It's Hard to Keep Up with the Splits Here": Irish-American Responses to the Outbreak of Conflict in Northern Ireland 1968–1974', *Irish Political Studies* 10 (1995).

—— *From Civil Rights to Armalites: Derry and the Birth of the Irish Troubles* (Cork: Cork University Press, 1997).

O'Doherty, E., *The IRA at War 1916 to the Present: An Illustrated History* (Cork: Mercier, 1985).

O'Doherty, M., *The Trouble with Guns: Republican Strategy and the Provisional IRA* (Belfast: Blackstaff Press, 1998).

O'Doherty, S., *The Volunteer: A Former IRA Man's True Story* (London: Fount, 1993).

O'Donnell, P., *The Gates Flew Open* (London: Jonathan Cape, 1932).

—— *The Knife* (Dublin: Irish Humanities Centre, 1980; 1st edn 1930).

—— *Monkeys in the Superstructure: Reminiscences of Peadar O'Donnell* (Galway: Salmon Publishing, 1986).

O'Donovan, D., *Kevin Barry and His Time* (Sandycove: Glendale, 1989).

Ó Drisceoil, D., *Peadar O'Donnell* (Cork: Cork University Press, 2001).

O'Duffy, B., 'Violence in Northern Ireland 1969–1994: Sectarian or Ethno-National?', *Ethnic and Racial Studies* 18, 4 (1995).

Ó Duibhir, C., *Sinn Féin: The First Election 1908* (Manorhamilton: Drumlin, 1993).

O'Faolain, S., *De Valera* (Harmondsworth: Penguin, 1939).

—— *The Irish* (West Drayton: Penguin, 1947).

O'Farrell, P., *Who's Who in the Irish War of Independence and Civil War 1916–1923* (Dublin: Lilliput, 1997).

O'Flaherty, L., *Insurrection* (Dublin: Wolfhound, 1993; 1st edn 1950).

O'Halpin, E., *Defending Ireland: The Irish State and its Enemies Since 1922* (Oxford: Oxford University Press, 1999).

O'Leary, B., 'The Nature of the Agreement', *Fordham International Law Journal* 22, 4 (1999).

—— and McGarry, J., *The Politics of Antagonism: Understanding Northern Ireland* (London: Athlone, 1993).

—— and McGarry, J., *Explaining Northern Ireland: Broken Images* (Oxford: Blackwell, 1995).

—— and McGarry, J., *Policing Northern Ireland: Proposals for a New Start* (Belfast: Blackstaff Press, 1999).

—— and McGarry, J. (eds), *The Future of Northern Ireland* (Oxford: Oxford University Press, 1990).

O'Leary, C., Elliott, S., and Wilford, R., *The Northern Ireland Assembly 1982–1986: A Constitutional Experiment* (London: Hurst, 1988).

O'Malley, E., *The Singing Flame* (Dublin: Anvil, 1978).

—— *On Another Man's Wound* (Dublin: Anvil, 1979; 1st edn 1936).

—— *Raids and Rallies* (Dublin: Anvil, 1982).

O'Malley, P., *Biting at the Grave: The Irish Hunger Strikes and the Politics of Despair* (Belfast: Blackstaff Press, 1990).

O'Neill, J., *Blood-Dark Track: A Family History* (London: Granta, 2000).

O'Neill, S., *Impartiality in Context: Grounding Justice in a Pluralist World* (Albany: State University of New York Press, 1997).

O'Neill, T., *The Autobiography of Terence O'Neill* (London: Rupert Hart-Davis, 1972).

O'Rahilly, A., *Winding the Clock: O'Rahilly and the 1916 Rising* (Dublin: Lilliput, 1991).

O'Reilly, D. (ed.), *Accepting the Challenge: The Memoirs of Michael Flannery* (Dublin: Irish Freedom Press, 2001).

Ormsby, F. (ed.), *The Collected Poems of John Hewitt* (Belfast: Blackstaff Press, 1991).

Paret, P., *Understanding War: Essays on Clausewitz and the History of Military Power* (Princeton: Princeton University Press, 1992).

Parker, J., *Death of a Hero: Captain Robert Nairac, GC, and the Undercover War in Northern Ireland* (London: Metro, 1999).

Paseta, S., *Before the Revolution: Nationalism, Social Change and Ireland's Catholic Elite, 1879–1922* (Cork: Cork University Press, 1999).

Patterson, H., *The Politics of Illusion: A Political History of the IRA* (London: Serif, 1997; 1st edn 1989).

—— 'Sean Lemass and the Ulster Question, 1959–65', *Journal of Contemporary History* 34, 1 (Jan. 1999).

Paulin, T., *The Wind Dog* (London: Faber and Faber, 1999).

Pearse, P. H., *Political Writings and Speeches* (Dublin: Phoenix, n.d.).

Pettitt, L., *Screening Ireland: Film and Television Representation* (Manchester: Manchester University Press, 2000).

Phoenix, E., *Northern Nationalism: Nationalist Politics, Partition and the Catholic Minority in Northern Ireland 1890–1940* (Belfast: Ulster Historical Foundation, 1994).

Pilgrim, J., 'The Provisionals', *Fortnight* (19 Feb. 1971).

Pimlott, B., *Harold Wilson* (London: HarperCollins, 1992).

—— *The Queen: A Biography of Elizabeth II* (London: HarperCollins, 1996).

Pollak, A. (ed.), *A Citizens' Inquiry: The Opsahl Report on Northern Ireland* (Dublin: Lilliput, 1993).

Porter, A. (ed.), *The Nineteenth Century* (Oxford History of the British Empire, vol. 3) (Oxford: Oxford University Press, 1999).

Porter, N. (ed.), *The Republican Ideal: Current Perspectives* (Belfast: Blackstaff Press, 1998).

Prior, J., *A Balance of Power* (London: Hamish Hamilton, 1986).

Purdie, B., 'Was the Civil Rights Movement a Republican/Communist Conspiracy?', *Irish Political Studies* 3 (1988).

—— *Politics in the Streets: The Origins of the Civil Rights Movement in Northern Ireland* (Belfast: Blackstaff Press, 1990).

Quinn, J., 'Theobald Wolfe Tone and the Historians', *Irish Historical Studies* 32, 125 (2000).

Quinn, R. J., *A Rebel Voice: A History of Belfast Republicanism 1925–1972* (Belfast: Belfast Cultural and Local History Group, 1999).

—— *The Troubles: A History of the Northern Ireland Conflict* (Belfast: Glenravel Publications, 2001).

Rea, D. (ed.), *Political Co-operation in Divided Societies: A Series of Papers Relevant to the Conflict in Northern Ireland* (Dublin: Gill and Macmillan, 1982).

Redmond, S., *Desmond Greaves and the Origins of the Civil Rights Movement in Northern Ireland* (London: Connolly Publications, 2000).

Reed, D., *Ireland: The Key to the British Revolution* (London: Larkin Publications, 1984).

Rees, M., *Northern Ireland: A Personal Perspective* (London: Methuen, 1985).

Regan, J. M., *The Irish Counter-Revolution 1921–1936: Treatyite Politics and Settlement in Independent Ireland* (Dublin: Gill and Macmillan, 1999).

—— 'Strangers in our Midst: Middling People, Revolution and Counter-Revolution in Twentieth-Century Ireland', *Radharc* 2 (2001).

Reid, P. R., *The Colditz Story* (London: Cassell, 2001; 1st edn 1952).

Rentoul, J., *Tony Blair* (London: Little, Brown, 1995).

Restorick, R., *Death of a Soldier: A Mother's Search for Peace in Northern Ireland* (Belfast: Blackstaff Press, 2000).

Ring, J., *Erskine Childers* (London: John Murray, 1996).

Roche, P. J., and Barton, B. (eds), *The Northern Ireland Question: Myth and Reality* (Aldershot: Avebury, 1991).

—— and Barton, B. (eds), *The Northern Ireland Question: Perspectives and Policies* (Aldershot: Avebury, 1994).

Rose, P., *How the Troubles Came to Northern Ireland* (Basingstoke: Palgrave, 2001; 1st edn 2000).

Routledge, P., *Public Servant, Secret Agent: The Elusive Life and Violent Death of Airey Neave* (London: Fourth Estate, 2002).

Rowan, B., *Behind the Lines: The Story of the IRA and Loyalist Ceasefires* (Belfast: Blackstaff Press, 1995).

Rowthorn, B., and Wayne, N., *Northern Ireland: The Political Economy of Conflict* (Cambridge: Polity, 1988).

Ruane, J., and Todd, J., *The Dynamics of Conflict in Northern Ireland: Power, Conflict and Emancipation* (Cambridge: Cambridge University Press, 1996).

—— and Todd, J., 'The Politics of Transition? Explaining Political Crises in the Implementation of the Belfast Good Friday Agreement', *Political Studies* 49, 5 (2001).

—— and Todd, J. (eds), *After the Good Friday Agreement: Analysing Political Change in Northern Ireland* (Dublin: UCD Press, 1999).

Ryan, F., *Easter Week and After* (Dublin: National Publicity Committee, n.d.).

Ryan, M., *The Tom Barry Story* (Dublin: Mercier, 1982).

—— *Liam Lynch: The Real Chief* (Dublin: Mercier, 1986).

Ryan, M., *War and Peace in Ireland: Britain and the IRA in the New World Order* (London: Pluto Press, 1994).

Ryder, C., *Inside the Maze: The Untold Story of the Northern Ireland Prison Service* (London: Methuen, 2000).

Said, E., *Culture and Imperialism* (London: Vintage, 1994; 1st edn 1993).

Sands, B., *The Diary of Bobby Sands* (Dublin: Sinn Féin, 1981).

—— *Prison Poems* (Dublin: Sinn Féin, 1981).

—— *One Day in My Life* (Cork: Mercier, 1982).

Savage, R., *Sean Lemass* (Dundalk: Dundalgan, 1999).

Scoular, C., *James Chichester-Clark: Prime Minister of Northern Ireland* (Killyleagh: Clive Scoular, 2000).

Sharrock, D., and Devenport, M., *Man of War, Man of Peace: The Unauthorised Biography of Gerry Adams* (London: Pan, 1998; 1st edn 1997).

Shaw, F., 'The Canon of Irish History: A Challenge', *Studies* 61, 242 (1972).

Sinn Féin, *Eire Nua is Local Democracy* (Dublin: Elo, 1974).

—— *A Scenario for Peace: A Discussion Paper* (Dublin: Sinn Féin, n.d.).

—— *Towards a Lasting Peace in Ireland* (Dublin: Sinn Féin, 1992).

Sinnott, R., *Irish Voters Decide: Voting Behaviour in Elections and Referendums Since 1918* (Manchester: Manchester University Press, 1995).

Skelly, J. M., 'Appeasement in Our Time: Conor Cruise O'Brien and the Peace Process in Northern Ireland', *Irish Studies in International Affairs* 10 (1999).

Skillen, C., 'Pravda's Provos: Russian and Soviet Manipulation of News from Ireland', *Irish Political Studies* 8 (1993).

Sluka, J. A., *Hearts and Minds, Water and Fish: Support for the IRA and INLA in a Northern Irish Ghetto* (Greenwich: JAI Press, 1989).

Smith, D. J., and Chambers, G., *Inequality in Northern Ireland* (Oxford: Oxford University Press, 1991).

Smith, M. L. R., *Fighting for Ireland? The Military Strategy of the Irish Republican Movement* (London: Routledge, 1997; 1st edn 1995).

Smyth, M., and Fay, M. (eds), *Personal Accounts from Northern Ireland's Troubles: Public Conflict, Private Loss* (London: Pluto Press, 2000).

Stalker, J., *Stalker* (London: Harrap, 1988).

Stationery Office, *The Irish Uprising, 1914–21: Papers from the British Parliamentary Archive* (London: Stationery Office, 2000).

Stephens, J., *The Insurrection in Dublin* (Gerrards Cross: Colin Smythe, 1992; 1st edn 1916).

Stevenson, J., *'We Wrecked the Place': Contemplating an End to the Northern Irish Troubles* (New York: Free Press, 1996).

Stradling, R. A., *The Irish and the Spanish Civil War 1936–1939* (Manchester: Mandolin, 1999).

Sunday Times Insight Team, *Ulster* (Harmondsworth: Penguin, 1972).

Sutton, M., *Bear in Mind These Dead: An Index of Deaths from the Conflict in Ireland 1969–1993* (Belfast: Beyond the Pale, 1994).

Sweeney, G., 'Irish Hunger Strikes and the Cult of Self-Sacrifice', *Journal of Contemporary History* 28 (1993).

Tanner, M., *Ireland's Holy Wars: The Struggle for a Nation's Soul, 1500–2000* (New Haven: Yale University Press, 2001).

Tarpey, M. V., 'Joseph McGarrity, Fighter for Irish Freedom', *Studia Hibernica* 11 (1971).

Taylor, P., *Provos: The IRA and Sinn Féin* (London: Bloomsbury, 1997).

—— *Loyalists* (London: Bloomsbury, 1999).

Thatcher, M., *The Downing Street Years* (London: HarperCollins, 1993).

—— *The Path to Power* (New York: HarperCollins, 1995).

Thompson, W. I., *The Imagination of an Insurrection: Dublin, Easter 1916 – A Study of an Ideological Movement* (West Stockbridge: Lindisfarne Press, 1982; 1st edn 1967).

Tóibín, B., *The Rising* (Dublin: New Island Books, 2001).

Tone, T. W., *Life of Theobald Wolfe Tone* (Dublin: Lilliput, 1998).

Toolis, K., *Rebel Hearts: Journeys within the IRA's Soul* (London: Picador, 1995).

Townshend, C., *The British Campaign in Ireland, 1919–1921: The Development of Political and Military Policies* (Oxford: Oxford University Press, 1975).

—— *Political Violence in Ireland: Government and Resistance since 1848* (Oxford: Oxford University Press, 1984; 1st edn 1983).

—— 'The Suppression of the Easter Rising', *Bullán* 1, 1 (1994).

—— *Ireland: The Twentieth Century* (London: Arnold, 1999).

—— (ed.), *Consensus in Ireland: Approaches and Recessions* (Oxford: Oxford University Press, 1988).

Trimble, D., *To Raise Up a New Northern Ireland: Articles and Speeches 1998–2000* (Belfast: Belfast Press, 2001).

Truscot, B., *Red Brick University* (Harmondsworth: Penguin, 1951; 1st edn 1943).

Tuck, R., *The Rights of War and Peace: Political Thought and the International Order from Grotius to Kant* (Oxford: Oxford University Press, 1999).

Urban, M., *Big Boys' Rules: The Secret Struggle Against the IRA* (London: Faber and Faber, 1992).

Uris, L., *Trinity* (London: Corgi, 1977; 1st edn 1976).

Valiulis, M. G., *Portrait of a Revolutionary: General Richard Mulcahy and the Founding of the Irish Free State* (Blackrock: Irish Academic Press, 1992).

Walker, G., *Intimate Strangers: Political and Cultural Interaction Between Scotland and Ulster in Modern Times* (Edinburgh: John Donald, 1995).

Walsh, D. P. J., *Bloody Sunday and the Rule of Law in Northern Ireland* (Basingstoke: Macmillan, 2000).

Walsh, P., *Irish Republicanism and Socialism: The Politics of the Republican Movement 1905 to 1994* (Belfast: Athol Books, 1994).

Ward, M., *Unmanageable Revolutionaries: Women and Irish Nationalism* (London: Pluto Press, 1983).

—— *Hanna Sheehy Skeffington: A Life* (Cork: Attic Press, 1997).

White, R. W., *Provisional Irish Republicans: An Oral and Interpretive History* (Westport: Greenwood Press, 1993).

—— 'The Irish Republican Army: An Assessment of Sectarianism', *Terrorism and Political Violence* 9, 1 (1997).

Whitelaw, W., *The Whitelaw Memoirs* (London: Aurum Press, 1989).

Whyte, J., *Church and State in Modern Ireland 1923–1979* (Dublin: Gill and Macmillan, 1984; 1st edn 1971).

—— *Interpreting Northern Ireland* (Oxford: Oxford University Press, 1990).

Whyte, N., *Science, Colonialism and Ireland* (Cork: Cork University Press, 1999).

Wichert, S., *Northern Ireland Since 1945* (London: Longman, 1991).

Wilde, O., *Complete Works of Oscar Wilde* (London: Heron Books, 1966).

Wilford, R. (ed.), *Aspects of the Belfast Agreement* (Oxford: Oxford University Press, 2001).

Wilkinson, P. (ed.), *British Perspectives on Terrorism* (London: George Allen and Unwin, 1981).

Williams, P., *The General: Godfather of Crime* (Dublin: O'Brien Press, 1998; 1st edn 1995).

Wilson, A. J., *Irish America and the Ulster Conflict 1968–1995* (Belfast: Blackstaff Press, 1995).

Wilson, G., *Marie: A Story from Enniskillen* (London: Marshall Pickering, 1990).

Winks, R. W. (ed.), *Historiography* (Oxford History of the British Empire, vol. 5) (Oxford: Oxford University Press, 1999).

Wright, F., *Northern Ireland: A Comparative Analysis* (Dublin: Gill and Macmillan, 1992; 1st edn 1987).

Wright, J., *Terrorist Propaganda: The Red Army Faction and the Provisional IRA, 1968–86* (Basingstoke: Macmillan, 1991).

Wright, P., and Greengrass, P., *Spycatcher* (New York: Dell, 1988; 1st edn 1987).

Yeates, P., *Lockout: Dublin 1913* (New York: Palgrave, 2000).

Yeats, W. B., *Yeats's Poems* (Dublin: Gill and Macmillan, 1989).

Index

Act of Union (1800), 22
Adair, Johnny 'Mad Dog', 281
Adams, Annie (Hannaway), 109
Adams, Dominic, 69, 109
Adams, Gerry: abstentionism break, 252; on
   Anglo-Irish Agreement, 242, 265, 311; on
   Belfast republicanism, 311; birth, 383; Blair
   meeting, 296; on Bloody Sunday, 153–4;
   Bodenstown speech, 217, 224; bodyguard,
   257; on British policy, 310; on Canary Wharf
   bomb, 290; Catholicism, 130, 347; on
   ceasefire, 287; on civil rights movement, 91,
   92; Connolly influence, 346;
   decommissioning issue, 325–6, 333–4; on
   Dublin Dáil, 309; on Easter Rising, 5;
   election campaign (1987), 246; election
   defeat (1992), 277, 278; election success
   (1997), 294; on Enniskillen, 255–6; on Falls
   Road curfew, 136; family background, 69,
   109–10, 111; on Good Friday Agreement,
   299, 300, 306; graveside orations, 112–13;
   Harrison on, 316; Hume relationship, 263–5,
   271, 287, 291, 308; hunger-striker meeting,
   202; on hunger strikes, 207; imprisonment,
   110, 162–3, 189, 197; influence, 132; IRA
   career, 105, 110; on IRA effectiveness, 351,
   383; on IRA truce (1975), 311; London
   Whitelaw meeting (1972), 157; on Long
   Kesh, 189, 190; on loyalists, 348; Mandelson
   on, 308; on Northern Ireland, 125, 245–6,
   339; O'Donnell comparison, 370; on
   Operation Motorman, 161; peace initiative,
   269–70, 273, 290, 303; on referendum, 301;
   on release of prisoners, 324; on republican
   objective, 280; on Restorick death, 293; on
   RUC, 100; on Sands, 196, 199, 200; on
   Shankill bomb, 282; on Sinn Féin, 350; Sinn
   Féin President, 110, 244, 249, 274, 364;

socialism, 216; on stalemate, 307; on
   Teebane killing, 277; Tone influence, 85; US
   visit, 273, 304; on violence, 343; Wolfe Tone
   Society, 85; wounded by UFF, 247; writing as
   'Brownie', 180, 181–2
Adams, Gerry (senior), 69, 78, 109
Adare, robbery shooting (1996), 291
Agate, Jeffrey, 219
Ahern, Bertie, 306
Ahtisaari, Martti, 329, 330, 331
Aiken, Frank, 35, 37
Aldershot, barracks bombing (1972), 175
Allan, James, 178
Alliance Party, 165, 302
Amsterdam, support for hunger strikers, 204
Anglo-Irish Agreement (1985), 240–3, 265, 311,
   336
Anglo-Irish Joint Declaration (1993), xxiv,
   271–3
Anglo-Irish Treaty (1921), 30–5, 45, 46, 214
An Phoblacht, 44, 47, 48
An Phoblacht (Provisional), 115, 203, 219, 222,
   242, 270, 276, 278, 279, 280, 286, 292–3,
   295, 301, 302, 310, 327, 331, 333, 337, 341,
   345, 356
An t-Óglách, 24
Apprentice Boys' parade, 102
Arlow, William, 178
Armagh: IRA strength, 380; killings (1975–76)
Armagh Jail, 194, 195, 196, 257
Armalite rifles, 116–17, 344
Armstrong, Patrick, 168
Arthurs, Declan, 254
Ashe, Thomas, 26
Atkins, Humphrey, 203
Atkinson, Joe, 56
Auxiliaries, 19

Index